THE AMERICAN ALPINE
JOURNAL
2005

Above: Ermanno Salvaterra nearing the summit of Cerro Torre. *Alessandro Beltrami*
Cover: Josh Wharton traversing (5.10+ A1) into the headwall on day 3, about 1,500m up the Azeem Ridge,
Great Trango, Pakistan. *Kelly Cordes*

Condor on Paso Superior, Patagonia (lower left). *Klemen Mali*
Oscar Perez (left) on Anké Asashe, Changi Tower (5,800m), Pakistan. *Cecilia Buil*
Stefan Glowacz and Markus Dorfleitner opening Last Exit Titlis in the Sustenpass, Switzerland. *Klaus Fengler*
Bean Bowers just before his 30-meter fall from the summit of Torre Egger (bottom). *Jonny Copp*

Paul McSorley on the west buttress of Aguja Rafael Juarez, Patagonia. *Jon Walsh*
Right: Ben Gilmore approaching the summit cornices on Arctic Rage, The Moose's Tooth, *Alaska.* *Kevin Mahoney*

Corporate Friends
of the
AMERICAN ALPINE JOURNAL

We thank the following for their generous financial

support of the 2005 AMERICAN ALPINE JOURNAL

Friends

OF THE

AMERICAN ALPINE JOURNAL

We thank the following for their generous financial support:

BENEFACTORS:

The H. Adams Carter Endowment Fund for the American Alpine Journal
Yvon Chouinard

PATRONS:

Ann Carter, Peter D. McGann, M.D.
Gregory Miller, Joseph E. Murphy, Jr.
Louis F. Reichardt, Steven Schwartz

SUPPORTERS:

Dr. C. Vernon Cooper, Jr., Neale E. Creamer
Jim Edwards, Richard E. Hoffman, M.D.
Z. Wayne Griffin, Jr., Michael John Lewis, Jr.
Verne R. Read, Peter L. Renz
Royal Shannon Robbins, William R. Stall
Scott Vander Voort, Michael Yokell

SPECIAL THANKS TO:

Robert J. Campbell
Kristi Jett
Louis W. Kasischke
Mary Ann Matthews
M. Craig McKibben
Dennis J. Meister
John M. Young

THE AMERICAN ALPINE JOURNAL

710 Tenth St. Suite 140, Golden, Colorado 80401
Telephone: (303) 384-0110 Fax: (303) 384-0111
E-mail: aaj@americanalpineclub.org

THE AMERICAN ALPINE JOURNAL
2005

VOLUME 47 ISSUE 79
CONTENTS

CLIMBS AND EXPEDITIONS

Including: When the Alps Cast Their Spell: Mountaineers of the Alpine Golden Age, *by Trevor Braham;* High Rocks and Ice: The Classic Mountain Photographs of Bob and Ira Spring, *by Ira Spring;* Mount Everest, Khumbu Himal, Rolwaling Himal I Khumbakarna Himal, *Satellite Image Map (1:1,000,000), by Jan Zurawski;* K2 and the Baltoro Glacier in the Karakoram, *Satellite Image Map (1:80,000), by Grzegorz Glazek;* Postcards From The Trailer Park, *by Cameron Burns;* Ways to the Sky: A Historical Guide to North American Mountaineering, *by Andy Selters;* Between a Rock and a Hard Place, *by Aron Ralston;* Longs Peak: The Story of Colorado's Favorite Fourteener, *by Dougald MacDonald;* Life and Limb: A True Story of Tragedy and Survival Against the Odds, *by Jamie Andrew;* Ice & Mixed Climbing: Modern Technique, *by Will Gadd;* The Big Open: On Foot Across Tibet's Chang Tang, *by Rick Ridgeway;* The Fellowship of Ghosts: A Journey Through the Mountains of Norway, *by Paul Watkins;* In the Ghost Country: A Lifetime Spent on the Edge, *by Peter Hillary and John Elder;* Everest Pioneer, the Photographs of Captain John Noel, *by Sandra Noel.*

Remembering Barry Corbet, William Preston Elfendahl, Russell Huse, Reese Martin, W. V. Graham Matthews II, Polly Prescott, Landon Gale Rockwell, Peter K. Schoening.

Dave MacLeod on the second ascent of Happy Tyroleans (IX,10), Northern Corries of Cairngorm, Scotland. *Dave Cuthbertson, www.cubbyimages.co.uk*

The American Alpine Journal

John Harlin III, *Editor*

Advisory Board
James Frush, *Managing Editor*
Rolando Garibotti, Mark Jenkins,
Dougald MacDonald, Mark Richey

Assistant Editor
Kelly Cordes

Art Director
Adele Hammond

Production Assistant
Lili Henzler

Contributing Editors
Steve Roper, *Features*
Lindsay Griffin, *Climbs & Expeditions*
Joe Kelsey, *Climbs & Expeditions*
David Stevenson, *Book Reviews*
Frederick O. Johnson, *Club Activities*

Cartographer
Martin Gamache, Alpine Mapping Guild

Translators
Konrad Kirch
Molly Loomis
Tamotsu Nakamura
Henry Pickford

Indexers
Ralph Ferrara, Eve Tallman

Regional Contacts
Malcolm Bass, *Scotland*; Danny Kost, *Wrangell-St. Elias*;
Drew Brayshaw & Don Serl, *Coast Mountains, BC*; Colin
Haley, *Washington Cascades*; Raphael Slawinski,
Canadian Rockies; Bill Wright, *Yosemite*; Antonio Gómez
Bohórquez and Richard Hidalgo, *Peru*; Rolando
Garibotti, *Patagonia*; Damien Gildea, *Antarctica*; Harish
Kapadia, *India*; Elizabeth Hawley, *Nepal*; Tamotsu
Nakamura, *Japanese expeditions*; Lindsay Griffin, *Earth*;
Mark Watson, *New Zealand*

With additional thanks to
Ghafoor and Karim Abdul, Dario Bracali,
Sam Chinnery, Tommy Caldwell, Jonny Copp,
Jeremy Frimer, Paul Fuller, Dan Gambino, Grzegorz
Glazek, Steve House, Saed Jan, Tomaz Jakofcic,
Roy Leggett, Vlado Linek, Bronson MacDonald,
Klemen Mali, Daryl Miller, Ian Parnell, Joe Puryear,
Joe Reichert, Beth Rodden, Matt Samet, Marcelo Scanu,
RJ Secor (get well soon!), The Spot, Jack Tackle,
Jon Walsh, Josh Wharton, Jeanne Young

THE AMERICAN ALPINE CLUB

OFFICIALS FOR THE YEAR 2005
*Directors ex-officio

HONORARY PRESIDENT
Robert H. Bates

PREFACE

"Alpinism is an art of survival," wrote Marko Prezelj, of Slovenia. "When it comes down to the question of life and death, there are no more ethical barriers for most of us. 'Leaving things' on the mountain has a final limit in leaving your body there."

Prezelj's comments came in response to a query I sent to a number of *American Alpine Journal* contributors last winter. I wanted to know what leading climbers worldwide consider acceptable to leave behind on a mountain. At least in North America, the backpacking community long ago adopted "Leave No Trace" principles. Today you can hike for days on American and Canadian trails and never see a single scrap of garbage. This concept is not unique to North America. Harish Kapadia, the long-time Honorary Editor of the *Himalayan Journal*, responded, "All climbers should carry back what they have used on a climb or a mountain. This is a well established principle for many years now."

So this is an accepted wilderness principle. But how often is it followed?

Kelly Cordes came home last summer from his first expedition to Pakistan shocked by what he witnessed. Cordes and Josh Wharton had carried their empty fuel canister for three dangerous days over the summit of Great Trango, only to find themselves picking up other people's garbage on the descent and later on nearby Nameless Tower. There was garbage up and down the gully leading to Nameless, and garbage stuffed in cracks at belays. "It was infuriating," Cordes wrote, "heaps of trash on the most beautiful rock tower in the world!"

Molly Loomis visited the remote Komorova Glacier in the Kokshaal-Too last summer, a place that only a handful of expeditions have visited, and she found piles of garbage, unburied toilet "pits" a meter from the stream, years-old food preserved in the cold stream, plastic and duct tape on the ground. Jon Otto, climbing in China last summer, says his team joked that "it was impossible to get lost since you just had to follow the line of garbage from base camp to camp one."

Low-altitude garbage should not be an issue today. Yoshitomi Okura, the senior director of the Japanese Alpine Club, informed me that The Himalayan Trust of Japan published the guidelines "Take in–Take out" over a decade ago. Kin-ichi Yamamori, the president of the Himalayan Association of Japan, wrote that a climbing party "has to depart from the base camp after cleaning the site as they arrived at it. If there is time and energy, it would be advisable to clean the remainders of other parties in the vicinity."

But my original query was not merely about base camps; I wanted to know if our supposed ethical principles apply to the climbing route itself. Is leaving a fixed rope somehow different than littering base camp because it's more difficult to get down? Mostly I wanted to learn what people considered acceptable on new routes—*AAJ* territory.

Occasionally a climber admitted to appreciating old gear. When Dan Mazur climbed the West Ridge of K2 he found old ropes, a ladder, a tent: "It was almost as if we were shaking the hands of the great mountaineers who had laid them." But that was truly old stuff, like Roman garbage becoming modern museum pieces. Kenton Cool, UK, didn't feel that way on his 2003 climb of Annapurna III. He had traveled halfway around the world to climb a new route and found the experience "disappointing. The lower buttress was covered in old rope…. There was no attempt to cut it off the mountain. Why not??? No one had been hurt, and the weather was okay."

Grievous examples abound, even among our most influential climbers. On a recent well-publicized single-push climb on Denali, three noted American alpinists abandoned equipment they no longer needed upon reaching the upper Cassin Ridge. A few years earlier, two well-known

Cascade climbers dumped their garbage, ropes, food, and fuel at the base of Cerro Torre's west face after their ascent. Does climbing a technically difficult route somehow justify littering in a way that trashing base camp does not?

Perhaps it's time to extend our debates about climbing style to something beyond the ascent. The condition of the mountain after we're done with it reflects not just our style, but also our ethical foundation.

It seems that everyone agrees that taking down fixed gear is the right thing to do when it's not dangerous. In the words of Sung-woo Kang, of Korea, "We should climb cleanly if we can, but when nature overwhelms us and leaves us no choice but to survive, we have no alternative but to leave gear behind." Fair enough, but one of the basic principles of "Leave No Trace" is to be prepared. In the words of the Tyrol Declaration of 2002, Article 8—Style: "The quality of the experience and how we solve a problem is more important than whether we solve it. We strive to leave no trace." The point being, if the climbers aren't good enough to take their ropes down, should they be there in the first place? As Yamamori put it, "Tactics and practices for equipment recovery should be taken into consideration in the initial stage of expedition planning. Costs for the high altitude porters [if needed to recover gear] must be included in the budget."

Perhaps the most publicly controversial climb of last year was the ascent of the north face of Jannu. The climb drew nearly universal admiration until it was learned that much of the equipment was left on the face. Then the talk started: "The Russians abandoned everything." "Disgusting." "This absolutely must be brought to the reader's attention."

But life on and off the wall is rarely simple. Though massive amounts of gear were abandoned, that doesn't mean the climbers didn't care. Nikolay Totmyanin wrote: "I went down last. We took down seven ropes above 7,400m, the portaledge of camp 7,400, two ropes above 7,000, the tent and equipment of camp 7,000, the portaledge of camp 6,700, some ropes between 5,600 and 7,000, and the tent and equipment of camp 5,600. There are a lot of old ropes and pitons from other expeditions up to 6,500, and the broken tent of an Uzbek expedition at 6,700. We have taken down the maximum possible at one time." Still, on a face this large, even that effort did not come close to getting the job done. Alexander Ruchkin wrote, "To my regret, the majority of cords are left on the route. I think we left about 50 ropes on the most abrupt and dangerous sites. It is left because many members of the team were sick and [worn out] to the limit. Further cleaning of the route was not safe for the team." And then he added, "The camp was left pure. I am for [leaving] valleys and mountains pure. And even routes, neither cords and hooks, nor iron cables and ladders, anything."

It seems we all want the same things: a clean mountain to climb, the summit under our feet, and to get home alive. And we all believe that the mountain should be left as pure as possible for the climbers who follow us. The questions are whether a clean mountain for future climbers is more important than the summit for ourselves, and if we find it worth the effort or risk it takes to clean up our own messes. The ethical answer seems easy on paper. But being clean in the mountains takes real work. Increasingly, climbers are deciding it's a necessity. As Urs Odermatt of Switzerland put it, "For me it's out of the question to leave any garbage behind. If somebody does, he's not a real alpinist. I have no respect, even if his 'new route' is something very hard."

Dave Morris, from Scotland and the president of the UIAA Mountain Protection Commission, put it even more succinctly, "No storm, no epic, no excuse."

The full text of letters from my correspondents will be placed at www.American AlpineClub.org/knowledge/aaj.asp.

JOHN HARLIN III

SUFFER WELL

Thirst and hunger on the Azeem Ridge, Great Trango, Pakistan

KELLY CORDES

Porters on the final day of the approach, from Paiju to Trango base camp. On the left is Great Trango Tower, with the upper half of what was to become the Azeem Ridge rising along the left side to the Southwest Summit. The snow-capped peak farther along the ridge to the right is the main summit of Great Trango Tower. The jagged peak to its right is the Trango Castle. Please note: the cover of this Journal is from the Azeem Ridge. *Kelly Cordes*

A faint reminder of words written a couple days earlier crept across my subconscious as our only fuel canister sputtered empty on Great Trango Tower. Josh Wharton and I were over halfway up—the easy half—the 7,400-vertical-foot southwest ridge with two ropes, a basic rack, and a single 28-pound pack. Ice-capped towers looming overhead cast immense shadows onto our base camp 4,000 feet below, as they did two nights before when the weather had cleared and we knew that, come morning, we'd attempt the biggest route of our lives. That night, with my nerves tingling but my mind strangely calm, I'd closed my journal with a simple note to myself. The words would be our blessing and nearly our curse: "Be mentally strong. Suffer well, it'll be worth it."

The first two days had gone smoothly—except for losing a quarter of our 20 cams on the second pitch when one side of our jury-rigged double gear sling came undone— and we'd made good time. The climbing often was easy enough for the second to climb with the pack rather than jumar, punctuated by a few difficult pitches and the occasional loose pitch (most of the death blocks remained perched on ledges). Toward the end of the second day the climbing steepened, with several 5.10 and 5.11 pitches, as we finished the lower-angle, broken portion of the route. On the last pitch of the day Josh was leading out of my view when I heard him yell:

"Kelly, send up the tape!"

"Huh?" I thought, but I stick to what I learned early on: leader is God. I tied the roll of tape to the tag line and sent it up. A few minutes later Josh yelled:

"Pull the tag line tight please!"

I did.

Azeem Ridge on Great Trango Tower, seen from up-glacier (Trango Glacier). Route begins in lower right and ascends the right skyline to the Southwest Summit (ca 6,250m sometimes called West Summit). Descent is marked. *Kelly Cordes*

"No, no, not that tight, a little less. Perfect, tie it off please!"

Josh, 30 feet above his last piece of pro, had come to a two-hole threader ladder (holes with threaded sleeves, drilled on some previous attempt). But we had only one hook. He taped the hook to the first hole, had me tension the tag line to help hold it in place, and fired past the "blank" section free at sketchy 5.11.

Our plan was all or nothing: we'd climb as light as possible, as fast as possible, and if things went to hell we'd descend. This spirit fueled my pre-trip training, and it seemed like a good plan—assuming things didn't go to hell too high up. We knew we could retreat from atop the "headwall," about 6,000 feet up, as a team of four Spanish climbers had done in 1990, and our American friends Timmy O'Neill and Miles Smart did in 2000. The Spaniards had fixed and sieged for three weeks, while making a movie before retreating, claiming to be only a few easy pitches from the top. (Our Slovenian friend Tomaz put it perfectly at base camp: "Of course.

That is what everybody says who does not summit.") Timmy and Miles had made an impressive lightweight attempt, but warned us that the crux might lie above. Indeed, when we hiked up-glacier for a view, it was obvious that considerable terrain—and not trivial terrain—remained above the previous highpoints. Only the most foreshortened view—or wishful thinking—could convince anyone otherwise.

When we reached the bivouac where our last fuel sputtered out, we never spoke of retreat. It was early still, we felt strong, and we'd melted enough snow to get us through the next morning. We'd surely find water melting from snowpatches higher up…. The truth is that it's always easy to find excuses to go down or not finish a route, but the weather was good, and we were still comfortable. Besides, our strategy relied on delusional optimism, what I term "disaster style" and Josh calls "safety fifth!" climbing. I gulped some water, curled into a ball inside my summer-weight down bag on a sloping rock under the starry Karakoram sky, and dozed off with a smile on my face.

* * *

Traveling to Pakistan had everything to do with style: the big picture of style, not just climbing. Looking beyond the propaganda-driven hype and deciding for ourselves whether or not we should come. Meeting people from cultures almost incomprehensible to us, but who had

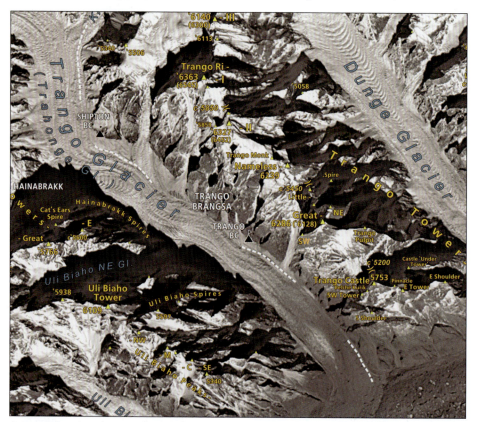

An extract from the Baltoro map by Grzegorz Glazek reviewed later in this Journal. Available in the U.S. from www.TrailStuff.com. *Grzegorz Glazek*

introspection, openness and warmth that seem too rare in our world. And

the climbing, of course it's about style, though I realize that some people couldn't care less. So long as they don't wreck the place and are honest about what they did, then fine—climb however you want. It's every individual's choice.

* * *

In the morning we packed our empty fuel canister and scant gear, and I traversed from our bivy alcove out right into a steep crack, blowing into my hands for warmth to start the third day. After two pitches a rubbly ramp led to the base of the headwall. I gazed down at the lake and the specks of tents at base camp, and wondered what our friends Ghafoor, our cook, and Karim, his assistant and little brother, were doing.

Josh took over leading and traversed, with aid and free-climbing, up and into the obvious vertical-to-overhanging crack splitting the headwall. The two-bolt Spanish anchors made the hanging belays easier—especially since many of the cams we lost on the first day were crucial sizes. Josh masterfully pieced it together,

Josh Wharton on easy terrain relatively low on day three. *Kelly Cordes*

alternately punching 20-foot runouts and aiding off marginal placements in the parallel crack. I jumared for short bursts then collapsed in a loud, gasping heap before continuing. The altitude was kicking my ass, perhaps because we'd only given a weak nod in the direction of acclimatization before the climb. Not surprisingly, Josh didn't seem bothered.

Atop the four-pitch headwall, Josh set an anchor beside a tattered cluster of old Friends, no bolts—surely from the Spaniards' 1990 hasty retreat in a storm. The route had narrowed and the crack systems dwindled, severely limiting routefinding options. For the last day and a half we'd been finding obvious signs of the 1990 team. We'd benefited from clipping their anchors (especially on the headwall) and knowing that retreat, though a horrible hassle—the Spanish had climbed 61 pitches—would still be possible. But when Josh ripped out that old anchor, the final sign of previous attempts, with the tug of one hand, we were definitely alone. And a long ways from the top.

I took over, leading steep cracks with occasional aid, to a small break with a tiny ledge and no obvious line. The sun hung low, and the miniscule ledge would make a miserable bivy.

Josh Wharton about to punch it up a 5.10+ off-width at ca 6,200m, with no gear big enough to fit, on day 4. Much to the pair's disappointment, the point above was not yet the summit. *Kelly Cordes*

I tensioned left around a corner and climbed a thin, unprotected face into a wild, wind-sculpted concave roof that jutted horizontally then downward, like a wave carved in stone. Traversing its left side and up a series of crumbly cracks, I reached a ledge of broken boulders as the sun set. We settled in for a cold and sloping bivy. I chipped chunks of ice into a tiny pile beside my head to suck on between fits of restless sleep. The summit had to be near.

* * *

A little over a year before, on a drunken night at the Fairview bar in Talkeetna, Alaska, British hardman Paul Ramsden told me something I've remembered almost every day since. Paul joked about how Americans spend so much time getting gear dialed, fussing about weight, and training. Paul thought we were missing the point: "The bottom line for hard alpinism," he said, "is you have to want to go up more than you want to go down, isn't it?"

* * *

First thing in the morning of our fourth day, Josh went to remove his headlamp. It was a micro LED lamp with a retractable elastic cable, much like a slingshot. It moved like a slingshot when it slipped from his grasp and disappeared. At least we still had the good torch, and the summit had to be close…. We packed, and Josh set off around the corner to the left. Much of the climbing blurs together in my mind, but there were steep cracks, icy cracks, tension traverses, runouts, and sections of snow—some climbed in rock shoes, some in "ice gear" (since it looked easy from below, we'd gone with Gore-Tex sneakers and ultralight aluminum strap-on crampons). The gendarmes seemed endless, and at one belay along the side, while Josh alternately aided and ran out steep rock on the face to regain the ridge, I scraped my fingers into a runnel of snow-ice tucked in a crack and brought the crystals to my mouth. Dabs of red spotted the white from the jam-like blood of my fingertips scraped raw over the past four days.

Smooth, overhanging rock receded from view, down both faces falling from the ridge. It would be suicide to rappel. I looked to the storm clouds brewing far enough to the south, then down at the speck that was base camp, 7,000-feet below, with simple detachment, and sucked on more snow.

Several hours later I sat, breathless at 20,000 feet, on a mound of sugar snow where we found the first sign of the big-wall teams who'd finished along the upper reaches of our ridge. In 1999 Russian and American teams made heavily-publicized, nearly month-long ascents of the face that dropped like a plumb line below us to the left. Their routes started up the gully from base camp on broken slabs, before tackling the impressive big-wall portion and, finally, the ridge. Josh volunteered to take over leading, and I lowered him to a notch, from where he traversed to the base a steep off-width, too wide for our gear. He placed a tipped-out cam that rattled out as he pulled into a layback and fired 20 feet to a belay ledge. Above, it looked blank and snow mushrooms capped the ridge. I now wonder about our mental states, as our photos make me think we should have gone straight up. No matter, Josh set off leading again, traversing around the corner onto the big-wall face in a mix of free and aid. Far to his left, Josh saw the only feature: a thin vein of ice in a right-facing corner. He connected desperate pendulums, lowers, and hard free traversing, eventually balancing himself below the corner. For his last gear, 35 feet above him and 25 feet to his right, he'd equalized a knifeblade piton and bird beak. He delicately removed his crampons from his harness, strapped the left one to his rock shoe, put his kiddie-toy of an ice axe (a "third tool" with the shaft cut down to save weight) in his left hand, and started climbing. He tapped up thin ice on his left side and smeared invisible dimples and crimped tiny edges on his right. After reaching the level of the dubious gear far to his right, he ran out another 35 difficult feet to a good ledge.

I swung around the corner and lowered out twice. Then, while I was freeing our stuck tag line, one of Josh's few pieces blew out. Soon after, I dropped my belay device. The remaining gear was easy to clean: I removed the knifeblade, lowered out on the beak, and jugged cleanly up the vertical big-wall face. Jugging the pitch blew my mind: the most incredible lead I've ever seen. I've since been asked if I think that lead was boldness or stupidity. To me, it's simple: calculated boldness with incredible skill. When I run it out on 5.9, nobody says I'm being stupid. We'd done enough sketchy climbing, tension traverses, and lower-outs already to make retreat improbable, terribly complex at best. Josh's crux lead sealed it. The way out was up and over. Besides, we had no reason to retreat. We contemplated continuing that evening—the hump above had to be the summit—but the spacious ledge was too tempting with nightfall so close.

We strung our eight-ounce emergency tarp close overhead for warmth, and watched the sun set from our room with a perfect view up-glacier to The Flame. Josh and Brian McMahon had made the first ascent of the incredible solitary spire in 2002. Almost everyone thought they were crazy for going that soon after 9/11, but their families and close friends supported them, and in Pakistan they were met with kindness and warmth. On our climb in 2004 Josh lay on the ledge, unable to stop looking at The Flame. They had endured 40 days of continual rain at base camp when finally, with only a week remaining in their trip, the skies cleared, and they were rewarded for their patience. Josh, only 23 at the time, led the final pitch, a 165-foot runout of 5.10+ slab to gain the narrow summit pinnacle.

As night fell, despite our exhaustion and thirst, we were optimistic. Summit: first thing in the morning. I ate an energy bar for dinner and chased it with an icicle. The clouds from the southwest were drawing closer. I cultivated a small pile of ice chips, placed it by my head and lay down for our fourth night.

Josh Wharton employing wishful thinking at the second bivy…their only remaining fuel was inside the lighter in his hand. *Kelly Cordes*

* * *

In the morning I traversed left past an overhanging chimney and onto an unprotectible slab of snow that grew thinner, barely covering the rock. My feet started to skate. I downclimbed, back to the chimney. In the back was a runnel of ice, and I arm-barred with one hand and swung my axe into the ice with the other, chopped through the overhanging cornice, and flopped onto the snow mound above. No summit. Shit. I brought Josh up and he sat in the snow while I sketched, almost fell, and made a hook move on a short steep rock face that led to sugar snow on another mound. Not the summit. I continued for another three pitches, up, down, around, climbing rock and snow, sometimes straddling the knife-edge like a happy cowboy until I scraped my way up a snowy slab onto the Southwest Summit. Without thinking I climbed over the top and down the other side to set an anchor. I was too exhausted—too focused—to notice our surroundings, what must be one of the grandest views on earth: Masherbrum, Gasherbrum IV, K2, and incredible unnamed, unclimbed spires rising from rubble-strewn glaciers snaking up and down the valleys like the rivers of ice that they are. It was around noon on our fifth day. We didn't even celebrate the top.

We rapped too hastily, too sick of the ridge, and so eager for safety that we nearly missed the hanging glacier that was crucial to our descent. The face below grew smooth, threatening to suck us into the overhanging big-wall abyss wrapping around from the right. We tensioned hard left on every rappel, cleaning ice from cracks and stuffing them with cams for anchors, but, as the wall blanked out, anchors became sparse. One rappel anchor was an RP backed by two shitty knifeblades. After five rappels we hit the hanging glacier. I began pulling our skinny rope, but as the other end rose off the glacier and up the wall, suddenly the ropes wouldn't budge. It was a sinister and challenging prank to remind us we weren't done yet, and the mountains are always in charge. I pulled harder.

"Shit," I said. "They're stuck."

Josh slumped forward and leaned his head against the ice. He mumbled a simple response: "Fuck."

We both pulled with all our remaining strength. Nothing. With the other end unsecured, dancing in the wind, we had no choice. There was 70 feet of our tag line beside us, so we cut it. Two-thousand five-hundred feet of 40- to 60-degree crevasse- and serac-riddled hanging glacier remained to traverse and descend. Below us, the glacier's bottom calved off a cliff for 3,000 feet. Our "disaster-style" "safety fifth!" ice gear and sneakers, with no snow or ice pro, meant one thing only. Before continuing, I stated the obvious: "No mistakes." If we stayed roped-in and one of us fell, barring the improbable one-person save, we'd likely both plummet. With little discussion, we tied in and continued down together.

* * *

A couple of tense hours later we collapsed on the terminal end of the glacier and guzzled water like two men who'd been lost in a desert. Suddenly I noticed how horribly I reeked of ammonia, and the pungent chemical-like taste in my mouth. It was our first water in over 48 hours, bubbling from the bottom of the glacier at 17,000 feet. I recalled my physiology, retained from many years ago: the nitrogen component of amino acids is stripped away and excreted as ammonia, so that the carbon skeletons can be metabolized. This happens when the body is forced to consume its own structural tissues for energy.

We soon scrambled—staggered, really—to a ledge atop the Trango Gully. All that remained was a 4,000-foot slog down to base camp. I gazed back up at Great Trango, slowly being engulfed by clouds. The weather window slammed shut like a door hitting us in the ass. Rain and snow would fall in a few hours. I was still in a hyper-focused, trying-to-keep-it-together state when Josh's words of congratulations and our embrace broke my trance. Inside I shifted, feeling a surge of emotion. It seemed fitting that it was only us, no hype, no web reports to send or sat-phone dispatches to make (especially since we didn't have one). There was, however, one spectator. As we stumbled down the loose gully, a lone figure, clad in tattered clothes and sandals, scrambled rapidly up toward us. It was Ghafoor, coming with the biggest smile I've ever seen and a huge hug for us both. I felt tears, like I was crying, but my body spared no moisture. Ghafoor placed glittery ribbons around our necks and grabbed our pack—he refused to let us take it down, "No, no, Sir, I carry, I carry!" (no matter what we said, he insisted on calling us "Sir") and set off at high speed, hopping over boulders, to prepare one helluva hot meal. Ghafoor had told us that he'd be watching from camp through our binoculars, though we doubted he'd be able to see us. Once we were high on the ridge, he hustled out to the nearest outpost, bought some Coca-Cola and, somehow, found some cheesy party favors. He and Karim had strung our camp with banners and home-made congratulatory signs, spelled in wonderfully broken English, and built stone-lined walkways from our tents to the cook-tent.

* * *

I lay around camp sleeping, resting, eating, drinking, trying to hydrate and recover, though I couldn't seem to regain my energy. My thoughts were mostly introspective, but I made some notes about our ascent:

We brought two ropes: a 9.1mm lead line and a 7.9mm tag line. We did no fixing. We carried no bolt kit. We started climbing at 9 a.m. on July 24 and summited at noon on July 28. The second jugged with the pack where it was steep, which was probably half of the route. We clipped fixed gear when we saw it—mostly belay bolts, and up to a half-dozen protection bolts—but did not use any of the fixed ropes abandoned from prior attempts. (After our descent we scrambled up and cleaned one that someone had abandoned at the start.) We carried off all of our garbage (empty fuel canister and food wrappers) but left a few protection pieces fixed along with five rap anchors (many cams) and, unfortunately—my only regret of our climb—our ropes that got stuck on our last rappel.

Our route starts on the lower right of the broad southwest buttress, at just under 4,000m, and climbs to the Southwest Summit (sometimes called West, ca 6,237m-6,250m depending on the map) of Great Trango Tower. This was 17 pitches beyond the highest traces we found from previous attempts. Josh led the hardest pitches, including five that were 5.11 (one included M6). My hardest leads were 5.10+ (and M5), and not as serious as Josh's. With 60m ropes and simul-climbing a handful of pitches on the lower half, we climbed 54 pitches. Twenty-five of the pitches were 5.10 or harder. I led 30 and Josh 24, but Josh was indisputably the ropegun, leading the hardest and most dangerous pitches. We named our route Azeem Ridge and rated it 5.11R/X M6 A2. Azeem is an Urdu word that means "great," in size or stature, and, more importantly, "great" as a greeting of fondness and respect between people. Azeem accurately summarizes our feelings about the wonderful people we met in the northern areas of Pakistan, people from Pakistan and several European countries. The widespread fear and propaganda at home is absurd and carries an ugliness disturbingly similar to racism in its de facto portrayal of all people in one entire region of the world as "bad." People need to quit listening to the Fox News and Bush regime drivel and do a little thinking for themselves.

* * *

One week later the weather cleared, so we trudged back up the heinous 4,000-foot choss gully to bivy at the col below Trango (a.k.a Nameless) Tower. I grew increasingly angry with a large Korean team—there had been a party of six attempting, unsuccessfully, to siege the Slovenian Route—as I collected their garbage, halfway filling a large plastic bag that, ironically, I found laying in the rubble. We had previously cleaned up much of their garbage (not all of it was theirs, but the frequent Korean lettering was a give-away) when hiking up and down the gully to acclimatize. How were they unable to carry away their trash, when there were six of them going up and down repeatedly for a month? The next day, on the Slovenian Route, we climbed to the Shoulder Camp (a.k.a. Sun Terrace), about one-third up the tower, by early afternoon and bivied. This camp is disgusting, a mess of garbage, too much for us to carry down. Some impact by climbers is unavoidable, emergencies happen, and safety issues arise. But I can't understand abandoning fixed lines everywhere and leaving piles of garbage. What was their excuse? I've assumed that everyone is drawn to the mountains for the same reasons I am: for their beauty, their magnificence. On Trango I realized that I was wrong.

We retreated early afternoon on the second day. At most belays we had found fresh garbage, with Korean labels, stuffed into cracks. We cleaned most of it, despite not coming to Pakistan to be their maid service. Anyway, according to our topo, we were somewhere near pitch 22, with a few steep pitches remaining—the cracks were icy and the going would be slow—followed by a few moderate ice and mixed pitches to reach the summit. The climbing itself had been beautiful: spectacular granite with great protection, on such an incredible spire. Storm clouds were coming in, but we have no excuses, the clouds were not upon us yet. We would have had to spend the night out if we continued, and we simply didn't want it badly enough, not then.

* * *

On August 16, after saying goodbye to our friends in base camp, we started walking toward Paiju. I couldn't stop turning around to catch another glimpse of Great Trango Tower in its massive and nearly incomprehensible grandeur. Our failure on Trango-Nameless didn't really bother me. Thoughts of Great Trango drifted through my mind, and I couldn't help but close my eyes, feel light, and notice the smile on my face.

I didn't care as much as I might have about the mysterious health funk I'd developed, smelling of ammonia during any physical exertion and having erratic swings in blood sugar. It continued on the trek out, and for months I'd be tired, napping, sleeping late, unable—or maybe just uninterested—in doing anything demanding. Maybe I'm getting old, or maybe I'm just enjoying an excuse to be lazy. Maybe I just can't stop thinking about those days on the Azeem Ridge, days that are blurry, surreal, and crystal clear all at the same time. Those four and a half days when Josh and I wanted to go up more than we wanted to go down.

SUMMARY OF STATISTICS

> AREA: Pakistan Karakoram, Trango Valley
>
> ASCENT: Southwest ridge of Great Trango Tower, Azeem Ridge (7,400' vertical, 5.11R/X A2 M6). Kelly Cordes and Josh Wharton. July 24-28, 2004.

A NOTE ON THE AUTHOR:

Kelly Cordes, 36, is assistant editor of The American Alpine Journal and lives in Estes Park, Colorado.

Kelly and Josh, near the bottom of the Nameless Gully descent after climbing the Azeem Ridge. Ghafoor, their friend and cook, had been watching them with binoculars from base camp, killed "Sheepy" for their celebration dinner, and hiked up the gully to meet them with refreshments and party favors. *Cordes-Abdul collection*

ARCTIC RAGE

Pushing through the storm on the east face of the Moose's Tooth, Alaska.

BEN GILMORE

The Moose's Tooth, showing Arctic Rage. *Kevin Mahoney*

"Ben, come out quick! You're missing sun hour!" Kevin's voice was muffled, as I was down in the snow cave chowing hot dogs, tortillas, and Nutella. Inertia was strong down in our subterranean home where gluttony and vices prevailed, but I couldn't miss the precious 50 minutes each day when the sun briefly shone on our camp. We were dug into a tight cirque on the Buckskin Glacier in late March, and only one small gap in the huge walls surrounding us allowed the sun's brief peek. It was turning out to be a bitterly cold and snowy trip.

I ducked out of the hole, groaning from a stiff back and squinting at the weak, cloud-filtered sunbeams reflecting everywhere on fresh powder. The awesome east face of Moose's Tooth loomed directly above us, and the line of our failed attempt a few days earlier was looking snowy and spindrifted.

"Man, we should get back up there," Kevin said. "We could be climbing right now!" This was Kevin's usual sun hour pep talk. He was driven on this trip. We were feeling some extra motivational angst for this climb after coming away empty-handed from three prior expeditions. Now we were three-quarters of the way through our sixteen days out here and morale was at a low point. We had been battered back once already, and it looked like we would have time for only one more go. Looking up at the massive face, I felt the familiar bowel flutter of intimidation.

"Don't you think it's a little too cold?" came my feeble response. "Maybe we should let the face shed a bit after all that new snow. I already had some whisky today. Let's wait another day and see if it warms up." This had been my voice-of-reason response for four days. But the subtext really said, "I'm not sure I want to go back up there, Kevin. Can't I just make you another hot dog?"

Kevin Mahoney and I had met in the mountains while we were both working as instructors for NOLS. We started climbing together in 1998 on a trip to Mt. Combatant in British Columbia's Waddington Range. I wasn't much of an ice climber back then, but our shared NOLS expedition training, love for classic rock, and taste for cheap beer made it obvious on that first trip that we had a good thing going. We've been on seven expeditions together since then and have had some surprising successes on big Alaskan routes. We're a good team, and Kevin has Jedi powers on ice. It's been one of those magical climbing partnerships that drives us both to climb above our best when we're tied in together. Besides, Kevin is always game to lead the hardest pitches, and I can shovel snow and break trail with the best of them.

We'd stood beneath the east face of the Moose's Tooth before, in September 2001, with Scott DeCapio, Steve House, and Mike Wood. On that trip the huge face just looked too difficult, so instead we climbed a great new route with House on the southeast face. But Kevin and I had looked at each other with raised eyebrows, and we stored the east-face potential in our memories. The face was no longer one of Alaska's "last great problems," as it was known in the 1970s and 80s, but there had only been two routes done on the immense wall. The first was the Dance of the Woo-Li Masters (VI 5.9 WI4+ A4), put up alpine style in 1981 by Jim Bridwell and Mugs Stump. Bridwell came back in 2001 with Spencer Pfingsten to add a variation called the Beast Pillar (VII A5 5.10b WI4+ M6).

It was a photo by Paul Roderick in Alpinist 4 that brought the idea back to us. It was exactly what we were looking for: a big unclimbed ice route in a beautiful remote setting right next to a fat base camp with no acclimatization necessary. The idea of climbing hard alpine routes has always been thrilling back in a warm house looking at photos over a few beers. That's how we have always picked climbing objectives; Kevin usually lures me in with ideas for some sick and challenging climbs, and then we look at photos and pick the one that looks the most compelling. In the comfort of home, with beer in my bloodstream, I'm always psyched to go along on anything. With the help of a Mugs Stump Award we were on our way.

Upon landing on the glacier on March 19, we immediately put in six hours of hard labor digging a huge snow cave for our base camp. It became the perfect kitchen/party room for decadent base-camp living. We styled it out with wide standing counters, bench seating, shelving, and a well-stocked entertainment center. The next morning we woke up amped with clear weather and frosty mixed big walls all around us, so we skied around on the glacier scoping

Ben Gilmore entering the Chimney Pitch, which marks the start of their new route after it branches off from Dance of the Woo-Li Masters. *Kevin Mahoney*

different angles of the route we wanted to try. The line looked huge and amazing. We could see ice in the back of dark chimneys that we hoped would connect all the way. I felt a stomach-churning mix of excitement and dread as I looked up through my binoculars. Strong forces told me to run back and hide in the cave for the duration, but a stronger pull toward the adventure and unknown kept me smiling. We skied back to camp to spend the rest of the afternoon racking gear, listening to music, and generally partying. That night I lay awake with a nervous racing pulse, listening to Kevin snore comfortably.

The next day by sunrise we had soloed 1,000 feet of snow and were pulling out the ropes for the first steep ground we would share with the Dance of the Woo-Li Masters. The weather was warm, and we labored on a Stairmaster workout from hell, post-holing and dragging ropes through deep, sticky snow. Just above the area where Bridwell and Stump's route traversed left, our wall reared up at steep angles broken by deep chimneys and smears of ice. I was still drooling and hyperventilating from the approach pitches, so thankfully I handed Kevin the first block of the real deal. He was soon out of sight, burrowed deeply into a tight, icy chimney. Occasionally, groans of despair would echo from the chimney, but the rope moved steadily. I judged that it was a hard lead by Kevin's constant grunting and sounds of crampons and picks sparking on rock. I was happy to top rope the pitch. This was serious stuff, and the climbing was fantastic with mixed stemming and just barely enough thin ice and protection. Kevin had found some protection in the rock, but most of it was the kind that you clip with a screamer and try to forget about. The ice was great for tool placements but generally too airy and snowy for decent screws. It often required serious mind control and careful weight distribution over four points to prevent shearing out one tool or crampon.

Ben Gilmore in the Duplex Bivy (the first bivy). *Kevin Mahoney*

Kevin's next pitch offered delicate and unconsolidated snow-ice leading up to a stance underneath a massive snow mushroom. Cold shadows had enveloped us 2,000 feet up the wall, and it was time to find something flat enough to lie down on. Kevin was frantically digging to find protection when suddenly one of his tools sheared into an empty void. We couldn't believe our incredible luck. After two more hours Kevin had hollowed out the snow mushroom, and we were brewing up in a spacious two-chambered bivy we dubbed the Duplex. That night I lay awake again all jumpy with nervous anticipation of leading out on the first block the next day. Kevin slept peacefully.

As we cooked and got ready in the morning, our bivy was a steamy orb brilliantly lit up by a red alpenglow that illuminated the thin walls of the snow mushroom. Blue skies outside gave me confidence to explore above, so I put the rack on and tunneled through to stand on the roof of our cave. Stretching from the roof of the mushroom, I was able to get a good stick in squeaky névé. Grateful that I'd opted to haul the pack on this pitch, I pulled onto the steep smear and carefully picked my way up to the base of a thinly iced corner. My picks bottomed out on rock all the way up the corner. I screamed two or three times, on the micro-edge of falling, but somehow I whimpered my way through and finished what we named the Balcony Exit Pitch (WI6+R) at a good stance. Kevin followed it quickly with his pack on.

Everything was getting drippy on us in the direct sun and warm temps. I debated with myself about asking Kevin to lead the next pitch, but I decided it would be just too chicken to do only one pitch for my "block." So I headed up onto the slushy vertical wall toward a dark off-width looming above. From the outside the off-width looked like it was filled with ice, but when I got a view from underneath I could see that it was only a thin film of frozen snow bridging the gap with fully formed cavity hoar crystals growing inside.

"Oh shit," I thought.

I got a sling around a chockstone in the base of the off-width for protection and stemmed up to see if any ice would hold my weight. Four or five times I flailed a bit higher, but my tools only sheared through into nothing. Rock climbing the verglassed foot-wide crack was out of the question, and I didn't fully trust the chockstone, so I had Kevin lower me back to the belay. It was still early with nice weather holding, so I convinced Kevin to go up and give it a try. He made many valiant attempts, hooking micro-edges and reaching higher in the crack only to slice through more loose crystals.

I lowered him down. We were both bummed. We'd never been shut down by something we couldn't at least aid. Suddenly, the day felt late and we thought of how little fuel was left for this limited progress. We noticed a vague line to the right of the off-width that might go with some aid, but we had already committed to going down. Four hours of rappelling and down-climbing to the glacier below brought us into a cold hell of failure and despair.

Down and out in base camp. Our decision to retreat proved to be a good one the next day when we woke up to heavy snow and much colder temperatures. The next six days were a blur of bad weather and cave time. Temperatures were in the negative numbers. The walls around us were plastered with snow, and the whole cirque remained clouded with a mist of spindrift. Kevin was like a caged animal, pacing back and forth in camp. We packed the runway each day to keep our chances for a pick-up alive. The angst-meter was reading extreme. I almost had to slip Percocet into Kevin's food to keep him down for a few days.

The weather improved slightly on March 29, so we skied out to try another objective, this one on the Bear's Tooth. We were pushing it going out so soon after the new snowfall, but with time short we went anyway. As we started up the snow cone underneath the face a cracking explosion sounded high above. An avalanche was coming down on us, but we couldn't tell how big yet. Our attempts to run out of its path were ludicrous. I tangled in my sled and fell down. Luckily, we were hit only by a powder blast, and we skied back to camp with our tail between our legs.

Now it was really getting down to the wire. The weather was better, but still snowy. I couldn't keep Kevin at bay with hot dogs any longer, so we decided to go up no matter what the next day, March 31. We would try our original objective and attempt to aid around the off-width.

In the morning we broke trail through two feet of fresh powder to reach the wall. There was still a mist of spindrift in the cirque, but it didn't seem to be snowing hard any more. Temps were much colder this time around, and our hands froze climbing the snow on the first 1,500 feet. There were advantages to going back up into now-familiar terrain, but it also meant that we had to re-lead each other's pitches. They had been hard enough following on a top rope already!

I completely lost my shit trying to find an anchor after leading Kevin's first chimney. I was cold, stressed out, had low blood sugar, and the constant spindrift made it hard to find the thin cracks we had used earlier for an anchor. Kevin waited patiently below while I screamed through every obscenity I knew until I was hoarse. Finally, an hour later, I had an anchor in place and Kevin was on his way up. I was so shamed by my psychotic raging breakdown that I managed to dig deep and lead Kevin's next delicate pitch up to the Duplex bivy.

That night was bitterly cold. I hung my wristwatch computer in the cave to record the temperature, but it soon faded and stopped working in the cold. Twenty-degree down sleeping bags were not cutting it. Kevin's side of the bivy had sustained major damage to the roof, so it was open to constantly pouring spindrift. Peeking out from my sleeping bag in the morning, I could see that he had been completely buried in snow overnight. As I started to get up to dig him out, the mound he was under cracked, and he butted his way out, gasping for air. He had been sleeping packed under two feet of spindrift!

We were both glad to leave that bivy but concerned about whether the aid around the off-width would go. Kevin fired off the Balcony Exit pitch without a problem in the brittle conditions. He was determined to do anything necessary on the Off-width Bypass Pitch. Forty feet of initial steep mixed climbing led to another 40 feet of gear-pulling and A2. We were elated. We had pulled around the off-width section and now moved on above, into new terrain.

I followed the pitch freestyle, hooking gear with my tools and taking tension with the rope. At the anchor we high-fived and reveled in climbing past our previous high point. Above us, a perfect runnel of WI 5 ice dripping out of a tight chimney tapered out of sight far above. Luckily, it was my lead since there was nowhere for the belayer to get protected under

Ben Gilmore starting the first pitch in the morning by tunneling through the roof and climbing up above onto the Balcony Exit Pitch (WI 6+R). *Kevin Mahoney*

this pitch. The Pipeline Pitch, as we ended up calling it, turned out to be the best 200-foot stretch of ice either of us had ever climbed. The perfect natural feature tapered from a three-foot chimney to a three-inch crack before disappearing and crossing over into another crack. I was having a blast on the lead, but my icefall gave Kevin a bloody beating down at the unprotected Pummeling Station belay.

Three more WI 4 pitches and some simulclimbing brought us to a small snow fluting that we investigated for snow-cave potential. It was thick enough to hollow out a nice, low-ceilinged cave. Now we had a secure bivy site, the Cocoon Cave, 3,000 feet up the wall where we could rest before and after a summit bid. Our down sleeping bags were wet and filling with ice clumps, but we snuggled in for a decent sleep with a starry sky outside.

The weather had changed 180 degrees by morning, and we woke to a full blizzard outside. We were in a new world, completely engulfed in spindrift. I took one look out the cave door and thought for sure we'd either wait it out or go down. Kevin was already outside stacking ropes.

Kevin Mahoney leading Shotgun Alley in full conditions on summit day. *Ben Gilmore*

"Uh, Kevin, what do you think about this weather?" I called out meekly. "Maybe we should talk about this a little."

"We have to give it a try," Kevin yelled over the wind. "This could be my last trip for a long time!"

"No problem, I wasn't saying I wanted to go down or anything," I lied. "Just wanted to make it a conscious decision. I've never kept going up in anything like this before!"

Kevin had the critical drive and leadership at that moment to keep us going. I decided to commit, and we were off and running against the tide of spindrift flowing down the face. Kevin entered a narrow couloir we dubbed Shotgun Alley on the second pitch, and he disappeared into the raging whiteout above. Communication was impossible, and the spindrift was so intense that Kevin couldn't stop to place an anchor. An unspoken trust was between us, so I climbed when the rope came tight. We simulclimbed until the 90-degree alley widened and the spindrift eased off. The whole time we couldn't look up at our tools, and the spindrift pressed heavily on our heads and shoulders, so we just swung blindly and climbed by feel.

The route followed spindrift-polished 70- to 90-degree couloirs for eight more pitches, all the way up to the overhanging summit cornices. Kevin led the whole day, and I followed with the pack. He found a gap in the cornices, and we mantled onto a flat area we figured was the summit. The storm was gaining force. It was hard to stand up in the strong winds and vertigo created by the whiteout. We feared getting lost now that we were on horizontal ground. We screamed congratulations, celebrated with a few quick photos, then downclimbed through the cornices and started the long journey down the route.

After nine rappels we bivied in the Cocoon Cave. Our bags were full of ice, but our spirits were high and we didn't care. The next morning the storm had slowed, so I took the rack and started rappelling down the rest of the face. My mission was to find anchors as fast as I could, but the snow and bottoming cracks made it difficult. I kept one tool out for the descent and beat half an inch of metal off the pick scraping and chopping in the search for one decent piece of gear per anchor. Eight hours later, we finally crossed the bergschrund and pulled the ropes for the last time. We had stashed our skis nearby, but now they were buried under tons of new snow. An hour and a half of digging and searching uncovered nothing, so we gave up and waded in snow up to our waists back to base camp.

We dug out the tent and cave from under three feet of new powder. It was great to be down, even better to have succeeded on the new route, but we feared now that we would be stuck for a while if the plane couldn't land with all the soft snow. It would have been nice to sleep in that next morning, but we woke up with discipline and spent six hours boot-packing a runway with the hope that the weather would allow a pick-up. Luckily, the skies cleared and our efforts paid off. Later that day we were drinking beers in Talkeetna, basking in the afterglow.

SUMMARY OF STATISTICS:

AREA: Alaska Range

ASCENT: Arctic Rage (4,500 feet, VI WI6+R A2) on the east face of The Moose's Tooth (10,355 ft.), Ben Gilmore and Kevin Mahoney, March 31-April 3, 2004.

A NOTE ABOUT THE AUTHOR:

Ben Gilmore learned how to climb while attending college in Maine. After graduating he began working for NOLS in 1994. Currently he is AMGA certified and guides for Exum Alpine Ascents Inernational, and International Mountain Climbing School. He has made first ascents from Fitz Roy to McKinley, climbed A5 on El Cap, and hiked the Lions Head Trail on Mt. Washington (20 laps in winter).

Kevin and Ben celebrating on the summit in a white out.
Ben Gilmore

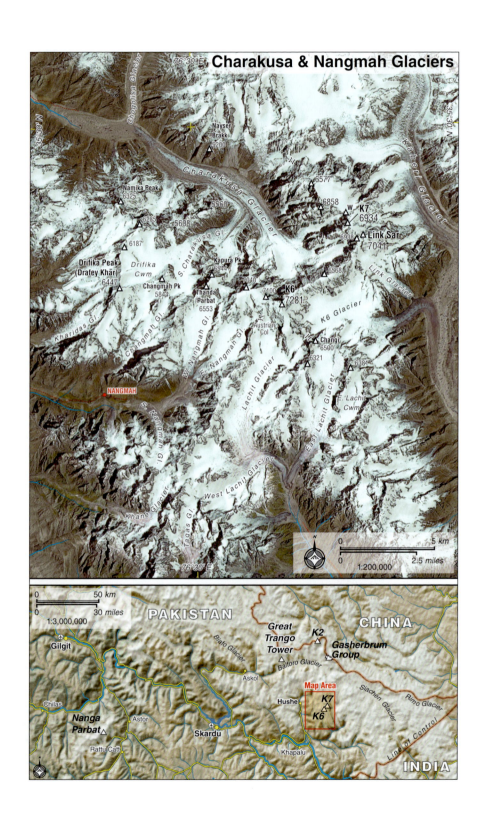

Charakusa & Nangmah Glaciers

76°30′E

35°30′N

Chogolisa Glacier

Kaberi Glacier

Charakusa Glacier

Nayser
Brakk
5200

6577

6858   W   K7
                 6934

Namika Peak
6325

5560   6938△   Link Sar
                                          7041

6265
5608

6187   Kapura Pk.
                             5544

Drifika Peak   S. Charakusa Gl.   6568
(Drafey Khar)   Drifika
6447   Cwm   7040   Link Glacier
         Changmah Pk   Thanda   7100   K6
         5844   Parbat   7281
Kharidas Gl.   6553   K6 Glacier

                     Austrian
                     Col   Changi
                                            6500
                              6321

              Changmah Gl.   6384

NANGMAH   E. Lachit
                                                    Cwm

         S. Nangmah Gl.   W. Nangmah Gl.   E. Nangmah Gl.   Lachit Glacier   East Lachit Glacier

                              West Lachit Glacier

Khane Glacier

Tagas Gl.

76°30′E

N

0   5 km

0   2.5 miles

1:200,000

---

0   50 km

0   30 miles

1:3,000,000

PAKISTAN   CHINA

                 Great
                 Trango   K2
                 Tower
Gilgit   Gasherbrum
         Biafo Glacier   Group

                 Baltoro Glacier

         Askol

Chilas   Map Area

                 Hushe   K7
Nanga   K6
Parbat   Siachen Glacier   Rimo Glacier

              Astor
                    Skardu   Line of Control

Rattu Catt.   Khapalu

                                                    INDIA

KARAKORAM SUMMER

A prolific month of new-routing in the Charakusa Valley, Pakistan.

STEVE HOUSE

Steve Swenson and Steve House on the summit of Nayser Brakk after climbing Tasty Talking. K6 and Kapura are in the background. *Marko Prezelj*

SEPTEMBER 2003, HUSHE VILLAGE, BALTISTAN

As I clean, dry, and pack expedition supplies into plastic drums, I review the climbing season that just ended, highlighted by a near-miss on K7 (6,934 meters) and the first ascent of Hajji Brakk (5,985 meters) (see AAJ 2004, ppg. 95-105). Packing the drums into a stone-and-mortar hut that I rent each year in Hushe Village, I take careful notes for next year's return. Five jugs for kerosene. Two pressure cookers. Folding table and eight chairs. Twenty-seven foam sleeping mats. Five dome tents. Two large canvas cooking tents. Hundreds of other things that an expedition requires, things that a group of Karakorum regulars, including myself, have accrued since 1999. The list fills 12 pages. I leave a lot in Pakistan, but I know I'll be using it.

JUNE 2004, HUSHE VILLAGE, BALTISTAN

Back again, on a sunny, dew-kissed morning in Hushe Village, in the foothills of the Karakoram. This time it's with Marko Prezelj (from Slovenia), Bruce Miller, Doug Chabot, Steve Swenson, and Jeff Hollenbaugh (all from the US). This is the best group of people that I could ever imagine going to the mountains with. Collectively we've been on more than 100 expeditions. Everyone is fit, healthy, and happy, and we hold permits for four mountains: unclimbed K6 West (7,021 meters); unclimbed Kapura Peak (6,544 meters); magnificent K7 (6,934 meters); and monstrous Nanga Parbat (8,125 meters). The first three peaks all lay within striking distance of the K7 base camp and should provide acclimatization for the end-goal, Nanga Parbat, which lies some 160 kilometers south of the K7 group.

My recent and frequent experience in the area have made me the logical choice to organize and lead the group. And things work like clockwork right into base camp. Soon we are stalking the scree slopes near base camp, hiking the Charakusa Glacier, and bouldering. The Charakusa Valley is perfectly suited to this type of expedition, with fun and interesting ways to acclimate. And there is nearly every type of climbing, from superb granite bouldering to super-alpine objectives to be reserved for the twenty-second century.

Nine days after arriving in base camp (at about 4,200 meters), I belay Marko and Steve up the final pitch of the superb route we name Tasty Talking. Of the 11 pitches, 10 of them have come in at 5.10, and the final pitch up an arête to the summit stands as one of the most memorable 5.8 leads of my life.

Two days later, Steve, Doug, and I cross the Charakusa Glacier to the Drifika Glacier. We set up our tent on a moraine on the right side of the Drifika, and the next day we ascend easy snowslopes on Kapura Peak's southwest flank. These slopes steepen to 50 degrees and turn to ice, so we get out our ice tools and gain a large snow ledge that we follow back to the mountain's west ridge.

At the ridge we negotiate a tricky section of seracs. We rope up and, with Steve leading, simul-climb for two ropelengths across snow-covered ice. On the far side we elect to keep the ropes on, and I lead off through deep snow to an eventual bivouac site at 6,160 meters, a place protected from the southwest wind. The sun sets on our last clear day. The views of Masherbrum, K2, the Gasherbrum group, and Chogolisa make us all feel resolute to spend the summer climbing in the incomparable Karakoram.

We awake to clouds and wind and the fourth of July. Our thoughts are far from watermelon and water sports. Instead, we are focused on getting up this mountain. I sense the need for momentum and grab the rope, tie in, and start off up the snowslopes above camp. After half an hour of trailbreaking I stop at the first technical section and hand the sharp end to Doug. He climbs a fine M4 pitch to the right of the ridgecrest and belays us up. While Doug climbs, Steve expresses concern that he wouldn't get his share of the leads as he felt that he might be the slowest of the three of us. "Well" I say, "in this group if you want to lead, you'd better speak up."

And so it was with assertion that Steve volunteered for the next pitch, a tricky lead along

Nayser Brakk, approximately 18,000 feet, first climbed in 1988 by a British team and repeated, solo, by Galen Rowell in 1998. Tasty Talking and No More Tasty Talking take the southeast ridge (the sharp ridge left of center). *Marko Prezelj*

Kapura Peak from basecamp. The Chabot-House-Swenson + Miller-Prezelj route climbed the right-hand skyline, which they reached from the other side. *Doug Chabot*

the left edge of the ridgecrest. We swap leads a few more times but the higher we get the worse the weather gets. By afternoon it's blowing and snowing hard, and I realize we are on the verge of deciding to descend.

I belay the boys to me and, without allowing a "descent conversation" to begin, grab the rack and start out on the seventh pitch. Higher, the eighth pitch follows a lovely ice runnel past the last visible rock. The next pitch climbs near-vertical Styrofoam-névé, perfect to climb but impossible to protect. I belay off pickets and ice tools under a six-meter overhanging wall. Starting the last pitch, I lever out a cooler-sized chunk of ice from a horizontal crack, then begin arm-barring the ice crack. This leads to steep snow where, with exaggerated breaths, the shafts of my tools sink as deep as I can stab them. The terrain suddenly goes horizontal and I am caught by surprise. With a mixture of joy and astonishment, I yell to Doug and Steve, "we're on the summit!"

They come up and it is true: In the storm we had not been able to discern summit from cloud, but now we can make out the skyline falling away from us to the north and south. Together we stand in the wind atop the giant corniced fin of Kapura Peak's summit.

A careful descent leads us back to camp where we find Marko, Bruce, and Jeff ensconced in their tent. The next morning we head down with Jeff, while Marko and Bruce retrace our route through continued stormy weather to the summit.

Back in camp, I ask our beloved cook Hajji Rasool what "Kapura" means. He giggles into his palms and looks down at his shoes. He is blushing and I am even more curious. Kapura Peak, when translated, means "goat-testicle mountain." We have a long laugh at the fact that our efforts had been for something so ignobly named.

Steve Swenson and Steve House descending Kapura Peak, with the summit in background. *Doug Chabot*

After 26 days in base camp I at last get the chance to make my first serious attempt on K7. The weather breaks and I set out in the afternoon and climb through the rock crux to make a bivouac at 5,200 meters. The next day, July 17, I climb to approximately 6,650 meters but turn back after spending considerable time figuring out how to negotiate the crux at 6,600 meters. I'm faced with less than two hours of light, more than two hours of climbing to the summit, and threatening-looking clouds approaching from the south.

I retreat, for my lightweight tactics don't allow for errors. I am carrying eight pounds of equipment. This includes: 80m x 5mm of rope to rappel, a lightweight harness, seven carabiners, one ice screw, one wire Abalakov-puller, six titanium pitons, three nuts, six slings, one 5m x 5mm cordalette, two ice tools, crampons, a titanium stove and small pot, 12 packages of energy gel, 4,000 calories of powdered energy shake, a headlamp, spare batteries, a three-ounce windshell, a synthetic DAS parka, two pairs of gloves, one pair of mittens, one hat, and a neck gaiter.

On July 24, seven days after my failed attempt, we record an expedition-high barometer reading in base camp, so we split off into three groups. Doug and Bruce awake early and depart to attempt an alpine-style ascent of the original Japanese route on K7. Later, Marko, Jeff, and Steve leave to attempt the west ridge of the unclimbed K7 West. And at five in the afternoon, after a day of napping and snacking, I leave base camp to try my route on the southwest face of K7.

My equipment did not change, though my timing did. This time I intend to make a single-push ascent from base camp. Starting in the afternoon allows me to do the technical rock climbing (5.6-5.10a) down low in the late-afternoon warmth. This leaves the easiest climbing to do in the dark. I plan on a late-morning brew stop around 6,500 meters and then to start the

K7 from Kapura, showing the House solo route on the left, and the Japanese Route on the right, which was alpine-climbed by Chabot and Miller. *Marko Prezelj*

hardest climbing at 6,600 meters fresh and in the warmest part of the day.

The plan works perfectly. The weather is flawless and I climb quickly throughout the night, stopping at mid-morning to brew and eat. I pass the aid crux by eleven, and the early afternoon sees me negotiating new and tedious terrain. I proceed carefully for the last 400 meters to the summit. Short mixed cruxes. Steep snow traverses. One collapsing cornice. At six, two hours before darkness, 100 meters of low-angled but snow-laden slope lies between me and the summit. The snow is waist-deep but I am determined to succeed. At 7:45 I reach the summit of K7, nearly 27 hours after I had started. I snap a few pictures of the crisp Karakoram skyline, carefully flip on my headlamp, and start back down.

I follow my tracks downward for most of the night. At sun-up, below 6,000 meters, I sit down on a small flat spot. Forty minutes later I awake with a very wet seat. At 10:45 I walk into base camp, almost 42 hours after I had left. I enjoy my first can of beer in a month, a welcome gift left by Marko.

Two days later Doug and Bruce return from their successful climb of K7 and the others return from K7 West, having been thwarted by dangerous snow conditions near the summit. On August 1 the porters arrive to take us back to Hushe and eventually Skardu, where we reorganize, sleep, and gorge on salad, apples, and grilled chickens for a week before loading up the jeeps for the Nanga Parbat leg of our Pakistani summer.

Steve Swenson and Jeff Hollenbaugh starting from the second bivi on the northwest ridge of K7 West. *Marko Prezelj*

SUMMARY OF STATISTICS:

AREA: Pakistan Karakoram, Charakusa Valley

ASCENTS:

Nayser Brakk (18,000ft.), southeast ridge: Tasty Talking (600m, III 5.10+). Steve House, Marko Prezelj, and Steve Swenson. June 30, 2004.

Nayser Brakk, southeast ridge: No More Tasty Talking (1,000+m, IV 5.10+). Bruce Miller and Marko Prezelj, June 31, 2004.

Nayser Brakk, British Route: solo ascent by Jeff Hollenbaugh. 5,000m peak immediately down from Nayser Brakk, south buttress: Jeff Hollenbaugh and Bruce Miller. July 1, 2004. Kapura Peak (21,500ft), first ascent, southwest face and west ridge (1,500m, V M4). July 3-4: Doug Chabot, Steve House, and Steve Swenson. July 4-5: Bruce Miller and Marko Prezelj.

Drifika, west ridge, attempt: Steve House, Jeff Hollenbaugh. July 8-11. Rock tower on southern flanks of K7 West, first ascent: Bruce Miller, Marko Prezelj. July 14, 2004.

K7 (6,934m), south face, new route (41:45-hour round trip, 2,400m, VI 5.10- M6 WI4 A2): Steve House, solo. July 24-25, 2004.

Looking down on the crux pitch of House's K7 route.   *Steve House*

K7, third ascent, first alpine style ascent Japanese route, plus new pitches (2,400m, VI M6 WI5+ A1): Doug Chabot and Bruce Miller. July 24-28, 2004.

K7 West (7,040m-unclimbed), northwest ridge, attempt (2,400m, VI M6 WI4): Jeff Hollenbaugh, Marko Prezelj, Steve Swenson. July 24-26, 2004.

Nanga Parbat, Mazeno Ridge, first ascent to intersection with Schell Route at Mazeno Col (6,940m): Doug Chabot and Steve Swenson. August 12-18, 2004.

Nanga Parbat, Direct Rupal Face attempt to 7,500m (VI M5 90° ice). Steve House and Bruce Miller. August 12-17, 2004.

For a more complete summary of the 2004 American-Slovenian expedition to Pakistan, please see Climbs & Expeditions, Pakistan in this Journal.

A NOTE ABOUT THE AUTHOR:

Steve House works as a mountain guide and as an ambassador for Patagonia. He has recently relocated to Bend, Oregon, where he is developing a taste for sport climbing. He has plans to return to Pakistan in the summer of 2005.

The Charakusa team except Prezelj. From left to right: Bruce Chabot, Cpt. Amin Raza, Steve House, Jeff Hollenbaugh, Steve Swenson, Bruce Miller, with Hajji Rasool holding House's birthday cake (his 34th). *Marko Prezelj*

K7 ALPINE STYLE

The Karakoram Summer continues with a rapid second ascent of a 20-year-old route that originally took 40 days to climb, Charakusa Valley, Pakistan.

DOUG CHABOT

Bruce Miller, silent but deadly, with K6 in background. *Doug Chabot*

We were climbing even lighter than we intended. I reached for a cam and realized Bruce had accidentally left two of them at base camp; this was one-fifth of our rack. It was day one, pitch one, already 900 meters up K7. Before the day was out Bruce dropped another, leaving us seven. There's no sense making a climb too easy by carrying more gear than necessary.

Bruce Miller and I had set our sights on the Japanese Route on K7 during one of our recons up the Charakusa Valley. Its golden granite turrets stacked one on top of the other

Bruce Miller low on K7, day one. *Doug Chabot*

looked enticing. The largest of these formations, aptly named the Fortress, is a 300-meter wall that was the crux of the Japanese ascent in 1984 and the high point of a British attempt in 1990. The Japanese took 40 days, using 450 bolts and pitons and 6,500 meters of rope. Bruce and I had three dinners, three fuel canisters, no bolts, and an ever-shrinking rack.

After a spell of bad weather, a false start, and an obsessive amount of re-racks, we left base camp at 3 a.m. on July 24. We were glad to be climbing together again. Over the years Bruce had become my main alpine climbing partner, with trips to Alaska and India under our belts. He's my secret weapon, falling into the "silent but deadly" category.

The first 900 meters consisted of a frightening-looking gully. Avalanches had scoured a 1.5-meter-deep half-pipe that we followed. We soloed upward on frozen snow, anxiously watching the sunrise. We needed to be out of this luge run before the sun warmed the terrain above. At 10 o'clock I was contemplating crossing the gully to easier ground when a huge wet slide launched over the cliffs above us and gouged out the runnel. So much for that idea. Instead, we decided to climb the rock bordering the chute. I grabbed the rack, noted the missing cams, and headed off on the first real pitch of the climb. The rock was high quality, with M6 moves and awkward stemming off the first belay. I led the rest of the day, finally reaching a snowy perch at 5,600 meters where the Japanese had put their Camp II. We expected to see loads of bolts and old fixed line from their climb, but passed only an occasional anchor.

Bruce was nauseous and had not eaten all day, a concern to us both. Additionally, the snow was dangerously soft, and the ice pitches leading to the Fortress were being hammered by slides. We opted to make camp, eat, rest, and leave in the wee hours of the frozen morning. To save weight, we had bought only one sleeping bag for us both. Spooning together, we slept restlessly.

At 2:30 a.m. I began climbing ice and snow to a ridge leading to the Fortress. We watched the sun rise again into a cloudless, breathless sky. We saw Masherbrum and Nanga Parbat for the first time, which further stoked us. A few pitches of M5 A0 climbing brought us to the base

Bruce climbing low on the Japanese route, K7, day one. *Doug Chabot*

of the Fortress, which Bruce aptly described as a "little big wall." We saw where the Japanese climbed, but it was out of the question. With so many bolts at their disposal we envisioned a bolt ladder, but instead they had climbed A3 seams. Not equipped for serious aid, we looked for a line that would go free.

Bruce, who up to this point was more silent than deadly, was feeling better and led off to the right in search of a weakness. Out of view and tucked in a hidden cleft was a 70-meter, Grade V+ ice chimney splitting the steepest part of the Fortress. The walls had no cracks and thus no protection. Bruce grabbed our four ice screws and headed up the meter-wide, occasionally overhanging flow. For the next hour he delicately climbed ice, placing three screws in 70 meters, saving one for the anchor. Sporty. Bruce commented with his dry wit that it is ridiculous to travel halfway around the world to spend only an hour doing the type of climbing he's good at. The next few pitches were mixed, with the crux of K7 being a poorly protected steep corner (M6) that we dubbed "The Miller Come Again Exit." With a new route up the Fortress, the climb was exceeding our expectations.

As the afternoon wore on, the snow got soft and we triggered wet slides. At one point Bruce sent a dump-truck load of snow onto the slope just a meter away from me. I was scared and contemplated how bad it would look for me, an avalanche forecaster, to die in a wet avalanche.

That evening we chopped out a tent platform under a cornice at 6,100 meters. The next morning dawned clear and we began negotiating the massive snow flutes that capped the buttress.

Doug Chabot leading on summit day of K7. *Bruce Miller*

After a traverse we could see that easier, faster climbing was below us. We reached it in five rappels. Two more pitches of ice climbing brought us to a huge bench at the same elevation as our last camp. This plateau was safe and luxurious and we spread our gear out to dry in the afternoon sun. We were going to the summit from here and needed a good rest.

Steve House had soloed K7 by an obvious, mostly unclimbed, line that passed below the Fortress and intersected the Japanese route at this plateau. He left the day after us and we were unsure of his progress until that afternoon when we saw his tracks leading up and then down again. We found out later we missed him by 12 hours.

The next day we were climbing by 2:30 a.m. Ice gave way to snow, and Steve's trailbreaking helped us conserve energy. After snaking along a snowy ridge, we came to a huge rock tower called the Gendarme. The Japanese had pioneered a route up this that involved 10 meters of A1, an ice slot protected by bolts, and then another A1 section. This 50-meter pitch was the key to accessing the upper slopes. Once again, Steve's four previous recons benefited us in routefinding. The pitches were mixed and we saw more evidence of the Japanese: bolt anchors and bleached fixed lines pointed the way.

At 3:03 p.m. Bruce and I stood on the summit; K7's third ascent. We were ecstatic and drank in the views. After a round of high-fives and self-portraits, we started down. Since we had brought only one rope, we were forced to do about 30 half-rope raps. We reached the bottom of the Gendarme by 7:30 and our tent at 11:15. Sleep came easily.

The next morning we descended Steve's route, which required hundreds of meters of downclimbing on ice and setting the occasional rappel. When we finally hit the safety of the glacier, we were elated and relieved to be down.

I have to hand it to the Japanese for their vision and stamina to pull off the first ascent. The fact that they were young and inexperienced university students on their first big climb makes it even more impressive. We found only a fraction of their bolts, and the only fixed rope we saw was on our summit day. My guess is that most of the ropes were avalanched off long

Bruce Miller on mushrooms descending from K7 summit. *Doug Chabot*

ago. The route Bruce and I did was a beautiful line with hard mixed climbing that's worthy of another ascent.

SUMMARY OF STATISTICS

AREA: Pakistan Karakoram, Charakusa Valley

ASCENT: Alpine-style ascent of the Japanese Route on K7 (6,934m) (2,400m, VI A1 M6 WI5+). Significant new pitches added on and below the Fortress. Bruce Miller and Doug Chabot. Four days to the summit, one down; July 24-28, 2004.

A NOTE ABOUT THE AUTHOR:

Born in New Jersey in 1964, Doug Chabot learned how to climb and ski at Prescott College. He migrated north in 1986 and made Bozeman, Montana his home. During the winter months he's director of the Gallatin National Forest Avalanche Center, while in the summer he works for Exum Mountain Guides in Grand Teton National Park.

THE DIRECT RUPAL FACE

Going broomless on Nanga Parbat's 4,000-meter Rupal Face, Pakistan.

BRUCE MILLER

The Rupal Face in the summer of 2003. At about 4,000 meters of vertical gain, the south face of Nanga Parbat is considered the world's biggest alpine wall. (1) Messner-Messner, 1970. (2) House-Miller attempt, 2004 (highpoint marked "x"). (3) Mexican-Polish, 1985 (Carsolie-Heinrich-Kuhuczka-Lobodzinski). *Arne Hodalic*

S teve House and I were two hours out of base camp and already over 600 meters up the new route of a lifetime. What that means on the Rupal Face of Nanga Parbat (8,125 meters) is that we were still below "cowline" and had 3,900 meters to go. In all of climbing, it doesn't get any bigger than the Rupal Face. I broke it down, convincing myself that the first third would be cruiser, a warm-up really, for the upper two-thirds of the face—which, by itself, was 600 meters higher than the biggest wall I'd ever climbed. But as we stepped off the braided network of cow singletrack onto the glacier, I realized that the next 300 meters of warm-up, a snow gully, was in a pile in front of us. On our recon we'd considered the possibility of it sliding. But we'd dismissed it as unlikely and hadn't been too concerned. Our obvious miscalculation—it had run so massively that a couple of hundred meters of it was completely devoid of snow, making it impassible—now seemed almost comic.

I made my first reality adjustment about the wall, which for 20 years now had been an iconic presence for me. In the mid 1980s I had read Reinhold Messner's provocative first book, *The Seventh Grade*. The last chapter recounted his 1970 first ascent of the Rupal Face with his brother Günther. My edition included a photo taken

Steve House beginning the mixed section that empties onto the Merkl Icefield. *Bruce Miller*

in the Merkl Gully of a goggled, snow-plastered Günther. What interested me was the small whiskbroom dangling inconspicuously from his harness. No one had ever told me about whiskbrooms. Armed with that secret Rupal knowledge, I attempted to sweep my way up more than one snow-covered route above my home in Boulder, Colorado. Steve, meanwhile, was gaining more relevant experience. He was actually attempting to climb Nanga Parbat (with ice tools) via the Schell Route as part of the 1990 Slovene expedition. He didn't summit, but the mountain, particularly the Rupal Face, made a lasting impression.

In 2004, while brooms continued to figure more prominently in my life than ice tools, Steve was training and plotting a new line up the center of the Rupal Face. Until a few months before our expedition, Steve had fully intended to solo his direct route. That changed when I learned of Steve's plan and invited myself along.

The shortest road from Skardu to Tarshing, at the base of the Rupal Valley, crosses the Deosai Plains, a grassy plateau reminding me of the Scottish Highlands. What makes the landscape unlike any other is the solitary presence of Nanga Parbat, the ninth-highest mountain in the world. As we dropped into the valleys closer to the peak, the high plains gave way to rolling hills. At one point we stopped where a couple of vans full of Pakistani men had pulled over.

They were taking photos, laughing, and picking flowers on the lush surrounding slopes. That's just the kind of beautiful country it is. It's a place where grown men frolic.

We arrived in Tarshing on August 9, sorted loads, gathered porters, and trekked up to Steve's old Slovene base camp at 3,580m the following day. After the first leg of our trip in the relatively treeless Charakusa Valley, the pine forests of the Rupal Valley felt like coming home. The next day Steve and I walked up to cowline and studied the face for a couple of hours. The upper half was obscured in clouds, but Steve saw enough to convince him I might be of use up there. I had only to see something to dissuade me from going, but I didn't. So, with a lot less discussion than we'd given to the relative merits of *Kill Bill I* and *II*, we committed ourselves to the climb.

On August 12, after a day of sorting gear, we walked out of base camp in tee shirts and tennies. Back at the avalanche debris we opted to climb the rock to the right of the former snow gully. Soloing a couple of hundred meters of 5.4 rock was a great way to start an 8,000m peak. At mid-day we were back in the gully, above where the slide had entered, kicking up 45° snow. There were no more surprises that day, just easy snow and ice that we followed back across the rock to the base of the first significant obstacle at 5,100m.

Early the next morning, after 60 meters of 60° to 70° ice, we were at the base of two runnels. Steve chose the thin right runnel, which appeared more difficult than the rotten left runnel, but offered the possibility of rock pro. He was half-right. The pitch was the hardest of the route

(M5), but he was able to place only a few decent pins. I removed the rest by hand. He led one more pitch that spit us out onto open 50° ice.

The sun had wrapped around by now, warming up the wall and bringing it down on us. Seracs that hung over the enormous right side of the Rupal Face were calving off regularly. We were far enough left, in the center of the face, to be fairly certain we were catching only the windblast of one such release. Still, I swung furiously to anchor myself before the cloud enveloped us. Objects falling from directly overhead were the real concern. Rock frisbees whistled past regularly, and wet snow slurries flowed down like intermittent waterfalls.

By mid-day further progress was out of the question. We set up the bivouac tent at 5,400m on a fin that offered some protection from all but a massive avalanche. Unfortunately, that was a real possibility. A complex serac wall, having the appearance of a benign

Steve House past the main difficulties on day two. *Bruce Miller*   ripple in the photos we'd used for planning, hung unpredictably 450 meters above us. Two hours earlier, while tracing the route, I had watched a torrent of wet snow spill over the imagined exit notch.

My nerves were shot and my anxiety had turned to resignation. "Steve," I said, "this is way outside my window of acceptable risk." I wanted to go down. Though respecting my opinion, he was completely unfazed by the situation. As we talked about options, one of which included him continuing solo, the sun left the face and it quieted down. I agreed that if we could reach the serac wall (where we had originally hoped to bivouac that night) before sunrise, negotiate it, and climb the entire slope above, we wouldn't leave ourselves too exposed. It was a messy decision on my part, but it's been my experience that alpinism is always messy. If I came down with only my bibs soiled I would consider myself lucky.

Our plan for August 14 was so unrealistic that it should have been a disaster…but it wasn't. Our partnership and the route both came together unexpectedly. As always,

Steve House on day three. *Bruce Miller*

on a serious route, I defer to the stronger climber when it's practical. I spent most of the day looking up at one of the strongest. It was no place for niceties such as "Whose lead is it?" We soloed 1,250 meters of mostly 50° to 60° ice that included 15 meters of dead vertical through the serac at sunrise. Steve finished the day leading two pitches that were, thankfully, easier than they had appeared in the planning photos. We were digging out a tent site at 6,750m on the Merkl Icefield before dark. Looking out at the clear Karakoram skyline, it was hard not to be optimistic.

The next morning we didn't get moving until first light. It had been a cold, miserable night sharing one 20° bag. We were dehydrated, our heads ached, our faces were ridiculously swollen from edema. Steve had vomited but reassured me that he often did this at high altitude (somehow this made sense at the time). Additionally, while asleep, his breathing had been disturbingly labored and irregular.

We climbed the southern edge of the Merkl Icefield to a monolithic rock wall that extended all the way over to the Merkl Gully. I led two pitches through an unlikely weakness in the wall. Steve led a third up to a stance, where with mock drama we cut our 70-meter rope in half. Any advantage the extra 35 meters might have provided us on our intended descent down the Schell Route was more than offset by its extra weight. In addition to half the rope, we ditched our two cams, some stoppers, and Steve's helmet.

We labored up another stretch of 50° snow and ice, now carrying the bare minimum we would need to summit and descend the other side. While a significant portion of the route had involved grinding up ice at a 55° angle, the steeper mixed climbing was always intricate enough to keep things interesting. Steve led another two scrappy pitches that were no exception. It was late afternoon when we stopped, exhausted, at the base of the last significant slope (at 7,200m) before the upper Messner Route.

Leaving for the summit early on August 16 we found that snow conditions were slightly better in the pre-dawn hours, but I was still up to my waist in places as I broke trail. Steve was lagging for the first time. As we approached mid-day, the 50° snow turned to ice. Steve's rests and my waits became more frequent. He was clearly having more than a bad day and I was serious-ly concerned. A chest infection, complicated by the altitude, was grinding him to a halt. There had been warning signs, but he had performed so well until now that they'd been easy to ignore.

At the end of the ice I scratched up the first sketchy 60 meters of a jumbled mixed section to put me near the upper Messner Route, above the Merkl Gully. I waited half an hour watching Steve draped over his axe. He was barely moving. Ghosts of past partners were talking to me. I climbed down to Steve and said, "You're going too slow. You're sick. You're not going to get any better here at 7,500." Steve admitted that, yes, he was hurting, but he thought he could recover —we could bivouac just below.

That was the moment I realized I hadn't really known him. Soloing K7, earlier in the trip, Steve had performed like someone without limits, physical or otherwise. It was beyond his understanding that he was, in fact, subject to some of the same limitations as less fanatical climbers. He was making decisions based mainly on the risk of not reaching the summit. The risk of dying was a secondary concern. I listed my priorities in the reverse order. That made us

Steve House descending the lower Messner Route.
Bruce Miller

a partnership perhaps essentially balanced for the Rupal Face, somewhere between bold and crazy. But we were tipping toward the latter. Finally I made the call because I thought, quite simply, he was dying. Reluctantly he accepted my last word: "down."

I quickly descended the 300 meters that had taken us all morning to climb. Steve said he'd be right behind me. He didn't show for an hour and a half. We exchanged some shouts, but I was still worried. The last time I was at that elevation was in 2002 on Ngozumpa Kang II, in Tibet. My partner Mike Bearzi fell to his death descending similar terrain (*AAJ* 2003, pg 116-123). My thoughts wandered to Mike and back to the present. Steve finally arrived and I asked what had taken him so long. "I must have fallen asleep," he answered. I learned later he was suffering from frustration, as much as infection. We continued down, retrieved the other half of our rope, and were back the Merkl Icefield bivouac before dark. The mountain was socked in with clouds now for the first time, and spindrift spilled over the tent all night.

The next 3,200 meters of descent weren't a complete unknown, but it was close. We had one oblique photo of the Messner Route. It was impossible to distinguish the ridges in the foreground from those in the background. First thing in the morning, we made our best guess and I started down the new terrain, setting anchors. Three raps later, spinning six meters out from the serac wall, I realized that no one had ever come up this way. We downclimbed 600 meters, and then started rapping again. I burned through our meager rack setting countless anchors to reach the Messner Route. There was consis-

Steve House and Bruce Miller on day three. *Bruce Miller*

tent rockfall, and I was hit more than once, without consequence. We continued down hundreds more meters of ice, never easy, through the clouds. I was getting sloppy by sunset when we got to cowline. At that point, though, it was over. At 10 p.m. we stumbled into base camp.

A few days later Steve was out doing "aerobic recovery tests." (It's four months later that I write this and I still haven't recovered!) I wished my friend luck, said goodbye to our LO, Captain Amin, and the staff, and headed home.

After another week and two courses of antibiotics, Steve walked back to the Rupal Face. Left to his own judgment, he turned around below cowline.

Before I left for Pakistan, friends had expressed more concern about anti-American extremists than they did about the dangers of the Rupal Face. We didn't experience anything but warmth and generosity from the people of northern Pakistan (except from the satellite phone company —some things are the same the world over). The only extremist I met was the one I tried to climb the Rupal Face with. And as for the Rupal Face itself…now there's cause for concern.

SUMMARY OF STATISTICS

AREA: Pakistan, Nanga Parbat

ATTEMPT: Nanga Parbat's Direct Rupal Face (VI M5 90° ice). Reached 7,500m on the 8,125m peak—4,000 meters up the 4,500-meter face. August 12-17, 2004. Steve House and Bruce Miller.

A NOTE ABOUT THE AUTHOR:
Bruce Miller, 41, lives with his wife Michelle and stepson Satchel in the Foothills above Boulder. Working as a carpenter has given him the freedom to make four trips to the Himalaya. He most enjoys cragging with friends in nearby Eldorado Canyon.

MAZENO RIDGE

Nanga Parbat's 10-kilometer ridge caps a multi-peak
Pakistan Summer, albeit without an 8,000m summit.

DOUG CHABOT

Steve Swenson skirting Peak 7,090 on the Mazeno Ridge. Mazeno Peak (7,120m) is the corniced peak behind him.
Doug Chabot

Steve Swenson pulled a photo out of his back pocket. "We should do this," he prodded, showing me the unclimbed Mazeno Ridge on Nanga Parbat. I couldn't take my eyes off the image and instantly agreed. A month later I did some research and panicked. I called Steve and yelled, "A 10-kilometer-long ridge at 7,000 meters? Eight summits? This is crazy! We can't do this!" Steve was unflappable. He's also one of the most accomplished alpinists I know. He overlooked my outburst and calmly reassured me that, yes, we certainly could do this.

After six weeks of climbing in the Charakusa Valley with Steve and four other friends, we were ready for Nanga Parbat. With a first ascent of Kapura Peak (6,544m) and an alpine-style ascent of K7 (6,954m) under my belt, I figured it was now or never.

Our arrival at base camp (3,600m) on August 9 was perfectly timed. Two weeks of little snow was followed by jet-stream winds. Three days later, under clear skies, we launched. Going alpine style, we took seven days of fuel and five days of food. Our gear was one 60-meter 8-mm rope and a rack of two pickets, three ice screws, six stoppers, six pins, and eight runners. We took no bolts and no other rope.

Thigh-deep snow, bad weather, and avalanches had stymied previous attempts on this ridge. It curves up and down like the tail of a dragon with eight distinct summits until it drops down to Mazeno Col, the intersection of the Schell Route. The first attempt was in 1979 by a French expedition. In 1992 Doug Scott and team climbed the first three peaks on the ridge. Scott came back in 1993 and again in 1995, but got no higher. The last attempt on the ridge had been by Wojciech Kurtyka and Erhard Loretan in 1997.

On August 12 we hiked to Advanced Base Camp at 4,900m. Along the way we met villagers who knew of the Mazeno from Scott's attempts. "You trying Doug Scott Route?" they'd ask. "Not possible. Schell Route much better." They looked at us like we were crazy. In their minds Scott had already proved that it couldn't be done.

The next morning we left at one o'clock and climbed moderate snow and ice to 6,200m. A three o'clock start the following morning quickly put us on the first summit of the ridge, at 6,880m, and gave us fine views of the Mazeno winding off into the distance. Conditions were excellent. Where other parties found deep snow, we found névé. We dispatched the first three peaks with ease and surpassed Scott's high point that morning. We chopped our second camp at 6,900m, quite pleased with ourselves; we might pull this off after all.

The stable weather eased our fears of getting pinned down on the route. Theoretically, we could reverse the ridge at any point. However, if one of us got sick or injured we couldn't realistically retreat. I wasn't too worried about sickness or injury (what climber is?), but storms would be another issue. The terrain is technical enough to make climbing in strong winds and bad weather almost impossible. A retreat would entail climbing back instead of simply rappelling. It was a committing route.

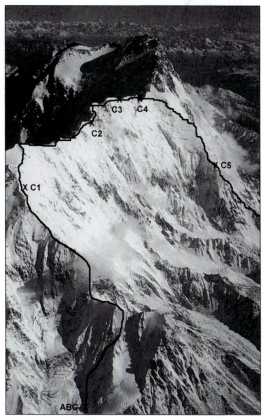

Nanga Parbat's 10-kilometer-long Mazeno Ridge from the air.
Robert Mantovani

Steve Swenson climbing around gendarmes at 6,000m. *Doug Chabot*

We awoke on the 15th to clear skies and started mixed climbing right out of the tent on Peak 7,060. Steve led and skirted the next peak, 7,090, via an ice traverse. We reached Mazeno Peak, marked 7,120 on the map, soon after. In 1986 a Spanish expedition had climbed the steep north face of Mazeno Peak to within 200 meters of the summit before a storm forced retreat. For us it was a simple walk-up and over the snow dome, as was the next one, Peak 7,100.

I was getting tired, but Steve was an absolute machine at this altitude. Besides a 10-kilometer-long ridge, most of the peaks required 500 meters of climbing up and then back down. With only one peak left before the Mazeno Col, we felt confident as we set up camp that afternoon. Peak 7,070 consisted of several rock towers, but I predicted we'd only need three hours to climb it. We could see the Schell Route and Nanga's summit, and we had enough food and fuel to reach the top. We optimistically planned a short day over 7,070 followed by two days of relatively non-technical climbing to the summit. Our optimism was quickly crushed.

The skies began clouding up that night and Steve came down with a respiratory infection. The hanky he carried said it all. It was grotesquely covered in blood and chunks of god-knows-what; I had to look away every time he pulled it out. He coughed most of the night and didn't get much rest. Because of Steve's condition, I led the entire next day, and it was our most difficult climbing. My prediction of three hours turned into a dozen hours, all of it on technical terrain. The climbing was spectacular but mentally and physically taxing. We climbed sections of M4, did numerous rappels off towers, and kept finding another summit after the last. We drug ourselves to the Mazeno Col in the last rays of sunlight, chopped out a platform, and set up the tent. I was wasted. The deteriorating weather, Steve's illness, and our general exhaustion all pointed to retreat.

Both of us had a restless night, and we knew going down the Schell Route was the right option. But our descent was anything but easy. We had heard fixed lines were in place on the technical section between camps I and II. Thinking we were going to cruise to base camp, we cached our extra food and fuel and our climbing rope. We envisioned climbing the Schell to the summit later and thought this cache would allow an even faster ascent. Leaving the rope was a decision we'd regret.

Three hundred meters below the cache, in poor visibility and soft snow, I fell into a crevasse up to my waist. From then on we roped up with our remaining cordalette and slings. At the end of the ridge we could see old anchors, but the fixed lines were gone. The weather was getting worse and we knew the avalanche danger would quickly increase if it snowed. Going back up to get the cached rope was an option, but it would've taken an enormous amount of energy and at least one full day. The terrain was too steep to downclimb so we searched for an old fixed line on the ridge. A strand snaked into the ice and after three hours of chopping we were proud owners of a 25-meter piece of braided line.

The next morning, with only 30 meters of visibility, we had a difficult time finding the descent. I had a digital picture on my camera—taken from base camp—and we referred to it often to pinpoint our location. We made good time simul-climbing but soon found ourselves in a steepening ice gully that forced us to rappel. With our rope we could do only ridiculously short 12-meter raps. Our lean rack dwindled as we set anchors, but luckily, after five abseils, we were able to downclimb once again. The rockfall was substantial, and at one point large blocks narrowly missed us. By the time we reached safety we had decided that ascending later was out of the question.

I think the last time the Schell Route was climbed was in 1992 by Doug Scott and team; this 12-year lapse helps explain the missing fixed lines.

The Mazeno Ridge was one of the greatest climbs of my life. Relatively safe from objective hazards, it was fully committing. Although Steve and I did not reach the summit, we feel fortunate to have climbed the Mazeno Ridge to its conclusion at the Schell Route, as well as four new summits over 7,000m. We hope this route sees other ascents. Just don't forget to bring a rope for the descent.

AREA: Pakistan Himalaya

ASCENT: Nanga Parbat, first ascent of the Mazeno Ridge to the junction of the Schell Route at 6,940m—a 10km-long ridge with an estimated 6,500m elevation gain, VI M4 AI3. Along the route, first ascents of Peaks 7060, 7120 (Mazeno Peak), 7100, and 7070. August 12-18, 2004. Doug Chabot and Steve Swenson.

A NOTE ABOUT THE AUTHOR:

Born in New Jersey in 1964, Doug Chabot learned how to climb and ski at Prescott College. He migrated north in 1986 and made Bozeman, Montana his home. During the winter months he's director of the Gallatin National Forest Avalanche Center, while in the summer he works for Exum Mountain Guides in Grand Teton National Park.

Doug Chabot and Steve Swenson in base camp just after coming down from the Mazeno Ridge. *Bruce Miller*

THE NORTH FACE OF JANNU

"It was like war, with teammates returning from the route as if from a battle. Jannu was showing its character." Nepal.

ALEXANDER RUCHKIN

The north face of Jannu. All photos courtesy of the Big Wall Russian-Way team.

Just two days after arriving at Jannu Base Camp on April 5, Alex Bolotov, Sergey Borisov, and Gennady Kirievsky began to work the bottom part of our route. We would use a trio of three-man parties, and our leader, Alexander Odintsov, planned to join us from time to time. Relieving each other, members of our team moved up quickly, setting up intermediate camps, with the vanguard changing when the following group approached. We gathered as a whole team only at the end of the expedition.

The first thing we had to do was renew last year's fixed ropes (in 2003 we had been defeated at 7,100 meters because of bad conditions). It's obviously dangerous to rely on worn-out ropes; therefore we climbed with our ice axes, gingerly using ascenders on the old ropes. There was very little snow on the route this time, and we found that last year's belay/anchor stations had deteriorated badly.

At the beginning of the route we had to pass quickly across the avalanche cone. Huge seracs fell from above, sometimes 20 times per day. Such blocks of ice broke into fine pieces and scattered over the whole cone. Also, on the bottom part it was necessary to carefully pass shattered rocks so as not to drop stones on those below.

Our safest camp was located at 5,600 meters, where rockfall and avalanches didn't touch us. We set up two big tents on a rocky ledge, where it was possible to rest before the next day's effort. A plateau at 5,700 meters was studded with crevasses, but we found the way between them and marked our path with wands. Fog and clouds came often at this altitude, and it was easy to lose the way and plunge into a crevasse. But our red wands led us in the right direction.

The nearness of the plateau, a windless corner, and the sun all combined to warm the ice, so our ice screws often melted out. The ropes, by contrast, melted five centimeters into the ice. Climbing the fixed ropes, I pulled out anchors seven times, and once fell four meters, but I was still hanging on the rope since the rope was melted into the ice. Belay anchors based on ice screws were also not reliable, and our troubles went on and on. I was lucky to survive.

It wasn't possible to set up a tent on the icy ridge at 6,500 meters; instead we had to set up a portaledge at about 6,675 meters on the rock. The weather was unpredictable, turning bad regularly every time we began to work on the route, and we had to "swim" in the snow like fish going against the current. In this way we won pitch after pitch.

On April 23 we reached 7,000 meters. Higher, we set up a portaledge just under a vertical wall. There was too little space to relax and have a good rest after the work. Terrible winds almost destroyed the poorly fixed portaledge, breaking the tubes, which could not be fixed. The heavy, wearisome work and struggle against a vertical wall had begun.

To reach 7,000 meters from base camp we had to climb three days by fixed ropes (52 pitches), carrying the necessary equipment, meals, gas, etc. It took us more than three hours to pass four vertical fixed ropes above 7,000 meters, with 10- to 15-kilogram loads, when we were already tired after the three-day ascent. To reduce the time on this part of the route we set up a portaledge at 7,200 meters. So we reached the bottom of the vertical wall in four days. But further progress was agonizingly slow, with some days showing zero gain. Some of us became very nervous when Bolotov's group, on a windy day, climbed only five meters of very difficult rock. Would it really be possible to climb the wall, which looks like El Capitan in its length and steepness, but above 7,000 meters?

I'll describe a typical morning up high. You get up at 5 a.m. on the portaledge. You have to force yourself hard to begin moving. All occurs slowly at this altitude, and you can almost watch the brain's impulses go down the nervous system and make the fingers move. The organism —like an old computer—thinks slowly and takes time to understand commands. It really needs a new processor! You melt ice, making water for breakfast, and drink, drink, drink. It's impossible to drink enough. Then preparation during a whole hour, and finally at 8 or 9 you leave the portaledge, hanging in space on the vertical wall. There is nothing to step on, only air. You are connected to the rope by two ascenders. The cold at once envelops you; it's everywhere and you find yourself suddenly in an unreal world. Most of the ropes don't touch the wall's surface, so you expend a lot of energy.

Mike Mikhailov at 7,300m on his way back up to "ABC."

The steep 700-meter granite wall would be a problem at low altitude, but it was much harder above 7,000 meters. To climb it we had to use our whole arsenal of techniques and equipment, and we looked like soldiers with lots of ammo. We could hardly move our bodies with all the hardware draped on us. And in the thin air we climbed slowly, centimeter by centimeter, solving difficult problems, like in a labyrinth, to find an optimum way, using barely visible cracks.

All cracks ended at a smooth, steep wall, and we had to use tiny curved nuts and copperheads pounded into shallow holes. Together with Mike Mikhailov, I climbed three and a half pitches up the face in four days. Nick Totmjanin and Mikhail Pershin ascended to 7,200 meters to relieve us—a kind of vertical changing of the guard.

We acclimatized slowly, and all of us had bad coughs. The doctor, as meticulous as a prison guard, watched over us. Having thus received medical treatment, and having

The north face route, showing camp locations. ABC was at 7,400m.

had a rest, having rehydrated, we went back upward. Meantime, Pershin and Totmjanin climbed two more ropelengths up the wall.

Five pitches of vertical terrain used up precious time needed for climbing further. So we moved the portaledge from 7,200 meters to 7,400 meters, and it became our Advanced Base Camp, where it would be possible to go to the top and back. It was only necessary to surmount the last 310 vertical meters.

The wall began to present surprises and provide work for our doctor, Mikhail Bakin. First, because of overwork, Pershin had a detached retina; he went down, almost blind. Second, while descending on the last rope, Totmjanin was hit by a stone, which broke his glasses and injured his head and a finger; his helmet had saved him and he remained efficient. Bolotov's group began to fall apart on the second day of work above 7,500 meters. A falling stone punched through Serguey Borisov helmet and into his head. A few hours later Alex Bolotov broke a rib after falling at an overhanging section. Their group went down, and the doctor surpervised by radio as Gennady Kirievsky treated the patients at Advanced Base Camp. It was like war, with teammates returning from the route as if from a battle. Jannu was showing its character.

On May 19 our group carried loads to the portaledge at 7,400 meters. Dmitry Pavlenko went down to 7,000 meters to rest a day and return with additional equipment. Mikhailov and I remained in the portaledge, hoping for further progress. The weather had turned bad and covered us with snow, and we had constantly to dump it from the portaledge so as not to be torn from the wall. The next day the weather had not improved, and we had to climb in a snowstorm.

Mike Mikhailov in the 7,400m ABC.

Our route passed through a wide chimney filled by snow; snow also covered all the equipment and cracks. Everything that accumulated on the wall above was dumped onto us. Whenever the sky quickly darkened it meant that an avalanche was coming, and we had time only to lower our heads. Our progress in such weather was like a turtle's: 30 meters of new ground per day, plus the ascent and descent on the fixed ropes. It took a lot of time to organize intermediate points and belay stations.

Three days we worked in the incessant snow. Mike Mikhailov heroically froze while belaying me practically without movement. In such terrible conditions we managed to win two pitches from the wall. During the fourth day Mike felt symptoms of pulmonary edema, and quickly headed down. It was sad that Mike, after working with me over most of the north wall and climbing almost the entire route, couldn't ascend the last 150 vertical meters. Together we had climbed the most complex and steepest part of the wall, even though he was not fully restored from the traumas received last autumn on Jannu. I never felt comfortable with the altitude, and I had to drive away the idea that I could be the next victim.

Only on the fourth day did the weather improve, after Mike had gone down and Dmitry Pavlenko had climbed up to my portaledge. It was just in time. I worked as the leader this day, too. Now the chimney angled to the left, in the direction of the ridge, and one of its walls was, of all things, less than vertical, though the rock was shattered. We could now climb faster. Pavlenko took over as leader for the next two days while I belayed him. It was very difficult to find places for the intermediate belay points because of all the loose rock.

We heard every evening by radio that we were close to the summit, that it was only three or so ropelengths to our goal. But the days ran on, and the top—like a mirage—moved further and further away. For equipment we had only the last three ropes and a few pieces of hardware. The steepness of the wall did not allow us to climb without ropes, and reaching the top became ever more problematic. If the angle would allow us to climb free and move connected with only one rope, we would do it. But it wasn't clear how much distance we still needed to climb, how many ropes were required, how difficult was the rock ahead, and whether we would have time to return. I had less and less strength. It was hard to climb the fixed ropes, and it seemed I already knew each section of rock. I was lost with the day count, and I knew the chances that I would reach the top decreased every hour. I had been above 7,400 meters now for seven days.

Our progress affected our teammates, several of whom began to ascend toward Advanced Base Camp. If we couldn't make it, some of them might have enough equipment and a chance to summit. But we still had a tiny chance, too.

The next day we planned our summit bid. Dmitry and I arose at 3 a.m., with the wind rattling our portaledge. We melted snow and hoped that the weather would calm down. Dmitry left the portaledge for five minutes and returned absolutely covered in snow. Avalanches fell from the wall like white rivers.

Our private space—1x2 meters in a portaledge—differed much from the world of stone and ice outside. We were separated by only a thin layer of fabric, but it saved us from the wind, cold, and snow. Our fragile world was easy to destroy. The huge mended hole in the ceiling and floor was a reminder of the stone that had flown through the portaledge. Dressed in all our

Alexander Ruchkin at 7,100m re-climbing old ground from 2003.

The summit of Jannu, at last.

equipment and ready to leave at any minute, we waited nearly four hours in the bad weather—and finally understood that we would not have enough time to make the summit.

We slept all day—if that qualifies as rest at this altitude. The sky cleared, and there appeared a chance to leave the next day. Borisov and Kirievsky waited at Camp III at 7,000 meters, ready to relieve us on the route, and Totmjanin and Bolotov had reached Camp II at 6,700 meters.

On May 26, at 2 a.m. and already on autopilot, in a half-dream state, we began to prepare breakfast: soup and tea. I was going to climb as the leader, not because I would like to be first to the top, but to do my best, and to blame only myself if we didn't summit. We left the por-taledge at 5 a.m., deciding to go without packs, instead hanging all the equipment on ourselves. We dressed in down jackets over the down one-piece suits and did not regret this, because it was very cold. The wind increased as the morning progressed. The ascent to the end of the fixed ropes took three hours, and soon I was going up the final terrain.

There was no time to dig out a chimney that was completely filled with snow, and when my inside leg slid out, I searched for another place and ascended there. It was too cold for gloves, but impossible to work with equipment using mittens. Hands freeze 10 times faster working with metal. I constantly shook my hands trying to warm them.

I climbed two technically simple mixed ropelengths with difficulty, having to rest after each step while trying to extract enough oxygen from the thin air (we did not take supplementary oxygen). Where was the top?

Concentrating our last forces, wading to our waists in snow and rolling in it as in a bog, we floated slowly upward. Finally, a steep firn slope led to the summit ridge. Even our crampons refused to hold because they had been so worn down during the climb on the wall.

I was not sure that the top was close. After a lot of days I had ceased to hope, and only having looked around did I understand that the snow peak on the right was Jannu's summit. At 3 p.m. I reached it.

On the horizon I saw Makalu, Lhotse, and Everest. The valleys below were shrouded by clouds, and only the 7,000- and 8,000-meter giants were floating like ships on an ocean of clouds, and I together with them. I shouted from happiness that we had climbed Jannu's north face. I set up a belay station and awaited Dmitry, who ascended by the fixed rope. There was no place to stay at the summit; I had to cut down the top with my ice axe, and we sat as on a horse. The wind beat on my face, burning it. We had climbed Jannu's north face! We embraced and soon headed downward.

Sergey Borisov and Gennady Kirievsky had ascended to the portaledge, where they met us. I felt symptoms of pulmonary edema by evening, and the doctor ordered me down; Gennady helped me, at night, down to 7,000 meters. At this camp there was oxygen, and it saved my life. Next day we continued to descend, and our teammates began to ascend to Advanced Base Camp; on May 28, Borisov, Kirievsky, and Totmjanin climbed to Jannu's summit.

SUMMARY OF STATISTICS:

AREA: Nepal, Kangchenjunga Himal, near Singalila range
ASCENT: Jannu (7,710m), north face, 72 vertical pitches, 3,250m, ABO+, VI A3+. Summit climbers: Dmitry Pavlenko, Alexander Ruchkin; May 28, 2004: Sergey Borisov, Gennady Kirievsky, and Nick Totmjanin. Leader: Alexander Odintsov. Other climbers: Mike Mikhailov, Mikhail Pershin. Doctor: Mikhail Bakin.

A NOTE ABOUT THE AUTHOR:

Alexander Ruchkin, born in 1963 in Kazakhstan (then USSR), is Russian and lives in Saint Petersburg. He started climbing in 1985 and works as a guide and organizer of expeditions and tourism. He is married, with two children. His big climbs include a new route on Big Sail Peak on Baffin Island, winter ascents of No Siesta on the Grandes Jorasses and other Mont Blanc massif testpieces, the Troll Wall in Norway, and various new routes on Ak Su in Kyrgyzstan.

GRANTS: This climb was sponsored by Panasonic and BASK.

MY PATH TO PARADISE

Finally, a direct route on Cerro Torre's east face.

ERMANNO SALVATERRA

The seriously foreshortened climber's eye view of Cerro Torre's east face, showing the direct line climbed in 2004. Torre Egger is the needle on the right. For a non-foreshortened perspective with all the route lines, see *AAJ* 2004, page 140. *Ermanno Salvaterra*

Alessandro jumaring on the 25th pitch. *Ermanno Salvaterra*

I clip another copperhead, then two rivets, and finally reach the last belay station of Cerro Torre's headwall. A few more moves up icy rock and I am there. Hard to believe, but we have done it! It is seven in the evening, and as I wait for my partners to jumar this last pitch I lean my head against the rock and cry, engulfed by happiness and emotion. My friends take longer than expected, for Giacomo has to descend 50 meters to free a jammed rope. I am almost happy about this, since it gives me more time to savor this special moment.

Once my partners arrive, we continue to the base of the summit snow mushroom, and calmly I lead the last pitch to reach the highest point of Cerro Torre. It's the fourth time I have had the pleasure of being here, but still we pause to appreciate the summit and it is close to nine o'clock by the time we take a few photos. The cold and wind quickly take their toll.

Five years it had taken me to complete this dream, to reach this, my very own version of paradise. The first to mention this project was Andrea Sarchi in 1985. It was a beautiful day on the glacier below Cerro Torre when he suggested that after completing the first winter ascent of the mountain we should give the east face a try. These are the type of things that one says when the weather is good and when one is fresh. However, after our winter ascent, which we carried out via the Compressor Route, we didn't speak again about this idea.

The English had already made a brave attempt in the prominent dihedral on the right side of the east face (1981), and Slovenes came soon after with the "Devil's Direttissima" (1986) on the left side of the east face, an ascent that helped further the myth of this dangerous face. In 1994 Conrad Anker and John Middendorf (USA) showed up pursuing a more direct line, and they were soon followed by Spaniards, Chileans, Poles, and some others as well. But none of these teams managed to climb very high. Years passed and the direct east face sat there, beautiful and virgin, waiting for somebody.

My dream took shape slowly, and when we were finally ready to depart on what would have been my first foray on the face, my partner broke his arm. This proved to be the first of many delays. In early October 1999, Mauro Mabboni and I finally stood at the base of the face. For me there is something special about this mountain; it makes me feel inspired and alive. We climbed 100 meters and then returned to base camp to wait for better weather. When we returned a few days later, we found signs of a large avalanche at the base of our proposed line. Mauro looked me straight in the eye. I immediately understood his feelings and did not insist on continuing. In 1994 Mauro had lost a close friend on Cerro Torre, and it was clear that he was hesitant to take on such an obviously risky enterprise on the same mountain. We quit and instead completed a major variation to the Compressor Route.

The portaledges at the final bivy (the "Last Sun Bivy").
Ermanno Salvaterra

Time passed and my dream refused to leave. I planned another attempt, and again, at the last minute, something didn't work. There were many other ideas floating around, projects in the Himalaya and elsewhere, but my mind was fixed on that lovely east face of Cerro Torre.

In 2001 I found myself again at the base of the east face. This time there were four of us: Walter Gobbi, Paolo Calzà, Mauro Giovanazzi, and me. For eight days we climbed in atrocious conditions, clenching our teeth, but after 800 meters we were forced to retreat when Walter and I almost died of propane poisoning inside our portaledge.

This attempt, though unsuccessful, became the foundation of my dream. Two years passed, but from the moment we started planning our return, months in advance, I dreamed about each aspect of our ascent. In mid-August 2004, after many months of planning, I was told "no" by my partners yet again. I decided that I had waited long enough. I was nearly 50, but physically I felt strong and still keen for this kind of adventure. Perhaps in the future it wouldn't feel the same, and so I felt that I couldn't wait. In two days I found new partners, not caring if they didn't have any previous Patagonian experience, or if in the end they didn't even lead a single pitch. What

Alessandro on the first headwall pitch of the Maestri Route. The Maestri Route ascends from the right. The direct east face ascends from the left. *Ermanno Salvaterra*

interested me most was that they were enthusiastic about what we were about to try.

Matteo was strong and perhaps a bit crazy. I barely knew him, having climbed with him only a few times. Giacomo Rossetti, who initially wanted to come with us to help carry loads, proved himself to be a capable individual, available to do anything at any time. Alessandro Beltrami, having just finished the mountain guide courses, lived only one kilometer from my house, and, in spite of not knowing him well, I came to like his simplicity. He was strong and unfazed by hard work and physical fatigue.

I was pleased to have assembled a team so quickly, and we left Italy on October 29. By November 2 we were already climbing the first few pitches. Our plan was to climb to a triangular snowfield some 300 meters up, and from then on stay on the wall in our portaledges.

Things are going well; even the weather seems to be giving us a hand. On the 6th, after having ferried several loads to the base of the wall, Alessandro and I climb past the snowfield to a spot where we decide to set up the portaledges. We have all agreed that Matteo and Giacomo would haul the equipment to that point, but it is three o'clock and they have not yet arrived. We begin to worry. Finally Giacomo appears over the lower lip of the snowfield. At the same time we see someone descending the glacier. Matteo has decided to retreat, but in spite of this Giacomo is more motivated than ever.

The alarm rings at four a.m., and at first light we are ready to go. By that evening we have managed to get all the gear to our first portaledge camp, just above the snowfield.

The next day, despite constant snowfall, we manage to climb 130 meters, returning to our tents satisfied with our progress. Next morning we reach the crux of the route, a steep section involving lots of difficult climbing. The weather makes climbing particularly difficult. On one of the harder bits I find a fixed rope that we left on our 2001 attempt. Tempted, I start jumaring up it, but after 20 meters, unable to protect myself due to the steepness of the wall, I decide to turn around. The rope is frayed and it's just too risky. Instead I climb the two pitches that take us to the "Dalai Lama," a flake of enormous proportions that is mostly detached from the wall ("lama" means flake in Italian).

By day's end we have been on the go for 22 hours, but we have managed to move our camp to the top of the flake. The following day brings beautiful weather, and we reach the 2001 high point. That time the weather was terrible, with wind so strong and violent, and with so much snow, that I could not tell where I was, or what was up and what was down. I cursed that whole day. I cursed Patagonia and everything that had led me to be here.

This time everything is different. Alec and Giac join me at the belay, and I continue upward with a difficult hooking move and some hard free climbing to reach a very comfortable belay station. The angle of the wall kicks back and that greatly encourages me. It feels like we are up on a sunny Mont Blanc. We eventually set up the portaledges at our high point, but before dinner I climb a further 30 meters. Dinner unfortunately takes a long time since our second stove died during the first bivouac.

The summit is not far now, and right above our heads looms the mysterious and intriguing chimney that could lead us to the north face, to a spot less than 100 meters below the summit, allowing us to complete a totally independent line. I climb a further two pitches until I can finally have a good look into this chimney. In the lower part the ice looks very aerated, and higher up there is another section that looks the same. I was hoping that this chimney would be like the one on Exocet on Cerro Stanhardt, but unfortunately this is not the case. It looks dangerous and very time consuming. When Alessandro arrives at the belay he has a good look as well and agrees that it seems too dangerous and that we should head up and left to join the Compressor Route at the base of the summit headwall.

I climb one more pitch under the constant bombardment of falling ice and manage to set up a belay under a small overhang. The following pitch is mixed and quickly turns into a full-on battle. In the second half I climb an ice smear that requires everything I have. The ice is porous and my tools keep popping off. One of the picks breaks, then I smash a finger, then I manage to drop a tool. Feeling very tired, I equalize three dubious ice screws and lower myself down to the belay. I convince Alessandro to give it a try, and he climbs a further 10 meters before we descend to our bivy. The weather has changed yet again and we are faced with constant spindrift. In the morning Giacomo suggests that we should take a rest day, but I know that on this mountain one rests only when one is safely on level ground.

We jumar up our ropes with the intent of pushing on to the summit. Alessandro finishes the pitch and then lets me lead on. One more pitch puts us at the base of the summit headwall, joining the Compressor Route. Now it feels as if we are in another world, one that is familiar and almost relaxing. Very quickly we climb to the compressor itself, and, after taking yet another souvenir from that controversial machine, I continue up the so-called "Bridwell Pitch." We have only one headlamp among the three of us, so we decide to spend the night in the vicinity of the summit. We dig a hole right under the mushroom and spend all night trying to keep our hands and feet warm. We have half a liter of orange juice, but it is one solid block. It's a cold night, and the thermometer shows minus 13 degrees Celsius. The wind does the rest.

Early in the morning we rappel to our portaledges, stopping to rest, eat, and drink. The weather is terrible and we spend the night worrying about what is falling on us and around us. This is our eighth and last night in the wall. In the morning, carrying heavy loads, we head down, reaching the base of the wall by evening. Our adventure is finished, but only when we reach Chalten do we realize what we have accomplished.

Each of us had his own whys, his own objectives, and his own dreams. I had this particular one, my very own little bit of paradise.

SUMMARY OF STATISTICS:

AREA: Argentina, Chalten Massif

ASCENTS: Cerro Torre: First ascent of the east face direct route, "Quinque Anni Ad Paradisum" (6b A2 100° ice) Alessandro Beltrami, Giacomo Rossetti, and Ermanno Salvaterra, November 2-15, 2004.

A NOTE ABOUT THE AUTHOR:

Ermanno Salvaterra was born in Pinzolo, Italy, in 1955, and still lives there. His family ran the XII Apostles Refuge, at 2,500m, and for that reason young Ermanno spent his summers playing in the high mountains, sneaking off for his first climb at the age of nine. Naturally, he became a ski instructor and mountain guide as a young adult. He has been climbing in Patagonia since 1982, including new routes on Cerro Torre, Cerro Standhardt, Punta Herron, Aguja Rafael, on the east face of Central Tower of Paine, as well as ascents of Fitz Roy, Aguja Guillaumet, Poincenot and the South Tower of Paine. Salvaterra now runs the XII Apostles Refuge, and continues to teach skiing,guide climbing, and play in the Brenta. Salvaterra now runs the XII Apostles Refuge, and continues to teach skiing, guide climbing, and play in the Brenta.

Translated from the Italian by Rolando Garibotti

Giacomo and Alessandro on the top of Cerro Torre. *Ermanno Salvaterra*

DIHEDRAL PERSPECTIVES

Lessons learned during my first decade of free climbing on El Capitan.

TOMMY CALDWELL

El Capitan, showing the Dihedral Wall route. *John Harlin III*

I really had no chance at being a dentist, lawyer, or anything generally considered respectable. In retrospect, becoming an adventure climber was inevitable. I was bred to crave the outdoors. My earliest memories are of long ski tours in the Rockies, getting blown off my feet by the wind or buried in a snow cave, and of sitting in El Cap Meadow with my sister watching my dad up on the wall—and dreaming of going up there someday. Sleeping in a tent or a van felt more like home than sleeping in a house. If my parents wanted a responsible son who would grow up to make money, they blew it by showing me the wonders of the mountains.

I can't say I blame them for raising me this way. In fact, I cannot imagine a better way to grow up. When my dad dragged me up Devil's Tower at age six, people thought he was insane and reckless, but I thought it was amazing, and it gave me a passion to experience and explore. When he took me to Bolivia to climb 20,000-foot peaks at age 14, people thought he was mean for taking me away from kids my own age. But climbing big mountains in far-off countries seemed more exciting than video games and movie marathons, and I came back with a willingness to suffer and work hard to accomplish goals. My father became my mentor and role model, and by the time I set off on my own, I was pretty set on the path of a climber. When I started big-wall free climbing, I already had many of the skills necessary.

In 1996, at age 18, I took my first trip up El Cap, with my dad. By this time I had climbed numerous 5.14 sport routes and naively figured that a route rated 13b wouldn't be that hard. But I hadn't a clue about the difficulties of big-wall free climbing and was in for a big surprise. Five days on the Salathé Wall left me battered and bruised. Afterward, free climbing such a huge face seemed ridiculous, something far beyond me. But I romanticize about ridiculous-sounding adventures. Free climbing El Cap became important to me, and I was determined to do whatever it took to get it done. Humbled, I changed my mental and physical approach, and my training. I learned that big-wall free climbing has many layers of difficulty, all equally important. The strongest climber is not necessarily the best, because logistical strategies and tricks matter just as much as brute strength—maybe more. Strong does not mean bulging muscles and iron fingers. It means the ability to endure significant pain and climb day after day without resting. It's also about knowing what is making you tired and learning how to minimize that. I changed my training to fit these needs, and to do everything to the point of pure exhaustion and pain.

Ten months after that first failed attempt on the Salathé, I started up again. This time, with new perspective and the discovery of a variation around one of the crux pitches, I freed the route, exhausted but hungry for more. It opened my eyes to possibilities I never knew existed. For the next five years I couldn't keep away from Yosemite. In the spring of 2000, I headed up the Muir Wall with my good friend Topher Donahue. The first four days we made great progress, nearly onsighting the bottom third of the route. But on day five Topher's wife got sick, and he had to head down to take care of her. At first I felt bummed, but it turned out to be the best thing that could have happened. Three days later I teamed up with Beth Rodden, my future wife, to try to free-climb Lurking Fear. Within a week I was completely head over heels for her. Together we climbed the most intense and remarkable slabs I have ever seen. The desire to impress one another and spend time together increased our willingness to suffer through sweltering temperatures and razor-sharp crimpers. We were having the time of our lives. We pushed ourselves hard and climbed until every fingertip bled; we invented new taping techniques to allow us to continue. We were a driven team that worked well. We both did some of our best climbing on Lurking Fear, and after two months of constant work we completed the first free ascent.

The next season I returned to the Muir Wall with another good friend, Nick Sagar. He was originally exclusively a sport climber and in more recent years had shifted his focus to bouldering. In the midst of previous sport-climbing trips together, I had convinced him to climb Moonlight Buttress and the Nose in a day, and that was his only real traditional climbing experience. Normally I'd be apprehensive about partnering with such a novice trad climber for an El Cap free-climb, but Nick learns fast. We did get off to a bit of a rocky start, though. Pitch one was a 5.9 flaring chimney that left Nick panting and battered. He almost threw in the towel right then.

Pitch 10 on the Dihedral Wall, 5.13c, an awkward flaring pitch that required powerful laybacking and ultra-flared fist jams. *Corey Rich*

On pitch two, a 5.12 layback, he yelled to me from a hundred feet above, "What color cam is it if my fingers fit all the way in the crack?" I wish I could say he was kidding, but he wasn't. True to form, after a few days he had it dialed: purple if your fingers go in all the way, gray if they go in part way. His sport climbing and bouldering background made him strong as hell and it paid off. After two weeks on the route, we topped out on Nick's second El Cap route and cracked open his celebratory home brew. It was his first free El Cap route and my third.

Five days after the Muir Wall I decided to try to free the Salathé in a day. Hans Florine and I started at three in the morning and after nine hours and 25 pitches, we were already looking at the crux headwall pitch. I was scraped up and cotton mouthed, but excited because I had never climbed that fast before. About two-thirds of the way up the pitch I had a full physical breakdown. I felt like a truck had hit me. It reminded me of the way I had felt the first time on the route with my dad. Aid climbing and jumaring at a crawl behind Hans to the top was all I could do. It became painfully clear that free-climbing El Cap in a day offers another whole set of challenges.

That winter I had a slight setback: I cut off my left index finger in a home remodeling accident. Feeling traumatized, I wondered if I would ever be able to climb anywhere near my previous level. But with the determination my dad taught me as a kid, I made it my mission to move forward and trained with more passion and dedication than ever. I returned with Beth to the Salathé the next spring, stronger and more driven. Surprisingly, I freed the route in a day on my first attempt.

Over the next couple of years I did two more El Cap free routes: the West Buttress with my wife and Zodiac with Topher. Both climbs were incredible, and helped me refine my big-wall free-climbing and address my El Cap addiction. I had seemingly found a formula that worked for getting me up these climbs, and I was ready to step it up another notch. Little did I know how big of a step I was to take.

"I don't know if I have this in me anymore." The Dihedral Wall pushed me to say these words for the first time in my climbing career. I have always subscribed to the theory that I cannot back down, even an inch, or I will never reach my true potential. But there I was, 1,800 feet up El Cap feeling like I might actually be at the end of my rope. My arms were seizing every time I lifted them above my head. Blood seeped from holes in my fingers, knees, elbows, shins, and forehead. I had been relentlessly abusing my body on this climb for over two months and was wrecked. Perseverance is great, but this was getting ridiculous. Several times I had spent more than an hour on a redpoint burn only to hopelessly pump out or have a foothold crumble, sending me down for more abuse. In fact I had fallen over a dozen times, having to reclimb pitches each time. Here I was only one pitch from almost sure success but feeling like I could go no further.

I had chosen the Dihedral Wall because it was one of the most obvious lines on El Cap. The first time I climbed it, I rope-soloed it as an aid route over three days because I wanted the experience of being alone on a wall. Freeing the Dihedral wasn't a new idea, as Alan Lester and Pete Takeda free-climbed 50 percent of it in the early nineties. Todd Skinner and Paul Piana also worked on it extensively in 2001 and 2002, pioneering the variations that would eventually link the complete free ascent. At first, it looked nearly impossible, but beautiful. Dihedrals soared on for hundreds of feet without a break. When the cracks petered out, face holds seemed to appear and were just big enough and close enough together to make me think it might go free. The dihedrals are surrounded by immense, featureless slabs that sometimes stretch uninterrupted for over 1,000 feet. Throughout the bottom half, the cracks are usually thin, only occasionally big enough to accept more than a fingertip. Higher they become bottomless and flaring. If it could somehow be climbed, it would be one of the most extraordinary free-climbs I had seen.

The Dihedral Wall consumed me. I climbed more intensely and for longer each day than I ever had before, four or five days a week from sunrise to sunset. On my biggest days I would start at five and climb from the ground to the end of the last hard pitch, 1,800 feet up, self-belayed on my fixed lines. I would then rappel to the ground by noon, eat lunch, and go bouldering until dark. Bloody stumps replaced my fingers, my toenails fell off, and my muscles were so constantly sore that I forgot what "normal" felt like. I imagined I looked like a grimacing 90-year-old hunchback.

The route raised my tolerance for pain and frustration, and taught me the true meaning of hard work. It also gave me great satisfaction, the intense feeling of living each day to its fullest. The sustained nature of the route seemed absurd. Of the first 15 pitches—out of 26 total—there was one 5.14, one 5.13d, three of 5.13c, three of 5.13b, and four of 5.12.

Since nobody could withstand the countless hours of belaying it would take to get me up this climb, at first I worked the route solo, which, with no distractions, enhanced my appreciation of the route's magnificence. I noticed every crevice, edge, and bulge. I memorized every feature,

Pitch six, 5.14. This was the crux pitch of the route, but was only the beginning of the major difficulties. *Corey Rich*

whether it was a gigantic dihedral or a hairline fracture. I took time to watch the swallows tackle each other in mid-air and plummet toward the ground, separating just before the treetops. I would catch myself saying out loud, "That is so cool." The view became etched in my mind, as did the thousands of moves I rehearsed. Silence no longer felt uncomfortable; I was alone with my thoughts and motivation.

After two months the route was starting to come together. I started to link long sections of pitches, then entire pitches, and pretty soon had top-roped most of the hard climbing. Soon I would be ready to attempt the route, so I developed a plan of attack. I decided to climb from stance to stance in a continuous ascent, because it was the best style I thought I could use.

There are climbers who spend countless hours debating style in an attempt to establish a pecking order, and honestly it reminds me of the reasons I did not like high school. I believe people should strive to do climbs in the best style they think possible for themselves, but refrain from criticizing others for what they choose to do. El Cap is for having fun and having an adventure, not for having fights and criticizing others. This does nothing but boost egos and show disrespect for people who share your passion. As long as you are not harming the rock or the route, and if you are honest about what you have done, you should be able to climb in whatever fashion you want.

For the final push, Beth and my friend Adam Stack offered to come along to belay and help in any way they could, giving me the moral, emotional and physical support that's as crucial to my success as any other aspect of climbing. Their generosity astounds me—they put aside their own lives to help me. I am lucky to have friends like that, and would never have free-climbed El Cap if it were not for them.

We started up for the redpoint at five o'clock on the morning of May 18. The weather was unseasonably cool and perfect for free-climbing. The wall looked ominous in the early morning light, and I could almost hear them challenging me. I started up the enormous face feeling very minute. The rock is polished, and the finger locks (from old piton scars) are far apart. Every time I reached from one finger lock to the next I feared that my feet would slip and I would go skidding down the wall until my 100-pound belayer got yanked up to the end of the anchor rope. But as the ground receded, I got into the swing of things. The climbing soon felt natural and I began to find the rhythm that I had discovered over the past weeks.

Months of conditioning paid off, and 5.12 was feeling like 5.10. The first four pitches took about an hour and a half, and I reached the crux pitch around eight o'clock. As I started the pitch my heart was racing and my body trembling. I laybacked up a foot-wide dihedral with no crack. There were almost never visible footholds, so the only way I was able to stay on the wall was to pinch the outside corner of the dihedral and press my feet hard against the wall. The rubber on my shoes was tested to the max, I felt strain in my back, strain in my fingers, and strain in my neck. The rock got steeper, but a crack appeared and gave me something relatively substantial to hold onto. With no feet in sight I had to continue climbing without pause. I tried to remember to relax, but my body started shaking. As the crack ended I made a full span right to a sloping ramp, smeared my right foot high, and dynoed for a shallow finger lock. I was beginning to get pumped and had to focus hard, compose myself, and then delicately traverse on barely visible holds to a belay stance. Once there I felt an overwhelming sense of relief. I had managed to do the crux of the route without falling. But I knew I still had a tremendous amount of hard climbing ahead.

For the next three days, climbing from dawn to dusk, I desperately fought my way up pitch after pitch. I fell many times; the route took its toll. By the end the first day I was bleeding from beneath most of my fingernails. On the second day my feet were so swollen I thought they might pop through my shoes. By noon on the third day I just wanted it all to be over. But I was almost done: only one hard pitch remained.

As I started up the pitch my body quivered with pain and fatigue. I had been concentrating for three days, and my mind was tired. A shallow groove led to a small layback crack and the final few feet of hard climbing. If I fell here, a fixed pin that was at least 20 years old and driven into mud would hopefully catch me. I did not want to test its integrity. I pressed my bloody fingertips against a tiny side pull and smeared my feet into a glassy dish. Just as my fingertips reached the opening my foot slipped. Panicking, I desperately pulled my foot back up, smeared it again, and slotted my hand into a bomber jam above. I reached the ledge, threw my hands in the air, and screamed as loudly as I could.

I was ecstatic. So much pain, suffering, and hard work goes into these climbs that when finished I feel indescribably fulfilled. It does not happen for me to this extent on hard sport routes or boulder problems; big-wall free-climbing is special in that way. Something about climbing thousands of feet, with tens of thousands of moves, sets it above anything else. Momentarily, I forgot about my countless wounds and aching feet—and that alone made all the suffering worth it.

Three weeks after completing the climb I was still visibly tired. My first day back climbing felt horrible. I felt lethargic for months but at the same time satisfied deep inside. The Dihedral Wall had forced me to work harder than ever before and helped me realize, once again, that climbing gives me energy, passion, and makes me feel more alive.

The Dihedral Wall was only one step in a long chain of events in my life as a climber. I am a free climber through and through. For me it's purity at its finest, demanding a level of focus and energy I have not found anywhere else. It combines the boldness and adventure that big-wall climbing has always possessed, with physical attributes that can be maintained only through dedication and passion.

Each of the six El Cap routes I have freed has taught me something new. Many people think that the major climbing problems have all been done, the big peaks climbed and the major lines conquered. I beg to differ. For me free-climbing has opened nearly endless potential. It gives a new generation the opportunity to explore and discover all over again. People are realizing that the great walls of the world may be possible to free-climb, and more people are embracing that every day. In the nineties maybe one free attempt took place on El Cap a year. These days you might find three, four, even five free parties up there at once. They may be pioneering a new line or climbing an existing one. I am sure this will soon expand to all the great-wall destinations of the world, and in many ways it already has. But I feel like the potential has barely been touched and that free-climbing will revolutionize big-wall climbing as we know it.

Free-climbing possesses a flow and movement that is addicting. I crave the burning in my fingertips, the pump in my forearms, and the puzzle of a crux sequence. Free-climbing requires less gear and is often faster, opening the door for huge alpine-style ascents and big link-ups. It's also a more natural way to climb and a more sustainable resource. Once established, a hard free route is usually unchanged by climbers, whereas most hard aid routes change a little with each hammer blow.

Pitch 8, 5.13c, which Caldwell calls "one of the most beautiful and amazing pitches of my life." It spit him off three times on the final push. *Corey Rich*

Pitch 12, 5.12c. Tommy Caldwell is pulling out of the most difficult section of off width he had ever encountered. This pitch "tested all my techniques." *Corey Rich*

Granted, most of these are just my observations and opinions, but I know this for sure: big-wall free-climbing has allowed me to live a fuller, more interesting life than I could have imagined. Anticipating a big Valley climb, I feel my pulse quicken, my body weightless, and my fingers tingling. Maybe it is the beauty of the immense glimmering walls, maybe it is the memories of numerous adventures and the dream of countless more, and maybe it is because Yosemite is where I fell in love with Beth. The Valley will always draw me back, though I doubt that I will ever do another climb as amazing as the Dihedral Wall. But then again you never know.

SUMMARY OF STATISTICS:

AREA: California, Yosemite Valley.

ASCENT: Dihedral Wall, 2,700', 26 pitches, VI 5.14 (the first 15 pitches alone contain one 5.14 pitch, one 5.13d, three 5.13c, three 5.13b, and four 5.12). Tommy Caldwell. May 19-22, 2004.

A NOTE ABOUT THE AUTHOR:

Tommy Caldwell, 27, grew up on the rocks. For the first 15 years of his life he spent his weekends and holidays traveling the U.S. climbing with his father. His father also took him to Europe and Bolivia to experience mountaineering. At the age of 15 he found his passion in sport and competition climbing. When he turned 18 he started traveling full time and climbed in Europe, Asia, Africa, and North and South Americas. He became obsessed with free-climbing El Cap after his first attempt in 1996. Now he has freed more routes on the Big Stone than any other climber; the routes include the Salathé Wall, the Muir Wall/Shaft Variation, Lurking Fear, West Buttress, and the Zodiac. He resides where he was raised, in Estes Park, Colorado.

THE INCREDIBLE HULK

Hitting the jackpot in the High Sierra, California

PETER CROFT

Venturi Effect, Pitch 4, The Book of Secrets: weird incut dykes and a crack that would suddenly appear and then vanish just as quickly. *Dave Nettle*

A t three in the morning I couldn't stand it anymore. Although we had set the alarm for five, I was just too wound up. Catnapping through the night, every hour or so I had checked the glowing face of my watch and then, turning slightly, looked up through my tent door at the hulking black silhouette of a wall that blocked out half the stars.

Without a moon, all the secrets of the wall lay hidden. The pitches we had climbed so far on earlier efforts I saw now in my mind's eye. A couple of them, steep blank corners of bewildering bridging, were easily the hardest free climbing yet done in the High Sierra. One of them, in particular, smacked me down completely on my first attempts. Just two days earlier I had managed to lead that pitch, arriving at the belay mystified, unable to remember any of the crux moves. Above our high point lurked a series of unknowns, and in the dark I imagined the best and the worst.

The Incredible Hulk, its summit a bit higher than 11,000 feet, lies just north of Yosemite National Park. Invisible from roads or other climbing areas, it sits at the head of a steep, trackless canyon. West facing and 1,500 feet high, the main wall has a big, cold feeling to it at first light, colder yet if the usual Hulk wind is blowing. Those strong winds are a double-edged sword, for although they can make an ascent a race to stay warm—or a nightmare to retreat from—they also scour the stone, with the result that the rock is the best I've seen in the range.

My first trips here were simply to repeat the two big classics, Positive Vibrations and the Red Dihedral. From those routes I glimpsed a number of unclimbed crack systems, a couple of them running the height of the wall. Awed by the place, I assumed that if they hadn't been done they must be hopeless to free climb. I don't know what I was thinking.

Intent on coffee, I wiggled out of my sleeping bag and tiptoed past Dave Nettle and Greg Epperson lying sound asleep in their respective bivy tents, immune, apparently, to the buzzing tension I felt. Dave, who had been with me on the first foray onto this route, had made scores of first ascents up and down the range and so, perhaps, could afford to be nonchalantly asleep. Greg, the master climbing photographer, had loads of big-wall experience, but on this trip photography would be his main focus, so he, too, could slumber on. I, on the other hand, was facing my first big new route in the High Sierra and any further attempt at sleep was useless. Over the past ten years I had combed the range for big traverses, climbing new ground here and there as I linked peaks together, but had never tried my hand at a first ascent up any of the big walls.

Our route followed the massive dihedrals just left of Positive Vibes, a line, I've since learned, that a number of people had been eyeing. Dave himself had had a stab at it some years before but had been stopped by steep, blank ground. Because of his work schedule it had now been several weeks since we had gone up to explore those corners. Back in early June of 2004 he and I climbed seven pitches, with Dave putting out a beast of an effort aiding up the crackless sixth and seventh pitches to place protection bolts. A week later Kevin Calder, a friend from Bishop, helped me find a more direct start to the route, following some unlikely but beautiful 5.11 cracks. Finally, just the day before yesterday Greg and I had climbed those seven pitches again to fix ropes for his photographic efforts. Although this time I managed to free climb to there, my optimism was tempered by the uncertainty above and the threat of thunderstorms that been pounding the mountains.

Behind our tents a large boulder formed a cave for our kitchen, and I hunkered down in the back of it with the warm glow of the stove and the smell of good coffee. Soon I heard the others stirring and I put another pot on. The day could begin.

We left camp in half light, hiked up steep talus, and began climbing 20 minutes later. Greg, loaded down with camera gear, became the jugging machine sprinting for position while

Dave and I swung leads up the first five pitches. After the initial lead of 5.10 the route stiffened up into 5.11 for a few hundred feet before steepening as we climbed out a large overhang to gain the main corner.

At the small ledge at the base of the sixth pitch I got ready for the first hard climbing. Wall exposure sunk in as I placed a small TCU and made the first wide stem. Here the rock reared up steeper at the same time as the left wall of the dihedral turned to glass. Bolts protected the rest of the pitch and it was a good thing, too. The back of the corner was truly blank; I doubted a rurp could punch its way in. Luckily, the right wall had a smattering of small edges, and I crimped on those when I could while bridging out on the polish to my left.

Once I'm way up off the ground, wide stemming is my favorite type of climbing. The climbing becomes increasingly multi-dimensional with arms and legs spanned wide across the two facets. Looking down in the middle of a hard move and seeing nothing but thin air, you become fully conscious of where you are.

Pulling up onto a small belay ledge, I was only too aware that the pressure was on. The pitch I had just done was full value 5.12, and the one above was a number grade harder than that. Even though I had climbed these pitches before, I had no recollection of the crux moves ahead, other than that they were maddeningly complex and delicate. Over my left shoulder thunderclouds were already building; with at least a half dozen pitches to go I felt there was simply no time for falling and flailing.

Without any preliminaries, the crux began with wide, wide bridging, at once both delicate and powerful. Often I was forced to make three or four intricate moves in order to position myself for one move up. Halfway up, the pitch eased off to 5.12, but the sustained climbing and tiny holds kept the intensity level amped up until the very end.

At the belay I shook my head in disbelief. I could remember none of the crux moves; my mind seemed more pumped than my forearms. Dave speedily arrived and slapped me on the back, grinning. Through the last two pitches he had French-freed the majority, yarding on quick draws and standing in slings. Now, though, he was eager to try the next pitch, another dihedral. Although this one started out blank, 30 feet up a finger crack appeared on the left wall.

We could see that black lichen and some loose flakes lined the crack above, so I aid climbed up to clean it. Mindful of the darkening clouds, I went as fast as I could, leapfrogging brass nuts and TCUs to near the top and then lowering and doing my best to prepare the pitch for Dave.

By the time we switched ends of the rope Dave was ready. My best guess about the pitch was that it would be something like 5.11+, if we were lucky. Dave likes to give the impression that his upper limit is 5.10+ which I know is bull but there was still no doubt he would be stretched. What followed was one of the best efforts I've seen in years. Insecure bridging, fingertip liebacking and horizontal full-body stems took him up into the finger crack. Gasping, he managed another 20 feet before pitching off.

After Dave lowered and cleaned the gear it was my turn. Still fooled by his modesty, I under-estimated the difficulty. In no time at all I was fighting for every inch, wrangling in gear and sucking thin air. I had hoped that once I reached the finger crack I'd be in there, but as soon as I did it angled away from the corner making the corner impossible to stem off of. There was little I could do but smear my feet on polished granite and crank on the thin jams.

As I climbed up onto a good ledge, I felt cooked. Belaying Dave with my heavy arms, I had new respect for his effort. The pitch had been much harder than I had guessed, probably

The west face of the Incredible Hulk, 1,500 feet tall, whose summit lies at just over 11,000 feet. The cliff is actually much wider than it appears in this photo. All known routes: (1) Blowhard (IV 5.12+); (2) Polish Route; (3) Airstream (V 5.13); (4) Sunspot (V 5.11); (5) Positive Vibrations (V 5.11); (6) Venturi Effect (V 5.12+); (7) Red Dihedral (IV 5.10). Route information supplied by Peter Croft. *Dave Nettle*

The sixth pitch of Airstream (5.12+)—little edges on the right wall, blank glass on the left. *Dave Nettle*

5.12+ or so. His underestimation of his abilities was laughable, for he had climbed deep into the difficulties.

Greg arrived at the ledge and helped haul the pack. His cheerful strength and efficiency on this wall helped make this one of the smoothest running and most enjoyable big climbs I've ever done.

The three of us gazed up at the route. The cracks got fatter now—finger and hand, fist and off-width. Dave led two pitches from there to the ridgecrest. One of them was brilliant, involving a wild overhanging face traverse from a hand crack to an arching corner. Pulling out of an overhanging off-width into the sun, he quickly ran the rope out to the ridge.

We climbed up and into the top of Positive Vibes, where beautiful sunlit finger and hand cracks took us to easy ground. Here it appeared that the thunderheads realized we would summit and decided to give up. The dark clouds turned lighter and the blue soon outweighed the gray. Several hundred feet of mid-fifth took us to a final steep corner and soon we were on top.

Sitting on the summit, the three of us took it all in. With the storm threat gone we were able to laugh at the earlier intensity. Now, we allowed ourselves to bask in what we had done. For Dave, another big new route, one that he had been dreaming about for years. Free climbing as much as he could, he had surpassed himself. Greg had photography as his main objective, alternately jumaring and climbing as was practical. The confident grin he sported on top confirmed that he had "got it." For me it was a summit of summits. This was the hardest big free climb that I had ever done and my first in the High Sierra. At that point I was quite sure that I was done with the Hulk. I had no idea.

In the days that followed, my thoughts kept returning to the Hulk, not so much to the route we had just done, which we named Airstream, but to the crack systems on either side. Back home in Bishop I came to realize that I cared nothing about Tuolumne and the Valley and next to nothing about the rest of the Sierra. I became obsessed; I knew it and reveled in it.

Before long I was back, this time with Scott Carson out of Salt Lake City. Jimmy Dean is what some call him, out of their reverential awe upon viewing his bratwurst-sized fingers. On the first day Scott and I went up to investigate the cracks right of Positive Vibes. Starting on that route, we climbed several hundred feet to a large ledge from which we could view a beautiful left-facing dihedral that was an integral part of our proposed route. Right away I saw that it was too thin; free-climbable perhaps but at an absurd grade. I wanted no part of some pitch I would have to work on for days. So we decided to continue up Positive Vibes, a worthy goal since Scott hadn't climbed the Hulk yet.

Two pitches higher I had a hunch. I got Scott to lower me out around the arête to view that stunning corner. The farther down I went, the higher my hopes became. A hidden crack came into view, as well as some horizontal dikes. Satisfied that it would go, I yelled up to stop lowering. Elated, I grappled my way back up, taking as much tension as Scott could give me to regain the belay. From there we decided to follow PV to the top and return the next day. Under warm, sunny skies we flew up the pitches, and Scott got his first view of Hulk perfection.

The next day we re-ascended the first five pitches of PV to the Bivy Ledge, a large slanting shelf some 600 feet up. From there we did a series of rappels down the new corner system to do some cleaning, in particular some big loose blocks up high and some munge down low.

By noon we were back down on the ledge at the top of the second pitch of PV and ready to give it a go. The first pitch involved an unlikely-looking traverse to a flaring crack. Hanging on with my left hand, I whacked a knifeblade up to the hilt. A couple of blind, fingery moves led around the corner into the crack where a long reach between flaring jams provided the crux. This plunked me down at the base of a tan-colored corner I had eyed the day before. Scott joined me at the semi-hanging belay and I re-racked, leaning heavily on brass nuts and tiny TCUs.

The next hundred feet provided us with perhaps the best bridging corner I've ever done. The main crack varied between 1/8 and 1/4 inches, but every 25 feet or so a splitter finger-hand crack swept out of the bed of the corner and out onto the left wall. Wild stemming took me by the thin sections until I could get a rest when I gained the splitter. Even with the periodic reprieves that the finger and hand jams provided, it was still one of the hardest bridging pitches I have done, and I barely made it to the belay without falling. I called this pitch the Book of Secrets because of its many unusual and surprising features.

Scott came up, raving about the quality, and we climbed a steep, thuggy lieback to the Bivy Ledge. We rapped off from there, thrilled at the quality of the climbing. Although what we had done amounted only to a three-pitch variation, I felt the doors swing open, not just to the possibility of a fully independent line but also to other prospects I had scoped. It seemed that on this cliff every time I reached an impasse a hold appeared or a crack opened up.

I felt as though my friends and I were playing a lottery with a huge jackpot and that we had winning tickets—and no one else was even bothering to play. I was the luckiest, though, because, while my friends were sporadically psyched, I was full time obsessed.

Dave was certainly the hungriest of my friends, with a great ability to think big. He and I had spoken about the possibilities of a free line right of PV, in particular the upper headwall cracks on the Macedonian Route, an old aid line from the seventies. Dave had had a go years

The third pitch of Airstream. Desperate looking, but full of hidden surprises (5.11). *Dave Nettle*

before but was turned back by ever-thinning finger cracks. Now, with the guts of an independent start in place, Dave and I decided to investigate that upper headwall.

Returning to the Bivy Ledge, he and I set out on the headwall, free climbing at first and then resorting to aid as the cracks pinched down and the angle steepened. We spent all day pulling on biners and standing in slings, cleaning off flakiness and loose blocks, including a massive guillotine flake that narrowly missed me when I pulled on it. Here and there we placed bolts, either for belays or for protection, but it was a small amount compared with the long blank sections we had had to deal with on Airstream. Although we didn't try to free the pitches, it was clear to me that the route would go. Bubbling with tentative enthusiasm, we reached a point a couple of hundred feet from the ridgecrest and rapped the 1,200 feet to the ground. We called this line the Venturi Effect out of deference to the windy nature of the place and because of the funnel-like finish to the headwall. Hiking out that evening, I grinned knowing that the pieces of the puzzle were there. I couldn't wait to get back and I didn't. The next few weeks were spent either going to the Hulk or planning to go there. Phoning friends in town, and then friends outside of town, I left stalker messages on a score of answering machines. Eventually one would pay off and I'd head back in.

My longtime friend Andrew Stevens stepped into the picture at this point and, with Dave's blessing, we went up to free the headwall. Beneath threatening skies we did just that, bullied by booming thunder and afternoon showers. Under the gun, flashing pitches became more than a game; it became critical strategy. As it was, we barely made it to the top of the headwall before weather dictated a retreat.

Andrew and I also made a stab at a line on the shady north face but retreated when we ran into crappy rock. We then shifted our attention to the prow at the far left side of the west face, an unlikely-looking line consisting of thin cracks and short blank sections. Unlike other Hulk routes, which tend to start off at a relatively low angle, this one began steep right out of the gate.

Starting on the nearby Polish Route, we angled up a few hundred feet and left to a ledge on the prow. After placing a few bolts, we climbed an incredible pitch face climbing up into a thin finger crack just left of the crest. The crux involved first knuckle finger jams while slapping up and heelhooking the bald arête. Toward the top of the pitch I ran out of the right-sized gear and had to face that heart-fluttering choice of going for it or jumping off. Too scared to jump and too pumped to hold on, I lunged for a jug and stuck it. Immediately I saw that no gear would go in, so I palmed the arête as high as I could--it was crap. I edged higher and clamped down, front-pointed on nothing footholds, and quickly stood up on the jug. Hyperventilating, I looked down at the exposure and at the fall I would have taken. I quickly laced up the crack in front of me.

The next pitch took a blind step around to the right side of the arête, where a perfect handcrack shot up for a long pitch to a ledge on the Polish Route. We followed this for a last long lead to the top. We called this route Blowhard.

More trips followed. Chris McNamara and I climbed the Venturi Effect to 3/4 height. Hans Steingartner and I did a direct start to Blowhard. I simply couldn't stay away. Somewhere in there, though, I injured my left elbow, and by early September, when Dave and I were ready to push to the top of Venturi, I knew I had to take a break. It was a heartbreaking decision to make and so I didn't make it.

The 5.13 third pitch of Airstream. Mind frazzlingly technical, toe numbingly footsy. *Dave Nettle*

Dave and I alpine started in on September 4. One way or another, this would be my last trip of the season to the Hulk. Either my elbow would cooperate and we'd make it or it wouldn't and I'd have to slink out with my tail between my legs, with a stack of "what ifs" to stew on over the winter.

If we were going to roll the dice, we at least wanted the stakes to be high, so we opted for a car-to-car ascent. Shorter days and the burly approach ensured that if it worked this would be the full package.

We started at the lowest point of the face, at the right side of a triangular slab. Dave led an initial awkward 5.11 pitch and I followed, babying my elbow as much as I could. I found I was able to hold on with my left arm but that cranking on it was tricky. Throughout the day this forced me into making bizarre sequences that allowed me to give the lion's share of the work to my right arm.

The landmarks of the route rolled by: the Book of Secrets, the Bivy Ledge, and then the headwall. The sun hit us halfway up this on a long 5.12 finger crack just below the ninth and final crux pitch. By now I was taking a mental note at the end of every pitch of how much farther we had to go, a sure sign that I was getting tired. The next lead involved three 5.12 cruxes with a heartbreaker move right at the end. I had one chance to get it right.

At the last crux I felt fried. The contorted efforts I had made in order to favor my elbow were now making themselves felt. Liebacking off rounded seams and stemming as wide as I could, I committed to the final moves to the belay. In the midst of it a foot skidded and both hands slipped. Teeth gritted, I held on and barely, barely made it. One more 11+ liebacking pitch took us through the Venturi to the top of the headwall.

Sitting on a wild belay perch and belaying Dave, I watched the sun get low in the sky. It was a clear metaphor for the end of the Hulk season, which was okay by me. We raced up the last four easier pitches, tagged the top and ripped down the descent. Hiking in the dark those last few miles was one of those descents I wished would never end.

I'd like to say that the plums are now picked, but I'd never get away with such a baldfaced lie. I can, however, take some solace in the fact that all the factors that have guarded the Sierra from overdevelopment are still in place. Strenuous approaches, thunderstorms, and thin air are just some of the defenses that make highcountry climbing what it is. But the host of variables that make alpine rock climbing distasteful to some make it nirvana to others. Last summer at the Hulk was clearly one of those right-place-at-the-right-time situations. Grades in the High Sierra had slipped far behind other California climbing areas (somewhere in the 11+\12- range), leaving the range ripe for picking plums. To a certain extent, Yosemite experienced a similar situation in the mid-1980s. At that time a number of luminaries predicted that the Valley was dead, that the rock was simply too smooth to be conducive to hard free climbing. Many believed it and shifted their focus to other areas with more featured rock. Now it's plain to see that smooth-featured, impossible-looking granite is often climbable. In the High Sierra there are granite walls hiding throughout the 150-mile length of the range. What am I saying? I should shut my trap.

SUMMARY OF STATISTICS:

> AREA: Northern Sierra Nevada, California
> PEAK: Incredible Hulk, 11,300 feet, west face
> ROUTES: Airstream (1,500 feet, V 5.13). Peter Croft, Greg Epperson, and Dave Nettle. July 3, 2004. Blowhard (800 feet, IV 5.12+). Peter Croft and Andrew Stevens. July 2004. Direct start: Peter Croft, Hans Steingartner. August 2004. Venturi Effect (1,500 feet, V 5.12+). Peter Croft and Dave Nettle. September 3, 2004.

A NOTE ABOUT THE AUTHOR:

Peter Croft is a Canadian living in Bishop, California, with his wife Karine. He works as a guide and have been climbing for about 25 years.

FREE HALLUCINATIONS

Defining a new game: "free aid" on the Hallucinogen Wall, in the Black Canyon of the Gunnison, Colorado.

JARED OGDEN

View of North Chasm View Wall with Hallucinogen shown. *Jeff Achey*

In 1980, four climbers must have been hallucinating when they set out for a new route in the Black Canyon of the Gunnison: their chosen wall looked impossibly blank. But when Bryan Becker, Ed Webster, Bruce Lella, and Jimmy Newberry topped out after a final push of eight days, they completed one of the hardest aid climbs in the world, the Hallucinogen Wall.

A free ascent of the Hallucinogen would be a dream climb for any Black Canyon aficionado, yet it had never seen an attempt. Many climbers overlook the Black Canyon because of its reputation for poor rock, which is fairly accurate. However, the Hallucinogen follows some of the best rock in the canyon. The route's reputation for horrific runouts and hard climbing was legendary, and any ascent, free or aid, is a mental and physical challenge.

Hoping the Hallucinogen would go free, in May 2003 I rappelled the top four pitches with Mike Sheppard to investigate. I tried freeing the bolt ladder on pitch 13 unsuccessfully. The overhanging face was fairly blank with more bolt ladders below, and the project seemed improbable. That fall I did another reconnaissance, with Topher Donahue, to the top of pitch 8, where we worked it out all free on follow. Things were looking better, but to free the whole route still seemed like a long shot.

I returned in March 2004 with Ryan Nelson on a three-day attempt that ended at the top of pitch 10 when heavy snowfall forced a retreat. On pitch 6 I bolted, on lead, a two-bolt, 40-foot, 5.12+ variation that avoided the pendulum used on the first ascent. On that attempt we freed every move on top-rope through pitch 10, but the remaining two pitches I hadn't yet seen and remained a mystery. We were thrilled with our progress yet terrified by the lack of protection for leading it as a free climb. Ed Webster, a prolific pioneer in the canyon, recently said that Hallucinogen was the hardest route—both mentally and physically—that he had done there. It was proving to be just as hard for us, too.

Hallucinogen follows an obvious corner system for five pitches, then breaks off into a blank-looking wall. Pitches 6 through 13 comprise the hardest aid done on the first ascent and involve extensive copperheading, hooking, and thin nailing. At pitch 14 the route joins a prominent crack and chimney system that reaches the top for a total of 16 pitches in 1,800 feet. The first-ascent party placed a high priority on minimal drilling (only 45 holes), thus creating extreme aid climbing with mind-numbing runouts. Today, as on the first ascent, the possibility of falling 70 feet or more is often present, adding to the character of the route. The route's dangerous reputation was appealing to us, but preserving the original character of the climb was more important than free climbing it.

Continuing our efforts during the spring, Ryan and I, with several ropes fixed, would rappel into the canyon and rehearse pitches 9–13 on top-rope, then jug out. The chore of rappelling in and jugging out, in addition to trying to free the pitches, was so taxing that we worked on it only two days a week. For the free climb we didn't change the original route by adding bolts or fixed gear of any kind, but we did remove some deadly blocks, broken fixed gear, and garbage, in addition to replacing 30 of the original bolts, some of which I pulled out with my fingertips. Working out the moves on top-rope felt secure, but the exposure never went away. The roar of the river 1,500 feet directly underfoot added to the intense interaction with the canyon.

Every pitch except one went free. Appropriately, it was pitch 13, the second Fear and Loathing Roof that we couldn't find a solution to. The 30-foot bolt ladder on the headwall at the end had a few blank sections, and after numerous attempts to piece together a free sequence we finally gave up. Had there been six or seven more holds, the pitch would have gone free. The entire route had gone free except for this short section—and to have it go at A0 wasn't acceptable.

The modified pick is a cut off pecker piton.
Topher Donahue

To solve this problem we decided to try leashless ice tools since the picks might hold onto dimples of rock too small for fingers. We chose leashless tools to maintain the difficulty associated with hard mixed climbs that are considered "free" climbs. Using a piece of 5mm cord, we tethered the tools to a shoulder sling so we wouldn't lose them if we fell. It was unlike anything we'd ever done before. The sequences linking the blanks went something like this: use a tool on a dimple while pasting rock shoes on smears, reach up for a sloping side pull with your hand, hit a crimp with the other hand, then reach with the tool again, match hands on the tool, more hand holds, and so on. This gave us "free" passage past the short blanks between the usable handholds. One hold was too small for the standard pick, so we customized it by bolting the head of a Pecker piton to the tip of the pick. This hold was the size of a ballpoint-pen tip, but the custom pick held and the pitch linked up.

On the first ascent, where they'd already established A5 hooking and copperheading, the leaders had resorted to drilling a bolt ladder on this section. Could they have avoided drilling as many bolts had they used free-aid? Our decision to apply dry tooling to the face compromised our "free" ascent, but could it be the solution to cleaner and freer routes of the future?

Bryan Becker explains his style of climbing on the first ascent of the Hallucinogen: "The game I liked to play was to place as few bolts as possible, hence my many hours dinking around on lead with equalizing hooks, blades, copperheads, etc., along with numerous little tension traverses and the sketchy style I have always referred to as 'fraid' climbing—using your fingers, toes, and marginal pieces simultaneously to move upward. 'Fraid' (obviously short for 'afraid') I believe accurately described my emotional state numerous times while in that mode on the climb. It was fun experimenting, and it was the hardest aid climb I'd done at that time in the Black."

Leashless mixed climbing has been accepted as a legitimate form of climbing at mixed crags and in the mountains to navigate terrain that would be otherwise too icy, cold, or impossible to free climb with bare hands and rock shoes. To us it seemed a natural progression to apply these techniques to the blank sections in order to "free" the pitch. However, "free" climbing is defined by climbing a face or crack using only your hands and feet, so technically this wasn't "free." Instead, it's a hybrid that we call "free-aid."

We think free-aid is an improvement on aid climbing because you can climb a face or crack that's too thin to free in the traditional sense, but it is still harder than simply clipping bolts or gear and walking up ladders. It's also faster than aid and less damaging to the rock than

Ryan Nelson on the end of pitch 13 in between hand holds. *Topher Donahue*

the repeated hammering in and out of pitons or drilling bolts. Free-aid also allows you to simultaneously distribute your weight across your tools and feet, making available holds that hooks might otherwise break. You can also use the picks to sidepull and undercling edges, techniques that are impractical or impossible in traditional aid.

Appalled critics like Alex Huber spoke out against free-aid, mentioning that El Capitan could look like mixed routes he'd seen in Europe that had broken or chipped holds if free-aid

Jared freeing pitch 12, 5.13-R. *Topher Donahue*

was used there. This is a fair argument, and both Ryan and I would never want such an atrocity to happen. Free-aid should never be brought to a free climb. The idea is to make aid climbing more efficient and cleaner so routes won't get damaged and less bolting will take place. Ironically it's the repeated use of pitons in cracks that has made routes on El Capitan possible to free climb.

In the early 1990s Charlie Fowler and Xavier Bongard did the first hammerless ascent of the Shield on El Capitan by using Black Diamond Spectre hooks (a short ice pick used for ice protection) in their arsenal of customized tools for clean protection. Is there any difference between hanging all your weight on a hand-placed Spectre hook (or aid hook for that matter) and free-aid using leashless ice tools and rock shoes? If not, then which is closer to free climbing or more difficult: free-aid climbing a face using leashless tools and hands while wearing rock shoes, or hanging in your harness and walking up ladders old-school style? Decide for yourself, but we're not the only ones trying this free-aid style. In 2004 Ivo Ninov was going to attempt the Shield using free-aid, however he never managed to due to crowding and logistics. In 2003 Steve House and Marko Prezelj climbed the north face of North Twin in the Canadian Rockies using ice tools on the rock to free climb past where others had aided. This shows the style has potential. Is free-aid the next step in the evolution of aid?

By mid-May we felt ready for a redpoint attempt. We had been building just as much mental fitness as physical for this climb. The lack of available protection meant that if we couldn't climb we also couldn't rest on the rope and were faced with a dangerous whipper. At night I'd lie awake running sequences through my head and what would happen to me if I fell. It was horrible, and my imagination was filled with visions of broken bones or worse. Physically we felt ready, but the mental game proved a much greater challenge.

On May 20, our first redpoint day, Ryan tried pitch 13 four times until he sent it. If we fell on any pitch, we would lower back to the belay, pull the rope, and re-lead it without falling.

A broken hold plus a few slips were frustrating and sapped his energy. But his success boosted our outlook for the rest of the climb since this pitch had been a huge question mark. We rated it D10+, the D replacing the M in mixed grades. The D (for dry) was the only way we could try to explain the difficulty. It's similar to M (mixed) ratings or a 5.13- pump. Perhaps introducing a new grading system is ridiculous, but we think it's very different from the M grades: wearing rock shoes, using face holds in tandem with tools, and obviously no ice.

Then I sent pitch 14 (5.12-) and tried pitch 12 (5.13-R). The protection at the first crux on pitch 12 is a RURP and a long string of manky fixed heads. Not inspiring. Then you traverse under and out a roof 20 feet over a knifeblade to a headwall for a 165-foot pitch, the longest crux on the climb. There are just enough holds on the bolted headwall, but I still blew off. I was too tired to try it again, so we settled into our bivy site at the bottom of pitch 12 (we had rapped in earlier that day with three days' worth of food and water).

We decided to do the pitches out of order over three consecutive days while living on the wall. We figured that if we started from the ground and failed up high due to fatigue it would mean failure for this season. The heat of summer was quickly approaching and we only had a three-day window. For us it was an acceptable compromise to the ground-up style we desired. For comparison, Todd Skinner's free ascent on Nameless Tower in Pakistan and Moby Dick on Ulamertorssuaq in Greenland were done in the same way and were accepted as free ascents. In the future we'd like to do it again from the ground, but we did the best we could under the circumstances. Indeed, our style of ascent could be improved upon and we hope in the future a team will onsight the route in a day or at least do it from the ground. Perhaps someone will free the whole thing! Like anything new in climbing it will evolve. Hallucinogen hasn't yet reached its final chapter.

The next morning I sent pitch 12 first try. I had broken a huge mental barrier because I hadn't been able to send the pitch clean on top-rope. With that momentum Ryan then sent pitch 9. He later recalled this pitch: "When I looked up at pitch 9 through the sunlight, all I could see were copperhead wires poking out through a sea of granite. The climbing on this pitch was beautiful. I moved quietly, trying not to disturb the crusty exfoliating edges I trusted my well being to, ignoring what I was clipping as I went. This pitch plagued my mind more than any other on the route, and my visualizations of potential mistakes were vivid reminders of the mindset I needed to be in during the send. What made me want to continue was the fact that Jared faced the same demons; he put his neck out and so would I."

Pitch 9 (5.13-R) is 100 feet of crimping ending with a technical roof and face. Only three bolts and a few worthless copperheads protect the entire pitch. The thought of pulling the crux 30 feet above the last bolt made us want to boot. Just two moves from the anchor Ryan's foot popped off. Somehow he stabbed for a crimp and clipped the anchor, avoiding a 70-footer! He said it was the scariest moment of his life.

Pitch 10 (5.13-R), the hooking pitch, is similar with 100 feet of crimping with only five bolts for protection, two of which are right next to each other. The crux is only 10 feet above the final bolt, but the sustained 5.12 climbing in between the previous three bolts makes the potential for taking a 70-footer an unpleasant reality. I hadn't done it on top-rope without a rest, so I was really gripped. I begged for mercy, crimped hard, and pulled it off. We were so stoked that our screams bounced all the way down the canyon. We finished the day with pitch 11 (5.12R) and both arrived at the bivy totally psyched that we hadn't fallen.

Having the hardest and most dangerous pitches behind us was a major relief.

Ryan cruxing on pitch 13. *Topher Donahue*

We celebrated with shots of whisky on our ledge. Neither of us had ever pushed that hard not to fall. We could have added bolts to make it safer, but that would have ruined the challenge. It would have left little to aspire to and certainly would have changed the character of the climb. By pushing ourselves to rise up and face those challenges, the rewards were deeply satisfying.

The final day we rapped with two ropes to the ground and quickly climbed through pitch 5. It had been over a month since I led pitch 6 (5.12+) and I nearly fell off. Ryan and I then sent pitches 7 (5.12b) and 8 (5.11+) and jugged up to the top of our ropes on pitch 14. Two pitches later we topped out successful. By chance, Jimmy Newberry (from the first ascent), who'd just stopped by for a look into the canyon on his way home, shared the moment with us.

As far as free-aid goes, we think it's got a place in the future. Applying free-aid to new routes, especially in the mountains, where cold and intense weather prevent free climbing, and aid climbing is too slow, may be its best application. Would a new route on Baffin Island done free-aid style receive praise or criticism? Is it right or wrong? I don't know. Bryan Becker believes that "almost all climbing—unless you go at it shoeless, naked and unroped—is aid. All gear helps, assists, and aids us in our ascents of whatever medium and location we choose."

Critics who don't climb mixed routes or understand the potential benefits of free-aid won't see the value and will probably disagree with the technique. Having open minds about style and ethics brought free-aid to our attention. Will it catch on? Maybe, but it might just die out like Spandex did. Perhaps it's our own pipe dream. We've climbed at the highest levels of mixed climbing and climbed lots of 5.13s, up to 13+, so we have respect for both mediums. We also have respect for pure aid climbing. In fact we like all disciplines of climbing no matter how dogmatic the practitioners. For us it was a natural progression to put mixed and aid climbing together on the Hallucinogen while maintaining a high degree of ethics and traditional free climbing. Ryan adds that he "has sympathy for those who oppose us on free-aid, and I can't blame them for not understanding our reasoning behind opening this style. The key for us was to drop all predefined biases that are associated with climbing's many disciplines. If you break down the concepts from alpinism, aid climbing, mixed climbing, and every other style of climbing you will find common threads that interweave and borrow traits from one another. Human nature has played a part in how we categorize and place rules for these styles, often causing a myopic outlook on how the sport can evolve. By dropping these notions and looking to objectivity as our guide, we found that free-aid worked to shed new light on pitch 13, and possibly opened doors for a freer, cleaner, and faster form of aid climbing."

Ed Webster recently commented that our greatest contribution to "freeing" the route was our "creative problem-solving in finding ways to free climb virtually the entire climb by going into brave new territory, conceptually and physically. Pushing the limits, all of them, that's what it's all about in the Black Canyon!" Bryan Becker adds, "What's most important is that we use our energies to get out and go to these beautiful and wild places that climbing takes us." We agree.

We did the Hallucinogen how we wanted to do it for ourselves, not because we were trying to introduce something new. If we had freed the route in the traditional free style perhaps no one would have even noticed. But because we used ice tools on a handful of moves on the 30-foot section it's become a controversial style. That's par for the course when you think about the introduction of V ratings and sport climbing. They too received criticism yet are now considered the cutting edge of modern free climbing. The Hallucinogen was scary as hell and you'd get really whacked if you fell at the wrong spot. We had to believe in ourselves to overcome those fears, and that was tough to do since the consequences of a fall could have ended our climbing altogether.

To this day I still get sweaty palms when I think about our experience on the Hallucinogen Wall. It's the hardest "free" climb we've ever done. Yeah, we've climbed harder pitches and done much longer routes, but those were hard in different ways. The level of risk involved at a high climbing standard is what really made it stand out and that was most exciting. The Black Canyon is full of adventure, whether you're hallucinating or just getting high on a rock!

Summary of Statistics:

Area: Black Canyon of the Gunnison, Colorado.

Ascent: Free Hallucinations (VI 5.13-R D10+), Jared Ogden and Ryan Nelson, May 20-22, 2004.

A Note About the Author:

Jared Ogden, 33, lives in Colorado not far from the Black Canyon. He has made first ascents from Patagonia to Pakistan, including Parallel Worlds on the Great Trango, and is one of America's most well-rounded climbers. He puts up new routes at or near the top standards in aid, mixed, alpine, free, expedition, speed, big wall, and now "free aid." He is has written a book, Big Wall Climbing: Elite Technique, *published by The Mountaineers books.*

Miriam O'Brien (later Underhill) in the Chamonix aiguilles in the 1920s. From: *Women Climbing: 200 Years of Achievement*

Going Manless

Looking back, forward, and inward 75 years after Miriam O'Brien Underhill's milestone all-female ascent of the Grépon in the French Alps.

MOLLY LOOMIS

"The Grépon has disappeared. Now that it has been done by two women alone, no self-respecting man can undertake it. A pity, too, because it used to be a very good climb." [1] Those were the words of French alpinist Etienne Bruhl in 1929 on the return of Miriam O'Brien Underhill and Alice Damesme from their successful manless ascent of the classic Alps test piece of the era, The Grepón. Women climbing "alone"—without the presence of a man—was in those days a scandalous act.

The year 2004 marked the 75th anniversary of American Underhill and Frenchwoman Damesme's ascent, a hallmark in the history of women's climbing. Although one other recorded "en cordée féminine" climb had taken place (Elizabeth Le Blond and Lady Evelyn McDonnell's winter traverse of Piz Palü on the Swiss-Italian border in 1900), in the late 1920s the Grépon was considered one of the Alps's toughest climbs; the daring and gall required for two women to climb a route as technical as the Grépon shocked the climbing community.

Despite prejudices and obstacles created by societal norms, women have followed Underhill's lead and succeeded in style on the world's most difficult routes: Alison Hargreaves blitzing the classic north faces of the Alps, Lynn Hill freeing The Nose in a day, and Ines Papert winning Overall First at the Ouray Ice Festival. And many of today's top female alpinists, like Abby Watkins, Karen McNeill, Heidi Wirtz, and Sue Nott, often choose to climb in all-women's teams, continuing Underhill's manless tradition. But, despite a long list of impressive ascents helping to dispel doubts about women's capabilities in the mountains, and the near-century that has passed since Underhill and Damesme's groundbreaking ascent, women remain a minority in the world's high places.

Why?

Even before Underhill, Lucy Walker, Anna and Ellen Pigeon, Katy Richardson, and Lily Bristow scaled peaks throughout the Alps (accompanied by guides or experienced men). Even now, 75 years after Underhill's ascent of the Grépon, when I'm with my girlfriends at a popular crag or high in the mountains, we still encounter comments ranging from complimentary and kind to condescending and rude, their message being that we are women and we are climbing, a combination unusual enough to warrant commentary.

Driven by an interest in climbing history, a curiosity to hear the perspectives and insight of my foremothers, and a belief that female voices aren't heard enough, I set out in search of their stories. With bivouac conversations and e-mail discussions with nearly two dozen leading climbers in today's small sorority of alpinists, I've tried to explore what keeps our numbers down and what the future holds for women in high places.

REASONS FOR CLIMBING EN CORDÉE FÉMININE:

Credit Where Credit is Due

Noted in 1957 as "undoubtedly the greatest lady climber that America has produced,"[2] Under-hill writes in her 1956 autobiography *Give Me the Hills* that she was drawn to the idea of man-less ascents as a means of proving to herself and others the depth of her climbing skill: "Very early I realized that the person who invariably climbs behind a good leader…may never really learn mountaineering at all and in any case enjoys only part of the varied delights and rewards of climbing…. He is, after all, only following…. If he is also the leader, the one who carries the supreme responsibility for the expedition, he tastes the supreme joys…. I saw no reason why women, *ipso facto*, should be incapable of leading a good climb…. But I did realize that if women were really to lead, that is, to take the entire responsibility for the climb, there couldn't be any man at all in the party. For back in the 1920s women were perhaps a bit more sheltered than they are today. In any emergency, particularly in an outdoor sport like mountaineering, what man wouldn't spring to the front to take over? I decided to try some climbs not only guideless but manless."[3]

Considering French climbing icon Catherine Destivelle's outstanding resumé of ascents in the Himalaya and the Alps, as well as rock and competition climbing, I was surprised when she told me, "When you climb a route

Miriam O'Brien Underhill.

with a man everyone says, 'Of course the guy does the job.' I have to accept that if I climb with a man." Although lauded as "one of the world's most accomplished all-around climbers,"[4] Destivelle, more than half a century after Underhill, has still been subjected to doubt.

Pacific Northwesterner Carla Firey, who made many impressive free ascents in the 1970s, didn't feel that she'd fully participated in the climbing experience unless she'd been on the sharp end: "If I don't participate in leading, I don't really count [the climb]. It's the leading that is really exciting."

Arlene Blum helped usher in relative acceptance in the 1970s for North American females on the world's highest peaks. After being denied admission onto multiple Denali expeditions ("I was told women could go as far as base camp. They didn't think women were strong enough to continue higher than that"), Blum took matters into her own hands, organizing an all-women's expedition up the peak in 1970. All six expedition members reached the summit. Blum subsequently spearheaded the well-publicized American Women's Himalayan Expedition to Annapurna I (26,540ft), and later a joint Indian-American Women's expedition up the virgin peak Bhrigunpanth in the Indian Himalaya.

When I asked Blum if she would organize something like the American Women's Himalayan Expedition now, she paused, then replied, "Probably not," citing the equality of men and women in the mountains today compared to when she was climbing.

Arlene Blum in 2005. *Annalise Blum*

Several of the women from Blum's era (she just turned 60) and earlier whom I contacted viewed "manless climbs" as a thing of the past—no longer a necessity, since women have proven they are capable of climbing at the same level as men.

To Blum the present number of females making significant ascents must seem astounding. The opportunities available to women climbers today weren't possible in the era of prejudice and doubt she experienced. But perhaps to her and her peers' surprise, many current climbers, both male and female, believe the vertical world still has a ways to grow before we've reached equality. We women may have proven we're capable, but many of those I contacted argue that our capability is still struggling for recognition. Many women seek all-women's expeditions to remind themselves and others of the female's capacity for climbing hard, without the shadow of doubt that a man in the team may cast on their abilities, either inadvertently by his own doing or by critical peers.

But climbing isn't just about proving yourself, of course: it's also fun. Many of today's most active female climbers climb "en cordée feéminine" simply because they enjoy the comfortable dynamic—the camaraderie—special to climbing in an all-women's team. By the same token, I suspect, many men prefer to climb with other guys.

Amy Bullard in 2003. *Sallie Shatz*

Special Dynamics

Amy Bullard received a copy of Blum's *Annapurna: A Woman's Place* when she turned 18, and remembers the inspiration it provided: "It gave me permission to climb in the big mountains."

In addition to first ascents in the Himalaya and Patagonia, and working as a mountain guide, Bullard, in 1999, led the first American women's expedition to attempt an 8,000-meter peak without supplemental oxygen or Sherpa climbing support. Three team members reached the summit.

"Cho Oyu felt so normal [compared to co-ed expeditions]. We didn't have to be so careful with what we said to each other, and we made decisions by

Monika Kambic-Mali in 2005. *Tanja Grmovsek*

consensus," she recalls. "We were criticized at base camp for bringing too much stuff up on the mountain, like sleeping bags to Camp Three, but in the end the guys slept in them while we were away!"

Coloradoan Heidi Wirtz, 36, who has participated in all-women's expeditions to China and Canada, and has several tough first ascents to her credit, like Bad Hair Day (VI 5.12-, all female team) on the South Howser Minaret and Quilombo (IV 5.11+ A1) in Patagonia, wrote to me, "I definitely think that it is way more inspiring to hear of two women getting after it together rather than a guy-girl team. I personally prefer climbing with women in the mountains. It feels a lot more empowering to me. Not to say that I don't have awesome male partners as well, but I feel more of a 'team' dynamics with a female partner."

New Zealander Karen McNeill, 35, who currently resides in Canada, admits candidly that climbing in an all-women's team often presents sponsorship opportunities—a point of distain among some males I know. But regardless of the publicity, McNeill, who has carried out manless expeditions to Patagonia, Greenland, British Columbia, India, Peru, and Nepal, has found she thrives when climbing in all-women teams. Most recently McNeil and her frequent partner Sue Nott completed the first all-women's ascent of McKinley's Cassin Ridge (Alaska Grade 5).

"Personally this is the best approach for me. I find men and women function differently. Being a woman we understand how each other works. We tend to be supportive, and there always seems room for discussion about the climb, direction, and decisions to be made. I haven't always found this with men. I have done my best climbs with women." Junko Tabei of Japan, best known as the first woman to scale Everest, has participated in an astounding 44 all-women's expeditions to high peaks around the world, including Shishapangma, Pobeda, McKinley, and the Eiger. Tabei, now 65, wrote me while climbing in Spain, "The satisfaction I get from women-only expeditions is greater than from mixed expeditions. When

the members have similar physical conditions, climbing becomes equal among them. It is much easier to be in a small tent with partners of the same sex, and I feel much happier when we overcome difficulties with only women."

The bottom line, as Wirtz, McNeill, and many others agreed, is that the ideal composition of a team comes down to what works best for the individual. Beth Rodden, 24, participated in a 1999 expedition to Madagascar with Lynn Hill, Kath Pyke, and Nancy Feagin, where they established the line Bravo Les Filles (5.12c A0). She told me, "Women can achieve their potential in any atmosphere depending on how hard they push themselves with their partner. If the individual believes that she

Junko Tabei. *Tabei collection in 2000.*

can only be pushed with other women, then there is the answer. Most of the time I climb better with men because they are stronger and therefore push me to aim higher." Rodden typically climbs with her husband Tommy Caldwell. She recently opened The Optimist (5.14b), the hardest climb to date established by an American woman.

Role Models

A highlight for McNeill from her Cassin success has been interest from other women climbers. "After the climb I've given a bunch of slideshows," she says. "Women come up to me and comment on how inspired they are to go into the mountains from seeing the show. To me that is the best part. I love it!" McNeill counts alpinists Anne Palmer, Pat Deavoll, and Brede Arkless as her own role models.

Abby Watkins in 2004. *Scott Wilson*

Abby Watkins, a certified Alpine Guide with the Association of Canadian Mountain Guides, is another firm believer in the importance of strong, accessible examples for female climbers. "The more successful role models there are out there," she says, "the more young women will be attracted to take the sport seriously. Being guided or taught by a man does not apply as directly as being guided or taught by a woman. Watching a man do something bears no significance to a woman—it simply does not apply to her."

I don't believe Watkins is referring to something as simplistic as a woman watching a man tie a knot, but she does verbalize something I've witnessed (and experienced) time and time again guiding, pointed out to me several years ago by a fellow guide, as experienced as I was old: "Women perform better when a woman guide is part of the team," he said, elaborating that excuses, whether silent or spoken, like "I'm not strong enough, tough enough, etc.; I'm a girl" are taken away. In front of their eyes a girl is succeeding.

For me it is more tangible, easily transferable, to watch a woman climb: I am in essence watching my own form—the form I most naturally, inherently relate to and identify with—and it doesn't stop at movement, but encompasses attitude and composure as well.

Kath Pyke, 39, who in addition to her ascent of Bravo Les Filles in Madagascar has made impressive first ascents in Iran, Pakistan, the United Kingdom, and the United States, believes a link exists between the media's portrayal of women climbers and the lack of accessible role models in the alpine realm. "Typically climbing media portray women with beautiful bodies achieving at sport climbing. Mountaineering involves a lot of grunt work that is rarely glamorous, and after a long demanding trip it may be difficult for people to discern if the climber is even female. It's rare that a journalist comes along on these trips and portrays these images. For a climber trying to transition from sport climbing to mountaineering there are few images, role models, or real people out there to talk to. Groups like Chicks With Picks and magazines like She Sends are doing a good job, but they don't reach enough people."

Founder and publisher emeritus of *She Sends*, Lizzy Scully, started the magazine in an attempt to address the void mentioned by Pyke. "I was a contributing editor for *Climbing* Magazine at the time [2002], and they wouldn't put more stuff in the magazine about women,"

Lizzy Scully and Heidi Wirtz, 2002. *Lizzy Scully*

she says (she clarifies that this has since changed). "I got frustrated and decided just to throw something together myself. It bummed me out to rarely see articles about and or by women. I wrote an article for the second issue of *Alpinist*, but I think I'm still the only woman to have an article about an alpine experience in that magazine."

Scully, who has organized all-women's expeditions to Canada, Pakistan, and India, often with Wirtz as a partner, says she was motivated to publish *She Sends* in part because she wanted "other women to see that women could climb big walls in foreign countries and organize expeditions." Scully continues, "I sought out great women climbers and great women who climbed because I wanted to be inspired. I figured *She Sends* would provide women such as myself with those role models."

It comes as no surprise that many climbers, including Scully, have been inspired by Lynn Hill, who stunned the climbing world with her one-day free ascent of El Capitan's Nose in 1994, a feat unrepeated by man or woman. Alison Osius, the only female president of the American Alpine Club (1998-1999), a former member of the U.S. Climbing Team, and a recipient of the AAC's Underhill Achievement Award for "outstanding mountaineering achievement," recalls the electrifying effect of Hill on women climbers, "Certainly women such as Mari Gingery or Barbara Devine in the 1970s, had been performing at a very high level before Lynn's era. But Lynn was so visible and did so many very hard climbs that it really normalized the idea of women doing them. After a while everyone realized that women can be strong climbers, that climbs are all different; they are often sequencey, and it's no big deal if a woman does a route first, in fact it happens all the time, and is to be expected."

THE VALUE OF FIRST FEMALE AND FIRST ALL-FEMALE ASCENTS

"A woman who has done good work in the scholastic world doesn't like to be called a good woman scholar," said Annie Smith Peck, one of the first women to make a career out of high-altitude mountaineering, to the *New York Times* in 1911. "Call her a good scholar and let it go at that. I have climbed 1,500 feet higher than any man in the United States. Don't call me a woman climber." [6]

Twenty years later, as the number of women leading routes in the Alps continued increasing, due largely to Underhill and Damesme's ascent of the Grépon and their subsequent climbs, representatives of Britain's Ladies Alpine Club wrote, "It is inconceivable that the average woman climber could ever compete with the average man, but the inequality is no longer so pronounced that any mountaineering feat by a woman should cause so much surprise. The time has come when a woman must no longer think it a matter of importance that she was the first or second of her sex to be taken up a difficult climb…. Can we hope that the day is not far off when our achievements will be judged on their own merits, rather than overpraised because we are women?"

Why is it then that three-quarters of a century later we still precede first-ascent information with "female" and "all-female"? Is it a marketing ploy to draw sponsorship to a climbing bum on a meager budget? Or does it have to do with a phrase in the previous paragraph: "*to be taken up* a difficult climb"—an easily missed indication of conditions which have hindered women's development in athletic endeavors? Is "First All-Female Ascent" a reminder that men's and women's backgrounds are different? Or do such distinctions divide us more than equalize us? I don't think there is one right answer, nor that the multiple answers are simple.

Kitty Calhoun, who has attempted numerous difficult first ascents around the world in co-ed teams, including the west face of Latok III and the west face of Middle Triple Peak, does not see a need to distinguish between first ascents and first female ascents, but she does appreciate its value for some. "No, I don't think there should be attention drawn to it," she says. "But for some girls it's important to have female role models. It's a good thing for articles to be written about women, so girls can have them."

Kathy Cosely, one of Calhoun's partners on the 1990 Makalu West Pillar expedition, estimates that 90 percent of her 28-year climbing career has been spent in the alpine zone. She believes she may have been the first North American woman to climb the North Face of the Eiger, Aconcagua's South Face, and Cerro Torre. She looks back on her and Mark Houston's ascent of Aconcagua's notorious South Face in 1992, accomplished in under two days. The wall is famed for its huge scale, dangerously loose rock, and seracs. "We bivied on the glacier and topped out in bright moonlight near midnight of our second day. It was very beautiful, and we felt satisfied that we'd done it as fast and as well as we could." As for Cerro Torre in 1998, "I was sort of trying to be the first woman on Cerro Torre, but missed it by a couple of months. An Italian woman, Rosanna Manfrini, beat me to it!"[8]

Recently, Slovenians Monica Kambic-Mali and Tanja Grmovsek completed what they considered to be the first all-female ascent of Cerro Torre. Kambic-Mali, who completed the first all-female ascent of Fitz Roy with Tina Di Batista (Slovensa), via the Franco-Argentine Route in 2004, describes their harrowing ascent up the Torre's Compressor Route's final pitches: "Just two pitches before the top I got hit by a block of ice dropped by English climbers above me. I saw the block falling and just had time to put my head down and got hit on my back. For more than five minutes I was in shock. After half an hour I thought, 'I have to go on,' and I did. My partner continued leading, and I followed jumaring very slowly, 20 centimeters each time, only using my left hand. It was very painful but I had to do it. I couldn't go down being so close to the top. I was just hoping the mushroom would not be too hard. Luckily it was very easy. My partner made good steps, and I could manage to the top finally! When I returned to Chalten, I went to the hospital [for] x-rays and they told me I had three ribs broken and that I had to rest for five weeks. But I climbed the Torre...."

In the gathering darkness at the top of the bolt ladder, shortly after the accident, Kambic-Mali and Grmorsek bypassed a few meters of copperhead-clipping by jumaring a rope brought up by the

Kitty Calhoun in 2004. *Susie Sutphin*

Kambic-Mali and Tanja Grmovsek in 2005.

Englishmen climbing above: a fact that in some climber's minds compromises their claim to a first all-female ascent.

In her post-expedition report Grmovsek writes, "In the end some climbs that I made with other women mean to me a bit more, because there was 'no cheating'; I had to do it all, solve all the problems by myself, so nobody could say I was pulled up by my climbing partner. To climb with an equal woman, to do a hard climb when you have to show all of your best and when you have to do it all by yourself is really a challenge."

Famed Polish alpinist Wanda Rutkiewicz wrestled with the ethics of first ascents and the definition of all-women's ascents. During the first all-women's winter ascent of the Matterhorn's north face (1978), she and her three teammates reached the summit; however, they were rescued shortly thereafter by a helicopter because one of the climbers was in critical condition. Rutkiewicz questioned the validity of their ascent, and feared that doubt would be cast by her peers.[9]

Rutkiewicz went on to summit eight of the fourteen 8,000m peaks, and made the first female ascent of K2, before she died on Kanchenjunga in 1992. From her experiences in the Himalaya, she pondered the legitimacy of a "women's expedition" that includes male Sherpas. In her much discussed paper *Women's Mountaineering in the Himalayas and Karakorum (in the last 25 years)*," presented at the 25th Jubilee of the Indian Mountaineering Federation, she stated, "All expeditions until 1981 to eight thousand meter peaks were not really women's expeditions, because Sherpas participated in each of them. Sherpas are also mountaineers. I do not see why it is necessary to make a distinction between the mixed men-women's expeditions and women's expeditions made with Sherpas."[10]

In 1994 she was posthumously awarded the King Albert Mountain Award for "her courageous, pioneering spirit in the development of feminine mountaineering and the exploration of the world's highest peaks for more than a quarter of a century."[11]

WHAT KEEPS WOMEN IN THE MINORITY?

Although a long list of examples proves women are capable of climbing the world's difficult routes, it is still a relatively small percentage who climb beyond the crags. I asked a number of today's women alpinists why. Their replies focused mostly on heavy loads, lack of exposure to successful role models, acceptance of risk, and motherhood.

Size and Natural Abilities

With a long list of first ascents and first female ascents in Patagonia, Pakistan, Kyrgyzstan, Baffin, and the United States, 5-foot 5-inch Steph Davis is no longer put off by the challenges of

Wanda Rutkiewicz.

weight and size that she once believed were hindrances. She often climbs with her husband Dean Potter, whom she describes as a "6-foot 5-inch giant," and sees challenges even for him: "I think that at first women can feel limited in alpinism by the amount of gear you must carry and use. But when I climb with Dean we are still limited by these things. After years of feeling physically disadvantaged because of the problem of carrying weight in alpine climbing, I have finally come to realize that *everyone* is limited by it. With alpinism there isn't really a certain limiting factor that is specific to women; some women are bigger and stronger than some men. Ultimately it's not even gender-based, just size and endurance."

McNeill adds, "We aren't built like men, and sometimes we focus on what we aren't, and that it's been a boys' club. We need to focus on what we are good at, and get out there because we like it. We are built differently. Often we can't carry as much on our backs as the guys. This is not a negative. As women we need to develop alternative approaches, whether this is climbing in teams of three to spread out the loads or by adopting the 'fast-and-light' approach."

Several women I interviewed hypothesize that the success many ladies have found sport climbing, helped by natural flexibility and gymnastic background, have kept them happily distracted in the lowlands.

"Women have a better chance of shining in comparison to men in sport climbing; that is, their physiological differences are not limitations to their success in sport climbing (in fact rather the opposite), in contrast to the alpine arena, where a certain amount of weight-toting and brute labor are required," writes Cosely in an e-mail. "Role models like Lynn Hill and others since have proven that in rock climbing the playing field is actually fairly level. This is less clear in high and difficult alpine climbing."

Children

At one time climbing was believed to cause dangerous pelvic disturbances and disrupt the menstrual cycle. [12] Fortunately, that was just a myth. But women who are serious climbers still have to wrestle with the mommy track, just as career women do. For many would-be mothers that choice affects their windows of opportunity for both climbing and childbearing, as well as the types of climbs they pursue.

"One unavoidable limiting factor for the advance of women in alpinism is the fact that alpinists reach their prime when they are in their late thirties/ early forties," explains Davis, 34. "Climbers often put off [having a child] during their twenties in order to travel and climb. Then it's now or never by the time they reach their thirties. It seems like every male alpinist I know has a wife and kids at home. For them it's great. They get to have the benefits of a family at home, and then go climb in the mountains. I have never met a female alpinist who has a husband and kids at home; it just doesn't work that way. For example, if I chose to have a child, Dean's lifestyle would not have to be affected at all. Mine, however, would change completely. So unless our society shifts radically, and I too can also have a husband and kids at home, this is something that

Steph Davis in 2004. *Dean Potter*

Lynn Hill in 1994. *Heinz Zak*

will always limit the numbers of hardcore women alpinists."

There are exceptions, of course, and the famous British soloist Alison Hargreaves comes to mind. Although she was criticized by many for the role reversal, her husband managed the home and small children while she climbed around the world, including Everest, during the early 1990s. But her home life was rare indeed. More typical (if the word "typical" applies) are women like Calhoun, Destivelle, and Hill, who have found that the responsibilities of motherhood have significantly changed their climbing careers. Calhoun and Destivelle, mothers of nine- and ten-year-old boys respectively, are reluctant to leave home for long periods. Meanwhile Hill (44), mother of a two-year-old son, has lost interest in remote, big wall objectives.

Destivelle concurs, at least temporarily: "When you have a project, you think about it all the time; you can't do that with a kid. It is difficult for me to focus on climbing until he is a little more independent. I don't want to leave him or go too far away from home right now." Destivelle anticipates returning to climbing once her son is older.

Catherine Freer, regarded in the 1980s as one of America's top alpinists, male or female, died in an avalanche or collapsed cornice at age 38, while attempting a second ascent of Mt. Logan's Hummingbird Ridge. Renny Jackson, Freer's partner on their first ascent of a difficult route on Cholatse's north face, recalls that Freer "wondered out loud on several occasions about not having enough time to do it all—alpinism and having a family life." But, he adds, "She was way better as a climber than most men at that time anyway. It just seemed natural that she should be doing what she was doing."

Some women, including Bullard and Cosley, have chosen to remain childless. "I think having children is a huge limiting factor for most women taking on big expeditions, and is one of the reasons that I don't want to have kids," says Bullard, 37. "I don't think I could keep my head in it if I knew I was responsible for someone else's welfare. I couldn't stand to be away either."

Acceptance of Risk

Lynn Hill wonders if there is a link between potential motherhood and a lower risk threshold amongst women climbers in comparison to men, a difference many elite women climbers recognize.

"Women are more reasonable risk-takers; they typically make a rational refusal to take unnecessary risk. I know how to handle a dangerous situation, but it's not what gives me pleasure —I don't seek it out. I know I am more cautious than many men," Hill says, pointing to her non-desire to solo climb as an example. She carefully qualifies her comments as generalizations. "Men are more likely to put everything on the line. I don't know if it's a cultural or biological thing. Maybe they feel more expendable?"

Wirtz states it bluntly, "Maybe women are smarter; they have more of a breeding instinct than a bacon drive."

Ironically, Destivelle, whose list of solo ascents includes the formidable famous north faces of the Alps in winter, admits "I hate to be scared and without a big safety margin, which is the case in alpine climbing: you will be scared." I asked if fear has ever crept in while soloing. "Well, that was not such a high level," she explained. In my silence over the telephone she must have realized how ridiculous her statement sounded to be a mortal. "Well, yeah, okay, it's a high level." We both laughed.

"As a generalization [men] can be classified as greater risk takers," notes Kath Pyke, "and women are generally more cautious." She points to research studies she read while working for the British Mountaineering Council [13] "Women can learn from this, although for some it will be innate."

Or could it be that a double standard still exists for the level of acceptable risk for women, what Arlene Blum once called the "supposed life-giving rather than life-risking sex" [14] ? And could this in turn reinforce even more cautious behavior?

Karen McNeill and Sue Nott's Cassin Ridge ascent of McKinley was criticized by some for pushing the limit too far. The pair ascended in abysmal conditions and was forced to spend a night on the summit. Abby Watkins commented, "If they had been men, there would have been less speculation about how far they hung it out to climb that route. I think perhaps when women do risk everything for a mountaineering goal, society frowns on them."

Watkins's suggestion of a double standard brings to mind Hargreaves's death on K2 in 1995. Hargreaves, mother to two, had recently made an ascent of Everest without bottled oxygen or Sherpa support (until then a feat accomplished only by Reinhold Messner, in 1978). After K2, she planned to climb Kangchenjunga, the world's third highest mountain, also without oxygen. Hargreaves was lambasted by many in the British media for undertaking such serious climbing objectives as the mother of young children. In a panel discussion at the 1994 Banff Mountain Film Festival in Canada, where Hargreaves was the opening speaker because of her first-ever (male or female) solo of all six great north faces of the Alps in a single summer, one guest recalls the audience "temporarily derailing" a panel discussion of women in adventure because they "were aghast that Alison would dare to mountain climb being the mother of two small children."

"I think a double standard still exists," commented Kitty Calhoun in a 2003 *Climbing* magazine article on the history of women climbing in the Karakoram. "It still seems more acceptable for a dad to be a climber." [15]

Calhoun has experienced her fair share of adversity in the alpine realm, a partner once calling her "the bivy queen." [16] "I'm most attracted to routes I am not sure that I can get up, ones that are technically challenging. Sure," she says, "there have been avalanches, times we ran out of food."

"Did these close calls ever lead you to reconsider alpine climbing?" I asked.

"No, it just makes me appreciate the small things in life again—things that we usually take for granted."

Double Standard—A Digression

Many see the question of a double standard from a different angle. A middle-aged, liberal official of the American Alpine Club was asked to comment on an

Alison Hargreaves. *Ed Douglas*

Catherine Destivelle in 1988. *John Harlin III*

earlier draft of this essay and embedded this comment in the manuscript: "Why is there such a double standard in women's climbing? I either know or know of every woman in this article. I doubt I would have heard of most of them if they were men, given their level of accomplishment. Sounds harsh, but it's true. I don't know the names of half the Americans doing good repeats in the mountains."

I was interested in what the women interviewed for this article would think of his statement; he seemed skeptical of their accomplishments, and his comment raised the bigger question of whether special attention should be given to women's climbing endeavors regardless of how they measure up to men's accomplishments.

Blum responded, "We tend to remember people because of things that make them stand out. For example, Eric Weinhemayer and Warren Harding are unforgettable. Excellence isn't necessarily memorable, because there are so many excellent climbers. It's the distinguishing characteristics that make us remember people. The other thought that comes to mind is that in Brazil, they are interested in what Brazilian climbers can do, African-Americans are interested in the accomplishments of African-Americans, so it seems reasonable that women would notice women's achievements."

"This all is extremely petty, comparing men and women and their accomplishments in the mountains," replied Calhoun with characteristic polite forthrightness. "Who cares? It is just nice for me sometimes to read articles written by women, about women. Almost all I ever read in the climbing genre is written by men about men."

I had consciously avoided male input to this article, in part for the reasons Calhoun alludes to. However, my letter to women climbers also fell into the mailbox of the Patagonian climber Rolando Garibotti, who was engaged in a parallel discussion with friends. Rolo wrote, "Without inspiration no particular field advances, so if magazines and journals don't give space to women's activity, even if this might involve needing to have double standards, there will be no push forward. Even if at times I might be a bit surprised or frustrated by it, I would rather see double standards being used, such as reporting the 'ordinary' all-female 12-hour Nose, than see no reporting at all. Equal opportunity should imply being exposed to the same type of inspirational role models, regardless of how those role models compare to the role models of the opposite sex. This I think is a necessary step towards further advancing gender equality.

"If in every sport there is a differentiation between men and women, why should we not have it in climbing? There are obvious physical differences between the sexes, and for the last couple of hundred years people have accepted this as a fact and in almost every sport have given credit to male and female achievements separately. While in the future this might perhaps eventually disappear, in climbing we should not fancy ourselves as being super avant-garde or progressive and try to push this type of agenda before sports such as running do. We should use the rules and yardsticks of the day, and crediting sports achievements of men and women separately is one of them. There might come a time when this will change, but we aren't there yet, and climbing is not the sport that will lead the way."

Acquired Taste?

Back to the big question: three-quarters of a century after Underhill's momentous ascent, why are our numbers still so small?

"Climbing in the mountains is like climbing a big wall," says Lizzy Scully. "It's a hell of a lot of work, and until you do it for many years it's uncomfortable and time consuming. Not to say that women don't work as hard as men, they obviously do. It's just that they haven't figured out the joys of working hard to climb big alpine routes. It's difficult to climb 'really hard' in the mountains because you have to be better rounded. These days the focus is on climbing hard routes (bouldering, sport), rather than on spending time in the mountains."

Karen McNeill in 2004. *Kim Csizmazia*

"I think it's hard for women to embrace alpinism, as opposed to rock climbing, for many reasons," concludes Steph Davis, who has always been in the minority as a female drawn to remote objectives. "When I think about alpine climbing, I think of really heavy packs, sleep deprivation, weird and dangerous snow, ice and rock, horrific body odor, and being exhausted/hot/wet/cold/scared. Most women are not naturally attracted to these things. Alpinism is much more experience-dependent, and there is zero glamour involved. It takes hard training, hard work, a strong mind, and a willingness to endure. Yet I would say these are all things that women excel at, physically and mentally, if they can get past the initial turn-offs (heavy packs, stinkiness, grovelly climbing, etc.) and the cultural feminine stereotypes of our current society. (Britney Spears and Nicole Kidman are not alpinist material.)"

THE FUTURE:
WHAT IT HOLDS AND HOW DIFFERENT WILL IT BE?

Although the majority of women I spoke with believe that the number of women pursuing sports perceived as high risk will never equal the number of male participants, there is overwhelming consensus that female alpinists will and can accomplish whatever they set their minds to.

"I see more and more women out there leading and taking responsibility for themselves in the mountains," notes Abby Watkins. "It is easier to find partners these days who are willing and capable of taking on a big mountain (or big ski tour, or big rock or ice climb). The more successful role models there are, the more young women will be inspired to take the sport seriously."

Karen McNeill, whom many view as a key player in alpinism's bright future, wrote me, "I believe we're on the verge of some big changes. Ines Papert will go climb some big alpine routes. This in turn will encourage other women to do the same. Often we need to see other women doing it; then we believe we can do it."

I wonder, 75 years from now, what will be the focus of a similar article about women in alpinism. Will tomorrow's top alpinists cite any of today's stars as those who provided them with inspiration? As lighter-weight and warmer gear evolves to meet female-specific needs, the pool of talent continues expanding, and our collective female climbing history keeps growing, what new heights will we reach? Will the tradition of manless climbs endure simply for the pure enjoyment found climbing "en cordée féminine"?

I don't know, of course. But I do know that exploring these questions will involve countless cold, wet bivies, deep sinker jams, the crunch of snow at dawn, and the vivid paint of alpenglow. It is only after thousands more women have experienced these joys that the answers will begin to take form. I hope we all are able to relish the process as much as the end result.

Additional thanks to Sibylle Hechtel, Gwen Moffat, Eliza Moran, Irena Mrak, and Barbara Washburn for helpful comments and stories.

A NOTE ABOUT THE AUTHOR:

Molly Loomis lives in Victor, Idaho, though she spends much of the year guiding and instructing throughout the western United States and currently for Alpine Ascents International and NOLS. Having participated in multiple "en cordée féminine" expeditions herself, she most recently traveled to Kyrgyzstan for a climbing and cultural exchange made possible through the generosity of the Anatoli Boukreev Memorial Fund.

BIBLIOGRAPHY:

1. Underhill, Miriam. *Give Me the Hills* p. 153.
2. By Sir Arnold Lunn in 1957, leading historian of Alpine mountaineering. Brown, Rebecca A. *Women on High* p. 220.
3. Underhill, Miriam. *Give Me the Hills* p. 144.
4. http://outside.away.com/banff/destivelle.html
5. DaSilva, Rachel. *Leading Out* p. 94
6. Brown, Rebecca A. *Women on High* p. 146.
7. Brown, Rebecca A. *Women on High* p. 218.
8. Manfrini was indeed the first woman to ascend Cerro Torre, however she did not do any of the leading.
9. Birkett, Bill and Bill Peascod. *Women Climbing: 200 Years of Achievement* p. 135.
10. Birkett, Bill and Bill Peascod. *Women Climbing: 200 Years of Achievement* p. 127.
11. www.king-albert-foundation.ch
12. Brown, Rebecca A. *Women on High* p. 40.
13. There are many U.S studies and papers such as the "*Failing at Fairness*" by Myra and David Sadker PhDs, "*Gender Leadership*" by Missy White, *Reviving Ophelia* by Mary Pipher PhD., and many others, backing the research results mentioned by Pyke.
14. DaSilva, Rachel. *Leading Out* p. 8.
15. Scully, Lizzy. "*In the Footsteps of Fanny: Women in the Karakoram.*" *Climbing* June 2003.
16. Waterman, Jonathan. *The Education of an Alpinist. Climbing* April 1988.

A Woman's Place is On Top

Selected highlights in women's alpinism.

Molly Loomis

1808: 18-year-old Marie Paradis (France) becomes the first woman to summit Mont Blanc (15,771').

1867: Frances Case and Mary Robinson make the first women's ascent of Mt. Hood, Oregon.

1871: Lucy Walker (Britain) becomes the first woman to summit the Matterhorn. Walker, a woman who pursued climbing with passion and determination, is considered by many to have been the first real female mountaineer.

1890: Fay Fuller becomes the first woman to summit Mt. Rainier, Washington.

1897: Annie Smith Peck scales El Pico de Orizaba (18,700') and Popocatépetl (17,883') in Mexico. These were the highest points yet reached by a woman.

1899: Fanny Bullock Workman (Britain), Karakoram pioneer, makes the first ascents of Mt. Bullock Workman (19,450'), Mt. Koser (21,000'), and Mt. Lungma (22,500')

1901: Beatrice Tomasson climbs the South Face of Marmolada in the Dolomites, one of the hardest climbs of the day.

1906: Workman ascends Pinnacle Peak (22,810') in the Nun Kun, India, the highest point yet reached by a woman.

1907: The Ladies' Alpine Club is formed in Britain. Elizabeth Le Blond is elected the club's first president.

1908: Peck makes the first ascent of Huascaran Norte (21,812') in Peru. A debate ensues between Peck and Workman as to whose peak is higher, and thereby which woman holds the female altitude record. Topographers, employed to substantiate claims, determine that Workman climbed higher.

1912: Dora Keen makes the first ascent of Mt. Blackburn (16,390'), the first ascent of an Alaskan peak by a woman.

1921: The Pinnacle Club, an all-women's rock climbing group, is formed in Britain. Mrs. Winthrop Young is the Club's first president.

1928: Miriam O'Brien participates in the first complete ascent of Les Aiguilles du Diable. In this same year she is the first female to lead the Grépon. The Grépon was then considered the most challenging climb in the Mont Blanc area.

1928: First ascent of the Dent Blanche's north ridge by Dorothy Pilley (Britain) and team.

1929: O'Brien (later Underhill) and Alice Damesme (France) make the first "manless" ascent of the Grépon, via the Mer de Glace face, ushering in an era of en cordée féminine.

1932: O'Brien and Damesme make the first all-women's ascent of the Matterhorn.

1933: Phyllis Munday (Canada), who with her husband Don made numerous lengthy exploratory expeditions in the Coast Range, makes the first ascent of Mt. Combatant in the Coast Range.

Mid 1930s: Loulou Boulaz (Switzerland) and Lulu Durand make the first female ascents of the Southwest Face of the Dent du Géant, the Requin, and the traverse of the Grands Charmoz and the Droites. Boulaz continues making first ascents and first female ascents throughout the Alps for a number of years.

1935: Boulaz makes the first female ascent of the Grand Jorasses Central Spur. She and her partner achieve the route's second ascent, two days after the first ascent.

1936: Boulaz completes the second ascent of the Petit Dru's North Face.

1938: Una Cameron is the first woman to ascend Mt. Kenya.

1947: Barbara Washburn makes the first female ascent of Mt. McKinley. Washburn is involved in several exploratory expeditions through the Alaska Range and makes several other first ascents and first female ascents of smaller Alaskan peaks.

1951: Gwen Goddard Moffat (Britain) makes the first free ascent of the Andrich Route on the Civetta and Via Tissi on Torre Trieste, both in the Dolomites, and the Marinella Couloirs on Monte Rosa in the Alps.

1953: Moffat becomes the first certified female climbing and mountaineering guide in Britain (and perhaps anywhere).

1953: Claude Kogan makes first ascent of Nun Kun (23,400') in the Himalaya.

1955: Kogan makes the first ascent of Ganesh Himal in the Indian Himalaya. Kogan is the first woman invited to speak before Britain's Alpine Club.

1961-1975: Every summer but one, Joan and Joe Firey, often with their daughter Carla, make multiple first ascents in Washington's Cascades, including Ghost Peak and the East Ridge of Mt. Terror.

1962: Austrian, British, Czechoslovakian, French, German, Dutch, Italian, Polish, Swiss, and Yugoslavian female climbers create the organization Rendezvous Hautes Montagnes to bring people together to share their love of climbing.

1962: Yvette Vaucher (Switzerland) makes the first female ascent of the North Face of the Eiger.

1966: Vaucher completes the first ascent of the Dent Blanche's North Face.

1967: Liz Robbins becomes the first woman to climb a Grade VI, with her ascent of Half Dome's Northwest Face.

1970: Junko Tabei (Japan) makes the first woman's ascent of Annapurna III (24,787').

1970: Grace Hoeman and Arlene Blum lead the first all-women's expedition to Denali. All six team members summit.

1973: Sibylle Hechtel and Anne Marie Rizzi complete what is believed to be the first all-women's ascent of a North American big wall: Washington's Column South Face (V 5.8 A1).

1973: Hechtel and Bev Johnson make the first all-women's ascent of El Capitan, via the Triple Direct (VI 5.8 A2-). Hechtel submits a report of their climb to the *American Alpine Journal* entitled "Walls Without Balls." The *AAJ* deems the title inappropriate and suggests "Keeping Abreast of El Cap" instead. Hechtel, unclear why the reference to female anatomy is appropriate while mention of male anatomy is not, refuses the change. The article is published as "Untitled."

1974: Eight Soviet women led by Elvira Shataeva become the first all-female team to reach the top of Peak Lenin (23,405'). However, the entire team perishes on the summit in a horrific storm.

1974: Vera Watson completes the first female solo ascent of Aconcagua (22,840').

1975: Tabei, at age 36, climbs Everest. It is the first female ascent of the peak and coincides with the International Year of the Woman.

1975: First all-women's ascent of and 8,000m peak, Gasherbrum II (26,362'), by Halina Kruger-Syrokomska and Anna Okopinska (Poland). As part of the same expedition Wanda Rutkiewicz and Alison Chadwick-Onyszkiewicz make the first ascent of Gasherbrum III (26,090') in a team that included two men.

1975: First all-female ascent of the Diamond on Long's Peak, by Molly Higgins Bruce, Steph Atwood, and Laurie Wood.

1978: First female winter ascent of the Matterhorn's North Face, by Rutkiewicz, Anna Czerwinska, Krystyna Palmowska, and Irena Kesa (Poland).

1978: First female ascent of Annapurna (26,545'), by Irene Miller and Vera Komarkova.

1981: Tabei makes the first female ascent of Shishapangma (26,286').

1982: First female ascent of Dhaulagiri (26,795'), by Belgian Lutgaarde Vivijs.

1983: First female ascent of Broad Peak by Czerwinska and Palmowska, self-supported, alpine style, without supplemental oxygen.

1983: 100 years after the first ascent of Aconcagua, Julia Ramirez of Chile leads the first all-female team to Aconcagua's summit.

1984: First female ascent of Nanga Parbat (26,657'), by Liliane Barrard (France).

1984: Catherine Freer climbs a difficult new route on Cholatse's north face with Renny Jackson and Todd Bibler.

1984: First female ascent of Cho Oyu (26,906') by Komarkova and Dina Sterbova (Czechoslovakia).

1986: Rutkiewicz completes the first female ascent of K2 (28,251'), via the Abruzzi Spur. Rutkiewicz previously organized an all-women's expedition to K2 in 1982.

1990: Calhoun summits Makalu (27,825') via the West Pillar, thus becoming the first woman to climb an 8,000m peak by a technically difficult route.

1993: Alison Hargreaves (Britian) solos the Alps' famous six north faces in a season.

1994: Lynn Hill repeats her free ascent of El Cap's Nose in a single day, a feat still unrepeated.

1995: Hargreaves makes the first unsupported female ascent of Everest without supplemental oxygen. Only Reinhold Messner had previously climbed Everest solo without oxygen.

1998: Abby Watkins, Vera Wong, and Nicola Woolford (Australia) make the first ascent of the highly technical Changi Tower (5,800m) and Marpo Brakk (5,000m) in the Karakoram.

1999: The first ascent of Bravo Les Filles (5.13d A0) in Madagascar, by Nancy Feagin, Hill, and Pyke, the hardest rock climb yet established by a women's team. (Beth Rodden had to leave early.)

2002: Lizzy Scully and Heidi Wirtz make the first ascent of Bad Hair Day (V 5.12-), in the Bugaboos, Canada.

2004: Monika Kambic-Mali (Argentina/Slovenia)and Tina Di Batista (Slovenia) make the first all-female ascent of Fitz Roy, via the Franco-Argentine route.

2004: Karen McNeill (New Zealand/Canada) and Sue Nott make the first female ascent of the Cassin Ridge on Mt. McKinley.

2004: Steph Davis free climbs El Capitan's Free Rider route (38 pitches, 5.13a) in a day.

2005: Ines Papert (Switzerland) is the first woman to win Overall First Place at the Ouray Ice Festival in Ouray, Colorado.

2005: Davis is the first woman to summit Torre Egger, as well as completing the peak's first one-day ascent, with Dean Potter.

2005: Kambic-Mali and Tanja Grmovsek (Slovenia) make the first all-female ascent of Cerro Torre.

UNDER THE WEATHER

Why is Scotland such a good training ground for much higher mountains?
Perhaps because an average winter day in Scotland offers more adventure
than a week of storms anywhere else.

SIMON RICHARDSON

The northeast face of Ben Nevis from just above the CIC Hut. North-East Buttress (IV,5) climbs the long left skyline ridge. Orion Face is the V-shaped ice face directly below the summit, flanked by Zero Gully on the right. The next major gully right that opens out into the funnel-shaped bowl is Point Five Gully. The lower section of Tower Ridge (IV,4) is the sunlit ridge rising up to the right. *Simon Richardson*

It was past two in the afternoon, blowing hard and snowing heavily. Roger climbed up to the stance and we took stock. Attempting a new route up the crest of Mitre Ridge, deep in the Scottish Cairngorm Mountains, we were battling on in a rising storm. It had taken six hours to climb the first three pitches. Scottish winter days are short, and we had less than three hours of daylight, but the line was just too good to give up. Logical and elegant, a succession of steep corners and unclimbed turfy grooves slotted together like a jigsaw puzzle all the way up the spine of the ridge.

I took the rack and continued straight up the crest, grateful that Roger had insisted I take a Warthog, as this was the only protection at one particularly awkward bulge. The natural winter way was a steep, right-facing corner that had accumulated a huge quantity of powder snow. The crack at its back was devoid of turf, so I liebacked up it on torqued ice tools with my crampons skating on the smooth rock. I badly misjudged it near the top and was on the point of falling when I found a crucial foothold. Panting heavily, I pulled on to the platform above just as the rope came tight. The next pitch was the last difficult one. I struggled up a steep corner, hand traversed on wilting arms to the crest of a tower, and stumbled in the gloom along the sharp ridge to belay in a col below a second tower. By the time Roger arrived it was dark and the urgency of the last few hours dissolved into the icy blackness.

Six hours later, we had finished the route and I trailed head down behind Roger as he kept us on the correct bearing. Conditions on the plateau were extreme, with gale-force winds and blinding spindrift. Our world was limited to the pools of light from our headtorches and the ever-shifting snow around our feet. We counted our paces to track our progress against the map and shouted out every hundredth step into the screaming wind. When we bumped into a prominent boulder we'd passed on the approach, the relief was immediate. We stumbled back down the glen and, elated, collapsed into our tent after 22 hours on the move.

Our ascent of The Cardinal on Beinn a'Bhuird was typical of many Scottish winter adventures. The 200-meter-long route had seven pitches of sustained mixed climbing, but technical difficulty was just one aspect of the experience. The 16-kilometer approach, the eight-hour winter day, the wild and unpredictable weather, and difficult navigation all provided equally important ingredients to the challenge. Overall it was more like doing a major alpine route than climbing on a minor crag.

THE SCOTTISH WINTER EXPERIENCE

During the summer the Cairngorms are a range of grassy, flat-topped hills, but like the rest of the Scottish Highlands they are transformed in winter and take on a seriousness way out of proportion to their size. Their summit plateaus collect huge quantities of snow that are swept by the prevailing westerly winds into deep-sided corries that were carved out by glaciers long ago. Their granite cliffs are cracked and vegetated and made for on-sight climbing. The cracks take protection readily and frozen turf has the consistency of plastic ice. When conditions are good, ice dribbles down corners, and powder snow and hoarfrost transform the dark granite walls and buttresses into white-frosted fantasy castles.

Scotland is a small country and more than half the landscape is mountainous. The mountains range from the rolling schist hills of the Southern Highlands to the spectacular sandstone summits of the Northwest Highlands. The Central Highlands comprise the rugged volcanic peaks around Glen Coe and Ben Nevis, while the Cairngorms lie in the center of the country and include the highest group of mountains in Scotland. The Hebrides Islands on the western seaboard are mountainous, too, and in a hard winter they can give spectacular climbing overlooking the sea. Most of these areas are accessible from Glasgow or Edinburgh in less than three hours, and are within weekend range of the English cities. On a good day during February and March the popular areas can take on a cosmopolitan air, and you are as likely to meet a climber from Slovenia or Spain as you are someone from Glasgow or Manchester.

Brian Shackleton leading the lower section of Orion Direct (V,5) Ben Nevis. The 400-meter route was first climbed by Jimmy Marshall and Robin Smith in 1960 by cutting steps. *Brian Findlay*

Unlike the Alps, very little fixed gear is found on Scottish cliffs, and bolts are shunned. Every route you climb is like doing a first ascent. Protection has to be placed on the lead, and belay spots can sometimes take half an hour to find. On the harder routes, three-hour leads of 30-meter pitches are common, as the leader fights to clear the rock to find gear placements. This ground-up approach maximizes the challenge of the cliffs, and the harder routes are always a race against time and the short winter day. Most ascents are made in weather where, in the Alps, you would not consider leaving the valley. The wind blows almost continuously, and it is often raining in the glens and snowing on the tops. Despite modern clothing and materials, one is nearly always damp. On longer routes a single push is far more effective than a multi-day ascent, as the weather is too poor to consider bivouacking. The sub-arctic climate is unforgiving, and it is always better to stay moving rather than stop.

It is the mental dimension that makes Scottish winter climbing so compelling. Solving the frozen puzzle of leading a pitch and finding protection is one aspect, but predicting conditions and selecting an appropriate route is the underlying challenge. Conditions change daily, and historically the most successful Scottish winter climbers have not been the strongest or most technically gifted, but those who have the knack of being in the right place at the right time. While many Scottish climbs are reliably in condition most winters, others take a particular sequence of events?snowfall, wind, thaw, and freeze?to form, and many climbers will wait years for their chosen route to come into condition.

A BRIEF HISTORY

Scottish winter climbing has a long history. The Victorians pioneered winter ascents of the great 500-meter-high ridges on Ben Nevis before the end of the 19th century, using long, unwieldy alpenstocks, clinker-shod laborers' boots, and short lengths of hemp rope. Even today, Tower Ridge (IV, 4, 1894) and Northeast Buttress (IV, 5, 1896) are respected climbs, with the latter sporting a short M4 crux near the top of the route. Step-cutting skills advanced, and Harold Raeburn took ice-climbing levels to WI3 levels with his ascent of Green Gully (IV, 4) on Ben Nevis in 1906. Fifty-odd years went by before ice-climbing standards advanced significantly, when Jimmy Marshall and Robin Smith brought step-cutting to its pinnacle in 1960 with a magnificent series of ascents on Ben Nevis, culminating in the first free ascent of Point Five Gully and the 400-meter-high Orion Direct (V, 5). These climbs were the preserve of the elite. Marshall and Smith wore crampons,

Victor Saunders on the second ascent of Pointless (VII,6), Ben Nevis. This very serious route typifies thin face climbing on Ben Nevis: very thin snow/ice overlying steep slabby walls with no protection. *Mick Fowler*

but step-cutting was still a slow, dangerous, and exhausting process, where a short axe was used to cut a ladder of handholds and steps in the ice. Further east, on the powder-covered rock of the Cairngorms, Tom Patey used nailed boots and a single axe to push mixed climbing standards up to M5 levels with Eagle Ridge (VI, 6, 1953); Parallel Buttress (VI, 6, 1956) on Lochnagar; and Scorpion (V, 6, 1952) on the Shelter Stone Crag.

Throughout the 1970s, the "curved axe revolution" advanced standards on ice, mainly on Ben Nevis. British climbers, well practiced on Nevis ice, applied their skills to great effect in the Alps and elsewhere. Perhaps the best example is the Colton-MacIntyre Route on the north face of the Grandes Jorasses (ED3, 1976). This very narrow couloir, Scottish in character, was undoubtedly the hardest ice climb in the Alps at the time. Another example was the application of Nevis-style thin face climbing to the north face of the Pelerins (ED2) by Rab Carrington and Al Rouse in February 1975. Toward the end of the decade, however, the focus began to slowly turn back toward mixed climbing, and during the early 1980s the art of "torquing" was developed. Mountaineers have jammed axe picks into rock cracks for centuries, but ironically it was the reversed curve "banana" picks, developed on the Continent for steep ice climbing, which proved to be perfectly suited to the technique of levering shafts to cam picks in narrow cracks. The vegetated cliffs of the Cairngorms are ideal for this type of climbing, for the deep cracks and rough rock hold the picks well, and there is a liberal supply of turf on all but the very steepest routes.

During the mid-1980s, the Aberdeen-based team of Colin MacLean and Andy Nisbet forged one of the strongest partnerships in the history of Scottish winter mountaineering. The bulk of their new routes were in the Cairngorms, but their first Grade VIII was away from home territory, some 100 kilometers to the west, in Glen Coe. Their winter ascent of the prominent corner line of Unicorn (VIII, 8) in Stob Coire nan Lochan in January 1985 proved controversial, as local climbers doubted whether a hoarfrosted ascent really counted as true winter conditions. The line of Unicorn occasionally forms as a thin ribbon of ice, but MacLean and Nisbet were applying Cairngorms techniques and attitudes developed over the previous few winters, where the key requirement for a route to be in winter condition is that it should be frozen and have a wintry appearance. These criteria are now accepted as the norm for high-standard mixed climbing across Scotland.

Three weeks later, the MacLean-Nisbet team went on to climb their greatest route, The Needle (VIII, 8) on Shelter Stone Crag. It took two weeks of continuous effort, scoping the best winter line and waiting for a settled spell of weather, before they made a two-day ascent. Twenty years on, the 250-meter-long climb still rates as one of Scotland's most demanding winter routes in terms of length and sustained difficulty. Last winter it saw its first one-day free ascent.

The way was now open for the other great challenges to fall. The following season, 1986, Kenny Spence succeeded on his third attempt to climb Centurion (VIII, 8) on Ben Nevis, with Spider MacKenzie. In the same season Nisbet and Sandy Allan linked up an ingenious line on the front face of the Central Gully Wall of Creag an Dubh Loch to give The Rattrap (VIII, 8). As more people became aware of the new techniques such as hooking edges and torquing, attention in the early 1990s shifted to the easily accessible Northern Corries of Cairn Gorm. Brian Davison, Graeme Ettle, and Nisbet were all involved in the action, resulting in a series of short technical routes including Big Daddy (VII, 8), The Vicar (VII, 8), and Prore (VII, 7). The late 1990s were primarily a time for consolidation, and these climbs introduced dozens of climbers to Grade VII routes. As climbers became fitter and more skilled, many of the big winter routes of the 1980s were repeated, and the one or two points of aid often used on the first ascents were eliminated.

STATE OF THE ART

Until the mid 1980s many of the harder mixed routes were winter ascents of summer lines, but as confidence has grown there has been an increased emphasis on seeking out winter-only lines. These are typically vegetated, wet and dripping in summer, but they are transformed by winter's grip into inspiring mixed climbing possibilities. Diedre of Sorrows (VIII, 8, 1986) on the Tough-Brown Face of Lochnagar was an early example of a cutting edge winter-only line, and more recently routes such as Magic Bow Wall (VIII, 8, 2001) and The Godfather (VIII, 8, 2002) in the Northwest Highlands have expanded this concept to create 300-meter-long routes of alpine proportions that have significant technical difficulty.

Today two distinct styles are emerging. The first is a continuation of the traditional approach, with an emphasis on climbing routes on-sight and ground-up. Attitudes to aid have now hardened, and ascents using rest points or direct aid are considered seriously flawed. As a result, Scotland can perhaps lay claim to the most stylistically pure form of mountaineering in the world. Some routes require multiple attempts over many seasons, such as Brian Davison's ascent of Mort on Lochnagar (IX, 9, 2000). This line involved 18 attempts over 15 years, and is widely considered to be the hardest traditional winter route in Scotland. The three-pitch climb involves technical and strenuous icy mixed climbing with poor protection and serious groundfall potential.

The second style is to pursue technical difficulty by applying modern rockclimbing techniques such as pre-inspection to shorter (often single-pitch) climbs. Dave MacLeod, one of Scotland's most talented rockclimbers, is at the forefront of this development with routes such as The Cathedral (X, 11, 2004) on The Cobbler. MacLeod climbed this 30-meter-high roof problem by placing the gear on the lead, and suggested that the overall difficulty was similar to a pre-protected M12 route. Some climbers are questioning whether The Cathedral represents the limit of what is possible using traditional Scottish winter ethics, and for standards to

Chris Cartwright enjoying the strange and typical ice conditions sculpted by wind, rain, and freeze on Ninus (III) in Coire Bhrochain, Braeriach, Cairngorms. *Simon Richardson*

progress, routes need to be pre-protected or practiced on a top rope. Although these techniques will drive up technical standards, the difficulty of the bigger traditional routes will always be dominated by the mountaineering challenges of longer approaches, lack of daylight, exposure to weather, and a strong determination to preserve the on-sight ethic.

THE FOWLER INFLUENCE

Mick Fowler, one of Britain's most successful alpinists, has had a prolific Scottish winter career. "The appeal of Scottish winter climbing is not something readily understood by the average person," he wrote in the 2002 Scottish Mountaineering Club Journal. "I have to admit that I struggled to come to terms with it. Conditions are fickle, early starts wearing and success comes only to those that persevere. Perhaps these are the attractions. Successes that are won too easily are inevitably those that are the least rewarding."

Fowler made his Scottish new-route debut in 1979 with the first winter ascent of The Shield Direct (VII, 7), a soaring line of icy chimneys on the Carn Dearg Buttress of Ben Nevis, with Victor Saunders. Fowler went on to climb a superb string of sensational icy mixed routes

The 200-meter-high Mitre Ridge in Garbh Choire on Beinn a'Bhuird. The Cardinal (VIII,8) takes the line of grooves up the crest of the buttress and was first climbed by Roger Webb and Simon Richardson in 1995. *Simon Richardson*

in the 1980s, mainly in the Northwest Highlands. Routes such as Tholl Gate (VI, 6, 1984), Gully of the Gods (VI, 6, 1983), and Great Overhanging Gully (VI, 7, 1984) are among the most sought-after winter routes in the country, and climbs such as Ice Bomb (VII, 7, 1988) on Beinn Dearg; Against All Odds (VII, 7, 1988) in Glen Coe; and Storr Gully (VII, 7, 2000) on the Isle of Skye, are still unrepeated. All these climbs take strong natural lines of daunting steepness and are predominately ice or icy mixed.

It was natural that Fowler should take his Scottish skills to the Greater Ranges. The first ascent of the technical southwest buttress of Taulliraju in Peru with Chris Watts in 1982 was his first major success, but the Golden Pillar of Spantik in the Karakoram, climbed with Victor Saunders five years later, was an eye-opener. Unquestionably this was one of the finest Himalayan routes of the decade and was very Scottish in character. Intricate routefinding, poor protection, and tenuous mixed climbing on powder-covered rock all contributed to the difficulty. "Prior experience of hard climbing in grim conditions helped enormously with this ascent," Fowler told me recently. "Scottish winter gave us the confidence to be bold and push on for pitch after pitch knowing that we could find protection in snow-blasted situations."

Spantik led to a series of outstanding first ascents on Taweche, Cerro Kishtwar, Changabang, and Siungang. These routes shared several common factors. They were mainly icy mixed climbs, the hard climbing was below 6,500 meters, and they could be climbed relatively fast in an alpine-style single push. But most importantly, perhaps, they were all intelligently chosen objectives that in many ways could be described as "super-Scottish" climbs.

SCOTTISH STYLE IN THE GREATER RANGES

The current generation of British alpinists has grown up with Mick Fowler's exploits, and his style very much defines the current British approach to climbing the Greater Ranges. There has been a shift of emphasis away from 7,000-meter-plus peaks or attempting technical rock routes at altitude. The recipe is simple. Combine Grade VII Scottish winter skills with good alpine experience, then go and attempt a mixed climb on a moderate-altitude peak. Ian Parnell and

Kenton Cool's near-free repeat of the Denali Diamond (2002), Nick Bullock and Al Powell's bold route on Jirishanca (2003), and Rich Cross and Jon Bracey's rapid ascent of the north face of Mt. Kennedy (2004) all point to the success of this approach.

One of the finest British successes of the 1990s was the first ascent of the north face of Changabang by Andy Cave and Brendan Murphy (1997). "Undoubtedly, having climbed hard mixed routes in Scotland helped us dispatch sections of the Changabang climb more quickly," recalls Cave. "We'd often made similar technical moves on previous climbs up north, and the ability to climb a long way above protection is also something that you learn in Scotland. Doing new routes in Scotland also breeds essential routefinding skills?a sense of where the line is going to lead. Climbing through bad weather is de rigueur in Scotland, too, something we did a lot of in India."

It would be simplistic to claim that experience with Scottish winter climbing is the underlying basis for these ascents. Proximity to Chamonix, good libraries, sharing of information, and an excellent expedition funding system also play their part. But many successful British climbers passionately cite Scottish winter experience as a key ingredient. "The weather and conditions that even novice Scottish winter climbers take as part and parcel of heading out into the hills really is unusual in world mountaineering," says Ian Parnell. "While we miss out on the scale and terrain, everything else about Scottish winter climbing is very close to the big-mountain experience. A hard day in Scotland is as tough as any you'll ever spend in the mountains. Even an easy day in Scotland you have to commit, whereas continental ice cragging you can amble up and decide when you get there whether you can be bothered or not."

The variety of climbing encountered on a Scottish winter route is another key factor, as Malcolm Bass, author of several new routes in Alaska, explains: "In an average Scottish winter season you climb all sorts of white stuff. Water ice, névé, powder, rime, verglas, lovely plastic squeaky ice, wet snow plastered on rock, turf and all sorts of intermediate material. If you waited for routes to be in perfect condition, you'd wait for decades. Winter climbing in Scotland is done, almost by definition, when the routes are "out of condition" in the traditional Alpine sense. You do your best to make a good choice of venue, walk in, and if it's white you climb something. You climb what you find in the corrie and on the route. I think this gives Scottish winter climbers an advantage in the big hills. When it snows all over your rock pitches you can go on. When the ice pitches melt out you can climb the running rock beneath, and powder-covered slabs come as no great surprise."

But it is not just the technical skills that are important. "It is your will that is most tested when climbing in Scotland," Patagonian winter expert Andy Kirkpatrick told me. "Conditions are never assured. The mountains can strip before your eyes as warm winds push north, and even when you find good conditions, climbing can prove impossible with hurricane winds and meters of rime and verglas. Once the top is reached?usually in the dark?there is the descent, testing the navigational skills of even the professional orienteer, especially in a whiteout with no pistes to follow or cable cars back to the valley. This means we Brits are optimists. We'll give any climb a go if we have fighting chance."

THE BEN NEVIS PLAYGROUND

Although there are hundreds of corries and winter cliffs across the Scottish Highlands, the great northeast face of Ben Nevis is the best known and has had the greatest influence on successive

Mick Fowler on the first ascent of Gully of the Gods (VI,6), Beinn Bhan, Applecross. This overhanging gully climb is a typical Fowler route and climbs through outrageous ground for the grade. It has become one of the most sought-after classic routes in the Northwest Highlands. *Fowler Collection*

generations of British alpinists. It is reliably in condition by January and for a few months onward and has the CIC Hut conveniently situated at its base. Climbing on the Ben is unique. Its cliffs are alpine in stature, and by virtue of their height and position near the west coast, they are exposed to the full force of North Atlantic weather. The resulting high level of precipitation, along with frequent changes in temperature and wind direction, allow ice to build rapidly and produce a winter climbing ground without equal in the country. While the mountain is best known for its Grade V gully climbs such as Point Five and Zero, it is the thin face routes such as Galactic Hitchhiker (VI, 5), Albatross (VI, 5), and Pointless (VII, 6) that climb the blank slabby walls in between?and these have the monster reputations.

Thin face routes rely on a buildup of snow-ice on steep slabs and are normally climbed when the covering is only two or three centimeters thick. Rarely does the pattern of freeze-thaw allow the snow-ice to form thicker than this, and, once one is committed, the climbing is a delicate game of mind control while balancing tip-toe up thinly iced slabs far above protection. The transitory nature of these climbs adds to their attraction, for it takes only one quick thaw to strip the routes, and they can disappear in a few hours.

Dave Hesleden, one of Britain's finest all-round climbers, explains: "Climbing on the Ben has had a big influence on my climbing. There's no fixed gear. You have to find protection and set up belays yourself. Routes like Orion Direct are big adventures?far more so than doing a Grade V+ icefall in the Alps where you can use screws and Abalakovs. The Ben is the most exacting climbing I've ever done. I would never dream of falling off. I'd be prepared to go for it and fall off in the Cairngorms, but never on Nevis."

Hesleden's comments reminded of the time I met Catherine Destivelle in the CIC Hut. She was making a reconnaissance trip with her husband to check out some climbs for a photo feature for Paris Match, but the weather had been poor and they had failed to do a single route.

The hut was full and Catherine joined in the general banter with grace and charm, but underneath you could sense that she was disappointed with her week. She visibly brightened when Robin Clothier, the hut guardian and renowned Nevis ice climber, suggested they follow him and Harvey Mullen up Orion Direct the next morning.

It was a preposterous suggestion. The mountain was very snowy and it was too early in the season for snow-ice to have formed on the uppermost slabs. Morning came dark and gray with low clouds and blowing spindrift; most climbers in the hut sensibly chose icefalls or mixed routes low on the mountain. Robin was undeterred, however, and soon after breakfast the four of them set off for the Orion Face. That evening, when I returned to the hut, everyone had returned safely and were now recounting the day's adventures over steaming mugs of tea. Catherine's eyes danced with delight as she described their climb.

They had followed Robin and Harvey up into the murky gloom of Observatory Gully, and when the slope steepened they roped up as two pairs and started climbing. There was no ice, just a 15-centimeter-thick layer of barely consolidated snow covering smooth slabs. There were no runners or belays. Routefinding was desperately difficult in the mist, but the marginal conditions meant that it was critical they took the easiest possible line. Blindly they followed Robin and Harvey across a delicate traverse that led right

Chris Cartwright making the first ascent of Cherokee Chimney (V,6), Garbh Choire Mor, Braeriach—one of the most remote crags in the Cairngorms. *Simon Richardson*

The Southeast Cliff of Fuar Tholl, Northwest Highlands. Tholl Gate (VI,6), climbed by Mick Fowler and Phil Butler in 1984, takes the central of the three ice streaks. This was the first climb on the face—there are now over a dozen routes. *Simon Richardson*

into the maze of exit gullies above. Every so often they could hear avalanches hissing down Zero Gully. When they got to the summit, Robin pointed instinctively through the swirling snow with his axes and they plunged down through the whiteout toward the descent route. "It was like nothing I've ever done before," Catherine told me later. "It's a climb I'll never forget."

INTERNATIONAL PERSPECTIVE

For international visitors, the most practical way to experience Scottish winter climbing is to attend one of the International Winter Meets organized by the British Mountaineering Council every other year. The meets are based in Glenmore Lodge, the Scottish Mountaineering Centre in Aviemore, at the foot of the Cairngorms. Guests are paired up with local climbers who have the necessary Scottish winter skills to direct their new friends to the routes, swing leads, and then get them back down to the valley again.

The meets have attracted many top climbers from around the world. Interestingly it is Slovenians such as Janez Jeglic, Andre Stremfelj, and Marko Prezelj who have been most at home in Scottish conditions. Prezelj first climbed in Scotland in March 1999 and notched up eight big routes, almost a lifetime's worth of hard Scottish classics, in a mere five days. The following summer he made a rapid, alpine-style repeat of the Golden Pillar of Spantik. "There's no doubt that my Scottish experience has improved my approach to mixed climbing," he told me. "Scottish routes are quite short compared to those in major areas, but the experience is very strong. It's a complex thing, but after experiencing the long approaches in Scotland, clearing snow off to place gear, climbing in bad weather, and coming back in the fog and wind, I now believe that many things are possible in the mountains. On Spantik I had the technical experience from Scotland, so I wasn't scared to make interesting moves without protection close by, and my Himalayan experience meant I wasn't scared about the altitude and size of the mountain. It was really good!"

The meets have also given Scottish climbers a greater understanding of what makes Scottish winter climbing unique compared to the rest of the world. "You get great training in Scotland for big mountains," British Columbia guru Don Serl told me recently. "You tend to be out in all weather, so bad weather is not unsettling. You know how to dress for it and how to cope with it. Most success in the big mountains depends first and foremost on being able to 'live' in the mountains, in any and all conditions. Here in the Coast Range and the Cascades, the problem is one of consistently bad weather coupled with extremely heavy snowfall and long approaches. If you get two mountain routes in over a winter, you're doing really well."

When you live in Scotland, the accessibility of the Scottish winter experience is easy to take for granted. Keen climbers will climb routes every weekend. There are probably few other places in the world where you can leave your bed early in the morning, have a full mountaineering experience, and be back in time for dinner.

But Scottish winter is far more than just training for big mountains. Some of the finest Scottish winter climbers rarely go elsewhere because Scotland gives them all the adventure, challenge, and commitment they need. The Scottish winter game can be frustrating and uncomfortable for much of the time, but when it works nothing can compare. As I write this in early January, a warm southwesterly is howling outside, the ice is falling off the crags, and the hills are being stripped by a deep thaw. I've failed on every route I have tried in the last month, but I know I'll be back on the crags as soon as it freezes again. Andy Kirkpatrick understands: "Every season, countless climbers make the pilgrimage to the Highlands, believing that it's better to take a shot and miss than never take the shot at all. Every now and again you'll score, and when you do there's no better place on the planet to climb."

A NOTE ON THE SCOTTISH WINTER GRADING SYSTEM

Scottish winter grades are used to describe the difficulties of all types of a winter route, whether it is ice, mixed, or snowed-up rock. Nowadays a two-tier system is used with Point Five Gully on Ben Nevis as the benchmark V, 5 climb. The Roman numeral describes the overall difficulty of the route and takes into account technical difficulty, the quality and quantity of protection, and how the sustained the climbing is. The Arabic numeral describes the technical difficulty of the hardest pitch. The contrast between the two grades gives an indication on the nature of the route. For example a V, 6 grade suggests a well-protected technical climb, while a grade of V, 4 implies a route that is technically easier but with limited protection and possibly poor belays. It is almost impossible to compare Scottish climbs with ice and mixed climbs elsewhere, but as a crude approximation Scottish technical grades are a generous grade easier than the equivalent M or WI grades in North America.

SUMMARY OF STATISTICS:

AREA: Scotland

ARTICLE: A survey of history, recent developments, and nature of winter climbing in Scotland.

A NOTE ABOUT THE AUTHOR:

Simon Richardson is a petroleum engineer who lives in Aberdeen, Scotland, with his wife and two children. Born in 1960, Simon has made first ascents of over 150 Grade V winter routes in the Scottish Highlands and is the author of the Ben Nevis guidebook.

KENYA'S ROCKS

Welcome to the remote crags of Kenya, where adventure rules.

ALEX FIKSMAN

An unclimbed cliff in the desert just outside of the Ndoto Mountains. It has been called the Shark Fin, but this may not be the local name. *Felix Berg*

It's easy to fall in love with Kenya, a country as diverse in landscapes as in cultures. The contrasts come at every turn, from suited businessmen in chauffer-driven mabenzis (Swahili slang for posh German class-distinguisher on wheels) to farmers living off their land, cattle, and goats as they have from the beginning of time; from glacier-studded Mt. Kenya to bush climbing on remote gneiss outcrops; from medium-wall adventure climbing to short classics frequented by the small Nairobi-based climbing community. Not many places in the world remain as wild as Kenya's crags, where you could walk past a herd of zebra on your way to the climb and the only thing that keeps you from your long-awaited reunion with a cold Tusker (exceptional Kenyan beer) might be an irritated 1,000-pound Cape buffalo.

Kenyan climbing entered the modern age in the 1970s when the strong British Ian Howell came to work in Kenya and found a 16-year-old Iain Allan showing great promise and enthusiasm. The routes they established were world class, and it was the Ia(i)ns who most explored the region's vast rock potential during nearly four decades.

Today, many of the gneiss domes jutting from semi-arid plains have seen varying degrees of development, but so much more remains to be done. Ololokwe, for example, is a two-kilometer-long cliff standing 400 meters high. Located about five hours' drive out of Nairobi, it has only a few established routes—enormous potential remains for hard sport routes and possibly some thin crack climbs. The

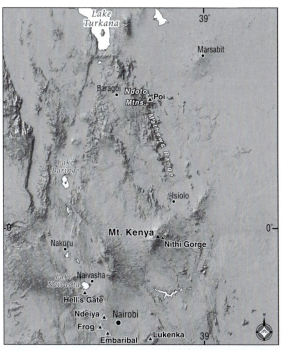

Northern Kenya map by *Martin Gamache*, Alpine Mapping Guild

vast quantity of rock around the country (there are about a dozen noteworthy cliffs with only the most obvious lines explored), combined with the small number of local climbers, translates into superb possibilities for new route potential, second ascents, and removal of aid on existing climbs. It should be mentioned that the Mountain Club of Kenya (www.mck.or.ke) has developed a clear bolting policy (which includes a moratorium on bolts in national parks); the club can also be a big help with suggestions

Samburu and Rendile warriors with Marnix Buonajuti (with the bouffant hairdo) about three hours into their hike toward Poi. *Felix Berg*

on logistics for climbing in outlying areas as well as finding climbing partners.

In the pages that follow, we decided to focus on three climbing areas that have received noteworthy development in the last couple of years: the 250-meter cliffs in the Nithi Gorge on the eastern approach on Mt. Kenya; the Ndoto Mountains in the Northern Frontier District, home to the longest sport route in Africa on the recently famed Poi cliff; and the Main Wall of Hell's Gate in the Rift Valley, 1.5 hours out of Nairobi—it was originally developed as the training ground for Nairobi climbers headed for Mt. Kenya and now stands in its own right awaiting the new generation of climbers.

THE NDOTO MOUNTAINS

There is a lot more to the Ndotos than the great Poi. Welcome to the lesser-known crags of Kenya's largest climbing area.

MARNIX BUONAJUTI

The Ndoto Mountains from the south, looking toward Poi. *Andrew Wielochowski, www.ewpnet.com*

The Ndotos are a remote cluster of mountains in the deserts of northern Kenya. Getting there is a grueling two-day drive through unruly country, but once you arrive you find yourself in one of the most beautiful and untouched places in the world. This area has many cliffs over 400 meters high, and has Kenya's biggest cliff, Poi, which stands a proud 700 meters tall.

The northern Ndoto Mountains around the town of Ngurunit are large forested or brush-covered hills with enormous gold and red gneiss blocks parked on top. There are a dozen or so cliff faces that exceed 300 meters in height, and many of these are as high as 500-600 meters and easily a kilometer wide. It is a hard hike to the base of many of these cliffs. This is because you need to walk uphill, in very warm humid weather (up to 35° Celsius in December), through some very thick thorny scrub, and then through forest to get to the bottom of the cliff. In addition to the dozen bigger walls, there are many smaller cliffs with easier approaches. There is also lots of bouldering. You could live in this area for three life times and not do the half of what is here.

Despite its amazing cliffs, the Ndotos region has received scant attention from climbers. This is for two reasons. First, the Ndoto Mountains are very remote. To get there you either need an expensive airplane charter or a two-day car drive through beautiful but harsh and uncompromising land. Second, the quality of the rock is not as good as it is in other adventure areas such as Greenland and Baffin Island. This makes the climbing a little on the dangerous side, and new routes require much cleaning.

In frozen realms, ice cracks the stone and protection is generally abundant. In northern Kenya the rock heats up during the day and cools at night, so that rather than cracking it just exfoliates. Where rain washes the face you get smooth featureless slabs (great friction climbing) with no protection for the entire height of the cliff. Where rain does not touch (overhangs), you get millions of flakes, most of them loose, and many of them really huge. These usually are not adequate for protection. In the Ndotos there are blank faces that are great for sport climbing, and rotten areas that are good for psycho climbing. There are a few cracks and enormous grooves on some of the cliffs; these are where you go for trad climbing. Be careful here, as many of these cracks have an exfoliating layer. Break it off as you climb up, or the protection could break out when you fall. Vegetation also can be a problem. Most of the plants are on the slabby top sections of the cliffs where they receive water runoff. In sum, trad climbing in the Ndotos is a little chossy, and sport climbing is not so steep, but five star.

To date there have been six successful expeditions to this area.

1983: Kenya residents Ron Corkhill and Andrew Wielochowski made a bold, totally traditional ground-up ascent of the right hand wall of Poi's east face. Original Route: E2/3, with some 50-meter runouts.

1999: British climbers Pat Littlejohn and John Barry did a ground-up ascent of a bold

View of Mt. Poi from the main Ndoto Ridge. There are no real "trails," but the Normal Route from the col down is a path used by locals. The climbing line leads to pitch 5 on two failed attempts on the "south crack" by Wielochowski. *Photo and information from Andrew Wielochowski*

The great east face/Gas Hole Face of Mt. Poi as seen from one hour's hike up the trail. (1) Doing A Dirty Eastern Groove (E5 6b trad and 5.12d sport, Berg-Buonajuti-Horsey-Nutter, 2003). (2) Story About Dancing Dogs (5.13b, Fonda-Gruden-Jeran-Koren-Sisernik, 2002). (3) True At First Light (5.13b, Bechtel-Milton-Piana-Skinner, 2000). (4) East Face, a.k.a. Wielochowski Route (E3, Corkhill-Wielochowski, 1983). *Felix Berg*

Poi from the north. (4) East Face/Wielochowski Route. (5) Dark Safari (E6 6b, Barry-Littlejohn, 1999). *Andrew Wielochowski*

crack system on the north wall of Poi. Dark Safari: E6 6b.

2000: Americans Steve Bechtel, Scott Milton, Paul Piana, and Todd Skinner rappel-bolted a sport route. True At First Light: 5.13b.

2002: The Slovenian team of Luka Fonda, Stanko Gruden, Matja Jeran, Goran Koren, and Rok Sisernik drilled another sport route from top to bottom. Story About Dancing Dogs: 5.13b.

2003: A mixed Kenyan and British team of Felix Berg, Marnix Buonajuti, Peter Horsey, and James Nutter did a ground-up mixed sport and traditional route on the groove of Poi's eastern face. Doing A Dirty Eastern Groove: E5 6b trad pitches and 5.12d sport.

2004: The British team of Toby Dunn, Alex Jakubowski, and Ben Winston, climbed on one of the smaller walls in the area, Manamonet: E5 6b.

There are still at least five walls of 400+ meters that have not yet been climbed.

Andrew Wielochowski on the first ascent of the east face on Poi. *Ron Corkhill*

THE MAXIMUM MIRACLE CENTRE

*In Kenya's Ndoto Mountains, it's not the climbing
you'll be telling stories about, it's the bush.*

BEN WINSTON

Enjoying the "out of character pitch" on Maximum Miracle Centre, Manamonet. *Ben Winston, www.BenWinston.co.uk*

"It's like a mini Yosemite," John Barry had said. "There are loads of walls dotted around, probably between 500 and 700 meters high. Just go. You'll have a great time…."

Memorable phrases have a habit of echoing around your head at the most inappropriate times, and up in the Northern Frontier District of Kenya, John's words, like the dried camel meat, kept repeating on me. Ian Howell, one of Kenya's greatest climbing pioneers, had another phrase that came back over and over again: "It's not the climbing you'll be telling stories about. It's the bush."

So sure enough, with three weeks at our disposal in the awesome Ngurunit Valley, Miles Gibson, Alex Jakubowski, Toby Dunn, and I thrashed through bushes and into some form of vegetative purgatory. Nowhere else have I seen plants that threaten to maim or kill. And nowhere do I ever want to see them again.

Manamonet in the Ndoto Mountains, showing the line of Maximum Miracle Centre. *Ben Winston*

The first objective of the trip was the incomparable prow on a mountain known as Baio. Pictures of this had piqued our excitement from the U.K., but the pictures failed to detail the bottom two thirds of the 500-meter wall. If they had, we would have known that it was composed of the same kind of bush that covers the valley floors, only vertical. Not an appealing prospect. Instead, we trooped to the bottom of another huge wall to try to break into the bottom of a crack system that split the face, only to be defeated by 60 meters of protection-free climbing on dustbin-lid flakes of rock that came off when you sneezed on them. Climbing in Ngurunit wasn't looking very much like fun.

It wasn't until we turned our attention to the next biggest wall in the valley that there was some prospect of salvation: a 450-meter corner system that took the wall at its highest point. Five days after chopping a path to the bottom and braving the killer bees that guarded the start, a battered Alex and Miles came back down having climbed pitches of vertical grass, committed to unstable lianas, and thrashed through spiky palms; but they had enjoyed one pitch ("the out of character pitch") of what is conventionally considered rock climbing. The Maximum Miracle Centre was the result, at XS (or E5) 6a, although "In Homage to Fowler" would have made a fine alternative name—or any combination of grade-A expletives heard from the valley floor during the ascent.

With something established in Ngurunit, we headed south to the slopes of Mt. Kenya for an appointment with the Temple [see Alex Jakubowski's article].

When we returned to the U.K. people invariably asked if we had "a good time," if the trip was "fun," or whether we "enjoyed ourselves." Initially, these were difficult questions. The scars of the ordeal were still fresh, our internal flora still unsettled, our bodies still recovering from five weeks with hardly a rest day between us. But now, as memories of the cobras and missionaries and deadly vegetation fade, as fingers and toes forget the nip of deep frozen nights, the answers to those questions have evolved. Yes, I now think, we did have a good time. And yes, there were bits of the trip that were hilarious fun. However, the other great question: "Would you go back?" is still in the balance.

(Adapted from www.PlanetFear.com)

NDOTO LOGISTICS

Advice to climbers headed for the Ngurunit Valley and beyond.

MARNIX BUONAJUTI

The Ndotos as seen from half way up Doing a Dirty Eastern Groove on Mt. Poi. There are a few cliffs of 400 meters in the background that are unclimbed; many of the crags are hidden behind the central mass of hills. *Felix Berg*

The major cliffs vary in their distance from the village of Ngurunit. This is important because Ngurunit provides your supply of food and water. The closest cliff is about a two-hour walk from the village and the furthest (Baio) is about 20km from town. The essential problem here is this: It is a hard walk to the base of any cliff (a few hot hours with no trails), so carrying gear up to your base camp is already a struggle. Carrying all the water and food you need for an expedition would be a monumental task, and I don't know where you would find so many water containers. So you are left with needing porters to come to your camp every few days with fresh water. The closer you are to Ngurunit, the easier getting food and water will be.

GEAR STORAGE

You can find someone with whom to leave gear in Ngurunit. Make a list of what you are leaving and be prepared to pay for the storage. Small but useful things like cutlery, lighters, and torches are likely to go missing, so you had best hang on to those. Be prepared to have all of your porters and all the people you meet asking you to give them your gear (especially camping gear and climbing ropes) as gifts. These people do not have much money and they can't believe how comparatively wealthy we are. This situation has been compounded by many of the foreign expeditions paying the porters very high rates and giving them all their sponsored gear at the expedition's end.

ORGANIZING FOOD, WATER AND PORTERS

When you get there you will need to make contact with a person who speaks both English and the local languages (Samburu and Rendil-e). He will be your middleman for organizing food, water, and porters. Treat this man well for he holds the keys to your pleasure and pain. I recommend Petro Lakada from Siangan village. He was a reliable man for us, and is also a very good cook. I paid him 1,50 Kenyan shillings ($2) a day for his translation and organizational services. The standard price for a porter in Kenya is about 600 to 800 shillings ($8-$10) for a full day's work. You will also want to employ a guide to show you any secret paths that might get you to the base of the cliffs. This man should be paid slightly less, unless he is carrying luggage for you. Water should be free (you just need to pay its transportation) and food is very cheap. 2,000-3,000 shillings ($25-$40) for a goat.

The hardest thing about these expeditions is the interaction with the people you employ. If you do not make written agreements with them before you start it is very likely that they will ask for more money at the end. They will expect a tip when your expedition is finished. This is reasonable, but make sure that all of your terms are clear before you start. I found that women made the best porters. They complain much less than the men, and are by far the tougher sex. The men will tell you that the bags are too heavy, and that their bodies hurt, and that they need water and food, etc, etc, but the women will do their job and that is it.

You may well be charged for camping or leaving your car in a village. The going rate for camping in Siangan in 2003 was 250 shillings ($3) per person per night. People live by barter in Kenya, so expect all prices asked to be about double what they are worth. The average Kenyan makes much less than 700 shillings ($9) per day; as cheap as this sounds by Western standards, be aware that you are actually paying them very well.

OF LOCALS AND CLIMBERS

The locals are okay climbers if we are polite to them. They like us because we bring a high income to their area and we are something of a curiosity. Be careful with scaring their livestock or walking through private compounds. Most of the people in the area are really friendly and very curious about foreigners. You will get a thousand offers for assistance. Unfortunately, on the drive to Ngurunit you may cross bandits and gunmen. Travel in a convoy of a few cars. Don't make visible fires while on the roadside at night, and if someone does hold you up be very polite and compliant.

THE NITHI GORGE

On the flanks of Mt. Kenya, just above the heather and chaparral vegetation zone, climbers walk right past some of the country's finest cliffs.

BOBBY MODEL

The Nithi Gorge, showing Opium Of the People (see report in Climbs & Expeditions in this Journal). *Bobby Model*

The eastern approach to the main peaks of Mt. Kenya follows the stunning Chogoria trail, which contours up the northern ridge of Gorges Valley. This route takes you to the highest point above the valley where it narrows and forms the gorge. There, on the plateau near Hall Tarns, sits Minto's Hut. A mere 10-minute walk takes you to the edge of The Temple, where the stunning Nithi Gorge plunges about 250 meters to the valley floor and Lake Michaelson below.

The gorge is a subsidiary trachytge plug that has been fractured into a worthy climbing objective. From the two highest points of Mt. Kenya (Batian, 5,199m; Nelion, 5,188m) one cannot

Alex Jakubowski wrapping up Angelfish on The Temple. *Ben Winston, www.BenWinston.co.uk*

help but notice this great stone crevasse. However, at this stage one usually is looking forward to a cold beer in Nairobi rather than climbing a lesser objective. For these reasons, and because of the summit-seeking orientation of most parties, this magnificent gorge has been ignored for over 33 years.

The Nithi Gorge saw its first technical climb in 1971, when Phil Snyder and Ian Howell established Ricochette. This route is at the narrowest point of the upper gorge, where it follows an obvious weakness up a groove to the base of a 60-meter chimney, which they climbed to the top.

Because the gorge is below the upper nival zone, lichen, helichrysum, and moss are common obstacles on the lower-angled rock. Despite this almost "African bush climbing" atmosphere, nightfall exposes climbers to alpine climbing conditions as temperatures drop below freezing.

Inspired by new route potential on a mountain that has seen most of its "gems" developed by the driven local duo Iain Allan and Ian Howell—as well as by the glitterati of visiting climbers—two separate teams ventured into the Nithi Gorge during the last days of 2004. Climbers based in Kenya, as well as a visiting "dream" team from the United Kingdom, added three new climbs to the gorge. Climbers from the Mountain Club of Kenya established a route in the narrow gorge to the left of *Ricochette*. The visiting climbers established two very proud lines that ascended the "prow" to produce some of the finest new routes in the country.

THE TEMPLE

Worshipping at Mt. Kenya's feet, the Nithi Gorge.

ALEXANDER JAKUBOWSKI

The Temple in the Nithi Gorge: Angelfish (left: E4 6a, Gibson-Jakubowski, 2004) and
Brew Up Audrey (E4 6b, Dunn-Winston, 2004). *Ben Winston, www.BenWinston.co.uk*

Flicking through a back issue of *High* magazine in the St. Govans Inn at Pembroke one night, I came across an article about climbing in Kenya written by UK South West legend Pat Littlejohn. The article celebrated the joys of free climbing on medium-sized walls in the Kenyan bush. It spoke of giant thorns, leopards, snakes, and acres upon acres of unclimbed rock. Staring out from the center spread was a huge, orange prow jutting out of the skirts of Mt. Kenya with the word "unclimbed" beneath it. I had found the Temple and I knew that I must worship there.

Six months later I found myself in Chogoria (2,000m), the last town to the west of Mt. Kenya. This is the start of the Chogoria route up to the Austrian Hut on Mt. Kenya, and a favorite with the more accomplished trekker. Supplies are best purchased in one of the bigger towns such as Nanyuki, where supermarkets can be found. However, porters and transport can be arranged with very little bother in Chogoria, where we hired a Land Rover to the park gates and Banda's, a cluster of trekkers' huts. From there it was a day's walk up to Lake Michaelson, where we camped, enjoying fresh water from the stream that runs down the valley. Lake Michaelson is the most beautiful place you will ever be.

Despite reports of a wall over 300 meters high, it turned out to be closer to 200 meters. In the next days our team of Toby Dun, Miles Gibson, Ben Winston, and me forced two lines up The Temple's wall. The first was the one I had seen in the magazine. It stands out from the left, from the right, and from in front. It is the corner in the arête and heads straight up into a roof. No climber could miss it, and certainly not the likes of Pat Littlejohn. Miles and I stepped up, and the first pitch fell easily until we came to a halt at a hairline corner crack. Miles led a spooky traverse left and then up (E4 6a) to put pay to this and finished at Littlejohn's old high point, which was marked by some abseil tat. The next pitch is the glory pitch, a long never-ending crack corner (E4 5c).

After that, the wall opens out and a new router is faced with a myriad of opportunity. We let the line take us and headed up and right for a further three pitches to emerge at the very point of the prow. We called the route Angelfish, but that's another story.

The next route, put up by Toby Dunn and Ben Winston, heads up to reach a crack system in the upper wall that can be seen all the way from Lake Michaelson. It starts up a dirty, loose corner at the far left end of the right side of the prow. This was followed by an incongruous pitch of technical and scary climbing at E5 6a, which required cleaning from pegs en route. The pegs were then eliminated and the pitch went free.

The route then launched up a further three pitches of outstanding crack climbing that ranged from body jamming through off width and down to thin fingers. It took some black bits, some orange bits, and some naughty bits. Just as with Angelfish, the upper wall provides a new router with endless possibilities. They, too, let the line take them and headed left, finishing up the final 10 meters of our route. Both routes are high quality expeditions and can be done in a long day each by a competent party. However, watch out for the wind and the cold. The minute the sun goes in and the wind picks up, you are transported from searing Africa to high altitude, sub-zero Mt. Kenya. This change is not as good as a rest.

The Temple holds endless opportunities for new routing. Some fairly amenable-looking lines on the right wings contrast with all-out finger-searing prizefights up the walls between the two established routes. Go there, enjoy, and say hello to those who sometimes descend from the sky to fish Lake Michaelson. We enjoyed trout for tea on New Year's Eve.

HELL'S GATE

*Near Kenya's largest city, huge hexagonal columns provide
lonely jamming and loads of potential.*

ALEX FIKSMAN

Hell's Gate. The Main Wall is on the left, watching misty weather coming in from Lake Narvashe. *Bobby Model*

Rising from the Rift Valley floor less than 100 kilometers from Nairobi is one of Kenya's
most spectacular climbing areas, Hell's Gate National Park. Just an hour and half outside
of Kenya's capital, Nairobi, this is also the most easily accessible multi-pitch climbing area
in the country, with many routes of excellent quality.

The climbs on the Main Wall of Hell's Gate mostly follow crack lines splitting polygonal or
hexagonal columns. They rise over 700 vertical feet. Excellent jamming and stemming on solid rock
(with some exceptions) forces the climber into wonderful positions overlooking vast populations

of wildlife on the valley floor. Thought-provoking sections of loose rock—especially on the top 100 feet of most routes—have kept the Main Wall out of reach of the majority of recreational climbers. Still, no climbing area in Kenya can provide as much satisfaction as a day out on the Main Wall at Hell's Gate.

Most of the significant route development in Hell's Gate took place in the middle to late 1970s, resulting in classics like Olympian (Iain Allan, Ian Howell, and Phil Snyder, 1972) and Future Shock (Iain Allan and Mark Savage, 1972). Currently there are over 40 routes on Main Wall alone and several dozen on the smaller crags. The last couple of years has seen renewed interest in Hell's Gate, which has resulted in removal of aid on several routes and the first completely free ascent of one of them.

The first route to be freed on Main Wall in the last 15 years was Sorcerer, originally established by Ian Howell and Iain Allan in 1975. This route featured 410 feet of climbing (Australian 17 A1). All four of the original pitches involved various amounts of aid (both pegs and nuts). On May 16, 2004 Bobby Model and I went out to explore the possibility of freeing the route. We did a lot of cleaning during this first attempt, and we managed to free climb all pitches except the first. Pitch 3 required a peg to protect the exposed move around the arête.

Nearly a month later, on June 12, Dave Zimmerman and I returned to free, which required a series of subtly engineered moves out of a short chimney on Pitch 1. The climbing provided excellent finger locks and hand jams. A serious "sting in the tail" completed the day with a slightly overhanging finish on loose rock 10 feet above a ledge and over 300 feet above the deck. For this reason, the original ascent received a Hell's Gate seriousness grading 4 out of

Alex Fiksman on the first free ascent of The Sorcerer, Hell's Gate. *Bobby Model*

possible 6. We graded the technical difficulty of the climb Australian 21, but only a few moves were of that standard, while most of the climbing was about 18 and 19.

Other routes that were cleaned of aid in 2004 and early 2005 include Capital Punishment, a 320-foot climb on Main Wall originally put up by Iain Allan and Ian Howell in 1976 at Australian 15 A3. It was cleaned of aid on two out of the three pitches when John Train and I attempted to do a free ascent of the route on March 5, 2005. Pitch 1 remains A3, with a 120-foot smooth wall with hairline cracks leading to the main corner. Although the climbing on Pitch 1 will go free, we have so-far found it impossible to protect the crux moves.

We had more success the following day when John and I removed aid on six out of seven pitches on The Zebra Wall, a 700-foot climb in the highest portion of Main Wall. The most impressive pitch (number 2) required John to fist jam through a wide corner crack into a superb chimney, exiting on the top of a pillar more than 200 feet above the valley floor.

Further aid removal is sure to continue, albeit at a slow pace owing to Kenya's abundance of climbing potential and paucity of people to take advantage of it. Despite its proximity to Nairobi, the Main Wall of Hell's Gate hosts few experienced climbers. Most local climbing takes place on the 120-foot Fishers Tower, where beginners and curious visitors to the park taste this wonderful rock in a most stunning setting.

NOTES ABOUT THE AUTHORS

Marnix Buonajuti was born in Kenya in 1980, to parents of Italian and Dutch origin. He started climbing at the age of 15 with a friend. At first he climbed mostly in Kenya, but as his passion grew he began to travel to different parts of the world in the all too familiar search for cliffs. His favourite way of experiencing climbing is to travel around the bush lands of Kenya exploring its multitude of unclimbed lines. When not at home in East Africa, Marnix can be found completing the last year of his Medical degree in London England.

Alex Fiksman was born in the ex-Soviet Union, educated in the United States, and arrived in Kenya in 1998 planning to stay only two years. He fell in love with the country and decided to remain. The climbing bug bit him as soon as he arrived in Kenya, and he's been committed to it ever since. He manages a successful safari company, Tropical Ice, and steals away to climb with the owner, Iain Allan, at every opportunity.

Alex Jakubowski spent his apprenticeship climbing out of his home town of Sheffield, England. He has been climbing for 15 years and has scratched his way up routes all around the world. He spends much of his spare time dodging big waves on the scary sea cliffs of South Wales and Cornwall.

Bobby Model grew up on a ranch near Cody, Wyoming. After turning adventure photography into his profession, he developed an interest in social and geopolitical interests as well. In order to cover Africa more effectively, he relocated to Nairobi in 2004, where he works as a professional photographer and is active with the Mountain Club of Kenya.

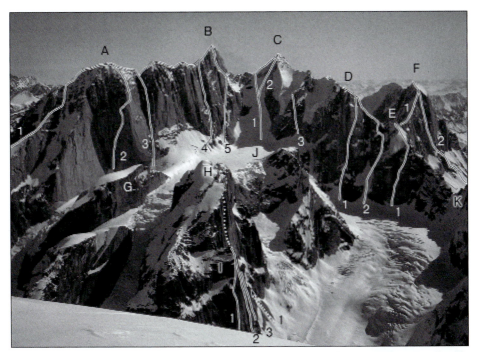

The south and west faces of the historic "Tooth" group, rising from the east side of Alaska's Ruth Gorge. All visible known routes are drawn, though numerous variations exist. See the Alaska section of Climbs and Expeditions for reports on the 2004 routes.

The Moose's Tooth, West Summit (**A**), 9,780'; Main Summit (**B**), 10,335': (1) West Ridge (5,200', V 80°, Bierl-Hasenkopf-Reichenegger-Welsch, 1964). (2) The Moose Antler (2,600', VI 5.8 WI4, Bocarde-Clark-Porter-Svenson, 1974). (3) Shaken, Not Stirred (2,600', V AI5, Crouch-Donini, 1997). (4) Ham and Eggs (2,900', V 5.9 WI4, Davies-Krakauer-Zinsser, 1975). (5) Levitation and Hail Marys (2,900', V M7 A0, Adamson-Stover, 2004).

The Bear Tooth (**C**), 10,070': (1) Original Route (2,600', 60°, Lunn-O'Neil-Young, 1973). (2) White Russian (2,600', 70°, Matusevych-Mytropan-Shuruyev, 2004). (3) Unforgiven (1,150', M5 WI6, James-Ramirez, 2004).

The Eye Tooth (**D**), ca 9,000': (1) West Pillar, The Dream in the Spirit of Mugs (3,300', V 5.10c, Bonapace-Haas-Orgler, 1994). (2) The Talkeetna Standard (3,300', 5.9 WI5, Hollenbaugh-House, 2003).

The Sugar Tooth (**E**), ca 8,000': (1) West Face (2,130', V 5.10+ A2, Bonapace-Haas-Orgler, 1994).

The Broken Tooth (**F**), 9,050': (1) West Ridge (1,970', IV 5.9, Bauman-Lewis, 1987). (2) Quinlan-Stump (1,970', 5.10+ A3, 1987).

The Incisor (**G**), ca 7,500'.

The Wisdom Tooth (**H**), 7,770': (1) Novocaine (2,600', 5.10 A2, Daniels-Davis-Gamble-Frontella, 1997).

The Stump (**I**), ca 6,600': (1) Goldfinger (1,800', IV 5.11a McNamara-Puryear, 2004). (2) Quinlan- Stump (1,800', 5.10 A2, 1991). (3) Game Boy (1,800', 5.11-, Neswadba-Orgler-Wutscher, 1995).

The Root Canal (**J**): The pocket glacier.

Espresso Gap (**K**): The col.

This photo is part of an extensive route documentation being prepared by Joe Puryear. Watch for publication coming soon. Visit www.americanalpineclub.org/knowledge/aaj.asp for an update on publication venue. Puryear has spent 11 long seasons climbing in the Alaska Range, and many of his images can be viewed at www.cascadeimages.com. He is the author of the upcoming book *Alaska Climbing: A Comprehensive Guide to 30 of the Best Routes in the Central Alaska Range*. Several Ruth Gorge routes can be found in his book. Visit www.supertopo.com for more information.

CLIMBS AND EXPEDITIONS

2005

Accounts from the various climbs and expeditions of the world are listed geographically from north to south and from west to east within the noted countries. We begin our coverage with the Contiguous United States and move to Alaska in order for the climbs in the Alaska's Wrangell Mountains to segue into the St. Elias climbs in Canada.

We encourage all climbers to submit accounts of notable activity, especially long new routes (generally defined as U.S. commitment Grade IV—full-day climbs—or longer). Please submit reports as early as possible (see Submissions Guidelines at the back of this Journal).

For conversions of meters to feet, multiply by 3.28; for feet to meters, multiply by 0.30.

Unless otherwise noted, all reports are from the 2004 calendar year.

NORTH AMERICA
CONTIGUOUS UNITED STATES

Washington

OLYMPIC NATIONAL PARK

Sawtooth Ridge, complete traverse. From August 7 to 9 Wayne Wallace and I made the first full traverse of the remote and rugged Sawtooth Ridge in the Olympic Mountains. Known for its relatively good rock (for volcanic), the ridge includes of 13 named peaks (some more like pinnacles) from Mt. Alpha to Mt. Lincoln. We climbed about 20 peaks and pinnacles, doing our best to stay as close as possible to the ridge and climbing northeast ridges or faces and rappelling southwest ridges and faces. Much of the climbing is on steep pillow lava of moderate grade, with above-average run-outs. The rappels were either off 3/8" webbing slung on horns or blocks or, in a few cases, the rope looped around a pointy summit.

The most popular peak is the highest, Mt. Cruiser (6,104'), which graces the cover of the Olympic Mountains guidebook and is generally considered the only worthy objective in the area. While we believe every summit had been touched, we are quite certain nobody had made the complete traverse in a single push. We approached 10 miles past Flapjack Lakes and Gladys Divide on a wet Saturday and ended up at the base of Alpha in dense clouds with zero visibility. We bivied and hoped the skies would clear that night, as forecast. They did, so we were up early and off.

Alpha had two peaks and offered the first view of the complicated traverse. We knew we were in for a great ride with exposure, and our excitement mounted as we rapped to the base of Cruiser. We chose the purest line by keeping on the ridge, and Wayne led the first of many steep, sparsely protected pitches. Next came an unnamed summit (Blob?), more exposed ridge, and then The Needle. The first pitch of the three Castle Spires was another steep, exposed arête with a memorable overhang. We ended the day by doing The Fin and The Horn. One of the most spectacular pitches was a monster chimney up the northeast face of The Fin. The Horn is not class 4, as rated in the guidebook! Unable to find snow to melt, we were forced to drop from the ridge almost 1,000' to get water. We found a pond and slept well under brilliant stars, in spite of relentless mosquitoes.

Wayne Wallace balances on a section of the Sawtooth Ridge near Mt. Cruiser. *David Parker*

The northern half of the Sawtooth ridge showing much of the ground covered on the second day of climbing. *David Parker*

Early the next day we ascended scree gullies back to the ridge where we had left it. The last day of climbing was slightly lower elevation, and there was considerable vegetation, mostly small pine trees, between pinnacles such as Tin Cans 1 & 2 (so named because we found old rusty cans near the summit), The Cleaver, Slab Tower, The Rectagon, Picture Pinnacle, The Trylon, and North Lincoln. We believe our routes up the northeast ridges of Slab Tower, The Rectagon, and Picture Pinnacle to be first ascents. After a complicated series of rappels off North Lincoln, we found the only (obvious!) descent gully, where we dropped our packs, made a quick scramble over to the true summit of Lincoln, returned, and finally dropped off the ridge around 2:00. The steep chute of dirt was puckering, but mellowed to scree, then talus and boulders, before we entered the forest and bushwhacked around a ridge and back to Flapjack Lakes. Slide alder and devil's club reminded us we weren't done yet. The 500' descent down cliffs to the lake was more of a controlled fall; we hung onto bushes and tree limbs until we almost splashed into the crystal water. A swim in the lake cooled and cleaned us for the 7.8-mile hike out to lukewarm beer and chips in the car. Fish and chips and a dozen Hood Canal oysters on the half shell fueled us for the drive home. Grade V 5.8R (old school). Gear: two ropes, medium rack to 3", several small pins, tat cord.

DAVID PARKER, *Bainbridge Island, WA*

CASCADE RANGE

Washington, summary of activity. [Note: this summary supplements individual reports, mostly of bigger routes, below—Ed.] Previously unreported were two ascents of Poster Peak, by probable new routes, in the summer of 2003. Poster Peak is shown on the Washington Pass quad as Point 7,565', one mile southeast of the Early Winters Spires. It is the terminating high point of the long but mostly flat ridge extending toward Copper Point from the Early Winters massif. Larry Goldie and Blue Bradley climbed the leftmost of the two prominent east-northeast buttresses, as seen from Highway 20 just below the hairpin turn. This high-quality moderate route, which they named Blue Buttress, makes for a great day out, with a one-hour approach. It traverses onto the nose of the buttress from the left on a broad ledge, 200 feet up and left from the toe. From there, staying true to the ridge crest on delightful, sound rock takes one right to the summit in about 12 pitches, the most difficult pitch being near the summit (III 5.7). Steve House free-soloed the rightmost of the two east-northeast buttresses in 45 minutes. The climbing is less continuous than on Blue Buttress but is 5.9 at its hardest. The route begins in a shallow depression on down-sloping, awkward climbing. Two pins are fixed on this first pitch. Subsequent parties have reported as many as 17 roped pitches (III 5.9). Descent for both routes is by a walk-off to the south to the base of the route.

In February 2004 Mt. Fury saw its first winter ascent, by a soloist from the Skagit Valley who prefers to remain anonymous. Mt. Fury was arguably the most impressive and obvious peak in the Cascades to have not been climbed in winter. The reclusive Pickets Range aficionado approached by following the Goodell Creek drainage all the way to Fury from Newhalem. In addition to the main summit, he climbed the West Peak, which is rarely climbed, even in summer.

Over February 19-20 Sky Sjue, Ross Peritore, and Corey Bloom made a ski descent of Mt. Buckner's North Face, making the first winter ascent of the route in the process. They approached up the Quien Sabe Glacier and through the Boston-Sahale col to gain the Boston Glacier.

On June 20 Mike Layton and Jordan Peters climbed a new route on the west face of Cutthroat Peak. They named the six-pitch route Community Service Project (III 5.8R), alluding to their altruistic discovery of the rock's low quality. The climb begins below a dihedral system, trends rightward avoiding blank headwalls and gullies, and finishes at the top of the second southwest gully.

On June 27 Layton and Eric Wolf climbed a new route, Der Dihedral, on the northeast face of Dragontail Peak. The route begins just uphill of the Northeast Couloir route, between the 1962 and 1972 northeast face routes, climbing seven new pitches up the dihedral before joining the Northeast Buttress route at about two-thirds height. Most of the dihedral was 5.8 or easier, but they rated the crux roof 5.10b.

On July 31 Layton and Eric Whirley made the long-awaited second ascent of the North

Face of Inspiration Peak, a.k.a. The Soviet Route. The pair approached by traversing around the east side of Little Mac Spire, and on the route found Soviet hardware relics left from the first ascent in 1977.

Immediately after returning from an attempt on K2, Chad Kellogg took advantage of his residual acclimatization to break his own Mt. Rainier speed record. On August 9 he climbed the Disappointment Cleaver in 4:59:01 Paradise-summit-Paradise.

On August 20-21 Brett Bergeron and Jens Klubberud climbed a new route on the north face and northwest rib of Katsuk Peak in the North Cascades. They reached the surprisingly large face by traversing the Katsuk glacier (the biggest in the area) from near the Kimtah-Katsuk col. The rock climbing began near, and just west of, two ribs and gained the summit ridge, where several more pitches led to the summit. The route began on beautifully polished granite and finished on more typical fractured Cascade volcanic rock. Bring crampons. III 5.6.

In October photographer John Scurlock launched a website (www.pbase.com/nolock) exhibiting some of the thousands of pictures he has taken of the Cascades over the past few winters. Scurlock flies solo around the Cascades in winter, in a self-built small airplane, taking high-resolution digital photographs. His contribution to the Cascades is comparable to Brad Washburn's to the Alaska Range. It comes at a fortuitous time, as winter climbing is gaining popularity in the Cascades, and this was a winter that provided fantastic climbing conditions, though horrible skiing.

Phil Fortier and Dave Burdick made what is likely the first winter ascent of Mt. Maude on December 23 in one long day, using a snowmobile to quickly cover the 23 miles of closed road. They ascended an obvious right-slanting couloir on the west face and descended by the south shoulder.

On February 2, 2005, Darin Berdinka and Dave Brannon made the first winter ascent of the Northeast Ridge of Whitechuck Mtn. Berdinka returned to Whitechuck on February 27 to make the first winter ascent of the East Face Couloir with Gene Pires and Justin Thibault. They found the reportedly undesirable summer climb to make a fantastic winter climb, with several pitches of water-ice runnels, sometimes no more than a foot wide.

Dan Aylward and Colin Haley made the first winter ascent of Mt. Triumph's spectacular Northeast Ridge on February 26-27, 2005. The climb consisted mostly of a steep, exposed snow-ridge, but included a few tricky mixed steps, with the crux encountered in the same place as in summer. They descended the southeast ridge.

On March 12, 2005, Craig Gyselinck and Ryan Painter made the first winter ascent of Mt. Thompson's West Ridge, encountering almost summer-like conditions.

Ade Miller and Stuart Taylor made the first winter ascent of Davis Peak's Northeast Couloir on March 13, 2005, a route that had thwarted attempts by other parties earlier in the winter. They experienced difficult mixed climbing low in the couloir and straightforward snow-climbing in its upper portion.

COLIN HALEY, *AAC*

Mt. Challenger, Poltergeist Pinnacle, East Face. On July 3 Dan Aylward and I hiked to Perfect Pass via Hannegan Pass/Easy Ridge. On the 4th we traversed around Challenger Arm and climbed a new route on the southernmost of the prominent subsummits between Challenger and Crooked Thumb. In keeping with the theme of Ghost and Phantom peaks, we dubbed this

Poltergeist Pinnacle. It is particularly distinctive because of a huge shield feature at the base that is streaked by hundreds of dikes that crisscross the face like bolts of lightning.

We picked our lines by aesthetics. Ignoring easier cracks to the left, which would have required a long traverse up higher, we gained the rock in a crisp dihedral just left of the shield. Twenty feet above the snow, Dan left the security of the corner, which blanked out 80 feet higher, and tiptoed rightward across parallel dikes for 40 feet to the very edge of the face. Wild face climbing past an overlap led to more featured climbing along the edge (55m, 5.9+ R).

The second pitch followed a clean easily-protected corner system with a small roof at mid-height (60m, 5.8). A third pitch traversed left after 10m, around two corners, to reach a weakness that breaks through to the top of the steep lower face (60m, 5.8). From an ample ledge we simul-climbed to the ridge crest. We started in the wide trough in the center of the face, then moved right onto a sharp buttress crest with solid rock and less snow (ca 270m, up to 5.7 but mostly low 5th).

We thought about descending directly to the west, but then decided that the easiest way down was up. We turned north and simul-climbed toward the summit of Challenger, which we reached in about an hour and a half. This was generally moderate, and the rock reasonable, though we made no attempt at a true crest traverse. We were interested in speed over purity, and cut below the endless gendarmes where possible. We did loop back up the standard route to the true summit (who can resist all those fixed pins?), which we tagged at about 7:45 p.m. Following the well-trodden track across the glacier, we were back in camp in just over an hour. The hike out the following day was memorable only for blisters. Grade: IV 5.9.

FORREST MURPHY

Burgundy Spire, Action Potential with variants, and Ultramega OK. On July 19, after an evening bacchanal at the Winthrop Pub, Mike Layton's and my approach time to the base of Burgundy had doubled to six hours. At the spire we beheld the impressive and unclimbed east aspect while thunderheads formed above the summit. We saw several options but started with a Bugaboo-like splitter crack and white granite first pitch, followed by a more complicated second pitch. The crux, lichen-filled pitch 3, was steep 5.10 fingers, until a clap of thunder ended our attempt. The next afternoon, after a downpour subsided, we returned. This time we were armed with sleep and a base camp at Burgundy Col. Despite the threat of residual storms, by 3:30 p.m. I linked the first two pitches in 60m, then Mike pulled the crux and cruised through cracks and flake systems to a belay atop pitch 3. We simul-climbed 90m through a crack-chimney system that cleaved the east face, and Mike topped out on Burgundy's north shoulder. I finished the last pitch via the Original Route (Beckey-Hane-Parrott, 1953) and reached the summit block, at 9:00 p.m. We smiled, congratulated each other, and rapped 800' off the north face to our camp at the col. We named the route Action Potential (III 5.10).

The next morning we established the Beautiful Hand Crack (5.10) variation to the first three pitches. Two days later Tom Smith and I completed the second free ascent and established a left-hand variation on pitch 6 that is now the suggested route. A topo can be found at www.cascadesclimbers.com.

On July 24 Tom and I returned, started up the first pitch of an independent line 10' right of Action Potential, shared the first belay, and cast off into a chimney, followed by a right-facing corner. The system continued via hand and finger cracks. Later, Tom aided a lichen-filled seam, then freed a difficult double-roof at 5.10c/d. Seconding I freed the newly cleaned seam and concluded that it should be 5.11. We continued on finger and hand crack systems with exposure and inspiring views of Vasaliki Ridge and the Silver Star Glacier drainage. Tom led the last spicy pitch and topped out on Burgundy's north shoulder. We followed the *Original Route* for a final pitch to the summit block, reaching it at 8:30 p.m. This route retained high quality climbing at a consistent 5.8-5.9 rating with a stellar 5.11 crux; it is the most attractive line that Burgundy has to offer. After two stuck-rope and one core-shot rockfall incidents, at 1:00 a.m. we returned to the highway and to beer chilling in Early Winters Creek. The route was done free of tat or bolts. Two Lost Arrows were placed at the crux belay and one remains. With climbing at 5.11 (5.10c/d A0) III+, seven pitches (5.8, 5.9, 5.8, 5.11, 5.9+, 5.9, 5.8), the route was named Ultramega OK.

MARK ALLEN, *AAC*

Chiwawa Mountain, Intravenous. Inspired by John Scurlock's photos of the northwest face, Dave Burdick and I snowmobiled and skied almost 30 miles up the Chiwawa River valley on March 5, 2005, to a bivy below the south side of Chiwawa Mountain. On the 6th we passed through the Chiwawa-Fortress col to below Chiwawa's northwest face, and made its first ascent by the distinct chimney that splits the face vertically in the center. The climb was mostly water-ice on the lower half, mostly mixed climbing on the upper half, and was done in five pitches with a 60m rope. The climbing was hard, but high quality: the best mixed climb I've ever done. Because of the route's needle-like nature, and how "high" we got from the superb climbing, we named it Intravenous (IV WI4+ M6).

COLIN HALEY, *AAC*

The northwest face of Chiwawa Mountain, showing Intravenous. *John Scurlock*

Mt. Stuart, Complete North Ridge, first winter ascent. Four bluebird days and stellar conditions in February 2005 allowed Colin Haley (20) and me (42) to finally climb Mt. Stuart's Complete North Ridge in winter. It was my 7th attempt in 17 years and Colin's 2nd in a month and a half. Five previous attempts over the years with Don Preiss had ended in true Cascade fashion with thigh-deep snow, high winds, rain, and/or sickness.

Colin Haley on the first pitch of Intravenous, Chiwawa Mountain. *Dave Burdick*

On the first day we parked one mile up the Eightmile Road and followed tracks to the bivy boulder at the base of the route. In December the route was plastered in snow, but this time the rock was dry and the snow had been replaced by nevé. The next day we aided two clean pitches and fixed our two ropes. On day 3 we slept through the alarm and started jugging at 6 a.m. We tossed one rope to the ground and continued on up some of the funnest climbing either of us has ever found in the Cascades. Mostly dry rock, nevé, and even the occasional thunker alpine ice took us to the North Ridge Notch just at sunset. None of the soul-destroying deep snow and wind of December.

After sleeping through the alarm, again, we climbed more alpine fun to the base of the Gendarme. I got the first pitch: steep, all aid with a few moves off the tools, but straightforward and the cracks mostly ice-free. Colin got the definite crux of the route: a 4" to 5" ice-choked crack, followed by insecure free moves, mixed with more aid. He stretched out our 47m rope to a comfy belay just as it became dark.

In brilliant moonlight we climbed for four more hours on easy ground, mixed with harder steps and one section of aid, until we topped out 100 horizontal feet from the summit. A short stroll to the top and we hit the watch at 11:15 p.m. It was so bright we could even see Rainier as we followed tracks down to the head of the Sherpa Glacier Couloir. We then downclimbed perfect nevé, descended the glacier, and set up the tent below the moraine. I got the cush job of melting snow, while Colin hoofed it back up to the bivy boulder to collect his ski poles, sleeping bag, and the rope we tossed. After a good sleep and leisurely brew we had a pleasant walk out.

Mark Bunker, *AAC*

1   2

Summit Chief Mountain, north face. On April 18 Colin Haley and I climbed a new snow and ice route (IV AI3) on Summit Chief Mountain's north face. The route climbs roughly 2,000' up the center of the face, connecting ramps between two major snowfields and finishing just right of the summit. The route begins at a bergschrund to the right of a small cliff below a left-leading ramp. The first half of the route ascends this ramp, which consists of mostly AI2-3 ice steps. This gains the first snowfield, which we

Summit Chief Mountain, north face, showing both 2004 new routes. (1) Burdick-Haley. (2) Hirst-Larson. Lower: Colin Haley on his new route *Dave Burdick (2)*

climbed for several hundred feet, before climbing left through a short rock band and onto the second snowfield. At the top of the second snowfield a narrow constriction with an AI2 ice step led rightward to the ridge crest. An easy scramble up broken rock led to the summit.

We descended the southwest gully, which begins just below the summit. We downclimbed until a rappel was necessary, with anchors on the right. Two 30m rappels reached the snow gully coming up from the col just west of the face. Our rack consisted of knifeblades, ice screws, and medium-sized cams.

DAVE BURDICK

Summit Chief Mountain, Alpine Chicken. Alpine ice climbing in Washington is so suck. From time to time, however, the weather does conspire to create decent enough conditions to grovel one's way up a face using crampons and ice tools. Such was the case in early spring as Rolf Larsen and I set off for an unclimbed line on the north face of Summit Chief.

Rolf and I thrutched up the first ice runnel for five pitches, enduring nearly constant spindrift bombardment from the snowfield above. The going on this lower section was mostly near-vertical and the most sustained portion of the climb. The climbing was never too desperate, but scary, as it often felt like the whole ice sheet would rip right off the face. And frequently parts of it did as the leader climbed past, making the climbing twice as hard for the follower. Belays and pro were hard to find and mostly involved the occasional screw, as well as scraping off a lot of ice and snow to find poor blade placements in the crumbly rock.

By early afternoon we reached the snowfield in the middle of the face. We were thankful to be past the source of the spindrift but now stared at an imposing blank section of steep, protectionless choss that held little snow and less ice. The pure line would continue through this choss, but I suggested to Rolf that we lacked a strong bargaining platform and might want to compromise. We traversed right to the adjacent runnel.

From there a couple of easier long pitches got us to the ridge. A manageable mixed pitch and a bold lead by Rolf up an extremely chossy runout arête got us back on our intended line, above the scary pitch we skipped. A few more lower-angle pitches of steep snow took us to a spot on the summit ridge where a steep pyramid of rock stood between the true summit and us. With the afternoon sun sinking low, but us still a hundred feet below the summit, Rolf and I called it a day.

After a short rappel down the south side of the peak, some downclimbing, and a traverse, we reached the rappel anchor established by Dave and Colin the weekend before during their first ascent of the face. The rest of the descent was straightforward and we made it back to our bivy before dark. We decided to call our climb Alpine Chicken (IV 5.8 AI3+).

PETER HIRST, *AAC*

Mt. Snoqualmie, Pineapple Express. On my third attempt this year, Roger Strong and I climbed the line of corners tracing up the longest part of the northwest face of Mt. Snoqualmie. We completed the climb on February 9, 2005. Located only an hour from Seattle, yet not visible from nearby Alpental ski area, the northwest face of Mt. Snoqualmie is the largest and steepest face in the region. The growing popularity of the New York Gully route (Cotter-Ruch, 1985) confirms the quality of this winter crag; there have been numerous repeats, a speed ascent, rope solo, and, finally, freeing of NYG's short aid pitch (*AAJ* 2004, p. 164).

Approach from the Alpental parking lot. Ascend the Phantom Slide to the northwestern shoulder of Mt. Snoqualmie. Drop into the Thunder Creek basin and traverse beneath the New York Gully area to the lowest toe of rock buttress. The approach takes one to three hours, depending on snow conditions. The first pitch starts just left of the lowest point of rock, climbing a thin slab of ice hidden in a long right-facing corner (WI3+R). After this pitch trend up left, pulling steep heather into a mixed gully leading to a tree belay beneath a rock headwall. The superb third pitch climbs the steep right-facing corner to a tree belay (M6 with good gear). Pitch four leads up and right into snow and trees. The next pitch squeezes through the trees and traverses right to a 5.8 rock step, which leads to a tree belay. Continue up easy mixed ground to a flat ledge beneath the huge headwall that guards the top of the northwest face. Traverse right easily along a spectacular ledge system to join the last two pitches of NYG. We did nine 60m pitches. Include a few thin pitons, cams to 3", and many slings. Pineapple Express (IV 5.8 M6 WI3+R).

DAN CAUTHORN

California

Yosemite Valley, various activity. Big wall free-climbing in Yosemite hasn't lost its appeal, and many impressive ascents were achieved in 2004. The Leaning Tower in particular has seen a lot of recent action, probably due to its more manageable length and more moderate grade (5.13a/b). Unreported from 2003, on October 24 Rob Miller made the second "free" ascent of the Tower. The route itself has not gone free, as the first pitch overhanging bolt ladder will "never go free." Hence, when someone "frees" the Leaning Tower, they are freeing everything above the first pitch. Miller partnered with Chris Van Leuven, who followed everything free but the boulder problem to Guano Ledge. It was Rob's 9th day of effort on the route.

On March 26 The Leaning Tower received its first "team redpoint" ascent by Justin Sjong (30) and Adam Stack (19). On May 27 this pair also made the first team redpoint of the Salathé Wall. Stack, who has redpointed Kryptonite

Central Scrutinizer, El Cap. Jacek Czyz on lead, Maciej Ciesielski belaying. *Tadeusz Montano Grzegorzewski*

(5.14c/d), felt the hardest pitch was the 5.11b slab low on the route. The pair climbed the Free Salathé Light version, avoiding the crux 19th pitch (5.13c/d), as have every party but Skinner-Piana and Herson. The pair are the 6th and 7th climbers to free every pitch of the Salathé, after Alex and Thomas Huber, Tommy Caldwell, Yuji Hurijama, and Jim Herson. Todd Skinner and Paul Piana are generally credited with the first free ascent of the Salathé, although both climbers did not free all the pitches, a more accepted style of the day (1988).

A week after Sjong-Stack's Leaning Tower ascent, Tommy Caldwell scored the first flash of this route, in just five hours. Previously, Yuji Hirayama onsighted routes of similar length and difficulty on Washington Column (Quantum Mechanic) and Sentinel Rock.

Freeing the Regular Northwest Face of Half Dome is still an uncommon feat, despite its relatively tame rating of 5.12a. One reason is that the route is probably harder than 5.12a. The consensus grade for the final ZigZag pitch is settling at 5.12b/c, but still a relatively moderate rating for high-end climbers. The route has devious sections that avoid two bolt ladders and a difficult 5.12 slab finish. On June 26 Phil Gruber of Boulder, Colorado, flashed the route free. I believe this is only the sixth or seventh free ascent and the first time it has been flashed. Not only that, but Phil climbed the 23-pitch, 2,000' face in only 9.5 hours, possibly the fastest free ascent as well. Technically, Phil had seen the route before, since he had previously climbed it with aid, while linking it with The Nose in less than 24 hours. However, Phil had never seen the Higbee Heedral before, one of the 5.12 cruxes. Phil called the final 5.12 slab the crux for him since he hadn't been climbing slabs. In fact, he trained by working 60-hour weeks in an office!

El Capitan received its first flash ascent, as well (not counting the 5.12a West Face and 5.10b East Buttress routes). Twins Mark and Mike Anderson climbed Free Rider, over a few days. Mike led or followed every pitch free first try, taking no falls, and led the crux 5.12d Huber Variation Pitch and 5.12c/d Dihedral pitch, just below the Salathé roof. They completed their ascent on May 8. The pair had climbed many of the pitches two years earlier, while doing a 30-hour aid ascent of the Salathé, but the aid line avoids many of the hardest free pitches on Free Rider. Perhaps their climb wasn't a flash by the strictest definition, but it is awfully close and the best to date.

The king of Yosemite big-wall free-climbing is still Tommy Caldwell. He already has first free ascents of Lurking Fear, West Buttress, and the Muir Wall (Shaft variation), and repeats of the Salathé Wall and Zodiac. Now, he's added possibly the most continuously difficult free climb in the world. On May 22 Caldwell completed the first free ascent of the Dihedral Wall. Belayed by his wife Beth Rodden and friend Adam Stack, Caldwell freed the route over four days. Pitches 6 through 10 were the crux, with every pitch 5.13b or harder. A few were 5.13c, one 5.13d, and the 6th pitch 5.14a--the first pitch on El Cap with this rating, though many consider the Changing Corners and Great Roof pitches on the Nose to be 5.14.

Another notable repeat was Justin Sjong and Steve Schneider's ascent of 5.13b Golden Gate on El Capitan, the fourth or fifth ascent of this 41-pitch Huber brothers testpiece. After backing off in May due to jingus fixed gear, the pair returned in June, added a bolt (with the Hubers' permission) and sent the route over six days.

Free-climbing on El Cap has been male-dominated, but Steph Davis added her mark in 2004. Steph Davis added her mark in 2004, becoming only the third woman to free-climb El Cap (the others being Rodden and Lynn Hill). After free-climbing Free Rider in April, Davis returned in late May to send the route in a day. Lynn Hill's sub-24-hour ascent of The Nose is the only other female one-day free ascent. Belayed by Heinz Zak, Davis freed the 38 pitches in 22:15.

But enough about free-climbing; what about speed-climbing? One name: Ammon McNeely. He did 11 speed-climbs on El Cap in 2004 and came away with nine records, the most prolific speed-climbing season ever. McNeely did the first one-day ascents of the Atlantic Ocean Wall (23:38) and Wall of Early Morning Light (23:43) with Brian McCray, and Never Never Land (16:00) and Horse Chute (20:39) with Chris McNamara. Other records included Iron Hawk (30:42) with Cedar Wright, Pacific Ocean Wall (33:02) with Ivo Ninov, and the 2nd ascent (and first one-day ascent) of Pressure Cooker (23:41), also with Ninov.

Heidi Wirtz and Vera Schulte-Pelkum teamed up for three female speed-climbing records. Training for a Half Dome-El Cap link-up, which they ran out of time to attempt, the tireless two-some climbed the West Face of Leaning Tower on June 17 in 5:15. Two days later they did the Regular Route on Half Dome in 5:19, and on June 23 they climbed the Nose in 12:15.

Yes, new routes are still being put up in Yosemite. Unreported from 2002, Kirsten Kremer, Greg Collins, and Paul Turecki put up The Twisted Road (19 pitches, VI 5.12-) on the southeast arête of Higher Watkins Pinnacle. They speculated that this could be the last major unclimbed wall in the Valley. The pinnacle is attached to the south face of Mt. Watkins, and the route follows the first seven pitches of Hook, Line, and Sinker before breaking left to ascend the pillar. The route took 16 days to establish from March to May.

In 2003, over ten-days, Hannah North, Tom Harper, and Tom Malzbender established an "alpine rock route" on Cloud's Rest, which they named My Favorite Things (15 pitches, IV 5.10-). Cloud's Rest is the largest unbroken sweep of granite in Yosemite, though few routes are documented on this huge, lower-angled slab. The route is accessed by descending Tenaya Canyon from the top. Information has been posted at www.mindspring.com/~thharper/FTTop.html.

A new route on Higher Cathedral Spire was mentioned on Supertopo.com. The route is 5.10 or easier, except for a 5.11+ hands pitch through a roof.

Cedar Wright, with Luis Rivera, did the first free ascents of both the Camp 4 Wall and the Arrowhead Wall. Wright onsighted these routes and graded them 5.11.

As a final Valley note, Jacek Czyz (46) and Maciej Ciesielski (28), both of Poland, did the second ascent of the VI 5.11 A4 Central Scrutinizer on El Cap. They repeated the 22-pitch route in six days.

In Tuolumne, in 2002, Sean Kriletich and Bob Jensen put up 5.11+R Separation Anxiety on Fairview Dome. It starts up Inverted Staircase, before breaking right to a dike. It follows this dike for a long way, before merging with the route Roseanne for the finish.

Also on Fairview Dome, Mike Schaefer established an eight-pitch, stiff 5.12 route, between Pièce de Résistance and Hemispheres. It was established top-down, the first route on Fairview done with "sport-climbing tactics." Schaefer writes, "I'm not sure if I should be ashamed or proud. It is one of the best climbs I have ever done. If it was not rap-bolted, it would have been a ground-up bolt ladder with poorly placed bolts and more than I placed. I do believe rap-bolting produced the better route with the fewer bolts. But I still struggle with the fact that it was me who brought rap-bolting to Fairview Dome."

BILL WRIGHT, *AAC, Satan's Minions Scrambling Club*

El Capitan, Dihedral Wall free ascent. In May, adding to his phenomenal list of El Capitan free routes, Tommy Caldwell freed the incredibly sustained Dihedral Wall (26 pitches, VI 5.14a), perhaps the most difficult free route on El Capitan. See Caldwell's feature on big-wall free climbing, earlier in this journal.

Hetch Hetchy Dome, Resurrection and In Memoriam. Hetch Hetchy is the next canyon northwest of Yosemite Valley. From Tuolumne Meadows, the Tuolumne River flows west into what used to be the "other valley." A bit smaller than Yosemite, but every bit as beautiful, Hetch Hetchy was composed of 1,000-2,000' foot walls of golden granite, waterfalls, meadows, animals, and of course native people. But it was stripped away from them, as a reservoir was built in the 1920s to provide water for San Francisco. Some say Congressional approval of this catastrophe caused John Muir to die of a broken heart. Now the empty walls fall away into the dark cold waters and the lost world below. Needless to say, if you're open to it, Hetch Hetchy carries a heavy vibe!

About eight years ago, when I was hiking through the area, it became apparent that at some point I would have to engulf myself on one of these mystical walls. One line in particular stood out. The line runs straight up the center of Hetch Hetchy Dome. About 1,800' high, the system splitting the golden headwall near the top of the dome is one of the most perfect lines I have ever seen. I later learned that Galen Rowell had done a route up this wall, and knew it had to be this line. It was, but at 5.9 A3. Since my goal was to free-climb the wall, I wasn't as crushed as I could have been.

In May Brian Ketron and I set out to free the line. The first 1,100' are vertical or less. The wall is then crossed by a massive ledge system and capped by a 700' headwall

Brian Ketron on Resurrection, pitch 18, 5.12c, Hetch Hetchy Dome. *Shawn Reeder*

above. We thought we would explode up the lower wall in a one-day push, freeing everything and fixing ropes to the upper wall, but were stopped at 800' by an unavoidable and unfreeable bolt ladder. We retreated and reevaluated, and over the course of many days linked a line up the lower headwall in 10 pitches, at 5.12a, half on run-out face and half up nice cracks. The crux was a bolted slabby arête. This new lower-wall route shared only about one pitch with the old Galen route, which turned out to be a blessing, as it followed a more direct line and provided better free-climbing. With more work we managed to link up the upper wall at 5.12c, the crux being an overhanging layback that led into a less-than-vertical, way-thin, slippery seam. The rest of the upper wall hosts a 5.9 pitch, a 5.11b, two 5.11+ pitches, a 5.12a, and a 5.10c final pitch. On the upper wall we stayed mostly on the original aid line, with only slight variations. With the prep work done and the entire wall fixed with ropes, we rapped, went home, and returned a week later for the first free ascent. Ketron and I completed the route in two days, both freeing every move, while Shawn Reeder jugged the lines above us and photoed the ordeal. Resurrection (17 pitches, V 5.12c) is five stars and the nicest free climb I've ever done. Pro: One full set of stoppers and one full set of cams from #00 Metolius to #3 Camalot.

In late June I returned with Jake Jones and freed the original line on the bottom wall up to the bolt ladder, then traversed into Resurrection to establish In Memoriam (11 pitches, IV 5.11d), which probably rates three stars. Pro: One full set of stoppers and one full set of cams from #0 Metolius to #4.5 Camalot. Both routes can be rapped with a single 70m rope.

SEAN JONES

SIERRA NEVADA

The Incredible Hulk, free routes. On July 3, Peter Croft, Dave Nettle, and Greg Epperson established Airstream (V 5.13), considered the most difficult free climb in the High Sierra. In August, Croft returned to the Incredible Hulk with Andrew Stevens and Hans Steingartner to put up Blowhard (IV 5.12+). Finally, on September 4 Croft and Nettle finished the season with another new route, The Venturi Effect (V 5.12+). See Croft's feature article in this journal for details.

East Fuller Butte, Eagle Buttress, and Eagle Dihedral free ascent. Dave Nettle and I may have made the first free ascent of Eagle Dihedral (IV 5.11- or 5.10 A2) on August 21. We freed the crux pitch after wiggling the original pitons out by hand. This route was established by Galen Rowell and Jerry Coe in 1971. This natural line starts with a sparsely protected groove chimney and ends with a steep, spectacular hand crack. Dave and I also established a new seven-pitch line left of Eagle Dihedral. Eagle Buttress (5.11+ A0) consists of well-protected face climbing that links natural features. The first pitch (some bolts) starts at the base of the 4th/5th class ramp of Eagle Dihedral. The line is almost free, except for 5 feet on the third pitch.

BRANDON THAU

Fuller Butte. (A) The Twisted Bit (5.12b, Drazin-Thau, 2001). (B) East Face (5.9 A1, Bartlett-Reid, 1979). (C) Cassam-Maciaszek (5.8, 1993). (D) Eagle Buttress (5.11+ A0, Nettle-Thau 2004). (E) Eagle Dihedral (5.11- or 5.9 A3 Coe-Rowell, 1971—FFA: Nettle-Thau, 2004). (F) Southern Yosemite Direct (5.10c A2+, Cassam-Didden-Maciaszek, 1994). (G) Walking With Walt (5.10d C2, Anderson-Rose, 2003). (H) Southeast Face (5.8 A2, Beckey-Donaldson-Stuart-Vennum, 1972). Photo, lines, and route info from Brandon Thau

Palisade Traverse, second continuous ascent. Our climb consisted of a complete traverse of the Sierra Crest from Southfork Pass to the summit of Mt. Agassiz, a distance of approximately eight miles. This route is notable not only for its length but also for its sustained elevation. At no point does the traverse drop below 13,000', and much of the climbing is at or above 14,000', making it, in all likelihood, the highest continuous stretch of alpine ridge in the continental United States.

As best we can determine this traverse had been climbed start to finish only once before, in 1979, by Palisade guide John Fischer and his client Gerry Adams. Although he and Adams apparently bypassed a few sections of the ridge crest during the last mile or so, this hardly detracts from their visionary achievement. Including these sections presented us with no exceptional difficulty, and we found that closely adhering to the crest along its entire length (with the

The Palisades Traverse follows the entire skyline in this photo. *Adam Penney*

minor exception of the "Dolphin Fin" between Thunderbolt and Winchell, which we skirted above the bergschrund) made for a satisfying route.

Partial traverses of the Palisades are not uncommon, and a good route description can be found in several guidebooks. However, logistics contributed greatly to our success. Since much of the climbing is fourth class and most obstacles go at 5.8, technical difficulty isn't the primary reason attempts at this traverse are unsuccessful. Weather, on the other hand, is decidedly an issue. Palisades storms may be mild by the standards of great ranges, but they're still unavoidable. Seven of our twelve days on the Crest (6/14-6/25) found us on the receiving end of frozen precipitation. This complicated the climb and added to its duration. Had we not been prepared for such delays, we too might have failed.

Like Fischer and Adams we placed supply caches at strategic points, each stocked with three to four days of food, fuel, and miscellaneous equipment. Establishing these caches was not a trivial undertaking—it required as much time and almost as much energy as the climb itself— but it kept our packs to a tolerable weight and more importantly, gave us the margin of extra time we needed not to be hurried. We remained well-hydrated, well-fed, and well-equipped, and inclement weather proved no more than a minor inconvenience.

The route is rated VI 5.9, but we feel competent parties have a reasonable chance of success, provided they allow sufficient time. The first ascent team's time of seven days is a tribute to the skill and stamina of its leader; lowlanders and weekenders (such as ourselves) should probably factor in a few more days. All in all, the Palisade Traverse is a magnificent climb that we highly recommend to aficionados of alpine adventure. We hope another 25 years won't pass before its next ascent.

SCOTT MCCOOK *and* ADAM PENNEY, *Columbia, South Carolina*

Birch Mountain, Bardini Route. This climb is hidden in plain sight. You can study the north face of Birch Mountain (13,665') from downtown Big Pine. But it took a decade of driving up to guide in the Palisades before I began to notice the huge dark face to the south, and two more decades to act on it.

The Bardini Route on Birch Mountain. *Doug Robinson*

In many ways Birch Mountain is the mirror of Temple Crag, just five miles away. Same dark granite, same bewildering complexity of ridges on a 2,400-foot face on a 13,000-foot mountain. A similar Dark Star-like buttress dominates the center of the face, and we went straight for it, even though it was hard to tell how it connected to which ridge above. Recon with a spotting scope failed to show the link-up, but did convince us to return in the spring, with snow covering the approach talus and meltable for the inevitable bivy. Meanwhile others noticed the face, and a couple of friends jumped us, climbing 5.10 up the buttress before rapping off in the face of darkness. Terry Kearney and I became more secretive and returned early, May 2-4. A jumble of loose blocks gave way to clean 5.6 up the buttress, incut holds even. Where it steepened, we cut left across the prominent corner to stay with the grade and came to a fine, unroped bivy atop the buttress. Several pitches took us over the prominent Twin Towers; we rapped off the second one. Here was the hidden junction with the upper ridge, striking but seriously harder. This early in the season we weren't yet tuned, and veered right, crossing two gullies on snow, chopping 5m off our new rope on another rap, and bivying again before finishing up another fine ridge straight to the summit. Backside glissading for 5,000' took us to burgers in Bishop.

Allan Bard and I had planned to do this climb a decade ago. When he died, my snapshot of the route was on his refrigerator. Ever since, it has been earmarked the Bardini. By sidestepping the direct upper ridge, and assiduously backing off other hard sections, this route barely noses out the grand traverse of the Whitney Skyline to become the easiest big route in the High Sierra (23 pitches, three on snow, and four raps, V 5.6). But fair warning: loose patches and routefinding make the Bardini more serious than it sounds. Soon there will be a direct.

DOUG ROBINSON, *AAC*

Birch Mountain, north ridge, attempt. In the summer, Seth Dilles and I were back again to do the first ascent of the complete north ridge, which we planned to call the Kramer Memorial Ridge [for history, see *AAJ* 2004, pp. 170-171]. I invited Doug Robinson to join us, only to learn that he had just climbed Birch [see above]. He climbed it with a client, spent a night at our 2003 high point, and continued. However, to avoid another bivouac, they bailed off the ridge and climbed another ridge to the summit. This left our prize, the complete 2,500' north ridge, unclimbed. We decided to go on a 24-hour alpine-style push. The climbing was challenging and adventuresome. Beautiful granite, interspersed with loose bands of granodiorite. But we ran out of water at about 3 p.m., ran out of food at 4 p.m., and ran out of energy at 7 p.m. We bailed 500' from the summit.

MIKE STRASSMAN

Mt. Whitney, If at First…. We began this route on the east face of Mt. Whitney in 1999, with 14-year-old Scott Thelan. We sat in a tent in the rain for 36 hours and got back on the face only to have the clouds come in. We accomplished one pitch before deciding that a hanging death flake made the cracks we were in too dangerous. I made a second attempt with my ex-wife, Jackie Carroll, in 2002. We opted for the farthest left crack system, where we could quickly gain the edge of the face. However, to save time we ventured way left on the south face, to easier ground, and cut back right to the edge of the face at the top of pitch 6. From here I followed a beautiful crack to a groove on the south face proper. Steep. Runout. We went down.

In the summer of 2003 I enlisted a ropegun, Seth Dilles. We fixed the first five pitches and waited for my wife. She would hike in the following day, and we all would send it to the top. However, she went to the wrong campsite. Since Seth was my ride home, I left and the ropes remained. Later that summer Seth and I enlisted extreme skier Johnny "Rotten" McGrath. The day after we arrived at base camp it rained, but it dawned clear the following day. Seth and I jugged the ropes, reached our high point, and got to work. Seth ran it out on 5.10 ground and then placed a bolt. Then the sky opened up, we were in a full blizzard, and we went down. On our fifth attempt, we got to our high point, and Seth ran it out to discover…no belay, no cracks, nowhere to go. He weaseled in something to back off and got back to the ledge. We went down and removed the ropes.

On the sixth attempt we gave ourselves seven days, but things did not go as planned. I was approached by a Whitney Trail hiker, who asked if we could porter a load for his daughter, who had a broken arm. We got the overloaded pack to their base camp, but my back was in spasms. We marched off toward the North Fork and camped beneath Pinnacle Ridge, where Seth dis-covered he still had some of the girl's stuff. He circumnavigated Wotan's Throne and arrived back in camp at 2 a.m. That was the sixth attempt.

On the seventh attempt Seth was determined to do it in a day, so we came in, fixed almost to our previous high point, and took a rest day. We awoke at 2 a.m. and were jugging away when the sun rose. From atop the original first pitch, we took a line left for several pitches, because it was easier than the original. From our highpoint Seth dashed around the corner into space. I sat and waited. Not a sound did I hear from him. I had hoped he was going to climb the outside of the dihedral we had spied from the ground. But as time passed, I imagined Seth out there, no pro, sketching out. What would the rescue scenario be if he fell? With one rope and a 5mm tag line, not pretty. However, he called off-belay, and I followed the most spectacular pitch I have ever climbed in the mountains. Sustained 5.10 on the outside edge of a dihedral, with 1,500' of air beneath me. A great pitch of hand cracks led through a roof, then an easy pitch, then a hail storm. I climbed into the dark and collapsed onto a ledge. Seth jugged, which was fine with me, because I was tired. We spent the rest of the night shivering.

The next day went quickly, as we climbed easy ground to the summit. We called our 2,800', V 5.10+ route If At First…. One of the finest routes in the Whitney region. This was my seventh first ascent on the nine pinnacles between Mt. Muir and Whitney.

MIKE STRASSMAN

Lone Pine Peak, Pathways Through to Space. V 5.10 A1. First ascent August 1, by Stephen Quale and Scotty Nelson. This route starts about 100' left of the huge inside corner on the south face. Climb a right-facing corner (marked by a prominent roof five pitches above) to the top of a pedestal. Continue up the right-facing dihedral (5.8) to a ledge with a bush. Climb the off-width splitter crack (5.8) to a belay ledge. Move to the left wall of the dihedral and climb double cracks (5.8) to a hanging belay at a bush, underneath the prominent roof. Move to the right, under the roof (A1) to another hanging belay, and climb the corner and chimney above for two or three pitches to a bolted belay stance at Dead Tree Terrace. Continue up Windhorse to the top. Protection to 5" is needed.

R.J. SECOR, *AAC*

Lone Pine Peak, The Streets of the Mountains. IV 5.10 A0. First ascent September 4-6, by Miguel Carmona and Joe LeMay. This route is on the far western side of the south face of Lone Pine Peak. Ascend the South Gully a short distance, then scramble up right across tree-covered ledges to a ledge with two large pine trees. Walk up a ramp into a slot just below a roof. Move right below the roof into a wide crescent crack (5.7) that ends on a ledge. Climb up and left along a groove into a slot (5.9), traverse to the right to a horn (5.10a), then up a wide layback flake to a hanging belay in a hole in the flake. Continue up to a left-facing inside corner (5.9) that ends at a ledge (descend down and left from the ledge to an excellent bivouac site). From the right end of the ledge, go up and left around a block and then back to the right into the corner, then continue up the face, passing over the first orange dike, and traverse into a wide chimney. Climb the chimney (5.9), followed by a layback up a flaky section into a left-facing corner. Stem up the corner for two pitches (5.8, 5.9) to easier climbing, with a huge chimney overhead; traverse to the right onto a big, loose platform. Move to the right into a left-facing corner, stemming and laybacking (5.9) to a narrow ledge. Easy aid then leads into a wide, loose 5.10 crack, ending with a belay from a large pedestal. Go to the right through ledges and the second orange dike (5.7) to another big ledge in the upper part of the left-facing inside corner. Face climb to the left before traversing back into the corner (5.7) and climbing up to an alcove on the right, beneath a huge roof. Climb the right side of the alcove (5.8) before moving left to a ledge. Easy climbing leads to a notch; go left through the notch and descend 50' before climbing over easy class 5 ledges for two pitches to the summit plateau.

R.J. SECOR, *AAC*

Arizona

Vermilion Cliffs, various activity. For the past five years Albert Newman of Flagstaff, with a dozen partners, including Jeff Kennedy and James Martin, has passionately pursued new route development in the Vermilion Cliffs of northern Arizona. Composed mostly of Navajo Sandstone, the cliffs reach heights up to 1,500' and stretch for over 20 miles at the head of the Grand Canyon. There are only six recorded technical routes in this sandbox, which includes the 1,400' spire named Tooth Rock, the tallest free-standing formation in Arizona.

Tooth Rock has four challenging routes, each with a colorful history. One of the finest desert climbing achievements took place in 1977, when the Lost Love route (1,400', V 5.9 A3) was climbed by Spencer McIntire and George Bain. This is one of the longest and most committing free routes in the state, besides offering 20' of dangerous aid. Matters in Motion (1,000', V 5.9 A3), by Jason Keith and Dave Insley in 1993, ascends the overhanging, tombstone-like north face and is rumored to be especially loose and scary. The prominent east-facing prow was begun in the 1980s by Flagstaff climbers Bain and Glenn Rink, who made it high onto the face, and completed in 1997 by Dougald MacDonald and Paul Gagner (V 5.10 A2).

Vermilion Cliffs climbers encounter a Zion-like rock, although much softer in places. Every route has sketchy sections. Add to this the complicated logistics of a big wall several miles into an area with no trails or water, and the adventure factor becomes high. In dozens of trips to the area we have encountered one hiking party, and no climbers.

Efforts by Newman and partners have resulted in three new routes. Red Dawn (700', IV 5.9 A3), 36° 42.5' N 111° 50.6' W (NAD83 datum), ascends the southernmost prow of the cliffs. The route features a healthy share of exciting nailing, a riveting bolt ladder, and steep free climbing, topping out to spectacular 100-mile views of the Colorado Plateau. The Albatross (1,100', V 5.9 C2), 36° 49.5' N 111° 41.5' W, follows a plumb-line splitter crack to the Mambo Ledge, one of the finest bivys anywhere. Another 300' of scrambling leads to a pendulum roof pitch with a thousand feet of air below. The route will become one of the most difficult free routes in Arizona. More Sand Than Stone (1,100', V 5.11 A1), 36°

The 1,400-foot Tooth Rock, in the Vermilion Cliffs, is the largest sandstone spire in North America and has had only 14-16 people on the summit (until 2003, there had been more men on the moon). All existing routes: More Sand than Stone (V 5.10 A1, Martin-Newman, 2004), climbs an impressive dihedral system up the south face (not shown). (1) Lost Love Route (V 5.9 A3, Bain-McIntire, 1977), follows a natural line of chimney systems up the southeast face. (2) East Prow Buttress (V 5.10 A2, Gagner-MacDonald, 1997) takes the most obvious line up the formation. (3) Matter in Motion (V 5.9 A2, Insley-Keith, 1993), one of the longest hard aid lines in the state goes up the north face (partially shown). *John Burcham*

50.2' N 111° 41.1' W, follows an impressive dihedral system up the south face of the Tooth and is in the process of being free-climbed.

The Vermilion Cliffs comprise a unique, fragile, and isolated wilderness. We have worked to minimize our impacts and hope that others will continue to do the same.

ALBERT NEWMAN *and* JEFF KENNEDY, *AAC*

Utah

The Desert, various activity. Many new routes were established in the Moab area by Joe Slansky, and in the Castle Valley area by Greg Child and partners. They were wall climbs under 400' in height. Further information is available at www.climbingmoab.com.

A significant new route is Excommunication (IV 5.13), by Greg Child on the Priest in Castle Valley. Says Child: "It is the only complete new route on the tower since the original Honeymoon Chimney ascent." The route follows the northwest edge of the Priest for two pitches, right on the arête, then breaks onto the overhanging calcite-covered north face for the crux pitch. Two more pitches back on the northwest edge lead to the summit. The route was climbed ground-up, with mainly bolt protection (though a rack is required) and was red-pointed over several days in October.

Steve "Crusher" Bartlett soloed The More You Jeep, The Less Intelligent You Are (2 pitches, III A3-), on the 190' free-standing Repo Man tower. The route begins under an obvious A-shaped chimney on the south side, and was completed on December 20. The tower is just before the Gemini Bridges in the Island in the Sky area southwest of Moab. Four-wheel-drive and high clearance is required for the approach.

Layne Potter and Paul Ross started off 2004 with a new route in March on the Pinnacle/ Weasel formation in the San Rafael Swell. They spent two days climbing an awkward and torturous groove system that ended at a feature they dubbed The Rooster, a prominent block visible from miles away. They also named the route The Rooster (400', 4 pitches, IV 5.8 C2 A1). Paul kept Layne on high alert, as he took two leader falls and provided much rock bombardment. It was a wake up call for their desert adventures, and Ross says he has the scars to prove it. The team next turned their attention to the massive slabs of the San Rafael's Eastern Reef. Layne, his son Sheridan, and Paul climbed The Grand Adventure (1,340', 7 pitches, III 5.8R). "The name says it all, a trip that will not disappoint those that like a wander into the unknown," said Ross. More routes on the Reef followed Layne and Paul's aim to complete 50 new climbs in this area before the end of 2004. They climbed several routes up steep sides of slot canyons that divide the various high-angle slab formations, including The Gordian Knot (530', III 5.9 C1) and, with Paul Gardner, Perhaps Not (560', III 5.9 C1). In May Paul Ross and his son, Andy, made a trip back to Weasel Spire in the northern part of the Swell and climbed, in a day and a half, a new route up the impressive south face. They named it Ozymandias (440', 6 pitches, IV 5.9 C2). In July, back on the Reef, Layne Potter and Paul continued their quest on the slabs with eight more climbs, including Fear Not (850', 6 pitches, III 5.8+R), Laugh Not (620', 4 pitches, III 5.8R), and Fall Not (970', 5 pitches, III 5.7R). On September 1, on their 45th new route on the Reef, Paul took a 40-foot fall when a small ledge he'd swung onto collapsed, leaving him with a broken ankle and an end to his season, a few routes short of his 50-route goal. He wrote, "To date there are 44 (and a half) routes on the Reef that give a total of 44,828 feet of climbing. Roll on, spring 2005."

ERIC BJØRNSTAD, *AAC*

ZION NATIONAL PARK

Zion, various ascents. On the southeast face of West Temple, from March 19-21, Bryan Bird, Brody and Jared Greer, and I put up The Big Lebowski (21 pitches, 5.10 C1). The route is characterized by clean crack climbing and lots of ledges. It ascends the obvious crack system in the white rock approximately 400' left of Getting Western. Chimneys, double crack systems, and a splitter offwidth (just right of the two striking splitters) make this route easy to see from Spring-dale. We bivied at pitches 7 and 11. To descend rap the route with two 60m ropes or go down the Mountaineering Route. It's grade V or VI ? (Hard to tell, when McCray climbs it free in a day.) [On April 13, Brian McCray and James Martin made a one-day, all-free ascent of the route in about 17 hours. They stopped at the ridge, forgoing the final 5.5 pitch to the summit—Ed.]

Bryan Bird and Joe French made the first ascent of the Southwest Ridge (9 pitches, IV 5.9R) on Mt. Spry on November 16. The bottom three pitches (5.8-5.9) are on good, black rock and are hidden from view, inside a chimney. Next, traverse a few hundred feet right to three pitches of obvious crack climbing (5.8), leading to a giant ledge (bighorn country) and the summit cone. Three pitches of interesting patina and slab climbing (5.9R) up the southwest prow gain the top. Walk off the summit cone, then, reverse the route by abseiling from trees and large bushes. Bird and French used two ropes, but other options exist.

On November 19 Bird and French climbed a new route, More than a Woman (10 pitches, IV 5.10+), on the southeast face of the Middle Mary. The route starts in the middle of the southeast face, marked by a hand crack that passes through three roofs. Start in the crack leading to these roofs, then take a right into a continuous crack system. Six pitches of good crack climbing (5.10+) lead to a couple of pitches of 4th class, then two more pitches of 5.8-5.9 to the top. The first-ascent party abseiled down the west ridge into the notch between the Middle Mary and the Left Mary and followed the standard descent for Gentlemen's Agreement (one rope will do). They mentioned, however, that the descent between Middle Mary and Right Mary might be better.

French and I, on November 12, established The Groper (7 pitches, IV 5.10+) on the east face of Mt. Moroni. The route can be identified by splitter double cracks in a patina headwall, just right of the smooth shield in the right-center face of Moroni. Four broken pitches of offwidths, chimneys, and gullies reach a big ledge with a tree. Traverse right to a black corner and a bolt belay, where the real climbing begins. Two pitches of exciting headwall climbing end on a ledge halfway up the formation. We rapped the route, although continuing to the top and down the Lady Mountain trail is also an option.

ERIC DRAPER

Angel's Landing, Lowe Route, first free ascent with variations. After a successful spring trip to Yosemite, I resolved to establish my own long free route, somewhere near my home in Utah. Zion was the obvious venue, and with some advice from the prolific Brian Smoot, I settled on the Lowe Route on the north face of Angel's Landing.

My first attempts were foiled by a short bolt ladder, but to my amazement, I found a series of holds to the left. Their mere existence on these sheer walls was unlikely, but that they would offer a route of passage seemed downright impossible. With optimistic naïvete I bolted three independent pitches, hoping they would be climbable.

I wanted to work on the route in October, but the one-two punch of a Master's thesis deadline and atrocious weather conspired against me. By the time I was ready to "send," it was November.

That late in the season, free-climbing on this sunless wall is barely tolerable for about six hours per day, when the mercury breaks 40°. A one-day ascent was out of the question. I resorted to the typical Zion "fix-and-fire" style. On November 21 I led half way up the route without falling. That night it snowed.

My naïve optimism was turning to cynical realism. My employer, the Air Force, was moving me to Colorado Springs in late December. My commute time to Zion was going to double, and I was sure the NPS would close the route soon for nesting raptors. As I was losing hope, a high pressure system moved in.

On December 11, my wife Janelle Anderson and I quickly climbed to my previous high point below the 8th pitch. I had TRed it a few times but had not successfully led this scary C3 pitch. I pulled through the strenuous roof moves, clipping three fixed pins. I milked a rest above the crux to warm my fingers and psyche up for the runout above, but was forced to move on by dwindling reserves in my calves. I strained to stay relaxed as I wiggled tiny nuts into the thin aid seam to protect the 12a moves, and I let out a scream of relief when I latched the final dyno, 15 feet above a #3 peenut.

Mike Anderson on the Lowe Route 5.13a R, Zion NP, UT. *Andrew Burr*

The next day we rapped in from the summit, and I quickly redpointed the first of the three new bolted pitches. The overhanging 10th pitch took me three tries to redpoint, and the delay was costly. I was unable to climb the final hard pitch, despite five or six desperate tries in waning light. We returned a third day and I climbed the last hard pitch on my first try, at 12c. The last four pitches were just a formality, and we were relieved to meet the warm rays of the sun on the summit. (15 pitches [3 new], V 5.13aR)

MICHAEL ANDERSON, *AAC*

Spearhead Mountain, Midevil Wall. From March 22-25 Ammon McNeely and I established Midevil Wall (V 5.9 A3+) over three days. The first day we climbed approach pitches to a killer bivy at the base of the wall. We climbed three pitches the next day and descended fixed lines to camp. On the third day we jugged, climbed three or four more pitches, summited after dark, and rappelled the route to base camp. This wall, on Spearhead, is directly across the canyon from Red Arch Mountain. The route connects faint, natural cracks with much apparently blank face. The face actually yielded amazing placements of stoppers, hooks, tri-cams, and Camalots in pockets, and some free-climbing. It's an improbable line which needed little drilling: three or four holes for pro, plus anchors at every belay. Photos and a topo can be found at www.rocknclimb.com.

BRIAN McCRAY

The Watchman, Cradle to Grave. In May Dave Jones and I climbed a new 10-pitch route on the northwest face of The Watchman. Our route, Cradle to Grave (V 5.11a C2), starts about 150' left of Hue & Cry. We started in a dark, somewhat hidden, left-facing corner. Chimneys and offwidths on great rock led to a squeeze section so tight that I had to remove my gear, including my harness, to get through. Higher, Dave led a short section of aid to the base of a beautiful crack with face holds. We followed this crack to the summit and a great top-out. Decent to the southwest took about an hour and a half and included three rappels.

BRIAN SMOOT

Colorado

Rocky Mountain National Park, summary. The RMNP summer alpine season was limited by exceptionally wet weather for Colorado. Although Tommy Caldwell and Topher Donahue made a first free ascent, at 5.13-, of Bilge (previously 5.8 A3) on the Ship's Prow at 12,000', perhaps the only long new route established in 2004 was a springtime mixed route.

Steve Su and Edward Corder climbed what seems to be a new line up the next cleft/chimney system to the right of Womb With a View, on Cathedral Wall. The line, fairly obvious though rarely forming on the sunny wall, offers over 800' of mostly mixed climbing, with a surprising "holy shit, Batman" passage behind a huge chockstone. The route, Tunnel Vision (M4+ WI4+), ends on a plateau with a walk-off descent. Su, Corder, and Andy Johnson were also active in scrapping together various ephemeral 1,000' ice and mixed lines near the gash splitting the south face of Dragon's Tail.

Unreported from 2003, Donahue and Scott Gillespie climbed a long-overlooked line, a striking crack just right of Hallet's Chimney, but left of the Love Route, on Hallet Peak's 1,000' north face. Bold is Love (5.10-) ascends perfect rock, albeit with the minimal protection typical of the face, and finishes in a large dihedral.

BLACK CANYON OF THE GUNNISON NATIONAL PARK

Hallucinogen Wall, dry-tool free ascent. In May Ryan Nelson and Jared Ogden made a hybrid free-aid ascent of the daunting Hallucinogen Wall (VI 5.10 A3+). Ogden and others had attempted to free the route previously (*AAJ* 2004, p. 180) but without success. Nelson and Ogden worked the route over several weeks, eventually climbing everything free except for the most desperate portions of pitch 13, where they employed controversial tactics by using ice tools to hook thin features on the dry rock. They made a variation to avoid the pendulum on pitch five but otherwise climbed the original line. Nelson and Ogden's ascent included regular (free) rock climbing up to 5.13-R; the dry-tooling section was rated D10+. See Ogden's feature article earlier in this Journal.

Charm School Boutique, repeat. Between The Journey Home and The Cruise on North Chasm View Wall, Jeff Achey found an improbable line called Charm School Boutique (5.12 A2+; *AAJ* 2004, pp. 180-181). In May, Steve Monks and I free-climbed it, with the aid pitch going at dicey 5.13-. Steve aided the pitch first and left the gear in place. After playing around on top-rope, I led it free. It could be done placing the gear, but not by me that day. Both of the hard pitches are gear intensive, with hand-placed beaks or crack 'n ups helpful on the 5.12 pitch, and the crux has mandatory 5.13- above a #2 RP.

A direct start from the Dylan Wall, a four-pitch 5.12- that leads to the beginning of the Charm School, has yet to be done. To link the two routes and place the gear at the crux would be a mighty day.

TOPHER DONAHUE

Tague Yer Time. South Chasm View Wall hides its secrets well. It took Jared Ogden and me many trips to work out a new line just right of Astrodog, and then another few trips to complete it. Tim Toula and Jim Olsen did the first two pitches and named the unfinished climb "Air is Free." They reported the second-pitch dihedral to be as good as any stemming corner on Devil's Tower. They're right. We did a variant start directly up to the corner to avoid a loose flake and continued up the same system. After the Two Boulder Bivy on Astrodog, the line follows thin cracks on the buttress to the right and finishes in discontinuous cracks under the South Chasm rappel line, even clipping a couple of the anchors.

A triple set of RPs is needed for the sustained thin cracks. The rock is excellent. There are six pitches of 5.12 and five of 5.11. We shared the ascent with the ashes of Cameron Tague and let them fly into the winds of the Black. We called the line Tague Yer Time (V 5.12), for the intricate nature of the climb and the spiritual leader of the first ascent team. It is arguably the best climb in the canyon.

TOPHER DONAHUE

BloodSport and various ascents. In the spring Zach Smith and I climbed a new route between Ament's Chimney and Kachina Wings. The IV 5.12b route is a sustained line worthy of repeats and should continue to improve with traffic. We found a faded sling anchor atop the 5.9+ crack variation to pitch one, indicating that the line had been previously investigated. Although Zach and I climbed a moderate, independent finish leading up and right from the top of pitch five, on the second ascent Brian McMahon and I found a better finish by sharing Trilogy's final 250'. On this ascent I also added a bolt to the crux pitch, eliminating ledge-fall potential. Neither the 5.9+ nor the independent finish are recommended. A topo can be found at the North Rim Ranger Station.

Also in the spring Phil Gruber and I made the second ascent, onsight in 10 hours, of the difficult new Tague Yer Time (V 5.12b/c). The climb is among the best and cleanest routes in the canyon and similar in difficulty and quality to Red Rock's Rainbow Wall.

In early fall Phil, with Ico DeZwart of New Zealand, made the first one-day, free ascent of the notorious V+ 5.12b Black Hole on South Chasm View Wall. Phil's climb, onsight, is only the third known ascent of this offwidth testpiece.

In October Thad Friday and I made the second enchainment of the so-called Black

Canyon Trifecta. Walking in the large footsteps of Black Canyon endurance pioneers Mike Pennings and Jeff Hollenbaugh, Thad and I linked, free, the Painted Wall's V 5.10+ Southern Arete, South Chasm View Wall's V 5.11+ Astrodog and the North Chasm View Wall's V 5.10+ Scenic Cruise in a 20:45 push. Both Mike and I feel that this link-up is more difficult than connecting Half Dome's Regular Route and El Cap's Nose in a day.

JOSH WHARTON, *AAC*

OTHER COLORADO AREAS

Mt. Silex, north face. In September 2000 Rex Wolters and I climbed a new 1,500', IV 5.10 A1 line on the north face of Mt. Silex in the San Juan Mountains. It follows an arête/buttress to the right of the large dihedral on the western side of the north face.

JOHN KELLEY

Tijeras, south face: (1) Southeast Face Route. (2) East Buttress Route. Both routes continue up the skyline to the summit. *Cameron Burns*

Tijeras Peak, new routes. On July 19, Cam Burns, of the Basalt Bigfoot Coalition, and I attempted to climb the crowning rock ridge that runs east-west on Tijeras Peak (13,604') in the Sangre de Cristo Range. We completed four pitches up the southeast buttress to gain the east ridge before rain and lightning forced a retreat.

We returned on September 11, attained our previous high point, and added an additional nine pitches of roped climbing, simul-climbing, and more than 500' of fourth class scrambling to the summit. This southeast buttress/east ridge combination (East Buttress Route) is on good rock, surprisingly easy, and nearly 3,000' long (IV 5.6).

On September 18 we returned and added the Southeast Face (1,500', III 5.7-5.8) route, starting left of the previous route and joining it at the summit of the second gendarme on the east ridge. The majority of this route is on loose rock, except of the upper pitches, where the rock is solid and exposed.

BENNY BACH, *AAC*

Wyoming

GRAND TETON NATIONAL PARK

Various ascents. In August 2001 an Appalachian State student named Chris and I climbed a new 800' variation to the High Route on the Enclosure. It parallels the High Route on the right and goes at IV 5.10+R/X.

In October 2001 Bob Webster and I made the first ascent of the Minor Fourth Couloir (2,000+', IV M6 WI5) on Mt. Moran. It's the couloir/chimney system to the right of the Pika Ridge on the northeast face.

In September 2002 Kevin Mahoney and I made the first ascent of Three Shots in the Dizzy Wind (600', IV M6) on the north face of the Enclosure. This route connects the Enclosure Couloir to the High Route, with around 2,200' of climbing total.

In November 2002 Steve Farrand and I climbed a new route on the east face of the Grand Teton. The Kelley-Farrand (IV WI5R/X) climbs the thin smear of ice just left of the Stettner Couloir. It connects with the left branch of the Stettner after three pitches and follows it to the top.

In December 2003 Matt Neuner and I put in a new ice line to the right of Guides' Wall. Tango Max (1,400', IV M6 WI6) is to the right of the right Tackle Pillar.

JOHN KELLEY

Grand Teton, Alex Lowe Memorial Route. On October 5 Mark Newcomb and I climbed a new route on the north face of the Grand Teton. The route ascends about 1,000' of new terrain, beginning just left of the start of the 1936 route. A wet late summer and fall brought the needed moisture, and then freezing temps above 10,000' froze things enough for an ascent, barely! The crux second pitch presented unclimbable chandelier ice with no protection, so I climbed into a womb-like feature, up the backside of the ice, and broke through to the other side. After pulling a small roof, I was on lower-angle and drier terrain. The womb was gushing with water, and I spent the next belay, thankful for a Reverso, wringing out my clothes and dumping water out of my boots. I slipped my boots back on just as a graupel storm began. Graupel showered down several locations on the north face, one of the most spectacular sights I have witnessed in the mountains. The deluge of graupel was also flowing down our line. But it stopped after 25 minutes, and we were able to continue. Several more beautiful pitches, including the nicest pitch of ice I have ever climbed in the mountains, a flowing WI5 pitch winding its way through the steep granite, brought us to the Hossack-McGowan. We continued up to the East Ridge and across the east face to the Ford Couloir and on to the summit.

STEPHEN KOCH, *AAC*

Idaho

Slick Rock, Scenic Traction. Slick Rock is a few miles northeast of McCall, about 100 miles north of Boise. This is a beautiful granite face, similar to the northwest face of Chief's Head (RMNP, CO) in style and smoothness, with the same limited gear. It's a tad bigger and much friendlier, however, being south-facing and less steep.

This climb (1,100', 5.9+) ascends the face 150' left of Slippery Slope in seven pitches. Fran Bagenal and I climbed it onsight on July 15, with bolts placed on the lead. The rock and the climbing are superb. Routefinding is tricky in places, and several pitches are run-out. We tried another new route on the cliff a few days later, taking the face right of the original classic Triple Cracks, but after a few run-out

Stephen Koch headed for the Alex Lowe Memorial Route on the Grand Teton. *Mark Newcomb*

moderate pitches discovered that someone had rap-bolted the entire face immediately left of us, to make a long and convenient clip-up.

Scenic Traction begins, about 80' left of Slippery Slope's start, with a scramble up a left-facing ramp/groove to a ledge. There is a large, rotten, bulging right-facing dihedral up left from this ledge. On the face above are two major vertical crack systems, 100' apart. The route stays between them, then takes the clean face above, heading to a large dead tree at the top.

1. Climb up cracks, then trend up right to a ledge system and an old two-bolt anchor beneath a long vertical crack (5.6, 180'). 2. Clip an old pin in the crack above, then angle up left into the middle of the steeper face. Climb straight past two bolts, then run it out to a ledge (5.9+R, 120'). 3. Continue up on easier terrain, then step right to another pair of older bolts (5.7, 80'). 4. Angle up left into the middle of the face, then straight up, with occasional gear. Belay after 180', under a Cadillac-size, two-foot thick, V-shaped flake. The belay is somewhat below, and 80 feet left of, a prominent left-facing dihedral with a lone tree. You will be directly under a large dead tree at the top of the cliff (5.8R, 180'). 5. Layback up and left around the V-shaped flake, then gain a small ledge and left-facing dihedral/flake. Up this, then run it out up a nice rippled face to a small ledge and two-bolt anchor (5.8R, 180'). 6. Continue up on never-ending dike ripples, passing occasional flakes for gear, and belay at a fat right-facing flake, just before the angle eases but just as the rope runs out (5.8R, 205'). 7. Continue to the top (190', 5.7). Gear: One each of cams from tiny to 3.5", with doubles of 0.75"-2.5". A few wires.

Slick Rock, with all known routes shown: (1) Scenic Traction (5.9+, Bagenal-Bartlett, 2004), done ground up, with run-out 5.7 and four bolts—two on the crux pitch, two at a belay. (2) Slippery Slope (5.10c, Chavez-Cronk-Gentry, 2001), excellent eight pitches, done ground up, bolt protection at crux sections, runouts on easier terrain—about 17 protection bolts, plus bolted belays. (3) Triple Cracks (5.7, Unknown), the classic original route, taking the obvious cracks up the center. (4) Memorial (5.8, Caudill-King-Queen, 2004), about 60 bolts, no gear needed, some bolts close to cracks. *Steve Bartlett*

Double ropes recommended.

More information: www.rockclimbing.com/routes/listArea.php?AreaID=970

STEVE BARTLETT

Jughandle Mountain, various routes. The northwest face of Jughandle Mountain (8,340') is directly above picturesque Louie Lake, near McCall, in the Salmon River Mountains. I ran across this face in 1999 during a hike with my kids. Over the last few years I've put up seven routes on the 600' face. The routes range from 5.10a-5.13b, some with minimal bolting. Four of the routes are 5.13s. They offer steep granite with sparse cracks, mostly face climbing. Some routes have runouts and ledge-fall potential, and the rock quality varies from good to dirty, but the setting of the wall is stunning and makes for an adventurous day out.

The most exciting routes include Wall of the Oceanman (5.13b), in the center of the wall, with a potentially very dangerous fall from the crux of the 5.12 third pitch. Brave Like a Girl (5.13b), four pitches, climbs through the yellow overhanging wall in the center, connecting with Oceanman on its third pitch. Brave like a Girl is a safer lead, though it is the most spectacular route on the wall. Dreamcatcher (5.13) is four pitches, with an awesome 100' thin crack at the crux. Renegade is a four-pitch 5.13a line with two steep boulder problems on the second pitch.

I established all routes ground-up, without top-rope inspections. I drilled bolts on lead, without using hooks. A big thanks to my friends and climbing partners, Mike Teschner, Jeff Smith, Sean Wolff, Brad Heller, and Adam Chitwood.

MIKE STOGER

Jughandle. (1) North/West Face (Stoger-Smith; 5.7, 5.10a, 5/10d, 5.10a, 2002). (2) Renegade (Stoger-Teschner, 5.10c, 5.13a, 5.10a, 5.5, 2003/2004). (3) North Face (Stoger-Smith, 5.10a, 5.9, 5.10a, 5.8, 2002). (4) Brave Like A Girl (Stoger-Teschner, 5.11+, 5.13b, 5.11+, 5.10, 2004). (5) Wall of the Oceanman (Stoger-Teschner, 5.13b, 5.12a, 5.12b, 5.11+, 5.10, 2003). (6) Dreamcatcher (Stoger-Teschner, 5.6, 5.13a, 5.10d, 5.11a, 2002/2003). *Mike Stoger*

Elephant's Perch, free ascents. During the summer I realized the free-climbing potential on the Elephant's Perch. A number of old aid routes, created on perfect granite in the 1970s and 80s, had not been free climbed. The Seagull, a nice 5.10 A3 line up the steepest part of the wall, came highly recommended by parties who had attempted to free it. I don't know details of their attempts, and since I did not lead the crux pitch free, I can't claim the first free ascent, just a free ascent of the A3 pitch with a top rope at 5.13+. The crux section offers an extreme layback sequence, with no chance to place gear in the hairline seam. Since a fixed-anchor ban exists, placing fixed protection is out of the question. A stronger or bolder climber than I might be able to run out this section from a decent piece of gear.

During the two-day effort Brad Heller and I added a direct start to the original traversing first pitches, instead following the great dihedral of the Seagull directly from the ground. Pitch three of the direct start begins with a difficult-to-protect 5.11a overhang, with belay-ledge-fall potential. Our version of the Seagull: 5.10a, 5.9, 5.11a, 5.11, 5.13+ (TR), 5.11+, 5.10, 5.10+, 5.10, 5.9, 5.9, 5.9.

To the right of The Seagull, King's Highway (5.9 A3) begins with a system of arching cracks, then crosses The Seagull at pitch 4. After it joins The Seagull, King's Highway's climbing eases off after a short overhanging section of 5.12-.

The difficulty of the free King's Highway is not more than 5.12. The first 5.12 pitch is a 170' perfect crack. The A3 pitch protects adequately with such gear as TCUs and follows an arching crack with some sketchy protection to three old bolts. The first-ascent party pendulumed into The Seagull here, but Doug Colwell and I followed the crack to a knifeblade placement (removed) and traversed on small holds to The Seagull's 5.11+ pitch.

I greatly admire the first-ascent parties of these beautiful climbs. Protecting them with the gear available that many years ago was quite an achievement. We are just followers in their footsteps.

MIKE STOGER

The Seagull (left) and King's Highway on Elephant Perch. *Mike Stoger*

Goat Perch, Weekend Warrior. On June 5 Dave Hopper and I made the first ascent of Weekend Warrior (IV 5.8 M1-2) on the Goat Perch, in the Sawtooth Mountains. The route followed the narrow, northeast-facing couloir between the Goat Perch and Eagle Perch for 400' of snow and ice, to 60°, before exiting south onto the north face of the Goat. A 50' pitch of easy mixed climbing led to the conspicuous dihedrals on the north face. The first rock pitch ascended the right dihedral, crossed the arête, and climbed the left dihedral, before reaching the bulging, wet, mossy crux of the route. The second pitch continued up left on steep rock to a small belay stance at a pine tree. Pitches three and four were class 4, negotiating steep, broken rock to a good platform just below the summit block. A scramble reached the high point. Two rappels and downclimbing to the west led to the top of couloir, which we rapped and downclimbed. This route may go better in late July when the couloir is firm and the rock up high drier. Good pro exists throughout; 16 hours round-trip to and from car.

STEVE LYSNE, *Boise, Idaho*

Hyndman Peak, Travis Michaelis Memorial Route. On May 14 Abe Dickerson and I climbed a very temporary ice route on the northeast face of Hyndman Peak in the Pioneer Range. We left a bivy at 10,400', below the northeast face, and climbed a 60° snow cone to the base of a delicate WI4 smear draining from a large snow bowl. The first pitch (60m) contained thin ice, a vertical curtain and spicy non-bonded eggshell ice. From a rock-anchor belay at the top of the first lead, we climbed two pitches of labor-intensive, 60° deep snow on the right side of the bowl to the base of a thin, rolling WI3 slab. The fourth pitch ascended this slab on the left to steep snow, and then thin ice runnels brought us to the crux headwall. We passed the M5 crux in two 30m pitches on thin ice runnels, an overhanging chimney, and a narrow ramp. These two pitches angled up left to a solid pin belay, in a corner below a snow ramp. From there a short, steep WI3 step gained a narrow, high-angle snow ramp. We followed this ramp for 60m, to a point where we crossed the northeast ridge into a steep, hanging, mixed rock-and-snow couloir. The last 120m followed this couloir directly to the summit. The left side of the couloir was a short rock wall and 50'-high cornices on the east ridge; a 10'-high rock rib on the right separated the couloir from the near-vertical north face. From the summit Abe and I scrambled down the east ridge and made one rappel into the Wildhorse Cirque, between Old Hyndman and Hyndman Peaks. A long, tiring slog along the base of the east face brought us to our snow-cave bivy after a 20-hour day.

The Travis Michaelis Memorial Route (1,800', M5 WI4R) is named in memory of our close friend and climbing partner who lost his life rescuing a dog from an abandoned mine shaft.

DEAN LORDS

Montana

Hyndman Peak, Pioneer Range, central Idaho. The Travis Michaelis Memorial Route (TMMR) takes the obvious ice smear flowing from the snow bowl, goes up the bowl, and continues to the summit following smears, runnels, and corners up the headwall above the snow bowl. This is the only route on the face. *Dean Lords*

Sheep Rock, various ascents. Between August 2002 and July 2004 I climbed eight new routes on Sheep Rock in Gallatin Canyon, 20 miles south of Bozeman. Sheep Rock is the first major formation seen when entering the canyon, on the west side. Each route was climbed ground-up, solo, mostly involving direct aid but with occasional sections of free-climbing.

Local climbers have been passing under Sheep Rock for years on their way to the solid gneissic climbs Gallatin Canyon is known for. The legend was that Sheep Rock was no good, that climbers of old had checked it out and demurred. Upon initial inspection I presumed they were correct. Sheep Rock is composed of less-than-solid limestone, with the lower 300' a mass of fractured blocks. But after this introductory terrorfest, the rock becomes sounder, and the angle diminishes from overhanging to less-than-vertical for the final half. The routes that flank the shifting sides of Sheep Rock require skills that can evade most, involving long stretches of pin pounding, and mandatory free climbing moves mixed with the occasional clean aid blessing. Demarcating a line out of the abstractness involves keeping a very open mind if one does not wish to lower oneself to drilling.

With large expanses of loose, collapsible rock, and wild, teetering, gothic formations, Sheep Rock presents a certain foreboding within its structure that does not allow for speed. Aspirants should allow for the trials that await them on any route attempt, and any attempt should be considered as an attempt on a Grade IV. As an example: I have had two hammers break, have had three ropes chopped by rock fall, and have taken a 40' ground fall...all on the same route!

BRAD CARPENTER

Beaverhead Mountains, traverse. On August 12, 2003, I finished a 1,362-mile journey that included a traverse of the Rocky Mountains. The journey was completed in segments involving kayaking, hiking, climbing, and mountain biking. I began in Montana on May 12, by kayaking

Sheep Rock, showing all routes. Ram Buttress: (1) Satan's Jewel Crown (500', 5.7 A3, 2004). (2) Hell and Tarnation (525', 5.6R A3-, 2002). (3) Jotunheim (400', 5.7 A3, 2003). Ewe Buttress: (4) Burning Bridges (425', 5.5 A4, 2003). (5) Milwaukee Direct (450', 5.6 A2+, 2003). (6) Saari Memorial Route (425', 5.6 A2+, 2003). (7) Blue Collar (400', 5.7 A2+, 2002). Kid Buttress: (8) Whitebread (325', 5.7X A2, 2002). All first ascents by Brad Carpenter, solo. *Brad Carpenter*

up the Missouri River from the Gates of the Mountains Wilderness, then across the Jefferson and Beaverhead drainages down the Salmon River and across the Bitterroot Valley to Lolo Pass. With friends I mountain biked 150 miles across the Bitterroot Range of northern Idaho and western Montana. I kayaked the Clearwater to the Snake, the Snake to the Columbia, down the Columbia to Wallula Gorge. Then I continued on my mountain bike until I rode onto the beach at Astoria, Oregon.

In late June 2003 I'd crossed the Rockies, but as a climber I wanted to be in the high mountains. I took a break from my westward journey and returned to traverse a portion of the spine of the Beaverhead Mountains, a subrange of the Bitterroots on the Continental Divide between Idaho and Montana. It took four days and reminded me of the Alaska Mountain Wilderness Classic race, with its endless route-finding while traversing mountain ranges with everything on your back. I started one section in the Big Hole Valley and climbed Peak 10,048', west of Pioneer Creek, then climbed to the CD and traversed west to Monument Peak (10,356'). I then descended to the col east of newly named Sacagawea Peak and hiked out to Salmon, Idaho.

There is a 2.5-mile-long cornice of ice and snow on the north side of the CD here. The route from Peak 10,048' to the CD is 5.3. In my research I could find no description of the route I climbed having been previously done. The rock is metamorphic and unstable. The most technical part is descending couloirs on the west face.

I first saw this range rising from the Salmon River Plains in 1971 when I was a young smokejumper returning from a fire. I wondered what it would be like to climb along the ridge. Now I know. (Note: a complete story and more information on this traverse can be found at www.sierraclub.org/lewisandclark/your_adventures/dixon/index.asp)

JERRY DIXON, *AAC*

Alaska

BROOKS RANGE

Arrigetch Peaks, Samurai Savitz and Rock Jock. Tim Kemple, Justin Sjong, and I flew to Bettles, where we met Max Hanft, the only local climber. He accompanied us on our journey into the Arrigetch. Our team, with a combined age of less than 100, was a constant comedy. This report may be somewhat vague, because we lost both our maps. We also ran out of food. We flew to Takahula Lake and hiked west along the river. We walked over a pass and started down the other side, hiking through a little stream. As we continued, the sides became steeper and rain fell. The sides became walls, and we were stuck walking down a fast-moving river, scrambling over boulders. At the bottom we turned right (north) and followed another river upstream. After three days, at the headwaters of that river, we set up base camp. I suggest that anyone else fly to Circle Lake and approach from there, over Independence Pass; it would be safer and quicker. (Other *AAJ* reports provide beta on this approach, though most people stop and climb before they reach the pass.) As you were coming down from Independence Pass, directly in front of you would be a 2,000-foot wall with a striking ridge that we called Samurai Savitz (5.10) [For a photo of Samurai Savitz see p. 72 of *Climbing* magazine #237, March 2005—Ed.]. We did it fast and light, 15 hours camp-to-camp. It has good rock and an easy descent. From the summit rap 10 feet and walk down the back. We also climbed the diamond-shaped wall seen in the middle as you stand in the meadow, facing north. We started just left of the center of the wall and climbed the right-facing dihedral to the big roof. We then followed wandering cracks to the summit. Rock Jock, 1,500' 5.11d, nine bolts. We descended the back side, on the right.

ADAM STACK

Angutikada (Old Man Mountain), first ascent in 1985. With Ron Watters, Deborah Dixon and I made our third attempt to climb Angutikada (Old Man Mountain) in March 1985. I have found no record of it having been climbed before. Angutikada rises 4,120' from the upper Kobuk River plains and lies on the Continental Divide, in the southern Brooks Range just north of the Arctic Circle. The Kuuvunmiut have used it to tell time since the last ice age. It stands out as a sentinel, and when the sun circles the sky in summer, not setting for months, time can be reckoned by the sun's position relative to the mountain.

   We mushed for two days to the base of the mountain in temperatures of -40°, then skied for a day and built a snow cave. On the fourth day we skied through a caribou herd on the slopes of Angutikada, and Ron and I climbed to the summit (5.3) as a rainbow arced through frost crystals. The view was magnificent, with the entire esplanade of the Brooks Range stretching from horizon to horizon. It was like looking into a mirror and seeing a reflection of myself in another lifetime, for I could see clearly the spot from which I had first beheld this magnificent country, on July 3, 1973, via parachute and the door of a DC-3 smokejumper.

JERRY S. DIXON, *AAC*

DeLong Mountains, exploration. In August Craig Deutche, Anne Machung, Jerry Weidler, and I established a new route across the DeLong Mountains from Howard Pass to Desperation Lake. We were studying the landscapes and ecology of Petroleum Reserve no4. From Kavaksurak we ascended the Ipnavik River to its source in the unexplored nexus of peaks and passes that eventually subside into the Makpik Drainage above Feniak Lake. We passed through the Holocene lake basins on the north side of the vast, complex Siniktaneyak Massif and made the first ascent of its summit above the central cirque. This expedition was part of a larger historical effort to comprehensively explore the entire Brooks Range.

DENNIS SCHMITT

ALASKA RANGE

Geographical note: While the well-known peaks in Denali National Park are often called "The Alaska Range," these peaks form just one part of the immense Alaska Range, which contains many significant subranges, including the Hayes and Delta ranges, and the Revelation, Kichatna, and Tordrillo Mountains.

HAYES RANGE

Nenana Mountain, Descent Gully and South Buttress. In March, with Fairbanks local Seth Adams, I followed rumors of granite and an unclimbed named summit to Nenana Mountain (2,402m) in the western Hayes Range. After 70km of skiing via the Yanert River, we discovered quite a bit of granite, up to 500m high. We climbed a broad snow couloir that was even easier than it looked. We dubbed it "Descent Gully," because it really wasn't a fun way up the mountain. I fancied a mixed route on the south buttress, but the next day was cold and windy, so we began our ski out. Skiing into a stiff headwind at -30°, I questioned the logic of my upcoming 800km drive for a 230km ski race in the Brooks Range.

But a rock line on the 500-meter south buttress had caught my attention, and in July I returned with Kevin Wright. We took a motor canoe as far as it would take us up the Nenana

The south buttress of Nenana, showing its first and only route. *Kevin Wright*

River, before abandoning it at the base of a canyon and walking. Less than 50km of hiking deposited us on the glacier, and after some rainy weather, we set out up our route. We swung leads up six pitches of quality 5.8 to a nice ledge, then ran the belay up three more pitches to the ridge. We unroped and scrambled along the ridge to the top of the summit boulder. The descent of the southeast face was loose but quick. It is worth noting that in the cirque to the right of our route is a high-quality wall with high-standard free climbing. On the edge of this cirque, we climbed a couple of nice 5.10 pitches before getting chased off by rain.

We have heard that perhaps a NOLS group previously climbed the peak via our July descent route, but otherwise no one seems to know of any prior ascents of Nenana.

JED BROWN, *AAC*

DELTA RANGE

Correction. The photo on p.188, *AAJ* 2004, was mislabeled. The peak is Mt. Kimball, not Mt. Balchen. In the accompanying report by Jeff Apple Benowitz, the route of ascent is incorrectly given as the southeast ridge. On Mt. Kimball, Benowitz and Gilmartin climbed the southwest ridge, as shown in the photo.

DENALI NATIONAL PARK

Denali National Park and Preserve, summary. Raindrops were falling at Kahiltna Basecamp the first week of May, as unusually and unpleasantly warm temperatures surprised early season climbers. Longtime mountaineers can't recall a season so balmy, with temperatures throughout Alaska breaking state records. As summer temperatures soared, most of the glaciers inside Denali National Park experienced considerable melt-out. Previous landing areas on many glaciers were riddled with crevasses running every direction, preventing landings after mid-July.

Denali's unpredictable potency once again became evident, when a massive rockslide at Windy Corner hurled down car-sized boulders. This unusual, colossal event killed climber Clint West, age 47, and severely injured two others on the rope, as they descended from the 14,200' camp. This is one of the few accidents in the history of Denali mountaineering where human error was not the key factor.

The grave of deceased mountaineer Gary Cole eroded and was partially exposed at the 17,200' high camp. Cole died in 1969 from HAPE and was buried in a shallow grave by a medical research team that was on the mountain at the time. The Alaska State Medical Examiner, the Alaska State Troopers, and the NPS Regional Director agreed to allow his reburial after his identification, with helpful information from the family. Gary Cole was lowered to the 14,200' camp and reburied by a National Park Service mountaineering patrol in a deep and undisclosed location. We can only speculate that these two unusual events, the massive rockslide and the discovery of human remains, were precipitated by the record-breaking temperatures.

In addition to our wonderful mountaineering volunteers, we were particularly fortunate to have a patrol of seasoned Grand Teton National Park climbing rangers, who performed several difficult life-saving rescues. Renny Jackson, former Denali mountaineering ranger, co-led the first patrol of the season, with Denali mountaineering ranger John Loomis. The experienced

Teton patrol members saved the life of an incapacitated Korean climber just above Denali Pass. They performed this rescue in "full weather conditions" with a strong pair of British climbers, Andy Perkins and Neil McNab, who were chosen for the 2004 Denali Pro Award for their contribution to this significant rescue.

Only a handful of new routes were completed in 2004, with little action on non-trade routes. On Denali only three popular routes were successfully climbed: the West Buttress, the West Rib and the Cassin Ridge (only two climbers). There were 1,275 climbers attempting Denali (1,173 on the West Buttress), with 51% reaching the summit. Only four people reached the summit of Foraker, all part of a NPS ranger patrol, and local knowledge does not recall anyone reaching the summit of Mt. Hunter!

The average trip length for an expedition on Mt. McKinley was 17.3 days, with the average age of a Denali climber being 37 years old. Continuing a gradual upward trend, women constituted 11% of the total climbers. Guided expeditions as a whole (including clients and guides) accounted for 33% of Denali mountaineers. No surprise that June was the busiest summit month, with 510 summits recorded. In May, 90 climbers summited; 56 in July. The liveliest days on the summit of Denali were June 4 (71 climbers), June 27 (48 climbers), and June 26 (42 climbers).

Climbers came from 42 nations. The top countries represented were United States (798), Canada (63), United Kingdom (52), Japan (48), Germany (39), and Spain (36).

Climbers can now access our newly updated mountaineering booklet in pdf format at www.nps.gov/dena. The English revision is complete, and we aim to get the information

Mt. McKinley's magnificent northwest faces. (1) Zanto's Riches (Riches-Zanto, 2001), continues along the Northwest Buttress to north summit. (2) Tranquillo Couloir (Lyall-Shlosar, 2004), joins Northwest Buttress, then traverses across the obvious hanging glacier in the center of the frame and returns to the 14,000' camp on the West Buttress route (right edge of frame), without summiting. *Joe Puryear*

translated into multiple languages within the next couple of years. Currently, international climbers can access the older version of the booklet in seven languages on our website.

DENALI NATIONAL PARK/TALKEETNA RANGER STATION

Mt. McKinley, northwest face, Father and Sons Wall, Tranquillo Couloir. On June 4 Steve Lyall and I left the14,000' camp on the West Buttress and descended to the lower Peters Glacier via the north side of Motorcycle Hill. Seven V-threads later we landed on the Peters Glacier with the intent of climbing one of two couloirs to the left of both the Father and Sons Wall and the jagged, funnel-shaped hanging glacier/snowfield just to its left (as seen from the West Buttress). The right couloir proved to have too much hanging serac at the top, and was devoid of ice in the middle, so we opted for the unclimbed left couloir. We soloed 4,000' up the initial couloir and through a glacial headwall, then onto the right side of a hanging snowfield, after which we arrived at the base of another ice couloir. We simul-climbed this couloir for 700', which took us directly to the summit of point 13,540' on the Northwest Buttress. We continued along the Northwest Buttress and Upper Peters Glacier, returning to our camp after 35 hours on the move. The route, which we dubbed the Tranquillo Couloir, involved 50-65° ice the entire way and was graded AK Grade 4, with 4,500' of new terrain and 7,000' of total terrain climbed. It's a quality, moderate climb.

ZACH SHLOSAR, *AAC*

East Kahiltna Peak, showing D.S. (left) and F.J.
Vince Anderson

East Kahiltna Peak, D.S. and F.J. Carl Tobin and I flew into the Southeast Fork of the Kahiltna Glacier. We skied to the East Fork, where we spent from May 3 to 12 exploring climbs. May 5 was clear and, despite our being tired from the ski to the East Fork, we decided to climb and not waste a good day. This proved to be a good idea, as we did our best climb that day. The route, which we called D.S. [this is an acronym; the original name is unprintable—Ed.], took us in about 600m to a break in a spur that jutted out from the southeast ridge of East Kahiltna Peak. The climb started on the right-hand side of the spur with a small, left-angling snow couloir. At the top of the couloir, where the snow angles up and around left onto a rock slab, we headed up into a right-facing corner. The climb follows thinly iced corner systems for most of its length. It was Chamonixesque. The ice was often between 10 and 30cm wide, and thin. Several pillars were wider, but steeper, with junky ice. The climbing was mixed, with a few dry-tooling sections. The crux was the last pitch, which was 90m long. It started with a narrow (5-10cm) section of ice. The upper pillar had snapped off, leaving a large ice roof. There was another ice roof above the main break point, making a double roof. This was technically difficult, though it protected well with an ice screw driven up into the bottom of the break point of the pillar. This section was definitely WI7, and there were several other sections of grade 6 (both mixed and WI) on the pitch as

Carl Tobin spreading wide on East Kahiltna Peak. *Vince Anderson*

well. There were also several other hard pitches, including another roof pitch with 6+ climbing. I really liked the grade 6 ice off-width pitch, which I did not have to lead. We completed the route in a 17.5-hour round trip. I give the route an ED2/3 rating, despite its length, for its technical difficulty.

On May 8 we climbed another route, F.J. [another acronym for an unprintable name—Ed.]. It was 1,200-1,300m long, reaching the summit of East Kahiltna Peak (13,440'), but did not have the sustained difficulties of D.S. F.J. follows a long, steep snow ramp on the east face, previously climbed by Pat Callis and Terry Kennedy (*AAJ* 1994, pp. 78-81). Where the Callis-Kennedy traverses left to continue on up snow slopes, we continued straight up through a steep rock band (to the right of Barry and Jonathan's variation [see below]). The 70m crux pitch involved a short 90° pillar followed by a lengthy section of thinly iced mixed climbing up a steep chimney. The climbing was technical, thin ice and dry-tooling on tenuous holds. It took something like two hours to lead. The following pitch, though technically easier, had some very cool dry-tooling up a chimney to gain a break in the rock buttress just right of the center of the face. From there, we continued on steep snow and alpine ice to the summit. We topped out with a rapidly approaching storm and immediately began our descent. There were 20 rappels with 75m ropes, after a 19-hour push.

VINCE ANDERSON, *AAC*

East Kahiltna Peak, Homage to Pat. On May 4, Jonny Blitz, Carl Tobin, Vince Anderson, and I pitched a small base camp on the East Fork of the Kahiltna Glacier, below the southeast face of East Kahiltna Peak (13,440'). Weather was good, so the next day Jonny and I launched onto the Callis-Kennedy (1993), climbing with the vision of going direct where the original route veered left to avoid difficulty. We established a fine six-pitch variation that included a beautiful, glassy-green WI5 pitch led by Blitz. Lack of acclimatization smacked us at the rejoining of the Callis-Kennedy, and we descended 3,500' to base camp. We named our variation Homage to Pat (WI5, 5.7 mixed) in honor of Pat Callis, Montanan Ice Prophet. Carl and "Big Vinnie" established the radical and intense D.S. on the same day, 700m down-glacier from us.

Hanging out at the Hilton during the ascent of Electric View, the Gargoyle. *Lars Mjaavatn*

It stormed, we rested. On May 8, Blitz and I attempted the proudest line, splitting that golden granite about 1km up-glacier from the Callis-Kennedy. We bailed from under a massive snow mushroom about halfway up, having climbed some incredible WI6/5.11 mixed ground. There was too much of the same above. On this same day, Carl and Vinnie went to the summit of East Kahiltna Peak via their F.J. Said Big Vinnie of the crux, "It was the most engaged that I have been on a mixed pitch in over a year...and it wasn't Musashi."

Barry Blanchard, *ACC, ACMG, CMC*

Ruth Gorge, route line photographs. Many route lines for the climbs described below can be found in Joseph Puryear's Moose's Tooth photograph on page 145 of this Journal.

Gargoyle, Electric View; Pt. 6,000', Phanerotime. In July, Jarle Kalland, Mads Lund, Steinar Holden, and I planned to go to the Kichatna Mountains, but snow conditions on the glaciers were too bad for landing. That's why we decided to go to Ruth Gorge. We climbed several routes, including new ascents on Pt. 6,000' (just north of Barrill) and the Gargoyle.

From July 5-13, we four established Electric View (5.11a A2+, 18 pitches) on the Gargoyle. Two-thirds of the climb involved aid, and the route is fantastic. Solid granite, superb cracks, lots of sun when there's good weather, not too hard, yet steep and airy.

On July 17-18, in 17 hours, Jarle Kalland and I established Phanerotime (5.11b A1, 7 pitches) on Pt. 6,000'. The first pitch had been done before, but from there it's a new route. The first two pitches are classic. Just a few moves on pitch three make the route A1, otherwise it's all free. Some pictures from the climb are at: www.njord.as (click Galleri and Alaska ekspedisjon). Drawings and route descriptions are at the Ranger Station in Talkeetna. We had a fantastic month in Alaska, and there are still lots of great climbs undone in the Ruth Gorge.

Lars Mjaavatn, *Norway*

Mt. Dickey, Snowpatrol. After hearing vague rumors concerning a gorge with mixed lines 5,000' high, half an hour from camp, Andy Sharpe and I packed a spare pair of socks and headed out to the Ruth to see what we could find.

We flew in and got dumped off below the south face of Dickey on March 28. Few places have the potential for instant impact like the Ruth. One minute you are trying to drown last night's beers with strong coffee in Talkeetna, and next thing you know that nice sun has been blotted out by walls of shear, ice-streaked granite towering up into the sky all around you. You can't even tell how big they are. There is nothing to scale them against. Everything is just huge. It took us all afternoon to set up camp because we couldn't keep our eyes from craning upwards. Does it link? Will it go? How strong you feeling? How much whisky we bring?

On April 1 we set off on a line of ice and snow gullies that ran almost continuously down from the summit of Dickey, just to the right of the 1974 Roberts-Rowell-Ward route up the southeast buttress. After ten 60m pitches we reached a good snowfield, dug out a good bivy and were soothed to sleep by the northern lights flickering over the west face of The Moose's Tooth. In the morning the previous day's good weather had been replaced by an ominous layer of lowering cloud. Two more pitches and the cloud hit. With it came

Snowpatrol takes the obvious couloir system all the way up Mt. Dickey. *Sam Chinnery*

the snow. We were aware that all the lovely ice and neve we had been climbing was there only because our line serves as the drain for 5,000' of steep granite above. What we didn't realize was just how little time you have after the first snowflake lands. Almost immediately spindrift started pouring down the gully with impressive force. Four hours later we could breathe and see again, after being virtually avalanched out the base of the gully. Dickey bites.

We waited patiently for stable weather. After seven days we got impatient and headed back up on the first moderately good day. We thought perhaps if we could get much higher on the first day, before the snow started, the force of the spindrift wouldn't be so great.

Between April 9 and 11 we made the first ascent of Snowpatrol (1,600m, VI WI5+). It involved approximately 40 pitches of climbing, mainly on neve, snow, and water ice, all three up to 90°, with some mixed pitches through the shale

An ice patch on Snowpatrol, Mt. Dickey. *Sam Chinnery*

band guarding the summit slopes. We climbed using a normal Scottish winter rack and one snow stake, which was invaluable. Although we used bivy bags, with a bit of digging we could have used a small tent. The climbing was excellent and sustained at an interesting level, with the crux pitches involving teetering round large snow mushrooms in the upper gully system. We climbed through heavy spindrift for the first two days, but were then granted some sun and summited to clear skies at 6 p.m. on the third day. Descent was down the normal west face route via 747 Pass, in deep but easy snow, and we arrived back in the Ruth at midnight.

The whole route was of high quality and in theory should be climbable early most seasons until mid-April. Just watch out for that snowfall.

SAM CHINNERY, *United Kingdom*

Ruth Gorge, Snowpatrol second ascent, Cornhole Couloir, and British invasion. It's late March and only six days into a three-week trip in the Ruth Gorge, with beautiful unclimbed lines towering in every direction, and my partner decides to throw in the towel. He misses his girlfriend. So here I am, watching Paul's Beaver plop into soft snow, and out tumble two clean-shaven Brits in bright new Gore-Tex suits. This is their first visit to the Ruth, and they crane their necks and mumble questions as we unload their kit and throw our gear in. I avoid answering their queries about the virgin lines. I promise to return in a week.

Back in Talkeetna my luck changed. Ben Gilmore and Kevin Mahoney returned from their epic first ascent on the Moose's Tooth [see feature article in this Journal], and despite having just knocked off one of the burliest routes in the range, Ben, a true hardman, only needed a three-day bender to prepare for more action. Paul landed us where I had left from seven days earlier. Andy and Sam, the Brits, were camped in the middle of the Gorge, and we noticed skis cached at the base of one of those magnificent lines on Dickey. The weather was unsettled. Three days later, at an unruly hour, we heard the pitter-pat of footsteps past our camp. The next day we collected their skis for them and called on their base camp. The Brits managed to bag a 5,000' continuous couloir weaving up the southeast buttress of Dickey, climbing for three days through almost continuous spindrift. Why aren't they more psyched? Andy chain-smoked cigarettes. "There was lots of snow up there," Sam explained.

Over the next week Ben and I dodged collapsing snow mushrooms while attempting several other unclimbed lines (I won't tell you, either!) and consumed all the alcohol. Returning tired and distraught to camp after another ass-kicking, we noticed two new tents. More Brits. What's with these guys? We met Guy and Owen. Turned out Guy had a bad back and was going home. Owen Samuel asked if we would consider collaborating. The three of us romped up a fun and probably undone couloir across the valley, on London Tower. It is the first continuous line left of Trailer Park, and is right of the larger snowfield that's used to access the two routes done by the Swiss and French in 2003. The route is mainly 50° snow, with a memorable "cornhole" chockstone crux. It ends on a beautiful gendarmed ridge. The Ruth Gorge is not lacking in hardman routes, but fun moderates like the Cornhole Couloir are in short supply.

With one week left, Ben, Owen, and I decided to investigate Sam and Andy's line, Snowpatrol. We split overnight gear into two loads, so the leader could climb packless. On the first day we managed about 3,000' and woke the next morning to building clouds. Climbing through pouring spindrift, we summited late on the second day. Despite complete darkness and full whiteout, Owen navigated us down to 747 Pass and our snow cave on the glacier.

Snowpatrol has miles of moderate terrain sprinkled with several grade 5 cruxes. But buyer beware: It's a long route, with tricky routefinding through the shale band on top. And there can be lots of snow up there.

FREDDIE WILKINSON, *New Hampshire*

The Stump, Goldfinger; Mt. Barrill, Cobra Pillar speed ascent. An extended Alaska season gave me the opportunity to climb 14 routes on 13 peaks with four different partners. Chris McNamara and I managed to squeeze out four climbs in the Ruth Gorge, including a speed ascent of the Cobra Pillar (27 pitches, VI 5.11a A2, Donini-Tackle, 1991) on Mt. Barrill and a new route on the Stump formation. The Gorge seemed relatively quiet this year, with few parties enjoying the excellent weather and unseasonably dry rock.

We flew into the Ruth Gorge on the rainy morning of June 13. We thought to warm up on a few shorter climbs, for our ultimate objective, the Cobra Pillar. But the weather improved slightly, and after gazing across at sunlit Mt. Barrill, Chris exclaimed, "I want to climb that— now!" So a few hours after landing, we were at the base of the route. After a frenzy of climbing, 15 hours and 10 minutes later we topped out. We used typical speed tactics: short fixing and the second jugging with a pack. We descended the northwest slopes and circled back around Barrill to our base camp. It was our first climb together: what a way to warm up.

After climbing Hut Tower and the Eye Tooth, we turned our attention to the red and golden walls of the Stump. This "small" 1,800-foot triangular face is a subpeak of the Wisdom Tooth, which sits just south of the Moose's Tooth. There, on June 25, we climbed a new route we called Goldfinger. The route takes the same start as an attempt by Mugs Stump and Steve Quinlan, beginning in the main dihedral on the left side of the face. After five pitches, the route breaks out right for a direct summit finish. We found a total of 12 pitches of sustained, moderate climbing on excellent granite, with a wild 5.11 roof crux on pitch 9. With easy access and a straightforward descent, it has the makings of a classic.

JOSEPH PURYEAR, *AAC*

Approaching the roof crux on Goldfinger, The Stump. *Joseph Puryear*

Moose's Tooth, Arctic Rage. From March 31–April 3, Ben Gilmore and Kevin Mahoney established Arctic Rage (4,500', VI WI6+R A2) on the massive east face of the Moose's Tooth. See Gilmore's feature earlier in this journal on their brilliant alpine-style ascent.

Moose's Tooth, Levitation and Hail Marys, and various activity. On May 26 and 27 Scott Adamson and I completed a new route on the south face of the Moose's Tooth. Following ice runnels, chimneys, and cracks, we found our way directly to the main (east) summit. Shortly after Talkeetna Air Taxi dropped us off on the Root Canal Glacier [the pocket glacier beneath the south face of the Moose's Tooth], we scrutinized our situation. Appearing like a siren one evening, in perfect light, a vertical ice-filled chimney caught our eye. The chimney, tucked away in a long corner system, was mid-height on the wall. It defined a huge pillar directly below the summit.

Scott Adamson with the chopped rope on the first attempt on Levitation and Hail Marys. *James Stover*

Earlier in our trip, we'd climbed Ham and Eggs on an "old-school style" tour from the Sheldon Amphitheater, rather than being flown to the Root Canal, as we later were for the other routes. (As an aside that may be of interest to anyone selecting a tentsite, when we were on H. & E., a Walmart-size serac calved from atop Dickey. The powder blast traveled a mile and a half across the Ruth Gorge, climbed the 2,500-foot approach and dusted our tentsite on the Root Canal.) Being neophytes and wanting another warm-up, we set our sights on The Unforgiven (M5 WI6), an excellent new mixed adventure that Anchorage fellows had put up the week before. Six killer full-length pitches of sustained mixed climbing brought us to a snowy arête leading to a subsummit of the Bear Tooth. Conditions being

Scott Adamson enjoying "The Sweetness" tension traverse on Levitation and Hail Marys. *James Stover*

what they were, we didn't continue to the subsummit but, in the interest of safety, rapped from excellent fixed stations and crawled back to the tent seven hours after we started. Scott felt ready for a go at our project, while I wanted to take another step first, finding comfort in a gradual progression to successively harder routes. We concluded that our imaginary line looked good and was in condition.

We waited for promising weather, and a few mornings later went to have a look. We wallowed through three feet of wet, unconsolidated snow and roped up to cross a southwest-facing avalanche slope leading to the base of the real climbing. We burned more time trying to free a pendulum two pitches above. Scott brought me to the belay and we conferred. Things were getting soggy, we were behind schedule, and we discovered four core shots in our two 8mm ropes. During our retreat we put another vicious shot smack in the middle of one rope. With snow pounding us, we crawled into the tent, soaked from the 60-70-degree heat.

Two days later we woke to a break in the storm. The weather was suspect, but we left camp at 3 a.m. with a light pack. With our track firmly laid we reached the ice ribbon in a few hours. Stretching our remaining 70m 9mm rope on most leads, we forged upward, finding steep ice, killer hand cracks, and good protection. There were two spots of overhanging M7 in the verglassed chimney around the fourth pitch, and a chossy 5.11 face sequence to enter the upper dihedral around pitch six. We topped out on the pillar in swirling clouds, hunkered down, and waited for the upper face to refreeze. We tried in vain to peer through the fog for a glimpse of what was to come. After a five-hour nap but no sign of where to go, we committed ourselves to a two-rope-length traverse into the upper face. They were the type of 5.8 pitches that defy grading: insecure and run-out. They gained us a huge corner we had been aiming for, just below the summit, but the corner lacked any discernable climbable features. So, feeling the need for haste as the storm intensified, we aimed for an escape route to the right. As I led through rivers of spindrift on very thin ice, my previous feelings of sun, fun, surf, and stone were replaced by more primal feelings.

The wind mellowed a bit as we reached the summit cornice and felt our way along, riding huge waves through an ephemeral white soup. Up and over the summit we went, searching for identifiable features that would bring us to the Ham and Egg rappels. We wandered in the clouds, feeling smaller and smaller as we descended, looking for something recognizable. Finally, facing a committing rappel, we realized we were lost and retraced our steps back up. The morning sun broke through and the clouds thinned, giving us a quick glimpse of our location. We did not recognize a single feature. Where's Denali? Where's Huntington? Where's the Ruth? Nothing looked familiar. I sat on the edge of the Moose's Tooth gazing at the Buckskin Glacier 4,000' below, swearing never to go again without a compass and map.

The storm's fury increased as we continued back up, then descended the correct way into the Ham and Eggs funnel. Anchors were buried and avalanches were frequent, requiring us to time our rappels to the periodic vomit flushing from the upper bowls. We arrived on the glacier and more 60-degree weather, with another trashed rope. I crawled in to the tent at nine o'clock, thirty hours after we had started.

Waking 24 hours later and taking inventory, we were three and a half weeks and three ropes down, with rising temperatures. We stomped out a sign for TAT and waited for our turn. Two days later, the decompression on the flight out was surreal. Trees, birds, other signs of life that had been gone for so long, all seemed so vibrant as we sorted gear in TAT's driveway.

We named our route Levitation and Hail Marys, after a good joke shared with one of the young bush pilots who flew for K2. We graded it V M7 A0 (for the pendulum), although I sense that grades mean nothing in this place. It was a fine outing, committing at the top with a quick decent. Long pitches, steep ice, good hand cracks, and painful knee bars characterize the meat and potatoes of the experience. We agreed that the Ruth was the rawest, most powerful area either of us had ever been to. The perfect place to find out how small you really are.

JAMES STOVER

Bear Tooth, White Russian. Taras Mytropan (Ukraine), Sergei Matusevich (Ukraine), and I climbed a direct line on the west face of the Bear Tooth. Starting from base camp on the Root Canal, we went straight toward the saddle between the Moose's Tooth and the Bear Tooth, bearing right soon after crossing the bergschrund. It's a short climb of five technical pitches, offering excellent ice up to 70°, snow, and mixed climbing. We did the route on April 27 and named it White Russian, Alaska grade II or III.

ALEKSEY SHURUYEV, *Krasnodar, Russia, with additions from* SERGEI MATUSEVICH, *Ukraine*

Bear Tooth, Unforgiven to serac base. On May 13 Gilly James and I climbed a gully on a west-facing buttress of the Bear Tooth [located to the right of the prominent hanging glacier southwest of the Bear Tooth summit—Ed]. Approach from the Root Canal, just past the broad snow couloir that separates the Moose's Tooth from the Bear Tooth. The route is approximately 350m and involves moderate mixed climbing and a short section of WI6 at mid-height. Enjoyable WI4 pitches in a chimney end near a serac that doesn't threaten the route. We descended from there on pins and horns. We named the route Unforgiven (M5 WI6).

IVAN RAMIREZ

Mooseskin Mountain, The Ass of Spades, and various attempts. First, I thank the American Alpine Club for considering awarding a young dirtbag a Mountain Fellowship Grant to go climbing. Marcus Donaldson and I flew out of Talkeetna on April 14 and landed on the Buckskin Glacier in early afternoon. I am unable to describe the sights and our feelings as we stepped out of the plane and gazed, slack-jawed, at the surrounding peaks.

After a day of reconnaissance, we found a small, beautiful line of ice on a small peak immediately north of the Broken Tooth. The next day we climbed two lovely pitches of moderate-to-hard mixed ice and rock in a nice system, until the weather closed in and we retreated.

Four or five tent-bound days followed, due to weather and snow conditions. On the first day of good weather we left in a predawn caffeinated stupor and skied to the base of a 3,000' line that we had spotted. It was on the south face of a pretty peak to the north, left of the prominent buttress and right of a large couloir. We later learned that this peak was called Mooseskin Mountain (Peak 8,300'; *AAJ* 2001, p. 211). We roped up and simul-climbed moderate 40°-50° snow that led over the bergschrund and a few mixed steps to the base of the first real challenges. Marcus made a nice lead through the difficulties, M4, to a good anchor and brought me up. I then took the lead and we simul-climbed again through more snow and small mixed bands. Marcus's next block led through rotten, shattered black rock, a little spicy, to another good anchor. I got a fun couple of pitches in the same rock, and Marcus then led us to the summit ridge. Once on the ridge I took the lead, and we were on the summit at 4 p.m. On the decent Marcus ripped a 15- by 30-foot cornice that left us a little shaken and happy we were roped-up. We named the route The Ass of Spades, in honor of the naked-lady playing cards that kept us entertained during the storm.

During our climb we had ample opportunity to check out the north face of the Moose's Tooth, but I was unable to spot a safe or even semi-safe line on the intimidating but gorgeous face. The east face's ice also looked out of condition, and we knew our chances of success were little to none. We therefore bailed, to attempt routes elsewhere in the range. After 28 days on the glacier and the trip of our lives, we flew out to Talkeetna and devoured five dinners between the two of us.

CHRIS DONHARL

Royal Tower, Canadian Bacon, and Thunder Mountain, Maxim. Shawn Huisman and I climbed two new routes during a two-week door-to-door trip to the Alaska Range. This was our first climbing trip to Alaska, and we consider ourselves lucky to have pulled off two first ascents in such a short time. Taking advantage of April's colder temperatures (though longer nights, but still only about six hours of darkness), we found conditions on sun-exposed faces to be perfect, with good snow, ice, and mixed.

The first route was a narrow gully on the 2,500' east face of Royal Tower in Little Switzerland. It is the gully line immediately left of Spam and Legs (*AAJ* 2002, p. 243). Our Canadian Bacon (ED1 M5 WI4) involved 3,000' of actual climbing up thin, foamy ice and steep mixed. Much of the ice was too snowy to accept ice screws, making for unnerving climbing, as picks threatened to slice through the vertical "sn'ice." We encountered four WI4 pitches separated by longer sections of alpine gully terrain. The mixed crux was a steep rock pitch that gained the southeast ridge. Once on the ridge, we cruised to the summit. We completed the route in a 17-hour round-trip with lots of simul-climbing. There are still a few interesting-looking ice and mixed objectives on Royal Tower, so get after it!

Two days later, we bumped over to the Tokositna Glacier and the base of the 3,500' south face of Thunder Mountain. In a 14-hour round-trip, we climbed a gully located on the left side of the south face [the major gully left of Ring of Fire—Ed].

A close up of the left side of the east face of Royal Tower in Little Switzerland. Canadian Bacon (Huisman-Isaac, 2004) takes the left gully. The middle gully is Spam and Legs (LeeElkin-Seifer, 2001), while the right gully is unclimbed. See *AAJ* 2001, p. 207 for more routes. *Sean Isaac*

Thunder Mountain (10,920'), south face: (1) Barlow-Hornby (1993). (2) Maxim (Huisman-Isaac, 2004) (no summit). (3) Ring of Fire (Cordes-DeCapio, 2001). (4) Dream Sacrifice (Hall-Lewis-Ramsden, 1997) (no summit; ascent to summit by Johnson-Leggett-Su, 2004). (5a) Bragg-Donini initial attempt, to junction with line 5 (2000). (5) Subsequent attempt (Bragg-Donini, 2000). (6) Deadbeat (Cordes-DeCapio, 2001). (6a) The Bums Lost variation (Johnson-Leggett-Su, 2004) (no summit). (7) Walk of the Schnitzelkings (Duepper-Traxler, 1999) (no summit). (8) Paikea's Journey (Johnson-Piggott, 2004) (no summit). *Kelly Cordes*

Maxim (ED1 M4 WI5) begins as a steep snow couloir that gradually pinches to fun ice and mixed climbing. The first crux negotiated steep ice, slightly overhanging at one point, around the left side of a truck-size chockstone. The last couple of pitches involved a two-foot wide, spotty thin-ice runnel leading to a prominent notch on the gendarmed summit ridge. Unseen from the glacier, this tight, shoulder-width goullotte provided the best climbing of the trip. We stopped here, instead of continuing along the corniced ridge to the summit. Incidentally, this gully had been rappelled after the first ascent of Dream Sacrifice.

SEAN ISAAC, *Canada*

Thunder Mountain, The Bums Lost variation, and Dream Sacrifice, repeat to summit. On May 15 Roy Leggett, Steve Su, and I began our first climbing trip to Alaska. Roy and I each received a fellowship grant from the AAC. We set our sights on Thunder Mountain and Mt. Huntington, both on the Tokositna glacier. We were greeted in Talkeetna by poor flying conditions and waited four days before flying to base camp. The weather was fickle, but we left the next day to climb Deadbeat (M6 WI5, Cordes-DeCapio, 2001). We headed out at 11 p.m. in questionable weather, hoping to get the route done before the weather turned. Steep snow and a few steep ice pitches led to a fork in the couloir, where Deadbeat hung a left (not the big lower fork where Walk of the Schnitzelkings goes right, but a less-distinct branch much farther up). Not knowing this, we climbed the right branch (more straight-up, versus Deadbeat's trend left) via a continuous ice passage that was consistently steep, mostly WI4. An interesting ice pitch led to a beautiful 75-degree ice slab, followed by a snow ridge/arête. More moderate mixed climbing and steep snow led to the ridge, where we stopped. Our variation, The Bums Lost, added 800' of new, fun climbing. We rapped the route and were back at base camp 24 hours after leaving.

Several days later we headed up Dream Sacrifice (ED2 Scottish 6, Hall-Lewis-Ramsden 1997). The first technical ice pitch was rotted out, and we bypassed it by climbing steep mixed ground to its left. Fortunately, Steve was psyched on the pitch, and Roy and I could breathe sighs of relief. A long section of moderate ice led to a steep ice vein up high. At the base of the ice we found fixed gear from Malcom Daly's 1999 accident. Steve commented about the fixed gear unaware of the accident. Roy and I figured it was best that he not know about the dramatic rescue and sent him off on lead. We climbed through the ice vein (WI5+ M6) in three pitches and then

Andy Johnson on the upper pitches of Dream Sacrifice, Thunder Mountain. This is near where Malcom Daly fell. *Roy Leggett*

found easy ground, where we rested and slept for two hours. Enjoyable snow slogging and ridge traversing brought us to the summit cornice of Thunder Mountain in deteriorating conditions. [This is the first ascent of Dream Sacrifice to continue to the summit—Ed.] On the way down, as clouds drifted in, we saw the phenomena of Brocken Specter. We also got fine views of Mts. Hunter, Foraker, and Providence before the weather closed in. In a whiteout we made it to the top of our rappels on The Bums Lost and were back in camp 31 hours after starting.

ANDY JOHNSON, *AAC*

Thunder Mountain, Paikea's Journey, and Mt. Providence, Divine Providence. Jeremy "Jay" Piggott of New Zealand and I based ourselves and friends on the southwest fork of the Tokositna Glacier during the last two weeks of May. We completed alpine-style first ascents on Thunder Mountain and Mt. Providence.

The route on Thunder Mountain's southeast face ascends a 1,000m couloir that was previously unexplored. It is to the east of all established lines, approached via the left side of the large couloir between Thunder and Providence. [This route is visible in the *AAJ* 2001, p. 205, photo. It begins above the horizontal sun-shadow line in the broad, glacial couloir on the right side and angles up left through the obvious weakness—Ed.] It sports 600m of 50°-65° snow, capped by 400m of steeper ice and mixed terrain. A corniced col in Thunder's gendarmed and extremely corniced eastern summit ridge marked the end of the route. The climbing included a beautiful one-meter-wide ice runnel, a great mixed pitch, and a vertical water-ice groove pouring from granite walls. We climbed Paikea's Journey (IV+ WI5 M5) in 17 hours round trip from base camp, including a four-hour wait at a rappel station for rockfall hazard to decrease.

Divine Providence (left) and the Hall-Lewis-Ramsden route (1997) on Mt. Providence. Nick Lewis notes: "there seemed to be a lot more snow on the lower section of the peak back in '97." *Samuel Johnson*

The line on the western half of Mt. Providence's 1,200m south face climbs a striking couloir and narrow-clefted rock buttress, via uninterrupted stellar ice and mixed ground, to reach Providence's corniced summit ridge. The route is to the left of the previous couloir route on Providence's south face. We found 300m of 40°-60° snow, followed by 900m of continuous ice and mixed terrain, mostly in the WI2-3 range, with several near-vertical ice pitches and a short, well-protected mixed crux in a steep corner. More ice might change this short but difficult mixed crux into a moderate ice pitch. We climbed Divine Providence (V WI4 M6) in 13 hours round trip from base camp.

SAMUEL JOHNSON, *Alaska*

KICHATNA SPIRES

Mt. Nevermore, The Perfect Storm. After a four-day snowy wait in Talkeetna, Paul Roderick of TAT flew Dai Lampard, Stuart McAleese, and me onto the Tatina Glacier in the Kichatna Spires around April 27. It was Stuart's and my third trip in three years to this amazing granite. Again, we came across nobody else. After the four-day storm, the faces were plastered with fresh snow, which also made crossing the col from the Tatina glacier to the Monolith glacier dangerous. Establishing camp between the west face of Middle Triple Peak and the east face of Mt. Nevermore, we started up the east face of Nevermore. Our line ascended the pillar on the farthest right of the kilometer-long face; it led straight to the summit. After two days spent fixing the first 200m, many pitches being climbed in waterfalls from melting snow, we started capsule-style. From the third day on, the weather was cold and snowy. For five days we climbed in bad weather. Generally the climbing followed a continuous crack up very steep walls. The rock was excellent. Most of the cracks needed to be cleaned of snow and ice. On the eighth day the weather improved, and we made quick progress, free climbing fantastic cracks. We found a perfect cave in which to pitch our small tent and, for once, enjoyed a comfortable bivy. The following day started fine, and we made the summit of Mt. Nevermore by 2 p.m. After 1,000m of hard-won climbing, the summit was a fine prize. Another route exists on this east face, but it did not continue to the summit, so we assume ours to be the first ascent of the face. The summit of Middle Triple Peak seemed only a stone's throw away. As we abseiled the wall, the weather deteriorated. Not wanting to be stuck in bad weather, we abseiled through the night and arrived in base camp at 5 a.m., 10 days after leaving. Later that day, Paul Roderick picked us up and deposited us in the Fairview Inn in Talkeetna for an evening of festivities. Perfect Storm, 1,000m, 25 pitches plus easy summit scrambling, E4 (UK) A1.

MIKE "TWID" TURNER, *United Kingdom*

Tatina Spire, Groundhog Day, and Mt. Haffner, attempt. British climbers Mark Reeves and Steve Sinfield visited the Tatina Glacier for a short stay in late May and June. Having waited five days in Talkeetna for the weather to improve enough to risk attempting a flight in, they were surprised by perfect blue skies during their first morning at base camp. After quickly packing, they headed north down the glacier to the far end of Mt. Haffner's west face, where they discovered a less-than-vertical granite slab. The pair climbed 14 pitches of British VS/HVS in wonderful sunshine, before the slab merged with the lower reaches of a snow basin, and the terrain became unpleasant. Increasing clouds and the water feature up which they were now climbing combined to force a retreat. At 6 p.m. they began rappelling and arrived on the glacier at 9:30. They regained base camp at midnight.

It rained most of the following day, but in late afternoon the two were able to inspect the small cirque near the head of the glacier that rises southwest to Flat Top Peak. On the broad south face of ca 2,500m Tatina Spire they spotted an unclimbed line right of the existing route, Alaskan Rose (Calder Stratford and Kevin Thaw, 1996: nine long free pitches with a crux of 5.11c R), which climbs a steep south-facing buttress to the top of a subsidiary summit south of the highest point of Tatina Spire. The British pair considered the line they had spotted, which rises ca 600m from the glacier, to be more suitable for a one-day free ascent. (The first ascent of the higher Tatina Spire was made in 1975 by Hooman Aprin, David Black, and Michael Graber via a multi-day route up the 700m southeast face at VI 5.9 A4.)

It rained for the next four days, but on the fifth the weather cleared, allowing Reeves and Sinfield to start up their proposed new line with 100m of static line, a 60m lead rope and another 60m of 8mm static. The first four pitches (VS to HVS) led to an undercut traverse out to a hanging corner. This corner gave three pitches of slightly damp E2/3, with a couple of aid moves on the first and around 10m of aid on the second (A0/A1). They climbed the remaining seven pitches (up to E3) and reached the top at 1 a.m. They rappelled the route in three hours and regained base camp shortly before 5 a.m. The 14-pitch route has been christened Groundhog Day and has difficulties of E3 5b/5c or 5.10c R and A0/A1.

With their hands trashed from jamming, the pair radioed for a flight and were picked up at the start of the unusual heat wave that affected all Alaska.

LINDSAY GRIFFIN, *Mountain INFO, CLIMB magazine*

Neacola Mountains

Chakachamna Peak, south face to near summit. Fred Beckey had his eye on a prominent 7,530'
peak in the Neacola Mountains for many years, but it remained entombed in his infamous
"Black Book." The peak is located three miles south of Lake Chakachamna and is visible on a
clear day, 90 miles to the west, from Anchorage and Turnagin Arm. The USGS Board on
Geographic Names has just recently officially accepted Fred's name of Chakachamna Peak.
(Map: USGS Tyonek (A-7), Alaska; Approximate coordinates: 61°09'N, 152°26'W)

A few years ago Fred and two partners flew onto the glacier on the south side of the
mountain. It was late in the day and the snow soft and unstable; Fred felt it was not a safe time
for a climb. But his partners felt otherwise and got two-thirds of the way up the couloir, till a
wet-snow avalanche swept one of them 1,000' down the couloir. The climber escaped with only
minor injuries, but the event marked the end of the attempt.

On the evening of June 12, after waiting out several stormy days in Anchorage, Brook
Alongi, Fred, and I were flown by helicopter onto an unnamed glacier on the south side of the
peak, under clear blue skies. Since weather windows tend to be short and far between in the
Neacola Mountains, we set up our tents and immediately started climbing the left-hand (western) of the two broad, 3,000' couloirs on the peak's south side. We had breathtaking views of
immense glaciers, the active volcanoes Spurr and Redoubt, and dozens of unclimbed peaks. We
climbed through the night using pickets for running belays up the 40-50° snow, arriving at the
col atop the couloir at 2:00 a.m. Fred was exhausted and waited there. I led a ropelength of
snowy mixed ground and belayed Brook up to me. We could see the summit 100' higher and a
few hundred yards away, but descended due to deteriorating weather and concern for our cold

The arrow points to the couloir climbed on the south face of Chakachamna Peak. *Eric "Pax" Fox*

and tired partner back at the col. We descended without incident and arrived at our tents late the next morning. More information about the climb, as well as a few pictures can be found at: www.cascadeclimbers.com/threadz/showflat.php/Cat/0/Number/371540/an//page/0/vc/1

Brook and I had hoped to sample some other climbing opportunities in the area, but the weather did not cooperate. We spent the next five days in the tents while rain, snow, and strong winds made even the most mundane outdoor activities unpleasant. When the weather finally broke, we called in our helicopter and flew back to Anchorage. I thought that after this trip there might be one less page in the Black Book, but on the flight out Fred was snapping pictures and saying, "*That* looks like a nice peak."

ERIC "PAX" FOX

CHUGACH AND WRANGELL MOUNTAINS

Heritage Point and Mt. Yukla. After five failed attempts with several partners, I joined with Dan Petrus to complete the first ascent of the north face of Heritage Point (3,600', VI M6 WI6 A2) in the Chugach Mountains. We took the most obvious ice smear in the center of the face for 14 long pitches. This put us on top of the big snow ledge at mid-height. We then traversed right for 400' to the large dihedral that splits the upper wall and followed it up and left to the top of the wall. Very sustained climbing! Out of 29 total pitches, 25 were M5 or harder. Over a dozen pitches were hard, runout M6. From the top of the face we traversed up left to the couloir separating Heritage Point from Little Bear. We descended this couloir on the last day of calendar winter of 2005. No summit.

In early April of this year, 2005, Dan Petrus and I climbed a line on the north face of Yukla in the Chugach Mountains. It's the obvious couloir that tops out on the northeast ridge to the left of the summit. This may have been the line taken previously by Richard Baranow. If so, I think Dan and I made the second ascent of both the face and the line. Anyway, it goes at V WI5, 3,600'.

JOHN KELLEY

Chugach Mountains, ski traverse. In April we skied from Valdez, Alaska, to the Glenn Highway by way of Mt. Thor and the Matanuska Glacier. We parked at the Valdez airport and slogged up the Valdez Glacier, over the steep Cashman Col, across the Tazlina and Science glaciers to the intimidating precipitation vortex of the Columbia Glacier. A corridor between Mt. Elusive and Mt. Valhalla offered a low-angle route up the east shoulder of Mt. Thor (12, 251'), the second highest peak in the Chugach. Wearing crampons we double-carried our kit down the aesthetic north ridge of Mt. Thor to the Sylvester Glacier. An easy 7,200' col linked us to the Powell Glacier and high glacial benches for 15 miles to the west branch of the Matanuska Glacier and out to the Glenn Highway. Our route gained about 19,000' over 98 miles. We talked with every Chugach climber and tourer we could, and they were all certain that our traverse had not been done before. But it's Alaska, and many trips don't get reported.

JOE STOCK AND DYLAN TAYLOR, *AAC*

Upper Powell Glacier and Upper Barnard Glacier, various ascents and ski descents. Mike Meekins flew Dave Kinsella (Ireland), Wilfred Glanznig (Austria), Wolfgang Huber (Austria), and me into the upper Powell Glacier on the north side of the Chugach Range on May 4. We set up camp at about 7,000' in the middle of the glacier. Dave and Wilfi then headed up the northeast ridge of Peak 9,845' and Wolfgang and I to the ridge southwest of Peak 9,138'. We reached a subsidiary peak of about 9,100' on the southwest ridge of Peak 9,138', and I made a ski descent via our route (Wolfi downclimbed). Dave reached Peak 9,845' (Wili skied back from 8,500') and attempted to ski the north face, but after encountering ice, instead skied the northeast ridge. On May 5 Dave, Wili, and Wolfi headed to Peak 9,570' at the head of the glacier and skied the south face, though they didn't reach the summit. On May 6 Wolfi and I attempted Peak 8,710'. We didn't reach its summit either, but skied a couloir on the east side of the peak. On May 7 Wili and Wolfi climbed a 9,400' peak northwest of camp and skied a couloir on its southwest face. Dave and I climbed the 9,200' peak southeast of camp to within 10m of its summit and skied the couloir on its northwest side. Wili and Wolfi repeated this couloir the following day, and Dave skied one just to its northeast (no summit). At the same time, I climbed Peak 9,138' by its northwest face and skied the same route in descent. On May 9 we all climbed Peak 9,570', at the head of the glacier, to within 20m of its summit. Dave, Wili, and Wolfi skied a couloir starting on its northeast shoulder, while I skied a direct line down its east face.

Paul Claus flew us into the upper Barnard Glacier in the Wrangells, just east of University Peak, on May 13. We set up camp at 7,200' in the middle of the glacier. I then climbed the west face of Peak 10,170' to where it flattens out at around 9,200' and skied down. On May 15 we all climbed the southeast face of the south ridge of Super Cub Peak to its apex at around 11,500' and skied it. On May 19 we climbed a 9,800' peak just south of a 9,695' spot height, southeast of camp, and descended by the obvious couloir on its south side.

Reviews of the previous ten *AAJs* and discussions with the pilots lead us to believe that none of the peaks that we climbed on, other than Super Cub Peak, had been climbed before. The ski descents were between 45° and 60°, exposed, and we believe they were firsts.

PHILLIP A INGLE, *Wales*

FAIRWEATHER RANGE

Various ascents and ski descents. The name, bestowed in 1778 by the range's discoverer, Captain James Cook, is itself a curiosity. The Fairweather Range experiences some of the world's worst weather, including over 100 annual inches of precipitation. It can snow during any month, as low as 6,000' during summer. Overcast days and rain predominate.

We flew in on April 20, planning to ascend the west ridge and ski the northwest face of Mt. Fairweather. The day after arriving on the Grand Plateau, though, we were treated to some of the best tent-flattening, snow-pummeling windstorms any of us had endured or wish to experience again. However, after eight days the sun emerged and allowed us to make a seven-hour push to the summit of Fairweather via the west ridge. This is the most accessible and shortest route up the peak. The primary objective hazard is a large serac on Fairweather's north face that looms over the approach to the west ridge. We skied the northwest face directly back onto the Grand Plateau. The skiing was never steeper than 45°, and the climbing was Alaska grade 3 to 4. As far as we know this was a first descent. Now, with a month to spare, we set out

Left is up (in crampons) and right is down (on skis) on Peak 12,300'. *BJ Brewer*

to climb and ski some adjacent peaks, including Mt. Root (12,860', 3,920m), Mt. Watson (12,516', 3,815m), and Peak 12,300'. We moved camp approximately five miles northwest, down the Grand Plateau and into an amazing cirque, close to all three peaks

Next up, a 3,200' face on Peak 12,300' looked to hold steep, albeit skiable, terrain. Our route up started with a short traverse, followed by a large bergschrund and a northwest-facing couloir on the left side of the west face. The climbing in the couloir was steep, with one 50' pitch of vertical ice. The couloir deposited us halfway to the summit. We continued up the face, still favoring the north, climbers's left, ridge. The climbing there was consistently 40°-50°. The summit is a small knife-edge ridge with great views north to Mt. St. Elias. We skied from the top, down a slope that was about 50° for the first 200-300' and then the low to mid 40s for the remainder of the descent. As far as we know this was a first descent. The climbing was Alaska grade 2/3+.

The 3,000-foot ski couloir on the south/southeast side of Mt. Watson. *BJ Brewer*

Mt. Watson has one of the most impressive couloirs any of us had ever seen. The line cuts into the south/southeast side of the mountain for 3,000'. This was to be our final climb. We accessed the couloir via snow ramps to the west, as the bottom cliffs out. We ascended the steep hallway, and descended the same way. The climbing was again Alaska grade 2/3+, with slush giving way to hard, granular snow as we ascended the 42°-47° couloir. To the best of our knowledge this was another first descent. We believe that our routes of ascent on Watson and 12,300' were also firsts, as we could find no documentation or sign of previous passage.

On May 17, with time to spare we packed our belongings and started walking back to Haines. The seven-day, 120-mile traverse was a whole other story in itself.

For further specific information contact the Yakutat District Ranger, Glacier Bay National Park/Preserve, P.O. Box 137 Yakutat, AK 99689 (907–784-3295) or the Glacier Bay Chief Ranger at (907) 697-2230. We flew in with Drake, a professional pilot from Haines. We recommend him and his services to anyone going into that area. Drake's Phone # is (907) 723-9475.

BJ BREWER, MAD DOG, *and* JAMIE LAIDLAW

ALASKA COAST MOUNTAINS

The southwest flank of Mt. Blachnitzky in the Juneau Icefield. The route wanders up snow on this face through haze from forest fire smoke. *Keith K. Daellenbach*

Various ascents. My father, Charles B. Daellenbach of Albany, Oregon, Scott McGee of Anchorage, Alaska, Fred Skemp III of La Crosse, Wisconsin, and I, of Portland, Oregon, took a helicopter transport from Juneau to the Gilkey Trench in the Coast Range of Alaska. We climbed the previously unclimbed Mt. Blachnitzky (6,552', N58°47'47" W134°23'38") on June 30 via the southwest cirque/south ridge (45° snow, class 3 rock) from a high camp at a previously unvisited tarn, which, located at 3,600' on the southwest flank, seemed like Shangri-la. Fred and I also climbed a route on the previously unclimbed Peak 6,500' (N58°48'17" W134°35'56"). The date was July 4, and we named the route the Independence Route. Our route took us from the Bucher Glacier up the north-northeast ridge, across 55° snow slopes of the northeast face, and finally up the southeast ridge, where we encountered 5.3 rock and WI2 ice.

Our egress off the Juneau Ice-field took us from the Gilkey Trench on a traverse into the north side of Avalanche Canyon, a river ford across the Avacan, and up the steep valley to the "high ice" of the Northwest Taku Glacier. From here, we skied towards Taku D (5,810', N58°42'17" W134°17'530"), a previously climbed peak at the confluence of the Taku and Matthes glaciers.

We all climbed this peak via the southwest ridge (class 3 rock). We spent the final enjoyable days of the expedition on backcountry skis, making our way off the southern end of the Icefield via the Taku, Southwest Taku, Norris, Lemon, and Ptarmigan glaciers, with a descent down Lemon Creek back to the capital of Alaska.

KEITH K. DAELLENBACH, *AAC*

Devil's Thumb, South Pillar, first free ascent. In July Carl Diedrich and I spent several weeks climbing and exploring around the Devil's Thumb. Our main objective was to free climb the imposing South Pillar of the Thumb. However, we felt we first should climb the classic East Ridge route as a warm-up and to investigate descent options. On July 12, with a forecast of clear skies and high pressure, we set out to climb the South Pillar. From camp at the foot of the East Ridge, we descended toward the Witches' Cauldron. Our plan to approach and climb the initial spur to the base of the pillar in a day proved to be excellent. The spur consists of low angle 5th-class rock that becomes steeper toward the base of the pillar. We bivouacked comfortably on the large ledges below the pillar.

We started up the pillar about 15m right of the crest and climbed a wandering three pitches that led us toward the obvious large, right-facing corner system just left of the crest. The towering, blocky corner offered four rope-stretching 60m pitches (5.9–5.10). (We found several rappel slings in the corner system.) These pitches deposited us on a narrow ledge that led right and back onto the exposed pillar crest. The following 60m pitch, brilliant climbing on excellent rock with small holds, left us at an exhilarating hanging belay at an obvious black band visible from afar. We were committed and began a race with the setting sun to the summit. A thrilling 5.10 flake, crack, and layback pitch ended on a large ledge, easing our minds, as well as the angle of the rock. Success seeming imminent, we comfortably climbed the corners angling toward a large roof. Peering around the roof to the right revealed easy face climbing, with a summit bivouac in sight. Continuing clear weather allowed for a morning of leisure. We spent several hours solving the world's problems, while visually feasting on this grand landscape of white wilderness. We spent the remainder of our trip exploring the glaciers and ridges around the Thumb.

Our free ascent of the South Pillar deviated from the original line (Bebie-Pilling, 1991) with two notable variations. We took the obvious corner system to the left of the pillar crest in preference to the original line. And, where the original line climbs the Quartz Ramp to the right of the crest, our line ascends directly up the crest. The South Pillar of Devil's Thumb as we climbed it comes in at V 5.10.

Air transport was provided by the wonderful folks at Temsco Helicopters. Also thanks to Dieter Klose for his hospitality and information.

PAUL ADAM HARAF

Devil's Thumb massif, everything. Four years ago on an expedition to nearby Oasis Peak, Dieter Klose planted a seed: the complete traverse of Devil's Thumb. This seed grew into a dream that blossomed into reality in July, as Andre Ike of Squamish, B.C. and I were deposited below the East Ridge of the Thumb by Temsco Helicopters. A week of mostly bad weather followed, with just enough sun to advance a camp and scope the logistics of our mission. Finally the skies

Cat's Ears

Witches' Tits

Devil's Thumb from the south. The East Ridge route is roughly the right skyline. Burkett Needle is the distant aiguille on the left, and Mt. Burkett the distant peak to its right. The lines were those followed by Ike and Walsh. *Jon Walsh*

Andre Ike waiting for the wind on the summit of Devil's Tower. *Jon Walsh*

cleared, and we set off with three days of food and high hopes for the splitter white granite we had seen from the heli and from our scoping mission. We ascended through a crevasse maze to the ridge below the Witches' Tits and climbed eight moderate pitches to the base of the steep, clean headwall. This lower ridge had been previously climbed by the late Guy Edwards and John Millar in 2002. We climbed a new route to right of theirs on the headwall: Witches' Cleavage (eight pitches, 5.11a) to the col between the Tits and then up the east ridge to the summit of the West Tit. We then rappelled to the col between the Tits, and climbed the west ridge of the East Tit in three long pitches of 5.8 to its virgin summit. Rappelling and downclimbing its razor east ridge brought us to a tight bivouac in the notch between the Tits and the Cat's Ears. The next day started with a 45m rappel down the wildly exposed north side to a crack system we believed had been climbed in 1996 by Chad McMullen and Simon Elias. We freed their route at 5.10 (previously 5.10a A1) in five pitches and found ourselves at the Cat's Brow (the notch between the Ears). Each Ear then yielded incredible 5.9 climbing on steep, knobby stone full of cracks and chicken heads that kept us grinning ear to ear. It was the second ascent of the lower Ear and the third ascent of the higher, which Guy had claimed to be the sharpest spire in the Coast Range. From these summits we could clearly see our final objective glowing in the afternoon sun: the almost finished and not quite free West Buttress of the Thumb. A few steep rappels and traversing landed us in the chossy gully between the Ears and the Thumb. However, while crossing the gully, we generated rockfall, and our rope took a core shot at its midpoint, leaving us with no choice but to descend. Eight raps, some downclimbing, and a five-star bivy later, we awoke to see the

Andre Ike jugging the northwest face of Cat's Ears Spire
Jon Walsh

spires cloaked in an eerie mist. A few more rappels, more downclimbing, and we were back at ABC. At 2 p.m. the heavens parted, and 36 hours of nonstop rain began. Our rope chopping was a blessing in disguise, as continuing or retreating from high on the West Buttress would have been epic. A couple of days later, the rain stopped and we awoke predawn to clear skies and the finest aurora we had ever seen. Despite a poor and worsening weather forecast, we grabbed our packs and charged up and down the complete East Ridge of the Thumb in 12.5-hours roundtrip, making us the first climbers to tick the Thumb and all its satellites. During the descent we called our pilot on VHF radio so he could pick us up before the fast-approaching storm socked us in for another week. He showed up right on time and whisked us back to civilization, just an hour before the slashing rain of another west coast storm engulfed the range. Significant accomplishments: FA Witches' Cleavage 5.11a 800m to summit of West Witches' Tit (3rd ascent of spire). FA of East Witches' Tit via Witches' Cleavage and West Ridge 5.11a 800m. FFA of North Face (Elias-McMullen) of Cat's Ears Spires, 5.10 300m from Ears/Tits col. Enchainment of the Witches' Tits and Cat's Ears. Second and Third ascents of the lower and higher Cat's Ears spires, respectively. First to climb the Thumb and all its satellites.

We thank Dieter Klose for his hospitality and those who contribute to the John Lauchlan award for making the trip possible: Mountain Equipment Coop, Integral Designs, Rocky Mountain Books, Explore magazine, and Arcteryx.

JON WALSH, GOLDEN, *British Columbia*

Canada

ST. ELIAS RANGE

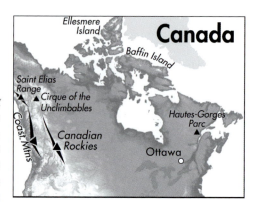

Kluane National Park Reserve, mountaineering summary and statistics. Mountaineering use was down by 50% in the St. Elias Ranges, with only 19 mountaineering expeditions registered. Fifty-four climbers and skiers spent 1,009 person-days in the St. Elias Range, the lowest use that the Park has seen in many years.

As usual Mt. Logan received the most attention, with eight parties attempting the King Trench route and six parties attempting the East Ridge route. Four groups reached one of Logan's main summits. Weather and tricky routefinding, due to open crevasses on the upper King Trench route, caused other parties to be unsuccessful. Climbers were also on Mt. Kennedy, Mt. Steele, King Peak, Pinnacle Peak, and Mt. Queen Mary.

Of note was a first ascent of the northwest face of Mt. Kennedy, by two British climbers [see report below]. They took three days to climb the face and descended by way of the Cathedral Glacier.

Also of note is an American team that climbed the East Ridge of King Peak. This was their fourth attempt at King Peak over a number of years and, they believe, the first time a woman has made the summit.

On a sad note, a Canadian was killed in a fall on a ski descent after climbing the East Peak of Mt. Logan. Recovery was not possible due to altitude and location.

Another death occurred during a planned traverse of the St. Elias Range by two Alaskan climbers. One member drowned after breaking through thin ice on Harlequin Lake only two days into their expedition.

Park staff took advantage of the heavy melt this summer and revisited the Project Snow Cornice camp established on the Seward Glacier by Walter Wood in 1948. A Parks Canada historian recorded part of the site, which will contribute to the human history of the St. Elias Range.

Anyone interested in mountaineering in Kluane National Park Reserve should contact the Mountaineering Warden, Kluane National Park Reserve, Box 5495, Haines Jct. Yukon, Y0B 1L0, call 867 634 7279, or fax 867 634 7277 and ask for a mountaineer's package. Or visit the Parks Canada web site at www.pc.gc.ca/kluane

RICK STALEY, *Park Warden, Kluane National Park Reserve*

Mt. Kennedy, northwest face. As a two-man team, Jon Bracey and I wanted a challenging mixed objective we could attempt alpine style, and the northwest face of Mt. Kennedy fit the bill perfectly. In 1996 Jack Tackle and Jack Roberts climbed their Pair of Jacks on this face, a difficult mixed line climbed in capsule style (see *AAJ* 1997; route photo p. 79, article pp. 80-91). However, bad weather and a dropped crampon forced a retreat from high on the wall, so this huge

2,000m face was still awaiting its first complete ascent.

We flew from Kluane Lake onto the Dusty Glacier on May 4. The next day dawned cloudy, with the threat of storm, but we decided to approach the face "for a look." A six-mile skin took us around onto the Kennedy Glacier, and the gods were with us, as the weather held off and the face was plastered. We spent the afternoon scoping the most obvious line on the face, the icy smears taken by the Jacks, which did, after all, deserve finishing.

Over the next three days we climbed the northwest face, finding excellent conditions. The bulk of the route was pure ice to Scottish 5, with several harder mixed pitches. We made a few variations on the Jacks line, one of which provided the mixed crux at hard Scottish 7. Where the Jacks were forced to descend the north spur, we continued directly through the second rock band on new ground, then straight to the summit via the upper icefield and north spur. The weather had held off until summit day, which was savagely cold and windy. We descended that night to sheltered ground on the Cathedral Glacier for our third (and first lying down) bivy. As food ran out we spent a couple of nervous days waiting for our pickup, but nothing could dampen the elation of climbing this incredible face, all within a week of leaving the U.K.

RICH CROSS, *United Kingdom*

BAFFIN ISLAND

Bylot and Baffin Islands, ascents and exploration. In May, Louise Jarry and I made a 30-day exploratory ski tour of 300km, with eight peak ascents, from the village of Pond Inlet, Nunavut Territory. On May 1 we were taken by snowmobile on a 5-hour ride to the west coast of Bylot Island, 21km east-southeast of Canada Point. Wishing to avoid polar bears, we moved north,

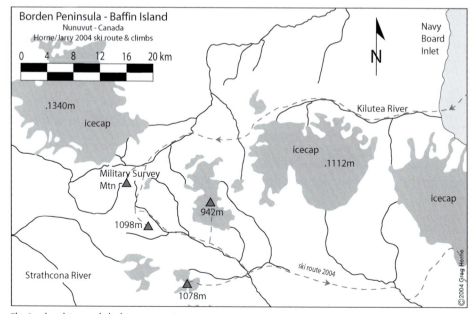

The Borden skiing and climbing route. *Greg Horne*

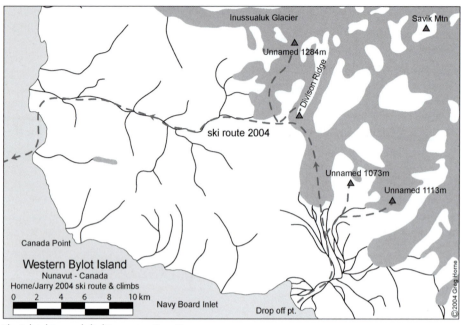

The Bylot skiing and climbing route. *Greg Horne*

Date	Peak	Elevation	Route	UTM Grid Reference[1]
May 3	Unnamed	1,073m	S-SW slopes	E0530843 N8136610
May 5	Unnamed	1,113m	W shoulder, gully & icecap	E0533760 N8134729
May 7	"Division Ridge"	720m	NNE ridge	E0526198 N8142491
May 8	Unnamed	1,284m	SW glacier	E0525960 N8147288
May 17	MSM NE summit	1,073m[2]	NE glacier & N ridge	E0445070 N8120266
May 17	MSM SW summit	1,073m[2]	E ridge from NE pk	E0444820 N8120071
May 19	Unnamed	1,098m	NW slopes & N ridge	E0448783 N8113379
May 21	Unnamed Icecap	942m	S slopes & ridge	E0457662 N8116298
May 23	Unnamed	1,084m, 1,078[3]	NE shoulder & E glacier	E0454616 N8105393

1 – Grid zone 17X, NAD 27
2 – Both summits read 1,105m by altimeter
3 – 1,078m is the spot elevation shown on 1:50,000 topo 48 D/3
All elevations and grid references are by a Garmin 12 GPS unit using the position averaging function.

Top, Borden: The view south from Peak 1,098m. Bottom, Bylot: The view of Tay Bay and Inussaluk Glacier from Peak 1,284m. *Greg Horne (2)*

inland, toward the toe of a 23km-long valley glacier flowing southwest from Savik Mountain. From a camp at 46m we ascended two peaks: a ski and scramble up Point 1,073m and a mainly ski ascent of Point 1,113m, which has an icecap summit.

We next skied up the valley glacier, then west up one of its tributaries to a 425m pass holding four lakes. We climbed the end of a long ridge that divides the tributary glaciers and climbed a tiny, 720m alpine summit by its north-northeast ridge. We called the long, narrow ridge Division Ridge because it separates two glaciers north as far as Point 1,357m. Next, in thick fog we skied from our lakes camp up the glacier to the northwest. It turned out to be one of those magical days when perseverance paid off. After several hours of whiteout navigation we broke through the cloud layer to blue skies and warm sun. We continued north up the glacier, skiing to the summit of a 1,284m ice-domed peak. There were impressive views down the Inussaluk Glacier and west to Tay Bay. Farther in the distance Baffin's Borden Peninsula was visible.

Leaving the mountains of Bylot was difficult, but we skied west from our lakes camp to Navy Board Inlet and crossed it (15km) to the mouth of the Kilutea River on Borden Peninsula. We saw five sets of bear tracks along this route. We followed the Kilutea upstream, bypassing a difficult headwall near its headwaters lake, and continued to the base of Military Survey Mountain (MSM) in five days of skiing. MSM is the only officially named peak in the northern interior of Borden Peninsula.

After more than a week of poor weather we were treated with improving views from MSM, neither summit of which had a cairn. In hindsight this seemed odd in the context of our next mountain climbed. Moving south we ski-ascended the next 1,000m peak, Peak 1,098m. On its summit we found a cairn, along with strips of bright fabric used for survey and air-photo work. Given that this peak is higher, has a cairn and survey fabric, and the labeled MSM has none of this, there may be map-labeling error.

Continuing southeast we detoured for a ski ascent of a 942m-high icecap peak 13km east-northeast of MSM. Our final ascent was of Point 1,078m, 17km southeast of MSM. This involved a pleasant ski across its east glacier. At approximately 832m we discovered what might be a human-built bivy rock wall, potentially prehistoric. Our plan had been to ski down the Mala River, but views of the lower Mala made us nervous. There might not have been enough snow left, so we traveled east, north of the Mala, through a series of side valleys and passes.

On our last night camping, May 29, it rained. Locals said spring arrived several weeks early. The next day we were picked up by snowmobile north of the mouth of the Mala River and returned to Pond Inlet. We thank The North Face Canada and Mountain Equipment Co-op, who generously supported this expedition.

GREG HORNE, *Alpine Club of Canada*

Exploration and various descents. The original premise of Brad Barlage's and my trip, from mid-April to mid-May, was to traverse from Pond Inlet, near the northern tip of Baffin Island, to Clyde River, 200 miles to the south. The idea was to use skis and traction kites to cover the large, open expanses of sea ice and link a series of fjords and passes through the heart of Baffin's Big Wall country. After an exploratory trip in 2002, we found the kiting and skiing to be so good that we were looking for bigger and better areas to experiment with.

Unfortunately, we got too much of what we were looking for. After a slow start, the kiting "improved" to the point that we were rocketing along at 30mph with loaded sleds. Much of Baffin's sea ice is smooth, but not all of it, including the patch of pressure ice that flipped one of our sleds into the air, scattered gear all over, and effectively put an end to our traversing dreams.

Brad Barlage searching for couloirs on Baffin Island after the kite skiing proved too much. *Andrew McLean*

Lacking a Plan B and still having three weeks, we began to improvise. The couloir skiing around Sam Ford Fjord and the Walker Spur had been stupendous, so we gambled a few weeks' salary on a Ski-Doo ride out to the Coutts Inlet and Nova Zembla Island area to seek out steep, splitter couloirs. This decision was based on looking at topo maps and trying to guess where good ones might be, a marginally successful strategy.

While they look similar on topo maps, the walls in the northern region aren't quite as high, as steep, or as plentiful as their southern cousins. There

Choice couloirs skied by Brad Barlage and Andrew McLean in 2004. *Andrew McLean*

are quite a few bulging shields of beautiful granite, but they tend to be split by smaller couloirs that either dead-end or are lower-angle and rocky. Most of the walls are in the 2,500' range, and the skiable lines are few and far between.

After a day attempting to climb the rounded massif of Qiajivik, the highest point in northern Baffin, we climbed and skied a nice south-facing line near the Qiajivik glacier terminus and dubbed it "Nanookie" in reference to polar bear tracks near its base. A day later we packed up and moved east, skiing the premier couloir of the trip along the way, a steep 3,500' north-facing line that we christened "Caribootie."

We spent the next week exploring the convergence area of Coutts Inlet, where we found four skiable lines. All four faced due east and had a sphincter-winking glaze of ice that didn't add comfort to the 45+° angle. The most gripping was the 50°, perfectly straight, narrow chute we named "Pagophile" (ice lover), followed by "Gnarwhal," "Arctic Turn," and "Terror Incognito."

In an attempt at something different, we later skinned over to the shores of Nova Zembla Island, where we weathered a bizarre arctic rain storm for days before finally climbing and skiing Nova Zembla's high point (which may not have an official name) via GPS in a virtual whiteout. The skiing was as bad as it gets: shallow, rotten snow, zero vis, warm, tons of rocks, and generally unpleasant.

ANDREW MCLEAN

Mt. Odin, south couloir ski descent. On April 17 Jim Surette, Ken Sauls, and I left our camp at the Windy Lake shelter, with our sights set on skiing a giant couloir which splits the south face of Mt. Odin. It was first climbed in 1974 by a French team and repeated in 2003 by Canadians, who recommended it as a spectacular descent. At 2,143m Odin is the tallest peak on Baffin Island. It took five hours to climb the couloir to a col at 1,640m. The snow at the bottom was rotten, but in the gully proper it turned solid and even had light powder in some sections. From the col it is another 500m of elevation gain to the summit, via the southwest ridge, with several sections of 5.7. The top part of the couloir is the steepest, at about 35°. The bottom part of the gully is choked with boulders, but we found a line which led all the way to the valley floor, for a total descent of about 1,550m (5,100'). According to my research, this is one of the longest ski descents in Auyuittuq National Park. The couloir will be in the best shape, for skiing or climbing, in April. Later in the season beware of rockfall.

MARK SYNNOTT, *AAC*

LOGAN MOUNTAINS

Vampire Spire, Nosferatu. It was about 4:30 in the afternoon when the three of us reached the oddly sloping ledge 100m from the summit of Vampire Spire. "No one's ever set foot on this ledge before," I observed as I crunched across the lichen-encrusted slab. This was our summit push. Doug had just struggled up a hideous bomb-bay squeeze chimney, making some of the strangest noises I have heard from the sharp end of the rope. We would do as many new pitches today as we

Ken Sauls ripping it on Mt. Odin, Baffin Island. *Mark Synnott*

had done since being dropped off in this wilderness two weeks previously. The weather was nice when Warren LaFave's helicopter departed, leaving five dirtbag American climbers stranded in the little alpine valley. This soon changed as rain and low-flying clouds, known as "mustard gas," settled in. I would be climbing with Doug La Farge, a friend from college, and John Sedelmeyer, a fellow Outward Bound instructor. Pat Goodman and Hank Jones were also there, with the intent of freeing a new route on the Vampire. We too had designs to free the Vamp, but our first goal was a first ascent.

During brief day-long intervals of relatively good weather, we pushed our route three pitches, averaging about one pitch a day. This part of our route was the crux. Pitch two features a splitter thin crack that took a triple set of brass nuts, plus a few hand-placed beaks. John did an excellent job on this lead, resisting the temptation to break out the

The south face of Mt. Odin, revealing part of its 5,000' couloir. *Mark Synnott*

hammer. There is a bolt to start the pitch, though, placed by Pat and Hank the previous year on their attempt. The bolt was justified, allowing passage through a blank section.

The third pitch consists of more thin nutting and a dicey pendulum into a wet seam. The seam soon turns into a finger-to-hand-size splitter. What made this lead so special for me was the hail storm that cut loose when I was halfway up. The chimney system above acted as a huge funnel, pouring millions of hailstones on my head. This spectacular pitch put us at the base of the aforementioned chimney pitch.

There was no way of knowing what the final pitches held in store. All we could see was the initial five-inch crack that arched under a big roof and out of sight, 70' feet above us. John racked everything. By the time he leap-frogged the big pieces to the lip of the roof, he had maybe two pieces of gear in. He kept threatening to belay, but eventually topped the pitch out. A short walk along a large, grassy ledge put us at the base of the lichen-covered 5.6R summit pitch.

On August 6 at 10:30 p.m. we stood on the summit of Vampire Spire. In the eerie sub-arctic twilight we surveyed the surrounding wilderness of peaks, glaciers, and cloud formations, which for the time being were behaving themselves. Our dream of establishing a new route on this fickle formation was now a reality. Our V 5.9 C2+ route, Nosferatu, follows the corner system immediately left of the main south face and, through two pendulums (to the right on the second pitch, left on the third), traverses out right under a bulge to the prominent crack system. It finishes through a wide crack system and tops out at the east side of the flat apron that surrounds the true summit. We placed some bolts at belays; otherwise our ascent was hammerless.

The south face of Vampire Spire showing the 2004 routes and one old. (1) The Dark Side (5.11, Goodman-Jones, 2004—first free ascent of the Vamp). (2) The Coffin (5.11 C1, Goodman-Jones, 2004. (3) Nosferatu (5.9 C2+, La Farge-Ludwig-Sedelmeyer, 2004. (4) The Undead (5.10+ A2+, Childress-Howard, 1999). (5) Sanguine Solution (5.11 A2+, Darkis-Goodman-Jackson, 1999). Routes 4, 5, and two more to the right are in a photo in AAJ 2000, pg. 226. Doug La Farge

Vampire Spire and the Fortress are the only substantial formations in the immediate area with quality climbing potential. A few miles down valley is the Phoenix, which has a number of established climbs. Doug La Farge

We spent the few hours of darkness on the lichen ledge, pretending to sleep, before rappelling the remainder of the route in a light rain.

RICH LUDWIG, *AAC*

The backside of the Vampire Spire, showing the end of The Dark Side. *Doug La Farge*

Vampire Spire, The Coffin and The Dark Side. On July 17 Pat Goodman and I began what seems to have become our annual journey to the Vampire region of Canada's Northwest Territories. A blown alternator left us stranded in Fort St. John, B.C., for three days, stretching the 70-hour drive into five days. This delay worked out to our advantage, allowing us to rendezvous with Doug La Farge, Rich Ludwig, and John Sedelmeyer at Warren LaFave's Inconnu Fishing Lodge and share the cost of the flight into the climbing area.

When we arrived, the weather was shaping up to be a repeat of the previous year. But after a week it cleared, allowing us to go climbing. Doug, Rich, and John began work on an aid route up the south face of Vampire Spire [Nosferatu, see above] that Pat and I had attempted last season. The following day Pat and I completed our new route, The Coffin (V 5.11 C1), which follows a striking large crack feature splitting the southwest face of the Vamp. To our dismay this route didn't go free, due to an eternally seeping roof.

Earlier, while circumnavigating the Spire, we saw what we believed could be a free route up the northwest face. On August 17 we completed a wandering climb on the northwest face following splitter dihedrals, overhanging fist cracks, and several moderate pitches, to establish The Dark Side (IV 5.11). We believe that ascent to be the first free and only one-day ascent of the formation.

HANK JONES

COAST MOUNTAINS

Coast Mountains, remote areas summary. 2004 was an astonishing year in the Coast Mountains, especially the Waddington Range. The new Waddington Guide was felt dramatically, with perhaps triple the usual number of climbers entering the range. Moreover, there was a shift in focus: with better information available, climbers chose objectives better suited to their talents and interests, rather than all lining up for the Bravo Glacier route on Mt. Waddington. More moderate mountaineers went to the Franklin, Upper Tellot, and Radiant Glaciers, while the "harder lads" settled in at Sunny Knob, Waddington-Combatant Col, and the upper Dais. The result was an outburst of climbing, the likes of which had never been seen in the Range.

At the moderate end of the spectrum, about a dozen people from the BC Mountaineering Club enjoyed numerous ascents on the Upper Tellot and around the Plummer Hut. A five-person Alpine Club of Canada party later did likewise. A 15-member party from Korea perhaps lacked glacier-travel skills necessary for the undertaking, and their stay was fairly short, but one wonders if their visit indicates a trend toward more foreign visitors. A four-man party from Britain spent a productive time at Rainy Knob, before a slip on snow on the South Ridge of Serra 2 resulted in an injured climber and the first helicopter long-line evacuation the Range has seen. One hopes this is not indicative of another trend. Finally, Chris Barner and Paul Rydeen from Vancouver Island made their annual foray into the Range, accompanied by four friends, the result being first ascents of both Couplet Towers and numerous other climbs in and around the Radiant cirque.

Hard repeat ascents abounded:
- Skywalk (600m, ED1 5.9) on Combatant was climbed three times, as was Kshatrya (735m, D+ 5.8).
- The Wiessner-House (770m, TD+ 5.8 60°) on Waddington had its eighth ascent (Jim Daubert, Bill Enger, Nick Ranicar, and Colin Wooldridge) and the Risse Route (800m, TD+ 5.8 snow/ice to 50°) its third (Jake Larson, Enger, Ranicar, Wooldridge).
- The South Ridge of Serra 2 (1,500m, TD 5.9 45°) almost turned into a trade route, with four or five ascents, two in a day.
- Serra 5 (1,450m, TD 5.8 mixed) received its fifth and sixth ascents (Doug Artman and Tom Reid; Mark Bunker and Colin Haley).
- Sundog (525m, ED1 5.11a) on the Blade (Justin Cassels and Ari Menitove) was repeated.
- And, in a seven-day tour de force, the complete Waddington Traverse (4,000m of ascent, 10km of travel, ED+ to 5.9 to 60°) got its first repeat, by Bunker and Haley.

There were also new routes, some relatively minor and not described here, but many of which were hard rock routes done in excellent style and sometimes astonishing speed.
- Janez Ales and Jia Condon established two new routes on the right side of the east face of Dragonback, the first being five pitches to 5.11, the second two pitches on a subsidiary righthand pillar at 5.11+.
- Andrew Boyd and Derek Flett established a route, with 300m of scrambling and simul-climbing, then six pitches to 5.10+, up crack systems on the west face of Denti form's West Peak. Later, in a fast day-trip from Sunny Knob and return to a bivy at the base, the pair climbed the rounded arête in the center of the west face of the Blade (11 pitches to 5.11 on good rock), with descent via Sundog.
- Justin Cassels, Ari Menitove, and John Simms climbed a new line, Drag Queen, on the southwest pillar of Stiletto, up a striking dihedral right of the existing line. [See report below.] Cassels and Menitove previously climbed the west face of Bicuspid Tower via a good six-pitch 5.11 line.
- Jeff Phillippe and Bret Sarnquist did a new four-pitch 5.10c route on the northeast

face of Phantom Tower. They previously made the second ascent of the Flavelle-Lane Couloir (980m, TD+ 5.8 55° [minor 90°]) on the Northwest Summit of Waddington and continued to the Main Summit by making the second ascent of the loose Northwest Ridge (220m, D 5.7). They also climbed the 630m, D+ South Face of Tiedemann Tower, with a beautiful 5.10c splitter variation on the middle pillar.

• Chris Atkinson and Kevin McLane established Line of Fire on the Northwest Peak of Combatant. This 14-pitch, stonefall-threatened ice line climbs a couloir immediately right of the Skywalk pillar, with bulges to 90° on pitches 11–14. Four pitches of rock to 5.9 then reach the summit.

• John Furneaux and Matt Maddaloni's new route on the southeast side of the Incisor was the highlight of the summer. See individual report below.

It was the most productive season in the Waddington Range since the days when the "old-timers" were knocking off first ascents.

Elsewhere in the Coast Mountains, the finest route of the summer was the Northeast Ridge of Mt. Talchako (3,037m), east of Ape Lake. [See individual report below.]

Chris Barner and Paul Rydeen climbed among the peaks at the head of Gillman Creek. This area south of Doran Creek had only previously been visited by John Clarke, who did several first ascents in 1974. Barner and Rydeen found excellent rock and fine lines, including one nine-pitch 5.9 that they likened to the East Ridge of Bugaboo Spire.

Jordan Peters, Andrew Rennie, and Don Serl walked into the Falls River valley. The highlight of the trip was the third ascent of the fine, and underestimated, 1964 National Pillar on Mt. Winstone (D+, scrambling plus 14 pitches to 5.8). Rennie and Serl later climbed a short but enjoyable rock route on the steep, crack-riddled granite of the southwest face of the Beehive.

In May, Gord Betenia, Drew Brayshaw, and Don Serl made yet another spring foray into the Niut Range. Basing themselves on a lovely 1,950m bench about 3.5km east of Quartz Peak (2,942m), they made a couple of ascents of 2,600m+ summits to the northwest of camp, then tackled Quartz. About 450m of 45°–55° neve on the east face led to a notch on the northeast ridge. This encompassed about 10 ropelengths of entertaining mixed snow and rock, with a few significant slab avalanches being kicked out of pockets on the right (lee) flank. Direct descent back into the access valley not being possible, they made a long descent involving 2.5km of ridge traverse southeast, a short rappel, 1,000m of descent east over another 2.5km to the lake at the head of Whitesaddle Creek, and finally a 350m ascent northwest back to camp. The outing consumed 22 hours (650m, D+ 5.8 M4 45°–55°).

DON SERL, *Alpine Club of Canada, AAC*

Southwest British Columbia (southern Coast Mountains and Canadian Cascades) summary. Although it was a great year for new routes in the Coast Mountains as a whole, 2004 was not particularly newsworthy in the southwest BC region, probably because the good weather took climbers further afield.

The Powell River and Vancouver Island regions were quiet, with some alpine activity ongoing but not much with respect to long routes or new alpine climbs. Squamish saw quite a lot of activity, which is being compiled by Kevin McLane for the latest edition of his guidebook, which should come out in spring 2005.

One of the biggest local alpine routes was the March new route and first winter ascent of a north face route on the remote and impressive Mt. Judge Howay. See details in the individual report, below.

Also in March, Drew Brayshaw and Fern Webb attempted a line on the east face of Arthur Seat Mountain, which had not seen climbers since the 1960s. After retreating in a snowstorm, Brayshaw returned solo in late May and climbed the entire route, which consisted of a system of ridges and gullies. The route length was approximately 1,400m, but only about six pitches featured technical climbing (mostly easy 5th class on loose rock, with a few moves up to 5.9); the remainder of the route was Class 2-4 scrambling on what was described as "good training for the Rockies," in other words, choss and rubble.

In late June, Jeremy Frimer and Cedric Zulauf (Swiss) climbed a prominent six-pitch flake chimney on the right side of the west face of South Nesakwatch Spire, at 5.10 C2, calling it Sublimation. Unaware of the earlier ascent, Craig McGee and partner made an ascent of more or less the same route in July, via a variant right-hand start. Craig returned later in the summer with Jim Martinello to free the line, which went at 5.11+/12- in seven short pitches. The free version is named Fairytales and Fantasies; McGee compared it to the best routes in the Bugaboos in terms of rock quality and purity of line. This brings the number of new routes and variations climbed in the Nesakwatch Spires since 2001 to nearly a dozen; a detailed topo will appear in the next edition of Fred Beckey's Cascade Alpine Guide.

Also in June, Don Serl, Jia Condon, and Janez Ales attempted the direct western arête of the Gnomon, a prominent tower on the Randy Stoltmann Buttress on Mt. Athelstan. After climbing a half dozen pitches to 5.8/9 on runout terrain, they traversed left to join the existing route Lillarete, which they followed to the top of the buttress. A few weeks later Jim Martinello and Damien Kelly made the ascent of the complete line to the summit of the Gnomon. They found several pitches of sparsely protected 5.10 climbing on good rock above the point where the earlier trio moved left. The full ascent of Gnomon Direct to the summit of Randy Stoltmann Buttress makes for a D+ IV 5.10R line that is close to 20 pitches long.

In the Cathedral Park area, Drew Brayshaw and Merran Fahlman climbed a short new route on the southwest face of Matriarch Mountain (PD II 5.8+) during an exploratory visit in June. They returned in late August to attempt a long aid line but were driven away by unseasonable snowstorms. As a consolation prize they visited the Anderson River Range and established a five-pitch PD III 5.8 line, Al-Pika Slabs, on the northeast face of Alpaca Peak, completing a line that Brayshaw had begun with John Simms 10 years previously.

Steven Harng and Reinhard Fabische continued to explore the southern Chehalis Range. On the southeast face of Stonerabbit Peak, they established a 600m line of 4th and easy 5th class slabs, notable for being one of the cleanest alpine climbs in the region. The potential for getting a lot of rock mileage unencumbered by a rope proved attractive, and the climb saw several repeat ascents within the season, a rarity for climbs in the local mountains.

In the Kookipi Creek drainage, Jordan Peters and Michael Layton revisited the large buttress on the unnamed peak on which they had established Back of Beyond in 2002. This time they climbed an eight-pitch line on the right side of the buttress, finding harder climbing and fewer continuous crack systems. Brambles Buttress Sky, named after a Philip Larkin poem, goes at D/D+ III 5.10 A1. A massive forest fire burnt through the Kookipi drainage several weeks later, cutting off access to the peaks and preventing any possibility of repeat ascents for the remainder of the season.

Finally, just before the Indian summer weather ended in early October, Drew Brayshaw, Steven Harng, and Don Serl snuck into a remote area north of the well-known Chehalis area to make the second ascent of Robertson Peak. This summit has had a reputation for inaccessibility since the first climb in 1978, and several parties had been defeated on the approach while attempting the second ascent. A new logging road in Tipella Creek diminishes the remoteness and makes a weekend ascent feasible; the area may see more interest in the near future, as parties attempt to climb before the now-inactive logging road becomes impassible.

DREW BRAYSHAW, *Canada, AAC*

Mt. Talchako, Northeast Ridge. In the last week of July, Fred Beckey (2003 Subaru), Drew Brayshaw (Chilliwack, B.C.), James Nakagami (Woodinville, WA), and I (Redmond, WA) flew from Hagensborg, B.C., with Richard Lapointe of West Coast Helicopters, to the northeastern edge of the Monarch Icefield, not far from the Talchako River and Jacobsen Creek.

We made a brilliant camp among small pines and a pond at 5,400' elevation. Across Jacobsen Creek to the south we had the great scenery of Beelzebub and Ratcliff peaks nearby.

The next morning Fred was still recovering from a back injury and was not able to climb, so Drew and I made an 11-hour roundtrip climb to the eastern of the four summits just north of Talchako Mountain. We then took a rest day.

James, Drew, and I headed out the following morning on the mosquito-inhaling, smoke-ingesting (from a forest fire raging to the east) hike to the bottom of the northeast ridge. This ridge is the most defined feature on the mountain and unmistakable from long distances, and was the obvious objective. We climbed about 16 pitches to a spectacular ledge, where we bivouacked with a view north to the Borealis and Ape peaks, while we had dinner and watched the sun set.

In the morning clouds were gathering. My previous trip's weather experiences told me to get moving. We did, and climbed a pitch of ice, then another on mixed ground, where we used one piton for safety. Between the two snow arêtes on the ridge, this rock section provided one of the more difficult sections. We reached the eastern summit in the early afternoon. After traversing to the central summit, we took a peek at the register and saw only two previous entries. The most recent was by George Whitmore, a member of first team to scale The Nose on El Cap, noting a climb in 1982 where he claimed "Indian priests hurled nude virgins over the northern precipice to propitiate the rain gods." If you say so! I can think of better things to do with nude virgins myself. Shortly after we arrived on top, the clouds started to dissipate and provided us with great views to the south.

The Northeast Ridge Route of Mt. Talchako. *Ray Borbon*

We descended the southwest gully; the peak's original route, then proceeded east back to our camp after crossing a small canyon with a waterfall.

It appears to me there could be a few more routes still worth doing on this peak for those interested. We rate our 1,000m route TD 5.8 60°.

RAY BORBON, *AAC*

Caroline Van Hemert packing next to the Sirocco on a dock on the Homathko River, about two kilometers upriver of Butte Inlet. *Patrick Farrell*

Mt. Waddington, possible variation and bushwhack from the sea. On July 28 Patrick Farrell and I began the approach to Mt. Waddington following the Mundays' first 1926 attempt via Coola Creek. This journey proved to be unusual in several ways. First, we approached overland, unsupported, from the ocean, a route that hasn't been reported since the late 1970s. We planned to approach from the water in a single push, without ferrying loads or receiving air assistance. Also, before arriving at our jump-off point, we sailed from Bellingham, WA in a 27' Catalina [sail boat] up Butte Inlet and the heavily silted Homathko River. At low tide the mudflats surrounding the mouth of the Homathko are too shallow even for a tiny skiff, so we pored over the tide book and hoped for the best, making headway at only a knot against the river's strong current. We moored our boat at a logging camp on the east side of the Homathko River, were shuttled across via skiff, and Chuck Burchill, the resident caretaker, brought us to the mouth of Coola Creek.

From here we planned to follow the recommendation in Don Serl's guidebook to the Waddington Range, which suggests that Scar Creek should be avoided at all costs, leaving Coola Creek as a supposedly favorable alternative. Our experience suggested otherwise [the good Mr. Serl prefers helicopters—Ed.]. We battled head-high devil's club and tightly woven thimbleberry and salmonberry bushes, growing on steep, previously clear-cut slopes. This disturbed Pacific Northwest rainforest proved to be so impenetrable that we took off our packs and rolled them ahead of us to pack down the thorny vegetation so we could climb atop it. At times in the horrendous terrain we made only a mile in over eight hours; sometimes one of us braced the other while trying to scramble up or over downed logs on the thrashed, uneven hillside.

After eventually reaching the glacier, we were unable to follow the suggested route, which skirted the edge of the glacier between the rock and ice, because of significant glacial retreat. The glacier was also far too broken up at its terminus to access, and thus we continued on through the forest and joined the Scar Creek approach route on top of the ridge leading to Pivot Dome. From here, we accessed the Waddington Glacier, and traveled without problems, other than being pinned down by weather at the Agur-Munday col at 9,100'. We dropped to the Corridor Glacier and wrapped around the impressive southwest face of Mt. Waddington to our final high camp, on the Dais Glacier at 7,000'. The next morning, July 4, we began our ascent under a nearly full moon, heading up the Dais Glacier to an alternate couloir line 150 yards to the right of the commonly ascended Dais Couloir. This route would not be visible from camp on Dais Glacier, lying between the Dais Couloir and prominent left-leaning couloirs to the right. Accessing the couloir presented a snow step of half a lead, followed by 650 feet of ice up to 50°. To our knowledge, this variation has not been previously climbed. We summitted the northwest peak that afternoon, under beautiful skies (alpine grade D).

Due to the unfavorable conditions of our approach route, we returned to the Homathko River via Scar Creek, despite the miserable reports we'd heard. The return to the Homathko River down the Scar Creek drainage, while very steep at times, offered much more feasible travel than Coola Creek, and we recommend this approach over the latter. During our 11-day trip we encountered no other people, only a cougar, brown bear, and wolverine.

CAROLINE VAN HEMERT

Mt. Combatant, The Incisor, The Smoke Show. John Furneaux, Paul Bride, and I made base camp on a protected ledge 500 feet above the Tiedemann Glacier on Day Trip Ridge, directly below the unclimbed 2,000' south face of the Incisor. We fixed five pitches, enabling us to work out the free moves on the first 1,000', 500' of which is an overhanging headwall. With one day of rest, John and I left camp at 6 a.m. on July 17 and climbed to our high point halfway up the tower in only two hours, leaving behind four 5.11 pitches, a 5.12b 200' offwidth, and a 5.13 face pitch that I managed with one fall. By 10 a.m. we reached the top of the Incisor, after more 5.10 and 5.11 pitches on gold alpine granite. We had accomplished our goal of a new route on the Incisor. We then linked into Belligerence for another 1,500' of sharp, difficult ridge, called the Jawbone, and climbed 1,000' more vertical rock to Mt. Combatant's summit, which we reached after 11.5 hours. We placed no bolts; several cruxes were protected by bird beaks. We rappelled to a snow shelf and traversed into the Combatant-Waddington col.

The south face of the Incisor is one of the grandest unexplored pillars of perfect granite I have seen. The potential for new hard aid or free routes is vast. The rock is similar to the upper ramparts of El Capitan. A savvy party could link vertical to overhanging features between Belligerence and our route to create something in the 5.11 to 5.12 range. There is at least 500 feet of unclimbed rock separating the two routes. You can put your rock shoes on at our safe and comfortable base camp, and there is ample snow there to fill your water needs. Good hunting!

MATT MADDALONI, Canada

Stiletto, Drag Queen. On July 26 Justin Cassels, Jonny Simms, and I started up a corner system on the Stiletto that Jon and his girlfriend Kinley had explored a few days earlier. Justin and I had also attempted the route, but we ran out of time trying to negotiate 40' of run-out face climbing (read: I was practicing my Elvis impersonation). This third time, though, we were determined. The route followed a striking corner system on the right side of the formation, right of the existing line on the southwest pillar, for 3.5 pitches of clean, sharp 5.10-5.11+ climbing. Exiting the corner proved to be the mental crux of the route, and requiring 40' of basically

Justin Cassels stemming on Pitch 3 of Drag Queen, the Stiletto. *Ari Menitove*

unprotected but brilliant 5.10- climbing. We resorted to aid for 12' in a steep corner, likely free-climbable at 5.12, and bivied on a huge ledge. We finished the next day via stacks of awesome 5.9 to 5.11- cracks separated by spacious belay ledges. We feel that this is an excellent route, with aesthetic climbing and decent rock. We placed no bolts, but left slings, stoppers, and a few pins on the rappels. About 2,000', V 5.11+R A2.

ARI MENITOVE, *AAC*

Stiletto, showing Drag Queen. *Ari Menitove*

Climbing the ski-descent route on Mt. Judge Howay.
Chris Kettles

The ascent and ski-descent route on Mt. Judge Howay.
Chris Kettles

Mt. Judge Howay, north face and ski descent. At the beginning of March, Scott Murray (U.S.) and I climbed and skied the north face of Mt. Judge Howay. Judge Howay is located in the Coast Mountains in Mount Judge Howay Provincial Park, which is directly north of Stave Lake and the town of Mission, British Columbia. The route was spotted by Scott in mid-February while flying his Cessna from Abbotsford to Pemberton; he noticed unusually large amounts of snowfall on the peak and speculated about the possibility of a ski line down the north face. On February 26 we flew a recon flight and confirmed the existence of a 6,000' climbing-skiing line. On February 28 we flew in by helicopter to northeast of the park and landed in a clearing near the river. We followed the creek up to the base of the north face, where we established a camp. We started climbing at 3 a.m. the next morning, March 1, soloing the route to the summit and skiing it in 11 hours total. The route begins in the Patterson-Bauer Couloir, between the two summits of the Judge, then veers left up a hidden ramp cutting across the north face of the main summit, joining the top of the 1991 route Weenies on Trial, which climbs the Judge's north buttress. The most difficult climbing is at the top of the ramp, requiring technical moves. The top of the ramp was the crux, and was the one section we rappelled on our descent. We skied the rest, with hard conditions and slopes in excess of 60°. This was the first winter ascent of the north face, the first ascent of the route, and the first time the mountain had been skied. Commitment level grade IV, climbing difficulty II/III.

CHRIS KETTLES, *Canada*

SELKIRK MOUNTAINS

Crumble Tower, When Hairy Met Scary; and Half Dome, Irregular Route. On August 9 Graham Rowbotham (Canada) and I made the first ascent of the limestone tower immediately south of Waldorf Tower in the Remillard Group of the Selkirk Mountains. We climbed the northwest buttress, which involved much face climbing on friable limestone with poor protection. Ten meters left of the toe of the buttress, the first pitch involved hairy climbing on decomposing rock in a prominent left-facing corner (5.9R). Next came the crux pitch: a 50m scary adventure into virtually crack-free, crumbly limestone (5.9+R/X). Six more pitches (to 5.7), generally following a chimney/gully left of the buttress crest, led to a shoulder below the final headwall. Beginning from a sandy ledge, the ninth pitch had neither a belay anchor nor any protection for the first 30m (5.8X). A final pitch led to the summit of this previously unnamed, unclimbed tower. We propose the name Crumble Tower and called our route When Hairy Met Scary (10 pitches, 5.9+R/X). We made five rockfall-threatened rappels down the north and west side of the peak to a bombarded muddy scree cone. Two days later, we climbed the northwest face of the granitic peak fittingly named Half Dome. Just right of the Death Slabs, we followed a faint buttress for three pitches (to 5.8) to where the terrain steepened. Three pitches (to 5.10a) led to a right-trending ramp, which we followed for two more pitches (5.7) to its abrupt end. The complex crux pitch followed thin cracks in an exposed setting (5.10c). We climbed another ramp up and right, curling onto the west face, to a multiple-pitch offwidth crack. I attempted to climb it but backed off, as I lacked sufficiently large protection or courage. We finished via three pitches of face and slab climbing 100m right of the offwidth (to 5.10a). We named our line The Irregular Route (13 pitches, 5.10c).

JEREMY FRIMER, *Canada*

Mt. MacDonald, Little Face, Prime Rib to summit ridge. Characterized by long, continuous rock ribs, numerous avalanche paths, frozen waterfalls in winter, and two pointy peaks, it's surprising how little traffic the north face of Mt. MacDonald has seen. Its lesser summit, known as the Little Face or Little MacDonald, has a particularly steep triangular wall. In 1974 the Waterman cousins opened a direttissima on the face in a three and a half day effort, but there had not been another successful party since. One obvious rib, just left of center on the face and more or less in a plumb line from a nipple on the ridge left of the summit, stands out, getting morning and afternoon light on long summer days.

On June 26 Squamish hardman Colin Moorhead and I left Golden at 3 a.m. with old Metallica blaring, and were approaching the rib by 4. An hour later we were back at the car, defeated by the raging Cannaught Creek. We started again, found a crossing, and two hours later were 2,100' above the road, at the base of the face. Three 5.8 rope-stretchers with a little simul-climbing put us below the first amazing pitch. An overhanging Yosemite-style squeeze chimney led to a splitter corner of sustained 5.10 finger and hand jams that led to a terrace where the rib juts out from the steep headwall above. From here we had a good view of the upper face and our intended line. The next two pitches were obvious: the left side of a 90m pinnacle, followed by a vertical blank face. With the weather looking marginal, we proceeded anyway despite the possibility of being dead-ended and getting wet. Sure enough, as I started leading

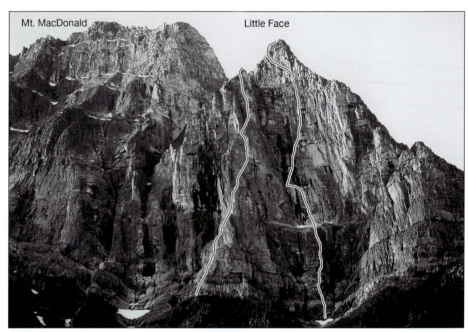

Mt. MacDonald and the Little Face. Left: Prime Rib (550m, 5.11b, Moorhead-Walsh, 2004). Right: North Face (600m, 5.8 A3, Waterman-Waterman, 1974). *Jon Walsh*

the sixth pitch, the rain began, but the 5.9 stemming and hand-jamming up this left-facing corner was too good to quit. As Colin reached my belay, the rain eased off.

We waited a few minutes for the stone to dry and continued. Fortunately, the quartzite was featured with just enough incut edges, as pitch seven was the key to the route. Colin found a diagonal line up this face, pounding in blades and Arrows for pro along the way, mostly from 5.10 stances. We left three pins in place in key spots for future ascents, although the crux section required a 20', 5.11a runout on small face holds. It was the only place, other than a few rappel stations, that required pitons. Five more pitches of sustained, technical, and exposed

Jon Walsh leading Pitch 4 on Prime Rib, Mt. MacDonald Little Face. *Colin Moorhead*

climbing brought us to the nipple on the ridge. Lightning was striking the neighboring peaks as we fired the last two pitches, but rain held off until we started rappelling. We rappelled our route, except that the final four raps are to climber's left of the ascent line. Eleven rappels, and we were back at our packs, tired, wet, and relieved. On the second-to-last rappel, the ropes stuck, and we had to climb and downclimb an extra pitch of wet slab in the dark: a two-hour exhausting task, given the state our bodies were in. With dying headlamps we groveled down to the highway through wet slide alder and arrived at the car 22 hours after leaving.

This was one of the best climbing days either of us had in 2004, and we highly recommend our route to others. Rack: 60m ropes, a double set of cams from #0 TCU to #3 Camalot, 1 #3.5 and 1 #4 Camalot, 1 set of nuts, 5 pitons. All belays are on good ledges.

With the route set for rappelling, competent climbers armed with the beta should shave several hours off our time—12 hours up and down should be enough, plus the approach. The ultimate, though, for a fit party might be to link Prime Rib, the Little MacDonald summit, the Northwest Ridge of Mt. MacDonald, and back to the car, in a day.

JON WALSH, *Canada*

PURCELL MOUNTAINS

BUGABOOS

Various free ascents. In July and August Nick Martino, Cedar Wright, and I freed two unrepeated aid lines on the Minaret of South Howser. On both the Italian Pillar (V 11+) and the Southwest Pillar (V 12- R/X) we created new pitches that wander from the original aid lines. Climbing in a team of three was interesting, with the leader clipping two 7.5mm ropes into each piece, and the seconds gingerly free-climbing, each on his own small line. Making first free ascents on such an inspiring, clean-cut, Half Dome-sized feature with two great friends was top-notch excitement. We climbed both lines "team free" (everyone free-climbing everything, no jugs), no falls, in 14 and 16 hours respectively, camp-to-camp.

We'd attempted the Southwest Pillar the year before, finding the first two pitches to be long, butt-cheek-clenching experiences. The route looks like a continuous 2,000' hand crack from camp, but it was a continuously hideous, hard-to-protect, flaring butt crack. It took us two years and some fixed copperheads to overcome.

The Italian Pillar, with wild but well-protected roof pulling, a dramatic "golden groove" crux last pitch (this variation to the original route goes up the middle of multiple parallel, arching cracks, with stemming and jamming between grooves), and a stone's throw from a five-star base camp, could become one of the more sought-after climbs in the Bugaboos. On the initial attempt by Cedar and I, we continued on through torrential rain and fog, fighting "team free" to the last pitch, before seeing the eyes of god and making a wrong turn. With dry rock and three people, we triple simul-climbed) for 500' and found the true finish. On both ascents we continued past the summit of the Minaret and along the 900' summit ridge (steps to 5.10) to the summit of the South Howser Tower itself.

Nick and Cedar also made the first free ascent of Lost Feather Pinnacle, which went in a day at 5.10 and involved a 5.9 down jump that was "definitely X" for the follower.

RENAN OZTURK, *AAC*

Duncan Burke on the sixth pitch of Back At Bob's, Lost Feather Pinnacle. *Chris Weidner*

Lost Feather Pinnacle, Back at Bob's. From August 11-20 Duncan Burke and I enjoyed excellent weather and conditions in Bugaboo Provincial Park. Driving north from Colorado, our main goal was to climb a new route in The Pigeon Feathers group, located east and slightly south of the Howser Massif. The Pigeon Feathers drew our attention for several reasons: walls up to 1,000' high that are virtually untouched, the low-to-medium commitment level of the routes, and their proximity to base camp.

Duncan and I crossed the East Creek Basin Glacier early on August 16 and arrived at the base of the east face of Lost Feather Pinnacle just as it caught the day's first light. An obvious, left-angling chimney system split the face, offering three long pitches of mostly moderate climbing with a steep 5.10a start, a few 5.9 boulder problems, and an overhanging 5.10b offwidth. We arrived at a huge ledge, where we unroped and moved the belay beneath a 5.10a squeeze chimney, the only portion of our line that it shares with the original route on the peak, called Lost Feather. Duncan continued up a vertical fist crack to a sloping ledge beneath the much steeper half of our route.

The overhanging triple cracks quickly turned into an aid pitch, which required every placement to be cleaned of lichen and flakes of granite. I made steady progress until I encountered The Guillotine, a 20-foot-tall flake that stopped my heart when it shifted as I placed a cam behind it. I eventually climbed to a tiny perch with bomber gear, beneath a soaring dihedral visible from camp in the East Creek Basin. The sun was sinking, our lead rope was stuck behind a flake 100' below, and we had no bivy gear. We retreated and returned two days later.

We quickly climbed to our high point. In morning shade Duncan led the dihedral, again in aiders due to the ubiquitous moss and lichen, which prohibited gear placements without extensive cleaning. To our delight, the intimidating feature went quickly at C1, and would be an incredible free pitch if cleaned. An offwidth roof nearly 1,000' above the glacier provided a tasty challenge, followed by overhanging fists, steep hands, a lower-angled squeeze chimney, and the summit.

We named the route Back At Bob's (7 pitches, IV 5.11 A2) in memory of Bob Enagonio of Canmore, Alberta who perished on a ski traverse from Rogers Pass to the Bugaboos in May. Bob's presence will always be felt in the mountains of Canada, especially in his favorite range, the Bugaboos.

CHRIS WEIDNER, *AAC*

CANADIAN ROCKIES

Canadian Rockies, summary. The big news of the summer of 2004 in the Canadian Rockies was a visit in July by the German soloist Frank Jourdan. He warmed up on the Greenwood-Jones (IV 5.8 A1) and the Supercouloir (IV 5.8) on the north faces of Mts. Temple and Deltaform, respectively, before moving on to the remote Mt. Assiniboine. There, he made the likely second ascent of the Cheesmond-Dick (V 5.9 A2) on the huge east face; a feat made especially bold by the summer heat and resulting intense rockfall.

Rockfall also marked a fine attempt in early August on the unrepeated Cheesmond-Blanchard a.k.a. the North Pillar (VI 5.10d A2) of North Twin. Chris Brazeau and Ian Welsted bivouacked below the 1,500m face, intent on a one-day ascent. Things did not pan out quite as planned, but by the end of first day they reached the Traverse of the Chickens ledge below the crux headwall, halving the time of the first-ascent team. Owing to a hot, dry summer, rockfall was especially intense, and only four pitches into the second day a falling stone broke Welsted's arm, dictating retreat. A stuck zip line and a chopped lead rope reduced the two to 25m rappels, and they spent another two nights on the mountain, leaving their entire rack before reaching bottom. Prior to heading up North Twin, Welsted had soloed the Emperor Ridge of Mt. Robson in a 33-hour trip car-to-car, including eight hours spent sitting out a whiteout on the summit.

On a more moderate note, in late July Dave Marra, Dana Ruddy, and Tom Schnugg made the first ascent of King's Couloir (III), an aesthetic 600m snow and ice route on the northwest face of Mt. Belanger, in the backcountry of the Fryatt Creek valley. In August Jason Thompson and Colin Woolridge made the first traverse of the three summits of the remote and rarely frequented South Goodsir (III 5.4), Goodsir Centre, and North Goodsir (III 5.4). During the same month, taking advantage of exceptionally dry conditions, Tim Haggerty, Ruddy, and Raphael Slawinski made the first car-to-car one-day ascent of Mt. Alberta, climbing the Japanese route (V 5.5) in 18 hours roundtrip.

On the pure rock climbing front, Shep Steiner recruited Scott Milton to make the first free ascent of Verstiegenheit (8 pitches, 5.12c) on Yamnuska. Steiner started the route eight years ago, drilling the bottom four pitches on lead and the top four on rappel. He had made a number of attempts at freeing the route, but until last summer all were repulsed by hard climbing, bad rock, and a high fear factor. Verstiegenheit now stands as the most demanding multi-pitch pure rock climb in the range.

A wet fall resulted in never-before-seen smears appearing everywhere, from Kananaskis Country to the Icefields Parkway, precipitating a flurry of first ascents. In November Chris Delworth, Dave Edgar, and Eamonn Walsh climbed The Silmarillion (150m, WI6X) up Storm Creek, linking thin ice and anemic pillars. The tireless Guy Lacelle, accompanied by a variety of partners, climbed two new routes in the cirque between Castle and Protection mountains: the aptly named Paradis Perdu (170 m, WI5), with Audrey Gariepy, Mathieu Audibert, and Heather Slowinski, and The Wicked Witch of the West (190m, M6R/X WI6R), with Rich Marshall. Other than Lacelle, no one was willing to make the four-to-five-hour approach more than once. Farther north, on Mt. Wilson, Jon Walsh and Paul McSorley attempted the often-looked-at line of ice in a bowl up and right of the popular Ice Nine. Climbing four pitches of rock the first day, they left ropes fixed. Returning the next day, they climbed the remainder of the route to establish Rivers of Babylon (480m, M6+ WI5+R), one of the finest creations of the season.

Blurring the line between waterfall and alpine climbing, Valeriy Babanov and Slawinski put up two new routes in December. Riders on the Storm (500m, WI4+) on the east face Mt. Sarrail in Kananaskis Country ascended a ribbon of snow-ice over three tiers to snowfields below the summit block. Darkness and bad weather prevented the pair from continuing to the summit. This striking but avalanche-prone line had been attempted in the fall of 1995 by Barry Blanchard and Mark Twight, who retreated in a storm after a couple of pitches. Farther north, Babanov and Slawinski established Aurora (600m, WI6) on the north face of Mt. Amery. From a camp below the face, classic north face terrain led to a spectacular finish: four pitches of intricate ice climbing up a series of pillars weeping from the edge of the summit seracs. In Slawinski's opinion, the final cascade stands out as one of the most beautiful waterfalls in the Rockies.

In February visiting Swiss climbers Michael Boos and Pierre Darbellay ventured onto the north face of the White Pyramid, home of the notorious unrepeated Reality Bath, established by Twight and Randy Rackliff in 1988. Although Reality Bath appeared to be formed, the seracs overhanging the route looked, if possible, even more threatening than usual. Instead Boos and Darbellay climbed a new and slightly safer line to the right, Dread Circus (500m, WI5+). Of note is the fact that Boos flew into Calgary the evening before dispatching the climb in a 17-hour effort car-to-car.

On the full-on alpine scene, in November Scott Semple, Greg Thaczuk, and Eamonn Walsh made the second ascent of Striving for the Moon (1,400m, WI6) on the east face of Mt. Temple, taking over 36 hours in a continuous push car-to-car. Semple and Thaczuk attempted the route earlier in the month, but after climbing through the technical sections, floundered in bottomless snow on the "easier" east ridge. In February a high pressure system descended on the range, spurring further action. Semple, Slawinski and Walsh took advantage of the fine weather and snow conditions to make the first winter ascent of Mt. Alberta. With even steep rock plastered in snow, they settled for the Japanese Route which, as a consequence of tactics which resembled unionized labor practices more than single-push alpinism, they climbed with one bivouac on the summit ridge. It was Slawinski's fourth time to the summit in as many years. Later the same week, Rob Owens and Mike Verwey made the third ascent of The Wild Thing (VI 5.9 A3 WI4) on the northeast face of Mt. Chephren. The two spent two nights and three full days on the route, finding that even with the full arsenal of new mixed techniques the route remained a serious challenge. In an eerie reenactment of Ward Robinson's misadventure on the first ascent, Owens took a long fall while leading the crux A3 chimney, losing one of his tools.

Unsettled weather and the departure of many of the activists to destinations ranging from Alaska to the Middle East meant a quiet end to the season. Of note was Babanov and Slawinski's first ascent of an often looked at but surprisingly moderate line on Mt. Andromeda. M31 (IV M3/4) ascends snowfields to the right of the classic Andromeda Strain to gain a hanging snow ramp, topping out on the very summit of the mountain.

RAPHAEL SLAWINSKI, *Canada, AAC*

Mt. Belanger, King's Couloir. Dave Marra and I were tossing back a few pints of Canada's finest at the Downstream Pub in Jasper and soon were jabbering about picking off a new midsummer ice route. When Dana Ruddy, fresh from a jaunt up Mt. Fryatt, came bounding into the bar with a digital camera and a shit-eating grin, our mission materialized. He showed us what appeared to be a stellar northwest line up Mt. Belanger (3,120m, immediately west of Fryatt). The adrenaline drip commenced.

The 30km approach needed trimming, and a portage across the Athabasca was our solution. We left Jasper at noon on July 22 with a borrowed, battered canoe strapped

Cruising up the King's Couloir on Mt. Belanger. *Tom Schnugg*

King's Couloir on Mt. Belanger. *Tom Schnugg*

to the roof of Dave's red beater wagon. Upon putting in, we discovered the vessel barely big enough for two boy scouts, and had to make two crossings. The river gods had their laugh: with little canoeing experience, shirts and shoes off, cameras in ziplock bags, we were beset by fast-flowing, frothy-frigid water that leapt furiously, filling the boat, and splashing us like a scalding cup of java in the crotch. Primal strokes, profanity, and hysterical laughter ferried us twice to the far side. The adventure had commenced.

A biblical squadron of mosquitoes escorted us beyond the Fryatt Hut to our base below the north face of Belanger. We powered down canned chili, and at 11 p.m. under summer twilight, surrendered to the proboscis onslaught and dove into our bivies. Four hours later we were en route to the northwest face under starry, windless skies. We trekked northwest through upward-sloping meadows onto a friendly moraine, which led to an obvious col. We continued toward Belanger until we had a complete view of the northwest glacier. Around 4:30 a.m. we spotted a short, steep talus descent from the col. This brought us to the edge of the northwest glacier proper and avoided a north face pocket glacier. We roped up and arrived by 6 a.m. at the base of the couloir.

The ice route is a right-leaning Y-shaped feature, with the lower section and the left upper arm facing northwest and receiving no sun. The aesthetics of this climb are matched by objective hazards, including rockfall and sloughing snow and ice high on the route itself, especially from the upper-right sun-kissed couloir. The first five to seven pitches consist of straightforward 55° ice. Given the playfulness of the gods, we stayed right, thereby protecting us from surprises they might throw our way from the hidden upper-right couloir. The crux came shortly after we entered the upper left section of the Y: 5m of vertical ice through a narrow gully. Above, we found a sustained slope of three to five pitches, 60°-65° at first but gradually getting steeper. There was no cornice, and we exited onto the ridge. The ridge was of a wide, low-angle snow ramp, leading to a 5m fourth-class rock climb to the snowy summit plateau. Royal views in all directions greeted us at the summit. Our spectacular but safe ascent to a place of such calm magnificence filled our "Why I climb" tanks full.

The obvious descent is the regular route down the southeast ridge. But we wanted to check out some other lines from the glacier below where we started, so we descended our ascent route, starting around 10 a.m., and were down to the glacier by 12:30. We made it back to the canoe just after sunset and crossed the river under starry skies. Despite the long approach, King's Couloir (600m), with its sustained line, objective hazards, and summit views, should be an absolute classic.

TOM SCHNUGG, *AAC*

Mt. Alberta, Japanese Route, first winter ascent. Ever since first scampering across Mt. Alberta's (3,619m) precipitous summit ridge, I had wondered what it would be like in winter. As the season progressed, I kept track of weather and avalanche forecasts. By mid-February, 2005, both were exceptionally good.

It was afternoon by the time Scott Semple, Eamonn Walsh, and I finally sorted gear, drove up the Parkway, and stepped into our skis. Winter transformed the familiar approach up Woolley Creek, the wide streambed seeming hemmed in by the snowy conifers. But travel was pleasant, until we came to Woolley Shoulder. The slope leading to it was blown clear, and we teetered up frozen scree, arms aching from poling. Daylight was fading when we crested the col, and all we could see of Alberta was a pale, cloud-enshrouded shape to the west.

Mt. Alberta, Japanese Route in winter. *Raphael Slawinski*

Not having had a proper look in the evening, we left the choice of route for breakfast. This gave us an excuse to sleep in. The cold lilac glow of a cloudless dawn revealed a mountain completely plastered in snow, even the headwall on the Northeast Ridge. We discussed the conditions, and decided on the Japanese Route. On February 19, as the sun's first rays lit up the summit, we were skiing down to the base of the east face. Recent avalanches had pounded the gullies and snowfields, and we booted up the debris, making a beeline for the Elephants' Asses. The air was cold but the sun was out, and at one point I found myself swinging tools clad in a T-shirt. After lunch on a snow fluting below the Asses, we continued soloing up the Japanese Gully, still mostly on snow, with small ice steps thrown in for variety. Just below the ridge we roped up, turned right, and weaved our way along the crest. Eamonn kept a straight face as he told Scott that if one of us fell off, the others should jump off the opposite side. "Is that safe?" Scott asked in disbelief. I was both pleased and disappointed at the absence of the expected double cornices. The ridge made up for it with delicate knife edges that had us shuffling sideways like crabs, snowed-up rock steps where crampons skated on black limestone, and a bitter wind that arced the rope over the east face and at every step whipped our faces with ice crystals.

The evening sun was painting the clouds a delicate pink when at last we stood on top. With the wind knifing through the parkas we had donned over all our other layers, we did not stay long, just long enough to thaw Scott's frozen chin. Then we turned around and headed down. A small scoop half an hour from the summit offered one of the few windless spots along the ridge, and we gratefully accepted its shelter for the night. Three people in a Bibler made for a tight squeeze, especially as one of them was Eamonn, but we were warm. It snowed during the night, and in the morning we woke surrounded by mist. Not until we were below the Elephants' Asses did we walk into sunshine, and realized that Alberta's summit cap was the only cloud in the sky. Back at the hut we decided to stay one more night on this the magical side of Woolley Shoulder. The following day we were back at the road in a mere three hours; the adventure was over. Or rather, this adventure was over. Though unseen beyond the Shoulder, Alberta is still there, beckoning.

RAPHAEL SLAWINSKI, *Canada, AAC*

Mt. Amery, Aurora. Mt. Amery (3,329m) is not the first mountain you notice while driving up the Icefields Parkway. But if you drive that road enough times, your eye will eventually be drawn to the broad stratified sweep of its north face, capped by a long hanging glacier. In winter two smears of ice form on the edges of the summit icecap. The left one peters out over a huge roof, but the right one usually forms completely. While the final cascade is definitely the attraction, the alpine face leading to it is not devoid of interest.

I filed the ice smear on Amery's north face away for future reference, but it was not until 2004 that I did something about it. Will Gadd and I made the half-day approach to the cirque below the face on a brilliant early April afternoon. While air temperatures were pleasant, one drawback of the coming spring was the open Alexandra

The Aurora route on Mt. Amery. *Raphael Slawinski*

Valeri Babanov starting up the first of four pitches on the final cascade on the Aurora route. Above were two pitches of WI6 and one of WI5. *Raphael Slawinski*

River, which necessitated hilarious barefoot crossings with a ski in each hand for balance. The following morning there was still no breath of wind; the only movement in the entire landscape was the unceasing spindrift down our chosen line. After waiting in vain for it to stop, Will finally just started up. Much of the ice was missing or detached, making for hard traditional mixed climbing. When I joined him at the belay, which for lack of a better spot was in the midst of the chilly torrent, we had both had enough. Leaving an expensive anchor, we ran away.

But I did not forget the view from the bowl below the face, with the frozen waterfall high above catching the last rays of the sun. Shortly after Christmas I went back, this time accompanied by Valeri Babanov. The approach was as long as I remembered, but this time the river was frozen. We camped in the shelter of the highest boulder, and at first light, around eight o'clock in December, I stood again at the base of the first pitch. There was more ice than in the spring, but it was steep and snowy, and picks and front points kept shearing through the insubstantial medium. Once over the bottom crux, we made good time up easier terrain, moderate ice pitches alternating with snow gullies and short mixed steps. A long traverse left took us to the base of the final column, an intricate structure of pillars and balconies plastered to the black rock of the summit headwall. I blithely estimated it at a couple of pitches. A couple of pitches later, as the violet light of winter dusk faded to black, I was belayed in a small cave halfway up the waterfall. We had come too far to turn around, so we continued into the night, linking overhanging chandeliers by headlamp.

Two hours after sundown I finally stood on low-angle ice, with the summit snow slopes stretching upward into the darkness. Moonlight glistened on seracs to my left, bathing an already weird scene in an otherworldly light; northern lights flashed in the sky. A keen west wind whipped across the landscape, and I retreated into the hood of my jacket. When Valeri rejoined me, we quickly agreed to declare the route finished, wind and cold winning out over magic and beauty. And so, foregoing a nighttime walk to the summit, we slid down the first of many rappels, eventually reaching camp well after midnight.

RAPHAEL SLAWINSKI, *Canada, AAC*

Mt. Wilson, Rivers of Babylon. On November 26 and 27 Paul McSorley and I climbed a new nine-pitch route on Mt. Wilson, in the bowl between Mixed Monster and Ice Nine. Rivers of Babylon is the central of three ice flows. The climbing is sustained, technical, and fun the entire way. It was also delicate and often run-out, requiring extra focus. For four pitches we climbed mostly rock, traversing left and right on weaknesses through the overhanging buttress, to gain the thin flow. The flow provided excellent thin ice and mixed climbing for another five pitches. Good screws were rare to nonexistent, but tool placements came easy. The rock is generally excellent by Rockies standards. We placed no bolts. We fixed three ropes on the first four pitches on day one, descended to Rampart Creek Hostel for the night, and the next day ascended our ropes and climbed the rest of the route. A one-day ascent would be an impressive feat, but doable by a strong party. The route is probably best earlier in the season and will be extremely dangerous when the avalanche hazard increases. Rack: 1 set of nuts, 2 sets of cams from 0.5" to 3.5" and 1 #4 Camalot, a few pitons, screws, 70m ropes recommended. 480m (400+m vertical), VI M6+ WI5+R.

JON WALSH, *Canada*

Mt. Assiniboine, Cheesmond-Dick second ascent solo, and various ascents. In July I traveled for the third time to Canada. In spite of bad conditions on the alpine faces I picked off a couple of good routes. After installing a bivy cache at Eiffel Lake I succeeded in climbing the Greenwood-Jones (V 5.8 A1, ca. 1400m, 1969) on the north face of Mt. Temple, then, after a bivouac at the cache, the Supercouloir (IV 5.8, Lowe-Jones, ca. 1200m, 1973) on Mt. Deltaform (the final pitches of which are especially brittle). Two and a half days later, when I was feeling more confident with this type of rock again, I headed to the glacier at the base of the east face of Assiniboine (the longest "20km" hike I ever did). This impressive mixed face was not in good shape either. After resting at the base I started climbing the Cheesmond-Dick (V 5.9 A2, ca. 1200m, 1982) at 2 a.m. I gained height pretty fast, but around 8:30 a.m. I got stuck just below the start of the upper, steeper sections because of intense rockfall. I searched for shelter and waited for dropping temperatures. At 4 p.m. (!) the rockfall abated and I kept going as fast as I could. In some sections, especially the steeper waterfall pitches, the snow and ice were almost gone. Therefore I was forced to climb very tricky, scary, loose, and wet mixed terrain with sketchy pro. A ramp system and a traverse to the left leads to a steep rock face which is usually the crux, but, compared to the lower sections, the rock was not too bad. Using free, aid, and dry-tool techniques I reached the easier exit slopes. A final, vertical, ice-and-soft-snow pitch through the cornice at the top made me shit my pants. The face took me 13 hours to climb (with the stop, 21 hours). Another longtime dream was fulfilled.

After some rest days and a 12-day visit to the remote Waddington Range, where I managed to solo three routes (the Flavelle-Lane route [980m, TD+ 55° 5.8] on Waddington; a possible new ca 650m, 5.9+ route left of Perseverance, on the south face of Combatant; and the Southwest Face [1,450m, TD+ 5.8] on Tiedemann), I headed farther north to the main goal of the trip: the 2,000-meter unclimbed northwest face of Devil's Thumb, the ultimate challenge for a fast solo push. From Petersburg I flew in, highly excited to look at the face, but what a mess: there was no snow and ice at all, only very broken and chossy-looking rock (especially in the lower part). I realized that there is no way to climb this vertical quarry. I left for Canada, where I sat in my car near the river ready to start another attempt on the north face of Mt. Alberta (which I had attempted in 1994, failing below the upper rock band, which scared me too much at the time)—but I hesitated. The last weeks had hurt my knees and back painfully. The stress of being alone in a lot of scary situations had blown my mind, and I decided to not go: I was not motivated or calm enough any more. I started the car, anxious to get back to life, to my friends, to share my beloved red wine…and realizing that once again, I had been lucky to survive.

FRANK JOURDAN, *Pforzheim, Germany*

Adapted from Alpinist *magazine, issue #9*

Greenland

EAST GREENLAND

North of Scorsbysund, Liverpool Land exploratory ski-moun-taineering. We aimed to investigate the ski potential of the coastal peaks of northeast Greenland. Liverpool Land was chosen for its interesting geography, high latitude, and relative accessibility via Constable Point airport. Our team of Phil Wickens, Keith Walton, Grant Jeffery, and I reached the peaks by dog-sled on the sea ice (two days), and made the return journey unsupported on ski through a chain of mountain passes punctuated by peaks climbed as day trips. We regularly moved the base camp with pulks (sledges) and carried all supplies for two weeks, with a further two weeks'

worth of food stashed on the way in. Our expedition lasted from April 21 to May 22.

The region is characterized by broad, flat glaciers leading up to a small ice cap, through which the peaks rise very steeply up to 1,430m. We found the snow pack to be very reliable, with only occasional surface sloughs, very little evidence of avalanche, and virtually no open crevasses. The glacier toes however are unstable and extremely tall. We suffered two weeks of very windy and unsettled conditions.

In the first fortnight, we ascended peaks around the Emmanuel Glacier, which included Pts 1,030m, 1,282m, 920m, 1,180m and 820m. All were achieved in good conditions and as day trips. Ascents were generally easier from the east, with some steep and icy sections. There was often a choice of ski descent lines including some enormous couloirs. Later we pushed passes between the Kolding, Age Nielsons, Grete and Hans Glaciers, and back to Scorsbysund, in some terrible conditions.

The area has great potential for new peaks and descent lines, although records are sketchy perhaps due to their low height. In good weather, many climbs could be made in a short time from a mobile base camp. Constable Point now has regular flights throughout the winter, making access to this area easy and costs relatively low. Contact Martin Munck at Nanu Travel (nanu@greennet.gl), the only outfitters based in Ittoqqortoormiit and run by local people. View our photos at http://www.offwidth.co.uk/greenland/gallery.shtml.

JEREMY THOMSON, *United Kingdom*

Knud Rasmussens Land, first ascents. Four British climbers, Geoff Bonney, Rosie Goolden, Mark Humpherys, and I, made nine first ascents from the Griffith Pugh Glacier. The team based itself on the glacier at 69° 10.741' N, 29° 9.029' W approximately 40km from the coast. Conditions throughout their stay in June were perfect and daylight uninterrupted.

The highlight of the expedition was the first ascent of Mt. Kellas (2,884m) via the narrow North Ridge (Alpine D). Following a short ski approach from their second camp, the team encountered typical conditions for the area with near perfect ice and névé interspersed with loose, friable rock. The narrow summit ridge gave stunning views of the ice cap to the north and an endless array of unclimbed peaks to the south. Other ascents included: One Down (2,750m); Pt Alice (2,316m); Kathleen (2,746m); Pearl (2,673m); Malago (2,788m); Pt Whymper (2,546m) and Gordon's Choice (2,680m).

This area has been something of a preserve for British climbers, who have visited the mountains of Knud Rasmussens Land five times in the last three years. However last year's expedition note that there is still enormous potential for first ascents in the lower grades.

JEREMY WINDSOR, *United Kingdom*

Watkins Mountains, two possible first ascents close to Gunnsbjorns Fjeld. Named by the Vikings "Hvitserk" or "White Shirt," Gunnbjørns Fjeld stands as the Arctic's highest mountain. Its 3,693m summit is not technically difficult to reach, but a good degree of mountaineering skill is still required. Our summit day was clear and cold, allowing stunning views of the surrounding Watkins Mountains and the distant Polar Plateau. I had only been in Greenland for three days and already I was so high. I could feel inside me that this was going to be another momentous trip.

The possibly virgin ridge of peak 3,535m (GPS: 3,421m) near Gunnbjørns Fjeld. *Nigel Vardy*

We then climbed two virgin peaks in two days—one ascending a long exposed ridge and another through deep snow before returning to base camp. The peaks are situated just south of Gunnbjorns Fjeld, one marked 3,535m, and the other a short distance to the north west and situated on the south west ridge of Gunnsbjorn Fjeld. We GPS heighted them at 3,421m (N68° 53.412' W29° 52.691'—via west ridge) and 3,265m (N68° 53.440' W29° 51.505'—via east ridge) respectively. The lower peak is not marked on any map. Few people have the opportunity to climb a virgin peak—to stand where no one else has been before and survey all below them. It's a wonderful experience and for me a very personal one. Being that first person does not fill me with pride or prowess, more an inner peace where I can find my soul again. Perhaps climbing itself is one of the world's great soul searchers. Other climbers who summited these peaks: Phil Poole, guide, and Liz Roche, UK, and Ulrich Goerlach and Wolfgang Schaub, Germany.

NIGEL VARDY, *United Kingdom*

Editor's Note: Claims that these two tops were previously unclimbed arise solely from the fact that they have not been registered with the Danish Polar Institute. Parties have traveled between them (crossing between GBF and Cone) since 1988 at least, but as they are rather more "bumps" than summits, it is possible they have been ignored until now. The team later traveled east to the Silk Road Glacier and made the second ascent of Outpost (2,848m).

Watkins Mountains, first ascents from the Fleece Glacier. Toward the end of May a British expedition comprising Jim Hall, Bob Kerr, Ros Murray and Rae Pritchard was landed on the Wooley Glacier at 2,400m and from here explored a previously unnamed side glacier to the east. This is the next glacier south of the Silk Road and it seemed appropriate to name it Fleece. Three probable first ascents were made: Pt 3,020m (dubbed Afternoon Peak), a subsidiary summit to the north west of Midnight Peak (first climbed by Scott Umpleby's five-person expedition in 1999). The grades of each were not much more than Alpine F and the climbs completed in ski mountaineering boots. Unsuccessful attempts were then made of the attractive Pt 2,725m further east down the glacier, and Julia (3,455m, the 7th highest peak in Greenland), which lies on the west side of the Wooley. Some of the team's original unclimbed objectives from the Wooley were apparently Peak (3,249m) on the south side of the glacier; Pt 2,908m (dubbed Wyvis) and its subsidiary (south west) top (2,750m: dubbed Minaret) on the north side of the glacier. It seems that many of the team's original objectives were climbed the previous month by a Royal Navy expedition, which was just leaving base camp as the four British climbers arrived.

The team completed their stay by moving base camp west to the foot of Gunnbjorns Fjeld (3,692m), the highest peak in the Arctic. From here they climbed both GBF and 3,682m Dome or Qaqqaq Kershaw, the second highest, both long days mainly on ski. [Compiled from Jim Hall's MEF expedition report.]

JIM HALL, *United Kingdom*

Mikis Fjord, ascent of Red Peak. Hoping to find anchorage in Kangerdlussuaq Fjord, which would give access to the Lemon Mountains etc, a small British team sailed in mid-May from Portsmouth, UK, via Iceland to the East Coast of Greenland. Bad weather and then the subsequent snapping in two of the boom, forcing the yacht to return to Iceland for repairs, caused delays. When they eventually reached their destination at the start of August, sea ice made penetrating the Kangerdlussuaq impractical and by the time an alternative venue, the Mikis Fjord nine kilometers east up the coast from Kangerdlussuaq, was reached, the five climbers on board, Tim Broad, Rob Jones, Steve Lodge, Peter Watson, and Stewart Wright, had only a week in which to achieve any ascents and were forced to concentrate on the mountains close to the head of the fjord. Unfortunately, the weather that week proved less than favorable, with gales to begin and sunshine appearing only at the end.

Two peaks were attempted from sea level. After climbing through an icefall (300m of climbing up to Scottish III/IV), a crevassed glacier was followed to 876m below the rocky pyramid of Mikis Peak (1,289m) on the south side of the fjord. A shattered rock wall of 100m led to the narrow and crumbly East Ridge but the team retreated around midnight at an altitude of ca 1,100m and returned in a 22-hour day. However, later they were able to climb 870m Red Peak, east of the fjord head, via a long glacier approach followed by scrambling on shattered rock to the broad summit. Two routes of ascent were taken: a dangerously loose gully on the South West Flank, and the rather more stable North Ridge.

PETER WATSON, *United Kingdom*

The north face of Tupilak, showing Lessons In Humility. *Klaus Fengler*

Schweizerland, Tupilak north face, Lessons in Humility. Before we left, Al Powell, the ultimate expert on East Greenland, told us: "If you're going to need fixed ropes, then leave the face up to someone who can climb it properly." Al had made an attempt on a direct line with Jon Bracey in the winter of 2001. They retreated and subsequently climbed the central depression in the face to the left, reaching the lowest point on the ridge that connects East and West Summits. Prior to this there had been at least one summer attempt on the face by an unknown party. Considering that Madagascar was an alternative choice for our expedition in 2004, our final decision to go to Greenland is difficult to understand.

At base camp on the 16th September Glacier, my father Walter Odermatt, Günter Wojta, Klaus Fengler, and I hadn't a clue about what we are getting into. Seven days before we had been chugging through the drift ice with an indigenous hunter in his small motorboat. There was so much ice we could hardly see the water. We placed base camp approximately five kilometers away from the face after five days of portering our gear.

The face of Tupilak looked higher, steeper, colder, wetter, and more brittle than I had imagined in my worst dreams. Do a bigwall free climb here? Forget it. But Klaus thought we could do it in 30 to 40 hours of non-stop climbing from the base camp to the summit and then back.

At 5 a.m. Fengler, Wojta and I crossed the bergschrund. On the rock we found very old nuts and a piton from a previous attempt. I led up brittle cracks while Klaus and Günter followed with jumars on a fixed rope. Time is the decisive factor on a 1,000m-high face when we have no bivouac gear.

After a while Klaus took over the lead for some demanding ropelengths of F6b difficulty, then we changed again. Günter would lead the upper part. The face was more difficult than we expected, and much longer. The rock became hell: extremely brittle—everything moved. A falling rock damaged the rope, which had to be repaired with a knot.

About half way up, a gigantic crack system led to below the summit icefield. Climbing was no longer so difficult, but the rock was still brittle and almost always wet because of the icefield. We thought we would reach the ice field much earlier, but it was nowhere in sight. Because we could only see the face from below, we had failed to consider the foreshortening. In reality, the upper part of a face is always much longer than the lower part appears. We used 70m and 80m ropes, but still there seemed to be no end to the cracks. The only way we knew we were gaining altitude was because the snow and ice on the face was constantly increasing.

Eventually we saw an edge above us. The ridge? Had we unknowingly climbed past the ice field by using a parallel crack system? After a 70-meter pitch, the big disappointment: This was just the beginning of the ice field. Would this ever end? We continued with crampons. It was becoming clear that we would have to bivouac—exactly what we had wanted to avoid. My optimism gave way to fear. How would we ever get down from here? The icefield was nearly 100 meters long, and 50°-60° hard ice. We only had three ice screws, and I needed two for the

Urs Odermatt briefly on quality rock during Lessons In Humility. *Klaus Fengler*

belay anchor, which meant a single screw to secure a 70m stretch of climbing. What does a body look like when it drops 60m into rock? I think of my family and move carefully. At the end of the icefield yet another disappointment: Instead of a ridge, the rock face towered up yet another 70 vertical meters to the ridge. The rock was even sandier, even more brittle. But giving up so close to our goal was out of the question.

I attempted to place protection every five to ten meters. I swore at myself, resolved never ever again to climb a north face. The rock was incredibly brittle. My nerves were so tense I could almost tear them to shreds. At the end of a rope-stretched 70m I reached a 20m "top" on the [previously climbed] West Ridge, which we christened "Tobias' Shoulder" in honor of our boat guide. It was 9 p.m. We had been underway for 20 hours. While waiting for the others I fell asleep. It was only a 40m difference in altitude to the Main (West) Summit (2,264m), but covered in difficult and dangerous ice. I was at my wits' end. I didn't care about the summit at all anymore. Günter and Klaus didn't want to go any further, either. We had climbed the face, but we would not reach the main summit. The Tupilak, which depicts evil spirits in Inuit mythology, could gloat, but no mountain in the world is worth risking your life for.

At 10 p.m. we began abseiling. I took the lead, placing two pitons every 70m for anchors.

Urs Odermatt on an ice field on Tupilak. *Klaus Fengler*

It grew dark. The ropes were patched together with knots in two places. Falling rock was a problem. We were fighting sleep. When the light returned we were still abseiling. The rope got stuck twice and I had to climb up without protection to get it loose. After ten hours of abseiling, we reached the lower ice fields. The rope got stuck here so firmly that we had to cut it with a knife. There was exactly enough rope remaining to abseil over the bergschrund. Through wet snow and between crevasses it took three hours to return to base camp. We had been underway for a total of 37 hours. I had just lived my dream.

We called our route Lessons in Humility: 900m high and 1,100m of climbing, F6b, 60° ice. Apart from our abseil pitons and the stuck rope, we left nothing behind. We used no fixed ropes or bolts and carried out all our trash. I also made a nice little first ascent with my 60 years old father. We called this Pik Walter and it is a summit above the Wall of Waiting at the end of the long South Ridge of Tupilak.

URS ODERMATT, *Switzerland*

CAPE FAREWELL REGION

Lindenows Fjord, Apostelens Tommelfinger, attempt on a new route. In 2003 German climbers, Steffen Laetsch, Jens and Michael Richter, and I from Dresden and Freital made an attempt at a new route on the 2,300m Apostelens Tommelfinger above the Lindenows Fjord in Cape Farewell (the first ascent of the Apostle's Thumb was made in July 1975 by the French climbers Maurice Barrard, Pierre Henri Feuillet, Dominique Marchal, Georges Narbaud, Yves Payrau, Michel Pellé, and Gérard Vellay via the 1,600m South Pillar. We traveled from Nanortalik in the boat Ketil and when we arrived the peak was covered in snow and in very bad shape. We first established a high camp below the wall. This required humping tons of equipment over a vertical gain of ca 1,000m from the fjord. The first few days of climbing were a real adventure as the snow melted on the Thumb and soaked us. Then the mountain woke up and showered us with stonefall. After seven days climbing we had fixed 800m of static and established a portaledge camp at the top of the ropes.

After a rest we spent seven days on the wall climbing from our portaledges toward the summit. To do so we needed to remove some of our ropes from the lower part of the wall, in order that we could fix above and return each night to the portaledges. On the last day, July 13, we found difficult and dangerous rock, so our progressed slowed. Then the weather turned nasty with storm and snow fall. We eventually had to give up just 20 meters below the summit icefield.

Back in our portaledges we planned to wait out the weather and make a second attempt. However, during that night we heard the noise of stonefall. One missile made a direct strike on our tent and hit Micheal's foot. It was obviously broken and we had to administer painkillers all night. It took the next three days to evacuate our casualty to base camp and in doing so we had to leave nearly all our equipment behind on the wall. In the end we put up a new but unfinished route on the highest peak in South Greenland. The line is ca 1,600 meters long and with difficulties up to VIII- A2 45°. We plan to return in 2005 and complete the route alpine style.

FRANK POLTE, *Germany*

Kangikitsoq Fjord, Tupilak Tower, Sandro e Vito; Lorenzo Peak, first ascent, Freedom Pillar route. "In the footsteps of Vikings" (Mark Richey, *AAJ* 2001) was the inspiration for our 2004 to trip in Greenland. In the first week of bad weather Sergio Dalla Longa, Rosa Morotti, Ennio Spiranelli, and I were in a state of dejection because of the quantity and ferocity of black flies and mosquitoes. Fortunately in the second week a splendid sun cheered up us.

On August 3 we climbed a new route on the north face of an unnamed peak (ca 1,900m) with access from the glacier behind "Tupilak Tower." We thought it was unviolated, but on top we found a plastic pack. Probably it was left by someone who had climbed an easy snow slope on the south face (with access from another fjord). We named our route Sandro e Vito (300m, 8 pitches, IV+) in memoriam to our friends who died 20 years ago on Monte Bianco (Italy).

On August 7 we made the first

The east face of Lorenzo Peak, showing the Freedom Pillar. *Giangi Angeloni*

ascent of 1,030m "Lorenzo Peak" (Giangi's newly born son) on the west side of Kangikitsoq Fjord. The route "Freedom Pillar" was 800m, 22 pitches, V+, 21 rappels) plus 250m of scrambling to the top, during three days of climbing on beautiful rock, with two bivouacs on good ledges and 200m of fixed rope.

GIANGI ANGELONI, *Italy*

Editor's note: This area came to prominence in 2000 when it was visited by Chris Bonington's Anglo-American team, which established some hard rock routes. However, it had been extensively explored as long ago as 1956 by Claude Kogan's expedition, which climbed 16 peaks, including three low summits on the west side of the Kangi-titsok, one of which could possibly be Pt 1,030m. Later, in 1975, David Walsh's Irish expedition approached the west side of the fjord from the south and climbed 12 peaks. Their Pt 1,900m to the south west of Tupilak Tower, climbed via a ca 1,300m snow/ice route at D, is likely the same as that climbed by the Italians and very possibly the same as Pt 1,990m climbed (at grade IV) by the 1956 team.

Ennio Spiranelli on the Freedom Pillar, Lorenzo Peak. *Giangi Angeloni*

Quvernit Island, seven virgin summits and nine new long granite routes. At the end of July a seven-member-strong group from Switzerland and Germany started on a six-week climbing expedition to the South of Greenland. The target of our group was first ascents of several 1,000-meter big walls in "big-wall" and "alpine-style" and afterward the attempt of a free ascent. The Base for our expedition was situated in the fjords around the islands Tornarssuk and Quvernit, near the Cape Farvel in the very South of Greenland, home of unexplored, exposed, and 1,400m granite towers. Some of the walls were even sticking out of the sea, sometimes only accessible by boat.

This lonely group of islands appears to have no recent history of climbing and it took some effort to get there with all the gear the group needed for the big-wall climbing. The team reached the base by boat in four hours from Nanortalik. We first explored the wild islands and then established the base camp close to the most beautiful towers. We believe that no one had climbed here before.

The Swiss and German group was comprised of brothers Jvan and Michi Tresch, Tom Holzhauser, Michi Wyser and his girlfriend Caro Morel from Switzerland; with "youngster" Wanja Reichel and myself completing the "German Team." Together we established nine new routes up to 5.12 (7c) and seven first-summit ascents in different teams. During our five weeks on Quvernit Island we were forced to rest only three days because of rain, which is incredible for South Greenland. We avoided placing bolts and we tried to climb all routes in one-day "single pushes."

Asiaq, Angagok (Ghetto Boys), and Tupilak. *Toni Lamprecht*

"Grön," 5.11 was the first new route of the Tresch brothers, followed by "Morel-Tower-Route," 5.10 (Holzhauser, Morel, Wyser) and "Angagoq," 5.11, along a 700-meter vertical wall with a bunch of hard off-width pitches, climbed by the team Tresch-Tresch-Reichel-Lamprecht. Afterward, due to the perfect weather and moderate temperatures, we established some really "classic" lines like the 900-meter-long big-wall route "Tupilak," 5.10 (Holzhauser-Wyser) and "Asiaq," 5.11 (Tresch-Tresch), climbed in "alpine style" in a day. One of the expedition's highlights was the 600-meter route "Ghetto-Boys," 5.12, by the team Tresch-Tresch-Reichel-Lamprecht, an absolutely "clean" free-climbed line to the summit of "Angagoq," with various pitches in the upper 5.10 and 5.12 range. Repeaters will find a big challenge

The view from saltwater, including Dos Canones. *Toni Lamprecht*

Immanaq and Gecko Tower. *Toni Lamprecht*

with vertical wall-climbing and cracks from finger, hand, fist, shoulder, body, to wide-off-width-size.

In the last week Wanja Reichel and I finally did "Immanaq" (the word for "maybe" in the Inuit language), 5.11, a more than 1,100-meter-long route summiting two peaks. For the access, climb, and rappel, we needed exactly 24 hours. A perfect finish was the nearly sport-climbing-like route "Dos Canones," 5.10 (Tresch-Tresch-Holzhauser), on a twin-peak-shaped tower. One of the most beauty-full crack-systems on the trip, which can be easily compared with Joshua Tree's climbs.

Our complete route list (heights quoted are the length of the climb): Grön, 5.11/A1, 700 meters (12 pitches), 1st ascent: Michi and Jvan Tresch, July 30. Morel-Turm-Nordwestwand, 5.10, 415 meters (10 pitches), 1st ascent: Caro Morel, Tom Holzhauser, Michi Wyser, August 5. Angagoq, 5.11, 700 meters (15 pitches), 1st ascent: Wanja Reichel, Toni Lamprecht, Michi and Jvan Tresch, August 7. Ghetto-Boys, 5.12, 700 meters (16 pitches), 1st ascent: Wanja Reichel, Toni Lamprecht, Michi und Jvan Tresch, August 12-13. Gecko-Turm-Nordostwand, 5.10, 750 meters (17 pitches), 1st ascent: Caro Morel, Tom Holzhauser, Michi Wyser, August 17. Immanaq, 5.11, 1,100 meters (20 pitches), 1st ascent: Wanja Reichel, Toni Lamprecht, September 1. Ajumaq, 5.10, 350 meters (5 pitches), 1st ascent: Wanja Reichel, Toni Lamprecht, September 1. Asiaq, 5.11, 620 meters (11 pitches), 1st ascent: Michi and Jvan Tresch, September 1. Tupilak, 5.10/A0, 930 meters (20 pitches), 1st ascent: Tom Holzhauser, Michi Wyser, September 1. Dos Canones, 5.11, 640 meters (10 pitches), 1st ascent: Tom Holzhauser, Michi and Jvan Tresch, September 4.

The members of the Greenland-expedition like to thank the German Alpine Club (especially the community Starnberg) for its support.

TONI LAMPRECHT, *Germany*

Pamiagdluk Island, new routes on the Baron and Baronet. Ross Cowie and Tim Marsh (UK) with Ronan Browner and Donie O'Sullivan (Ireland) traveled via Nanortalik to Pamiagdluk Island where they set up camp at the now established Baroness Base Camp on the west shore. They first made an ascent of the South Ridge of the Baron, a striking 1,340m spire conspicuous from the Torssukatak Fjord, which like other British parties they believed to be still unclimbed. Cowie with Marsh, climbed a different line to the other pair and although a lower pitch on one of the routes was British E3 6a, it could have easily been avoided and a grade of E1 5b is more accurate for the 600m of climbing. As they triumphantly approached the summit on the afternoon of the 2nd July they were somewhat deflated to discover a big cairn and old rusty peg.

[Ed note: while rock climbing in the Cape Farewell region has certainly come of age in the last decade or so, the area has been visited since the 1950s. In 1956 Claude Kogan's primarily French expedition to the Kangikitsoq region further north stopped off at Pamiagdluk. They climbed Pt 1,240m, now known as Qaqarssuaq, in the north of the island and christened the impressive double-summited spire, now known as the Baron, Le Grande Aiguille. They made a reconnaissance from the north and it seems the peak was most likely climbed the following year by another French expedition, which summited six new peaks on Pamiagdluk. This team also approached from the north and refer to it, not without reason, as The Dru. It was certainly climbed again from the northeast in 1978 or 1981 by Irish mountaineers, Ray Finlay and Roy Hudson, who found the French cairn. The peak will have a local Greenlandic name, but this has yet to be discovered.]

Working from a camp below the south southwest face, three more routes were added. After some preparation of the lower central section, where ropes were left fixed, the team established two new routes on the 14th July. Browner and O'Sullivan climbed more or less directly up the centre of the face, cutting through a ramp that slants up right across the whole wall at around half-height, and created the 17-pitch Amphibian. This had two crux E5 6a pitches but was sustained, with nine of the pitches being E2 and above. In the meantime Cowie and Marsh had climbed up to the right end of the ramp, then moved up and right into a huge diedre. After a total of 11 pitches they reached the upper South Ridge, where four more easy rope lengths led to the summit. The Red Dihedral had eight pitches of E2 and above with a crux of E3 6a. Both routes suffered from dampness in parts and as the pairs coincided on the summit they were able to make a communal rappel down the middle of the face, arriving back at camp after a 20-hour day. Two days later Cowie and Marsh returned to follow the ramp left across the face to the North Ridge and up this via an easy scramble to the summit. The climbing was not sustained but the middle of the ramp had a section of E4 6b, while a 35m pitch just before the end, led by Marsh, featured thin moves across a slab with negligible gear and a hard thin crack, giving it an overall grade of E6 6b. Gandhi's Ramp involves 16 pitches to the ridge plus 150m of scrambling. As the two sat on the summit two rather surprised climbers suddenly appeared. Another larger British expedition had arrived on the East Coast, also half expecting to make the first ascent of the Baron. However, the two new climbers were somewhat comforted to hear they were several decades late rather than just minutes.

Meanwhile Browner and O'Sullivan had re-located to below the North West Face of the Baron's lower western summit, dubbed The Baronet. On the 17th July they climbed the obvious cleft up the centre of the face above the half-way ledge. Reaching the ledge involved six pitches up to E3 6a, while above the terrain involved off width cracks (Friend 6) and a crux wet square cut groove at E4 6a. The 13 pitch route was climbed quickly and the pair were able to return to camp, pack and descend to the fjord the same day. No bolts were carried and only one peg was placed on the entire trip.

ROSS COWIE, *United Kingdom*

Pamiagdluk Island, new routes on the Baron and Baronet. About two weeks after the Anglo-Irish team mentioned above, a seven-member British team set up Base camp to the south west of the Baron, two to three hours above the Baroness Base Camp. From here, nine routes were climbed. Most of these were located on the lower flanks of both the Baron and Baronet and did not go to the summit. Leanne Callaghan and Glenda Huxter climbed three new routes. On the pinkish-orange South East Face of the Baron, a steep triangular wall right of the South Ridge, the pair put up Free Will (370m, 12 pitches, E3 5c) following an impressive line up a huge diagonal crack system to reach the crest of the South Ridge, which was descended by rappel. This ascent took place on the 3rd August. On the 15th they climbed a prominent corner system on the South East Face of the Baronet to create The Cams, the Cams (300m, seven pitches, E2 5c). This ended at the midway terrace and as the rock on the upper section of this face is not very appealing, none of the routes established here continued to the summit. A week later the same pair put up the Supercrack of Greenland (170m, four pitches, E3 5c) a superb and sustained crackline to the right of The Cams. They also repeated the Cowie/Marsh route Red Dihedral and the South Ridge, as did everyone else on the expedition, which they found excellent, particularly the Dihedral; a superb route of classic status. Their route up the south ridge involved two pitches of E2 5c, passing an in situ bolt.

Tim Neill and Louise Wilkinson repeated Little Foxy (one pitch: E3 6a) to the right of Supercrack, a line first climbed in 2001 by Tom Briggs. They then moved 50m left of Supercrack and re-climbed another Tom Briggs pitch (55m, E5 6b), then extended it for a further five pitches to the midway terrace to create 21st Century Arctic Fox (250m). A small crag below the face also yielded Life of Riley (100m: two-pitches: E2 5c). With Tim Riley they also attempted the big banana-shaped groove 150m right of Supercrack, climbing 10 pitches and nearly two-thirds of the way up the face at E3 5c and A1 before dangerously poised blocks in an inescapable corner blocked further progress.

Neill and Riley followed Callaghan and Huxter up Red Dihedral but just below the summit a falling rock struck Riley hard. He sustained chest injuries but was tidily evacuated to Base Camp by the rest of the team. A further five days went by before a passing boat could be attracted and Riley rescued.

Matt Perrier and Jude Spancken repeated several routes and added The Pink Power Tower, a seven-pitch crack system in a corner on the South East Face of the Baron, finishing on top a tower. Neill and Wilkinson repeated the E4/5 6a route, praising the quality and suggesting it was better than Astroman in Yosemite. One bolt was placed at most belays.

LEANNE CALLAGHAN, *United Kingdom*

Pamiagdluk Island, Kangerdluarssuk Fjord, Baron and other peaks, new routes, exploring, and mapmaking. On July 8, 12 members of the Karabiner Mountaineering Club left the UK on the complex journey to Pamiagdluk Island, near Cape Farewell, South Greenland. The idea had been to mark the 60th anniversary of the club with an Expedition, choosing an area that would attract a good sample of the club. Our objectives were to explore and establish new rock and mountaineering routes of all grades on the western side of Kangerdluarssuk Fjord, which runs into the center of the island. It had not been used as an approach before, so all we had to go on was an aerial photograph. Interesting targets looked like the steep southwest-facing wall of point 1,300m off the head of Kangerdluarssuk, with the quite well-known 1,340m summit of

The Baron and Butler area as seen from the east (Pt 1,300). Names without quote marks are those used by previous expeditions and are in common use. Names in quotes were used by the KMC to identify various features from the valley floor. Terrace: continuous ledge system giving access on the east side. "B Gully": easy snow gully giving access to the main ridge and terrace. "C Gully": possible access route. "Shelob's ridge": KMC exploratory climb (very scary). A Buttress: possible target for routes. B Buttress: several routes possible, with one KMC route on it— Bone Idyll. Question Mark: mistaken for the Mark until the KMC party worked out where it had to be. Information and photo from *David Bone*

The south face of the Baron. *David Bone*

the Baron offering new routes from the east. All previous attempts (the exact history was unknown when we left) having been from the island's western side. Peaks southward of the Baron looked to be first ascents, and there was new route potential all round the 1,300m-1,030m massif, with just two previous known routes on the east.

The team, myself (leader), Duncan Lee, Scott Sadler, Al Metelko, Rob Allen, Ian Heginbotham, Anna Neubert, Steve Cheslett, Jennifer Varley, Julie O'Regan, Karel Prochazka, and Helena Bestova, eventually arrived on July 11 to a coating of new snow after the famous Greenland weather had given an unscheduled visit to the Arctic Circle. We enjoyed a few fine days at the start, achieving many of our most-wanted aims, before an extended period of indifferent/poor conditions made big targets difficult to achieve. Fine weather

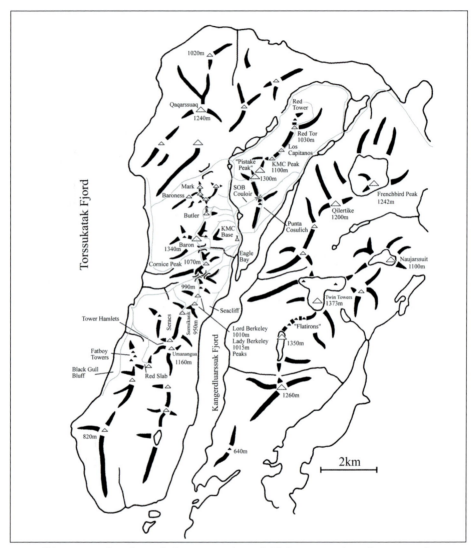

Pamaigdluk West map, based on multiple sources and KMC field observation, places the Baron on the correct island. *David Bone*

before leaving the island on August 2 (return to UK on 8th) allowed attempts on only a few of the many identified projects, so there's still much to go at here. The expedition overlapped 3 other British teams active on the western side, and we added four routes to the total on the Baron.

Highlights of the explorations include:

Two routes Baron Greenback, ca 900 meters, E1, and Baron Münchausen, E3 (not to summit) on the Baron from the south, and a mountaineering route (AD) from the north [most likely the route of the first ascent by French in 1957: see elsewhere—Ed]. A 260m route Drop

Peak 1,300m from the southwest, near base camp. *David Bone*

the Dead Donkey, E2 on the "Baron's Appendage" east ridge. A mountaineering route (D+) on point 1,300m's south ridge to a 1,250m foretop (lack of ice gear and scary rock on the summit inhibited progress). A mountaineering route (AD) to point 1,030m, christened "Red Tor," and south along the ridge toward Pt 1,300, ending at "KMC peak," 1,100m (likely first visits). A route Bone Idyll (665m, E3) on a buttress on the terminal northeast spur from the Baroness. A six-pitch E3 start to the west face of Pt 1,300m foretop, abandoned by rain. Exploration on the exotic ridge south of the Baron, giving Cornice and Lord & Lady Berkeley peaks (AD-). More information can be found at www.karabiner.org/expeditions.

DAVID BONE, *KMC, United Kingdom*

Pamiagdluk East, first ascents and repeats. During two weeks of perfect weather in the second half of August Daniela and Hans-Jochen Hägele with Andreas and Sandra Holle repeated several of the routes put up by the 1994 Bayerland and 1996 Freisinger expeditions, and added one or two of their own. Setting up Base Camp in the valley leading west from the shores of Anordli-utsup Iua towards Twin Pillar, they started with Naujarssuit (ca 1,100m), first climbed in 1994, where they put up Stümerkante (eight pitches: VI-). Then it was the concave South Face of Frenchbird (1,242m) where they repeated Haute Cuisine (15 pitches: VIII-). On the Red Wall (ca 1,050m), which lies south west of Qilerdike at the head of the valley, they repeated Nordlicht (VII+ and A2) as far as the 10th pitch then rappelled. Turning their attentions towards the islands highest peak, 1,373m Twin Pillar, they climbed the 10-pitch Vereinsausflug (VII+). Later, the Holles climbed Aurora (12 pitches: all free at VII+/VIII-) on Qilerdike (1,200m) to the end of the difficulties. The day before they were due to leave the Hägeles added another route to the

South Face of Frenchbird with Kurz vor Knapp (nine pitches: VII-).

LINDSAY GRIFFIN, Mountain INFO Editor, CLIMB magazine

Tasermiut Fjord, Ketil Pyramid, new route. I arrived in the area at the end of July, hoping to be the first climber to solo a new big wall route. I was surprised to find eight teams with a total of 30 climbers at Base Camp, though by the start of the second week of August most of these had departed. My plan had been to add another route to the South West Face of Nalumasortoq but I found the small glacier on the approach rather too crevassed to cross safely on his own and instead turned further north to Ketil Pyramid, a ca 400m-high spire one kilometre southwest of Ketil's 2,010m main summit, accessed via the Uiluit Qaqa Valley and far removed from other climbers. It is ca 1,600m and most probably first climbed via its easy East Face (300m, III) in 1960 by British mountaineers, Wally Keay and Roger Wallis.

I spent till the start of August ferrying all my equipment up the trackless 1,350m of height gain to the base of the South Face. The South Pillar of Ketil Pyramid was reportedly climbed in the 1980s by a Swiss team to give 11 pitches from UIAA V to VI+ [although unconfirmed this is likely to have been members from the Christian Dalphin/Michel Piola team, which put up a new route on the West Face of Ketil in 1984. The Pillar was certainly repeated in 1987 by three Danes and a Swede—Micheal Hjorth et al—in 1987]. However, the sheer south face to the right and the more slabby southwest face on the left remained untouched.

Adopting fixed rope tactics I began climbing up the center of the face on the 1st August and after six days climbing was just 20m below the east ridge. The climbing had been excellent, following diedres, cracks, and slabs in absolutely perfect granite. Then wind and rain prevented movement above base camp for four days and it wasn't until the 18th that I could finish the route and rappel the wall. Lost Friends is 425m and 10 pitches up to 65m each. Around half the route required aid (I carried a lot of equipment, including 54 Friends, 20 hooks, and 21 copperheads) and some bolts were placed. The difficulties were not severe, with the route felt to warrant an American grade of V 5.10a A3c.

THOMAS TIVADAR, Munich, Germany

Tasermiut Fjord, Nalumasortoq, Prowed and Free; Ulamertorssuaq, Moby Dick, speed ascent. On July 2 Nathan Martin and I started our 34-day expedition to the Tasermiut fiord in southern Greenland by climbing the dead-straight 2,500-foot route Non C'e Due Senza Tre (V 5.11+) on the right pillar of Nalumasortoq. We made it within 200 feet of the summit in a day before retreating in the dark. It was awesome. The following day it started to rain and continued for the next 12 days. Kind-of-a-bummer. After three days of clear weather we started up the central pillar by following the first eight pitches to the 2003 highpoint that Nathan reached with Tim O'Neil on a previous expedition. From here we followed excellent hand-to-finger cracks that would lead to the summit; however, three difficult pitches required cleaning, forcing us to hang on gear and forfeiting the free ascent on that attempt. We reached the summit at sunset and rappelled the route confident that another attempt would lead to a successful free ascent. Then it rained for 16 days straight. What a buzz-kill that was.

Eventually the skies and our heads cleared and on August 2 we completed our stunning 2,000-foot route, Prowed and Free (V+ 5.12+), all-free-in-a-day without using fixed ropes or jumars; a first for this area. The dead-vertical route is stacked with hard crack climbing including five pitches of 5.12 in a row starting at pitch 8 with two of them racking in at 5.12+. It was amazing that everything came together at the last minute on such a gem. It was hard to pioneer this route in this style, and we hope future ascents will follow suit. Someone's gotta onsight this thing!

Totally stoked and high, with one day left before pickup, we set out on August 4 and climbed the classic route Moby Dick (VI 5.13-), on the 3,000-foot Ulamertorssuaq. We managed to race up the climb in 11 hours and 56 minutes, free climbing most of the route. The potential for more free routes in the area, 5.14 and beyond, is practically unlimited and is highly recommended. The granite is reminiscent of Tuolumne characterized by superb and endless cracks, knobby faces and surreal environment making for remarkable conditions. In 6 weeks we climbed only 4 days, but those were four of the best days ever!

JARED OGDEN, *AAC*

Tasermiut Fjord, Ulamertorssuaq and Ketil, first ascents. Eight young French climbers on their first expedition were in the area from the end of June to early August. Jérôme Masoundabe, Benoît Montfort, Magali Salle and Rémy Sifilio, all from the Pyrenees, climbed Moby Dick on Ulamertorssuaq from the 15th-17th July. They started up the route without sleeping bags or portaledges, reaching the good ledge at the top of pitch 15 on the first day. Next day they gained the narrow ledge at the top of pitch 28, and reached the summit the following morning, rappelling the route from the existing anchors. Their next objective was Nalumasortoq and on the 30th, together with Pierre Labbre, they started up the Original British Route on the southwest face of the Left Pillar (7b+ or 7a and A2). Ropes were fixed to the top of the 8th pitch, then on the 1st August these were re-ascended and a portaledge camp established at the top of pitch 10. On the second they continued up a superb series of jamming cracks and diedres, reached the top and descended to their camp for the night.

The other three members of this party, Frédéric Degoulet, Rémi Sabot, and Francois-Régis Thévenet from Lyon, had more ambitious plans, first tackling a new route up the tapering tower leading to the West Summit (1,830m) of Ulamertorssuaq, right of the characteristic barrel-shaped buttress. The first ascent of this pillar took place in 2000 when Canadians, Jia Condon and Rich Prohaska, climbed What's Bred in the Bone, a 1,100m line with 29 pitches, only two of which required aid (A2+). The rest gave fine free difficulties up to 5.10+, notably in the middle to upper sections where the climb followed a prominent right facing diedre, though some of this was interspersed with poor rock.

The Canadians climbed onto the right side of the pillar having first gained the top of the large hanging serac formation at its base. However two years previously an Icelandic team had tried to avoid the seracs by starting up the first few pitches of L'inespérée on the main face (Daudet/Robert, 1996), then working up right across the intervening depression to reach the pillar. They found serious stonefall in the depression so retreated.

The three French, who took a similar start, appear to have experienced the same problems. At the second portaledge camp stonefall ripped through the fly while they were ensconced one night and they later were lucky to escape a huge volley while jumaring back up to Camp 3. Higher, one of the climbers pulled off a large flake directly above the belayers but fortunately managed to hold on and throw it clear. The trio had started up the wall to the right of L'Inesperée, close to the seracs, moved right on to the snow field at its top, then climbed compact slabby rock just left of the central depression until they could traverse across it and reach the pillar a little below half-height (at approximately pitch 13). From here the wall steepens and the difficulties increased. A series of diedres and a final exposed arête led direct to the summit, keeping left of the Canadian route until eventually joining it at the last belay. Twelve days were spent climbing, with eight nights spent on the wall in a portaledge. The summit was reached late in the day on the 3rd July. Due to the perfect weather throughout, the climb was named Le Temps de L'innocence and gave 29 pitches with difficulties up to 7a+ A1 and C1 (although there is only one aid pitch).

After a suitable rest, which coincided with a period of bad weather, these three moved north to Ketil, a spectacular peak is best known for its big routes on the 1,200m West Face, where they planned to add a third route to the less well-known South Face. They began on the 15th and spent three days fixing the first 350m. A capsule style attempt was then driven back by storm and it wasn't until the 30th that they were able to jug the ropes and continue with a portaledge for four more days to the summit. Clémence de l'Ogre (1,000m, 22 pitches, of which four required aid: 7a A1 and C1) is the first direct line up the face, climbing more or less up the center where there is a vague prow in the upper section. The Original Route to the summit of Ketil (TD, V and VI) was done as long ago as 1974 by an Austrian party that started up a couloir on the North West Face and eventually traversed around to the upper South Face from where they reached the summit. It was descended one year later by the French team of Agier, Amy, Lemoine and Walter, who climbed the complete South Face at TD+ (VI) with one bivouac, although this is reported to be a devious line connecting ledge systems with paths of least resistance.

LINDSAY GRIFFIN, Mountain INFO Editor, CLIMB magazine

WEST GREENLAND

Nutarmuit Island, Ullukkut. Originally I had wanted to climb a formation on Qaersorssuaq Island, however on the July boat ride there we saw that my topo map was not entirely accurate. So a quick change in plans, and Donny Alexander and I were on the island of Nutarmuit. While scouting out lines on the abundance of rock in the area, we climbed an easy 1,000-foot snow couloir. We then climbed a 400-foot 5.9 route. The next day we tried soloing a ridgeline. About 600 feet up we got into loose 5.8 rock that looked like it was going to dead-end under a headwall. So 600 feet of down-climbing followed.

After a week of rain in the tent we stared climbing a 1,200-foot wall. The approach had an 800-foot snowfield which was steep enough you not want to fall, followed by 300 feet of really loose 4th class. However after that point the rock became awesome and the climbing stellar. It was raining, so the rock was wet and the thin seams were muddy, making our progress slow at times.

After 600 feet we got to the pillar that we had been aiming for. We were very happy to see that the crack at the base was not an off-width. It still turned out to be an awkward lead. The inch-and-a-half crack ended by busting free moves off a hook, body weight knife blades, micro-stoppers, and blind stoppers going around a bulging corner. Then it went to #5 Camalots, more bulges, and a loose flake behind the pillar. Though I made a few unladylike comments while leading, it was one of the single best aid pitches I have ever led.

Our last day was a 23-hour push. Donny led the rest of the pillar mostly free (5.10b).

Ullukkut on Nutarmuit Island. *Lynnea Anderson*

As he was hauling our bag I heard a ding, ding, ding, I looked up just in time to see a couple of bolts taking a flight back to the ground. When I got up to our bag I was able to find three bolts, which ended up being the magic number. Two more pitches and we were at the summit. We could see that the next storm was going to hit soon, so it was a quick stay before we headed back down.

After drilling three single bolt rap anchors we were back at our established anchors, where there was food and water. I don't know that many people have enjoyed water as much as we did (because of a miscommunication we had been climbing for over 20 hours without water). Half an hour after we got back to camp the storm hit and we were happily eating more food and drinking hot tea. Since we climbed a lot in the middle of the night, we named the route Ullukkut, which is Greenlandic for, In The Daytime. We rated the route V 5.10c A2+.

The next sunny day we went back to the ridge that we had bailed from earlier. We soloed a different line that was a 2,000-foot 5.8 alpine route. After that the weather caused a bit of an epic. The expedition tent did not hold up to the winds, so we had to bail down to the ocean to get picked up. One wet night and a chilly morning later we were on our way back to Upernavik.

More cancelled flights, another $1,000 for luggage (putting the total at over $3,000), and we were on our way to France to enjoy food (which did not include canned fish or oatmeal), red wine, and daily hot showers. Thank you to the American Alpine Club's REI Challenge and The Obesity Treatment Center for helping make the trip possible.

LYNNEA ANDERSON, *AAC*

West Coast, various first ascents. The 10m fiberglass yacht Dodo's Delight, skippered by Bob Shepton again visited the West Coast. After sailing from Scotland to Godthab (Nuuk) via Cape Farewell, the crew progressed a short distance to 65°N and anchored in the ca 25km Kangerd-luarssugssauq Fjord. The climbing here is not technical but the scale is big with difficult route finding and often loose and bouldery terrain. Unusually poor summer weather in 2004 also hindered activity. On the 25th July Keith Geddes and Shepton climbed Pt 1,650m east of the fjord head. This had been climbed before but almost certainly not from the west. The ascent involved a 30km round trip and took 28 hours. Shepton, now being in his late 60s, was really quite pleased.

On the 27th Geddes, Shepton and Phil Ham made the first ascent of Mt. Stevenson (1,115m) via a Perfect Mountain Day. On the same day Emily Brooks and Nigel Harrison made the first ascent of 1,430m Mt. Peters, a fine peak climbed by the northern glacier.

The team then took the boat further up the coast to 71°N and into the northern end of Uummaanaq Fjord to reach Akuliarusinguaq Peninsular, an area previously explored by myself in both 1998 and 2001. The principal objectives here were four remaining unclimbed peaks of more than 2,000m. Attempts were not successful at first, though ascents were made of Pt 1,815m, a little to the north west of spot height 1,790, and several peaks on the nearby island of Qeqertarssuaq (Nugatsiaq): Pt 1,511m (previously climbed); two adjacent unnamed summits, and four summits (Pt 1,735m, Spot height 1,750m, 1,645m Twin 1 and 1,715m Twin 2) lying on an east to west ridge in the northern sector of the island. Then, over the 13th-14th August, Shepton made the first ascent of Solo Snow Dome (2,065m) on the peninsula via an easy but energy-sapping snow ridge. In all 14 peaks were climbed and 12 of these were believed to be previously virgin.

The boat then moved further north to Upernavik, where there was a change of crew. It then continued up the coastline with the intention of seeing how far north it was possible to sail a fiberglass yacht. Dodo's Delight eventually reached 78° 32'N in Nares Strait above Etah, probably as far north up the Greenland coast as any ordinary yacht has been. Returning south, the boat moored close to Thule, from where Polly Murray and Tash Wright made the first east to west ski traverse of Herbert Island (77° 25'N), ca 30km of exacting soft snow at an average altitude of 850m, completed from the 20th-23rd September.

BOB SHEPTON, *Scotland*

Mexico

NUEVO LEON

The Muñeca, La Muñequita. This 5,000' peak, 30 miles west of the Potrero Chico, was previously unclimbed because of the vertical sandstone cap-stone (100' to 300', depending on which side). However, there are several good-looking cracks on every side, and in October Rochelle Rochon, Hervey Peña, and I took the obvious splitter on the west face. The route, La Muñequita, was grade III 5.8, and we rapped the low point back to the north ridge. Full rack and single rope.

ALEX CATLIN

El Potrero Chico, Feral Dover Ridge and Monster Truck. Feral Dover Ridge (15 pitches, 5.10dX, Cindy Tolle and I, September) starts on Dope Ninja and follows the ridge for 2,000' to the summit of the Sense of Religion Wall (it's essentially a continuation of Dope Ninja). Full rack. Rap Devotion.

Monster Truck (20 pitches, 5.9R, Dane Bass and I, October) starts on the Central Scrutinizer and follows the ridge 2,500' to the summit of El Toro. Full rack up to two inches. Rap Timewave Zero.

ALEX CATLIN

El Potrero Chico, Battle Royale. Going to Mexico was perhaps the best decision I ever made. It is a land of happy people, cheap beer, and soaring limestone walls. What more could a climber ask for? Arriving at Homero's campground, I flipped through the flimsy guidebook, marking the climbs I was hoping to try during my visit. One route name that kept popping into my head was Battle Royale. It wasn't the name itself that intrigued me, but the word printed next to it, "PROJECT."

A few days later I was begging my best friend Big Al to join me on an adventure left unfinished, the adventure of Battle Royale. He was hesitant, as he had never done a multi-pitch climb, but enjoyed the thought of smoking Mexi-weed in such an exposed position. He smiled, and we started up the route that afternoon. The climb is located on the left side of the Potrero just as you walk into the park. It's the last climb on the far right side of the Club Mex Wall. In the mid 1990s Kurt Smith and Ned Harris put in countless hours on this masterpiece. Cleaning, gluing, and bolting on this terrain is far from easy, and they put in more work than I could have imagined, but they never found the opportunity to complete the ascent.

The rock leading to the route is low angle and choppy, so we opted for a three-pitch variation which climbs diagonally from left to right, adding three technical rope-stretching pitches of mid-5.12, a beautiful climb in its own right. This variation ends at a belay station that we dubbed "The Station." At this point climbers can rappel back to the ground and call it good, or continue up the steeper direct line to the top, a.k.a. Battle Royale [these upper pitches are

5.13a, 5.13c, 5.12b, 5.13b, 5.10a—Ed.]. Big Al and I thought it was worth the peek. We pulled off all the moves and set up a top-rope on the three hard pitches. After working the moves and sequences, we pulled the ropes and lowered to the ground from The Station, leaving one fixed line. We returned three or four times and attempted the crux pitches, without success. Each late-February day the sun would glare down, and we would be forced off the wall by dehydration. Finally, on day five, the sky was mercifully cloudy, and Big Al and I decided it was our best shot for a full ground up ascent.

We started with four chocolate bars, one bottle of water, and 15 quick draws. As we got higher our confidence increased, and we grew stronger with each bolt. The climbing felt good and our motivation was high. The route requires nothing more than strong crimp strength and good footwork. The crux came on the fifth pitch, very thin and pumpy, but the adventure is minimal as it is well protected. Nearly all falls are clean and safe, which is great if that's what you're into. I gritted my teeth and punched through the most demanding part of the climb. Only three pitches remained, and the cloudy sky held strong. The sixth pitch ended in a small magical cave. After a water break, we easily strolled the final pitches to a jaw-dropping view and a moment of reflection.

It's fucked up really, how people give me credit for the first free ascent, when really all I did was climb the route, just like anyone else would have. I happened to be at the right place at the right time. Sure it took some work, but the real heroes are the guys who envisioned the line and took the initiative to create it. Without them it would be another blank wall among countless blank walls. They should be the ones writing this, not the skinny sport weenie with strong fingers and a faggy toothbrush who had the route handed to him on a silver platter. I'm not proud that I made the first ascent, no more proud than if I had made the 51st ascent. I enjoyed the climb for what it was, and it made for one of my most memorable days in the vertical world, but mostly I admire the climbers who sacrificed so much to make this type of climbing possible. The location and position of the climb is hard to beat, and we should not celebrate only the ascent, but that there is a route existing at all. It was a gift and I'm thankful.

SONNIE TROTTER

Cerro Picachos, various new routes. This granite area off Hwy 85, 50 miles north of Monterrey, is as beautiful as it is wild. I will not even attempt to give directions. Go to Sombreretillo and ask the locals. Three- to four-hour walk in. The climbing is concentrated on the south and central peaks.

Jimmy Carse and I established several new routes, the longest being Lila (5.11cR/X), which climbs the 800' east face of the south peak in six pitches. Start on the slabs, climb the right-facing dihedral to the summit block (5.10) and follow a very thin seam out right. Where the seam ends, climb straight up to a belay 11c/d R/X. (A few knifeblades would take the danger out of this pitch.) Traverse back left to a crack that leads to the summit (5.10d). Thin to medium rack. There is an old ladder system that descends the south ridge and east face.

[Catlin and Carse also climbed four-pitch new routes on the northwest buttress and west dihedral of the south peak. On the central peak the pair climbed three new four-pitch routes, and Carse and Ralph Vega added another—Ed.]

ALEX CATLIN

El Pico Erin, Xiuhtecuhtli. Xiuhtecuhtli is named for the God of Fire of the Nahuatl Cultures. The route, located in La Huasteca Canyon on El Pico Erin, is almost 500m high. Erin is beside the sacred wall of Tatewari, Grandfather Fire to the Hiucholes.

Our expedition began December 27, 2004 and ended January 18, 2005. We started working on the route seven days after our arrival and finished on January 17. We were interested in the route mostly because La Huasteca Canyon is a sacred place for our people and ancestors; they believe it was where life started. We had never been there, but knew we had to go work on something special. The climb is not as weird as the shape of the limestone elsewhere in the canyon; fire seems to be everywhere when the sun is coming up and going down. Lots of walls are like big thin flames that come out of the desert. Another tripping issue is the peak, with its symmetric pyramidal shape, the same formations on both sides of the wall. It gives the impression of being in front of a giant sphinx.

Our route could be rated 5.10+ or 5.11-, but the main difficulty is the rough terrain of the last pitches and the length of the runouts, sometimes of 10 or 15m. The route tends to be an adventure, rather than a multi-pitch sport climb, and we bolted on lead. Nevertheless, no trad equipment is required, as everything is set with big bolts and huge anchors. The nine pitches are up to 60m long, so a pair of 60m ropes is essential. Our route begins with three pitches in the middle of the face and some left-to-right fourth class to gain a ledge. On the far right end of the ledge is a big, black, vertical wall with bolts. This is our route. It's very obvious and the easiest route on the wall to find. It can be climbed in one day, though an early start is recommended. The best season to visit is in autumn and winter; the area is in the Mexican desert, and in summer not only can the sun be a problem, but also snakes and scorpions.

Our story is simple. We were looking for something big in our lives, and none of us had ever created a multi-pitch route. Three boys and a girl with not a lot of years (ages 21-27) or experience, we started feeling magic materializing around us. The people we met helped us with everything we needed, from equipment and food to motivation. We were in the right place and time, with the right people, and the Universe did its thing and conspired to help us succeed. We have more stories that include killer falling rocks, portaledges collapsing in the middle of the night, big conglomerates of feelings such as fear, happiness, bravery, and uncertainty, but nothing you can't figure out if you climb Xiuhtecuhtli.

DANIEL CASTILLO, PABLO FORTES, MARISOL MONTERRUBIO, MARCOS MADRAZO, *Mexico*

Peru

CORDILLERA BLANCA

Caraz II, Australian Route and Salida Directa de Los Gordos. Early season snowfalls in the Cordillera Blanca created unstable conditions in the mountains. Most of the "action" was taking place in the bars of Huaraz. Undeterred, two small teams set off for the Laguna Parón area, hoping to find something not covered in snow.

From the summit of Pisco the French team of Damien Astoul, Mathieu Detrie, Gaspard Petiot, and Basile Petiot spied the east face of Caraz II, shining in the morning sunlight. The Australian team of Matt Scholes and Ant Morgan caught the same vision on their way to the Artesonraju moraine camp. The east face has three prominent couloirs, offering initial steep climbing, finishing at the overhanging summit headwall.

On July 21 the French team left their high camp on the heavily crevassed glacier, breaking a trail through knee-deep snow on their way to the left-hand couloir, which is directly below the summit. They encountered fantastic ice conditions on the lower pitches (90°), and continued up easier ice and snow, arriving at the headwall at dusk. The four spent the night in a small tent with a stove and two sleeping bags. The next morning Basile led the loose, overhanging crux first pitch of the headwall (6a A2), having to clear large blocks. They again encountered loose rock on the next two pitches, before climbing unconsolidated snow to the summit. [This describes a complete and slightly more direct finish to the 1997 Superduper Couloir route/ attempt. From the top of the couloir the '97 team traversed, before climbing the left-hand margin of the headwall, continued along the ridge, but did not summit. The photo in the *AAJ* 2002, p. 299, mistakenly shows the '97 route continuing directly up the headwall. The Caraz II photo presented here corrects this error and also shows the 2002 British variation/attempt, previously unreported in the *AAJ*, which also stopped short of the summit—Ed.] Eight rappels on two 100m ropes brought the Frenchmen safely back to their high camp. Superduper Couloir— Salida Directa de Los Gordos (700m, ED 6a A2 90°-95°ice).

Leaving just after midnight on the 24th, the Australians took advantage of the Frenchmen's trail on their way to the right-hand couloir. After crossing the 'shrund, they encountered styrofoam snow and a single ice step (WI3) before moving left, about 350m up, out of the couloir onto the rib between the right and central couloirs. The next seven pitches ranged from beautiful rock and ice to the infamous Peruvian honeycomb snow.

The Australians arrived at the summit headwall to find a 35m pitch of clean, solid rock guarding the final snow slopes. With no bivy gear but a promising forecast, they decided to continue up. The pitch had to be broken into two, due to a minimal rack. The first went at V+ (20m) and the second at A2. It was dark and windy by the time the Australians reached the summit slopes. They found a snow mushroom offering protection and settled down just under the summit. The next morning the pair climbed a short pitch to the summit, before rappelling the French route. Australian Route (720m, ED1 V+ A2 WI3).

ANTHONY MORGAN, *Australia*

Parón, Bartonellosis to summit mushroom. Owen Samuel, Mike Pescod, Tony Barton, and I set off up the Santa Cruz Valley on June 2, two days after arriving in Peru. We set up a camp at 4,700m on the moraine ridge below the northeast face of Artesonraju, in the Quebrada Arteson. After checking out both the unclimbed northwest face of Millishraju (5,500m) and the north face of Parón we decided on the latter because the former was a very complex, seraced face. We watched Parón for two days and saw two potential "ice" lines melt in the summer sun. We decided that our line would last, but it needed a night ascent to minimize falling rock and ice.

On June 5 at 9 p.m. we set off for the base of the route, marked by a chimney angling up and left. (Tony was not acclimatizing well, so it was just three of us.) The glacier was easy to cross, and we started up the first chimney pitch (Samuel's Cleft) before midnight. We found excellent ice, of about grade IV/V Scottish, with occasional loose rock steps. Above the chimney easier-angled snow slopes traversed back right, then a

Caraz II (6,020m), east face (sometimes mistakenly called the south or southeast face). Confusion has existed regarding the locations of the lines on the left. This photo corrects the error drawn into the finish of the Superduper Couloir as shown in the *AAJ* 2002 (and incorrectly listed as 1998). The correct finish in the photo above has been verified by the original ascensionists. (1) Northeast Ridge (Huber-Koch, 1955). (2) Fisher-Sheldrake-Warfield, 1986 (no summit). (3) Superduper Couloir (Coull-Kendrick-Morton, 1997) (no summit). (4) Jost-Mlinar (2001). (5) Barton-Carter-Winterbottom (2002) (no summit). (6) Salida Directa de Los Gordos (Astoul-Detrie-Petiot-Petiot, 2004). (7) Australian Route (Morgan-Scholes, 2004). *Matt Scholes*

rocky groove led into another left-slanting ice chimney. Daybreak brought us to the final funnel directly under the summit. We completed the 10-pitch ascent at 10:30 a.m., just below the final summit snow mushroom, which we did not attempt due to the conditions. We abseiled the west face to the Parón Glacier, traversed through interesting seraced terrain, and ascended back to the Artesonraju col and an easy descent to camp, where we arrived 20 hours after leaving. We named the 400m, TD+ route after a disease which is transmitted by a sand fly common high in the Peruvian Andes. We were paranoid that its bites might be infecting us. Tony Barton was the impetus behind us being in this valley climbing this route. He has spent several summers in Peru, checking out potential new routes.

NICK CARTER, *United Kingdom*

The popular east face of La Esfinge, showing the 2004 Killa Quillay route. Over a dozen routes exist on this face.
Antonio Gómez-Bohórquez

La Esfinge, Killa Quillay and variation. From July 24-31, Spanish climbers Ángel Olmos, Antonio L. Liria, and José M. Cancho climbed the east face via a new 17-pitch route, Killa Quillay (700m, VI 6b+ A2), located between Cruz del Sur (Bole-Karo, 2000) and the Original Route (Bohórquez-García, 1985). Killa Quillay was repeated (date unknown) by Basque Aritz Labiano and Belgian Michael le Comte, with a leftward deviation on the upper portion, toward Volverás a mí (Polanco-Olivera-Madrid-de la Cal, 1987), before reuniting with Killa Quillay.

ANTONIO GÓMEZ-BOHÓRQUEZ, *Spain*

Yanawaca, attempt. Last May two Mexican friends, Carlos Bazua Morales and Emiliano Villanueva Rabotnikof, and I traveled to the Cordillera Blanca with the idea of opening a new route on the wall known as Yanawaka (also called Peña Negra, ca 4,900m). From Huaraz, we traveled by truck to the Quebrada de Parón. Once there we took two days to explore and study the wall. Our base camp was under a big boulder in the moraine on the approach to the wall, about 15 minutes from the northwest face. After deciding where to start, we fixed three ropes and pulled the two "pigs" to the third belay. We then rested, because two members had the flu.

Five days later, on June 1, we returned, jugged the three pitches, opened pitch four, and bivouacked. The next day we opened only one more pitch, and on the following day two more pitches in excellent, vertical granite cracks, with both free and aid climbing. Our fourth day back on the wall started with easy face climbing to a ridge and finished with pitch nine in an excellent dihedral. Day five brought exposed free climbing on the ridge, face climbing into a dihedral, and a long pitch 12. We continued up 4th class terrain between trees and continued on class 2 terrain. On day six we hiked up more class 2 to the 13th belay, then climbed a dirty crack to an old, dry tree. Pitch 15 involved a 5.7 hand crack that got us to the top of the big pillar at 4,408m. We had climbed 735m (VI 5.10 A2) but decided to descend. Two of us had strong coughs, and we had only two days more of food and water. We bivouacked at pitch 13 and on day seven began rappelling at 11 a.m., reaching the base at 9 p.m. The next day we left the beautiful Quebrada de Parón. Another 600m of unclimbed vertical rock remains below the top of the wall. We estimate five more days of climbing, and another two to descend.

LUIS CARLOS GARCÍA AYALA, *Mexico*

The attempt on Yanawaka (also called Peña Negra, ca 4,900m) in the Quebrada de Parón. The 600m wall above is still virgin. *Carlos Garcia*

Pisco Este, south face to summit ridge. In mid-June I went to the East Peak of Pisco via Laguna 69 and a faint trail up the left side of the moraine. After reaching a high point, the trail descends steeply for 100m to a tiny pond, where I put up my tent, at the only possible place in the area. I followed a line to the right of the face as seen from the glacier, where the glacier was not very crevassed or complicated (and the crevasses were clearly visible). Reaching the face wasn't difficult except for the last bit, where I had to cross snow bridges across large crevasses which, as far as I could see, sliced the glacier beneath the whole south face.

The face, which is perhaps 300-350m high, provided all kinds of snow conditions. In the lower part I climbed 50-60° snow, before entering a narrow gully right of an evident rock spur. To enter it, however, I had to climb a 3-4m mixed section of 80° M4. There was then good ice and hard snow up to 70°, but mostly around 60°-65°, until the route enters a small bowl with 55° powder. The final mixed wall, though less than 100m, presented difficulties much harder than anything else on the route. First it was rock (80° M5), reasonably solid with many cracks and features, then a serac with short sections of 90°, and finally a longer 80° section that finished on the ridge to the left of, and some 10m below, the summit. I reached the summit ridge at 11 a.m. I did not climb to the summit, which was overhanging ice and snow. The route is exposed to objective danger, as everything falling from the summit is funneled into the gully, but during the climb nothing came down. To descend I downclimbed and rappelled, from Abalakovs, in a gully down the short north face to the glacier, until I could easily traverse down to the little col between Pisco West and East. There I placed a piton and made eight rappels (using a single 45m rope) to the south, from slings around rocks and a few Abalakov threads. But it's mainly a rock wall, of perhaps 150m, and more pitons would be preferable. I traversed the glacier beneath the south face to my starting point.

ADAM KOVACS, *Sweden*

Chacraraju Oeste (6,112m), north face. (1) Terray et al (Davaille-Gaudin-Jenny-Martin-Sennelier-Souriac-Terray, 1956). (2) The Lord of the Towers (El Señor de las Torres, Monasterio-Kovac-Kozjek, 2004) ends at junction with original Terray route (1956) on ridge, at middle summit. (3) Hapala-Husicka (exact line unknown, 1986). (4) Ortenburger et al (Abrons-Doody-Frost-Ortenburger, 1964). *Pavle Kozjek*

Chacraraju Oeste, The Lord of the Towers, to middle summit. On July 8 and 9 Marjan Kovac and I (both from Slovenia) and Aritza Monasterio (Basque, living in Huaraz) opened a new route, The Lord of the Towers (ED+) on Chacraraju Oeste (6,112m), north face, in a lightweight single-day-and-night push from tent to tent.

We started from Huaraz on July 5 and established a base camp in the Paria Valley on the east side of the Cordillera Blanca. There we spent another day in bad weather, exploring the complicated approach to the north face of Chacraraju. The upper part of the Paria Valley is surrounded by glacial walls and exposed to seracs from the Chacraraju icefield.

The approach to the wall, on July 7, took nine hours. We had to climb difficult, mossy rocks, find a way across water gullies below an icefield, and finally hurry through the icefield by the only possible line, which lay below serac towers. The weather deteriorated, and we found a place for the tent during a snow storm in the evening. Nice weather the next

The 10-meter ice wall leading to the ridge on The Lord of the Towers, Chacraraju Oeste. *Pavle Kozjek*

day surprised us. At 8 a.m. we began climbing a direct line on the buttress on the left side of the face. We found old pitons and ropes on the first pitches. After four pitches of excellent rock climbing (6a A1) we traversed right to the ice-field. Conditions there were mostly bad (wet new snow) until the wall became steeper, but then the first ice gully ended in overhanging mushrooms.

With another traverse we reached another gully, and after 10m of vertical icefall we reached mixed ground (M4-5) on the ridge. By then it was night, and we climbed with headlamps. The last rock barrier appeared to be overhanging, with no weak points visible in the dark. With another traverse, to the left, we reached a vertical corner, which combined standard Andean pow-der, smooth rock, snow mushrooms, and poor protection. Reaching the top wasn't technically the hardest part of the route, but was nevertheless the crux. On top there was no ice for an anchor, only deep powder. I prepared "something" with my axes. While my partners followed together,

In the upper ice slopes of The Lord of the Towers, Chacraraju Oeste. *Pavle Kozjek*

with one headlamp, Marjan slipped, pulling Aritza off. I had difficulty holding both without real protection, but after a few dramatic moments we stood on top at about 10 p.m. We rappeled immediately, having trouble with cold, dehydration, and jammed ropes. After a 24-hour push, by morning we were again below the north face and by midnight at our base camp. The next day we continued back to Huaraz.

New route: The Lord of the Towers (El Señor de las Torres, 800m, ED+ 6a A1 AI6 55°-70°(90° max)), follows the obvious buttress left of the main summit and reaches the original 1956 route on the ridge. It took 14 hours of climbing. We couldn't find information about the old ropes at the beginning of the route. Other routes on this side: Terray et al (1956), Ortenburger et al (1964), Hapala-Husicka (1986).

PAVLE KOZJEK, *Slovenia*

Hualcán Peak 5,350m (Nevado Libron), east ridge, and Huichganga, south ridge. On July 10 Dave Sykes and I (both British) made what may be the first ascent of a peak that is in the vicinity of Hualcán. The peak is on the northeast ridge of Hualcán and, although unnamed to our knowl-edge, has the spot height of 5,350m. [This peak was reportedly climbed from the south in 1973, but unnamed. It seems possible, however, based on the geography, terrain, and the 1973 team's report, that they may have climbed the next peak along the ridge to the east. If Peak 5,350m was previously unclimbed, Barton and Sykes have suggested the name Nevado Libron (Laguna Libron is below the peak) —Ed.].

I noticed this peak previously, when I was in the Quebrada Cancaracá Grande with an M.E.F.-sponsored expedition. However, we approached from the Quebrada Huichganga and climbed the mountain by its east ridge. An easy glacier led to the ridge and straightforward climbing to the foot of the difficulties. These consisted of five pitches of up to Scottish IV mixed (AD+). We gained the summit, though not a view, as we climbed in typically Scottish conditions of thick clouds and intermittent snowfall. We descended the south face. Four abseils and an easy traverse of the glacier put us back on our ascent route. It is perhaps worth noting that point 5,267m, named on some maps as Nevado Huichganga, appears to have been first climbed on June 25, 2002. Steve Head and Glen Stelzl climbed its south ridge at PD. I cannot find any more info regarding this part of the Blanca, despite a fair bit of digging.

ANTHONY BARTON, *United Kingdom*

Hatun Ulloc, Karma de Los Condores. On August 29 Wayne Crill and I completed a new route on the previously unclimbed 350m south face of Hatun Ulloc in the Quebrada Ishinca. Four large, impressive rock buttresses rise ominously from the forested slopes of the north side of the quebrada, guarding the entrance to the Ishinca Valley. Hatun Ulloc (Quechua for "Big Sprout") is the third, tower-like buttress visible above the Huascarán National Park entrance station. The base of the face is at about 4,120m.

We first viewed these impressive rock features en route to Ishinca base camp with Jeff Jackson in August 2003. The allure of a first ascent on steep, clean granite with abundant crack features and relatively minimal vegetation was all we needed to abandon our La Esfinge plans and spend the last days of our trip attempting the south face of Hatun Ulloc. Our 2003 efforts got us up 120m, our four pitches of 5.9+ to 5.11 including classic hands, fingers, steep dihedrals, and deep chimneys and bringing us to a vegetated ledge. We returned in late August 2004 with Jeff Jackson and Jon Herrera from Austin, Texas. After fixing lines to the vegetated ledge, we spent four days aiding and cleaning, before Jeff and Jon returned to the States. With half the manpower and time running out, we recruited a Huaracino [Huaraz local] and Casa de Guia aspirant named Oscar Negreiros Cerna. Our new team continued from our existing highpoint, three pitches above the ledge. We started each day before dawn, to catch the two hours of sun before being hampered by the frigid, gale-force winds that raged almost daily. We initially aided the

The Karma de Los Condores route on Hatun Ulloc. *Kevin Gallagher*

upper pitches, then cleaned loose rock, dangerous chockstones, and steel-wool-like vegetation, leaving beautiful splitter cracks. On August 29 we reached the flat sidewalk-like summit of the face after six long pitches on the upper headwall, leaving us one day for attempting the entire route in a single push. Free climbing attempts ground to a halt on pitch six, the "Roofer Madness" pitch. We will return early in 2005 to complete a free ascent of this route, which we believe could become a popular classic. We named the route Karma de los Condores because of the Andean condors that regularly flew by and inspired our ascent. Route Description: Karma de los Condores (350m, IV 5.11 A2+). Three pitches ascend to the ledge: one of two alternate 5.9+ starting pitches, a beautiful continuous 5.11 pitch, and a 9+ chimney/tunneling pitch. Six more pitches reach the top of the face. The first two pitches above the ledge climb steep face and cracks, at 5.10+, to "Roofer Madness." This pitch will probably go free at hard 5.11. The final three pitches were A2+ and have yet to be freed, but appear to be in the 5.11 range.

KEVIN GALLAGHER, *Eldorado Springs, Colorado*

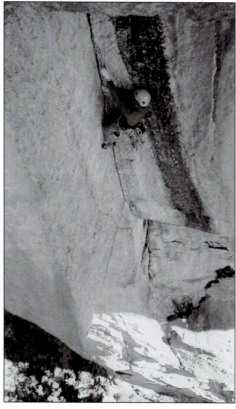

Wayne Crill on the Karma de Los Condores route on Hatun Ulloc. *Oscar Negreiros Cerna*

Oschapalca, new route and various activity. After acclimatizing by guiding the Normal Route (PD) on Pisco (5,752m), the North Ridge (AD-) of Vallunaraju (5,686m), and the Normal Route (PD+/AD-) to the north summit (6,664m) of Huascarán, Chilean climber Andrés Zegers teamed up with German partner David Bruder to make the first ascent of the Northwest Face (TD) of Oschapalca (5,881m). The new line follows an ice runnel and involves 10 pitches of ice up to 65° and three mixed sections. The crux was the last, vertical, soft-snow wall, which they negotiated by digging through a cornice. The route was established alpine-style in an 11-hour round trip from moraine camp at about 4,800 meters.

Andrés and David then established a new speed record for the east face of La Esfinge (5,327m), climbing the 1985 Normal Route (750m) all free and onsight in 3:57. The previous record for the route had been a few minutes under seven hours. Although the route was originally rated 5.11+, Andrés felt the grade rather easy by Yosemite standards and suggests 5.10+. The ascents of Oschapalca, La Esfinge and Huascarán were made in one week in late July.

The team still had energy to go for a speed ascent of El Escudo (D+), a direct route to the South Summit (6,768m) of Huascarán. They started from the village of Musho (3,050m) and went for the summit in a long, super-fast single push that lasted for 14:30, during which they climbed more than 3,600 meters of ice and hard snow up to 60°. The round trip time from Musho was 23:57 (they lost a couple of hours searching for a spot to pass the rimaye on the descent), which makes this the first one-day ascent of El Escudo.

Reported by Andrés Zegers to Jose Ignacio Morales for Escalando
Reprinted from Alpinist *magazine, www.alpinist.com*

Jangyaraju, south face. As part of a program for aspirant guides run by the Mountain Guide Association of Peru (AGMP), a 400m route was established on the south face of Jangyaraju (5,675m) on October 20, 2003. The route ascends the right-side of the hanging glacier in the center of the face, continuing up on an ice runnel that begins on the top-right margin of the hanging glacier. This runnel angles back left, joining the runnel that rises from the center of the hanging glacier. The route then traverses left along the summit cornices. The first ascent was made by Aritza Monasterio, Peter Alvarado, and Darwin Jamamca. Beto Toledo, Paolo Zaconet, Pedro Huaman, and Joseli Callupe then repeated the route, rated TD+ (50°-65° [90° max]).

The AGMP Route on the south face of Jangyaraju. *Richard Hidalgo*

Information supplied by RICHARD HIDALGO

Huamashraju, various routes. Huamashraju (a.k.a. Wamashraju 5,434m) is located southeast of Huaraz, just above the village of Janku. On its west face there is a vertical 200m wall, the base of which is at around 5,000m. The wall reaches a summit ridge that is 4th class rock and snow. While the peak's ridges and snow routes have seen climbers for several decades, rock climbing on the steep west face has not been documented until recently. The first reported climb of the face was by Ken Sims and Maura Hanning in 1998. The pair climbed two routes, the MK Route (III 5.9) and the Sims-Hanning Route (IV 5.9+). The Sims-Hanning takes a line up the middle of the wall. The MK Route is farther left, taking the obvious line just left of the large roof system that is left of the Sims-Hanning Route. It is right of the Sims-Jackson Route (described below). Sims reports that the Sims-Hanning is the best route, with long, clean cracks and a short offwidth midway up. After reaching the top of the west face, Sims and Hanning climbed to the summit

Huamashraju, west face: (1) Thai Express, 2000. (2): Sims-Jackson Route, 2000. (3) MK Route, 1998. (4) Sims-Hanning Route, 1998. (4') Sohn-Barlow Variation, 2004. *Ken Sims*

along the face's northern skyline ridge. They then descended this ridge until about half-way down, at which point they rappelled into the gully on the back side of the face. They followed the gully to an obvious notch in the north ridge; the notch led around to the bottom of the west face. They do not recommended this gully, as it is steep and loose, with lots of rock fall potential; Sims has subsequently been descending by the north ridge.

In 2000 Sims returned to Huamashraju with Dennis Jackson. They climbed two routes on the left side of the wall (Thai Express, farthest left, and the Sims-Jackson), both being 5.7-5.9 and finishing at the obvious notch left of the MK Route. On the former they were accompanied by Naresuan Butthuam, the owner of a Thai restaurant in Huaraz. Sims and Jackson also completed several climbs on the shorter walls on the left side of the cirque seen during the approach to the west face. These one- and two-pitch climbs, on a rock feature that resembles a ship's prow, include a superb 5.9+ finger-to-hand crack up the prominent arête.

In June 2004 Brian Sohn and Chris Barlow climbed a line up the middle of the wall, closely following the Sims-Hanning Route but moving left on a sloping ledge, below the short, steep dihedral that leads to the obvious offwidth of the Sims-Hanning Route. They took a slightly easier pitch to a lower point on the summit ridge (Sohn-Barlow Variation). Sohn and Barlow also climbed the north ridge to the summit. They then descended directly down the middle of the west face, rappelling most of face in the dark and leaving much of their rack. Sohn and Barlow subsequently reclimbed the wall and established a rappel route down the west face. This rappel route is to the south of the Sims-Hanning Route, beginning at the wall's highest point (bolt and sling anchor), and involves four double-rope rappels down corners. Some traversing on ledges is required to reach anchors. (The rappel-route topo is available at Zarela's hostel in Huaraz).

KEN SIMS *and* CHRIS BARLOW, *AAC*

Cordillera Blanca, other information. New route activity was below normal in 2004, presumably because of atypical unsettled weather and conditions. The following information supplements the new routes individually reported above.

On the south face of Chacraraju Este (6,001m) Nick Bullock (U.K.) and Adam Kovacs (Sweden) established a new finish to the Jaeger Route. They climbed most of the route unroped, belaying only their three-pitch variation, which continues straight up to the ridge (but without reaching the summit) where the Jaeger route traverses right. This variation parallels the 1984 Peruvian-Spanish line, exiting to the next point right on the summit ridge The three difficult and poorly-protected (especially considering their anemic rack) pitches rated Scottish VI,7; VI,6; V,5—the first two mixed and the third on poor ice and snow. The pair descended their line, reaching camp 20 hours after starting.

The ever-popular rock walls of La Esfinge (5,325m) saw numerous ascents, mostly of the Original Route (Bohórquez-García, 1985). There was, however, one new route and variation (see report, above). Also, Welcome to the Slabs of Koricancha (V 5.13b, Beranek-Linek-Staruch, 2003), surely the hardest free climb on Esfinge, received its second ascent. Americans Steve Schneider, Heather Baer, and 14 year-old (no, not a typo) Scott Cory climbed the route in two days in August, with Schneider leading (and on-sighting) all but one pitch—Cory led (redpoint) the 5.12a eighth pitch, and followed all but one (5.12a pitch seven) of the others clean.

Alpamayo in 2004: (1) Canal Central. (2) Ferrari. *Koky Castañeda/File A. G. Bohórquez*

In the Ishinca Valley, in addition to the climbers on Hatun Ulloc (see report above), a French team is rumored to have been active nearby. A Basque team was active as well, but details of their rotues are not available. There were also rumors of two climbers establishing a possible new route on the northeast face of Huandoy Sur, but again details could not be obtained. Given the spectrum of climbers visiting the Cordillera Blanca, from a variety of countries and speaking many languages, complete new-route information proves difficult to obtain. Climbers assuming they've climbed a new route should research their route's history as thoroughly as possible.

Information regarding the correct naming and history of popular routes on the southwest face of Alpamayo (5,947m), based on original-account research, has been provided by noted Cordillera Blanca researcher and historian Antonio Gómez Bohórquez (author of the authoritative 2003 book *Cordillera Blanca, Escaladas, Parte Norte* ISBN 84-607-7937-8).

What is often called the Ferrari Route is actually the Central Couloir (Canal Central); the first recorded ascent was made in 1983 by R. Renaud, his client Susana, J. Gálvez, and Bohórquez. It's possible that this route was actually first climbed in 1979 by R. Rield and R. Pöltner. Regardless, the true Ferrari Route is two couloirs right of the Central Couloir and is more difficult, longer, and changed significantly in 1995 after a massive collapse of the lower portion. It follows the couloir almost directly below the summit, beginning from the low point of the bergschrund, and is what has been called the French Couloir or French Direct (based on Nicolas Jaeger's 1977 second ascent; Frenchmen Beriol and Lay were killed there by serac fall in 1980) and erroneously believed to be different from the Ferrari Route. Credit for the first ascent has been attributed to North Americans W.A. Barker and S. Connolly, but actually belongs to C. Ferrari, P. Negri, A. Zioa, D. Borgonovo, P. Castelnovo, and S. Liati, in 1975.

Two fatalities in the Blanca in 2004 were reported. Matej Mosnik died after a 30m crevasse fall on Copa Norte on July 14. Peruvian guide Eder Sabino Cacha was killed in an avalanche while skiing the lower portion of Tocllaraju's normal, western slope, route on June 10.

Compiled primarily with information from ANTONIO GÓMEZ BOHÓRQUEZ *and* RICHARD HIDALGO

CORDILLERA HUAYHUASH

Siula Chico, A Scream of Silence, to summit ridge. Our five-member Slovene expedition to the Cordillera Huayhuash had plans for a direct line on the southeast face of Jirishanca and a new line on the southeast face of Siula Chico. However, two members had health problems, so only three of us were active. We set up base camp Lake Carhuacocha, reached from Queropalca. My brother Anze, Ziga Ster, and I, on July 25, climbed to the middle of Jirishanca's southeast face, but turned back because the wall was too difficult and objectively dangerous, and the weather was bad. [Their direct attempt shared a common start with Fear and Loathing (see photo *AAJ* 2004, p. 48), but after continuing left above the entry couloir (where F&L goes right), they climbed ice and mixed terrain

Siulas Chico and Grande: (1) Northeast Ridge of Siula Chico and South Ridge of Siula Grande (Obster-Scholz-Sturm, 1966); the first ascensionists climbed Grande's North Ridge (first climbed in 1936, not visible in this image), descended into the Grande-Chico col, made the FA of Chico, returned to the col and again climbed Grande. (2) A Scream of Silence (Marence-Marence, 2004) (no summit). (3) Southern Discomfort (Burbee-Frimer-van der Spek, 2001) (no summit). (4) Southeast Spur (Baehler-Défago-Schaffter, 1981).

trending back right, above and parallel to the 2003 line, to the base of the major (unclimbed) square rock headwall in the center of the face. They climbed along the right edge of the headwall, retreating from just above its half-height—Ed.]

Four days later we approached the southeast face of Siula Chico in eight hours of glacier walking and climbing. We pitched a tent and spent a day watching the wall. The direct line on Siula Chico had too little snow, so we decided to try a gully between Siula Chico and Siula Grande. We had time for only a quick ascent. The next day, August 1, at 3 a.m. my brother and I started up the wall, while Ziga stayed in the tent, not feeling well. We took only one rucksack, with equipment for only one day. At the beginning we had problems with deep snow, but on the steeper part of the line conditions were good. The key was the wall's 200m central part, with steep icefall climbing (70°-90°). The upper part, a nice couloir, brought us to a saddle between Siulas Grande and Chico. We then climbed for 11 hours. We tried to cross to Siula Chico, but the ridge was too dangerous and difficult. After gaining 50m in two hours, we turned around. At 8 p.m. we were again at the tent, 19 hours after leaving. The route's 14 pitches are all ice and snow. Conditions were mostly good, except for the first pitch (deep snow) and the last pitch of the central part (bad ice mixed with empty snow). The route is composed of three parts: a 200m snowfield (60°-70°), a 200m icefall (70°-90°) and a 200m couloir (65°-85°).

We named the route, A Scream of Silence (5+/VI, 60°-90°, 600m), a memorial route for our good friend Matej Mosnik who died on Copa in the Cordillera Blanca in July.

TINE MARENCE, *Slovenia*

Nevado Llongote (5,781m), south face: (1) Possible route of the 1963 Spanish first ascent. (2) Los Pecados se Rien! (Auvet-Clouet-Drouet-Villecourt, 2002) (did not continue to summit). (3) Longue, Haute, et Magnifico (Clouet-Drouet, 2002). (4) Lima-Limon (Hidalgo-Mejia, 2004). (5) Hidalgo-Mejia's 2004 descent route. (6) I-Célines [East Ridge] (Auvet-Villecourt, 2002). Photo and route lines from *Richard Hidalgo*

Cᴏʀᴅɪʟʟᴇʀᴀ Cᴇɴᴛʀᴀʟ

Nevado Llongote, Lima-Limon. The day after setting up base camp by Laguna Llongote in the Zona Yauyos, Guillermo Meija and I checked the approach to our intended route, an ice line directly up the south face to the summit of Llongote (5,781m), and carried gear to the glacier. On October 16 we started at midnight and reached the glacier in three hours. The first part of the route was easy slopes to the first icefall (good ice, 70°- 80°).We climbed together to more icefalls (80°), which led to the key ice wall. The condition of the ice was good, with steps of 90° and 95°. Above, deep, bad snow slopes (65°-70°) proved difficult and dangerous, but we gained the summit at 6 p.m. We started to rappel the southeast face (between our route and the 2002 French route on the east ridge), but could not continue due to rockfall. We bivouacked 100m below the summit. The next day we continued rappelling and arrived at base camp at 4:30 p.m. It's a very nice route (Lima-Limon, 600m, ED 70°-80° {95° max}) but might be better earlier in the season.

Rɪᴄʜᴀʀᴅ Hɪᴅᴀʟɢᴏ, *Peru*

Cᴏʀᴅɪʟʟᴇʀᴀ Vɪʟᴄᴀɴᴏᴛᴀ

Various ascents. Our expedition included Stanko Mihev, Franc and Janeta Pusnik, Samo Rupreht, Matjaz Prislan, Marko Anzelak, Igor Plesivcnik, Peter Naglia, Peter Jeromel, and me as leader. We started from Malma on June 30, with 20 horses for the 15km trek to our 4,625m base camp. On July 4 we established ABC at 5,050m, on a glacier below the south face of Colque Cruz and Jatunriti.

On July 8 we attempted Nevado Carhuaco Puncu, one group from the northwest, another group from the south side. Mihev, the Pusniks, Rupreht, Anzelak, and Naglia made an ascent from the northwest of a 5,525m sub-peak of Carhuaco Puncu that we think was unclimbed and

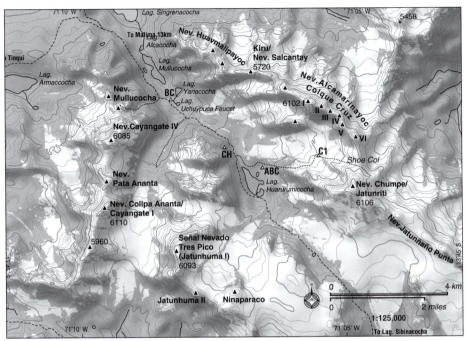

Map of the Vilcanota Range by *Martin Gamache*, Alpine Mapping Guild

we called it Slovenski Turn. Jeromel,Pris-lan, Plesivcnik, and I reached 5,450m on the ridge below Nevado Carhuaco Puncu from the west side.

On July 10 Mihev, Pusnik, Rupreht, Prislan, Jeromel, and I went to ABC to climb Jatunriti. The next day we bivouacked at 5,450m on a glacier, in a lot of powdery snow. On July 12 we reached Shoe Col (5,775m), from which Mihev and I, and Pusnik and Prislan, climbed the northeast side of Jatunriti. We reached the top at 2 p.m. The final 250m were ice and snow averaging 50°-70°, with a maximum of 80°. We called the route, "Nauci se Loviti Sanje" (Aprende a Atrapar Los Sueños). We rappelled the route.

The same day, alone, Peter Jeromelj climbed a new route on the

The Slovenski Turn (Slovene Tower), as named and perhaps first climbed by the Slovene team in 2004. *Boris Santner*

southeast face of Nevado Jatuncampa (5,700m). He named the route Anina Smer, rating it II/III (UIAA rock) with snow and ice to 45°(avg)/70°(max).

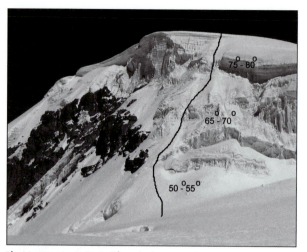

75 - 80°

65 - 70°

50 - 55°

The Nauci se Loviti Sanje (Slovenian) route on Jatunriti. *Boris Santner*

On July 13 Anzelak and Naglia made an ascent, from the north side, of Nevado Mullu-cocha (5,400m). On July 16 we cleaned up base camp and left.

BORIS SANTNER, *Alpinisticni klub Ravne, Slovenia*

Various ascents. The Anglo-Scottish Vilcanota Expedition 2004 had as its primary objective the south face of Colque Cruz 1 (6,102m). Our leader, Dave Wilkinson, had made two earlier expeditions to the Vilcanota, in the 1980s, but we were unaware of the attempt by Peter Carse and Amy Bullard (*AAJ* 2004, pp. 293-294). We arrived at the idyllic base camp (4,600m) on July 14 after an easy two-day walk from Tinqui. There is a good track on the right, when ascending, of the large glacier on the south side of the Colque Cruz peaks, which enabled us to put a temporary camp nearer our objective. After a tedious crossing of the moraine-covered glacier we found a surprisingly easy, and apparently safe, icy corridor, close to the rocky buttresses of Nevado Ichu Ananta, giving access to a glacier bay under the south face of Colque Cruz I. Unfortunately this glacier had a deep cover of unstable new soft snow. We climbed to the col between Colque Cruz I and Ichu Ananta (5,720m) but concluded that the south face of Colque Cruz I was not in a climbable condition. Accordingly, on July 23, we climbed Ichu Ananta from the col, by a short face and an easy mixed ridge to a splendid viewpoint.

After a rest at base camp we split into two parties. D es Rubens and Steve Kennedy ascended a very fine mixed rock and snow ridge (the "Scottish Ridge") rising from near base camp to the west peak (ca 5,650m) of Kiru (5,720m). They bivouacked a little above the top of the rock section (about 400m of Scottish Grade II climbing). The following day, July 29, they climbed the complex snowy section of the ridge, which sported a variety of typically Andean formations: huge mushrooms, massive icicles, and bottomless voids. This section included pitches of Scottish Grade V. They reached a broad and almost horizontal ridge near the summit, but the snow was waist deep, so they descended before reaching the summit.

Meanwhile, Dave Wilkinson and I ascended the glacier between the Cayangate and Jatunhuma groups and turned left up the glacier between Nevado Ninaparaco and Jatuncampa. We pitched camp at about 5,100m, above the lower icefall of this glacier. The next day, July 29, we crossed to below the north face of Ninaparaco and ascended it by a line we had spotted the previous day. The summit we reached (ca 5,930m) is a subsidiary summit of Jatunhuma (also known as Pico Tres), about 1 km northeast of the main summit. The route involved an initial deviation east and back west to get onto a glacier shelf below the main face, then a climb of about 150m up ice spattered with large quantities of debris from seracs above. To escape the line of fire we moved left across a mixed rock and ice section to reach a broad snowfield that

The "Scottish Ridge," indicated by the line drawn on Peak ca 5,650m along the Colque Cruz ridge. *Desmond Rubens*

narrows to a gully near the summit. The snow was composed of "steps" of the nieves penitentes type, making the climbing easier than it would otherwise have been at this angle. We reached the summit late in the afternoon and were benighted on the descent, spending a cold, uncomfortable night at about 5,700m. However, after a slow descent we regained base camp with no further dramas.

As far as we know all three climbs were first ascents. The expedition was very professionally supported by Cusco agents Atalante Quechua (operaciones@atalantequechua.com), whom we strongly recommended to anyone wishing to climb in Peru.

GEOFF COHEN, *Scottish Mountaineering Club*

Bolivia

CORDILLERA APOLOBAMBA

Cololo (5,915m); Chaupi Orco northern summit (6,000m); Katantica Central (5,610m); new routes and repeats. During July resident French guide Alain Mesili and visiting Brazilian guide Waldemar Niclevicz spent almost two weeks climbing several routes in this partially explored range in northern Bolivia, straddling the Peruvian border. Mesili and Niclevicz climbed a possible new route on the northeast face of the striking pyramid, Cololo, at 5,915m the second highest peak in the Apolobamba. Approaching via Kotani Lake (4,760m) to the east, then following the glaciers below Khala Phusi (5,465m), they reached the bottom of the virgin east face (unsuccessfully attempted by a British party in 1997), where a 250m-high couloir separates the face from the northeast ridge. This line gave good climbing over névé, soft snow, and ice up to 70°. It was graded Alpine D+.

Cololo (aka Ccachura) lies roughly in the center of the range but south of the Pelechuco road that divides the Apolobamba into its northern and southern sectors. It was first climbed in 1957 by a team from the German Alpine Club, via a circuitous route involving the south face and part of the west ridge. The West Ridge itself (D), perhaps the finest route on the mountain, was first climbed in 1988 by David Hick and Michael Smith (UK), while the rocky North Ridge (D- III, 65°) fell to Pam Holt, David Tyson, and David Woodcock the following year.

Mesili and Niclevicz repeated an existing route on the east face of Chaupi Orco's northern summit (6,000m). They encountered dangerous conditions, with a thin film of névé over deep wind-blown snow. This route lies to the right of the Central Couloir, climbed in August 1995 by a team of young Germans led by Alexander Ritzer, and was rated AD AI 2. Mesili also reports that the Normal Route up the East Ridge of Chaupi Orco (6,044m), the highest peak of the Apolobamba, is almost impossible to reach, as the approach via the northern flank is over rotten ice and is threatened by unstable seracs.

The Chaupi Orco Massif, which straddles the Peru-Bolivian border, is geographically complex and has traditionally led to parties confusing the north and main summits, resulting in ambiguous route descriptions, orientations, and ascents. The first ascent of the main summit (via the East Ridge) was made in 1957, at AD, by the Germans Werner Karl, Hans Richter, and Hans Wimmer, during the first recorded mountaineering expedition to the Apolobamba.

On Katantica Central (5,610m), which lies just north of the Pelechuco road in the northern Apolobamba, Mesili and Niclevicz repeated the Original 1968 German Route (Karl Gross-Dieter Hain), which involved easy climbing to a steep exit on the east-southeast face. They also climbed the West Ridge (Brain-Flood-Wiggin, 1997; AD+, 65°).

LINDSAY GRIFFIN, *Mountain INFO, CLIMB magazine*

CORDILLERA REAL

Overview and new routes. During 2004 there were significantly fewer climbers in Bolivia than in previous years. Political instability may have contributed, as in September 2003 many visitors were stranded in the town of Sorata, in the northern Cordillera Real. Local Aymara protestors, angry at the government's plan to privatize and export Bolivia's rich gas reserves, blocked the access roads from the highland town of Achacachi to Sorata (140km northwest of La Paz). Visitors were stranded for up to two weeks, and finally when the Bolivian Army forcibly opened the road there were armed clashes with the protestors, and buses were shot at and stoned. Looting in Sorata and eviction of the authorities complicated a tense situation. Then in October popular protests in La Paz and the nearby city of El Alto left a toll of 80 to 100 deaths. The corrupt president, Gonzalo Sanchez de Losada, escaped to the US, and the vice president Carlos Mesa assumed the leadership. During the first few months of the year there were widespread road blocks and protests, and many embassies advised foreigners against visiting the country. The situation improved following a nationwide referendum on the July 18, which gave the government popular support.

Furthermore, 2004 was a very dry year with the Bolivian Andes experiencing little precipitation during the monsoon months. The big mixed ice/rock walls were quite bare, exposed to rockfall, and often threatened by seracs. The weather, however, was predictably stable.

I know of only one fatality, an Argentinean solo climber who slipped and fell several hundred meters on the country's highest peak, Sajama (6,549m). A party of Australians managed to get lost on the country's most popular and straightforward mountain, Huayna Potosi (6,088m), but were rescued.

Several new routes were established by Bolivian-New Zealand guide and psychiatrist Erik Monasterio and New Zealand climber Mike Brown. Their MEF and New Zealand Alpine Club-supported "Wiphala Expedition" spent mid-July to mid-August in the northern Cordillera Real.

Monasterio and Brown acclimatized by climbing a new route on the subsidiary peak on the western side of the Illampu-Ancohuma Massif, south of the Laguna Glacier Base Camp. DAV Map Pt. 5,573m had one previous ascent, in 1991 via the long southwest rock ridge, Rebeldia de los Condores (Enz-Rauch, reported in High Mountain INFO July 1999). From the town of Sorata the pair took two days to reach a high camp at 4,700m. On July 23 at 6 a.m., without bivouac equipment and with only two liters of water, they set off and reached the base of the wall two hours later. The route started approximately 400m northeast of the Enz-Rauch Route and ascended directly up the west face. It ascended the left-hand (north) wall of an obvious gully. After the first pitch (60m), the pair was forced back into the gully, simul-climbing for 300m and again ascending the line of least resistance on the face to the left of the gully. By evening they had climbed 14 pitches and, still not within sight of the summit, were forced to sit out the night in temperatures down to -20C. Brown initially exhibited pronounced symptoms of altitude sickness, but he improved through the night. The next day they completed the route in four more pitches, merging onto the glacier west of Ancohuma. As the pair had not carried ice-climbing equipment, they were forced to cross 200m of glacier by cutting steps into the ice. They rappelled onto the moraine and descended to the Laguna Glaciar Base Camp (base camp for the normal route on Ancohuma). The route, named Aclimatizacion, was long, very cold, exposed, and dangerous, as it was threatened by frequent rockfall. It required eighteen 60m pitches, with a crux of 6a (French) rock and an overall American alpine grade of V (French TD). The hitherto unnamed peak was christened Pico Wiphala. The Wiphala is the multi-coloured Inca Flag that symbolizes the wisdom of the wind and is carried by locals in their protests and search for justice and equality.

On August 1, climbing from a high camp at ca 5,400m on the eastern aspect of the Illampu-Pico del Norte Massif, the pair attempted the southeast ridge of Pico del Norte (6,070m). Newly exposed unstable granite boulders on the ridge were extremely dangerous. Fear and a nostalgic attachment to life prevailed, and the attempt was abandoned after four pitches. The pair rappelled off the east face, before crossing a basin of thigh deep snow. On the same day they climbed a new route on the south face of Gorra de Hielo (5,760m). The 300m route followed an old avalanche gully and provided superb ice conditions. It was graded American alpine IV (French D+), AI4. Argentineans G. Minotti, M. Falconer, and L. Bromessard, who repeated the route a week later, confirmed the grade.

From the same high camp at ca 5,400m, on August 3 they climbed an excellent three-pitch new route (F6b, 6a, 5), on the rock spires running east from Aguja Yacuma (6,072m). The route ascended the unclimbed east face of the first major tower south of the Mesili-Sanchez Pass, between Illampu and the Yacuma Group.

The impressive rock peaks of PK 24, a.k.a. Punta Badile and Pico Emma Maria, lie east-northeast of Pico del Norte and Gorra del Hielo. There is some dispute as to the altitude and position of Pico Emma Maria; in Jill Neate's book, Mountaineering In The Andes (Royal Geographical Soc., 2nd Edition 1994), it is wrongfully described as Point 5,715m (this is most likely Pico Esperanza), and on the DAV Map it is given an altitude of 5,531m. This obvious rock tower, clearly visible from the village of Cocoyo, had its first recorded ascent, via the southwest ridge, in August 1953 by the legendary climbers Hans Ertl and A. Hundhammer. In 1983 A. Mesili and C. Hutson added a second route, the East Buttress, a mixed route graded French TD. There have been, to the author's knowledge, no other recorded ascents. On August 6 (Bolivia's Day of Independence) Monasterio and Brown approached the peak, climbing directly up from the Cocoyo-Jahuira River (DAV Map) to establish a camp at the foot of the east face at ca 5,000m. The attempt nearly came to a premature end, as locals set fire to the grass fields directly beneath Pico Emma Maria. The valley became engulfed in thick, acrid smoke, and the pair stumbled blindly through the choking fumes to eventually find their base camp. On August 7 the smoke cleared, and the climbers struggled on with severe throat and eye irritations. The route ascended the southeast face, and the climbing was varied and sustained, over solid and compact granite of complex architecture, with roofs, dihedrals, and delicate corner systems, often choked with ice. Conditions deteriorated through the day, and by 2 p.m. the pair was caught in a snowstorm. They reached the summit in whiteout and stormy conditions at 5 p.m. Struggling with poor visibility and frozen ropes, the pair rappelled into the night, leaving pitons, wires, and slings. They finally reached camp at 11 p.m. The route (Humo e Independencia) was 500m long and required 11 sustained 60m pitches (max F6c, A0).

ERIK MONASTERIO, *Bolivia-New Zealand (with additional information from* LINDSAY GRIFFIN, *Mountain INFO, CLIMB magazine)*

CORDILLERA QUIMSA CRUZ

New routes and information. A six-member British expedition organized by Sarah Griffin visited the Gigante Grande Group in June and July, establishing base camp at the northern end of Lake Larum Khota. From here they made eight ascents, two of which were possibly new. These were the West Face of Cerro Sofia (5,720m), the summit immediately north of Gigante Grande, by Matt Freear, Griffin, Tim Moss, and Ted Saunders, at AD+, and the South Face of a subsidiary peak immediately northeast of Torre Jihuna (5,740m) by Freear and Griffin. The former was a slope of wonderfully compact névé. The climbers separated on the summit, one descending the loose north ridge, the other the mostly snowy north face. The second new route proved the hardest of the expedition, climbing a 300m ice slope topped by steep deep snow, with a descent of the mixed rock/snow east ridge. The expedition visited four other summits in the valley, and the team notes that the new 1:50,000 color maps of the region (obtained from the Bolivia Insituto Geographico Militar in La Paz) are largely clear and reliable.

Unfortunately, ascents in the Quimsa Cruz have been poorly documented, and a lot of climbing from the 1960s and '70s was unrecorded. In addition numerous parties have recorded routes on mountains that they named themselves but not indicated the exact location. As Yossi Brain stated in his Bolivia climbing guide, "There is more confusion over names and heights in the Quimsa Cruz than in any other area in Bolivia."

For this reason Sarah Griffin has begun a long-term project to collate information on climbing in the region and is making a global appeal to the mountaineering community by setting up a website. Through this it should be possible for any climber to add pictures and information relating to ascents in the area. As the site grows it could become the point of reference for climbing in the Quimsa Cruz. Visit www.quimsacruz.info or write to sarah@quimsacruz.info.

LINDSAY GRIFFIN, *Mountain INFO, CLIMB magazine*

Argentina and Chile

NORTHERN ANDES, ARGENTINA

Various ascents. In March Marcelo Brandán, Nicolás Pantaleón, and Angel Ireba made the second or third ascent to the subsidiary summit (6,600m, S27°02'12.4" W68°17'37.8") of Incahuasi, reaching it from a route previously used to ascend the highest summit but not the lower. The group erected base camp at 4,620m S27° 00' 29.3" W68° 15' 51.2". They ascended the northeast ridge to the second camp at 5,800m, then attacked the summit in the morning, with very low temperatures. They needed crampons and boots to negotiatesteep ice near the summit. Incahuasi is one of the world's highest volcanoes, and its summit holds the second highest ruins in the world. Its name means "Inca's House." They descended to base camp and then did the second ascent of Volcan Rojo del Incahuasi and Volcan Negro del Incahuasi (see *AAJ* 2001, p. 291).

In this same area Dario Bracali ascended, solo, Chucula, a volcano of 5,760m (S26° 46' W69° 59') in November. On the summit he found a six-foot-tall cairn. I investigated and found that Chucula is also known by the ancient names Peladito or Nevado Negro Muerto, and the cairn is a waypoint erected by German Walther Penck ca 1910. This was the third ascent.

MARCELO SCANU, *Buenos Aires, Argentina*

Cerro Chepical, first ascent and Cerro Fandango, ascent. In February 2005 Antonio Pontoriero and I erected a camp on the southwest shores of the salty Laguna Brava (Fierce Lagoon). Nearby were Inca ruins, the Inca Trail, and a wrecked airplane that crashed transporting race horses some 40 years ago. When a horse of the region wins a race, it's said that it's "the son of the horse that fell from the sky."

The weather was unstable, but on February 14 we ascended Cerro Chepical (4,646m, S28°23' 00.8" W68°55' 49.2"), a peak used as reference for many decades, although it was a virgin peak. On February 16 I ascended, solo, a summit known as Cerro Fandango (5,173m, S28°22'03.9" W68°58' 30.3") by its east face. On the top I found some Inca ruins, including a stone wall used to cut the wind. Behind the wall they made sacrifices and burned offerings. The next day, after a small snowfall, we left.

MARCELO SCANU, *Buenos Aires, Argentina*

Cerro de la Aguada, ascent and historical note. A group of Argentinean climbers of the Club Andino Mar del Plata and Janajman (Salta) ascended this 5,810m volcano that is near the massive Antofalla (6,409m). The ascent commemorated the 100th anniversary of the first ascent by Fritz

Reichert, considered one of the fathers of Argentinean mountaineering. The team was directed by Guillermo Almaraz and consisted of Antonio Moreno, Juan Speroni and Alejandro Gimenez. They erected base camp at 3,300m and another camp at 5,000m. They summited on August 28, in the Southern Hemisphere winter. On the top they found Inca ceremonial ruins but no traces from Reichert. The group thinks that he might have ascended another minor summit or a different mountain. Andean authority Evelio Echevarria says that this is improbable, so the mystery remains unsolved.

MARCELO SCANU, *Buenos Aires, Argentina*

Cerro El Cóndor, addendum. On p. 302 of the *AAJ* 2004, El Cóndor is mentioned in the title of Alexander von Gotz's report, but we mistakenly deleted his brief mention of their El Cóndor ascent. Von Gotz and companions climbed to the north summit (6,356m or 6,373m, depending on the map; 6,440m on their GPS) of the peak, where they found no trace of previous passage. El Cóndor's south summit, which maps indicate as being lower, appeared to be clearly higher. This observation supports the assertions of Henri Barret and Marcelo Scanu, who also believe the south summit to be higher. See *AAJ* 2002, p. 314, for more information.

Ten years of exploration in the Puna de Atacama. During the last decade, exploratory mountaineering has achieved importance in the Puna de Atacama, a high plateau (altiplano) at about 3,500m in northern Argentina and Chile. This Andean region, one of the least explored corners of the world, is a desert featuring vast salt plains and the world's highest volcanoes. The Incas invaded it about 500 years ago and left many archeological remains, even atop mountains over 6,000m high.

Before 1994 only pioneers, such as the 1937 Polish team Mathias Rebitsch, Johan Reinhard, Philippe Reuter, and members of the Club Andino Tucumán, visited this isolated region. Since then, exploration has become intense and fructiferous. The 6,500ers have been the main objective, but other notable ascents have also been achieved.

Greg Horne (Canada) published a brief guide in a specialized magazine after climbing some of the highest peaks in summer 1995. Between 1999 and 2005 Henri Barret (France) explored the least known part of the Puna, the northern section of the Argentine province of Catamarca, and made the first ascents of Vallecitos (6,168m), Colorados (6,053m), Condor (6,373m), Cumbre del Laudo (6,152m), the western summit (6,326m) of the volcano Antofalla, and Aguas Dulces (5,642m). In 1999 Alex Von Gotz (Germany) and some partners opened routes on Walter Penck (6,658m) from the south and Bonete (6,759m) from the west. The following year John Biggar (Scotland) led the first ascent of Baboso (6,070m), situated due south of Laguna del Inca Pillo, in La Rioja (Argentina).

Jaime Suarez (Mendoza, Argentina) has organized several expeditions, climbing many of the highest summits. They opened new routes on Bonete (from the southwest, actual normal [meaning it is now the "normal route" on the mountain], 1996), Incahuasi (6,638m, from the north, 1996), Tres Cruces Sur (6,749m, from the southeast, 2001), Walter Penck (from the southeast, actual normal, 2000) and ATA peak (6,497m, from the northwest, 1998). The Grupo Rosarino de Alta Montaña made the outstanding first ascent of the south face of Tres Cruces Sur (from the southwest, 2000) and the first winter ascent of Patos (6,239m, 2001). Fernando Santamaría and other mountaineers from Mendoza made the first winter ascent of Incahuasi in 2003.

Several expeditions organized in the coastal Argentinean town of Mar del Plata between 1998 and 2005 opened new routes on Pissis (6,882m, from the north, actual normal), Tres Cruces Sur (from the south, direct), Vallecito (from the northeast), Antofalla (6,440m, from the north, with partners from Mendoza and Salta)[Antofalla's elevation differs depending on the map.—Ed.], and Bonete (from the west-southwest). They also achieved the first modern ascents of Aguada (5,810m) and Archibarca (5,629m), near Antofalla, and Inca del Mar (5,135m), near Laguna de los Aparejos. At the top of these three mountains they found Inca ruins. They also made the first ascents of the last remaining virgin local summits above 6,500m: Pissis's west summit (6,775m), Walter Penck's south summit (6,575m) and Bonete's west summit (6,501m).

While gathering information for the first climbing guide to the Andes' thirteen 6,500ers, between 2000 and 2003 Dario Bracali (Argentina) climbed all the local main summits higher than 6,500m in a simple and fast style. Meanwhile, he explored the area, helping to establish the most direct approaches, and made the first ascent of Lampallo (4,975m), in the Chaschuil Valley.

In a decade of exploration many of the most obvious routes to the highest peaks of the Puna have been climbed. Now it is time for first ascents of subsidiary peaks, harder or less accessible routes, and winter ascents.

GUILLERMO ALMARAZ, *Mar del Plata, Argentina*

CENTRAL ANDES, CHILE

Punta Italia, Direct West Face. This fine mountain had its first ascent in 1934 by Italians Gervasutti and Binaghi. Some routes were established on the 4,863m peak since then, the last being completed on December 21 by Chileans Andrea Garrido, Valentina Rota, Rodrigo Ponce, and David Valdés. They established base camp on the moraine between the glaciers Mesón Alto and Loma Larga. From there it took four to five hours to reach Camp 1. From Camp 1 to the summit, the route (800m, D 35° 5.8) begins with 400m of 35° snow and ice to the base of the west face. It then ascends a chimney and a 20m dihedral of class II/III rock, before continuing up the 400m face, with eight rope lengths up to 5.8 and a final 70m of II/III to the summit.

MARCELO SCANU, *Buenos Aires, Argentina.*

North Tower of Rengo, Séptimo Arte. In February 2005 Francisco Rojas, Dario Arancibia, and I opened a new route, using capsule style, on the North Tower of Rengo, an almost unknown granite peak located in the central Andes of Chile. It is the biggest tower in the valley, but there are other walls and spires around. In fact, just in front of the North Tower there is another huge wall called Solarium, which has trad routes up to 11 pitches, 5.11a, all of them characterized by perfect rock, little protection, and (because of its north orientation) no vegetation. Between these two main features is a little forest, which makes a kind of base camp.

Rengo is a little town 150km south of Santiago. From there it's another 50km to the east, by a very bad road, to arrive to the walls. The good news is you can arrive there by car, so the only walking you will do is 100m from there to the walls. The bad news is there are horses there, and they sometimes have the bad habit of walking over your tent.

Up and down the valley are smaller cliffs, but still big enough to offer a lifetime of climbing. If you consider that at present there are at most only 20 routes, the potential of the area is clear.

It is en route to a copper mine that is still in the exploration phase. Further climbing development will depend on the mine's access policy once mining begins.

Our route's name is Séptimo Arte (19 pitches, 650m, 5.9 A2+). It's the fourth route in the tower, but the first on the hard left section of the wall (there's still lots of space for new routes to the left of our line) and the first to go from the ground to the summit.

We began February 10, fixing ropes to bypass overhangs and roofs, in rock of average quality. For the first two days we were helped by Felipe González Donoso, who led the most difficult pitch (A2+). After 250m we arrived at the middle section, where we established a bivouac in 5th-class terrain. Then we retrieved our ropes and fixed them again in the upper section, this time being able to climb free all the pitches. We summited on the 18th after a summit push from the bivouac.

RODRIGO FICA, *Abriendo Huella, Chile*

The North Tower of Rengo, showing its first route, Séptimo Arte. *Rodrigo Fica*

Torres del Brujo, El Condor. Elena Davila, Riccardo Redaelli, and I finally reached Santiago, Chile on December 20 after a long flight from Milan. Our goal was to open a new route in the Azufre River Valley, home of the extraordinary Torres del Brujo. We reached the town of San Fernando by train and bought provisions that would see us through the ten days we expected to spend at base camp. On December 21 we met Don Segundo, who provided two mules and accompanied us to base camp. Since we didn't have much equipment (a few friends, six pitons, nuts, and ten 8mm bolts), two mules would suffice. We reached base camp after two days of walking and a worrisome river fording. The place was fantastic!

On December 23 we reconnoitered the area and promptly observed a beautiful granite pillar furrowed by clean dihedrals and cracks. The pillar was about an hour and a half from base camp, on the virgin walls in front of Torres del Brujo. The approach was tortuous, but the trade-off was not having to cross the glacier, which would prove demanding and dangerous, because elevated temperatures triggered constant avalanches. The next day we fixed the first two pitches. The ascent seemed doable and the climb so far was both unhindered and uncomplicated. We decided to only use bolts to equip belays.

Christmas is a holiday, but for us it was mainly a day of rest. We had equipped 150 meters, halfway to the top of the pillar. From there, a ridge of huge, unsteady boulders leads to the summit. We decided to end our ascent by reaching the top of the pillar the following day.

On December 27 we left our tents and faced a nasty surprise: the weather had changed. We couldn't see more than 5m in the heavy fog. The mountains had disappeared! We were forced to take a rest. Our spirits dropped along with the temperature. But it improved that evening, and the morning after was stupendous. We finished the route, leaving the belays well equipped. We descended the route and returned to base camp satisfied. We named the route El Condor (V 5.9 A1, 300m) after one of them flew overhead during our homecoming.

SILVESTRO STUCCHI, PONTERANIC, ITALY

Adapted from Alpinist *magazine, www.alpinist.com*

Torres del Brujo, Aprendiz del Brujo, Grand Illusion, and other activity. The Torres del Brujo area is situated in the Chilean Andes, south of Santiago, in the massif of Cerro Portillo (4,850m). The starting point is the small town San Fernando, located in the province Region VI, 150km from the capital. From San Fernando turn toward Termas del Flaco. At first the road is good, then dusty. After 50km continue from the statue Piedra de la Virgen, upstream of Rio Azufre and Rio San Jose, to Glacier Universidad and the Torres del Brujo base camp.

In February 2005 five Slovak mountaineers visited this area. The group consisted of Dusan Beranek (club: Metropol Kosice), Jozef Kristin (club: HK Filozof Bratislava), Juraj Podebradsky (club: Slavia UK Bratislava), Rastislav Simko (club: HK Sitno Banska Stiavnica), and I, Vlado Linek (club: HK Filozof Bratislava). Our goal was to repeat and, if possible, free climb the route Clandestino (9+[UIAA] A0) on Falso Brujo and to make first ascents in the Torres del Brujo massif.

After a two-day approach we reached base camp below Torres del Brujo, close to Glacier Universidad. There were Spanish and Italian mountaineers there too, and they did some routes. The approach glacier to Brujo was in bad condition, and it was necessary to use picks and crampons. The weather was stable and very hot. According to local people, it was a La Niña year in Chile. The glacier was changing every day. Because of the dangerous glacier, the Italians and Spaniards decided to climb on lower walls that had a good approach, while we found a way

Jozef Kristin on the third pitch of Grand Illusion. *Vlado Linek*

across the complex glacier. The approach from base camp to the face took four hours. We started sleeping on a moraine, close to the glacier, that was two and a half hours from the wall.

On February 13–14, Dusan Beranek and Juraj Podebradsky did probably the third ascent of Clandestino, at 7c+ A0. It is 13 pitches (7b, 6c+, 6b, 7c+ A0, 7a, 7a A0, 7b, 7a+, 7a+, 7c+, 7a+, 6a+, 7b) and 400m. During the ascent Rastislav Simko filmed their progress. Their initial plan to climb Clandestino free was not realized. The fourth pitch, graded 7c+ A0, would be climbed free at 8a+ or so, the A0 in the 6th pitch is too smooth for free climbing, and the 10th at 7c+ AF has a very hard start [AF, "all free," is a designation for a pitch on which a climber led all the moves free, but could not achieve a continuous redpoint or onsight. Perhaps the climber fell or had to rest on gear, yet did not resort to pulling on gear for upward progress—Ed.]. Dusan Beranek was not able to imagine how to make some of the moves. They finished the route at 6 p.m. the second day. Free Clandestino is a challenge for the future.

Aprendiz del Brujo, showing: (1) Reflexión Vertical, 5.11d (Farias-Heitmann). (2) Grand Illussion, 310m, 8 pitches, 9/9+ AF (Jozef Kristín, Vladimír Linek, Juraj Podebradsky, 2005). (3) Un poco Patagonia, 5.10d (Veit Uhlig). Vlado Linek

Jozef Kristin and I worked on new route in the central part of Aprendiz del Brujo. The granite is good, very hard, similar to the rock in Yosemite Valley. In the northeast face there are obvious crack systems. We decided for a line in the center of the wall. From February 12–14 we climbed three pitches (a chimney, a pillar, and nice slab) and joined a crack system that goes through a big overhang and continues to the upper part of the face.

On February 15 Dusan Beranek and Rastislav Simko left for home, while Juraj Podebradsky joined Jozef and me. On February 17 and 18 we finished the route and reached the summit of Aprendiz del Brujo. The fourth, fifth, and sixth pitches have nice crack climbing, and the last two pitches are easier slabs and the summit ridge. The route is 310m long and was climbed in 8 pitches.

On February 20 we climbed all of the route free and graded the pitches 6+, 7-, 8-, 9/9+ AF, 8, 8-, 5+, 7-. We climbed all pitches redpoint or pinkpoint, except for the 4th. The 4th pitch involves an overhanging corner crossed by a big roof. Juraj Podebradsky did it AF. We named the 310m route Grand Illusion, because the crux pitch resembles the route with the same name on Sugarloaf, in California: bad hands and no feet. We hand-drilled 30 bolts, 17 for belays and 13 on pitches. We recommend taking 15 quickdraws, two sets of cams, and a set of nuts. We wanted to try the crux pitch again, but falling rock damaged the crampons we left on the glacier, and we were not able to return.

There are several routes on the towers Aprendiz del Brujo and Falso Brujo from 300m to 500m long. In 2004 and 2005 local climber Juanjo Fernandez, from Santiago, did routes there, but we have no information about his climbs. Italian and Spanish mountaineers also did routes there this year.

VLADO LINEK, *Slovak Mountaineering Union JAMES and Mountaineering Club Filozof Bratislava*

CENTRAL ANDES, ARGENTINA

Aconcagua, 2004-2005 season overview. From December 15, 2004 to March 15, 2005 there were 6,490 visitors, less than the preceding year. There were fewer trekkers, but more climbers and more ascents. There was also less snow and serious concern regarding rising temperatures and melting glaciers. Park facilities were improved and 20 tons of garbage brought down.

Four climbers died. Two French died on the south wall in a big storm, a German on the Polish Glacier, and a Brazilian on the normal route. He summited at night and died of exposure. There were two other climber deaths in the region, one in Mercedario, San Juan and other in Pissis, Catamarca.

As an interesting sidelight, a backpack lost two years ago by an Argentinean climber was found by the police and returned to its owner. The pack contained lots of equipment and euros. After the two years the money was worth three times its value in Argentinean money. A good investment!

MARCELO SCANU, *Buenos Aires, Argentina*

Uruguayan rugby team plane crash of 1972, new discovery. On February 12, 2005 Mario Perez (an Argentinean horse guide) and I made a historical discovery related to the famous crash in the Andes of a Uruguayan plane chartered by a rugby team in 1972. This story gained world-wide fame after 16 people survived 72 days on the frozen slopes with nothing to eat except the bodies of their dead teammates. It was made even more famous by the best-selling book, Alive.

I visited the well-known crash site in the Cordillera Occidental and decided to explore up the mountain looking for the point where the airplane must have initially hit. As Perez and I climbed up we found parts of the airplane that seemed to indicate that the plane actually crashed in a different gully than previously believed. As I followed this hunch I found a coat, glasses, and the wallet belonging to one of the survivors, Eduardo Strauch. These were almost 3,000 vertical feet above the place where the fuselage came to rest and the survivors had lived their odyssey.

Eduardo had taken his coat off when he boarded the plane 32 years ago. He had his wallet in his inner pocket, and he put his glasses on the outer pocket. When the airplane hit a saddle in the mountains it broke into two pieces. The inside of the plane decompressed and the coat that Eduardo had put on the overhead shelf flew out into the snow, not to be found until 2005. The wallet, somewhat protected by the coat, was in relatively good shape. The wallet had IDs with recognizable photographs. This discovery showed that the plane actually came down a different gully than previously believed, one that is actually steeper and narrower. It also connected me with Eduardo Strauch; we have since become good friends and are working on a few projects together.

On February 12, I continued on to climb an unnamed 15,400' peak to get a view of what Roberto Canessa and Fernando Parrado saw in 1972 as they reached the saddle that would allow them down into Chile. My climb involved a couple of short sections of technical climbing on ice and frozen dirt. I photographed, apparently for the first time, the view that the two boys had when they reached a lower saddle of that peak. This had special significance to the boys since that was probably the first

Ricardo Peña in front of the memorial of piled rocks, a cross, airplane parts, clothing, and memorabilia that has been brought up by the survivors to honor those who died. Their remains are buried about six feet away at a spot marked by another cross. *Mario Perez*

The view presented to Parrado and Roberto Canessa after climbing partway up the 15,400' peak above the crash site. These are the mountains they spent 10 days crossing, living off human flesh. *Ricardo Peña*

time they realized they were in fact in the middle of the Andes and not on the western edge as they had thought for more than 60 days. In spite of this realization, and showing incredible courage, they headed west in a 10-day expedition and reached civilization 71 days after the crash.

Eduardo Strauch and I, along with many of the survivors, are now planning an exploratory expedition and documentary film to the site, in search of more evidence and a repeat (by me and possibly Roberto Canessa) of the historical climb and trek out to Chile. This is with the purpose of clarifying the events and honoring and commemorating the 35th anniversary of this incredible event.

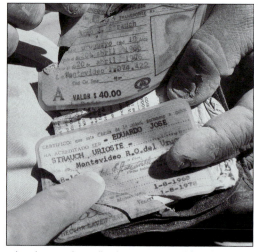

Eduardo Strauch's wallet, lost in 1972 and found in 2005. *Ricardo Peña*

RICARDO PEÑA

NORTHERN PATAGONIA, CHILE

Cerro Trinidad, Velebit. This route was fun, but not as hard as others in this region. Ivica Matkovic and I were in the area for only a short time in January, and began with six days of constant rain. Nearing the end of our time limit, we decided not to start working on a really big route, and found the north face of Cerro Trinidad. It was interesting enough and looked climbable in the time we had.

We started the route twice. On January 26 we climbed 150 meters and rappelled off in heavy rain. Returning from this attempt, Seb Grieve told us that it was dangerous to be on the face in the rain, especially in crack systems and chimneys, because these features quickly transform into waterfalls.

On January 31 we had better luck and climbed the route in one long day. Velebit (550m, V 6c+ [5.11c] A1), is mostly free with a short aid section in a chimney. We placed bolts at the belays and placed five more for protection on the route. The aid section, when a party has more time, will be possible to climb free.

BORIS CUJIC, *Sveta Nedelja, Croatia*
Adapted from Alpinist *magazine, www.alpinist.com*

San Lorenzo, first winter ascent. In July Chilean andinistas Pablo Besser, Camilo Rada, and Manuel Bugueño completed the first winter ascent, by the Agostini Route, of Monte San Lorenzo (3,706m), Patagonia's second-highest summit, in Chile's XI Region. The team established a base camp at the Tony Rorhen Hut (next to the old Agostini Hut), after pulling heavy loads on snow sleds through the native alerce woods for six days. They then established an advanced camp in Brecha de La Cornisa at 2,400m. They intended to establish an advanced camp before the summit push, but the continuing good weather prompted them to go for the top from La Cornisa, alpine style.

The next morning, after several hours of hiking in fresh snow, expedition member Marcelo Camus had to turn back due to a knee injury. Pablo, Camilo, and Manuel continued, passing an exposed serac barrier en route to the north summit ridge. To reach the main summit they had to surmount the north summit and descend to a snowfield before climbing up again. Alas, they encountered the huge summit ice mushroom as darkness fell. Encouraged by good weather, they descended to the snowfield below the summit and bivouacked in a snow cave. Temperatures dropped as low as –30° C during the night. The next morning they went back up, climbed the mushroom, and finally gained the summit on July 16 at 1:30 p.m. It was Pablo Besser's third attempt to climb San Lorenzo; with this ascent Camilo Rada has ticked Patagonia's two highest summits in winter (the highest being Monte San Valentín, 4,058m).

Reported by PABLO BESSER *to* JOSE IGNACIO MORALES *for Escalando*

Adapted from Alpinist *magazine, www.alpinist.com*

NORTHERN PATAGONIA. ARGENTINA.

Lake District, Bariloche, Cerro Catedral. The granite spires around Refugio Frey in Cerro Catedral provide great rock climbing, with routes ranging from one to ten pitches in a beautiful alpine environment. Routes tend to be mixed, requiring an average rack and having bolts in featureless sections. Many routes tend to be run-out and adventurous. Between mid-February and mid-March 2005, I replaced 270 old self-drive bolts, many of which had homemade hangers, with new 12mm stainless steel bolts and hangers (Triplex-Fixe combo). Euro-style self-drive bolts are notorious for being unreliable and having low holding power. These kind of bolts have been used in this area since the late 1980s and continue to be used by a few people. I hope that this bolt-replacement initiative will help first ascensionists realize the importance of stainless steel bolts and hangers instead of self-drives or zinc-plated bolts, which have a short life span. I replaced bolt-for-bolt, not adding extras, and in several instances chopped bolts that had been added after the first ascent without the first ascensionist's consent. Many thanks to Fixe USA for selling me the bolts and hangers at wholesale cost, and to my friends Lynn and MFT for loaning me drills and extra batteries.

ROLANDO GARIBOTTI, *Club Andino Bariloche*

SOUTHERN PATAGONIA, ARGENTINA

CHALTEN MASSIF

Season overview. The Fitz Roy and Cerro Torre massifs saw a ferocious amount of activity this season, particularly during a long spell of good weather in late January and early February. This is the third time in the last few years that an unusually long good-weather spell occurred, always around the same time of year. This might be another indication of global warming. Despite George Bush's denial of human responsibility for global warming, weather conditions in Patagonia, and elsewhere, are changing at a pace that hardly seems natural.

In addition to climbs reported individually below, many impressive repeats and new variations were made. Englishmen Leo Houlding and Kevin Thaw climbed Poincenot from the west, starting via an unclimbed ramp below the Carrington-Rouse route to join the Fonrouge-Rosasco route, which they followed to the summit. There they bivied before descending the following day. Later Houlding and Thaw completed the 5th ascent of the Goretta Pillar to the summit of Fitz Roy, which they reached via the Casarotto Route and Kearney-Knight variation. They started from Rio Blanco base camp around 2 a.m. and summited at 8 p.m. the following day, returning to base camp in mid-afternoon of their third day. They took a minimalist approach, carrying no stove, bivi gear, or alpine boots, and taking only one ice axe and one set of strap-on aluminum crampons between them. They free-climbed everything except a pendulum to avoid icy cracks. They rapped the route in poor conditions through the second night.

American Aaron Martin became the fourth person to solo Cerro Torre. (Previous solo ascents were by Pedrini 1985, Whimp 1993, Potter 2002. Potter and Martin are the only ones to have done the ascent on-sight.) He roped up only for the Bridwell Pitch on the upper headwall, but found scary mixed climbing low on the route while climbing in crampons over his approach shoes. (Yes, he climbed Cerro Torre in sneakers!) Martin fixed his rope at the compressor, then climbed to the end of his rope, at which point he tied it off to his only ice screw and continued toward the summit. A body length or so from the summit he found unconsolidated snow and decided to retreat. He left the Noruegos advanced camp at 2:30 a.m. and reached the top around 1 p.m., completing the ascent in 16 hours roundtrip. During his stay in the area, Martin, with American Jacob Schmitz, made the second ascent of the Canadian Route on Cerro Fitz Roy (see below). Schmitz dropped his climbing shoes early on, so Martin led every pitch, completing the ascent in 36 hours roundtrip from base camp. Earlier the two had attempted the Casarotto Route, with the Kearney-Knight variation, reaching the top of the Goretta Pillar from which they retreated after a cold bivy.

On Aguja Poincenot, Italian Elio Orlandi and Argentinians Horacio Codo and Lucas Fava made the second ascent of the Potter-Davis route (2001) on the north face, making a slight variation at the top, where they avoided the prominent roof by climbing up and right for the last two pitches.

Argentinian/Slovene Monika Kambic-Mali and Slovene Tanja Grmovsek completed the first all-female ascent of Cerro Torre, which they climbed via the Compressor Route. Right below the compressor, two pitches from the top, Kambic-Mali was hit by falling ice and broke several ribs. With Kambic-Mali in severe pain but unwilling to give up, Kambic-Mali and Grmovsek were aided by a British team who fixed their ropes. While Kambic-Mali jumared, Grmovsek climbed protecting herself with the fixed rope, but on the Bridwell Pitch was forced to pull on the fixed line a couple of times because the rivet and copperhead placements were out of her reach. It should be noted that Kambic-Mali, with Tina Di Batista, is also responsible for the first all-female ascent of Fitz Roy, which they accomplished in 2003.

In August 2004 Canadian Sean Isaac and American Will Mayo made the second winter ascent of Aguja Guillaumet, via the Amy Couloir (350m, III 5.8 55°).

After their ascent of a new route on the west pillar of Paine Chico (see below), Slovenes Tomaz Jakofcic and Grega Lacen moved to the Chalten massif, where they climbed Ipermermoz (600m, 6c, Giordani-Levitti, 1996) on the north face of Aguja Mermoz, completing what might have been the first free ascent. Earlier in the season Argentinians Horacio Codo and Walter Rosssini also climbed this route. Later Jakofcic, with American Josh Wharton, made a rare ascent of Corallo (450m, 7a+ A0, Leoni-Salvaterra, 1994) on Aguja Rafael Juarez.

On another note, in December 2004 the National Parks Administration of Argentina approved a measure instating a US $200 per person climbing fee for Cerro Fitz Roy and its out-lying peaks, which includes the Cerro Torre group. There was an immediate strong reaction against this measure, both from mountaineers and park rangers. Before the new regulation could be enacted, in late January the National Parks Administration temporarily suspended it until they could study the matter further. Since that study is on-going, it is important to make our voices heard. Please send an e-mail to fitzroy_chalten@yahoo.com to receive more infor-mation, including a list of reasons to oppose this measure, as well as a list of addresses of Park Service officials to e-mail.

ROLANDO GARIBOTTI, *Club Andino Bariloche*

Cerro Torre, Quinque Anni ad Paradisum. Italian climbers Alessandro Beltrami, Giacomo Rossetti, and Ermanno Salvaterra climbed a new route on the 4,000' east face of Cerro Torre in November 2004. Salvaterra first climbed Cerro Torre in 1983, and has been one of the area's most devout climbers. See his feature article earlier in this Journal.

Cerro Torre, Slovenian Start variation, and Aguja Poincenot, Italian Route, first integral ascent. On January 17, 2005, our small team from Slovenia, Patagonian veteran Silvo Karo, my wife Tanja Grmovsek, and Monika Kambic-Mali, and I settled down in Campo de Agostini. Our plan was to climb fast and light and to adjust our goals as the weather permitted. A window of good weather was forecast for January 19. The forecasts, which Thomas Huber was getting from Innsbruck (big thanks to him and Innsbruck's meteorologist), were a big help. On the night of the 19th we left Campo De Agostini and went directly to the base of Aguja Saint Exupery's west face. Silvo and I warmed up on a very nice route, Chiaro di Luna (800m, 6c), which we climbed in six hours (plus three hours to rappel). At 3 o'clock in the morning we returned to Agostini, after 23 hours on foot.

After more bad weather Silvo and I climbed the Anglo-American route (450m, 6b, Boysen-Braithwaite-Dickinson-Reid-Sylvester, 1974) on the west face of Aguja Rafael Juarez, in strong winds and snow showers, mostly in boots, on January 26 from Polacos.

At the end of January an unusually long and warm spell of weather set in. We moved our high camp to Noruegos and, and on January 31 Silvo and I started our planed line: the Slovenian Start on Cerro Torre. With only rock- and ice-climbing equipment, power bars, and a bottle of water, we started climbing at first daylight. We climbed the route Rubio y Azul (350m, 6c, Salvaterra, 1994) to the summit of Torre de la Media Luna. We continued on virgin terrain, climbing a few pitches up to 6c+ and passing the Three Sisters towers, as we named the first three towers above Torre de la Media Luna. Then we made a 40m rappel, climbed another pitch back to the ridge and continued on an easier ridge (UIAA III/VI) for more than 500m, passing an obvious 30m spire that we named Torrisimo. After another rappel we were at base of Torre Pereyra. We climbed 300m (6c+) in fine cracks and corners to its summit. We then traversed another 100m down the ridge and after a short rappel were on the Col of Patience, meeting climbers who already climbed the Torre. We had been climbing for about 11 hours. We drank a bit, left some cams, and at 5 p.m. started up the Compressor Route. We made good time on the first wet pitch, but conditions worsened, with more snow and ice, forcing us to climb in

From left to right: Cerro Adela Norte, Cerro Torre, Torre Egger, Punta Herron, Cerro Standhardt. 2004-05 climbing activity shown: (1) Slovenian Start (Grmovsek-Karo 2005); (2) Compressor Route (Alimonta-Claus-Maestri, 1970); (3) Quinque Anni ad Paradisum (Beltrami-Rossetti-Salvaterra, 2004); (4) Italian (De Dona-Giongo 1980) and Titanic (Giarolli-Orlandi, 1987) route combination (first climbed by Martin-O'Neill, 2000); (5) Davis-Potter (2005); (6) Standhardt to Egger traverse (Huber-Schnarf, 2005) involving: (6a) Festerville (Martin-O'Neill, 2000), (6b) Spigolo dei Bimbi (Cavallaro-Salvaterra-Vidi, 1991). Photo and route information from *Rolando Garibotti*

Silvo Karo on the Italian Route on Poincenot. *Andrej Grmovsek*

boots and crampons. We enjoyed the last sunlight on the monumental bolt traverse. We continued through the night, climbing tricky, mixed corners. After we passed the Ice Towers, freezing, stormy winds slowed us. We enjoyed the first sunlight at the base of the headwall and at 10:30 a.m. stood on the summit of Torre, in a sunny, almost cloudless day, with a wonderful view. We climbed our line in 28 continuous hours, gaining about 1,700m in altitude and climbing more than 3km of rock and ice. Silvo summited Torre for the second time, 19 years after his first. We rappelled the Compressor Route, which was now very wet, finishing our roundtrip at 7 p.m. in Noruegos.

We waited for the girls, also climbing on Torre, and together we went to Chalten to celebrate. But the weather became nice again, and we had to return to the mountains. On February 6 Silvo and I moved from Agostini to a bivouac above Laguna Sucia, our goal being to make the second ascent of the Italian Route on the east-southeast pillar of Poincenot (900m, 6c A3, Bortoli-Carnati-Colombo, 1986), light and fast, in alpine style, and as free as possible. The route was climbed by a large Italian expedition 19 years ago, over two years, with fixed lines from bottom to top. Checking the topo, we thought the many pitches of A1 or 6a A1 would probably go free and fast, so we planned a one-day or day-and-a-half marathon. On the morning of February 7 we crossed the dangerous glacier to the base of Poincenot's south wall. We started the first few easy pitches not earlier than at 9 a.m. When we came to the first aid pitch, we could only stare at the smooth, vertical and overhanging wall looming more than 400m above us, with only a few features. Luckily, the Italians left many of pitons, aiders, bolt kits, and lots of fixed rope on a ledge. We took the rustic aiders (we didn't take ours because we thought we would not aid much) and some pitons. Half of the next 10 pitches were thin cracks, flakes, and slabs, which required time-consuming (though not technically hard) nailing and aid climbing. The other half of the pitches were awesome free climbing (to 6c) on huge flakes and in corners. We arrived at a good bivouac ledge just before dark. The next day we climbed the last aid pitch and continued on easier terrain, free climbing to 6c for about 450m to join the classic Irish Route (Cochrane-Whillans, 1962), on which we continued for another 350m to the summit of Aguja Poincenot, reaching it at 3 p.m. We'd done the second ascent of this elegant but quite hard route (I don't think many of the aid pitches could be free-climbed). We'd also made the first integral ascent (the Italians didn't climb to the summit). We rappelled the route and crossed the glacier through the night to our Laguna Sucia bivouac.

With this forth summit, I finished an intensive, successful three weeks in Patagonia. My holidays were over and I had to fly back home. But I will always remember my first trip to sunny Patagonia.

ANDREJ GRMOVSEK, *Slovenia*

Cerro Standhardt, Punta Herron, Torre Egger, traverse. I came to Patagonia this year with the primary goal of climbing Torre Egger. After a month of bad weather, at the beginning of February Stefan Siegrist and I made our first attempt. We started at night for the col between Standhardt and Bifida, traversed the great ramp on the east face of Standhardt, and reached the icy gully of Tobogan (Garibotti-Karo, 1999) after two raps. We climbed Tobogan and at sunrise stood on the Col dei Sogni, between Standhardt and Punta Herron. Hours later we reached the summit of Herron via Spigolo dei Bimbi (Cavallaro-Salvaterra-Vidi, 1991), but wind and bad conditions forced us to descend without standing on the great peak named Torre Egger.

Stefan went home, but I had four more weeks. Eventually I partnered with Andi Schnarf (Switzerland) and 22 year-old Rok Zalokar (Slovenia). The three of us made an attempt, starting as I did with Stefan, but after Herron we descended Tobogan to the serac, traversed it to the left, then followed the Italian Route (De Dona-Giongo, 1980) on Egger (a lot of old ropes and fixed gear up to the col). This attempt ended 20m below the summit of Egger. We could feel it, we were almost there, but warm conditions made it impossible to climb the final icy mushroom. No Egger, I thought, not this year.

Although another weather window materialized a week later, I had no real motivation for Egger again. Instead, Andi and I climbed Cerro Standhardt via Festerville (5.11, Martin-O'Neill, 2000), starting at 2 a.m. and gaining the summit at 3 p.m. Conditions were much better than the week before; a little colder, the ice a little better. Egger looks great from there. I saw a glow in Andi's eyes and knew his thoughts were the same as mine. Three hours later we reached the Col dei Sogni, the col of dreams, and my thoughts and dreams where one summit ahead, on the Egger!

We reached the summit of Punta Herron at sunset for its fifth ascent (sixth, if the Italians actually did make the first), including my ascents with Stefan and with Andi and Rok. We tried to sleep at the col between Herron and Egger, but it was too cold. (We called it the Col de Lux, feeling privileged to name it because we think we were the first humans on it, We found no trace of the Italians here or above, in contrast to all of the fixed ropes and gear below.) We started climbing at 4 a.m., via a great 5.10 slab with bad protection on a cold and windy night. The climbing got easier, and the ice on the mushroom was better than it had been a week before. At

7:30 a.m. my dream became reality: we were on the top of Egger. We could see the footsteps of Dean Potter and Steph Davis, who had reached the summit the day before.

Descending, via Titanic, wasn't much fun, but once back in Noruegos camp, Dean, Steph, and I clasped our worked hands in celebration. We still couldn't believe that we climbed our big dream! But the dreams will go on.

I extend special thanks to Karl Gabl from Innsbruck, Austria, who gave us perfect weather forecasts. All Patagonia climbers benefited from them. Karl was the real hero in this season of Patagonia climbing!

THOMAS HUBER, *Germany*

Thomas Huber on a 5.10 pitch of the Martin-O'Neill route (Festerville) on Cerro Standhardt. *Andi Schnarf*

Historical Note: Regarding the 1980 Italian Route (De Dona-Giongo) on Egger, Huber writes, "I [cannot say] if they climbed it or not. I just will say, what I saw and found (and didn't find)...but for sure I will have an opinion." Huber notes the conspicuous absence of any trace of passage at the Herron-Egger col, or on the 5.10 slabs from the col to the summit, nor visible descent anchors from the col to the top of Egger. This, notes Huber, sharply contrasts with the abundance of fixed ropes and gear on the lower portion of the Italian Route. However, several clarifications need to be made. The fixed ropes and gear on the lower portion were left by teams that attempted the route before De Dona and Giongo, including a large British team led by Leo Dickinson in 1974 and a large expedition from New Zealand in 1975 (Punta Herron is named after one of the members of this team, Philip Herron, who died at the base of Torre Egger when he fell into a crevasse). De Dona and Giongo claim to have climbed alpine style, therefore it is not surprising that in the upper portion of the route gear would be sparse. In an article published in the Italian journal Scandere in 1980 (p. 33), Giongo writes: "In the slabs below the summit mushroom we place three bolts, as irrefutable proof of our passage."

Huber and Schnarf dancing on the summit of Torre Egger, with Steph Davis and Dean Potter's tracks behind. *Thomas Huber*

On the same page a photograph shows De Dona and Giongo climbing a mushroom-like formation in cloudy conditions, with a caption that reads: "Climbing the summit mushroom, a few meters below the summit." While Huber's findings cast some doubt on De Dona and Giongo's claims, further investigation is required.

Torre Egger, near miss and monster fall. In early February, Jonny Copp, Josh Wharton, and I joined forces to climb in the Cerro Torre and Fitzroy area. We set our sights on Torre Egger. It had only seen one alpine-style ascent, its last ascent three years ago. We agreed on the east prow, combining the Italian (De Dona-Giongo, 1980) and Titanic routes (Giarolli-Orlandi, 1987), in an alpine-style single push. [This link up (950m ED+ VI 5.10b A2 90°) was first climbed by Martin and O'Neill in 2002—Ed.]

We climbed the route in three massive blocks, each of us enjoying a good share of the leading. The climbing on the first six pitches (Italian Route) follows a large dike, and is mostly loose and moderate. Venturing onto the Titanic, the bottom half of which is indistinct, we simply followed a natural line to the large snow arête a little over halfway up. This section of the route, again, was loose and moderate. Above the snow arête, we found better rock on steeper terrain. We retreated to a ledge at the base of the snow arête, from five pitches above, due to waterfalls. Opting to cover the terrain during a cooler time of day and arrive quickly at the conditions-dependent crux mushroom, we left our bivy at 3 a.m. Josh repeated the five pitches he had originally led, and we continued, battling verglas and extremely loose blocks on traversing terrain. We made the base of the mushroom at 8:00 a.m. It seems that Torre Egger's mushroom is larger and more overhung than those of its neighbors Cerro Torre and Cerro Standhardt. One rope length up an easy ice ramp deposited us within a pitch of the summit. Above our position was a narrow tube through the overhang. Being short on time, this was to be our way to the top in the increasing morning heat.

The lead was wild and involved. Having to excavate as much as climb, but with overhanging stemming and chimneying, I delicately wiggled through the overhang. After 20 more feet of vertical slush, I traversed up and right onto a fin, a mere three meters from the very top. As I began to mantle, the fin detached. I began to fall. The screamer sling attached to the ice screw five meters below me broke, sending

After the fall. Bean Bowers recovering after his 30m fall from Torre Egger's summit mushroom. See color photo in the front of this Journal for the pre-fall photo. *Jonny Copp*

me over and outside of my tube in a 30m fall. Luckily my trail line flipped me upside down, and Jonny's melted-out V-thread anchor broke, launching him into space, so that I landed with all 26 spikes skyward on a dynamic counterbalanced belay. As the mushroom fell apart above and around us, we decided that it was time to go.

Although we do not consider that we truly attained the summit, it will remain to all of us the most eventful and lucky non-summit to date. And, hell, if you can't have the summit itself, might as well take a piece with you.

BEAN BOWERS

Cerro Standhardt, Potter Route and other firsts. I arrived in El Chalten on January 29 to meet Dean Potter, who had been in Patagonia for a month and had a high camp set up at Noruegos, for the Torre group. The weather turned good the minute I got there, and eight hours after I arrived in camp we were climbing a new route, alpine style, on Cerro Standhardt. We started at dawn on January 30 and summited the mushroom in the early afternoon. Several pitches of full-on (clean) aid and the fact that it was an obvious line convinced us we were climbing Motivaciones Mixtas (900m, 5.10d A2 85°, Chaverri-Plaza, 1993), which had not been finished to the summit. Later we discovered we had done a new route to the right of Motivaciones Mixtas, which we called the Potter Route. [The Potter Route climbs the steep 200m upper east face headwall, which it reaches from the col north of the peak via the prominent snow-ramps of Exocet. The Potter Route and the unfinished Motivaciones Mixtas likely share some ground—Ed.]

Next we made an arduous failing attempt to link the Italian Route to Titanic on Torre Egger. Torre Egger had only seen six ascents, so we really wanted to get up it. However, conditions were terrible. We roasted in the sun as we climbed, then the route became a waterfall, and we got soaking wet. We spent a miserable bivy on a sloping rock fin waiting for dawn to bring better conditions, but it didn't get colder. We then got bombarded by half the summit mushroom, trying to fight our way up to the top. Completely drenched, we managed to get 20m below the disintegrating mushroom, but could not get up the mushy, overhanging snow to the summit. We descended in more waterfalls. The day was no fun, but at least no one died.

We descended to Campo Bridwell (Campo De Agostini) to recover. Using a spotting scope to find a better path up the nasty summit mushroom, Dean saw a promising line more to the west. A few days later in the next weather window, we tried for Torre Egger again. We went Yosemite-style, carrying 22 Clif Bars, a liter of water, Gore-Tex and a bivy sack, two ice tools, and one set of crampons. Starting in the evening we climbed and summited in 23 hours, making the first one-day ascent of Torre Egger, as well as the first female ascent. We lost one rope less than halfway down the descent and spent a miserably cold night crouched together waiting for light, before making endless raps with the remaining rope.

We went up the glacier one last time, during another perfect three days of weather in the first days of March. One of Dean's dreams has been to make the first BASE jump in Patagonia. We climbed the Bridwell-Stszewski on El Mocho, and Dean jumped, making it down to the glacier in mere seconds. I got to spend hours rappelling alone, with no traumatic incidents except for having to cut another stuck rope.

STEPH DAVIS

Fitz Roy, new route attempt. We made two trips to Patagonia to climb the Northwest Pillar of Fitz Roy. On the first trip the team consisted of Nicolas Fabbri, Jérôme Huet, and me. We three returned in late 2004, adding a feminine touch in the person of Véronique Barbier.

On our first expedition the weather, wind in particular, was so horrible that we fled. We abandoned our ropes and the pitons on the route. We returned ready for storms but had a month of fine weather, with only three or four windy days. It was so hot that we were often dehydrated. We turned back at the Third Tower, which seemed very blank. We were tired and dehydrated and found no ledges for sleeping; we had no portaledge.

The route follows the ridge that borders the left side of the Supercanaleta. The ridge consists of three pillars and a final section that apparently is shared with the Afanassieff Route. We equipped

Pierrick Keller on the artificial pitch of the Second Tower. *Keller Collection*

the first pillar with fixed ropes. It's easy artificial climbing (A1/A2), combined with free passages to 6b, on excellent rock. We then climbed the second pillar. There are mixed passages at M5, one artificial pitch of A2, and nice free and rather difficult (6b/c) pitches. They are extremely exposed, with poor rock and anchors. The upper part of the second pillar consists of five little towers, each about 10m high, the last one being a little more difficult (aid). The line then heads for a third, 150m, tower, which we did not climb. There is apparently only one possible route, a crack that is large at the start, gets narrower, and ends at a slab.

The whole route would cover some 1,800m. We climbed in 44 pitches. There would have been 10 more pitches before we reached the Afanassieff Route. We left 10 bolts and a number of anchors that we used on our way down.

Here is a beautiful project,which we offer to anyone who feels up to it. We will not be back. Whose turn is it?

PIERRICK KELLER, *France (translated by Konrad Kirch)*

Fitz Roy, Canadian Route; Aguja Rafael Juarez, Comono; other firsts and new variations. There was excitement among the climbers at El Chalten in the fourth week of January 2005. The barometer was finally rising after three weeks of stormy weather. Paul McSorley and I had just arrived, and found ourselves scrambling to get in position for Fitz Roy. Within a few days we were setting out from Paso Superior with two days of food, bivy gear, and intentions of finding a new route on the south or east face. We topped out on the Brecha de los Italianos, saw a system of right-facing corners just left of the Boris Simoncic Route (Biscak-Fabjan-Lenarcic, 1985), and knew it was our line. We crossed the small bowl, roped up below the 'schrund, and started climbing at around one p.m. Recent storms had left ice on ledges, and sometimes cracks, for the entire route. Afternoon shade on the south face made our hands too numb to free climb much harder than 5.9, and we climbed in mountain boots rather than rock shoes. Two pitches of easy mixed up a left-trending ramp brought us to a 5.9 square-cut corner with double cracks. A finger crack connected it to the next right-facing corner, which turned out to be the technical crux of the route. We aided this eight-meter section on small nuts (A1)—it would probably be 5.12 free—and continued up easier terrain with a mix of aid and free, aiming for a long laser-cut corner. A 5.9

The Canadian Route on Fitz Roy. *Jon Walsh*

squeeze for 15m behind a triangular flake landed us at the base of the "Enduro Corner." This perfect pitch of fingers and hands was sustained for 60m (though too cold for us to free) and required the belayer to unclip from the anchor so the leader could make the ledge at the top. The best pitch of the route, it would probably be mid-5.11 free. Another 30m right-facing corner brought us to terraced ledges, where we hacked out a bivy site. Sunshine the next morning made free climbing with rock shoes pleasanter, as we cruised up a long ramp system below a steep wall on our left. A short offwidth put us on the summit slopes, and we were soon enjoying T-shirt conditions on top. The descent went smoothly, as we rapped the Franco-Argentine and made it back to Paso Superior with daylight to spare. About 10 days later, in much warmer conditions, Aaron Martin and Jacob Schmitz, both from California, made the second ascent. Using short fixing, they climbed from the bergschrund to the summit in seven hours with Aaron leading every

Starting up the Enduro Corner on the Canadian Route, Fitz Roy. *Jon Walsh*

pitch and freeing 85% at 5.10 and under. We agreed on the quality of the route (Canadian Route, 5.10 A1, 500m new) and felt it would be a better alternative to its popular neighbor (the Franco-Argentine) for a party looking for a clean line without fixed ropes and manky old poorly equalized fixed anchors. A standard double rack is all that's needed, as a perfect nut or cam is never more than a body length away.

A week later we turned to rock climbs on the west side of the Fitz Roy group. From the Polacos bivouac Paul and I made the probable second ascent, first free, and first integral (to summit) ascent of the complete west buttress of Rafael Juarez (Crouch-Donini, 1996, who retreated from the junction with the 1974 Anglo-American route, four pitches from the top). We found four pitches of solid 5.10 and many of 5.4 to 5.9, which we mostly simul-climbed. A fun day on great rock.

Another week later, after resupplying, we found ourselves back at Polacos. However, Paul twisted his knee and was forced to rest for a few weeks. Not wanting to miss a good weather window, I decided to rope-solo the beautiful north face of Rafael Juarez. With no information as to what had been climbed, I started up the right side of a red pillar, and after couple of false starts due to unstable weather, I had two ropes fixed. The first 120m were mostly 5.9 to 5.10-, except midway up the second pitch, where a left-facing squeeze chimney led to a hand crack through a roof (probably 5.11 free). The barometer finally rose, and I ascended my ropes and climbed six more pitches, for a total of eight 60m pitches up, then about two pitches of easy traversing on the east face. I reached the summit in 12 hours. Further research suggested the first four pitches (240m; 5.9, A1, 5.9, 5.10-), to the top of the red pillar, were new (I called the line Comono), and then I followed Artebelleza (Clauss-Von Birckhahn, 2002) and the Anker-Piola route (1989) to the top.

Again I stashed my gear at Polacos, and returned a week later with Andrés Zegers of Chile and Isaac Cortes of Catalonia. The three of us had just recently met and had never climbed together, but we were psyched and the weather was perfect. The next morning (February 27) we were at the base of the south face of Aguja Desmochada, cursing ourselves for

The Train Track Cracks on Rafael Juarez. *Jon Walsh*

Climbing Rafael Juarez, with a view of St. Exupery. *Jon Walsh*

forgetting the food bag. Fuck it! We don't need food: the face is too beautiful! With no previous-route info, we climbed five amazing pitches, all 5.10 but for a short 5.11+ offwidth on the third pitch, just left of El Facón. At the horizontal break a third of the way up, we traversed to El Facón and merged with it for two long pitches of gritty 5.11a hands and fingers. We then moved left into the big left-facing corner and climbed the overhanging wall for 120m of A1. We then merged again with El Facón (Bowers-Bransby-Tresch, 2004) and followed it through the night, topping out on the summit at 10 a.m., for the third ascent of Desmochada. We called our variation Dieta del Lagarto, and it will go free at around 5.12+. A #5 Camalot was key for the upper pitches and likely made the difference for us. We rappelled the route, as we had found an old 8mm rope near the base and used it to sling horns and make other rap anchors. After 36.5 hours we made it back to our bivy and gorged ourselves on the treats we had forgotten on the climb. It was one of the best adventures we had ever had.

Aguja Rafael Juarez, north face. (1) Artebelleza (6c, Clauss-Von Birckhahn, 2002). (2) Comono (6a A1, Walsh, 2005). (3) Corallo (7a+ A0, Leoni-Salvaterra, 1994). The right skyline ridge, as reached from the obvious crack leading to the lowpoint notch, is the Anglo-American route (6b, Boysen-Braithwaite-Dickinson-Reid-Sylvester, 1974). Jon Walsh

Jon Walsh, *Canada*

Agujas Saint Exupery, Rafael Juarez, and Poincenot, traverse. Beginning on February 18 Jonny Copp and I enchained Saint Exupery, Aguja Rafael Juarez, and Aguja Poincenot in a 52-hour roundtrip from Polacos high camp. After oversleeping we left Polacos at 10 a.m. and climbed Exupery via the classic Chiaro di Luna (V 5.11-). We then descended along the north side of Exupery to gain the knife-edge ridge connecting Exupery with Rafael. After a few spectacular but moderate pitches along the knife-edge, we discovered a fantastic bivouac at 10 p.m., just below Rafael's upper spire. In the morning we climbed the few remaining pitches to Rafael's summit via the Anglo-American Route (IV 5.11-) and then descended that route to the base of Poincenot's south face. During the descent we encountered friendly Germans, who advised us of bad weather forecast for the following day. Abandoning our hope of free-climbing Judgment Day on the steepest portion of Poincenot's south face, we turned to the Fonrouge-Rosasco (V+ 5.11, 1968). After another bivouac at the junction of the Carrington-Rouse and the Fonrouge-Rosasco, we reached the summit of Poincenot early the next morning and descended (via the Carrington-Rouse) into the building wind to Polacos. We made the traverse with a single small pack between us, climbing free on lead and second, apart from a few of the Fonrouge's steeper pitches. When we began, we had quietly hoped we might be able to continue all the way to the summit of Fitz Roy; this would be possible

From left to right: Cerro Fitz Roy, Aguja de la Silla, Aguja Desmochada, Aguja Kakito, Aguja Poincenot, Aguja Rafael Juarez, Aguja Saint Exupery, Aguja de L'S, Mojon Rojo. 2004-05 climbing activity shown: (1) Exupery to Poincenot traverse (Copp-Wharton, 2005) involving: (1a) Chiaro di Luna (Giordani-Manfrini-Valentini, 1987); (1b) Anglo-American route (Boysen-Braithwaite-Dickinson-Reid-Sylvester, 1974); (1c) Fonrouge-Rosasco (1968). (2) French attempt (Barbier-Fabbri-Huet-Keller, 2004). Photo and route information from *Rolando Garibotti*

with a bit more good weather, less sleep, and a better alarm clock. The other obvious addition would be putting Aguja de L'S into the mix to create a monster route, which would include five of the Fitz Roy massif's classic summits.

JOSH WHARTON, *AAC*

Fitz Roy and Cerro Torre massifs, various ascents. Between mid-January and early March a young team of Slovene climbers, including me, visited the Fitz Roy and Cerro Torre massifs, spending a total of 40 days accomplishing a series of important ascents.

On January 24 Rok Zalokar, Aljaz Tratnik, and I tried to climb the Casarotto Route (Casarotto, solo, 1979) on Fitz Roy, but finding poor snow conditions on the glacier and approach couloirs, as well as ice-covered rock,

Jonny Copp on the Chiaro De Luna segment of the Agujas Saint Exupery, Rafael, and Poincenot traverse. *Josh Wharton*

we returned to Chalten to drink a beer and have a few days of rest.

On our second attempt, on January 29, we started from Paso at 2 a.m. and, finding good snow, reached the "jammed block" at the base of the Goretta Pillar by 7 a.m. We started climbing at 8 a.m. and by 3 p.m. reached the tenth pitch of the Kearney-Knight variation to the Casarotto Route. We felt that our pace for a team of three was not bad and therefore decided to climb the Chimichurri y Tortas Fritas (Locher-Pedrini, 1985) variation on the upper west side of the pillar. After a few unsuccessful attempts to find the right line, we bivied. The following day we climbed our own variation (400m, 7a A1), following a crack system just right of Chimichurri y Tortas Fritas, to the top of the pillar, which we reached by 3 p.m. Icy cracks slowed our pace above, as we continued on toward the summit of Fitz Roy. We made a second bivy 200m below the summit, which we reached the following morning by 10 a.m. We descended via the Franco-Argentine, traversing the mountain and returning to Paso Superior by 5 p.m.

Our ascent was done in alpine style, with no fixed ropes. We called our new variation on the upper half of the pillar the "Young Jerks" (400m). Ours was the fourth ascent of the Goretta Pillar to the top of Fitz Roy [Previous ascents: Casarotto 1979, Kearney-Knight 1984, Harvey-Donahue 1993—Ed.] One day later, British Leo Houlding and Kevin Thaw made the 5th ascent.

Around the same time, Aljaz Tratnik and Jason Lakey (USA) climbed the Red Pillar (Albert-Arnold, 1999) on the east face of Aguja Mermoz but were turned back two pitches below the top by strong winds. Later Rok Zalokar, Aljaz Tratnik and Tanja Grmovsek (Slovenia) climbed the Italian Route (Buscaini-Candot-Metzeltin-Romano-Sinigoi, 1968) on east face of Aguja Saint Exupery.

Later yet, Klemen Mali and I climbed Guillamet and traversed south along the ridge to the col between Guillaumet and Mermoz. [Guillaumet had been traversed by Carrington and Rouse in 1976 (from north to south) and by Bresba, Dominguez, and Luthi in 1990 (from south to north)—Ed.] From the col we climbed Mermoz via the first ascent route (Cuiñas-Olaechea-Vieiro, 1974) to reach the summit. By adding the Mermoz, this was the first link up of Aguja Guillaumet and Aguja Mermoz. From the base of Guillaumet's northeast pillar (Paso Guillaumet) to the summit of Mermoz took us 11.5 hours.

Everything was a great experience, with great climbs and good parties in Chalten.

ROK SISERNIK, *Ljubljana, Slovenia*

Saint Exupery, correction. In the photo of Aguja Saint Exupery's west and northwest faces, on p. 315 of the 2004 *AAJ*, the route lines are reversed. Chiaro di Luna is actually the line on the left, and Tical is on the right.

HIELO CONTINENTAL

Cerro Dos Cuernos, first ascent. The Cordon Mariano Moreno is a range located in the middle of the Southern Patagonia Icecap, 25km southwest of Cerro Torre. During October and November, Karen McNeill, Amy Bullard, and I skied in to this range and climbed Cerro Dos Cuernos (3,074m). We believe this was the first ascent.

Our goal was a ski traverse of the Southern Patagonian Icecap from Paso Marconi to Estancia Christina on Lago Argentino, with three weeks spent on the east side of the Cordon

Mariano Moreno, attempting three new routes on the Dos Cumbres/Dos Cuernos face. We chose these routes based on Rolando Garibotti's photos. A Swiss/German team climbed the East Pillar to the South Summit of Dos Cumbres in 2000. We altered our plan in Chalten after Park Ranger Adrian Falcone showed us recent photographs of the icecap, revealing vast expanses of bare ice along the southern portion of our route.

On October 22 we began shuttling our gear up to Paso Marconi from Piedra del Fraile, then spent several stormy days in the shelter of the new Chilean refugio located at 490942S, 730822W on the north side of the pass. From the pass we traveled on skis, pulling sleds for 32km, to our base camp between Nunatak Viedma and the Cordon Mariano Moreno.

This season the east side of the range from Dos Cumbres to Punta Brava was composed of steep, loose rock, with numerous ice lines and nearly continuous seracs guarding the ridgeline. On sunny days temperatures reached nearly 60° F in the shade at our camp, and the range was continuously active with falling debris. We decided on the only safe route we could see: up the southeast ridge of unnamed P2,800m and up the north ridge of Dos Cuernos to the summit.

Although many days had fine weather, we experienced a couple of storms at our camp, with high winds, snow, and even rain. We retreated from several attempts before being successful on November 15. The route we took, although long (1,524m elevation gain and 5km long), was relatively safe, scenic, and moderate. We encountered chossy rock to 4th class, snow to 45°, and ice to WI2. We found passage through the summit mushroom on the northwest side. It took us nine hours for the ascent from our camp, and five hours to descend the same way. We left our base camp on November 16, retraced our approach route through Paso Marconi, and arrived back in El Chalten on the 20th.

PETER CARSE, *AAC*

Dos Cumbres (3,049m): (1) Dauer-Siegrist-Warthl, 2000. Dos Cuernos (3,074m): (2) Bullard-Carse-McNeill, 2004.
Peter Carse

Cerro Murallón, attempt. The following has been condensed from a press release provided by Glowacz's publicist in response to our request for information:

"Gone with the Wind" Part 1, featuring Stefan Glowacz and Robert Jasper. Top of the Murallón north buttress in sight, but out of reach: a two-man team consisting of Jasper and Glowacz—both part of a small elite of world-class expedition climbers—after an intense nine-week struggle, just barely failed to reach their goal.

Prologue. Stefan Glowacz and Robert Jasper once again [*AAJ* 2004, pp. 318-320] set out for Argentina in October. Their objective: another first ascent on Mt. Murallón (2,831m), this time on its mighty north face. There are certainly countless better-known goals, for instance in the Himalaya. However, exceptional climbers have been increasingly seeking challenges on peaks so remote that hardly anybody would risk attempting an ascent. Mt. Murallón, for instance, is situated in the middle of the Patagonian ice cap and is exposed to notorious blizzards. Not even the smallest of bushes provides shelter.

The Approach—a Torturous Adventure. Stefan Glowacz and Robert Jasper, with photographer Klaus Fengler, had to carry 200kg of freeze-dried food to the start of the climb. There were an additional 40 liters of petrol, 500m of fixed rope, climbing material, and three tents to carry. In the Himalaya expeditions are accompanied by coolies, porters, cooks, liaison officers, and doctors. On Murallón external help is out of the question. On the trek in, the small team was accompanied by mountain guide Hans Martin Götz, journalist Tobias Hatje, and cameraman Sebastian Tischler. The team set up base camp under overhanging rocks beneath the north buttress.

A Once in a Lifetime Experience. Two days later Glowacz and Jasper started climbing. On the first day they covered 200m, a good start. By day five they had reached the headwall. The following day, climbing two demanding free pitches and two on aid, the team worked its way to a point 200m from the summit. Then luck left with the arrival of a dreaded Patagonian blizzard. Their tents buckled under the wind, and Jasper, Glowacz, and Fengler were forced to retreat for miles to Refugio Pascale, a small tin hut.

Rome Was Not Built in a Day. Precious time elapsed while they waited for better weather. Desperate, but also full of hope, Jasper and Glowacz made another attempt at the summit but found their fixed ropes torn to shreds. Rocks and chunks of ice flew horizontally through the air. Glowacz and Jasper retreated: a brutal trek back to civilization. The projected route on Murallón already has its name: "Vom Winde verweht"—Gone with the Wind. To date it has 21 pitches, 17 of which were climbed free, four with aid. Their rating suggestion is 7c/A?. The team thinks the aid pitches should go free under favorable conditions.

In October 2005 Glowacz and Jasper want to return to Patagonia and to Murallón—to a route they consider the "line of their lives."

Mayr Nell Public Relations, Germany

SOUTHERN PATAGONIA, CHILE

TORRES DEL PAINE NATIONAL PARK

North Tower of Paine, new route. In February 2002 John Rzeczycki and I climbed a new route that went to the north summit of the North Tower in Torres del Paine Park. The route starts on the right side of the west face and shares the first pitch with what I think is El Caballo del Diablo (Lloyd-Pritchard, 1992), then continues straight up dihedrals for 600' where we crossed El Caballo del Diablo on a large ledge. We continued traversing toward the notch and summited via the south face after nine or ten pitches and some simul-climbing. The route went all free except for a fall on the crux pitch. The pitch was freed at 5.11 by the second on top rope. The first 500' were previously climbed by a party from Montana.

RALPH FERRARA, *AAC*

Paine Chico, Eol. I first saw the west face of Paine Chico (also called Cerro Almirante Nieto's west summit) in late 2002, when I was climbing on the east side of the Torres. I was surprised that there were no routes I knew of on the awesome-looking rock face. I found out that although thousands of people have seen this bastion (it's the part of famous Mirador lookout), nobody had touched it. The idea for next year was there.

I returned to the park on December 1, 2003, and attempted the northwest pillar, then tried the west arête nine times [*AAJ* 2004, pp. 320-321. In that report, what's here called the west arête was referred to as the southwest ridge. This feature in fact faces west, if not northwest—Ed.]

This year Grega Lacen and I decided to come later in the season, expecting better weather in January and February. The ice ramp that led to the real climbing on Paine Chico was gone, so we made our base camp on the other side, in the Bader Valley, on January 9. After nine days of bad weather, the pressure rose on the evening of the 18th, and the weather looked promising. We started from base camp at 3:30 a.m. and after four hours of steep approach started climbing. It went smoothly, and we were at the high point of our last year's attempts at 2 p.m. The weather then started to get worse, and the wind was already strong, but we'd had enough of trying this windy arête, so we continued. A few hours later we found a solution to the steep upper part, and at 6 p.m. we reached the summit of Paine Chico in clouds and strong wind. Rappelling the most wind-exposed route in the region was a horror show, especially at night. We reached the base of the arête, with just half of the rope left, soon after midnight and reached base camp at 3:30 a.m. The round trip took us 24 hours of hard work. We named the route Eol and rated it V 5.11- (650m). We climbed in pure alpine style.

TOMAZ JAKOFCIC, *Slovenia*

Cuerno Oeste/Este, correction. A report on p. 323 of the 2004 *AAJ* describes climbing on Cuerno Oeste. The climbers could not be contacted for confirmation, but we assume they meant Cuerno Este, as there is no Cuerno Oeste.

SOUTH OF PAINE

Cerro Ladrillero, first ascent. Patagonia is a land that challenges you to be patient, where waiting for the window is key and, because of that, waiting becomes a skill that is useful for getting prepared for when the opportunity comes. This we did while waiting for a chance to climb Cerro Ladrillero, an unclimbed, magnificent, glacier-covered peak similar to Mt. Rainier (Jack Miller, *AAJ* 1977, p. 58).

At 51 degrees south latitude, in the Magellan region, south of the Skyring Sound, is the Isla Riesco. This beautiful peak is on Isla Riesco's west side. It has been admired for many years, mostly from the ocean, but the common adverse weather and the reputation of swamps on the approach have kept climbers from the summit. After spending a month scouting a good route and approach, while persistent wind and snow made it impossible to attempt the peak, we decided to return.

Paine Chico, showing Eol. *Tomaz Jakofcic*

This time we were a group from a NOLS Patagonia mountaineering course: students Jeff Worken, Andrew Ramsay, Taylor Kettler, Tristan Stetson, Simon Koster, Charlie Parker, Colin O'Brady, Paul Dante, Rick Rudolf, David Olson, Jeff Bulligton, Chip Hayes, David Ferreira, and Sam Tyler; and instructors Phillip Schneider, Galen Dossin, and I. We arrived on two big Zodiacs and got to shore on the far southwest side of the Riesco Island, in a little bay called Puerto Cascade on the map. We were left with a month of food, fuel, and equipment. On day 8 the weather showed signs of improvement, so that night we prepared to attempt the peak in a hard two-day push. The next day we made a high snow camp, 2km northwest of Peak 990m, 0.5 km east of the valley between Peaks 990m and 931m, and 5.5 km southeast of the summit of Ladrillero. The following day, November 10, was clear. We traveled west until reaching the start of the main south ridge of Cerro Ladrillero. From there we traveled up for around half km to a big, snow-glacier-covered plateau, from which we continued pretty much straight north to the summit. After eight hours of straightforward glacier travel, the entire group reached the summit of Cerro Ladrillero (1,722m), a classic rimed formation with a fantastic view. We were already in the company of strong winds. When we arrived back at camp, at 19:30, a new bad weather system had moved in, and the sky was getting dark fast, but we were happy with what we'd done in the two-day weather window. The rest of the month we explored satisfied with having climbed a significant new peak and running another course in an exploratory area.

CHRISTIAN STEIDLE, *Chile*

TIERRA DEL FUEGO

Yorkminster Group, exploration and Monte Vavel attempt. In February Krzysztof Wielicki, Jacek Fluder, Wlodzimierz Szczesny, and I, after traveling for 80 hours from Poland, set up base camp in the remote glacier valley of the Cordillera Darwin, Tierra del Fuego. It was a beautiful place, by the shore of the eastern gulf of Bahia Parry, opposite the side of the fjord where the 1971

New Zealand expedition installed their base camp. Berries were plentiful, as well as firewood and running water.

To get there we chartered a boat in Porvenir for $3,500. We swore that next time we would hire the helicopter to avoid this sailing in madness (and sickness). As we had just two weeks for exploring, we focused only on the unexplored west side of the Darwin Glacier. We intended to climb the 3.5km-long north crest, a logical way to the summit of Monte Vavel, which is west of the main peak of the Yorkminster group.

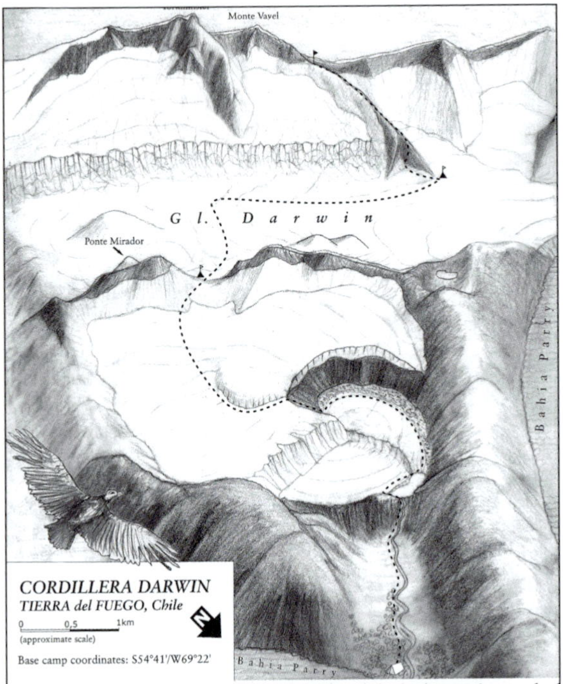

Monte Vavel
Gl. Darwin
Ponte Mirador
Bahia Parry
CORDILLERA DARWIN
TIERRA del FUEGO, Chile
0 0,5 1km
(approximate scale)
Base camp coordinates: S54°41'/W69°22'
Bahia Parry

Polish expedition approach to Monte Vavel and the highest point reached
ANDRZEJ ŚMIAŁY

After a couple of days struggling to the "pass with the view" and after a few more to get to the foot of our goal, we had only two days complete the route. After six hours of easy but tricky climbing (we left 50m of fixed rope on the lower, rocky part of the crest), we were forced to go down because of a storm. We reached the icy col just below the huge rock wall (main difficulties). We left one Piranha tool, pitons, and carabiners.

During our short stay we enjoyed just one full sunny day. The rest was more or less cloudy and windy, with rain and snow. The temperature was 7°–15°C during the day and about minus 5°C at night.

There is a good place to spend a night on the "pass with the view," even during a hurricane. Go to the south side of the pass and dig a snow cave. During our stay we noticed three condors, the only signs of life in that region. In exploring the area close to the pass, we got to the top of the isolated lower summit of the mountain bordering the pass on the south. We called it Punte Mirador as there is a good view of the entire area of the Darwin Glacier.

Although the mountains in this region are only up to 2,400m high, they rise from the sea. For that reason one should be prepared for at least two days and a couple kilometers of tricky climbing, weather permitting.

ANDRZEJ SMIALY, *Polish Alpine Club*

Antarctica

SENTINEL RANGE

VINSON MASSIF

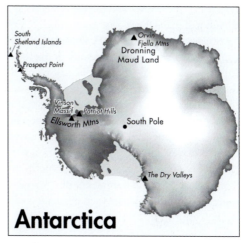

Vinson, summary, record numbers and new route. Over 120 people attempted Vinson Massif this season, far surpassing the previous record of 78 attempts set in 2000-01. This year only two people failed to summit, giving a success rate of nearly 99%. Though the weather this season was not always good, it was never terrible, with no major storms at any time. The Vinson expeditions supported by Antarctic Logistics & Expeditions (ALE) are now around 15 days total in duration, longer than in previous seasons, which gives people more time to acclimatize, rest and wait out bad weather.

The extra time also allows teams to attempt other objectives, if they are up to it and the weather complies. This season several teams took short day-trips out from various camps and four teams attempted Mt. Shinn (4,661m) from Camp 3. Three of the four were successful—a Spanish soloist, the two ALE guides Heather Morning and Neil Stephenson and a guided team from Alpine Ascents International led by Todd Passey. AAI Guide Vern Tejas spent most of the season on the mountain, leading four separate ascents. One of these ascents included Johnny Strange, at 13 years old the youngest person to summit Vinson. New Zealander Guy Cotter, owner and head guide of Adventure Consultants, doubled as marriage celebrant on December 8 to two of his group who tied the knot on the summit. On a more serious note, at least two climbers had roped crevasse falls on the section leading up to Camp 3 and one climber had a minor fall on Mt. Shinn. The Vinson route between Camp 2 and Camp 3, beneath the headwall, passed through significant avalanche debris this year, emanating from the seracs up to the right on Vinson. The opposing seracs on Shinn also calved several times, on one occasion strafing the route below the headwall shortly after climbers had passed through. The objective danger of this route is not insignificant and is not improving.

Only two expeditions attempted anything new in the Massif this season: the Omega

Remember this picture next time you hear how "safe" it is on Vinson. The leading edge of the avalanche is 30m from the track of the normal route at this point; 30 minutes earlier about eight people had walked right through here (7 p.m., Jan. 4, 2005). *Damien Gildea*

GPS team (see below) and the experienced Spanish climber Miguel Angel Vidal. Miguel and friends had made the second ascent of the 1999 Anker route on the right side of the West Face Ice Stream in December 2003. During that time they had scouted and attempted the obvious couloir at the right-most extremity of the rocky section of the main West Face, just left of the Ice Stream. Returning this year, he first climbed a minor route with Maria Jesus "Chus" Lago at the far left end of the West Face, up a short, moderate snow slope to reach the Vinson normal route. Maria descended, having already summited via the normal route some days earlier, so Miguel then went to the summit from that point on December 28.

On December 31 Miguel left his camp down on the Branscomb Glacier and approached the main face alone. Eight and a half hours later he reached the top via the 1,800m Banana Friendship Gully, overcoming much poor snow and several rock sections. His route took him up to and behind a small but obvious gendarme high on the face and over to the normal route on Vinson, which he then descended without going to the summit, arriving in Camp 3 at 11:30 pm.

DAMIEN GILDEA, *Australia, AAC*

Jaca Peak (3,372m), southeast face; Vinson West, Galfrío Route; Mt. Vinson (4,897m), Friendship Banana Gully to Branscomb ridge. On December 23 Chus (María Jesús) Lago and I attempted a new route on Vinson West face, but our backpacks were too heavy and our progress too slow. After climbing 600 meters, we decided to change our strategy. Chus Lago summited Vinson on her 40th birthday (Christmas), while I had to turn back due to the -30°C cold, accompanied by strong winds. On December 26, I moved to the southwest ridge of Mt. Shinn to explore a possible route there. Afterward I traversed to Jaca Peak (3,372m) and climbed it following a straight line up to the summit through the southeast face. Jaca Peak was first climbed in 1995 by a Spanish team, consisting of a group of the Military High Mountain patrol and the "Al Filo de lo Imposible" TV documentary team.

The main section of the west face of Mt. Vinson. (1) Linear Accelerator (Jay Smith, 1994). (2) Banana Friendship Gully (Miguel Angel Vidal, 2004). (3) Rudi's Runway (Rudiger Lang, 1991). *Damien Gildea*

On December 27 Chus and I climbed together a new route on the southern edge of Vinson West's rocky wall. It took us eight hours to climb 1,000 vertical meters on a rock spur. We named the new route "Galfrío" as a tribute to the expedition sponsor. The route includes some difficulties on ice and mixed terrain up to UIAA IV and 45° to 55° ice. The last 200 meters offered the most difficult section, as the climb progressed on very hard blue ice and unstable snow.

On December 28, I climbed the four-km-long Branscomb Ridge, past the point where it joins the new Galfrío route, up to the main summit of that ridge.

On December 31 I climbed a new route on Mt. Vinson following an unmistakable banana-shaped couloir that crosses Vinson's west face. Therefore, I named the new itinerary "Friendship Banana Gully." It took me 8.5 hours to climb 1,700 vertical meters from the foot of the wall to the Branscomb Ridge at 4,400m. The new route follows 50°-55° slopes on alternatively crusted and loose snow, along with some rock outcrops. There were some mixed sections up to IV. I found no ice at all, just some patches of hard snow.

MIGUEL ANGEL VIDAL, *Spain*

Vinson, new height (4,892m), first ascents of sub-peaks, many new peak names. As the name implies, Vinson Massif is a large bulk of mountain with numerous summits. Though the main summit, first climbed in December 1966, has now had over 950 ascents, all but one of the other high summits, arranged around a high plateau, were unclimbed until this season. The Omega High Antarctic GPS Expedition aimed to climb and measure as many of these peaks as possible, to ascertain the height-order of these summit peaks and to resolve other topographical issues with a view to producing a new and more accurate map of the Massif in 2006. Damien Gildea of Australia and Rodrigo Fica of Chile, who both climbed and measured nearby Mt. Shinn in December 2001, returned with young Chilean climber Camilo Rada for this year's work. Camilo would also record weather data to ascertain the suitability of high Antarctic mountains for future infrared telescope sites.

The Omega team flew to the mountain on November 16 after a two-week weather delay at Patriot Hills. Alone on the mountain, they ferried 50 days of food and fuel to Camp 2 over the next week, established Camp 3 on November 25 and made the season's first summit of Vinson on the 28th. The three set a tent a few meters below the summit and spent seven hours

The south faces of Vinson Massif, Kershaw Peak, and Unnamed Peak 4,822m from the summit of Long Top (4,841m). In the distant right background is the summit of Mt. Tyree (4,852m). *Damien Gildea*

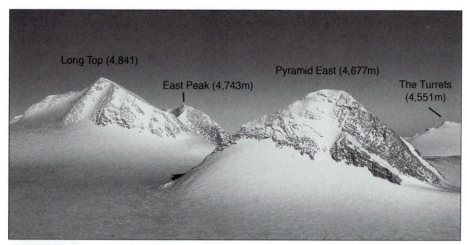

Looking east from the summit of Pyramid South (4,634m), across the Vinson High Plateau to Long Top, East Peak, Pyramid East, and The Turrets. All peaks received their first ascent in December 2004 by the Omega GPS team. *Damien Gildea*

there without sleeping bags, waiting for the GPS to run in its position atop the highest piece of solid rock. Operating data collectors for recording temperature and relative humidity, they later discovered temperatures reached -46°C that night. The GPS data was processed via satellite phone, laptop and the AUSPOS website to give a new height of 4,892m—5m lower than the previous official USGS height, but within the margin of error associated with that older figure.

On November 30 the trio climbed and measured Peak Kershaw, the obvious peak to the left of Vinson seen by all those doing the normal route to the highest peak. A first ascent of this peak was claimed by Britons Sundheep Dhillon and Andre Hedger on December 15, 1992 but it may well have been climbed in December 1989 by Canadian Rob Mitchell, who mistook it for the highest point, only learning his mistake later (see *Climbing* No.128 Oct/Nov 1991 p.120). Dhillon and Hedger coined the name "Kershaw" in memory of Giles Kershaw, one of the founders of Adventure Network International (ANI), who opened up the area to private expeditions in the late 1980s. Giles was killed in a gyrocopter accident on the Antarctic Peninsula in 1991. Gildea, Fica, and Rada ran the GPS on the highest point—an ice crest, just below which was a green ski pole stuck in the ice, presumably left by the Brits. The height was later found to be 4,865m—only 27m lower than the main summit of Vinson. The Omega team considered this a testament to the skill of the USGS personnel who made the original map of the area, correctly pinpointing the true summit of Vinson amongst so many close contenders and in a field where "official" altitudes are often incorrect by much more than 27m.

Requiring very good weather for their work on the high plateau, the Omega team waited at Camp 3 until December 8 when they traveled up the normal Vinson route until just before the final pyramid, then continued straight south through a narrow but easy col that leads out on to the high plateau south of Vinson's main summit. Crossing the plateau they made camp in the evening and immediately attempted the high peak to the southwest. This peak is visible from Vinson BC and has been eyed by dozens of wishful climbers over the years. It was attempted by a Spanish team in January 1995 who climbed the nearby Pico Principe de Asturias. The Spanish thought this big peak to be 4,860m, named it Monte Espana, and attempted it via a route similar to that used for Asturias, but failed some distance from the summit. The Omega team ascended the narrow south ridge of the peak, getting good views of the terrain to the southwest of Vinson, and summited just before midnight. Gildea suggested changing the name to International Peak in honor of all the nationalities that had passed underneath the mountain in the last 15 years and because the Spanish had not actually climbed it when they named it. They left the GPS running for around 10 hours until it was retrieved by Fica the next morning.

Immediately after that Rada and Gildea set off for a nearby sharp peak they named Sphinx Peak, due to its appearance from the north. Fica later joined them and belayed Gildea to a soft, crumbling, and wildly exposed summit, too small to stand on, where he placed the GPS. Fica and Rada returned to retrieve the unit later that night. Continuing straight away, they joined Gildea en route to another nearby sub-peak which they named Pyramid South due its appearance and location on the plateau. This was an easy ascent up a steep snow-ice slope to a very useful flat rock summit, where they placed the GPS just after midnight, having now reached the top of three previously unclimbed peaks in 24 hours.

After a long sleep Gildea retrieved the receiver alone, then joined up with Rada and Fica to move camp across the plateau closer to their next objectives. First the team climbed Pyramid East by both the west and south faces on snow and rock, then after retrieving the GPS from that summit, Gildea and Rada climbed Long Top on December 11 via its broad south face. Long Top is the peak often seen in the background of the summit photos of Vinson summiteers. It is a large peak with a long summit ridge, the highest point a crenellated rocky spine at the southern end. Here Rada and Gildea

Camilo Rada (Chile) on the summit of The Turrets (4,551m). In the background is East Peak (4,743m), with the unclimbed east ridge of Vinson dropping down to the right. *Damien Gildea*

The west face of Sphinx Peak (4,729m) showing the Fica-Gildea-Rada route. *Damien Gildea*

The southwest face of Mt. Epperly (4,359m) and west face of Mt. Shinn (4,661m) from the summit of Pico Jaca.
Damien Gildea

experienced extreme wind gusts over 120km/h while setting up the GPS. Fica soloed the peak later that night, in similar conditions, to retrieve the unit. The data showed that Long Top had been the highest unclimbed peak in Antarctica (though not an independent mountain). Immediately after Fica returned to the tent, they all packed up and plodded back across the plateau in increasing winds through the narrow col and back down the normal Vinson route to reach Camp 3 at 2:30am on December 12.

Waiting through variable weather, the Omega team did not go high again until December 26, when they left camp and made very fast time to the col before passing through it, collecting a cache from the previous trip, crossing the plateau again, but this time descending down and around to the south of Long Top to a flat area at the southeastern extremity of the high plateau. Immediately Rada and Gildea set off and summited an outcrop they named The Turrets—three rocky points on the extreme south eastern edge of the plateau overlooking the Dater Glacier. On the existing USGS maps this feature appears to be a snow peak possibly as high as the rocky sub-peak to its north. However, when on location it is obvious that this is not so—The Turrets are barely a peak at all, whereas the rocky sub-peak to the north is quite impressive. Correcting these types of discrepancies or misrepresentations on the current map was one of the main aims of the Omega expedition and was carried out in the name of improving and contributing to the greater body of Antarctic geographical knowledge. The drop-off to the east from The Turrets is quite steep and would provide some of Vinson's hardest climbing if ascended directly from the Dater Glacier.

Fica soon retrieved the GPS and he and Rada immediately set off and summited the bigger rocky peak to the north, which we had named East Peak. Climbed via an easy ridge connecting it to the back of Long Top, East Peak is quite steep on other sides and is in fact the terminus of the long and impressive east ridge of Vinson—the last major feature in the Massif that remains unclimbed. Gildea later retrieved the unit alone and upon returning to camp all three set off in deteriorating weather to return via the col to Camp 3 late on December 28th.

Over the next few days Fica and Rada climbed two minor points north of Vinson main summit. Manana Point (climbed and named by Dhillon and Hedger in 1992) is on the ridge running parallel to the normal route above Camp 3 on the left. Branscomb Point is the highest point of the Branscomb Ridge, which is the top of the main west face and runs parallel to the normal route, but on the climber's right as s/he ascends the upper cwm.

With all the major sub-peaks climbed and measured, Gildea set off on January 1 to summit Vinson and collect a second set of data. The work on the summit was conducted in extreme winds and Gildea was forced to descend via the less windy western side of the summit pyramid, going down a broad bowl and traversing around the western side past Branscomb Point to rejoin the normal route, on the way seeing Miguel Angel Vidal's tracks from his ascent of the west face the previous day. On this occasion the GPS ran for over 10hrs and reconfirmed the earlier figure of 4,892m. Fica retrieved the unit on January 2nd and later that day all three of the Omega team walked across the Vinson-Shinn col from Camp 3 to the eastern extremity of the col, where they ascended a very small peak that gives fantastic views north down the eastern side of the range. Having run the GPS for an hour they returned to Camp 3 in the early hours of January 3. That evening they packed up Camp 3—where they had stayed for over one month—and descended to Camp 2. After erecting the tent at Camp 2 the trio set off and made the third ascent of Pico Jaca, a rocky peak west of the main massif, on a ridge running parallel to the upper Branscomb. This peak is seen by all who descend from Camp 3 on Vinson but was only climbed first in 1995 by the Spanish team (mentioned previously) then for the second time by Miguel Angel Vidal around Christmas this season. The peak has a very sharp summit and gives wonderful views north down the western side of the range, past Epperly, Tyree, and Gardner.

Returning from Pico Jaca, after running the GPS for an hour, the Omega team slept briefly then awoke to pack the entire expedition load, including over 25kg of human waste, onto their sleds, eventually pulling into Vinson BC late in the evening of January 5, from where they flew out the next day.

Heights of the Vinson Massif:
Main Summit: 4,892m
Kershaw Peak: 4,865m
Long Top: 4,841m
Unnamed Peak: 4,822m
International Peak: 4,790m
East Peak: 4743m
Sphinx Peak: 4,729m
Pyramid East: 4,677m
Pyramid South: 4,634m
The Turrets: 4,551m

Note: These names are unofficial and were assigned merely to aid in the efficient running of the expedition and relevant communication. There is currently no intention for them to be officially submitted for consideration by any Antarctic Place Names Committee.

For more information see: www.theomegafoundation.org

DAMIEN GILDEA, *Australia, AAC*

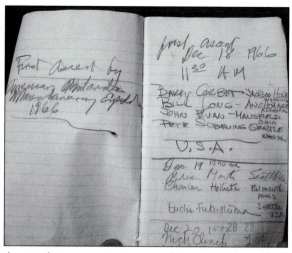

The original Vinson summit register, now safely removed. *Damien Gildea*

Vinson, summit register removed. On January 1, 2005 I removed the summit register book from the aluminum cylinder in which it had been housed for decades. The book was full, no longer useable, and I felt it would be too tempting a prize for a thief, given some recent similar problems in Antarctica. I photographed all the pages and passed the book to ALE in Punta Arenas, where it was placed in safekeeping. Subsequent correspondence with Nick Clinch, who led the first ascent in 1966, and John Evans, who summited first with Barry Corbet, indicates that the museum of the American Alpine Club is the best resting place for the book. Given that it was often hidden by snow, or that conditions dictated against stopping to write in it, the book is far from an accurate register of Vinson summiteers, but it is certainly a valuable and historic artifact that needs to be well preserved. A replacement register is being organized and will include a photocopy of the original first and second pages, showing the first signatories from December 1966.

DAMIEN GILDEA, *Australia, AAC*

THE PENINSULA

LIVINGSTON ISLAND

Tangra Mountains, Komini Peak, west slope new rock route. Komini (774m: 62°39'10.1"S, 60°07'05.7" W) is one of the minor peaks on the side ridge descending northward from Levski Peak in the Tangra Mountains, which are situated on Livingston Island, South Shetland Islands. The peak lies above Huron Glacier to the north and two of its tributaries on the east and west. The western slope of Komini is a rock wall of 212m vertical height and average steepness of 48°. The wall was climbed for the first time by Lyubomir Ivanov during the Bulgarian survey Tangra 2004/05 expedition, exploring remote areas in eastern Livingston Island from November 28, 2004 until January 8, 2005. The ascent started from the survey base camp Academia located on the upper Huron Glacier at the foot of Zograf Peak. The base camp area itself is accessible by an 11-13 km overland route running eastward from the Bulgarian base St. Kliment Ohridski or the Spanish base Juan Carlos Primero via Willan Saddle and Orpheus Gate. The peak was

Northern slopes of Levski Peak and Lyaskovets Peak as seen from near Camp Academia. The new route on Komini Peak climbes the rock buttress above the arrow. *Lyubomir Ivanov*

climbed on December 21, 2004 for the purposes of GPS surveying and compiling a photographic documentation of geographical features in eastern Livingston Island. The route first led from Camp Academia for three km eastward over Huron Glacier along the foot of Zograf Peak, through a pass towards the tributary of Huron Glacier flowing between Lyaskovets Peak and Levski Peak, then across the tributary to reach the foot of Komini. The glacier surface is solid firn suitable for walking or skiing, albeit fractured by visible and hidden crevasses. The wall (UIAA III) was free soloed, its surface providing holds that are mostly unstable. Indeed, the rock is highly fissile due to the wet climate, with several freezing-thawing cycles typically happening within one day even.

LYUBOMIR IVANOV, *Bulgaria*

Tangra Mountains, Lyaskovets Peak, first ascent; Zograf Peak, first ascent. Lyaskovets (62°39'48.5" S, 60°08'34.7" W) is a peak of elevation 1,473 m in the 30km-long Tangra Mountains situated on Livingston Island. It is bounded by Catalunyan Saddle, separating it from the summit of Mt. Friesland to the west, Shipka saddle separating it from Levski Peak to the east, and Macy Glacier to the south. A side ridge descending northward overlooks Huron Glacier, ending up in Zograf Peak. The conspicuous adjacent landmark of the Sphynx is a fantastic rock-cored ice formation in Catalunyan Saddle. Lyaskovets was climbed for the first time during the Tangra 2004/05 survey by a two-man team comprising Dr. Lyubomir Ivanov, Bulgarian Academy of Sciences, participant in four Antarctic expeditions and chairman of the Bulgarian Antarctic Place-names Commission, and Doychin Vasilev, alpinist, filmmaker, and climber of five 8,000-meter peaks

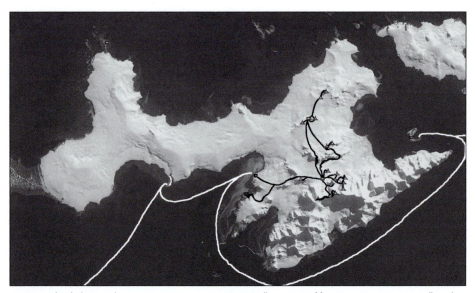

Livingston Island, showing the survey route. Imagery is SPOT satellite mosaic of four Pancromatic images collected on 30th March 1991. Orthorectification used horizontal control and elevation from British Antarctic Survey South Shetland Islands 1:200000 sheets W62-58 and W62-60 (1956) made by Institut Cartogràfic de Catalunya and Departament de Geodinàmica i Geofísica, Universitat de Barcelona (1992). (Original image was color.)

including Mt. Everest. The ascent started from Camp Academia, the survey base camp located on the Huron Glacier at elevation of 541m close to the base of Zograf Peak. The base camp area itself is accessible either by helicopter or—as in our case—by skiing an 11-13 km overland route leading eastward from the Bulgarian base St. Kliment Ohridski or the Spanish base Juan Carlos Primero via Willan Saddle and Orpheus Gate. The peak was climbed on December 14, 2004 for the purposes of GPS surveying and compiling a photographic documentation of geographical features in eastern Livingston Island. The route taken from Camp Academia up to Catalunyan Saddle (1,260 m) is four km of solid but crevassed firn surface. Lyaskovets is completely glaciated, with precipitous west, south and east slopes, so the ascent route (UIAA III) first traversed the west slope until the north slope was reached, from where the summit—itself split by a crevasse—was easily reached. Any fall during the crossing of the western slope would have likely resulted in serious injury or death. Common risks derive from unstable snow bridges on the route to Catalunyan Saddle, as well as from the notoriously bad local weather—changeable, windy, humid and sunless. Temperatures are rather constant—at that elevation around 0°C in summer, with wind chill temperatures some 5°-10°C lower on the average. Whiteouts are frequent, and blizzards can occur at any time of the year. The ascent was made on a rare day of perfect weather, allowing for magnificent views to the Antarctic Mainland 120 km away across the Bransfield Strait.

The satellite Zograf Peak (1,011m: 62°39'06.4" S, 60°08'54.1" W) was ascended by Lyubomir Ivanov in blizzard weather conditions on December 31 by way of the saddle between Lyaskovets and Zograf. That UIAA II route is heavily crevassed all the way to the glaciated summit.

LYUBOMIR IVANOV, *Bulgaria*

Vidin Heights, Melnik Peak, Melnik Ridge, first ascent. Miziya Peak (604m: 62°36'06.4" S, 60°09'11.2" W) is the main summit of Vidin Heights, a cluster of peaks, nunataks, and hills extending eight km in the northeast extremity of Livingston Island. Miziya was climbed for the first time by Lyubomir Ivanov during the Bulgarian survey expedition. The ascent started from the bivouac at Leslie Hill, set up after man-sledding 10 km north from the survey base camp Academia on the upper Huron Glacier, by way of Wörner Gap and then crossing Bowles Ridge and upper Kaliakra Glacier. Miziya Peak was climbed on December 25, 2004. The route of ascent went five km from Leslie Hill via Leslie Gap to a 481m peak and 453m knoll in the southwest extremity of Vidin Heights. From here Miziya itself was gained. The peak is completely glaciated, with a precipitous east slope overlooking Kaliakra Glacier, and a gentle albeit crevassed west slope (UIAA II), which was ascended.

The two-man team of Lyubomir Ivanov and Doychin Vasilev returned from Leslie Hill to Camp Academia on December 28 by a more easterly 14km route crossing Kaliakra Glacier, Yankov Saddle (575m) between Bowles Ridge and Melnik Ridge, then sledding down Struma Glacier to reach Huron Glacier via the pass between Atanasoff Nunatak and Maritsa Peak on the eastern Bowles Ridge. In the process, they made a UIAA II diversion from Yankov Saddle to climb Melnik Peak (696m), the summit of the two km-long Melnik Ridge situated north of the eastern Bowles Ridge. The peak is glaciated except for the precipitous northern slope overlooking Kaliakra Glacier.

LYUBOMIR IVANOV, *Bulgaria*

Approaching the 2,200m south face of Mt. Francais on Anvers Island. The attempted route went up the icefall on the left side of the mountain. *Phil Wickens*

The Peninsula; attempts and ascents on Anvers, Brabant, and Wiencke islands. A team of primarily British climbers aboard Alun Hubbard's yacht Gambo, was prevented by heavy sea ice from reaching its main objective of the Arrowsmith Peninsula. Instead it concentrated on making ascents on the more frequented Anvers, Brabant, and Wiencke Islands. From December 28, 2004 to February 8, 2005 a number of attempts/ascents were made in the region of Anvers and Wiencke. Two attempts on new routes were made on Mt. Francais, Anvers Island. On the first Alan Gear, Nico Lhomme, and Phil Wickens climbed 1,000m of a new line up the southeast face, hoping to reach the south ridge. They retreated on the upper slopes due to category 5 avalanche conditions and a rather ominous feeling created by large collection of seracs above. The second involved Gear, Hubbard, and Souness, who made an attempt at a new route over Mt. Rennie but gave up in poor weather and awful snow. The first named team also attempted a new route up the northeast slope of Mt. Williams but turned back 100m below the summit due to an impassable crevasse. Their attempt at a possible new route up the east face of Shewry Peak was also thwarted, this time only 50m from the summit due to fragile overhanging cornices and snow mushrooms.

On Wiencke Island three attempts to make the first traverse of the Seven Sisters of Fief were all thwarted by bad weather, but Lhomme and Wickens climbed a short new route up a gully on the northwest flank of Noble Peak (AD+) and then skied back down it for 200m of 45°. Gear and Wickens made two attempts on The Wall before a third, via the East Face icefall and North Ridge (AD-: a possible first ascent) brought them to the summit. Several ascents and ski descents were made of the popular Jabet Peak, while the minor summit of Doumer Hill on Doumer Island was also climbed via the East Ridge at PD.

On the way home the team stopped off for four days on Brabant Island where three attempts on the South Face of Mt. Bulcke (1,030m) failed but Tim Hall and Souness made the second ascent of Mt. Cherry. Notably, one or two of the ascents on Wiencke were photographed from the air, Tim Hall shooting the pictures while making the first successful paramotor flight in Antarctica.

PHIL WICKENS, *United Kingdom*

SOUTH GEORGIA

Larsen Harbour to Royal Bay traverse and first ascent of Peak 5,680'. Using Skip Novak's yacht Pelagic to make the sea crossing from Ushuaia via the Falkland Islands to South Georgia, Julian Freeman-Attwood, Rich Haworth, Novak and Crag Jones were dropped at Larsen Harbour in the Drygalski Fjord near the south eastern tip of the island. From here the plan was to sled via the Phillipi, Graae, Harmer, Novosilski, and Spenceley Glaciers to the Ross Pass and then down the Ross Glacier to a pick-up in Little Moltke Harbour, Royal Bay. On route it was hoped that an attempt could be made on one of the bigger unclimbed peaks that flank the Spenceley.

Leaving the boat on the January 13, 2005, the four experienced fairly typical South Georgia weather and were tent bound for several days before reaching a camp at the Novosilski-Spenceley col on the night of the 20th. The 21st dawned clear and despite obvious poor snow conditions they decided to attempt the nearby Mt. Baume (6,272' and unclimbed). The East Ridge looked long and crenellated, while the North Face glacier was plainly swept by serac fall in its lower section. However, a rocky ridge on the left side of the face appeared to offer a route on to the upper part of the glacier, above the seracs. The four set off for what they thought would be a one day ascent but the route up the east flank of the buttress involved nine pitches of ice and mixed up to Scottish IV with little protection. By the time they reached a point level with the upper seracs it was 5 p.m. and here it became apparent that they were only half way up the face. As neither stove nor bivouac gear had been taken, they decided to descend.

On the 23rd and still in fine weather, Haworth, Novak and Jones made the first ascent of Peak 5,680', which lies north west of Baume. The East Ridge gave an easy three-and-a-half hour ascent. Later that day a classic South Georgia gale arrived and the team had to break camp and transfer to a hastily dug snow cave until the morning of the 26th. During this period an inner tent took flight and was never seen again. With no good forecast imminent, the four continued their journey to the Ross Pass and down to Royal Bay, where they arrived on the 26th. Freeman-Attwood, who had traveled the section below Ross Pass some 15 years ago, was astonished by the glacial recession. The last 40% of the glacier was now dry and riddled with crevasses, where before it had been skiable more or less all the way. The party note that climbing on this highly glaciated island requires permission from the Government of South Georgia and the South Sandwich Islands, a permit fee of £1,000 and the requirement of a dedicated vessel, with which the climbers must always have communication, remaining at the island for the whole time the party is ashore.

JULIAN FREEMAN-ATTWOOD, *United Kingdom*

David Fasel and Tom Chamberlain on a buttress above the Nordenskjold glacier with Paget (far right) & Buzen Point in the background.   *Alun Hubbard*

Mt. Paget and other attempts. From February to May 2005 a multi-national team of climbers sailed the yacht Gambo from Ushuaia in Argentina to King Edward Point in South Georgia, and then back to Pireapolis in Uruguay. The team, which included Tom Chamberlain (UK), David Fasel (Switzerland), Daniel Haywood (UK), Tim Hall (UK), the yacht skipper Alun Hubbard (UK), and additional (non-climbing) crew members Alastair Gunn (UK) and Rory Williams (US) attempted various ascents on this highly glaciated sub-Antarctic island. Not atypical South Georgia weather thwarted any major achievements, though there were some near misses. While based between Husvik and Grytviken the climbers made three attempts on the unclimbed Quad 5 and Mt. Paulsen, and the once-previously climbed Mt. Spaaman (1,940m). All failed due to either weather or poor rock. On the way to Spaaman one party managed to make an ascent of the previously climbed Admiralty Peak. A total of 14 days were spent attempting a previous Hubbard nemesis, the unclimbed east ridge of Paget, the highest peak on the island and also the highest on British soil. One of these nearly made the top. However, they did make the first ascent of a 7,000' subsidiary summit of Paget, which has been named Buzen Point. Shortly after getting down from one attempt on Paget, the climbers experienced a classic South Georgia blow, caused by the rapid onset of a 929mb low pressure at sea level. Things got a trifle breezy and the roof was blown off the British Antarctic Survey hut at King Edward Point, one of the more sheltered locations on the island.

ALUN HUBBARD, *Wales*

Africa

MOROCCO

Atlas Mountains, Taghia, Oujdad peak (2,695 m), Barracuda. In the remote High Atlas Mountains, the Polish team of Eliza Kubarska, Borek Szybinski, and me free climbed a new multi-pitch route Barracuda (600m, 7c+max, 7a+ oblig). The climb runs through vertical and slightly overhanging slabs all protected with bolts (some runouts occur). Almost half of the route is harder than French 7.

Barracuda was opened using ground-up style where combined free and aid climbing tactics helped during bolt installations. Sky hooks and Aliens were the only useful aid stuff during this ascent. We started this climb as a sky hook novices and at the top of the mountain we were joking that we should start a Sky Hook Dance Academy business.

After over two weeks of bolting efforts interrupted by snowfall, rain, and diseases caused by dirty water (despite using pills and water filters), we hung one portaledge and a small hammock 200 m above Taghia canyon to stop the daily exhausting run from the village of Taghia (1.5 hours of airy approach on moving "sheep bridges" with potential 200m fall to the canyon).

Then we free climbed entire route. Today Barracuda is one of the hardest routes in Taghia Cirque. It goes through beautiful airy slabs of Oujdad Peak (2,695 m) rising directly above Taghia village. Even though 7c+ grade isn't "hard" anymore for today experts, different kinds of problems will appear. The rock in Taghia is sharp and skin-destroying. To free climb the whole big wall in one push could be painful (a barracuda is a "sharp and hard" fish, after all).

To climb Barracuda you need double 50m ropes, 15 quickdraws, 2 medium cams (only for the top

Eliza Kubarska delicately handling sharp holds on Baraccuda, south face of Oujdad, Taghia. *David Kaszliowski/StudioWspin.com.pl*

massif, but not necessary). If you want to rappel along the route, be careful because some belays are almost 50m from one another.

This part of Atlas reminds one more of the Alps than other desert African ranges (like the Todra Gorge); the peaks around are often 3,000m high. The second highest peak of the Atlas, Jebel M'Goun, is very close. Some of the walls are 800m high. The best seasons for climbing here are May-June and September-October. Some people come here to climb north faces and canyons even in summer.

Taghia is a beautiful, remote village high (1,900m) in the mountains, 90 km from the closest town, Azilal. To get there you need to travel using a Land Rover (to Zaouia Ahansal village), and then a two-hour walk with your stuff on the back of a mule. The Taghia area is home to the Berber people, who are very polite and hospitable. There are two shelters (gite d'étape) in the

A foreshortened view of the Barracuda route on the south face of Oujdad.

village. The deep canyons and red limestone walls create breathtaking scenery.

This place has lots of unclimbed walls. After two days of trekking our team found at least five major projects for 600m-long free routes. But we haven't seen even half of the Taghia walls. There seems to be the beginning of a climbing boom for Taghia. After of years of silence, strong teams of explorers have begun to come here.

DAVID KASZLIKOWSKI, *Poland*

The north face of Oujdad, Taghia.

Atlas Mountains, Taghia, Jbel Tagoujimt N' Tsouaint, Tamdoine. At the end of September the team of three Catalonians (Jordi Jambert Dorca, Moisés Llado Dorca, David Font Ventura) and one Mexican (me) drove from Girona, Spain, to Algeciras. Once there we crossed by ferry to Ceuta and passed the border into Morocco. Eventually we continued by dirt road to Zaouia

Berber hospitality in Zahouia. *David Kaszliowski, Studio/Wspin.com.pl (3)*

The north face of Jbel Tagoujimt N' Tsouaint in Taghia. The Tamdoine route is mostly hidden, but finishes up the left skyline. *David Kaszliowski/StudioWspin.com.pl*

Ahansal, where we left the truck and hired three donkeys to carry our gear two hours to the base camp of Taghia.

After studying the walls (there are so many) we decided to attempt the north wall of Jbel Tagoujimt N' Tsouaiant, an 885m limestone cliff. First we studied all the routes opened already. We detected one virgin line, a beautiful long crack diagonaling to the left (our route runs on the left side of Barracuda's line). The route start with an easy long traverse to the left by natural ledges with some vegetation. We reached the base of the wall behind a cave. After climbing the first three pitches and fixing ropes, we descended and built a Tyrolean traverse. It rained the next day. In two days of climbing we made three more pitches in amazing rock; all the protection was natural and we placed bolts only for the belays. Our second bivouac was in hammocks on top of pitch 7. In three more pitches of free climbing with good crack protection we found a good bivouac ledge.

We decided to leave all the weight on the ledge above pitch 10, and after reaching the top to rappel and sleep on the bivy ledge. On the fourth day we climbed the rest of the wall. In three more pitches plus easier ground, all four of us reached the top. Our new line is called Tamdoine, which means "Eagles" in the Berber language (774m, 17 pitches, VI 5.12b A1). During our last night on the wall we watched four eagles dancing on the air under the beautiful sunset and the different colors of the sky.

LUIS CARLOS GARCÍA AYALA, *Mexico*

Stairway to Heaven, 11 moderate pitches of intense bliss, on Anergui Upper Crag, Tafraoute. *Chris Bonington*

Anti Atlas, Tafraoute, new routes. It was a brilliant week of doing new routes on the quartzite around Tafraoute. Our last route was 340m, around 5.7 in difficulty with spectacular climbing. The complete team was Joe Brown, Claude Davies, Mike Mortimer, Joe (Morty) Smith, Pete Turnbull, Derek Walker, and myself. Joe, Pete and Claude have been coming here for 12 years and I'm a comparative new boy with only four to my credit. During all that time not a bolt has been placed and hardly any pitons.

Mike and I only had a week, but the others had already been there for a week when we arrived. The climbing is superb, especially for aging climbers—all but Mike were grandfathers. The quartzite rock of the area yields spectacular and very steep lines with good holds and on the whole good clean rock.

Mike and I completed two new routes: The Eagle's Perch on Anergui Upper Crag (140m, 5a), and The Baron's Largesse—Joe (The Baron) Brown pointed us at it—on Crag U, Upper (140m, 5a). The final route we did was one of the best I have done in Morocco: Stairway to Heaven, on Anergui Upper Crag (340m, 11 pitches, 4c).

There is now a guide book written by Claude Davies: *Climbing in the Moroccan Anti-Atlas* (Cicerone, 2004, ISBN 1-85284-412-4). [Another report suggested that various UK climbers recommend the services of a local outfitter detailed at http://trekmorocco.squarespace.com—Ed.]

CHRIS BONINGTON, *Alpine Club*

Uganda

Rwenzori Mountains, Mt. Stanley (Margherita Peak, 5,109m), west face, new route. In July, Steve Roach—44-year-old rocket scientist for NASA, orator of Robert Service ballads, experienced mountaineer, and Vedauwoo-trained offwidth aficionado—seven members of the Mountain Club of Uganda, and I accomplished a remarkably fun expedition to the fabled Mountains of the Moon.

The Mountains of the Moon—named site-unseen by second century Greek geographer Ptolemy and since then discovered to be one of the sources of the Nile, the world's longest river

Mark Jenkins finding tropical ice while it's still there on the west face (Congo side) of Mt. Stanley's Margherita Peak. *Steve Roach*

(4,132 miles)—rise smack on the equator along the border of Uganda and Congo. There are 18 individual peaks that rise to over 4,600m, including the triple-summits of both Mt. Speke and Mt. Stanley. The former was named for the persevering explorer John Hannings Speke, who discovered Lake Victoria in 1863, and the latter for Henry Stanley, a diabolically cruel man who found his ethical opposite, Dr. Livingstone, in 1871 dying in present-day Tanzania.

The four-day hike into the range is one of the most magnificent on earth. Surrounded by *giant* groundsel and *giant* lobelia and *giant* heather, it's as if you have stumbled into the Jurassic Park of flora. The giant groundsel, 25 feet tall, resembled Joshua trees with enormous, artichoke-like balls atop their furred branches. The giant lobelia, purplish spires of hair, stood up like blind gnomes in the swamp; a forest of giant heather hovered to either side resembling medieval leather-clad soldiers. It was the land of Little Shop of Horrors. At any moment I expected a giant groundsel to reach out and grab me, or a three-foot rosetta to spread its labial leaves and speak.

On the third day, leaving from the John Matte hut, Steve Roach, Greg Smith, Loren Hostetter, and myself managed to summit Vittorio Emanuele (4,890m), the highest peak of Mt. Speke via the original Shipton/Tilman route—once heavily snow-encrusted, now merely a rock scramble—and glissade moss back down to the Bujuku hut by dusk.

Two days later, leaving from the Elena hut in two roped parties—Steve Roach, Glenda Hostetter, Mike Barnett; Greg Smith, Loren Hostetter, myself—climbed Margherita (5,109m), the highest peak of Mt. Stanley and the third highest on the African continent, via the traditional route (easy glacier travel, one pitch of icy rock).

The following morning whilst the Mountain Club of Uganda team members descended, Steve Roach and I summited Mt. Savoia (4,977m), via a direct ascent of the Coronation glacier. With three summits for reconnaissance, we were now prepared for our secret goal.

Before our trip, I'd emailed Henry Osmaston, author of the long out-of-print 1972 classic *Guide to the Ruwenzori: The Mountains of the Moon*. Osmaston was the most dedicated climber of the Mountain Club of Uganda during its golden years, the 1950-60s. In my note I suggested that there appeared to be room for a new route on the west face of Mt. Stanley.

Osmaston, 84-years-young and living in Cumbria, UK, responded: "I think all you say is correct. The rock should be clean of moss and probably stones as it is so steep. But it is entirely in the Congo.... A bullet-proof jacket would be an important addition to your kit. I don't advise it."

For almost 20 years, between 1980 and 2000, Uganda and the Congo were at war (the causes of which are so convoluted as to dismay even Africans). By the mid-90s, Congolese rebels were using the Rwenzori mountains as a guerilla redoubt, periodically descending into Ugandan villages to murder, rape, and steal food and supplies. In July of 1997 the Ugandan government closed the entire park and sent in the military. Trail by trail, valley by valley, the rebels were removed.

Rwenzori Mountains National Park was reopened in July 2001 and an armed, radio-carrying ranger accompanies every expedition. No one really knew what was going on now on the other side of the border: the last documented ascent of the west face of Margherita was in 1956.

"I say we go have a look," I said.

"I say we might get ourselves killed," replied Steve, which didn't mean he didn't want to go.

From Osmaston's guide, it appeared that no one had made a complete traverse of the Stanley Plateau. There was once a cabin, the Moraine hut, down on the Congo side, but even Osmaston didn't know if it still existed. We figured we'd shoot for this hut, get a peek of the west face if we were lucky, and go from there.

An alpine start was requisite, but it was snowing hard the next morning and we scooched back down in our bags. By nine it was snowing only lightly and we set out, retracing our own steps up the Stanley Plateau, then veering left toward the pass. By chance, a hole opened up in the clouds and we spotted what we thought was a tiny hut, then the hole closed up. We crossed the invisible border and descended the west Stanley glacier until it disappeared, forcing us to rap down rock ravines. We were in the Congo.

As the mist momentarily cleared, we again spied the hut on the ridgeline...and two people standing beside it! We were speechless. This was the last thing we wanted. I thought we might be imagining things and stared through the wisps of white with all my might. I was trying to determine whether they were armed.

We slipped down into the scree and continued toward the hut.

"Are they moving?" Steve's voice was a wee higher than normal.

"No. They're not moving."

The mist rolled in, the guerillas disappeared, and we kept on. We were approaching like cats now, silent, shoulders tensed, creeping low to the ground through the boulders. The mist blew off again.

"They haven't moved one bit," I whispered.

Steve burst out laughing so loud I jerked. "Nope. They sure haven't. Might be because one's a cairn and the other one's a giant groundsel."

The hut was empty, but still in solid condition. We ate lunch inside with the door open for the little we could see of the west face of Mt. Stanley. The top 1,500 feet were engulfed in dark-bellied clouds. The glaciers, the icefalls, the three summits, we could see none of it.

Steve struck out up the face first, and I followed, both of us scrambling along steep, verglassed granite. Gaining what we presumed was the Alexander glacier, we roped up and simul-climbed, only occasionally sinking an ice screw.

For the next three hours we climbed continuously. The ice was 50°-60° and we could never see more than 100 feet above us, so we never knew where we were going, other than straight up. The last two pitches to the summit were a gothic castle of ice—turrets, moats, curtained walls. Standing on top the fog was so thick we could barely see each other.

The following day Steve and I descended to the Kitandara hut, but not before I soloed the south ridge of Alexandra (another peak of Mt. Stanley) via a new line of crumbling, dripping 5.8 rock and ice which is definitely not worth repeating. From Kitandara we walked all the way out in one day.

Only 50 years ago the Mountains of the Moon were heavily glaciated but, due to global warming, they will likely be devoid of all ice—like Mt. Kenya and Kilimanjaro—within the next 10-20 years. If you have dreams of climbing snow and ice in Africa, go now. Ptolemy will soon be rolling in his grave.

MARK JENKINS, *AAC*

Kenya

Mt. Kenya, Pt. John, new rock routes. December weather is still unstable: sunny warm days can switch with high winds, lots of rain, and snow above 4,000m. My first time on the peak, during the 2002 Christmas break, brought icy conditions on the high peaks, so after doing some of the ice gullies Will Frost and I looked for some steep climbing. The southwest face of Pt. John (4,880m) was an obvious goal. We went for the until-then unrepeated 1975 Allan-Howell route, back then climbed in three days at A3. Our free climbing idea was smashed by the first pitch, and finally we were happy to reach the top of the 300m high and 50m overhanging route after 12 hours of aid (A1) and free climbing (including a 5.11a offwidth chimney). It would take me until 2004 to climb a free route through that face.

In December 2003 I climbed another steep aid climb (180m, 5.9 A1+) on Migiot Peak (4,700m) named Electional Day as it was the 27th—the day Kenya had its first democratic election. On that peak Markus Grisshammer and I added a new route Flying Friends (200m, 5.10d) in February 2003. It had nice well-protected crack climbing. The best season for the south side of Mt. Kenya is between January and March. In 2003 I spent most of that time climbing some of the great classics on Bation (5,200m), Nelion (5,180m), and Pt. John (4,880m). August and September is the season for the north side of the peak, which also offers superb climbing.

In March 2004 I spent another 10 days on Mt. Kenya (as acclimatization for an Everest expedition). Thanks to Bongo Woodly, the National Park warden, I could train the rescue team of the National Park in climbing. With one of the rangers, Charles Kamau, I climbed a new route on the right-hand side of the Pt. John southwest face. Luckily all the pitches went free (one redpoint, the rest onsight), and so the impressive southwest face got its first free climb at a grade of 5.11c. Pitch 1: Starts at right end of southwest face, left of smooth slabs, through a corner to a steep layback, over slighty overhanging bulge (40m, 5.10d). Pitch 2: Traverse face right to join a corner system. Follow that to climb an overhang to less steep terrain (50m, 5.11c). Then two slab pitches (5.9) lead to easier climbing (5.7/8) another 100m to join the southwest ridge.

FELIX BERG, *Kenya Mountain Club*

Mt. Kenya's Pt. John (4,880m). (1) Northwest Ridge (350m, 5.10d A1). A nice exposed climb, often repeated. All but one pitch have been free climbed (5.10d) by Markus Grisshammer and Felix Berg (and maybe others). There remains a finger crack, which might go free at a high grade (5.13?). First ascent: 5.9 A2, Baillie-Phillips, 1964. (2) West Face (350m, 5.8 A4, Drlik-Plachecky, 1980). (3) Southwest Face Allan-Howell (300m, 5.11a A1). Very adventurous, overhanging climbing. Only one repeat (Berg-Frost, 2003); might go free. First ascent: A3, Allan-Howell, 1977. (4) Southwest Face Berg-Kamau (300m, 5.11c, 2004). (5) Southwest Ridge (300m, 5.7). Starts on the other side of the mountain and then traverses to the southwest ridge (right-hand ridge on the photo). Migiot Peak (4,700m) is in front of the northwest ridge of Pt. John. It has two new climbs Election Day (180m, 5.9 A2, Berg solo, 2003) and Flying Friends (200m, 5.10d, Berg-Grisshammer, 2003). Photo and information from *Felix Berg*

Nithi Gorge, Opium of the People. Alex Fiksman and I climbed a new route in the Nithi Gorge over two days in December. The initial goal was to climb the "prow" at the mouth of the gorge (which was climbed a few weeks later by a team from the UK—see the Temple report by Alex Jakubowski). However, due to unstable weather we decided to climb what appeared to be a less committing route a hundred meters to the left of the original route (*Ricochette*) climbed in 1971. Also climbing with us were visiting climbers William Hair and Peter Storp. However, after spending considerable time on a discontinuous and frightening line, they decided to take advantage of an excellent boulder near base camp.

We started climbing a series of right facing corners, which brought us to a large grassy ledge about 80 meters above the ground. As clouds moved in, we placed two pegs and retreated to spend the remainder of the day tent bound. The following morning we re-climbed to our high point quickly and continued up a series of left facing corners. Three very loose and scary pitches brought us to the top. As we walked down, the clouds opened up as expected. The next day we moved up to climb on the main peaks.

We named our route Opium Of the People and rated it 5.10b. Two pegs were fixed at the top of pitch three. The base has been marked with an obvious cairn. [See "The Nithi Gorge" feature article in this Journal for a route line photograph.]

BOBBY MODEL, *AAC, Mountain Club of Kenya*

Ndoto Mountains, Poi, Doing A Dirty Eastern Groove. During July of 2003, we climbed a new 17-pitch route up the east face of Mt. Poi in the Ndoto Mountains of northern Kenya. Our team consisted of four university students from around the world: Felix Berg from Germany, Peter Horsey and myself from Kenya, and James Nutter from England.

The route follows a groove line for most of its length up the cliff. The rock quality varies from excellent to frankly dangerous. The route was climbed in a mostly traditional style with bolts being placed at the belays and in areas where the rock quality was too poor for regular gear or run-out climbing. The climbing is extremely atmospheric, with 17-pitches carrying you high above the desert floor. There are plenty of vultures flying back and forth along the cliff to check on the state of their prospective meal.

We named the route Doing a Dirty Eastern Groove. The hardest traditional pitch is graded English E4 6a and the hardest sport pitch goes at about French 7c (5.12d). [For a route-line photo, logistics on climbing in the Ndotos, and survey of Kenyan climbing, see the feature articles earlier in this Journal.]

MARNIX BUONAJUTI, *Kenya Mountain Club*

Ndoto Mountains, Poi, Story About Dancing Dogs. In 2002 the Slovenian team of Luka Fonda, Stanko Gruden, Matja Jeran, Goran Koren, and Rok Sisernik drilled a sport route from top to bottom and climbed it at 5.13b. For more information about the route, visit www.Kenya2002.org. For the route line, see feature article "The Ndoto Mountains" earlier in this Journal.

Ndoto Mountains, Manamonet, Maximum Miracle Centre. The British team of Toby Dunn, Alex Jakubowski, and Ben Winston, climbed a virgin wall, Manamonet: E5 6b. See "Maximum Miracle Centre" feature article earlier in this Journal.

Madagascar

Tsaranoro Atsimo, Avanà. Between October 1 and 7 Italians Paolo Stoppini, Paolo Tombini, Alberto Zucchetti, and I climbed a new route on the east pillar of Tsaranoro Atsimo. We christened out route Avanà, which in the local language means rainbow. We climbed 10 pitches with difficulties up to 7a+ (5.12a) covering some 500m of vertical gain. We encountered perfect granite along steep blank slabs that we protected by placing a total of 104 bolts—84 for protection and 20 for belays. We climbed ground-up placing bolts using a power drill and drilling from hooks or stances. It took us four days to complete our climb, and it was Stoppini and Zuchetti who did most of the leading. We had many problems with the batteries of our power drill, one of which exploded at one point. It was very difficult to re-charge them, so on our last day, with just one pitch to go, we were forced to carry a 10-pound gas-powered drill up the route. Avanà is a fairly serious route, considering that the bolts are quite distant from each other and there is no natural protection to be found.

SANDRO BORINI, *Italy (translated by Rolando Garibotti)*

Scotland

Scottish winter season summary. Late January 2005. The last vestiges of a pathetic wet snowfall are swept from the hills by yet another howling, warm, maritime wind. Temperatures on the sodden summits rise to 6°C. Only a handful of interesting routes have been snatched in the brief cold spells, and the first summary of Scottish winter climbing for the *AAJ* is not looking very exciting.

Six weeks later. Mid March, and the picture could not be more different. A cold Northerly air stream becomes established in mid February bringing snow and low freezing levels. Brief thaws keep the water moving for ice formation. The cold spell continues until early March as psyched climbers from all over the world arrive in Scotland for the International Winter Climbing Meet. World-class talent, local knowledge, great conditions. The scene is set for one of the most magnificent weeks of winter climbing in Scottish history.

Simon Richardson's article earlier in this Journal has set Scottish winter climbing in the world context. This, the first annual summary, will provide a quick overview of some of the most significant routes climbed this winter. These annual summaries won't seek to be anything like definitive: over 135 new winter routes were recorded in 2003-2004. For comprehensive coverage and route descriptions the reader is referred to the annual *Scottish Mountaineering Club Journal.*

Winter climbing in Scotland is very varied, and becoming more so. Until recently most recorded routes ranged in length between 50m and 400m. Over recent winters some highly technical, shorter routes have been climbed and recorded. A couple of these (Logical Progression and The Tempest) have been sport or M style (pre-placed gear and top roping), but in the last two winters ground up ascents have been made of some short (less than 40m) but very hard lines. (E.g. The Cathedral on the Cobbler: X, 11, climbed by Dave MacLeod in January 2004). These summaries will have an overt bias to reporting longer routes on the bigger cliffs. This is not because the shorter routes are in any sense less significant (they will be among the most influential climbs done), but because this is the *American ALPINE Journal*, and the longer climbs have a more alpine character.

Ben Nevis is the most famous Scottish winter venue. Three kilometers of cliffs reaching 500m in height provide the setting for the greatest concentration of winter climbs in Scotland. The Ben (there are actually a great many Bens in Scotland—it means hill) is best known worldwide for its magnificent ice climbs, such as Point Five and Zero Gullies, Orion Face, and Galactic Hitchhiker. But the last decade has seen an explosion in mixed climbing on the steep and overhanging snow plastered grooves, chimneys, and corners. The charge was led by Simon Richardson and Chris Cartwright with the first ascent in 1996 of Cornucopia (VII, 9) a puzzling smooth corner on the right wall of Number Three Gully. This test piece received its 4th and 5th ascents during the Winter Meet courtesy of Bruno Sourzac (France) and Dave Hesleden (UK) then Stanislav Havanec (Czech) and Ian Parnell (UK). A few meters to the right and before the Winter Meet Cartwright and Richardson added Archangel, a bold, sustained, and strenuous VIII,7 that they had been watching since 1996—it's so steep that it rarely catches much snow.

Predicting good conditions is a key skill in Scottish winter climbing, and it was this ability that enabled Erik Brunskill and Gareth Hughes to make the first winter ascent of the summer rock climb Strident Edge high up on the Ben's South Trident Buttress. Winter ascents of Summer

Bruno Sourzac on pitch 4 during the first ascent of Extasy (VIII,8), Creag Meagaidh. This was the standout route of the International Winter Meet and possibly the most difficult onsight first ascent climbed to date in Scotland. *Dave Hesleden*

climbs depend on them being adequately "white"—that is plastered with enough snow to make conventional rock climbing impossible. Brunskill and Hughes needed to wait till the day after a huge Westerly storm had wrought havoc across the UK and dumped masses of powder snow over the Ben. This did the trick and they enjoyed a well plastered VI,7. Another new route that required snowy conditions was Godspell (VII,8) an overhanging chimney cutting through the headwall of The Castle (Kelly Cordes, USA, and Simon Richardson). This was just one of many fine first ascents made during the Winter Meet.

Creag Meagaidh lies 35 km North East of Ben Nevis. Being further from the sea it depends more on water ice from drainage and snowmelt to form its classic ice lines. Its usual attraction lies in long moderate ice climbs like The Pumpkin (300m, V,4) and Centre Post (400m, III). When in condition it's a busy place to climb, which is probably a good thing as trail breaking through deep snow up the long gradual walk in is especially tiresome. Two major icy lines were added to the mountain during the Winter Meet. Eye Candy (200m, VII,7, Primoz Hostnik/Slovenia, and Es Tressider and Guy Robertson/UK) takes hanging ramps to the right of Smiths Gully. On the same wall, but slightly to the right another international creation, Extasy (245m, VIII,8) appears to be an extremely serious line. Five pitches feature technical 8 climbing. The gear is non-existent. It may well be undergraded. If so it could be the first Grade IX climbed onsight in Scotland. (Other routes as hard or harder have required multiple attempts or abseil inspection). A major tour de force for the thin ice master Dave Hesleden and guest Bruno Sourzac.

The North-West Highlands of Scotland fill three climbing guidebooks. The term is used to refer to all the hills and corries north and west of the Great Glen, a watery line (including

Loch Ness) slanting across the country from the foot of Ben Nevis to the east coast at Inverness, just north of the Cairngorms. The North-West is a superb area for exploratory climbing. It is rare to see another party, and on many cliffs you are guaranteed solitude. Rock types vary, but sandstone and quartzite predominate giving a different feel from the climbing further south. The sandstone cliffs are very vegetated, giving great mixed climbing possibilities, and small springs cause great bosses and flows of ice to spring forth from improbably steep blank rock sections. Guy Robertson is a North-West aficionado and in January he and Alastair Robertson made the long tramp into the remote Coire Ghranda of Beinn Dearg. They set to work up a much fancied line to the left of Mick Fowler's 1988 route Ice Bomb (VII,7). A tuft (a small patch of frozen moss or turf—vital for progress on many mixed climbs) ripped and sent Alastair into a 15m fall. The pair persevered and Final Destination (VIII, 7) was the result. The International Winter Meet also made an impression on the North-West with second (Hesleden and Sourzac) and third (Sam Chinnery/UK and Steve House/USA) ascents of Snoopy (VII,7) on Fuar Tholl's magnificent sandstone tombstone Mainreachan Buttress. Snoopy was first climbed in winter by Chris Dale and Andy Nisbet in 1998, and features bold thin ice climbing and a vital spring fed ice column.

The Northern Corries of Cairn Gorm have long been a forcing ground for technical standards. A ski road runs high up Cairn Gorm making for a short walk in. Good paths and popularity make the crags feel friendly. The whole of the day's physical and mental energy can be applied to the route. The cliff bases here are high, and most routes require only powder or rime, so wintry conditions can often be found. The routes are short, and many are hard. In February Dave MacLeod, Scotland's most talented all round climber with hard trad., boulder, winter and sport routes to his name, raised the Northern Corries bar again. The Hurting is a 35m Summer E4 6a. Having inspected the route twice on abseil MacLeod attempted the line ground up in full winter conditions. The lower section is very poorly protected—a ground fall is clearly possible. The route continues on baggy torques, tenuous hooks, and tiny tufts. Crampons try to settle on the rounded granite edges. Every move is at least technical 9. Sadly, MacLeod fell from near the top on his first attempt, the fall held by a small cam, not the most reliable protection in icy conditions. A couple of weeks later he was back, and, in a howling wind that kept blowing his feet from the smeary edges, he fought his way cleanly to the top. The grade of XI,11 reflects the sustained technical difficulty and groundfall potential.

At first sight The Hurting and Extasy are very different types of Scottish winter route. One abseil inspected, the other climbed onsight. One very short, the other quite long. One requires cutting edge technical skills, the other unparalleled boldness. But there is much in common too between these climbs. Both are bold, both technical. Both required their ascentionists to wait until conditions were right. Both required the vision to see a potential winter line where others hadn't, and the belief to get on the line and push it out to the top. The diversity of winter climbing in Scotland is part of its compelling appeal. Climbing a steep ice line on the Ben in April feels a million miles away from a powder-choked groove on Lochnagar in December. The diversity of the developments this year shows the robust good health of Scottish winter climbing, and how much more there is to do.

And we always get long periods of great conditions in which to do it!

MALCOLM BASS, *The Alpine Club*

Norway

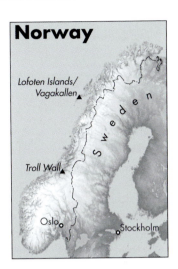

Norway

Lofoten Islands/
Vagakallen▲

Troll Wall▲

Oslo○

Stockholm○

Romsdal, Mongejura (1,200m), southwest face, El Pinche Borrego. In July David Font Ventura, Jordi Cañigueral Vilá, Jordi Servosa Roca, and I took about to open a new route in Norway. The first idea was to try to open a route on the Troll wall but the weather and the conditions this season were not good. Also, the only possible line we saw only was about 300m and then would intercept another route. So we changed the objective to the wall of Mongejura 1,200m, this has a southwest face and dries faster. We fixed four pitches and prepared two haulbags (the Pigs) and two portaledges, 40 liters of water, and food for seven days.

After four days of rain it was still raining. So the first day we could only open one pitch and put the bivy under a roof. The second day we could open two pitches in the rain. The third day we had sun and could climb two pitches on aid climbing, one of which was A3+. The next three days were mostly sunny, then the weather changed again and we decided to push the next day until we get off the wall. After the last hard pitches, we climbed 300m of third class to the only bivouac ledge, after 20 hours of activity.

El Pinche Borrego (905m, VI 5.10d A3+) has some pitches of aid and the rest is free climbing, with posibilities to free the whole route. It would be good for this to get a repetition.

LUIS CARLOS GARCÍA AYALA,
Mexico

Mongejura's southwest face, with El Pinche Borrego. *Carlos Garcia*

Kyrgyzstan

PAMIR ALAI

KARAVSHIN

Yellow Wall, possible new route. Our 21-day expedition to the Karavshin Valley last July was during one of the rainiest summers the Kyrgyz shepherds said they had seen in a long time. Despite this and numerous difficulties with border patrols, having the right permit, meeting our mule transport, climbing with partners that I had just met through the internet, and the worst of all a broken right hand, we still managed to escape with some stories to tell. Unfortunately, most of them were not climbing related. Dining with the Kyrgyz shepherd families over meals of bread, rice, chai, and sour milk balls was an interesting experience. But nothing beats doing machine gun practice with the Kyrgyz military, or watching them fire their AK-47s at the surrounding big walls, supposedly patrolling for IMU (Islamic Movement of Uzbekistan) insurgents.

Nonetheless, we had this rain-soaked valley of gargantuan granite walls to ourselves for the first two weeks. We spent the first day exploring a line up Little Asan, a small formation in front of Mt. Asan (a beautiful 3,000' cliff), on the left side of the Kara Su valley. However, after four pitches, we discovered that the beautiful crack we had spotted from the ground was chock full of grass, so we descended to the ground. Day two was spent climbing the "Diagonal Route", the presumed "classic" line up the Yellow Wall. Unsure of what Russian "5B" was supposed to mean, we over prepared for this route by fixing the first 1000', and bringing way too much gear. The crux is probably only 5.10, but the route climbs up a chossy, wet, approach ramp for about eight pitches just to gain halfway-decent climbing. It was on this climb that I discovered my right hand was not just sore; it was broken. This forced me to do everything left-handed. We found Tommy and Beth's portaledge (I'm assuming it's their A5 ledge) about one third of the way up the Diagonal Route just barely hanging on, apparently having fallen from its perch higher up after being shot at so much. Not surprising, the Kyrgyz military seemed to have been using it for target practice and we saw them fire quite a few rounds at

The Yellow Wall, showing its possible new, and in any case newly equipped route (not to summit). *Chris Harkness*

the surrounding walls when we were there too. Haulbags and fixed lines are still hanging up there. Ken and Stewart finished up the climb the next day while I explored the beautiful Ak Su valley alone.

Afterward, the rain fell consistently every day, leaving only afternoon windows of climbable weather. Due to the rain and having one injured climber, we decided to abandon our hopes of climbing Mt. Asan and settle for a smaller, more escapable objective on the Yellow Wall. We decided to try out a line that Ken had spotted on the first day of recon that followed the left side of the wall up a trail of disconnected crack systems and beautiful dihedrals. With about four to five hours a day to climb (if that) we poured all efforts into this route, climbing siege style. We were further encouraged when the Ukrainian National Climbing Team, the apparent climbing authorities of the area, arrived at base camp and told us we were doing a new route. However, we later discovered some ancient pitons on the last pitch. We cleaned it up a lot, and installed two-bolt anchors at every belay. In my opinion, this route should provide a much more enjoyable and aesthetic one-day warm-up route than the Diagonal Route, and will be easy to descend. In addition, any climber who summits the Yellow Wall will have a safe and clear way to get off the wall by following the shoulder from the summit down and west for about four low-angled pitches (easy fifth class; rappels possible) until seeing our last anchor—a bolt and piton (instead of having to downclimb sections like Ken and Stewart did after topping out on the Diagonal Wall). The route: Everything is Normal (1200', 5.10b, A2, Chris Harkness, Stewart Matthiesen, and Ken Zemach).

CHRIS HARKNESS

PAMIR

Zaalayskiy Ridge, exploration, first ascents and new routes. On July 22 a team from the UK, including a US citizen now working in Scotland, set off for Kyrgyzstan. The team consisted of Ian Arnold, Ken Findlay, Paul Hudson, Paul Lyons, Will Parsons (all UK), Susan Jensen (USA) and Shaun the Sheep. Shaun was a toy "Wallace and Grommit" sheep and was on the trip to

Various ascent routes as seen from above ABC1: (1) Peak of the Long White Cloud. (2) Whaleback. (3) Professor Peak. *Paul Hudson*

raise money for the Alpine Fund, a charity started some years ago by Garth Willis, an American working in Kyrgyzstan. The Alpine Fund helps disadvantaged and orphaned children make the most of themselves and uses the hills and mountain environment as a tool to make this happen.

The team chose a less frequented area of the Pamir south of Sary Tash and east of the main road leading from south Sary Tash into Tajikistan. A little further east along the range is the triple-border point of Kyrgyzstan, Tajikistan, and China. The venue was chosen to fit a one month's vacation, all that half the team could manage. A direct flight from Heathrow, London, to Almaty (Kazakhstan) via Astana Airlines, a drive to Bishkek (Kyrgyzstan), and another flight of a couple of hours landed us in Osh. From Osh it was a day's drive to our area of the Zaalayskiy Ridge.

There were some initial difficulties when we found out that the in-country company had placed our base camp in the wrong place and we had to negotiate its relocation. Subsequently, base camp was not quite in the right place and few of us used it much during our stay, spending most of our time at two advanced base camps, designated in this report ABC1 and 2, from where we explored two different valleys. The best venture from ABC1 was a two-day excursion to Charity Peak. After a night spent on a ridge south of Krazha and descent to the adjoining valley the following morning, Susan Jensen and Ian Arnold took a serac-threatened lower route while Will Parsons, Ken Findlay, Shaun, and I chose a lovely hard névé ramp. We joined forces higher on the ridge. Named Andy's Route, after Andy Bennett, a friend of Ian's killed in an Alpine accident in 1990, the climb varied between a snow plod and some exciting bits and pieces, where ice or rock jutted out. A grade of Alpine PD/AD seemed appropriate.

From ABC2 the two main excursions were to a pair of hills opposite the camp and a five-day excursion to a side valley that Ian had spotted when he and I took a stroll out on the first day. The two hills across the river from ABC2 were climbed on August 10 and 11. Cold Foot Peak was climbed of the day the team crossed the river and Professor Peak the day after.

The best outings from "Ian's Valley" were a first ascent by Ken Findlay and Will Parsons of Karena Peak, where the soft snow and sections of loose rock gave them one or two moments to think about, and a new route on Cold Sunrise Peak.

On the evening of the 16th we climbed to a high bivouac site in order to access one of the higher peaks in this little cirque. Up at midnight, we edged our way upward among the ice and rock outcrops with only Will seeming to know where he was going. Out in the lead he made good progress between icefalls and rock. At 4 a.m. Will, Paul Lyons, and Ken took a rest, as Paul needed a toilet break. Sue, Ian, and I carried on up towards the ridge and by doing so missed the pantomime of the trip. Paul tried to access his bottom through a climbing harness, water-proof salopettes, fleece salopettes, and underpants. All on a 70° ice slope. It seems that all the various pieces of clothing had to be removed in different directions and Paul's struggles brought Ken and Will to their knees with laughter. After that event Paul L., Will, and Ken started up the slope following our lights and began to close the gap, until Paul began to ask for more and more rests and in the end started to fall asleep resting on his axe.

Will and Ken realized that Paul was suffering from an altitude problem and decided they needed to get him down. A shouted conversation later and it was agreed that the three below could adequately deal with the situation, leaving those up above free to continue. The descending trio started down immediately, but after a few rope lengths Paul recovered enough for them to stop their dangerous descent and wait until first light. Hacking a ledge on which to sit, Will then got them all to start the digit wiggling procedure that so many mountaineers know. Ian and Susan continued pulling me along and as the sun rose we gained the final section and much to my relief soon stood on the summit of Cold Sunrise Peak. This was our last peak. Fortunately, Paul Lyons recovered as soon as he lost height, and apart from being tired was fit and well. The following day, the 18th, we started our journey back to base camp and finally flew back to the UK on the 23rd.

The team, well Shaun really, was sponsored for each hill he ascended and raised around £1,500 for the Kyrgyz charity. The following ascents were achieved: from ABC1 Whaleback (1st Ascent 4,456m—F); Peak of the Long White Cloud (1st Ascent 4,452m—PD); Charity Peak (1st Ascent 4,982m—PD/AD); Krazha Peak (1st UK/US ascent 4,592m—PD); White Top Rock (1st UK/US ascent 4,347m—PD-). From ABC2 Cold Feet Peak (1st ascent 4,550m—PD-); Marmot Peak (1st ascent 4,005m—walk); Karena Peak (1st Ascent 5,052m—PD+); Professor Peak* (1st British Ascent 4,840m—PD); Fossil Peak** (1st British/US Ascent 5,116m—PD); Cold Sunrise Peak** (New Route; 1st British/US Ascent 5,505m—PD+/AD). While I have found, as yet, no written evidence for previous ascents of any of the peaks excepting Krazha and White Top Rock, the asterisks show which tops had evidence of previous ascents. ** signifies clear evidence, while * stands for less clear evidence. We took the evidence as small cairns left on the summits. On Professor Peak it was unclear if the stone pile was man-made or a natural effect of weathering.

PAUL HUDSON, *United Kingdom*

TIEN SHAN

WESTERN KOKSHAAL TOO

Kyzyl Asker, second ascent; new routes on Great Walls of China, Ochre Wall, Panfilovski Division. Guy Robertson and I returned to Kyrgyzstan's Western Kokshaal-Too in late August, intent on finishing what we had started in 2002 on the unclimbed southeast face of Kyzyl Asker (5,842m). With us we brought extra firepower in the form of Pete Benson, and base camp conviviality in the form of Robin Thomas and Matt Halls. Matt and Robin planned to climb anything that took their fancy, while Guy, Pete, and I planned to tackle the southeast face as a three. In 2002 the problem had been the line thawing at the slightest hint of sunshine. Although it was colder this time around, thawing still proved a significant problem, and we left without having attempted our intended route. It is difficult to know the best time to attempt this route. You could go in September and get lucky, or you could simply try it in bad

Kyzyl Asker (left) and Panfilovski Division. (1) Robertson-Tresidder attempt (ended at the x, 2002). (2) Pete and Matt's Couloir (Benson-Halls, 2004). (3) Haggis Supper (500m, WI5+, Benson-Robertson-Tresidder, 2004). *Es Tresidder*

The first route on the Great Walls of China: Border Control (Robertson-Tresidder). *Garth Willis*

The Ochre Wall. (1) Ak Saitan (600m, 5.10+ A3+ 85°, Buil-Cabo-Castro-Latorre, 2002). (2) Fire and Ice (Scottish VII, Benson-Tresidder, 2004). (3) Beef Cake (600m, M5 WI4, Isaac-DeCapio, 2001). *Es Tresidder*

weather when it is not thawing but the likelihood of heavy spindrift is very high. February March is a good time for climbing in the Ala Archa and might be an option on Kyzyl Asker, but it will be very cold and getting to the mountain would be very difficult. Instead we added four new routes to the surrounding walls, and a new route on Kyzyl Asker to make the second ascent of the mountain. We stayed in the area till September 21.

Guy, Pete and I climbed a technical icy line on the south face of Panfilovski Division (ca 5,400m), the neighboring peak to Kyzyl Asker, early in the trip. In bad weather and continuous spindrift we climbed four fine technical pitches of pure ice and mixed. Higher up on the route we moved together up moderate but insecure ground before reaching easy ground approximately 200m below the summit. From here we descended a broad gully on Abalakov threads. We named the route Haggis Supper (500m, WI5+). After this the weather cleared for five days. Matt and Robin added a new gully line to the south face of Pik Jerry Garcia (ca 5,200m), climbing the crux ice before the sun hit them.

Guy and I made the first ascent of the Great Walls of China, finding a superbly sustained icy mixed line, which provided 13 long pitches, only three of which were easier than Scottish V (WI4)! The crux pitches involved thin ice, with some rock climbing on the more discontinuous sections. Border Control (WI 5, Scottish VII/VIII, A1) was born [thought not to the summit—Ed.].

On this wall there is massive potential for high standard icy mixed lines. The rock climbing also looks superb, but on closer inspection anything that gets the sun is very dangerous due to rockfall. This may be why routes have not been climbed before (people who have expressed an interest have thought of doing them as big wall aid/free rock routes. The Great Walls face east, but because there are pillars you can climb on northerly aspects. Each pillar has several stellar north-facing lines; ours was perhaps the easiest. The climbing might not be any harder on the others, but it would certainly be more sustained! Parties wishing to repeat our route would be advised to take bivouac gear, as there is the world's best bivi cave at the top of the hard climbing. This would make bagging the summit feasible and complete the route (we climbed for 20 hours with no water after bursting our water container on a crampon at the base of the route, so by the time we reached the ridge we just wanted to get down).

While we were recovering, Pete and Matt climbed a devious route to make the second known ascent of Kyzyl Asker. They avoided the problematic seracs on the north face by traversing onto the face above them from the east col, gained via a gully on the south flank (one pitch of Scottish VI). From the top of the gully there was a steep icy traverse above a big drop to reach the north face proper, after which it was quite easy-angled and was more or less skied in both directions apart from the summit slopes, which were too steep.

Last up, Pete and I added a route to the Ochre Walls, climbing an obvious ice smear to the left of the DeCapio-Isaac route Beefcake (600m, IV, M5 WI4, 2001). This offered superb icy mixed climbing up to Scottish VII on a bitterly cold day. We reached the unnamed summit at dusk. After a night out at a notorious Bishkek nightclub, Fire and Ice seemed an appropriate name.

It would seem that late August/early September offers the best chance for stable weather in this region. In July/August 2002, as two teams, we made four attempts on routes. This year, as two teams, the weather allowed us to make eight new route attempts!

ES TRESIDDER, *United Kingdom*

Pik Sabor, new route attempt and repeat of north ridge. In 2003 the Groupe Militaire de Haute Montagne suffered a tragic loss when two well-known members, Antoine de Choudens and Philippe Renard, were killed while acclimatizing for an alpine style ascent of the South West Face of Xixabangma. The group re-gathered in 2004 and planned an attempt on the coveted south east face of Kyzyl Asker. However, the heavy costs imposed by the Chinese and an eventual denial to allow the team to cross the border, meant a change of plan and the climbers opted for a new route on Pik Sabor (4,850m), an impressive rock bastion on the ridge south of the Ochre Walls and opposite the end of Kyzyl Asker's unclimbed north ridge. The first ascent of this peak took place in 1985 when Kasbek Valiev's team climbed a big wall route up the West Southwest Rib (the same expedition on which he also made the first ascent of Kyzyl Asker via the 1,500m west face). Unable to drive to their proposed base camp at the start of July due to boggy ground, the team was forced to ferry loads 15km to an advanced base three kilometres short of Sabor's 700m-high west face. Bad weather proved a constant hassle (early in the trip it deposited one-and-a-half metres of snow in base camp over a two-day period) and it wasn't until the 22nd that the climbers could embark on a new line up the west face, fixing the first 150m (approximately seven pitches) before Guillaume Baillargé, Manu Pellissier and Francois Savary set off with a portaledge. The granite was magnificent but the cracks proved either wet or chocked with ice. Above the end of the ropes the three only managed four pitches over the next two days, nice F5c cracks having to be climbed laboriously at A2. Then, at a point roughly half-way up the wall, a storm moved in and three very wet and bedraggled climbers were forced to retreat to base.

In the meantime the other two on the expedition, Lionnel Albrieux and Thomas Faucheur, repeated the 2002 British Route on the North Ridge (Neal Crampton/Blair Fyffe, 10th-11th August 2002: c800m: TD+: Scottish 6). The French pair climbed the route in a long day on the 31st. A day or two later Baillargé, Pellissier and Savary also climbed the line (which they report as 500m) in less than 12 hours, finding it mostly mixed up to M5. The weather continued poor until the French left the area, having experienced only two fine days in the 20 at or above base.

LINDSAY GRIFFIN, Mountain INFO editor, CLIMB magazine

Pik Yurnos, second ascent. With help from the Anatoli Boukreev Memorial Fund, Melis Coady and I spent several weeks during August and September climbing in Kyrgyzstan. After climbing several snow, rock, and ice routes in Ala Archa National Park, outside the country's capital of Bishkek, we headed south to the West Kokshaal-Too and Komorova Glacier, situated on the Kyrgyz-Chinese border.

On August 26 we made the second ascent of the peak located next to Pik Ecstasy, via a series of ice couloirs on the east-southeast aspect. We topped out in deteriorating conditions and descended the peak's north ridge in a whiteout. We dubbed the route Dreaming of Wild Elephants (estimated grade: III AI4).

Snow peaks from left to right: Pik Gronky (FA: Edwards-Isaac, 1998), Pik Yurnos (FA: Beckwith-Edwards-Isaac, 1998), Pik Ecstasy (FA: Beckwith-Edwards-Isaac, 1998). Pik Begger (FA: Edwards, 1998) is just right of Pik Ecstasy, out of the photo. *Molly Loomis*

Molly Loomis celebrating sunrise on the Komarova. *Melis Coady*

On August 3rd we had also attempted a prominent unclimbed peak two mountains north of 52 Years of American Duct Tape. Two-thirds of the way up the north ridge, we retreated due to unstable snow conditions. We then returned to the Ala Archa in late September.

MOLLY LOOMIS, *AAC*

BORKOLDOY

Central Borkoldoy, exploration and various first ascents. The central area of the Borkoldoy range in southeast Kyrgyzstan is a group of superb "alpine" peaks that are well-defended on every side by chains of slightly lower mountains. They are north of the Dankova group in the West Kok-shaal-Too. It has been traveled by a few trekking groups in recent years, but other than one (unsuccessful) attempt by a Russian team on the highest peak (5,170m) there are no known records of previous mountaineering expeditions. Our ISM expedition in September (Adrian Nelhams, Vladimir Komissarov, and I (guides); Ben Box, Steve Brown, James Bruton, Dr. Tom Fox, Phil Naybour, George Ormerod, John Porter, and Nick Wheatley) expected to approach on foot using horses for carrying camp equipment. However, with all our manpower we were able to open up an old geologists' road made in Soviet times. This led to a broad river delta, which was drivable for 20km to a base camp at 3,570m, where all the main glaciers terminate, making it a fantastic base for exploration.

After reconnaissance, ABC was set up at 4,240m on the right-hand branch of the double-headed glacier running southward (we later named this Ilbirs Glacier, after snow-leopard tracks were discovered). Ascents were made of Pk Ilbirs (5,017m, PD+), the big dominant peak on the right side; the obvious rock pyramid on the east side (Zoob Barsa, 4,685m, PD+), and a traverse of Trident Peak (AD) just north of Pk Ilbirs. One team explored the glacier to the west and climbed Pk 4,857m by its west ridge.

Overlooking base camp were rock walls between 100-500m high. These proved to be made of excellent solid limestone and gave two fine routes (E2 and HVS). For the second "foray," ABCs were set up on the east branch of Ilbirs glacier and the base of Pk 5,170m. Several summits above

Ilbirs E were climbed, including the excellent Dvoinay Vershina ("Twin Peak," 5,041m). The forepeak of Pk 5,170m gave a pleasant excursion to 4,915m (named Sakchi—Sentry), then a serious attempt was made on Pk 5,170m via a couloir on the west flank to the north ridge. At ca 5,000m the ridge became seriously knife-edged and corniced, and the attempt was abandoned. Three smaller summits on the opposite side of the glacier gave easier days before the expedition decamped. All in all it was a very enjoyable trip to the most remote mountains any of the team had visited (ca 200km to nearest proper village). Sightings of the rare Marco Polo sheep and seeing prints of the exceptionally rare snow leopard were a great privilege.

PAT LITTLEJOHN, *United Kingdom*

Pk Ilbirs (5,017m), climbed via the right-hand ridge. *James Brunton*

The still-virgin Pk 5,170m and its "Servant." *James Brunton*

Kuilu Range, first ascents. Gaizka Bilbao and Belen Menedez from Spain, with Amando Niño de Rivera (Mexico) and Gerard van der Berg (Holland), climbed two new routes in the Karator Valley of the Kuilu Range, first visited by an ISM expedition in 2000. The ascents took place between August 8 and September 5 and were named Controlador Aereo and Zoolander. No further information.

Servei General d'Infomacio de Muntanya, Spain

Djungart Range, first recorded visit and exploration. After an acclimatization ascent in the Ala Archa, Graham Sutton and I traveled from Bishkek via Karakol to At Jailoo (2,655m). From there we were able to make a 25-minute flight by helicopter to a base camp at 3,060m in the previously unvisited Djungart Range of the Tien Shan (Kyrghyz Map K-44-XIX: N 41 44' 32.6", E 78 56' 52.5"). We arrived on August 1.

Our aim was to explore the region and make the first ascent of its highest peak, Pt. 5,318m. Running south from base camp, two parallel valleys flank the east and west sides of this peak; we reconnoitered both. We first established an Advanced Base at 3,545m in the eastern valley, and on the 7th we climbed a gully on the flank of Pt 5,318m that connected with the western valley. We reached a height of 4,150m over scree and boulders. Sutton and I then walked further up valley to ca 4,000m, but found no obvious way forwarded through complex moraine and steep hanging glaciers. We dismantled advanced base and a few days later sited another camp at 3,500m in the western valley, later inspecting this valley to 4,000m before returning to base. On the 17th we made a 35-minute flight to Karkara, after which we returned to Bishkek via a night in Karakol. Throughout our stay the weather was exceptionally warm, with rain up to 4,000m. Any snow encountered was old and rotten, and there were regular late afternoon storms. Exploration revealed steep rocky terrain (for which we had no gear) interrupted by hanging glaciers, which due to large crevasses and avalanche danger we considered unsafe. Only border zone permits were needed to visit this area; these were easily arranged for $10 per person by ITMC in Bishkek (one month's notice needed). Gifts of cigarettes, watermelons, and fresh fruit were greatly appreciated by the border guards.

INGRID CROSSLAND, *United Kingdom*

Khan Tengri, mulitiple deaths. Sometimes referred to as one of the most beautiful mountains in the world, 6,995m Khan Tengri in the Tien Shan claimed the lives of no less than 12 climbers last summer. Its most formidable aspect is an almost 2,000m-high north face with many formidable mixed routes of the highest grade; apparently none have been climbed by non-CIS parties. On July 18 top Polish mountaineers Janusz Golab and Grzegorz Skorek were retreating in a storm from a probable new route up the center of this face. Skorek appears to have rappelled to a ledge and called to Golab that the rope was free. When Golab arrived there was no sign of either Skorek or the ledge. His body was later found at the foot of the face. Golab made a further nine rappels with minimal gear to escape the mountain, three times being hit by avalanches that seriously injured his leg. The talented Skorek was the son of the equally renowned Janusz Skorek (first ascent Thalay Sagar's northeast ridge), who had been a regular climbing partner of the famous Jerzy Kukuczka.

Traditionally, the classic route to Khan Tengri ascends the trough of the Semenovski Glacier from the South Inylchek to gain the west ridge at a 5,800m col east of Pik Chapiev (6,371m). Unfortunately, between ca 4,500 and 5,200m it is threatened by serac fall from both sides. In August 1993 an enormous avalanche, emanating from a huge serac band on Chapiev, obliterated this section of the glacier, killing the celebrated Soviet Valeri Khrischaty and two British climbers. Since that time it has become more usual to reach the west ridge from the north; this is longer but objectively much safer. However, ascents from the south have still been made on a regular basis.

Almost exactly 11 years to the day from the time of this accident a large group of climbers (reportedly 40-50) from many different nationalities set off up the Semenovski Glacier. At 6:00 a.m. a huge ice avalanche swept down the flanks and into this group. Five Czechs, three Russians, and three Ukrainians were killed and many others were injured, some seriously. Casualties were evacuated by Kyrghyz helicopter pilots who were forced to carry out rescue operations at night to minimize further risk from avalanche.

LINDSAY GRIFFIN, *Mountain INFO Editor, CLIMB Magazine*

Pakistan

Pakistan, peak fees. We are pleased to inform all clients, friends, the mountaineering community and adventure enthusiasts, particularly climbers, that the Government of Pakistan has decided to continue with the 50% concession in Royalty fee during 2005, thanks to the last minute meeting of The Alpine Club President, Mr. Nazir Sabir with the Federal Minister and Secretary, Ministry of Tourism on February 10, 2005. Initially this concession was given to all climbing expeditions during 2002/2004 in celebration of the Year of Mountains, Nanga Parbat, and K2 Golden Jubilee. Another incentive given for peaks anywhere in the Himalayan-Karakoram belt was a total elimination of the royalty, permit, and L.O. fee to climb peaks up to 6,500m; efforts are being made to raise the same concession to peaks up to 7,000m.

Mr. Nazir Sabir has been in the forefront of pushing for these and many more incentives to encourage foreign climbers into Pakistan during these past years, even before he took over the Alpine Club. We hope that many adventure seekers from all over the world will take full advantage of these incentives in the coming season and the years to follow.

MUSHIR ANWAR, *Nazir Sabir Expeditions, Pakistan*

HIMALAYA

NANGA PARBAT RANGE

Nanga Parbat, Mazeno Ridge, Rupal Face attempt. Steve House (leader), Doug Chabot, Bruce Miller, and I traveled from the Charakusa Valley [see report later in this section] to Nanga Parbat (26,660 ft) base camp below the Rupal (south) Face arriving in base camp on August 9. On August 12-18 Chabot and I did the first ascent of the 6.2-mile-long Mazeno Ridge on Nanga Parbat to where the ridge ends at the Mazeno Col and intersects the Schell Route at 6,940m [see feature article earlier in this Journal for story and route-line photo]. This climb involved a day to get to an advanced base camp at 5,000m, a second day to climb to a bivouac at 6,200m on the long south ridge of the First Mazeno Peak and another three days to traverse the ridge to where it intersects the Schell Route at the Mazeno Col. Due to fatigue and deteriorating weather, Chabot and I then descended the Schell Route without going to the summit of Nanga Parbat. The intent was to return back up the Schell Route when the weather was better in order to complete the ascent of Nanga Parbat. But because of poor conditions on the descent of the Schell Route, we decided not to go back up that route to finish going to the summit.

On August 12-17, House and Miller attempted a bold new route on the Rupal Face between the Messner Route and the Polish Route [see another feature article earlier in this Journal for story and route line photo].

On August 22 Chabot, Miller, and I left base camp for home. House remained to attempt the Rupal Face again solo. But on August 27 House returned to Islamabad after initiating a solo attempt on the Rupal Face that did not get very high.

STEVE SWENSON, *AAC*

HINDU RAJ

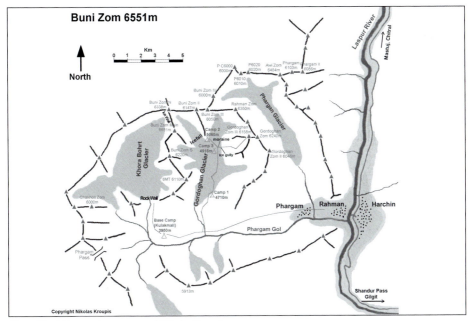

Map of Buni Zom region courtesy of *Nikolas Kroupis*.

Gordoghan Zom III, Buni Zom Mountain. Nikolas Kroupis and I first went to the Buni Zom range in July 2002 without any knowledge of the terrain and the geography of the peaks. Two years later (May-June) our goal remained the same, to climb Buni Zom Main Peak (6,551m). This time the two of us, with two more Greek climbers, Panos Sakellaris and Babis Politis, headed for the mountain. We started with two days light trek from the last village (Phargam) following the Phargam gol, and established our base camp at Kulakmali (3,950m). Hoping to get over the 300-meter rock wall that leads to the Khorabort glacier, our plan was to cross the glacier and reach the summit via a 300-meter ice face to the north ridge.

Unfortunately our efforts were cut off by very demanding rock climbing of nearly 150 meters. Bad weather and water coming from melted snow, from above, made the climbing route wet and even more difficult. We decided to go back and reach the summit from Gordoghan Glacier passing over Buni Zom North peak, as a New Zealand team did on the first ascent in 1957. We trekked back half way to Phargam village and met the foot of Gordoghan Glacier. Sakellaris and Politis trekked back to Phargam village and left for Chitral.

With the help of three porters, Kroupis and I scaled up to 4,700m and set a camp.

We arranged for the porters to come early the next morning to continue our way on the glacier. On the next day we were at 5,100m, having crossed the whole Gordoghan glacier, when we came before a dangerous net of crevasses hidden by fresh snow. It proved impossible to find a way through these crevasses. We set a second camp at 5,065m near the icefall. Next day we tried to continue but finally turned back and we set a camp at 4,915m and came up with the alternative plan of climbing Gordoghan Zom I (6,240m). At 03:30 on June 9 we set out for Gordoghan Zom I. We followed a cone moraine that leads to an ice gully (N36 08' 40.1"–E72 21'31.9"). The route passes a moraine situated almost at the middle of the length of the Gordoghan glacier, and continues to the West face of Gordoghan Zom III. We left the Gordoghan Glacier behind us and took the ice gully that leads to a big snow-covered slope. The summit is not visible from this point. The peak that can be seen ahead has the Gordoghan Zom I summit behind it and on its left. We continued our way for this peak believing that this was Ghordogan Zom. Finally we reached a slope covered by thick ice between 40° and 50°. From this point we saw that there was a higher peak behind this first one. The last 200 meters were exhausting. At 11:00, Nikolas reached this first peak (N36 08' 59.2" - E72 22' 51.5" at 6,158m altitude GPS reading). This peak is not signed in Japanese 1:150,000 maps so we gave the name Gordoghan Zom III. Gordoghan Zom I is connected with this peak by a very narrow ridge about 300 meters long. This abrupt ridge is formed by eroded rock with some places covered by snow and had been impossible to be passed by a solo climber. Nikolas met me lower on the slope. It was 13:30 when we reached our tent and crawled in with exhaustion. We covered the 1,240 meters to the peak in 6 hours and we needed another 4 hours to come back. The snow condition had not been very good due to the early season. The best time to climb in the Buni Zom mountain range is in August.

GEORGE ZARDALIDIS, *Greece*

Editor's Note: Gordoghan III has possibly been climbed three times before during attempts on Gordoghan I: in 1965 by Germans, Alfred Koch and Ernst Lainer (climbed to the Main Summit via an unspecified route, though thought to have been the West Face/Ridge), and subsequently by Japanese in 1968 and 1970 (they stopped at this summit during attempts on the Main Peak). However, the Greek ascent is interesting in that the mountains north of Chitral, close to the Afghan border, were considered very much a no-go area for foreigners after the terrorist strikes of 2001. The pair climbed, there also without problem in 2002, when they reached 6,050m on Gordoghan Zom (6,240m and the fifth highest peak in the range).

KARAKORAM

BATURA MUZTAGH

Sakar Sar, second ascent. Kunihiko Sato made a solo ascent of the 6,272m Sakar Sar via the southeast ridge. This remote peak, which lies on the Afghan border in the northern Batura Muztagh and is approached via the Chapursan and Sakarjerab Valleys, gained its first and, until last year, only ascent from Miyazawa Akira's four-member Japanese expedition, which climbed the southeast flank, finishing up a snow ridge. It appears that Sato's route was more or less the same.

TAMOTSU NAKAMURA, *Japanese Alpine News*

HISPAR MUZTAGH

Hispar Sar, attempt. On September 17 the British Hispar Sar Expedition 2004 (Andy Parkin and myself) set up a base camp at Yutmal (a small ablation valley on the north of the Hispar Glacier to the west of the Yutmaru Glacier), after a two-and-a-half day approach from Hispar Village. Our objective, the southwest face of Hispar Sar (6,400m), lay within sight to the east across the Yutmaru Glacier. From the 19th to the 24th we carried out various reconnaissance/acclimatization outings and set up an Advanced Base Camp on a small un-named glacier below the face. The 25th was spent in base camp celebrating Andy's 50th birthday. On September 26 we returned to advanced base and the following day began climbing the blatantly obvious couloir to the right of the center of the face. Over a four-day period of variable weather we climbed the couloir, exiting by a steep ridge to the right to gain a shoulder approximately 300 meters (reasonably angled snow slopes) from the top. Unfortunately, an accident on the first cramped bivouac had resulted in most of the food, the brew kit, and a spare can of gas being dropped. A storm set in on the night of the 30th/1st and with only vapor left in the remaining gas cylinder, we were forced to descend the couloir in the morning. We made an orderly set of abseils to the glacier despite frequent and increasingly large spindrift avalanches sweeping down the couloir. At the base of the route we found the three stuff-bags of food, gas, and brewing material, which we enjoyed at the advanced base camp that evening. The return to base camp on the 2nd turned into an epic after we got disorientated on the Yutmaru Glacier in a storm. We eventually reached camp just before nightfall and commenced the walk-out on October 4.

The route (1,100m, ED) gave some superb climbing up runnels and cascades of steep ice, between easier angled basins, with the hardest climbing exiting the couloir at the top. The peak still awaits a first ascent to the summit. The team benefited from the concession of 2002, lifting the height at which peak fees are paid from 6,000m to 6,500m. Freed from the bureaucratic hassle and expense of obtaining a permit, this was the most hassle-free trip either of us has taken to Pakistan. We advise others to take advantage of this wonderful concession while it lasts!

SIMON YATES, *United Kingdom*

RAKAPOSHI RANGE

Spantik, ascent of 1987 British Descent Route. A small Japanese expedition climbed 7,028m Spantik from the northwest, repeating the Descent Route used by Mick Fowler and Victor Saunders after their historic ascent of the Golden Pillar in 1987. The line follows a prominent snow and ice spur well right of the Pillar to reach the plateau and upper southwest ridge at ca 6,500m. It was also used for descent by the 2000 French-Slovenian-Russian expedition that repeated the British Route and added a second line to the Pillar.

Kazuya Hiraide, Ms. Kei Taniguchi, and Kazuo Tobita acclimatized on Rash Phari (5,058m) before establishing Base Camp below the face on the June 25. On the 28th they set up Camp 1 on the North West Spur at 5,500m and on the July 8 Camp 2 on the plateau after fixing 150 meters of rope through the serac wall at the top of the spur. Tobita remained here on the 9th while Taniguchi and Tobita ploughed their way up deep snow and through poor weather to the summit, relocating their camp later the same day by GPS.

The Japanese report two other expeditions active on this side of the mountain (probably Austrian and Spanish); one attempting the Golden Pillar itself and one the Descent Route. Both of these are believed to have failed.

TAMOTSU NAKAMURA, *Japanese Alpine News*

PANMAH MUZTAGH

Latok V (6,190m), attempt. Motomu Omiya with two other companions made his fourth attempt on this unclimbed 6,190m summit, which stands at the end of the southeast ridge of Latok III. Omiya, who made the first ascent of Latok IV in 1980, attempted V in 1999, 2000, and 2003 via the South Face, reaching high on the mountain on each occasion and in 2003 getting to within 70 meters of the summit. Last year he again reached 6,100m but failed to reach the highest point.

TAMOTSU NAKAMURA, *Japanese Alpine News*

Editor's note: there is some confusion in the naming of these peaks: the 1999 attempt was definitely on the south face of a peak previously climbed just a few days earlier by the Huber brothers, who refer to it as Latok IV (ca 6,450m).

TRANGO GROUP

Shipton Spire, new routes and attempts. The expedition of the Slovak Mountaineering Union was in Pakistan from July 17 to September 8. Our main goal was to climb Shipton Spire and some surrounding peaks. The expedition had 10 members: leader Igor Koller, vice-leader myself (Vladimir Linek), doctor Ivan Zila, members Gabo Cmarik, Martin Heuger, Dodo Kopold, Dino Kuran, Miro Mrava, Jozef Santus, and Brano Turcek. We received perfect services from the trekking agency Blue Sky Treks & Tours. From Islamabad we traveled two days to Skardu by microbus via the Karakoram Highway and continued by jeeps to Askole; from there we walked three days to base camp at 4,400m on the Trango Glacier below Uli Biaho, two hours from Shipton Spire. Quick progress in hot weather with altitude difference of 1,500m caused health problems for some members. Base camp was on a very nice grass meadow.

During our five weeks' stay the weather was almost always bad, with snow and rain in base camp. There were only nine days of good weather divided into three short periods. According to local people this summer was the worst during the last 20 years. In spite of this fact one Slovak team summited Shipton Spire, another team did a hard first ascent on central part of the face, and the next three climbers were close to finishing a new line on the right side. So it is possible to say that this expedition was successful. Our ascents:

Kopold, Kuran, and Santus did the first repetition of Khanadan Buttress (McMahon-Wharton, 2002), alpine style in two days. On the first attempt during the first period of good weather Kuran, Santus, and Zila slept in the middle of the mixed southwest face. Dino Kuran was stopped by an offwidth crack that he was not able to protect. The snowy face in this part was quite dangerous. They decided to quit the climb. After long thinking and preparation they returned to this route during the second good period of weather. This time the team consisted of Kopold, Kuran, and Santus with tubes to protect the offwidth crack. They completed the route and were on the top of Shipton Spire on August 15 at 19:00, joining the small list of about 20 climbers who have reached the summit. After that they rappelled down partway to a bivy, then returned to base the next day. During the descent they had a good luck in a big rockfall avalanche: only a broken helmet and some small wounds.

The couple Miro Mrava and Brano Turcek wanted to make a first ascent on the left part of Shipton Spire, where there are still no routes. They found the approach terrible via a dangerous glacier, so they decided to change their goal (maybe this is the reason why there is no route there). They chose a line in the central part of the face between Women and Chalk (Mauro Bubu Bole, 2001), and Akelarre (Eskibel-Larranaga-Ortiz, 2000) below the main couloir on the top. They started climbing on July 28. The first two pitches went to a big tower. From the top of this tower they climbed up via plain slabs to a crack system 100 meters above. During the periods of good and bad weather they climbed during

Shipton Spire: (1) The Khanadan Buttress (1,300m, 5.11X C1, McMahon-Wharton, USA, 2002). First repeat by Dodo Kopold, Dino Kuran, Jozef Santus, Slovakia, 2004. (2) Knocking on Heaven's Door (1,000m, 17 pitches, VIII A4, Miro Mrava and Brano Turcek, Slovakia, 2004). (3) Akelarre (1,150m, VI 5.10d A4, Eskibel-Larranaga-Ortiz, Spain, 2000). (3a) American attempt (1,100m, 5.10 A4 60°, Bebie-Boyd-Collum-Selters, USA, 1992). (4) Ship of Fools (1,300m, 5.11 WI6 A2, Ogden-Synnott, 1997). (5) Slovak attempt (800m, 17 pitches, VIII A3, Gabo Cmarik, Igor Koller, Vladimir Linek, 2004). (6) Bulgarian variant (Strahil Geshev, Milkana Ruseva, and Stanimir Zhelyazdov, 2004). (7) Women and Chalk (1,150m, 29 pitches, 5.13b, Bole, 2001). (8) Baltese Falcon, 1,350m, 36 pitches, 5.11 A4, Boyd-Child-Foweraker, USA/Australia, 1996). (9) Inshallah (1,350m, 30 pitches, 5.12a A1, Davis-Harvey-Shaw, 1998). Photo, route lines, and information by *Vlado Linek*.

eight days to above the huge triangle overhang two-thirds of the way up the face. On the 15th they committed to the face and built a portaledge camp named Tatry. They were 300 meters below the ramp leading to the right.

The next day, on the12th pitch, Miro was badly wounded by a falling rock. They decided to stop their climb and returned to base camp. After healing in base camp they returned to the face on August 22. During the next two days only Brano was able to climb, Miro was on belay, and on the 24th they climbed several pitches on the ramp and joined the Spanish route, Akelarre, that evening. Because of Miro's injuries, they decided not to continue to the summit. They named the route Knocking on Heaven's Door. It is pity that they did not knock on the top of

Shipton. (Knocking on Heaven's Door, 1,000m, 17 pitches, 8 A4, Miro Mrava and Brano Turcek; two bolts on belays, seven bolts on pitches).

The next team, consisting of Gabo Cmarik, Igor Koller, and me, tried to make the first ascent of the right part of the face. The first pitch is the same as Ship of Fools (Ogden-Synnott, 1997). Then we broke out right to the overhanging face. After seven days of climbing we had fixed 10 pitches for 400 meters of height gained. We climbed mostly free, so had to wait for sunny weather. Finally, 11 days before departure from base camp to Askole, we decided to climb in any weather.

During the first three days of good weather we established a portaledge camp below the big roof (perfect protection from falling rocks) and climbed three pitches in a big overhang. During the next seven days the weather was very bad; it was snowing and raining and the situation was complicated by the illness of Gabo Cmarik. We had to spend one day with a rescue operation, lowering Gabo down the face. Igor Koller and I climbed again on the face on August 30, one day before departure from base camp. We fought bad weather on the upper part of the face during hard aid climbing through big overhangs, and finally three meters below the easier terrain and 70 meters below the ramp where we would join Ship of Fools, we finished our ascent at 5,600m because of huge waterfalls on the face. We had climbed 17 hard pitches graded up to 8 A3, which was about 95% of the line.

Besides these three ascents we made several attempts that failed because of bad weather or health problems. Dodo Kopold and Martin Heuger tried to make a first ascent on Cat's Ears Spire; Kuran and Santus tried to repeat the American Route on Hainabrakk Tower; and again Kopold and Heuger tried to climb Trango III.

This region has perfect possibilities for new hard rock and mixed first ascents. We want to return to the Baltoro Glacier in 2005 to finish our climbs.

Other climbers on Shipton Spire in 2004 included:

Two Spanish climbers, Oriol Anglada and Toti Solé, arrived at base camp July 10. They tried to climb Inshallah (Davis-Harvey-Shaw, 1998), reaching Camp 3, but due to several rock-falls and bad weather they decided to end the climb and left for home July 23.

Three Bulgarian mountaineers, Strahil Geshev, Milkana Ruseva (wife of the Bulgarian mountaineer Nikolai Petkov, who summited Mt. Everest in 2004), and Stanimir Zhelyazdov did a new variant to Ship of Fools. They started via the American attempt Bebie-Boyd-Collum-Selters (1992), and from the top of the tower they turned to the right; after six new pitches they joined Ship of Fools. Due to bad weather they did not finish the climb, and on August 10 they left for home.

VLADO LINEK, *Slovakia, Slovak Mountaineering Union*

Shipton Spire, new route attempt. Bulgarians Milkana Ruseva, Dimitar Tzolov, Stanimir Zhelyazkov, and I climbed a variation start to Ship of Fools. We started up the face between Akelarre and the 1992 American attempt, joined the former, and after climbing a total of six pitches to the top of the first tower broke out right, climbing seven new free pitches (UIAA VI+, IX-/7b, V+, V+, VI, VI+, V+) to a big ledge, where we established a second camp. Six meters up to the right we joined Ship of Fools and continued up this for another six pitches before having to call it a day and leave for home. The crux IX- pitch was a 50-meter diedre with an off-width crack (two protection bolts) and was followed by several chimney pitches, some of which were dirty and dangerous. Due to poor weather we were only able to climb on eight of the ca 30 days.

STRAHIL GESHEV, *Bulgaria*

Great Trango Tower, southwest buttress, Azeem Ridge. Josh Wharton's and my route starts on the lower right of the broad southwest buttress at just under 4,000m, and climbs to the SW Summit (ca 6,237-6,250m, depending on the map) of Great Trango Tower. This was 17 pitches beyond the highest anchors we found from previous attempts by other parties in 1990 and 2000. We climbed 54 pitches with 60m ropes and simulclimbing a handful of pitches on the lower half. Twenty-five of the pitches were 5.10 or harder. We named the route Azeem Ridge and rated it 5.11R/X M6 A2. Azeem is an Urdu word that means "great," in size or stature, and, more importantly, "great" as a greeting of fondness and respect between people. Azeem accurately summarizes our feelings about the wonderful people we met in the northern areas of Pakistan.

We did no fixing and carried no bolt kit. We started climbing around 9 a.m. on July 24 and summited around noon on July 28. The second jugged with the pack where it was steep, which was probably half of the route. We clipped fixed gear from previous attempts when we saw it—mostly belay bolts, and up to a half-dozen protection bolts—but we did not use any of the fixed ropes we saw disappointingly abandoned along the route (after our descent, we scrambled up and cleaned one that someone had fixed and abandoned at the start). We carried off all of our garbage (empty fuel canister and food wrappers) but left a few protection pieces fixed along with five rap anchors (many cams) and our ropes that got stuck on our final rappel. [A complete account of this climb can be found in the Features section of this *AAJ*.]

KELLY CORDES, *AAC*

Trango Monk, first ascent; Peak 4,700m (Garda Peak), first ascent, Karakoram Khush; Nameless Tower, Eternal Flame, alpine-style ascent; rock routes in valley. From August 2 through September 28, Klemen Mali, Miha Valic, and I, all from Slovenia, climbed in the Trango group. Our main target was supposed to be the southwest ridge of Great Trango Tower. However, just a few days before our departure, we heard that the ridge had been climbed by Americans Josh Wharton and Kelly Cordes. It was a great disappointment for us, but we knew that there are a lot of other mountains around there, and enough work for us to do. When we arrived at base camp the weather was good, so we started with acclimatization. Five days after we arrived, Valic and I climbed Great Trango Tower (6,287m) by the Selters-Woolums Route on the north flank (ice and snow up to 80°, mainly 40°-60°). After

Peak 4,700m (Garda Peak), showing the line of the Slovenian first ascent. *Tomaz Jakofcic*

Sadu (right) and Piyar, Piyar (Love, Love), both 350-meter routes on a rock tower near base camp. *Tomaz Jakofcic*

that the bad weather lasted for two weeks. In this period of unstable weather Valic and I climbed Sadu (350m, 6b+ A1) on a rock pillar near BC. We thought that we were climbing a new route but later we recognized a picture in a climbing magazine about the French route of 2003 [Antoine and Sandrine de Choudens: 350m and seven pitches: 6c: the Slovenians made a variant to this route]. On September 3 the weather started to improve and that day all three of us climbed a new peak half an hour from base camp. We named the route Karakoram Khush (Karakoram Pleasure) (300m, 6b A0) and the peak became Garda Peak (4,700m). Next day we climbed another new route left of Sadu, and gave it the name Piyar, piyar (Love, love…) (350m, 6b+ A0). This route and Sadu were quite hard because of sandy rock and cracks filled with mud and grass.

After one rest day, on September 5 we started from base camp early in the morning. After four hours in an unpleasant scree gully we reached the north col of Nameless Tower and started climbing on the east face of the virgin Trango Monk (5,850m). There was a lot of snow and ice in the lower part, so climbed very slowly. We bivied on the good ledge on the south face and before the night we fixed our two ropes up to the obvious shoulder below the summit tower. Next day we found the only crack in the summit tower and at noon reached the sharp summit. On the same day we descended to base camp. The name of our route is Chota Badla, which means Small Revenge and is dedicated to our friend Josh Wharton who "stole from us" the southwest ridge of Great Trango; Josh had tried Trango Monk three times in the past. The route is rated (450m, 6b A2 70°).

The Chota Badla ("Small Revenge") route, which was the first ascent of the Monk (5,850m). *Tomaz Jacofcic*

After that we could take just one day of rest because Miha's time in base camp was running out. So the next day we went to the south col and in three days we made the first alpine style ascent of Eternal Flame (1,000m, 6c+ A2) to the top of Trango Tower (6,251m). We bivied on the shoulder and on the ledge after pitch 23. We chose the slower but surer two-bivouac tactic because we knew all previous alpine-style attempts had ended near the summit when they ran out of time. We reached the summit on September 11 at 1 p.m. We reached base camp after five hours of rappelling and sliding down the couloir. We climbed the route on our first try.

There have been a lot of attempts on this route, but as far as I know the only successful ascents (after the first ascent by Albert-Güllich-Stiegler-Sykora in 1989) were the Spanish in 1998, Germans in 2000, and Swiss in 2003. [Ed note: other attempts on this route during 2004 reached the junction with the British Route or in some cases the summit ridge.]

TOMAZ JAKOFCIC, *Slovenia*

Trango Tower, variation start to Sun Terrace. A Korean team more or less repeated a new start to the Sun Terrace pioneered by another Korean expedition in 2003 (two members of this were on the 2004 trip). This line climbs the lower west face to the Sun Terrace directly below the prow of Eternal Flame and left of the classic Slovenian start. There are 10 pitches: three on rock (5.10a and A3+); four on ice (to WI 4); three mixed (to M5). Although our team completed this line without the use of fixed rope, it was badly threatened by falling rock and ice due to the high temperatures at the time. From the Terrace our team fixed ca 250 meters of rope up the Slovenian Route and reached a height of 6,120m but couldn't finish due to the large quantities of snow and ice above.

DAE-HOON YOON, *Korea*

Trango Tower, attempted second ascent, solo. The highly experienced big wall climber Alfredo Madinabeitia (Norwegian Route on Great Trango, Amin Brakk, etc) attempted to make the second ascent, solo, of the Swiss-French Route on the West Pillar (Patrick Delale–Michel Fouquet–Michel Piola–Stéphane Schaffter, 1987 after an attempt by some of the party the previous year: 1,100m, 25 pitches, 6c A4). Madinabeitia fixed the initial section on the 13th July but was forced down by bad weather. He set off again capsule style on the 25th and eventually climbed 14 pitches over 17 days, though he was confined to the portaledge on 11 of those days. This more or less brought him to the big snow terrace at around half-height. Realizing he was not going to reach the summit, he started to descend on the 11th August; a lengthy process with 80kg of equipment. To his high point the Spaniard had climbed pitches of 6c and A4, though there is a hint he might have found the A4 a trifle overgraded.

LINDSAY GRIFFIN, *Mountain INFO, CLIMB Magazine*

BALTORO MUZTAGH

K2, various ascents and records in the anniversary year. July 31, 2004 marked the 50th Anniversary of the first ascent of 8,611m K2 by Achille Compagnoni and Lino Lacedelli from Ardito Desio's Italian expedition. To mark the occasion, 11 expeditions bought permits. One of these, a Korean

"Clean Up" expedition (an interesting and welcome development given that Korean expeditions are often criticized for their lack of tidiness in the mountains), met with early disaster. On or before June 11 three of these climbers, Hwa-Hyong Lee, Jae-Young Kim, and Kyong-Kyu Pae were at their Camp 1 on the mountain when an avalanche overwhelmed them. All were found dead in their sleeping bags.

K2 had not been climbed since José Garce's ascent on July 22, 2001. Reasons for this involve the threat of terrorism, weather, and most of all the collapse of the serac forming one side of the Bottleneck at ca 8,300m. The Bottleneck is a leftward slanting snow/ice ramp between a big serac barrier high on the Abruzzi Spur and the rocks bordering the South Face. Serac fall sometime after 2001 made the lower section of the Bottleneck much more difficult and dangerous, stopping climbers in 2002 and 2003.

By the summer of 2004 things had settled down in this area but for a long time it still appeared as if it was going to be another non-year for K2. Then toward the end of July a fine spell of weather coincided with many climbers in position for a summit push. During the night of the 25th-26th nine climbers set off from the top camp at the Shoulder and progressed slowly upward, the Bottleneck proving passable but very difficult and time consuming.

Silvio Mondinella (his 11th 8,000m peak) and Karl Unterkircher led a team of five Italians to the summit, although the work through the Bottleneck, general trail breaking through deep snow, and the fixing of ropes (this year ropes appear to have been fixed through the Bottleneck and up the final slopes above, leading to K2 being almost fixed from base to summit), was shared with the Basque climber, Ivan Vallejo, from the Al Filo de lo Imposible team. Fittingly, given the year, the Italians were first to summit and one of them, Michele Compagnoni, is the grandson of the first ascensionist. Last to summit, at around 5:30 p.m., was the second pair of four Basques, Juanito Oiazabal, and Edurne Pasaban. With her ascent (and safe descent), 30-year old Pasaban became the leading female 8,000m peak collector, having now climbed seven of the 14 giants. Only the late Wanda Rutkiewicz climbed more. In addition, the Basque mountaineer is the solitary living female to have summited K2 and has now climbed five out of the six highest summits in the world. Remarkably, this success has come in just four years.

Pasaban regained her tent on the Shoulder at around midnight, 24 hours after leaving, but Oiarzabal never showed. He was subsequently discovered sitting in the snow only 100m above camp by more Basque climbers leaving for their summit attempt on the 27th. Many summiteers and others on the mountain rallied to evacuate Oiarzabal and Pasaban, who had both sustained frostbitten feet. Pasaban eventually lost two toes but Oiarzabal's condition was much worse. Back in Spain medics were unable to save any of his toes and he is making a slow recovery. However, with his ascent, this highly experienced 48-year old Basque became only the third person to climb K2 twice, the two others being Josef Raconcaj (1983 North Ridge; 1996 Abruzzi) and Shera Jangbu (2000 Basque Route/SSE Spur; 2001 Abruzzi). He also set a record of climbing to an 8,000m summit no less than 21 times.

On the 27th and benefiting enormously from the opened trail, more climbers summited, including six members of Sam Druk's China-Tibet expedition, members of which have now climbed 12 of the 14 8,000m peaks. The 28th saw another batch including 65-year old Carlos Soria, who became the oldest summiteer and the only man to have climbed three 8,000m peaks over the age of 60, and Mario Lacedelli, a nephew of the first ascensionist. By the time four Japanese and their two Sherpas had reached the top on August 7, a total of 47 climbers had summited during the season but, notably, only 19 of these climbed without oxygen, a far cry from former years when climbing K2 with bottled gas was simply not the done thing.

Sadly, three more people died high on the mountain in a similar scenario to the 1986 disaster. On the 28th Davoud Khadem Asl from Iran and the experienced Sergei Sokolov from Russia were camped on the Shoulder. Unlike their teammate, Alexander Gubaev, they hadn't left for the summit that morning but decided to wait another night to see if the weather would improve (it had gradually deteriorated overnight). It is thought that Gubaev, climbing without oxygen, reached the top (the first mountaineer from Kyrgyzstan to reach any 8,000m summit) but he did not return. Asl and Sokolov could not be persuaded to go down and were subsequently trapped by a big storm. They didn't attempt to descend until August 1, after which nothing more was heard from them. Some of the remaining climbers at Base Camp mounted a rescue but were forced to abandon their attempt due to heavy snowfall.

One more climber was to summit, bringing the total for the season to 48 and the overall total to 246 ascents. This was the Catalan, Jordi Corominas, achieving what was undoubtedly the finest ascent on K2, or any Pakistan 8,000m peak last year, the second ascent of the Magic Line (see below).

LINDSAY GRIFFIN, *Mountain INFO, CLIMB Magazine*

K2, Magic Line, second ascent, death. On August 16th Oscar Cadiach and Manel de la Matta joined the summit bid along with Jordi Corominas from their last Camp at 8,100m. The first two decided to turn around at 10:00, from 8,300m, due to cold and exhaustion. After a short rest in the tent at 8,100m, Oscar and Manel descended together back to Camp 3 (7,500m), on the Pulpit glacier. They reached Camp 3 at 16:00 and spent the night there. Jordi Corominas reached the summit in a solo bid at 24:00. He descended the Abruzzi, finally stopping to rest in Camp 3 after 30 hours of continuous effort.

The next morning Manel and Oscar kept descending. Despite the increasing bad weather and their exhaustion, they were both happy and content. On their way down, they talked about future projects and new climbs to attempt in the next months. They slept in Camp 2 (6,900m). The next morning, Wednesday, they climbed back down to Camp 1 [approx. 6,300m] on the Negrotto Col, which they reached early.

It was then when Manel, for the first time, began to complain of acute abdominal pain. It prevented him from breathing normally. His anguish increased in the next hours. Oscar, always by his side in the tent, helped Manel to re-hydrate, eat, and keep warm. Communication with BC was broken by then, as the severe cold had exhausted the batteries in the climbers' radio. But Wednesday evening at 20:00, Oscar was able to send a short SOS: "Help Negrotto," over the radio. One hour later, in the middle of a snowstorm, Valen Giró, along with Baltí Ghulam, set of from BC with some food and medical supplies. The high avalanche risk forced them to retreat shortly after. At 3:00 in the morning August 19 they left BC again to climb up to C1 on the Magic Line.

Meanwhile, in Camp 1 at Negrotto Coll, at 4:30 a.m. on August 19, Manel de la Matta passed away in Oscar's arms.

The Spanish Federation of Climbing and Mountaineering have raised controversy in the past two years, refusing to give out their annual award due to "lack of good enough climbing." But this year, the federation decided, was different: There was one expedition worthy of receiving its annual award, the Spanish version of France's Piolet d'Or: The ascent of K2's Magic Line.

The "Piolet de Oro" award has no monetary price attached, although some small grants are given each year to other outstanding climbs accomplished by Spaniards. Manel de la Matta was awarded a post mortem "Creu de Sant Jordi" (Saint George's Cross) medal reserved for outstanding people and dignitaries in Catalonia, where Manel lived.

Adapted from ExplorersWeb.com

Gasherbrum III (7,952m), second ascent. On June 17 Alberto Iñurrategi, Jon Beloki, and I arrived at Gasherbrum base camp; we wanted to attempt G-IV by the northeast original route, but by July 12 we were tired of the bad weather and the deep track on the Gasherbrum plateau, so we decided to attempt G-III instead. On the 25th we camped on C-4 of G-II with a lot of other people, and the next day we followed the 1975 Polish Route on the south east face of G-III. On the first hard pitch we found a titanium piton, the only trace of previous climbers. I turned back 200 meters below the summit, but my partners reached the main summit at 10:30 a.m., 29 years after the first (and only) ascent.

JOSE CARLOS TAMAYO, *Spain*

MASHERBRUM RANGE

For a map of the region around the Nangma and Charakusa glaciers, please see page 32 in this AAJ.

CHARAKUSA VALLEY

Chogolisa Glacier region; Pointed Peak (ca 5,400m), Peak 5,300m; Chogolisa Catedral, Pilastro Kekka (4,500m); Raven's Peak, Chogolisa Shield (ca 5,300m); various new routes. We left for Pakistan in our usual style, six people without prefixed goals wanting explore and to climb as we do in the Alps. Initially we wanted to go to the Kondus and Saltoro valleys, but we were denied a permit a month before departure. So we moved ourselves to the Hushe where we had already climbed in 1998 and 1999 (Charakusa, Honbrok, and Khridas valleys with eight new routes). After two days of trekking we were on the Chogolisa Glacier, where we climbed four new routes on nearly unknown mountains. We only found signs of one ascent on Peak 5,300 and some anchors along the southwest ridge of Raven's Peak. All our first ascents were made alpine style. The team was Maurizio Giordani, Ezio

Crested and Pointed Peaks, showing the southwest face–west ridge route (Giordani-Maspes-Paoletto). *Hervé Barmasse*

Marlier, Hervé Barmasse, Nancy Paoletto, Giovanni Pagnoncelli, and myself. Our ascents:

Pointed Peak (a.k.a. Peak 5,300m but ca 5,400m) Northwest face and west ridge. New route: 800m, snow + 9 pitches rock (V+) and mixed. Giordani-Maspes-Paoletto, June 11. (Barmasse-Marlier-Pagnoncelli stopped two pitches from the summit). The summit was first climbed by another team, we think from the other face (English?).

Chogolisa Catedral, East Face, Pilastro Kekka (4,500m). First Ascent: 300m (8 pitches)—max VI+/A1 – 1 bolt (belay). Marlier-Maspes-Pagnoncelli, June 13.

Raven's Peak and Sheep's Peak, showing the south face route (Barmasse-Giordani) on Sheep's Peak and Luna Caprese (Barmasse-Maspes-Pagnoncelli) on Raven's Peak. The dashed line is the Hardwick-Littlejohn route (1987). *Hervé Barmasse*

Sheep Peak (ca 6,000m). South face, first ascent: 1,200m, snow and two pitches mixed. Barmasse-Giordani, June 17.

Raven's Peak, Chogolisa Shield (ca 5,300m). South face, new route: Luna Caprese, 1,000m (22 pitches)—max VIII-. Climbed all free, on sight and without bolts. Alpine style (1 bivouac on the wall) after fixing first 4 pitches. Barmasse-Maspes-Pagnoncelli, June 28-29. Six or seven pitches of the Hardwick-Littlejohn 1987 route (ED sup) (see *Mountain* magazine 120, March/April 1988). [Ed note: Raven's and Pointed Peaks lie on the north side of the Buesten glacier, a side glacier flowing west into the Chogolisa. Pointed Peak lies on the south side of this same glacier opposite Raven's.]

LUCA MASPES, *Italy*

K7, south face new route and repeat of Japanese Route; Nayser Brakk, southeast ridge, Tasty Talking, No More Tasty Talking; Kapura, west ridge; K7 West, attempt. The expedition included Americans Steve House (leader), Doug Chabot, Bruce Miller, Jeff Hollenbaugh, and myself, and Slovenian Marko Prezelj. We had permits for Kapura Peak (6,544m—unclimbed), K6 West (7,040m—unclimbed), and K7 (6,934m), all in this valley. We acclimatized by doing a number of rock climbs early in the trip. On June 28 Chabot and I climbed the British Route on Nayser Brakk (18,000ft), and Hollenbaugh and Miller attempted a new route on Nayser Brakk via the southwest ridge. On June 29 House and Prezelj also climbed the British route on Nayser Brakk. On June 30 House, Prezelj, and I completed a new route up the southeast ridge of Nayser Brakk (Tasty Talking—600m, III 5.10+) that started at a notch on the ridge part way up the peak. A couple of days later Miller and Prezelj added more pitches to this route by doing a start on the buttress right from base of the peak above the glacier (No More Tasty Talking—1,000+m, IV 5.10+). On July 1, Hollenbaugh and Miller climbed the south buttress on a 5,000m peak immediately down valley from Nayser Brakk.

During the period from–July 2 July 6 the expedition made the first ascent of Kapura Peak. On July 2, Chabot, House, and I climbed to an advanced base camp (ca 5,000m) on the glacier west of Kapura, and Hollenbaugh, Miller, and Prezelj set out from base camp to ABC the following day. Chabot, House, and I set out from ABC on July 3 and climbed the snow slopes of the southwest face of Kapura to gain a snow traverse leading to the west shoulder. The top of the shoulder provided a bivy site (6,100m). The next day we encountered technical difficulties on the west ridge above the bivy that included mixed terrain and a corniced ridge. With snowfall and limited visibility Chabot, House, and I reached the summit and returned to our bivy just at dark (1,500m, V M4). Hollenbaugh, Miller, and Prezelj reached the bivy on July 4, and Miller and Prezelj repeated the west ridge the following day. Chabot, Hollenbaugh, House, and I returned to base camp on July 5, and Miller and Prezelj arrived at base camp the following day.

On July 8–July 11 Steve and Jeff attempted Drifika but were not able to reach the summit via the original west ridge route because of bad weather.

On July 14 Miller and Prezelj did the first ascent of a rock tower below the south west face of K7 (Pt 4,900m: Difficult Life, 650m: 6c+ and A0).

On July 16 Jeff Hollenbaugh soloed the British Route on Nayser Brakk.

Starting late on July 24, Steve House made a solo first ascent of the south face of K7 in a single push in 41 hours base camp to base camp (2,400m, VI 5.10- WI4 M6 A2), making the second ascent of K7. Also starting on July 24, Chabot and Miller repeated the original 1984 Japanese route on K7 alpine style to do the third ascent of the peak in a five-day effort from base camp to base camp. They added many new pitches including a new route up the Fortress, a 300-meter buttress. The difficulties included overhanging ice and hard mixed climbing (2400m, VI WI5+ M6 A1). They descended House's route to the glacier arriving in base camp on July 28.

Hollenbaugh, Prezelj, and I attempted the northwest ridge of K7 West (unclimbed) on July 24th. On that date we climbed from base camp up the valley west of the glacier that is below the northwest ridge and then dropped down a couloir at the head of the glacier to a bivy at a col at the base of the northwest ridge. We followed this route to avoid being exposed to dangerous ice cliffs above this glacier. The next day we climbed some difficult mixed ground on the west face, which we ascended to gain the northwest ridge. We left a second bivy on the ridge crest on July 26, but were stopped several hundred meters shy of the summit by unconsolidated snow. We turned back after Prezelj triggered a small slab avalanche. We were safe, but the avalanche took my pack for a 1,000-meter ride to the glacier. We found extensive evidence from the 1982 Japanese attempt of the same route in the form of bolts, pins, and fixed cable ladders. During our 2,400-meter climb we experienced difficulties of WI4 M6. [Several articles, photos, and a map from this expedition are in the Features section of this Journal.]

STEVE SWENSON, *AAC*

NANGMA VALLEY

Amin Brakk, partial new route. The Russian Extreme Project, comprising climbers Sergey Kovalev, Alexander Lastochkin, Valery Rozov and Arcady Seregin with cameramen Lev Dorfman and Dmitry Lifanov, climbed a partial new route on the ca 1,250m West Face of Amin Brakk. Rozov, as is usual in these projects, made a sensational BASE jump from high on the wall. The team chose a prominent line towards the right side of the face between Sol Solet (1,650m of climbing and 22 pitches, 6c+ A5, 34 days is capsule style: Pep Masip–Miguel Puigdomenech–Silvia Vidal, 1999) and Czech Express (7b+ A3 70°, Marek Holecek–Filip Silhan–David Stastny, 1999). Starting in the same vicinity as Sol Solet, the Russians soon broke out right and appear to have climbed very close to or on the lower section of Namkor (1,550m, 31 pitches, 6b+ A5, Adolfo Mandinabeitia–Juan Miranda, 2000:), before breaking out right again to follow a parallel line that would lead them directly to the summit, crossing back through Namkor close to the top. The Russians spent 22 days on the route; the first 11 fixing rope. During this time one pitch, linking two cracks systems, had to be more or less entirely bolted and skyhooked. Later, a large rock fall, released in the warmth of the afternoon, smashed a section of rope, which had to be replaced.

Setting off around July 12 they made an 11-day round trip to the summit in capsule style. However, of the 33 days spent in the valley, all but three were plagued by either rain or snow, and prolonged bad weather hit when they were a little over half-height, forcing a traverse right to the Czech Route and a faster finish to the summit. The top was reached on July 19 in a blizzard, the Russians having negotiated deep snow and mixed ground in the upper section and climbing a total of 31 pitches, mainly on aid up to A3. Although the amount of significant new ground climbed on this route is perhaps relatively small, the team ascent was yet another successful achievement for former Soviet climbers in their astonishingly productive year of 2004 (Jannu, Everest, etc.).

On the 22nd Rozov made his jump from a point where the rock wall meets the easier-angled upper ridge ca 300m below the summit. This was a soul-searching experience for Rozov, as the wall is not totally vertical and at least one protruding ledge system had to be cleared. He finally decided to go for it and skillfully cleared the ledge in his winged suit for a 1,000m (and 30 seconds) flight to the glacier: "the sensations after landing were simply inexpressible. It seemed I had gone for a spin in a time machine. After so many days living on a vertical wall, suddenly to arrive below on a horizontal, safe site, able to do whatever and go where you liked, was fantastic."

ANNA PIUNOVA/VALERY ROZOV *and the Russian Extreme Project*

K 5,944m (Korada Peak), first ascent, Bostjan Arcon Memorial Route; Drifika (6,447m), White River Route; Drifika, southeast face attempt; valley rock route, Autobahn to Amsterdam. There are many interesting rock towers and mixed faces in the Nangma Valley. Members of the expedition were Gregor Blazic, Matija "Matic" Jost, Zlatko Koren, Vladimir "Vlado" Makarovic (all four of us from Slovenia), and Hussein, our cook from Pakistan. Our main goal was to climb a new route in Shinju (a.k.a. Shinju or Shjingu) Charpa (Great Tower, 5,800m) in alpine style, but for various reasons we never set foot on its walls. We spent 39 days in our base camp or above. In this period there were 11 sunny days. We managed to climb three new routes as listed below.

Autobahn to Amsterdam: Nice short rock climb—convenient as entertainment during rainy days. Rocky slabs near base camp. 170 meters vertical gain (bottom 3,900m, top 4,070m). UIAA graded pitches: VI, A1/ V, III, IV. Six hours, July 31, by Gregor Blazic and Matija Jost.

First ascent of K 5,944m (Korada Peak), via Bostjan Arcon Memorial Route. Serious ice climb with 60-meter rock band in the middle. We made probably the first ascent of the mountain, and we suggest the name Korada Peak for it. The route is harder than the Swiss Route on Les Courtes. We climbed it alpine style. Elevation gain: 750 meters (bottom 5,200m, summit

The south face of Drifika (6,477m) as seen from Korada Peak (K 5,944m). (A) summit of Drifika. (B) 5,300m saddle camp. (E) south ridge. (C) east ridge (Dutch attempt in 2001). (D) north ridge (Japanese 1978—50° snow and ice). (G) Slovenian attempt to 6,300m (Blazic-Jost-Koren-Makarovic, 2004). (F) White River Route (1,200m, D+, 40°-60° snow and ice, Blazic-Jost-Makarovic, 2004, alpine style). (H) Spanish (Basque) attempt in 2004; X marks accident site. Photo and route information from *Matic Jost*

The view from the 5,300m saddle under the south ridge of Drifika (6,447m). (B) Kapura (6,566m). (C) K6 West (7,040m). (E) K6 Main (7,281m). (A) K 5,944m on the ridge connecting Drifika (left—out of picture) and Amin Brakk (right—out of picture). (D) Bostjan Arcon Memorial Route (750 m, TD+, some rock + snow/ice 40°-75°, Gregor Blazic, Matija Jost, Vladimir Makarovic, 2004, alpine style). Because local people don't have any name for this peak we suggest Korada Peak. Photo and route information from *Matic Jost*

5,944m). TD+ UIAA V, snow and alpine ice. Ascent 15 hours, descent 10 hours, August 6-7, by Gregor Blazic, Matija Jost, Vladimir Makarovic.

Drifika (6,447m), White River Route: Probably the first route on this face. Maybe some day it will be the normal route from Nangma Valley. We climbed it alpine style ascent. We finished our route 20 meters below the summit on the north ridge. At that point we witnessed the tragic accident of the Spanish expedition about 600 meters below us, on the southeast face. 1,200 meters vertical gain (bottom 5,200m, north ridge 6,400m). D+, snow and alpine ice from 400 to 600 meters, and one point at 900 meters. Mix II (UIAA) and one point V (UIAA). 16 hours ascent, 12 hours descent, August 12-14, by Gregor Blazic, Matija Jost, Vladimir Makarovic.

Beside those ascents we made a strong attempt on left side of southeast face of Drifika on July 26-27, but we were forced to retreat at 6,300m.

MATIJA 'MATIC' JOST, *Slovenia*

Zang Brakk (4,800m), southwest face, Hasta la Vista David. Between August 10 and 13, Silvestro Stucchi, Anna Lazzarini, Enea Colnago, and I climbed a new route on the southwest face of Zang Brakk. Our route follows the most obvious line up the center of the face, climbing a series of cracks and slabs up the lower portion that is less than vertical. On the second half, where the wall becomes vertical, we climbed a series of fairly obvious dihedrals. The quality of the rock we encountered was generally superb. The slabs are very compact and do not offer many options for protection. The cracks tend to be very shallow and thin, and only take knifeblades, which were difficult to place, and occasionally an angle piton. We placed one bolt and one piton in each belay, which in turn we used on the descent, and placed only two other bolts in between pitches.

In bad weather we fixed the lower 200 meters, and camped in a broad grassy ledge that we dubbed "il giardino" (the garden). In less than ideal weather we fixed another 120 meters of rope above this point, and on the 13th, under a bright blue sky, we climbed the remaining 430 meters to the summit.

We named the route Hasta la Vista David (750m, VI+ A1) in honor of a climber on an expedition from Navarra (Spain) with whom we shared basecamp; he died during an attempt on Drifika (6,447m)

ELENA DAVILA, *Bergamo, Italy*
Translated by Rolando Garibotti

Zang Brakk (4,800m), showing Hasta la Vista David. *Elena Davila*

Zang Brakk (4,800m), Ali Baba, Ali Baba's Hadsch Variation; Shingu Charpa (Great Tower), attempt. At the end of June our team of Ines Bozic Skok and Janez Skok (Slovenia), and Hannes Mair and I (Austria), established base camp under the Great Tower (Shingu Charpa). After a few days of acclimatization and rock scouting, we carried a tent and equipment under the 600-meter wall of Zang Brakk to climb in two independent parties. My intention was to climb a new route in pure style, free, in one push, and not using any bolts or fixing any ropes. We knew of four routes, all put up in at least nine days, and mostly aid climbing. For Hannes and myself our first pick was a steep, impressive line right of the Spanish Route. Ines and Janez decided to try an easier looking line on the southwest face.

The cracks were looking great and appeared to give way to free climbing. But after the first pitch I realized it would be much harder than expected. The rock quality did not have so much in common with my anticipated dreams of great Karakoram granite—I had heard it was like El Cap—but what was this first scary layer on the rock's surface? Often loose and sandy, and why did Mother Nature fill so many cracks with dirt? Lastly, why did so many nice finger and hand cracks end in a thin knife blade seam or, even worse, in a blank section?

I guess that's the adventure part of the game. I gave it my best and climbed some demanding pitches up to 7c onsight. Then we bivvied in a corner halfway up. The next day started with a scary chimney, which led after 30 meters into an even scarier offwidth crack, in which a #6 Friend sometimes refused to work. After all this struggling the crack turned out to

Zang Brakk: (1) Hasta la Vista David (6a A1, 2004). (2) Ali Baba (6c+/7a A1, 2004—free until the Korean route Left Hand). (3) Ali Baba's Hadsch (7b+, 2004). (4) Ramchekor (5.10 A2,1998). (5) Left Hand (VI 5.9 A4-, 2000). (6) Right Hand (VI 5.9 A3+, 2000). (7) Ganyips (6a A3, 1998). (8) Free attempt (7c, 2004). Photo, lines, and information from *Hannes Mair* and *Michael Mayer*

be a damned knife blade seam. Aiding was not an option for us, so after I down climbed the pitch we decided to bail.

Our cook Ali welcomed us with all his warm hospitality, a cup of chai and the question, "Summit? Success?"… "No summit, no success." He told us he would pray more for us.

Janez and Ines were successful on their new route, Ali Baba. The top four pitches were shared with the Korean Route. They reached the top of the Korean Route in the afternoon of the second day; it ends several meters under the real summit because of a blank section. Janez onsighted new ground up to 7a, and used some aid only on the last four pitches (Korean Route).

Two days later, on July 3, Hannes and I were again under the wall with a big dream: to free climb the southwest face in one day. We started early and climbed the first easy pitch of Janez and Ines's new route Ali Baba in unstable weather. For the next 300 meters we headed up a crack system to the right of Ali Baba; it seemed to be slightly harder, with one 7a+ and a few 6c and 6b pitches. Before the traverse to the Korean Route it started drizzling again, but maybe Ali's praying helped our luck because it stopped. Inshallah!

The hardest part was still in front of us and Janez's suggested grading was three pitches of 6c/A0 and one A1. A one-day onsight ascent was enough of a challenge, but the real challenge was to ignore this unreliable layer of rock—laybacking without trusting your feet or the friction makes life as a free climber much harder. Hannes put it to the test seconding a 7a+ pitch when a TV-sized block, which he was using for a handhold, let loose, taking him along for the ride.

After this close call we pushed upward, climbing three more long pitches (7a+, 7b, 7b+). After these tenuous pitches we reached the prayer flags and there I realized that a small dream had come true. I looked over and took in the small Nangma Valley, and then I looked to the big north ridge of the Great Tower…yet to be climbed.

The next dream laid in front us. A few days later, together with the Slovenians, we found ourselves attempting the north ridge, only to be weighed down with heavy loads and volumes of loose rock. We scrambled and traversed our way up, and as we stared at the rock that loomed over us we woke up from our free climbing dream. Sadly, not all dreams are what they seem.

MICHAEL MAYR, *Austria*

Denbor Brakk (4,800m), southwest face, Bloody Mary. In July, after a period of bad weather in the valley, Vasek Satava and Pavel Jonak packed their gear and found themselves at the southwest face of Denbor Brakk (Nangma Valley). They then attempted the unclimbed left pillar of the three on the southwest face. They had some trouble with the first pitches, which were full of vegetation. They aimed at a roof with a hand crack close to the headwall, which they reached after four days of climbing. The crack turned out to be an off width. They could use only one Camalot for protection, and the weather made it worse, so they thought a descent to basecamp was the best decision. Both climbers returned at last, reclimbed their ropes up the first 10 pitches and at the end of the second day had added another. They then climbed the remaining five pitches to the summit. They called the route Bloody Mary, 14 pitches, IX- A2.

Denbor Brakk showing the new Bloody Mary route. The summit to the left is Nawaz Brakk. *Pavel Jonak*

JAN KREISINGER, *Czech Republic*

Changi Tower (5,800m), south face, Anké Asashe. The expedition was completed by Nestor Ayerbe, Oscar Perez, and myself, all from Huesca, northern Spain. Our mountain club, Peña Guara, supported the expedition. On July 21 we arrived at the 4,200m base camp in bad weather. During the next days we looked for a new line on the south face. The clouds didn't help us very much. Finally we chose a line and started carrying the loads to the base, at 4,600m. The approach was only one hour from our base camp, up a pretty comfortable hill full of edelweiss and cows. On the 26th and 27th we had good weather and climbed five pitches going slightly left, 300 meters up to 5.11-. On the last pitch I found a bolt from an old attempt, possibly used for rappelling. But we didn't find any signs of passage before this, so possibly the attempt was to the left of our line. When I arrived at the end of the pitch I realized that we should rappel down to a gully to continue the route. Perhaps that was the cause of the old retreat. We rappeled 25 meters to the gully and established the Camp 1 at 4,900m. We rappelled down the gully and left fixed ropes up to Camp 1. Bad weather arrived and we had to stop for eight days. On August 6 we returned to the wall. We fixed five more pitches up to 5.10c and A2, and hauled everything in two days. August 8: at night it started snowing and we came down again, leaving our ropes fixed. After some days of bad weather, we went up again on the 11th, but when we arrived at Camp 1 it started snowing again. We knew that the wall has a gully where is possible to gain the col and the main tower, so we decided to carry everything to establish Camp 2 and at least do some work in this horrible weather. We walked up the gully for three hours and left all our bivy stuff at 5,250m.

On August 13 we jumared up the ropes and climbed three pitches. We expected to arrive at the gully that day, but a section of aid climbing (A3) slowed us very much, and we only

The south face of Changi Tower (5,800m), showing the Anké Asashe route. This joins the Basque route in the upper section on the headwall pillar (more Changi Tower routes in *AAJ* 1999 p. 395 and *AAJ* 2000 p. 347). *Cecilia Buil*

Splendid granite high on Anké Asashe, Changi Tower. *Cecilia Buil*

managed to arrive at a big ledge where we had to bivy (5,300m). We were only carrying a tent as a bivy equipment, and we only had bread, no water; we passed a cold and hungry night. The next day we traversed right on the big ledge looking for the more obvious way to arrive at the col. We found the line opened by some Spaniards in 1999 called Ludopatia (see *AAJ* 2000) and followed it for two pitches to the col. We arrived at Camp 2 very dehydrated and hungry. The next three days we climbed and fixed ropes on the tower until the storm returned. It was technical climbing, with lots of aid and free up to 5.10+.

After eight more days of bad weather we decided to go up again despite the falling snow, just because we had to leave soon. We didn't know if we would finish the route or just remove the ropes. We slept at Camp 2 on August 25. At 3 a.m. we started climbing, arriving at the col at 4 a.m. (5,400m). We followed Ludopatia most of the time, although we did some variations. It was snowing; sometimes the clouds enveloped us, sometimes the wind dissolved them and froze us. Nobody mentioned going down, so we continued up. The sloping ledges were covered in fresh snow and made even the easiest climbing scary. Then Oscar finished the route at the south summit in the middle of the storm. We didn't reach the main summit; it would have required 80 meters or so of easy snow walking [Editor's note: 80m of vertical height gain but some distance horizontally]. After eight rappels and some hours more between the clouds, we arrived at camp 2 at 9 p.m. We left one bolt and 5 pins in the entire route at the belays to rappel down the tower. Anké Asashe is 1,150 meters, 24 pitches, VI 5.11 A3.

CECILIA BUIL, PEÑA GUARA, *Spain*

Roungkhanchan 1 (4,600m), north wall; Troubles, Cough and Fever. During August, Marco Zebochin, Stefano Zaleri, and I (all members of GARS— part of Società Alpina delle Giulie, the local branch of Italian Alpine Club) climbed a new route on Roungkhanchan 1 (4,600m) north wall. This wall had never been climbed before; our route, Troubles, Cough and Fever, is the first on the wall. It is on good rock, 540 meters long (14 pitches) of grade 6b+ and some aid (A1). Recommended climbing gear: Two 60m ropes, 12 quick draws, cams, and pitons. The pitches are equipped with bolts, but cams and pitons are still required. The route is equipped for rappels, but it is possible to return to base camp by walking on easy terrain directly from the top. We used about 100 bolts (each belay stand is equipped with a minimum of two bolts).

The line of Troubles, Cough and Fever on the north wall of Roungkhanchan I. *Dario Crosato*

To reach the cliff you have to travel from Skardu to Kande village by jeep. From there it is one day of walking up the Nangma Valley to the base camp on a beautiful and comfortable grass-covered clearing along the river. The wall is located on the right side of the valley (the same side as the Great Tower). To reach the cliff, follow the moraine (formed by the K6 glacier) on the right side and then walk to the base of the big dihedral of the Roungkhanchan 1.

This valley offers many possibilities for new routes even if the rock is not always perfect. During our stay we met other parties from Slovenia, Spain, Canada, and Italy that were successfully engaged in climbing new projects.

DARIO CROSATO, *Società Alpina delle Giulie, Italy*

The great and crappy north ridge of Shingu Charpa (5,600m). The American attempt (Davis-McCray-Offenbacher-Warren, 2001) went up the line on the right and bailed down the left line. The Austrian-Slovenian attempt (Mair-Mayr-Skok-Skok, 2004) gained the ridge up the left line, but did not ascend further. The Canadian attempt (Edgar-Geisler, 2004) climbed the right-hand line and continued to its highpoint. The original Korean route climbed the obvious couloir to its top, than angled left up the rock/mixed wall to the summit. Photo and route info from *Chris Geisler*

Shingu Charpa (Great Tower, 5,600m, north ridge attempt. Dave Edgar and I traveled to the Nangma Valley this past summer with our eyes set on the impressive unclimbed north ridge of Shingu (Shjingu) Charpa, east of the small village of Kande. The north ridge is an amazing visual feature. However, its rock quality and vegetated nature detracted significantly from our experience, as it did for others who attempted it this year. Nonetheless we made three attempts, each time hoping to take two to three days roundtrip, which allowed us to dispense with sleeping gear other than a tiny tarp and an insulated jacket each. Our first attempt had us almost to the American highpoint (Nils Davis, Brian McCray, Todd Offenbacher, and Brenton Warren, 2001) in one day. Without a bolt kit, I was forced to rappel 60 meters off of a single purple TCU during our descent after a cold snowy night. The cracks were most often shallow and almost always packed with hard dirt. This meant that even featureless sections might have the odd tuft of grass poking out of a tiny seam. It was only a mater of time before the tufts would rip out under our feet, but they helped us continue on.

The weather during our stay was generally poor, and during the sessions of good weather one of us was usually too sick to get out of bed. We did manage to make some headway despite our poor luck. We made better time during our second attempt, reaching the American highpoint with an hour and a half of daylight to spare. Despite making variations to avoid some dicey places on our first go, I still got to jumar a rope weighted directly off of Dave's waist. With descent info from our US friends, we headed off the left side, and were able to safely return to camp in the dark, faster than down the ridge itself. The following day it poured rain.

Finally we had run out of time and we needed to make a last attempt before catching our plane home. The weather had not quite settled, but we thought it was worth a try. Now familiar with the opening terrain up to 10a, we left camp at midnight, climbing a few hours in the dark. We made great time despite climbing through a light blizzard, and headed into new terrain. Unfortunately the blizzard picked up, so we hunkered down beneath a large boulder, burrowing a tight space for two. A small meal and some intimate snuggling got us through the night. Thankful for our 20 minutes of sleep, we struggled out of our barricade the following morning and headed upward again. Several pitches further we found ourselves on a small ledge, looking up at another 3,000 feet, having already climbed approximately 22 60-meter pitches. We decided to head down. We were in no state to continue the pitches with no protection and unsubstantial belays. We returned to camp safely and headed out of the valley a couple of days later.

The Nangma is a very beautiful valley, and we recommend making a visit, however we found the rock to be mostly unconducive to free climbing, though it does seem to support prolonged aid climbing projects. We were disappointed with Shingu Charpa's ridge, given our expectations of a long, quality rock climb. It is certainly a stiff challenge that won't give in easily. Best of luck to those who are still inspired!

We are thankful for the generous support of Mountain Equipment Coop, who assisted us both financially and with gear. They were willing to stand behind us even though attempting this long steep ridge in a lightweight style might mean returning empty handed. We are also thankful for the Mugs Stump Award and Helly Hansen–ACC Mountain Adventure Award, as these also made our trip possible.

CHRIS GEISLER, *Vancouver, Canada*

India

HIMALAYA

Overview of foreign expeditions. There was a marginal increase in the number of foreign expeditions to the Indian Himalaya—40 teams compared to 35 teams that climbed last year. The Ladakh area received 14 expeditions, mostly to the Nun-Kun massif and many to Stok Kangri—an easy walk-up to 6,000m opposite Leh. Stok Kangri now has the reputation of being the most climbed 6,000m peak in the world!

The Kumaon Range received five teams and the best climbs were achieved here. Martin Moran (UK) continued his love affair with the Indian Himalaya and made a fine ascent of Chiring We (6,559m), last climbed 25 years ago. The British climbed Adi Kailash and made a ascent nearby. Saf Minal (6,911m), on the edge of the Northern Nanda Devi Sanctuary, was climbed by an American-British team. The ascent, by a new route, came after a long gap, last having been climbed by a Japanese team in 1975.

The Gangotri area continued to remain most popular, with 10 teams climbing there, and the adjoining Garhwal received six teams. Peaks like Thalay Sagar, Arwa Spire, and Bhagirathi continued to attract mountaineers.

Lastly, in the Himachal Pradesh easy peaks like Manali Peak, Friendship, and KR group were climbed several times. Several teams climbed in the Miyar Nala of Lahaul. An Indo-British team trekked in the relatively unknown areas of the Pangi valleys of Lahaul. Visiting less-frequented valleys, they crossed high passes and brought back memorable photos as reference for future climbers.

Overview of Indian expeditions. A total of 65 expeditions from India climbed in the mountains. West Bengal led in numbers with 42 teams, followed by 10 teams from Maharashtra. The Indian Mountaineering Foundation organized four expeditions (two all women teams). Uttaranchal received 35 teams, followed by the Himachal Pradesh with 26, Ladakh with three, and Sikkim with one.

The major event for the Indian Himalaya was exploration of the Tsangpo-Siang Bend from the southern approaches. A team of three Indians made a route through thick forest of the Arunachal Pradesh and reached the Line of Control between India and China, where the Tsangpo enters India to be called the Siang. The same river is called Brahmaputra as it flows into the plains of Assam. The full exploration of the Tsangpo gorge was thus completed.

An Indian army team climbed Kangchenjunga from Nepal and flagged off the celebrations for the 50th Anniversary of the first ascent of the peak to be held in 2005.

HARISH KAPADIA, *Honorary Editor, The Himalayan Journal*

MIYAR NALA

Miyar Valley, upper glacier exploration and short new routes. A four-strong party from England and Scotland (Graham Little, Jim Lowther, Kevin Kelly, and myself) visited the Miyar Valley in May. The area offers large granite walls in a mountain setting. Various parties have been to the area since it first came to prominence after a visit by an Italian team in 1992. Most teams have established base camps at the snout of the Miyar Glacier and climbed in the adjacent valleys. Previous trips have given a variety of names to side glaciers that already have local names. We journeyed further up the Miyar Glacier to the junction with the Jangpar Glacier, which we explored and found to offer some impressive mountain big wall potential.

May seemed to be too early to attempt technical rock climbing, as ledges held much snow from an unseasonably late fall (the heaviest for 25 years), which was melting and flowing down the rock walls. We climbed two snow routes. On one, we dropped a pack after completing the difficult climbing; this forced a retreat short of the summit. We climbed three rock routes on slabs and spires nearer base camp. In brief:

Christina Peak, 5,420m (GL, JL May 14), by south face at PD.

South face of Pt 5,960m (BD, KK), retreat from 5,800m after dropping a rucksack.

Lammergier Spike 5350m (GL, JL May 22), Alpine D.

First ascent of 600m+ rock route on slabs above Khai Got on east side of Miyar Nala (BD, KK), UIAA VI.

Many of the currently available maps of the Miyar Nala and the glacier area are generally small scale and often of poor quality. The sketch maps produced by the Slovenian and Italian expeditions, while useful, are often not topographically very accurate. Some of the heights claimed for climbed peaks are exaggerated.

There is also mounting confusion over the names of the glaciers that lie to the east of the Miyar Nala/Glacier. Dali Got below the snout of Miyar Glacier has been the site of several expedition base camps and as such is a useful reference point. The following names have been used, with our favored versions (which are often local names) given first, followed by alternatives.

Glaciers linking to the Miyar Glacier:

Jangpar Glacier (no alternatives): the final glacier to join the Miyar Glacier (about 6 km above Dali Got at its snout).

Glaciers not linking to the Miyar Glacier:

Dali Glacier (Spaghetti Glacier, Thunder Glacier): lies directly above Dali Got.

Chhudong Glacier (Tawa Glacier): lies just over 1 km down the valley from Dali Got.

Takdung Glacier (Nameless Glacier): lies 4 km down the valley from Dali Got.

BRIAN DAVISON, *United Kingdom*

Miyar Valley, Neverseen Tower (5,700m), Mai Blau. Eloi Callado and I arrived there at the beginning of September, and after setting up our base camp (4,800m) at the glacier's moraine we started carrying the stuff to the base of the wall (5,050m). To reach the base we had to cross the glacier and climb a 400-meter snow ramp (35°-40°). We put up a new route called Mai Blau (in Catalan that means Never Blue) on the west face. It was a natural line that combines cracks and slabs. The route name reflects the bad weather: the sky was never blue. Last summer the monsoon had been bad and the post-monsoon was not much better. The sky sometimes cleared in the morning, but it would cloud over and snow in the afternoon.

We climbed in "capsule style," setting two camps on the wall (at the second and fifth belays). We spent 13 days living on the wall (12 bivis) to climb 13 pitches, some of them longer than 70 meters, graded A3+/6b/70° (890 meters climbed, not counting the snow ramp). On the summit day we climbed alpine style the last four pitches and the final Ca 150m snow ridge. But before the final attack on the summit, we rested two days on the portaledge because of the weather.

We rapped down the route (there are bolts only at belays) from summit to the second camp, and the next day continued to the base of the wall. After this journey a three-day non-stop snowfall started. We were stuck for the next two weeks at the base camp glacier without the possibility of walking down to the main valley. It was time to return home, but we couldn't move, and conditions in base camp were harder than on the wall. We had 1.5 meters of new snow, and problems with cooking in the tent in base camp. We waited to leave until the weather changed. We were in a remote zone, and during five weeks in the valley, we didn't see anybody. Just some sheepherders during the first trekking days. That's all!

It's difficult to find porters in the area, so we brought them from Manali (the most important town in the area). But to return to Manali we needed to cross a road pass (Rothang Pass, 4,800m) that is at the same altitude as base camp. We were afraid that the road could be closed because of the snowfall. But snowplows were working there, and with a 4-wheel-drive car we could have crossed it. The problem was that our driver decided to turn back before crossing it, so we finished our adventure hitchhiking on a truck.

SILVIA VIDAL, *Spain*

Neverseen Tower (5,700m). (1) Italian route (Di Vincenzo-Marcheggiani-Miele, 1992—reported in *AAJ* 1997). (2) Mai Blau (Callado-Vidal, 2004). (3) Spanish/Catalan attempts (Casablancas-Llongueras, 1999, 2001). *Xavi Llongueras SGIM*

Eloi Callado starting the epic snow-filled hike out from Neverseen Tower. *Silvia Vidal*

Castle Peak subsidiary summits, first ascents. Roberto Iannilli and Domenco Perri left Rome on July 27th, spent several stressful days in Delhi trying to regain their missing baggage and then experienced more delays above Manali, when a heavy storm washed out the road over the Rohtang Pass and 13 porters had to be hired to transport all their gear to the far side. From a base camp at 4,000m in the Miyar they hoped to attempt the big west-facing rock wall on the unnamed 6,000m+ peak at the head of the Spaghetti Glacier (Iannilli had climbed ca 400m of this in 2003 and the left side of the face was climbed a little later the same year to a 5,845m fore-summit—christened Mahindra— by Slovaks Dodo Kopold and Ivan Stefanski; see *AAJ* 2004). However, the wall was plastered with snow and ice, so the pair changed their objective to a lower sub summit of Castle Peak, overlooking the main valley.

After establishing an Advance Base at 4,650m, the Italian pair attempted the west face, very compact in the lower section to a large ledge system, then a more featured headwall above. On August 5 they climbed a 480m crack system to the ledge. A White Chocolate Croissant was graded UIAA VI. On the 9th, after a couple of rainy days, they made a light and fast attempt on a more direct line to the right but on the headwall it started to rain and the pair retreated, having to sit out the night with no gear at 5,000m. On the 12th they started up the face once more, this time with bivouac equipment. After a night on the ledge, they reached the summit on the 13th, having climbed 1,500m (18 pitches) to 6c. They named the summit Iris Peak (5,400m) and the new route, which they rappelled, Mustang Café.

On the 19th Iannilli soloed another route more to the left, ending on a lower subsidiary summit. This was about 5,000m in altitude and named David62's Nose. The 13-pitch route (740m of climbing) was named Prot House and had difficulties up to 7a+. The same day two young French women, Margherite Arpin and Aurèlie Delage, arrived in the valley and while they were waiting for their third compatriot to show up in several days time, they joined Iannilli and Perri for a fourth route up a wonderful crack line on David62's Nose. Delage and Iannilli alternated leads on the 13-pitch (590m) climb, which they named Shim-Nak (6b). Iannilli suggests that the altitudes quoted by the Slovak team for Castle Peak and the subsidiary summit on the north flank reached by The Sharp Knife of Tolerance (2002), are greatly exaggerated. The Italians placed only two bolts (on one compact slab pitch) during their stay, relying on nuts, cams, and pegs for belays and protection.

ROBERTO IANNILLI, *Italy*

CHANDRA BHAGA RANGE

CB-14 (6,078m), plane wreckage found. An Indian (Bengal) team led by Anal Das climbed this peak on 19th of August. Summit climbers were Swaraj Ghosh, Ajoy Mondal, Subrata Banerjee, Sanjay Ghosh, Moloy Mukherjee, and Arindam Mukherjee with three high altitude porters. They made a rare ascent of the west ridge to the summit. On their approach to the mountain this large team comprising of 14 members located the wreckage of a plane, which had crashed here in 1968. They reported the matter to the nearest authorities and in a large recovery effort many parts of the plane were brought back and a major mystery was thus solved.

HARISH KAPADIA, *Honorary Editor, The Himalayan Journal*

SPITI

Khhang Shiling on left and Shigri Parvat from Khamengar valley in Spiti. *Divyesh Muni.*

Khhang Shiling (6,360m), first ascent. A three-member team sponsored by The Himalayan Club made the first ascent of Khhang Shiling peak (6,360m–20,866') on 19th September assisted by Sherpa Lakhpa Bhote. ("Khhang Shiling" means "Snow Mountain of four ridges"). The team consisted of Vineeta Muni, Shripad Sapkal, and me. We explored the Khamengar Valley in Spiti, a rarely visited area in Himachal Pradesh. The peak Khhang Shiling is a prominent mountain at the head of the Khamengar Valley.

Dibbibokri Pyramid, from a col on Khhang Shiling. *Divyesh Muni*

We approached from Mikkim near Kaja to reach base camp (4,320m) in three days. ABC was at 5,160m. We established Camp 1 at 5,880m in a basin formed between a large rock feature and the Shigri Parvat massif. We climbed along the glacier until a bergschrund below the col between Shigri Parvat and Khhang Shiling. It was decided not to attempt Shigri Parvat since the entire route to the peak was over steep but loose rocks with a constant barrage of rockfall down the face. The route on Khhang Shiling looked promising, so we dumped rope and some hardware at the col and returned to C1.

Next day Vineeta, Shripad, Sherpa Lakhpa, and I left for the summit by 7 a.m. Although the route was not very steep, we had to fix three rope-lengths due to the hard ice below the thin layer of snow. A strong wind increased the wind chill and all of us were very cold. We ran short of rope to fix the last two rope-lengths and carefully belayed each other to the top.

We started our return journey on 23rd September. Since we did not attempt Shigri Parvat, we had a few days to spare and decided to trek across the Pin Parvati pass into Kullu, which brought us to the traditional route to Manali.

DIVYESH MUNI, *The Himalayan Club, India*

UTTARANCHAL

Uttaranchal, new regulations. While the world is opening its doors to mountaineers and mountain lovers, the news from the new Uttaranchal State in India is distressing. The state contains some of the most beautiful areas in the Indian Himalaya, with peaks like Nanda Devi, Kamet, and Shivling. The Uttaranchal State has imposed severe restrictions on climbing and imposed special royalty charges for mountaineers to pay (minimum US $1,400). This is in addition to charges payable to the Indian Mountaineering Foundation. Moreover special and separate permission (red tape!) must be obtained from the officials in the state, forest department, and local authorities. At least half the porters must be employed from local villages, and each village is to be paid a fee as you trek through it. The forest department is to be paid a special fee to camp on their land. Several foreign expeditions (notably a Spanish team on Shivling) were charged these extra fees in 2004. Indian mountaineers and trekkers are also not spared, and for the first time Indian teams will have to pay peak fees to climb a peak in their country. After many discussions, negotiations, and protests, which were brushed aside, the state government has decided to impose these rules for the 2005 season. Please check full details, rates and addresses for formalities at www.indmount.org.

HARISH KAPADIA, *Honorary Editor, The Himalayan Journal*

GARHWAL

Bhagirathi III (6,454m), direct southwest pillar, Stairway to Heaven. From the summit of Shivling in 1996 I saw the challenge: to find a direct route on the ridge of Bhagirathi III, because the southwest pillar route by the Scottish team of 1982 didn't follow the actual ridgeline of the southwest pillar. I wanted to master the route with free climbing and in alpine style. I wanted the route to be difficult and challenging, but Jörg Pflugmacher and I, both from Bavaria, also wanted to exclude any unpredictable risks to our lives. This is why we used bolts at belay stations and at dangerous points in free climbing—the style was similar to Wolfgang Güllich's on Nameless Tower in Pakistan.

On my 2001 expedition with Robert Jasper we started from the west face basin. The conditions were very bad: considerable snow and ice. The difficulty from the start to the pillar's ridge (10 pitches) was M7+. In the 2004 expedition we started from the foot of the direct southwest pillar and free-climbed more than 30 pitches of 5a to 7b (French scale), with the exception of two pitches that might be a real challenge to any climber who repeats our route. Due to a snowstorm in the upper region we couldn't climb higher on the iced slabs and had to move to another crack system with the help of a pendulum traverse. More information can be found (in German) at www.expeditionsberg-steigen.de. Please see "Berichte" (reports) for photographs of the 2001 and 2004 expeditions. [Additional details also in Lindsay Griffin's summary, below—Ed.]

WALTER HÖLZLER, *Germany*

Bhagarathi III, direct southwest pillar, Stairway to Heaven. In 2000 and 2001 Walter Hölzler attempted the direct southwest Pillar of Bhagarathi III, left of the now quasi-classic 1982 Barton-Shaw Route (also called the Scottish Route). On the second attempt, with Robert Jasper, Reiner Treppte, and Jochen Schmoll, and operating from a portaledge camp at around mid-height, he reached a high point (with Treppte) of ca 5,800m, estimated to be ca 100m or so short of the end of the major rock climbing difficulties. Bad weather forced them down.

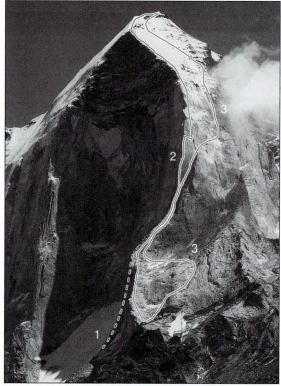

Bhagirathi III. (1) Direct Pillar (Hözler-Jasper, 2001). (2) Stairway to Heaven (Hözler-Pflugmacher, 2004). (3) Barton-Shaw Route (a.k.a. Scottish Route, 1982). *Walter Hözler*

The 2001 team started climbing from the left side of the crest, but on his return in May 2004 with Jörg Pflugmacher, Holzler began up the right side of the pillar and first fixed 400m of rope to a point about one-third of the way up the crest. After removing their ropes to use higher up the route, the German pair then set off for a six-day capsule style ascent, hauling a portaledge. On the 19th of May they left the ledge at 5 a.m. and began climbing in increasingly misty conditions. After a total of 30 pitches from the bottom of the route, they reached the shale band, which forms the final 400m of the line. Setting off up this at 2 p.m. unroped, they decided to make a turn-around time of 3:30. Climbing loose ground of UIAA II and III they continued to the summit, reaching it at 4 p.m. They were back at the portaledge by 10 p.m. The route took a total of nine days. Two other parties attempted the Barton-Shaw Route but were unsuccessful.

LINDSAY GRIFFIN, *Mountain INFO, CLIMB magazine*

Thalay Sagar (6,904m), northwest ridge, Harvest Moon. The northwest ridge attracted us because it was an evident line: the buttress looks like a wave from base camp, and the massive granite pillar at 6,400m provides a taste of challenge. We were also curious to see firsthand why nobody had climbed this route before. This turned out to be a perfect expedition for us. The culture mix was very fun: We were four who spoke German, one French, and one English: Stephan Siegrist, Ralph Weber, and me from Switzerland; Thomas Senf from Germany; cameramen Rob Frost from the U.K. who went till the pillar; and cameraman Zvonimir Pisonic from France who went till ABC. It was sometimes a bit confusing, but great team work. The crew (cook, help cook and liaison officer) were very helpful and gave a lot of flavor to the base camp life,

Thalay Sagar's Harvest Moon route on the northwest ridge. A photo with all the other route lines on the north face of Thalay Sagar is on pg. 84, *AAJ 2004. Denis Burdet*

especially Dava our cook. All we knew was that the itinerary had been attempted in 1987 by a Spanish Expedition (O. Cadiach, J.Camprubi und X-Pérez-Gil). When we built C2 we found an old belay station. This was the last sign of the Spanish team.

The difficulties were bigger than expected. The first buttress ("Shadow Buttress") was already steep, and the ice thin or very snowy. The perpetual spindrift and the absolute absence of sun make this part pretty demanding. The crux was the "Purgatory Pillar," which was massive with flakes and no obvious cracks. The pillar was very exposed to the west wind, and the temperatures were variable (from quite cold to extremely cold)—we always climbed with gloves. The use of hooks and beaks was obligatory, and the climb quite delicate at this elevation. Everything

High on Harvest Moon, Thalay Sagar. *Denis Burdet* (2)

worked very well, and it is always a great reward to reach this summit, especially the first time by a new route and without injuries. It was a really great experience for all of us.

Summary: "Harvest Moon," 1,400m, 6a WI5 M5+ A3; 11 days of climbing and two camps on the face. We fixed rope until C2 at the top of the pillar, and went for the summit in one day from C2. We reached the base camp (4,750m) on August 29 and did the portage to ABC (5,300m) on September 2. We reached camp 1 (5,750m) the 6th, and C2 (6,300m) the 18th. We reached the summit on the 27th, and the 1st of October we were back to Gangotri.

DENIS BURDET, *Switzerland*

Satling Sui (5,060m), first ascent, Jatra; Point Walker (5,260m), new route. After a three-day approach following the Bhilangna Valley on the south side of Thalay Sagar, Chris Semmel, Matthias Huber, and I reached our base camp (3,720m) beside the lateral moraine of the Phatling glacier. Our aim was to explore the mountains around the Satling Glacier ("Satling" meaning "Seven Phalli"), which had only been visited once before, in 2002 by an English expedition. After two days of checking out possibilities we decided to focus on an unclimbed granite needle on the northern side of the Satling Glacier. Our ABC was established at 4,550m, some 250 vertical meters below the bottom of the face. It took us three days (having to wait out a period of heavy snowfall in basecamp) to open our line up the southwest face. We named the 12-pitch route Jatra ("pilgrimage"). We climbed it on 1st, 6th, and 7th of October, and graded it UIAA VIII/1p.a. The summit not having been baptized before, we suggest the name "Satling Sui" ("Sui"

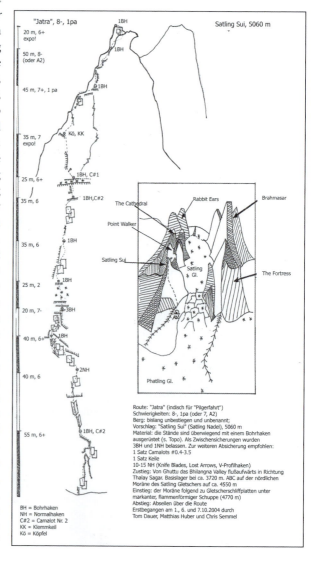

meaning "needle"). After a rest day we opened the "Central Couloir" (6 pitches, UIAA V M5) on the west face of Point Walker, which had been ascended once in 2002 via the east ridge. Our expedition was sponsored by Marmot.

TOM DAUER, *Weyarn, Germany*

Janhkuth, west face attempt. The main goal of the expedition was to make the first ascent of a 6,805m peak known as Janhkuth, north west of Chaukhamba. Only one other party has attempted to climb this mountain: the Austrians, Josef Jochler, and Christian Zenz, in 2002. Their attempt was stymied by inclement weather to such an extent that the climbers barely left Base Camp. Like Jochler and Zenz's attempt, our expedition proved unsuccessful in attaining the summit.

After establishing base camp at Sudenban (4,535m) on the lateral moraine of the Gangotri Glacier, Malcolm Bass (UK), Marty Beare (NZ), Andy Brown (UK), Pat Deavoll (NZ) and Paul Figg (UK) used five porters to help place a "dump camp" at 4,635m. They then ferried loads to an Advanced Camp (5,000m) at the base of the Maiandi Bamak. For this their snow shoes proved invaluable. By September 27 the New Zealand couple had three weeks food at Advanced Camp, while the three British, opting for a "lighter-loads, more-mileage" approach, took until October 4, though during this time all the climbers reached a Camp 1 at 5,230m on the Maiandi Bamak below the West Face of Janhkuth.

After a spell of heavy snowfall, Beare and Deavoll started up the central couloir on the west face at midnight on October 6. They climbed for 12 hours up 45° deep snow to camp at 5,700m. Next morning they continued up steeper ground, including two pitches of 80° ice, and after another 12 or more hours reached the crest of the South Ridge at 6,400m. That night Deavoll developed a bad headache. In addition a big electrical storm hit the mountain, though the heavy snowfall was at lower altitudes. Next morning Beare reached 6,500m on a horizontal section of the ridge leading to mixed ground beneath the summit and then returned to camp. He estimated another two days would probably be required to reach the top. Unfortunately, Deavoll continued to deteriorate and by evening was vomiting. The following morning was cold and with Deavoll clearly very ill the pair had no option but to descend (10 rappels from Abalakovs, then down-climbing).

Meanwhile at 10pm on the 6th, Bass, Brown and Figg left Camp 1 and climbed mixed ground up a buttress line to the right of the central couloir, reaching a point roughly level with the first New Zealand camp (ca 5,700m). The storm during the evening of the 7th deposited far more snow at this altitude and at midnight they decided to descend before retreat became impossible due to building avalanche danger.

By the 10th heavy snowfall and cold temperatures had arrived and it was obvious further climbing was out of the question. The team had a difficult time stripping their camps and breaking a trail down to Tapovan so that porters could reach base camp but by the 18th they had made it safely to the road at Gangotri.

MARTY BEARE, *New Zealand, and* MALCOLM BASS, *United Kingdom*

Chaukhamba III (6,974m) and IV (6,853m). An Indian expedition (Nehru Institute of Mountaineering) led by Col. Ashok Abbey made the first attempt on these unclimbed peaks. The team consisted of instructors from the Institute. A high point of 6,300m on the western flank was reached on 8 July. The weather conditions were generally poor.

HARISH KAPADIA, *Honorary Editor,*
The Himalayan Journal

Saf Minal (6,911m), northwest face. John Varco (U.S.) and I (UK) made the first ascent of the northwest face of Saf Minal (6,911m) in the Indian Garhwal reaching the summit on October 5. Unlike its sister peaks Kalanka and Changabang with their 1,700m near-vertical faces of immaculate granite, Saf Minal is the twisted relative. The peak looks like a cross between K2 and G IV, and its near-2,000-meter sweep of black shale and loose mixed climbing offers a dark challenge. After acclimatizing to 5,500m on a small foothill, we set about our ascent in pure alpine style with no reconnaissance, fixed ropes, or camps.

Saf Minal's northwest face, Parnell-Varco route. John Varco

We took the most striking line on the face, starting up a distinctive ridge before sustained mixed climbing on rock of dubious quality and over snow-covered slabs led to a system of ice couloirs in the upper part of the face. Following three days of reasonable weather, conditions deteriorated, trapping us in our partially erect tent. After 36 hours of cramped torment we opted to climb in the continuing storm, reaching the west ridge in the dark only 200 meters below the summit. To our surprise, the following morning brought perfect weather for our successful summit push, with cloudless views into China and the secretive Nanda Devi Sanctuary.

Having climbed in lightweight alpine style, things became even more interesting on our descent when the poor rock and traversing nature of the line took its toll. We staggered into base camp after two days of abseiling and tricky downclimbing, a cut rope, running out of food, and with only one stopper and a couple of cams remaining of our rack. I lost over 25 pounds on the ascent.

A cozy bivouac on Saf Minal. Ian Parnell

This climb was probably the most expensive but rewarding diet plan we've ever followed.

As far as we know this is the only ascent from the north side. A Japanese team made the first ascent from the easy snowy south side in 1975, and we know of no ascent since.

IAN PARNELL, *United Kingdom*

Ian Parnell on Saf Minal. *John Varco*

Ian Parnell on Saf Minal, with Kalanka and Changabang behind. *John Varco*

KUMAON

Little Kailash, showing the first ascent route on the southwest ridge. *Andy Perkins*

Little Kailash from Jolingkong, during a 2002 attempt from the north. *Martin Moran*

Andy Perkins leading the southwest ridge of Little Kailash. *Paul Zuchowski*

Adi (a.k.a. Chota or Little) Kailash (5,925m), first ascent; Nikarchu Qilla (The Fortress of Nikarchu, 5,750m), first ascent. An international team of climbers has made the first ascent of Adi (aka Chota or Little) Kailash (5,925m). The mountain is located close to both the Tibetan and Nepali borders of India in the restricted Inner Line area, and is revered due to its similarity to the famous holy mountain of Kailash in nearby Tibet. This guided expedition organised by Martin Moran Mountaineering and led by Martin Welch and myself also made the first ascent of a nearby mountain we named Nikarchu Qilla (The Fortress of Nikarchu) at 5,750m.

Tim Woodward (UK), Jason Hubert (Scotland), Paul Zuchowski (USA), Martin Welch (Scotland), Diarmid Hearns (Scotland), Jack Pearse (UK), Amanda George (Scotland), and I (UK) made the first ascent of Little Kailash by the southwest ridge on October 8 in perfect weather in seven hours from our ABC at 5,400m. The route was around alpine PD+/AD-. Out of respect to local sensitivities, we stopped a few meters short of the summit, and no fixed rope was left on the route.

Welch, Woodward, Hearns, Pearse, George and Gustavo Fierro-Carrion (Ecuador) also made the first ascent of Nikarchu Qilla (5,750m), which is located 3 km northeast of the unclimbed Nikurch Rama (5,995m). This alpine-style ascent was made by the southwest face from a camp at 5,200m at alpine F in about 7 hours, and the team also stopped a few meters below the summit.

ANDY PERKINS, *United Kingdom*

Chiring We (6,599m), second ascent. Chiring We is situated at the head of the Kalabaland glacier and is not frequently visited by mountaineers. The first ascent was achieved in 1979 by a team from Mumbai under the leadership of Harish Kapadia. The 12 member-team led by Martin Moran completed the second ascent 25 years later. They followed the west ridge (route of first ascent) after establishing four camps above base camp, and the summit was reached on 26th September. The nine summiteers were Martin Moran, Alex Moran, Jonathan Preston, Liam Warren, Paul Watson, Stuart Reid, Christopher Wheatley, Geoffrey Dawson and Christopher Harle.

HARISH KAPADIA, *Honorary Editor, The Himalayan Journal*

SIKKIM

Tingchen Kang (6,010 m), bureaucratic problems. An Indian (Bengal) team led by AVM A. K. Bhattacharya and sponsored by the Himalayan Club from Kolkatta climbed this peak on 6th November. The summiteers were Subrata Chakraborty with Sherpa Pasang Phutar. They followed the northwest face. The team had an exciting journey and was walked out in bureaucratic hassles by the Sikkim Government. They paid Rs. 5000/- for the liaison officer but no LO turned out until the end. As per the current rules a LO is required both for foreign and Indian expeditions. The Sikkim Government has certainly made it difficult for mountaineers and trekkers. [This team probably used a new northwest approach to reach the upper west ridge, which was first climbed by an Indo-British Military expedition in 1998 and used by Roger Payne and Julie-Ann Clyma in spring 2005 for the peak's third ascent—Ed.]

HARISH KAPADIA, *Honorary Editor, The Himalayan Journal*

EASTERN ARUNACHAL PRADESH

Tsangpo Gorge, exploration from India. Motup Chewang, Wing Cdr. V K Sashindran, and I traveled from the Brahmaputra along the Siang River to the Tsangpo Gorge where it enters the Indian territory. Though a few parties have explored the "Great Tsangpo Bend" in the north (Pemako area in Tibet) there are no records available of approaching the bend from India to the border of India-China. After the 1962 war with China the area was out of bounds. Now in 2004 a team of three Indians reached it from the Indian side, the entry point of the river into India, thus

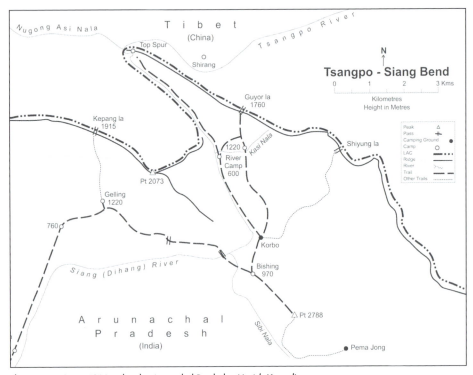

The Tsangpo-Siang "S" Bend in the Arunachal Pradesh. *Harish Kapadia*

completing the final exploration of the Tsangpo.

The Tsangpo (as it is called in Tibet) originates near Lake Manasarovar at the foot of Kailash. After a long journey eastward via Lhasa, it reaches eastern Tibet. Here its progress is blocked by the great massifs Namcha Barwa and Gyala Peri. The river takes a huge turn between these peaks. This has been termed as the "Great Tsangpo Bend." It was the goal of several explorations from early days. The Pundit explorer Kinthup was one of the first to reach the gorge (in disguise) and he observed the "Rainbow Waterfall" where this mighty river falls. Here onwards the Tsangpo descends steeply southward on the Tibetan plateau to the Himalayan divide leading to the McMahon Line and India.

As the river enters Indian territory at 580m (in Arunachal Pradesh) it takes two "U" loops, which can be called the "Tsangpo/Siang Bend." In Arunachal Pradesh it is called by different names like the Siang and Dihang and is joined by various tributaries. On reaching the Assam plains it is joined by the Dibang and Lohit rivers and onward is called the Brahmaputra River. Due to the various names and vast terrain it covers, it had been a matter of discussion whether the Tsangpo is the same river as the Siang and whether it flows into the Brahmaputra or into the Irrawaddy further east. This was finally solved by modern map makers and satellite imageries.

Our 2004 exploration party traveled from Dibrugarh, crossing the Bramaputra by a two-hour ferry ride to the northern bank. Traveling via Itanagar (to obtain "Inner Line" permits), we followed the road via Ziro, Daporijo to Along. We reached Tuting in two days of further travel, in all covering 985 km by vehicles. We then trekked to Kopu, Bona, Gelling, and Bissing, the last village on the Tsangpo. We crossed many precarious foot suspension bridges over the Tsangpo, known here as the Siang. From Bishing we climbed a peak of about 3,200m and had a wonderful view of the Namcha Barwa and Gyala Peri massifs.

From Bishing we descended to banks of the Siang and old Korbo village and soon had to climb steeply across several ridges to camp in the forest near the Kasi nala. It was an experience to cut through very thick forest with undergrowth. Two local guides led the way hacking a route through inhospitable jungles. Though we had to be most careful, the excellent clear weather allowed us to enjoy everything except the leeches, snakes, and malaria infested insects.

From this camp, we followed similar terrain, then climbed steeply to Guyor La (1,760m) on the Line of Actual Control (LAC). The pass was covered by thick forest and offered no view but it was a historic moment for we civilians to reach here. By late afternoon we descended to the Kasi nala camp. Next day we hacked a route through forest leading down steeply to the banks of the Siang. We followed the route along the Siang. A two-kilometer wide and about 150m-high rock cliff barred the way, with the Siang's water rushing at its foot, blocking passage. We climbed high along the edge of the cliff, and after covering a difficult patch with ropes, we again hacked a route through forest above to traverse and descend on the other side. Going over rocky terrain we finally reached the spot where the Tsangpo takes two "U" loops and enters India. We photographed it extensively, with a background of mountains, hills, and a river in Tibet. After retuning to the camp on the Siang, we returned along the riverbank to Bishing, crossing steep cliffs and exposed rocks. We returned via the same route back to Tuting and drove back via Along to Dibrugarh. Our expedition took place between November 16 and December 7.

We dedicated our expedition to the memory of my son, Lt. Nawang Kapadia of the 4th Battalion of the Third Gorkha Rifles, who died fighting Pakistan-based terrorists in 2000.

HARISH KAPADIA, *Honorary Editor, The Himalayan Journal*

Nepal

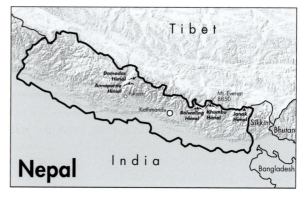

Travel update for Nepal, spring 2005. Tourism arrivals in Nepal continue to plummet due to increasing violence surrounding the growing Maoist insurgency, and the February 1st royal takeover of political control of the country. According to the Nepal Tourism Board, tourist arrivals during the spring climbing season are down 34 percent from last year. The country continues to be crippled by frequent transportation strikes and blockades of urban areas by Maoist guerillas.

In a bold move that brought intense scrutiny from the international community, Nepal's King Gyanendra seized control of country and the Royal Nepal Army in what has been equated to a "bloodless coup." The King cited great domestic instability and the inability of the democratic government to properly address the Maoist insurgency as justification for his actions. He vowed to quickly restore peace to the country and to put an end to the civil war, which has now claimed over 11,000 lives. Since his takeover, scores of human rights activists and protesters have been arrested, and Nepal now tops the list for the highest number of kidnappings and disappearances in the world.

Despite the growing conflict, tourists have not been deliberately harmed by either Maoist insurgents or security forces thus far. A well-publicized exception to this occurred when a Russian expedition was attacked by Maoists armed with homemade grenades as they traveled toward Tibet for an attempt on Everest from the north. Two climbers were injured, and the attack was credited to the fact that the group was traveling unaccompanied during a known national transportation strike. For trekkers and climbers, paying "taxes" to local Maoist factions along popular trekking routes has become commonplace across the country, and trekkers in the Everest region have become accustomed to encountering security forces on their frequent armed patrols.

In summary, travel to and around Nepal is still very possible and relatively safe. Mountainous regions of the country—especially the Khumbu valley leading to Everest—are quite removed from the civil conflict, as are the tourist centers of Kathmandu. Travelers need to be prepared for frequent and inconvenient hassles such as transportation strikes, vehicle searches, tightened security, etc. Travel outside of popular trekking routes and during times of civil conflict should also be avoided. The political situation in Nepal is, like other places in the region, becoming increasingly unstable and could potentially become dangerous. Travelers should do their homework before they travel abroad, register with their embassy, and be prepared to change plans at the last minute.

BEN AYERS, *Porters Progress, AAC*

MUSTANG REGION

DAMODAR HIMAL

Gaugiri, second ascent of southwest ridge. On August 27 Austrians Johannes Mihatsch, Anna and Edmund Wirbel, together with Guna Bahadur Tamang and Pisail Tamang made the fourth overall ascent of Gaugiri (6,110m) but the second ascent of the original route up the south west ridge climbed in May 2002 by Peter Ackroyd and Jim Frush. This peak lies more or less on the Mustang-Tibet border well north (15-18km) of the main area of the Damodar.

ELIZABETH HAWLEY, *AAC Honorary Member, Nepal*

Peak 6,350m, first ascent. Although he had a permit to climb 6,110m Gaugiri, Kiyoshi Ishii from Japan did not attempt the mountain. Instead he moved further east and climbed an unnamed peak over the border in Tibet. The ascent of this 6,350m summit was made via the east ridge on July 7 with Kumar Rai and Panima Sherpa.

ELIZABETH HAWLEY, *AAC Honorary Member, Nepal*

Chhiv Himal (6,650m), first ascent; Saribung (6,328m), second ascent, new route. Four members of the Japanese Alpine Club, Student Section, made the first ascent of Chhiv Himal (6,650m) on September 18, 2004. On the following day, all five members of the expedition reached the summit of Saribung (6,328m) via a new route; it was the second ascent of the peak.

Chiiv Himal's north face. The route followed the left skyline. *Kenichiro Kato*

The Kingdom of Mustang is a frontier region that well preserves an old form of Tibetan Buddhist culture. The Damodar mountain group is located in the eastern part of Mustang. At Ghami, our caravan shifted away from the main route, instead heading toward the east, following a tributary of the Kali Gandaki. After crossing three passes over 5,000m, the magnificent Damodar Himal appeared. It had been a nine-day trek from Jomson (including one rest day).

With Khumjungar Himal (6,759m) as the main peak, the group of mountains encircles the Namta Khola glacier in a horseshoe formation. One wing of the mountains heads in a northeast direction toward the border with Tibet. The newly opened Chhiv Himal (6,650m) is an independent (and previously unclimbed) peak located in the southeast area of Khumjungar Himal.

The expedition was comprised of team leader, Takeshi Wada (23), Chiba University Alpine Club. Deputy-Leader: Takeo Yoshinaga (23), Waseda University Alpine Club. Team Members: Kenichiro Kato (23), Rikkio University Alpine Club; Yuko Shibata (22), Gakushuin University Alpine Club; Mitsuhiro Kosei (19), Waseda University Alpine Club. The ascent was planned and executed with no assistance from climbing Sherpas.

On September 8, we set up the Base Camp (5,250m) at the end of the glacier that flows northeastward from the foot of Chhiv Himal. We made Camp 1 at 5,650m, on September 11. To reach C2 from C1 it is necessary to cross the glacier, which is about 1km wide at the crossing point. The whole glacier field was filled with seracs, some of which were 20m tall. As the sun rises, the bottom part of Pk 6,225m became dangerous because of the frequency of falling rock from the ridge. In addition, the snow plateau that leads to the west face of Saribung was potentially dangerous with hidden crevasses. Therefore, we made Camp 2 on the col (6,170m) between Chhiv Himal and Saribung, on September 15.

The northwest face of Chhiv Himal is shrouded with snow due to the strong wind, while its eastward side is rocky. Our route was on the ridge that came down northeastward from the peak. It continued for three roped pitches to a four-pitch 60° snow wall. On top of the wall the ridge became flat and continued to the summit. At this point (6,450m), we returned to C2. On September 17 all five team members started from C2. We continued along the gentle upper ridge, which became knife-edged and developed a cornice. At a 6,610m top, with almost all our snow pickets and fixed ropes used and the weather becoming worse, we returned to C2.

On September 18 four team members retrieved some of the fixed ropes for use on the final ridge to the summit. From 6,610m the party carefully followed the knife-edged ridge of snow, which was sometimes elusive in a whiteout. At 13:15 four team members reached the broad snow stance of the summit: the first ascent of Chhiv Himal. We had fixed approximately 850 meters of rope.

On September 19 all five team members left C2 to the summit of Saribung along the south [west] ridge. As the south face of Saribung is fortified by rock walls and several crevasses, we proceeded carefully, fixing seven pitches of rope. At 12:30 all five team members had made the second ascent of the peak, via a new route. The first ascent of Saribung was made by Americans Jim Frush and Peter Ackroyd in 2003.

KENICHIRO KATO, *Rikkio University Alpine Club*

Adapted from Japanese Alpine News, TAMOTSU NAKAMURA, Editor

Unnamed peaks 6,084m (Namy) and 6,130m (Yury), first ascents. I got a permit for Gajiang (6,111m), as it attracted me strongly. It soars like Machhapuchare in a less-frequented area of Damodar Himal. However, this peak had very steep slopes. In spite of four days of exploration (October 20-23), I could not find any viable climbing route, so I gave up the plan [Mr. Kato is reported to have reached ca 5,600m, but still some considerable distance from the summit, on the south east ridge after first attempting the north ridge]. Instead, I was able to climb two unnamed peaks, 6,084m and 6,130m respectively.

Unnamed peak 6,084 (I called it Namy Peak) October 24-26: The snow-covered Namy Peak is located to the south of Jomson Himal and is the highest in this area. We went from BC to Labse Khola to the north and set up ABC (5,000m) at the end of a glacier. Then we set up C1 at 5,200m on the right of the moraine. There we could see the mountain ridges extending to the top. On the way, we stopped using the climbing rope under a cornice, and plodded in the knee-deep snow. On the summit, I had my picture taken with Gajiang in the background. I measured the location of this mountain using GPS. I saw Pokarkan, which I first ascended two year before, to the east. The date of arrival at the summit: October 26. GPS data: 28°49'18.8"N, 84°08'14.1"E; H 6,094m.

Unnamed peak 6,130m (I called it Yury Peak) October 29-30: The peak, snow-capped on the southern side, is at the dividing point of the Labse Khola Massif. From ABC (5,000m) we followed the moraine on the left and reached the foot of Yury Peak. We climbed the rock ridge between a waterfall and a valley, then followed the valley and went up 100 meters to a gully on the left side. Then we set up C1 (5,480m) on a flat ridge at the top of the gully. Looking up from C1, we caught a glimpse of the white snow on the summit beyond on a rock ridge. Above C1 there was a steep slope of 25°-30°, with small rocks and little snow. My feet slipped many times on the rocks, but I carefully climbed, minding the falling rocks. 200 meters below the summit there was much snow, but I managed to reach the top. There was little space there and only one person could stand. From the top, I was able to see Jomson Himal in the south and, in the north, Khumjungar Himal, which is the highest mountain in the Damodar area. We took pictures and measured the location of this mountain using GPS, then returned to C1. The date of arrival at the summit: October 30. GPS data: 28°51'12.2"N, 84°07'23.1"E; H 6,143m. The team: Leader: Koichi Kato (63); Sherpa: Pasang Tamang (36).

KOICHI KATO, JAPAN

*Adapted from Japanese Alpine News, TAMOTSU NAKAMURA, *Editor*

Purkhang, first ascent. A large Japanese team and its Sherpas made the first ascent of Purkhang (6,120m), which lies in the Purkhang Himal south west of the main Damodar across the head-waters of the Labse Khola (west of the Teri La). The expedition climbed the west ridge on August 16 with Satoru Endo, Hiroyasu Hatsushika, Yuichiro Ishihara, Teruyuki Iwasaki, Chizuko Kono, Teruaki Kubo, Kazuko Takano, Hiroshi Yumoto and Sherpas, Ang Kami, Da Chhemba, Geru, Lhakpa, Ongchu and Pem Tenji.

ELIZABETH HAWLEY, *AAC Honorary Member, Nepal, and* TAMOTSU NAKAMURA, *Japanese Alpine News.*

MANANG REGION

Purkhang, first ascent. In the summer, a Japanese party was successful on Purkhang (6,120m) in Manang district north of a popular so-called trekking peak, Chulu West. Of its 11 members, eight, plus six Sherpas, succeeded via the west ridge on August 18. Above their only high camp at 5,450m, they first had to cross numerous crevasses—they used a ladder to negotiate one—surmount an icefall, and, at 5,700m, climb a 100-meter high 65° ice wall. They had a long summit day: they left high camp at 3:40 a.m., were on the summit at 2:45 p.m., and returned to high camp at 8:00 p.m.

ELIZABETH HAWLEY, *AAC Honorary Member, Nepal*

ANNAPURNA HIMAL

Annapurna Central Summit, ascent. A Russian, Boris Korshunov, whose age has been reported as between 68 and 70. set out from the top camp on the Standard (French) Route up the north face of Annapurna on the 28th May. However, he slanted up left too early on the long snow plod to the summit and arrived by mistake at Annapurna's Central Summit (8,051m). Although he was disappointed, he is perhaps only the 15th person to reach this summit, making the sixth overall ascent (three Germans on the first ascent in 1980 via a line on the North Face left of the Dutch Rib, two Poles in 1981 via the South Face, two Spanish in 1984 also via the South Face, two Swiss in 1984 via the East Ridge, and one Korean plus four Sherpas making the first winter ascent via the Dutch Rib in December 1984; on their repeat of the East Ridge in 2002, Iñurrategi and Lafaille traversed below this summit on the north flank). He is perhaps the only person to reach this top via the French Route.

PAMARI (LAPCHE KANG) HIMAL

Lapche Valley, reconnaissance. In order to find a place that is utterly unknown and to satisfy my curiosity, I decided to visit the unfrequented Lapche Valley, a small but independent mountain group located roughly 100 km northeast of Kathmandu. It lies between Jugal and Rolwaling Himal, or more specifically between the rivers Bhote Khosi (Po chu) and Tamba Khosi (Lapche Khola). Likely no serious attempts have been made to climb any peaks here, probably because the tiny 6,000m peaks of this region were not considered worth climbing. Long ago Kenneth Mason wrote a few lines on the existence of Lapche Kang in the classic book on Himalayan exploration *Abode of Snow*, but nothing more. Available maps include those from the Nepalese survey bureau and the AfvH's series, both in 1:50,000 scale. The former, we discovered, is relatively correct in its details; the latter is less reliable. Both are outdated in some points, e.g. the main path along the valley was partly on the opposite side, the glaciers have shrunk considerably, etc.

The way to Lapche Khan in the confined area surrounding Lapche Khola valley, actually starts at Lamabagar, one full day drive from Kathmandu through Charikot up to Singati (a terrible dirt load in its final part), followed by two days' walk along the trekking route to Rolwaling. From Lamabagar on a wide alluvial flat, you can look ahead to a huge narrow gorge geographically isolating the upper area. This area's cultural isolation later became clear. Visitors, such as alien mountaineers, are an encumbrance to them, and even the notorious

Maoists have been shut out from this high valley area, which is an exclusive autonomous locality.

We were a five-man party, all aged over 60, with the assistance of two Sherpas and 14 porters. Our target peak for our April-May expedition was located at the head of Phurkum Khola, a tributary of Lapche Khola. Two major peaks surround this bleak valley: Jobo Bamare (5,918m) and Chomo Pamari (6,109m). They are named on the maps and are known to some extent, and we suspected them to have been climbed already. But on close examination both of these beautifully shaped peaks look difficult, only fit for expedition-style climbs. We wanted a relatively unknown peak that could be easily climbed in a short period. Just from map-readings, we focused on a 5,811m peak at the junction of the ridge where Chomo Pamari stood and the branch ridge extending to Jobo Bamare. After three days' march from Lamabagar, we saw that this virgin mountain was a nice triangular snowcapped peak easily accessible through mere glacier climbs.

Little can be said about our climbing, however, because we were interrupted at C1 by a group of villagers and monks who came up from Lapchegau, the main village in this area. They insisted that nobody was allowed to climb the sacred mountains within their territory, and they said that sinful people who tried to violate the mountains' divinity must pay a financial penalty. We had confirmation that the Nepalese authorities allowed our mountaineering trip in this area within the framework of our trekking permit, but it seemed this region was half a half century behind, and too remote for such logic to hold. Eventually we gave up and did not go higher than circa 5,300m. Afterward we visited Lapchegau Monastery to negotiate a return visit for climbing.

There we found ourselves "back to the future." It was possible to communicate with people on mutually understandable basis. We received a friendly welcome (as we had paid a discounted penalty) by some monks and villagers, including a monastery staff member well educated in India who was renovating the Monastery backed by an international foundation. Thanks to his assistance, we learned that they were ready to accept tourists for pilgrimage purposes, and also other visitors could freely walk around and climb any peaks in their domain. The condition was only to show respect by holding a Puja and paying a decent donation beforehand, as otherwise they believed calamities would follow. So, it was an error in our procedures that made them lose face. This seems to confirm the fact that mountaineers have been seldom seen here.

We enjoyed this still-primitive valley country with somber villages and people living in traditional Tibetan style, with nothing for visitors like shops and lodges, and many splendid mountains above. There are five tributary valleys stretching to surrounding ramparts of mostly 5,000m class peaks. Each would be a good place to set up a base camp from where one could ascend virgin summits less than 1,000m elevation from the valley bottom. There are only three peaks over 6,000m in addition to the two already referred to; the highest one (6,065m) of the Ralin Himal group is a marvelous white massif. I do not hesitate to pick it as the new target for my next visit.

What a nice experience to have roamed around such remote mountains located near the old approach route to Mt. Everest but well behind the crowded realms of Everest today.

KEI KURACHI, *Japan*

*Adapted from Japanese Alpine News, TAMOTSU NAKAMURA, *Editor*

KHUMBU REGION

ROLWALING HIMAL

Chekigo attempt. Opened in 2002 as a trekking peak, 6,257m Chekigo, which lies east northeast of Beding in the Rolwaling Valley, was attempted by a French commercially organized party in 2004. After the usual problems with Maoists, they were able to reach about 6,000m on the summit ridge of this fine, fluted snow and ice pyramid. Chekigo has no recorded ascent but is thought to have been climbed by a route of around AD+ in standard. It was first attempted as long ago as 1955 by Alf Gregory's Merseyside expedition.

Tengi Ragi Tau (6,943m), north ridge, attempt. Tengi Ragi Tau is one of the peaks of the Seventh Goddess in the Rolwaling Himal; its pyramidal peak can be seen from Namche Bazaar. When the Nepal government opened this mountain in 2002, the Japanese Alpine Club (JAC) planned to organize a Senior Expedition to this mountain in pre-monsoon 2003. Tengi Ragi Tau was an ideal target for seniors who wished to climb a virgin peak because it features easy approaches, an appropriate altitude, and a manageable route for seniors without bottled oxygen. This mountain, however, was climbed for the first time via the southeast face (Tesi Lapche La side) by another Japanese team in December 2002. The party was composed of 6 senior members, who were 59 years old on average, with 6 climbing Sherpas and 4 kitchen staff.

On 25th April we set off from base camp at around 4,700m below the glacial moraine descending from the pyramidal peak of Pamalka (6,344m). Over the next week we reached C2 at the saddle between Pamalka and Langmoche Ri, but were blocked by deep snow and high winds. On 3rd May, we set off from base camp to attempt an alternative new route. Arriving at C2, however, strong wind again stopped our upward progress. On 5th May we started trail breaking, this time along the highest point on an easy slope, which fortunately led us to crusty parts. Then the slope led steeply upwards to a point at 6,100m from where we climbed a couloir located in the middle of the snow flank of Langmoche Ri. We progressed smoothly along the route with five fixed ropes, following this couloir which becomes increasingly steep until thin ice-covered slabs appeared above at 6,250m. A young Sherpa tried to surmount this difficult section for almost one hour while we were exposed in the couloir to continuous blasts of chilling spindrift avalanches. Our Sirdar also tried to tackle these slabs for a while, but climbed down with discouraging words, saying that these icy slabs could not be managed because of the impossibility of piton placement. Knowing not what to do next, we climbed down to C2.

We wanted to try to find a possible route to the east side of the flank even with the limited ropes and food remaining at C2. But our Sherpas were completely discouraged with these failures on the west ribs and the technically difficult couloir route. Unhappily, we realized that our physical competence as seniors was not strong enough to establish another new route by ourselves without support from the Sherpas, which was not forthcoming.

On 10th May, we cleaned the site of our base camp for the return journey back to Lukla. Leader: Ryouzai Nakahara (61); Climbing Leader: Masayoshi Fujii (57); Climbing Members: Minoru Tsubakuro (61), Isao Iguchi (59), Yoshimoto Naruse (57), Hisa Naruse (57).

MASAYOSHI FUJII, *Japan Alpine Club*
Adapted from Japanese Alpine News, TAMOTSU NAKAMURA, *Editor*

Langmoche Ri (6,811m), attempt. Langmoche Ri lies northwest of the Khumbu village of Thami. Two Americans, William ("Rusty") Escapule and Tom Togami, first went to acclimatize on nearby Parchermo. There had been heavy snowfall for two days just before they got there, and the day after their arrival a huge avalanche swept nine people—three Americans, three Frenchmen and three Nepalis—down its north face. Escapule and Togami joined in the strenuous rescue effort. They were now very tired when they went to look at Langmoche Ri, and besides, the snow conditions were too dangerous to try for the summit. They made no attempt to go above base camp, but it is a "beautiful mountain, a great mountain to climb."

ELIZABETH HAWLEY, *AAC Honorary Member, Nepal*

Tangi Ragi Tau South (Pahamlahaka) ascents and possible new route. Although they were unable to make any serious attempt on their main objective, the North Pillar/Face of Teng Kang Poche, a group of young French climbers were able to achieve several ascents on Tangi Ragi Tau South (aka Pahamlahaka: ca 6,187m), which lies on the opposite side of the main valley.

At the end of October Jean-Marc Clerc, Martial Dumas and Erwan le Lann climbed the south ridge with two bivouacs. This gave ca 1,700m of climbing up a fine rock ridge in its lower section, finishing with 500-600m of easy snow/mixed. The French found difficulties up to 6b+.

This route was first climbed in October 2002 by Radek Lienerth and Alexandr Toloch, who also took three days, named it Like a Dhal Bhat, and found the difficulties to be ED1 VII- and 75°. This pair from the Czech Republic then descended the south east ridge in its entirety, taking about six hours and estimating the grade as Alpine D+. It is thought the French also descended this route.

Later, Maxime Belleville, Philippe Coudray, Julien Herry, Nicolas Potard and Xavier Vimal made the probable first ascent of the south west ridge, which they likened in style to Route Major on Mont Blanc. From a bivouac at the foot, they first climbed rock at F4 and 5, made another bivouac at ca 5,800m, crossed steps of 80°-85° with the steepest section just below the summit and then made a third bivouac on the descent of the south east ridge. The route was named Le Sourire de Migma (after a local trekking lodge proprietor).

LINDSAY GRIFFIN, *Mountain INFO, CLIMB magazine*

MAHALANGUR HIMAL

Teng Kang Poche, ascent of the north west face (not to summit), Edge of Darkness. On October 22 British climbers Nick Bullock and Nick Carter left the tea-house at Thengbo situated approximately five hours west of Namche Bazaar, making a bivouac at the base of the ca 1,600m unclimbed north west face of Teng Kang Poche (6,500m). Teng Kang Poche is a striking mountain situated between the more well know peaks of Parcharmo and Kwangde. The north west face is massive, resembling the Droites North Face in the Mont Blanc Range

The two set out at 2 a.m. on the 23rd having already tested the initial snow cone for avalanche risk. Previously on the trip, while attempting to complete Bullock's solo route from 2003, Love and Hate on the north east face, the pair triggered two avalanches at 5,400m and had to make a careful retreat. This proved an intense 12-hour outing, which neither climber wished to repeat.

Finding the snow conditions acceptable, they continued to climb through the night, simu-soloing, and following a deep runnel furrowed by spindrift and hemmed in by rock-walls. The runnel had regular steps of Scottish Grade III and was interspersed with snow slopes of Scottish II, much resembling Tower Gully on Ben Nevis but on a grand scale.

At the top of the runnel section the slope opened out with patches of névé, deep snow and powder. The steep steps increased in regularity. These steps were approximately 65°-70°, with the average angle of the face at approximately 50°-60°. A slight left to right line was followed.

At daybreak the pair continued a more direct line following much the same type of ground as below. The weather at this point was very cold and clear, causing some concern. Even with the warmest boots and gloves, feet and fingers had to be constantly warmed to reduce the risk of frostbite.

At 12:30 p.m., a height of 5,900m had been reached; 1,300 meters of climbing in 10 hours. Above, the summit ridge was 300m away but with what appeared to be steeper, more technical ground above, and with no obvious place for a bivi site, they decided to take an early finish and cut a ledge in the top of a snow fluting. At 3pm they settled down for a rest and some food. Neither carried a bivi bag but they had a prototype single-skin Pertex bivi tent supplied by Outdoor Designs.

At 7 a.m. on the 24th the two started to climb and the angle of the face increased immediately, approximately 70° on average. Rock belays were sought to the right of the line, although due to the compact nature of the rock these were difficult to find. The climbing also became more tenuous with the increase in angle and the snow took on a very Peruvian feel. Protection on lead was virtually non-existent. Occasionally a driven-in ice hook or a dug out ice-screw could be placed if the ice, covering steep slabs, was thick enough. Lengthening sections of 80° powder-covered, hard-ice now had to be climbed (Scottish 1V). The grade of the climbing had no real relevance at this point, as within seconds of climbing one of the steep sections, hands and feet were wooden, making the whole experience more interesting. A race for a rest point where frozen digits could be re-warmed became the crux of the pitch. A long, rising traverse right, (approximately 50m beneath the summit crest) was led by Carter at a grade of Scottish 1V 80°.

Bullock led the final pitch, which consisted of much digging, chopping, burrowing and levitation. (Ungradable and one for the Peruvian connoisseur: 85°). He finished on the crest of the west ridge in the dark at 7:00 p.m. Carter joined Bullock and the pair cut a shelf/cave beneath a mushroom, completing the task at 8:30 p.m. The height was 6,210m and this final 300m of climbing had taken 12 hours.

Through the second day it had become obvious that the west ridge was going to present some very special techniques to try and forge a way onto the summit proper, which stood approximately 1 km away (and now clearly visible from the bivouac, as they were higher than the lowest point of the west ridge). With this in mind the pair decided to leave this joy to some other more deserving party.

After a particularly cool evening the descent was started at 7 a.m. on the 25th. This was virtually the same line as that used in ascent. The top half of the face was descended by rappel, with rock, ice and snow anchors all utilised. The weather chose this point to turn, causing some concern as large powder avalanches poured down the face. (Bullock was buried by one such avalanche while hanging from the end of the abseil rope, having unconnected from the end and about to start down climbing).

Fortunately the snow abated but the slopes now gave cause for concern, as they were freshly loaded with powder snow. The bottom half of the face was down climbed with speed, and it was with relief that the two safely reached the base, 12 hours from starting their descent, at 7 p.m. An overall grade for the route, Edge of Darkness, was thought to be TD+/ED1 Scottish 1V, 1,600m.

NICK BULLOCK, *United Kingdom*

Pasang Lhamu Chuli (Jasamba, Cho Aui) (7,351m), attempt. A six-member Slovenian team led by Uros Samec went up a new line on this mountain just south of Cho Oyu. Although it is officially called Pasang Lhamu Chuli, it used to be known as Jasamba or Cho Aui, and has been successfully climbed twice from its west side. This autumn's group attacked it from the south, up the southeast face to the south ridge.

Their route presented technical difficulties in the mid-section of the face above a big snowfield; here they encountered rock and thin ice leading to a 60° couloir, which in turn led to the summit ridge. The first part of the ridge was also a problem: it was narrow, covered with snow, in one section badly corniced, and was 90° at its beginning. But three members, Rok Blagus, Samo-Matiija Kremelj and Samec climbed the face, pitched a camp there and two days later, on October 24, were on the summit.

ELIZABETH HAWLEY, *AAC Honorary Member, Nepal*

Nangpai Gosum I new route; Dazampa Tse, first ascent. In the middle of October Slovenian expedition made first ascent of Nangapi Gosum 1 (7,351m) or Pasang Lhamu Peak from the southeast (Nepal side) and also made first ascent of Dazampa Tse (6,295m).

Slovenian team (Urban Azman, Tadej Golob, Uros Samec, Samo Krmelj, Rok Blagus, doctor Zare Guzej and me Urban Golob as expedition leader) set up Base camp near Sumna glacier, one hour from traditional way of yak caravan from Tibet over Nangpa La to Namche Bazar. On the same place was also Base camp of American team in 2002 when the southeast side of the mountain was an objective. However, Americans found themselves in the crossfire during acclimatization near Nangpa La and went immediately home without really trying the mountain. On October 5, two days after reaching base camp, ABC (5,555m) was established at the foot of the southeast face. In the time of unpredictable weather a party of Uros Samec, Samo Krmelj and Rok Blagus acclimatized twice in the chosen route on southeast face because there are no easier mountains suitable for acclimatization in the neighborhood. On the first acclimatization they climbed to 6,100m, slept there and equipped rappels for more easy descent from summit push. On October 17 after period of bad weather (when I had to leave the Base Camp because of pneumonia and went home) they reached 6,400m, slept in the tent and go back to Base Camp next day. On the 22nd they went for summit push from Base Camp and next day they started from ABC at 1 a.m. One long day they needed to climb to the south ridge (6,650m) and rested there one day in the tent and look for the route on complicated ridge. On the 24th they started from their tent at 2 a.m. and reached the summit at 9 a.m. in high winds and very low temperatures. Almost immediately they turned back descended to tent and continued their way down to ABC. They reached the foot of the southeast face at the evening making 19 rappels from the ridge. They named their ascent *Slovenian route VI*, 5 M, 1550 meters.

Meanwhile, on the 18th another party of Tadej Golob and Urban Azman climbed the southwest face of Dzasampa Tse (6,295m), south of Nangpai Gosum 1. They started from the south col at 6 a.m. and reached the top after almost seven hours of mostly unroped climbing on slopes of 55°-65° and one mixed pitch of 40 meters. They named the first ascent route as *Mali princ* and rated it at TD+, 5 M, 600m.

Until our expedition there was just two ascents of this highest peak of Nangpai Gosum group. First ascent was made by Japanese expedition in 1986 on northwest ridge starting from Tibet and in 1996 when an international expedition made the integral northwest ridge starting the climb on Nangpa La.

URBAN GOLOB, *Slovenia*

Losar waterfall, one-day ascent. In February Conrad Anker and I did what may be the first one-day ascent of the famous "Losar" waterfall across from Namche Bazar in the Khumbu. We bivouacked at the bottom of the valley and climbed the 2,400-foot waterfall in 16 hours round trip. After hearing stories from many parties that told of strong climbers having trouble on the descent, we opted to take 70-meter ropes and rappel. The plan worked perfectly. Most of the climb is less than vertical with a couple of burly vertical pitches at the end. We didn't do any simul-climbing on the technical terrain, and I was pretty sick at the time; so it is reasonable for any solid team to go for a one-day ascent—provided they are efficient with installing V-threads to get down.

TOPHER DONAHUE, *AAC*

Ama Dablam, crowds on normal route. In the view of many, there were too many people on Ama Dablam (6,812m) last autumn. Some Ama Dablam teams were very small with just a member or two and perhaps one Sherpa. And not all of the 29 expeditions were on the mountain at the same time—they were spread out over a month—but they did bunch up at times. Two expeditions consisted of 30 and 31 members each; the larger one, led by American Dan Mazur, was assisted by nine Sherpas.

Mazur's expedition sent a total of 38 people to the top over seven days. On a single day, October 24, which was just when a number of other parties were also summiting or trying to, this team put seven members and three Sherpas on the summit.

Henry Todd, the British leader of the second largest team, had 30 members and two Sherpas in his party. The members arrived at base camp and left the mountain at different times, and of his 19 successful members, plus two Sherpas—who went to the top three times—18 summited on six different days between October 26 and November 17. He said he tried to minimize the impact of his sizable group by, for example, not pitching tents that would be left empty much of the time while taking up space badly needed by other climbers, and by having his members summit in relatively small numbers each day. Furthermore, his team was based at a camp apart from others' bases. Finally, when some of his members arrived at Ama Dablam, other expeditions had already moved off the mountain.

Nevertheless, there were complaints. At one bottleneck a German team's leader and

Mazur's deputy leader attempted to speed up the progress of slow clients by hauling their rucksacks up by rope. This problem greatly delayed the German team's arriving at the second and third camps. Also, an American climber was almost been hit by a falling rock loosened by a climber above him. His own group could not pitch a second or third camp because no space was available; they were not only ones who had to skip a camp, usually camp 2, sometimes making for debilitating long summit days, and long waits at the mountain's bottlenecks.

The leader of an international expedition, Luis Benitez from the U.S., summarized the general situation on Ama Dablam in harsh terms: "too many teams were not led properly or responsibly [and] too cheaply." He said that some teams' Sherpas took food, fuel, and even a set of crampons from others' tents for their own members. One leader reportedly apologized for the stolen crampons, but others were apparently unaware of what their Sherpas were doing. Benitez says that the Nepalese tourism ministry must restrict the number of Ama Dablam permits it grants in a season because the mountain is getting so overcrowded that it has "almost reached critical mass." However, the government is most unlikely to act on his advice, since the fees are a major source of its foreign exchange earnings, and foreign climbers' expenditures are extremely important to their Sherpas, to the trekking agencies who assist teams, and to the many lodge keepers in mountainous areas.

In contrast, there were nearly twice as many teams on Cho Oyu (8,201m) but they did not have this kind of crowding problem. There was a lot more space, with none of Ama Dablam's narrow-ridge bottlenecks to confront them.

ELIZABETH HAWLEY, *AAC Honorary Member, Nepal*

Everest, north face, new route. Elizabeth Hawley's account of the Russian new route on the north face of Everest, along with commentary from Yuri Koshelenko, a team member, is in the Tibet section of this *AAJ*.

Everest, 2004 summary. During spring 2003, in the 50th anniversary season of Everest's first ascent, a record number of men and women had turned up to climb to its summit, and it was assumed that the numbers would decrease after that. Wrong assumption. The number of teams was slightly less, but not the number of climbers. In May 2003 a mere 260 people, foreigners and Nepalese, men, women, and one 15-year-old child, stood on the summit of Everest, and on a single day, May 22, 114 people summited. In 2004 the overall total rose considerably, to 319 people. However, they were more evenly scattered over various days this time, with just 61 on the busiest day, May 16.

Last spring's Everest teams also exceeded those of a year ago in a tragic way: the number of climbers' deaths. Last year, only three people died, all of them men and two of these were Sherpas. This year no Sherpa perished, but seven other climbers, including two women, did: five had just been to the summit, another was trying to rescue two of these summiters, and the seventh collapsed while struggling to surmount the final 150 meters to the top. On the North Col route were a Bulgarian, Hristo Hristov (who was one of his country's best mountaineers and in 2003 climbed a hard new route on the north face of Thalay Sagar); another Bulgarian, Mariana Maslaova, who never reached the top; two South Korean summiters, Jang Min and Park Mu-Taek, and Baek Joon-Ho, their leader, who climbed up from their highest camp to save them and then also died; and a 63-year-old Japanese woman, Shoko Ota (the second oldest woman to reach the summit). The only death on the South Col route was the American summiter, Nils Antzana.

There were only two teams on Everest last autumn: Dutch and Ukrainian. Both were on Tibet's standard route via the North Col, and both were unsuccessful due to too much snow and not enough fixed ropes. A major problem for these Everest climbers was that there was nobody else around: there were none of the big commercial expeditions that come in the spring, with numerous Sherpas to establish the route by fixing hundreds of meters of rope most of the way to the top.

ELIZABETH HAWLEY, *AAC Honorary Member, Nepal*

Everest, uncommon events on standard routes. In the spring a Greek expedition sent one climbing team to the north side and another to the south to carry to the top their flags of the 2004 Greek Summer Olympic Games. They were the first Greek expedition ever to attempt Everest, and both parties succeeded in planting their flags at the highest spot on earth.

Another team on the north side had a novel sendoff. It was the first to go to Everest from the Indian navy, so the Indian defense minister, George Fernandes; the navy chief of staff, Admiral Madhvendra Singh; the expedition leader, a submariner, Commander Satyabrata Dam, and the 13 other expedition members got into a Russian-built submarine and submerged to a depth of about 75 meters in the Arabian Sea for the official launching ceremony.

Sherpas on the normal climbing route from the Nepalese side included one with a prosthesis on his leg, and another who claimed a new speed record in his ascent. Nawang Sherpa, 32, lost his left leg below the knee in a motorcycle accident six years ago, but that didn't prevent him from getting to the top of the world this spring with an American, Thomas McMillan, who had arranged for him to have a high-quality U.S.-made prosthesis fitted three years after his accident. Nawang went to Everest last year and climbed as far as camp 2, testing his artificial leg. Now he was back, and with McMillan and three other Sherpas became the second amputee ever to reach the summit. (The first was an American, Tom Whittaker, who summited six years earlier, but Nawang had lost much more of his leg than Whittaker had.)

The speed climber was Pemba Dorje, who claims he raced up the 3,500 vertical meters from base camp on the Khumbu Glacier to the summit in only 8 hours and 8 minutes during the night of 20/21 May, climbing entirely alone and using artificial oxygen only above the last camp at 7,900 meters.

For this 27-year-old climber, it was his third ascent. He was now well acclimatized: he had just made his second ascent by the same route on the morning of the 16th in the company of a Swiss, Rupert Heider, and two other Sherpas. Furthermore, he said, he had spent about six months training intensively in Kathmandu before arriving at base camp on April 7. Nearly every day, he had cycled at least eight kilometers and jogged from one edge of the city to another; he had also gone rock climbing.

The announcement of this astonishing feat was received with some skepticism and was immediately challenged at base camp. In a satellite telephone interview with a newspaper reporter in Kathmandu, Lhakpa Gelu Sherpa renewed a controversy they had last year. Pemba Dorje made his first speed-ascent last spring and reported then that it took him 12 hours and 45 minutes to climb from bottom to top. Lhakpa Gelu said four days later that he himself had just spent only 10 hours and 56 minutes to do the entire ascent. Pemba Dorje charged Lhakpa

Gelu with lying and insisted that it was he who had made the fastest ascent. Lhakpa Gelu countered with evidence to support his own timings, and after investigation, Nepal's tourism ministry concluded that this man's claim to the record was valid. This spring again, the ministry was looking into the validity of a speed-climb claim and in the meantime was not revealing which specific details they were trying to check, nor what information he had given them.

Some details do seem to merit looking into since, unfortunately for him, no one else was on the summit with him—indeed, no one else was on the summit at any time on the 21st—so there was no one to confirm what time he was there or any other details. Pemba Dorje said that when he stood on the summit at 2:00 a.m. that day, he saw lights from two or three headlamps of climbers coming up from the Tibetan side. Based on his knowledge of that side from the first time he had climbed Everest, he judged these climbers to be a little above the highest camp, which is normally at 8,300m.

But there are two problems with this: there almost certainly were no climbers above that altitude at 2:00 a.m.; on the 21st there was one man, a Bulgarian searching for his missing teammate, and he was there at around 5:30-6:00 a.m., when it was no longer dark. And even if there had been someone, that person could not be seen from the summit, according to others who have climbed to the top themselves. They explain that a small ridge not far below the summit obscures a view of anyone in the 8,300m area of the north side.

The skepticism that was voiced when the news of Pemba Dorje's ascent broke was not based on these factors, which were not generally known, but on the question of whether anyone could lop four and a half hours off his own elapsed time of a year before. He said he had put himself through a rigorous training regime, but could that have cut his time by one-third? [His ascent was later ratified by the Ministry of Tourism.—Ed.]

One record that no one disputed was set by a well known modest Sherpa, Apa, who in the spring achieved his 14th Everest ascent at the age of 42. His nearest rival, Chuwang Nima Sherpa, who is five years younger, scored his 11th success last spring. Apa may not be unusually fast, but he is very strong. He has said that he does not climb Everest to set any kind of record, but to earn good money to support his family by doing the only kind of work he knows.

Another record in number of ascents was set by an American, Gheorghe Dijmarescu, who has acquired the habit of climbing Everest in the spring via the standard Tibetan-side route [his wife, 31-year-old Lhakpa Sherpa, also reached the summit to become the only woman to have climbed Everest four times—Ed.]. He became the only non-Sherpa to have gone to the summit every year for six consecutive years.

A useful permanent improvement to the standard northern route was a new ladder placed at the bottom of the Second Step at about 8,600m. It was installed by an expedition led by Russell Brice, a leader of teams on this route every spring. His ladder is wider than the old one, which was put there by Chinese climbers in 1975, and significantly longer. The old one was four or five meters long; the new one is eight meters.

ELIZABETH HAWLEY, *AAC Honorary Member, Nepal*

MAHALANGUR SOUTH

Kusum Kanguru (6,367m), south ridge, new route attempt. From the 10th of November until the 21st of November Young Chet and I from Alaska attempted to climb the "Dream Pillar" [see Venables' note to follow] on the south ridge of Kusum Kanguru. We were star struck when we first learned of a huge shining granite pillar at 6,000m in such a spectacular location. The pillar was rumored to be of top quality. Young Chet and I were rearing to go.

The "Dream Pillar" line was first climbed by Stephen Venables and Dick Renshaw (with Brian Davison as far as the crest of the south ridge on their first attempt), in November 1991. In 2000 American youths Bart Paul and Fredrick Wilkinson (both 20 years old) climbed a new route to the top of the "Dream Pillar," bivvied, and descended the next day due to high

Kusum Kangri's north face, (1) "Dream Pillar" (Renshaw-Venables, 1991). (2) Chet-Poacher, 2004 attempt. *Shakey Poacher*

winds on the summit ridge. They were no more than a couple hundred meters from the summit. Since then, the only other groups I've heard of attempting this aspect were a Slovenian team and an American team on the southwest face. The Slovenians gave up on their original new-route line in the middle of the face, and then turned back low on Venables' line due to constant rock-fall. About the Americans, I've only heard rumors from the local villagers that they succeeded. Needless to say, this side of the mountain has seen hardly any traffic, and this became painfully obvious when our guesstimate of two days to base camp up the Thado Khosi valley turned into five days of ridiculous bushwhacking through extremely thick and cliffed-out bamboo forest. Luckily we had a guy who knew the way, because otherwise it would have taken a lot longer. Future climbers should take with them a local who knows the whole way to base camp.

We arrived at base camp with only six days left for climbing before our flight home. A day spent watching the face revealed the same problem faced by the Slovenians: constant rockfall. Due to the face's aspect and T-shirt weather at 5,000m, the lower portion of our chosen line (the Venables route) was too risky for Young Chet and I unless we did the preliminary pitches in the night and reached the arête a quarter of the way up to the pillar before 9:30 a.m., when the sun reaches the face.

The next morning we climbed the snow slopes to the start of the technical climbing, only to find that there was still rock falling from the face, just not the huge blocks-of-death seen and heard from our base camp a mile away during the sun-baked hours. These were smaller fist-sized stones falling with quite a bit of velocity. Sadly we abandoned our main objective and dragged our heels back to camp. The Dream Pillar loomed above us like a T-bone steak dangling in front of a dog's face, just out of reach. We spent the rest of the day scanning for an alternate line. With three days left we hurried out of camp early the next morning and started up our new line. We climbed some nice mixed terrain onto easy snow, but the sun beat on us and our packs were too heavy. We were not moving fast enough, so we descended the next day and missed our flight anyways.

This aspect has a lot of potential. All of the lines look high quality and fun as hell. You just have to manage the rockfall better than we did, which means move faster, climb strategically, and maybe go during colder times of the year. We saw a bunch of sick water ice in the area.

SHAKEY POACHER, *Alaska*

Stephen Venables (now president of the Alpine Club) comments: "Dream Pillar" was the title editor Ed Webster gave to the article I did for Ascent *(1997, AAC Press). Now it seems to be THE DREAM PILLAR. It was a lovely bit of rock climbing, but let's not overstate the case. My intention in 1991 was to climb the southwest face direct, but we were deterred by rockfall. Hence the sneaky line up the side, leading to the south ridge. The rockfall WAS bad at the bottom of the face, but, apart from the first few pitches on our route, which we did at daybreak, we were completely safe. Perhaps global warming has made this face worse, like so many others around the world? Perhaps it is time for winter ascents. The southwest face direct would be a great route. Our route was also a very nice climb—good mixed climbing, some beautiful rock climbing, and quite a mushroomy snow/ice ridge to finish. And a truly spectacular summit. Some "trekking" peak! As to the approach: I think we were the first people to cut a trail up the valley, but it took three days, not five.*

MAHALANGUR EAST - BARUN SECTION

Baruntse North (Khali Himal) (7,057m), north face, Ciao Patrick. It was very, very difficult. We gave it all we had, and finally we reached our goal. The north face of Khali Himal, or Baruntse North, is big, vertical, dangerous, and intimidating. We knew that we would have to use all of

our capacities and strength to succeed on that face. For four days we struggled against the wind and the cold through a mixed climb of ice and rock. For four days we were three people sleeping in a two-man tent. We never managed to find a good place for camp, and we slept with our legs hanging out in the void. We used ice screws, rock pitons, ice axes, cams, and nuts to climb the complicated wall, but the real challenge was the wind and the cold. We had 120 km/h wind blowing during the

Baruntse North, north face. (1) Czech route (Leitermann-Otta-Pekarek, 1994). (2) Ciao Patrick (Moro-Tassi-Urubko, 2004). (3) Descent route for both parties. *Simone Moro* entire climb, even on the summit. We were very happy to reach our summit through this new route. Next, we spent 12 hours rappelling on single ice screws 20 times.

We called the route Ciao Patrick in dedication to the recently perished climber Patrick Berhault. He was our friend and now our legend. Details: 2,550m, of which the last 1,350m were in alpine style [the height of the northwest face itself is ca 1,500m]. Three camps. Difficulty of M6+, often on bare rock and loose gravel. The maximum difficulties on rock; 5+/6. The maximum difficulties on ice;

Camos Tassi and Denis Urubko on the cold north face of Baruntse North. *Simone Moro*

between 70° and 90°, thin ice covering granite plates exposed to northwest. Three intermediate camps and four bivouacs. Summited on May 4 by Simone Moro, Bruno "Camos" Tassi, and Denis Urubko. Descent 12 hours, with 20 full double rappels on the wall.

SIMONE MORO, *Italy*

MAHALANGUR EAST: MAKALU SECTION

Makalu, southeast ridge integral attempt. In spring a 14-member British Services expedition hoped to climb the south east ridge integral and arriving at the usual 4,700m base camp on April 8, first investigated the south east glacier approach. However, recession had made reaching the first ice fall too dangerous and they opted for the longer route over the lower continuation of the ridge, which bends south and runs down the east side of the Barun Valley opposite base camp. This was first pioneered by Doug Scott on his three major attempts at an Alpine style traverse of Makalu in the early 1980s and involves crossing Peak 6,260m and then Peak 6,825m before a long and almost horizontal snow arête leads to the South Col.

The team placed Camp 1 at 5,700m, from where they pushed out the route to the crest of the ridge at ca 6,100m, the last 200m fixed with rope. An intermediate camp was established at ca 6,100m on the far side of the first peak, while the team, with a little Sherpa support, fixed more rope above. Snowfall either hampered or completely curtailed progress toward 6,825m during the entire latter part of April and it wasn't until May 7 that Camp 2 was established close to the South Col and ca 200m below the summit of 6,825m. By the 10th, ropes had been fixed to 7,100m.

Strong winds then made progress difficult but on the 15th Camp 3 was placed at 7,300m. The next few days saw more rope fixed up the 45°-50° ridge leading to the Black Gendarme but around the 20th there was snowfall, burying the ropes. Although acclimatized and poised for a summit attempt, time was running out and as conditions now seemed relatively unstable, the team members made the decision to abandon the route on the 24th, having reached a high point of ca 7,500m.

COLIN SCOTT, *United Kingdom*

Makalu, southeast ridge ascent. After they had abandoned their attempt on the northeast ridge from Tibet, reported elsewhere, Frenchmen Yannick Graziani, Christian Trommsdorff, and Patrick Wagnon decided to try the southeast ridge. It had been in sight during their attempt on the northeast ridge, looked less laden with snow and by that stage was known to have a British party in-situ, fixing ropes. Packing big sacks, they walked up the straightforward glacier southeast of Makalu, crossed the ca 5,500m col on the frontier between the end of the true southeast ridge and Peak 6,100m (immediately northwest of 6,477m Peak 3), then descended the far side in the direction of the Standard Barun Base Camp. Before reaching this, at a height of ca 5,250m, they climbed to the lower continuation of the southeast ridge. Two days after leaving their Tibetan Base, all three were at the British Camp 1. Here, they joined forces with the British climbers, helping to fix ropes up to 7,300m, where Camp 3 was installed around the May 14. Relations between both teams were good from the outset and by the 15th the three French had descended and were walking all the way back to their Tibetan Base Camp to enjoy a good rest.

They were not back at Camp 1 until the 22nd (approximately 12 hours travel from their Tibet Base Camp). The following day they climbed to the British Intermediate Camp, where the weather promptly turned bad again. Trommsdorff and Wagnon decided to descend to Base for two nights but Graziani chose to wait. All three were united on the 25th and as the weather looked promising, they moved to Camp 2 the following day. The day after they reached Camp 3 (7,300m) and proceeded to dig out a tent left from nearly three weeks previously. It had not snowed for four days and conditions seemed good with little or no risk of avalanche. In the back of their minds was the hope that they could complete the route in a single push from here and traverse the summit, descending the Normal Route via the Makalu La.

On the 28th they moved up the ridge (ca 55° with a final mixed pitch) to 7,600m, where a descent can be made to the Eastern Cwm. Here, they first called for a weather forecast, were told the next three days would be fine, and then climbed down to the snowy amphitheatre, leaving 150m of rope fixed to safeguard their return. Underfoot conditions in the Cwm proved quite good and they moved up to camp at 7,600m.

During that night the wind approached 100km/hour and as they had only brought the inner tent and two sleeping bags between three, it was grim. Fortunately, at sunrise the wind stopped. Leaving at 9:00 a.m., all three reached the back of the Cwm at 7,800m (and one kilometer from the tent) in two hours. The weather was excellent and the temperature relatively mild as they climbed up to the rimaye at 8,050m with Graziani, who was moving strongly, in the lead. Here, Trommsdorff turned back, leaving the others to continue. The slope above, deep snow over slabby rock, was strenuous and at 4:00 p.m. Wagnon turned back from a height of ca 8,250m. Graziani reached the ridge, then overcoming a 30m rock step (about III), continued up the corniced arête to arrive at the highest point around 4:30 p.m. A grueling and even more strenuous descent followed, until at 8:00 p.m., just before nightfall, he regained his two companions in the tent. Next day, the 30th, all three made an exhausting climb down to the British intermediate camp, finding most of the ropes and their small cache of food and equipment had been removed. After a hard night, Base Camp was reached in heavy rain. The trio then had to make two hard days' walk back over the frontier to Kharta, in order to be on schedule for their flights home. This would appear to be the first time the lower south east ridge has been continued to the summit but the entire crest, super-integral, has yet to have an ascent.

PATRICK WAGNON, *France*

KANGCHENJUNGA REGION

JANAK HIMAL

Janak (Outlier Peak) (7,044m), attempt. In November two members of a Romanian team led by Constantine Lacatusu were the first to climb on to Janak above the upper plateau of the Broken Glacier. This summit west of Jongsang was referred to as Outlier Peak by climber-explorers of the early 20th century. Their plan was to scale this peak north-northwest of Kangchenjunga on Nepal's border with Tibet via its southwest ridge, but they managed to get no farther than a rock tower close to the bottom of the ridge.

On 11 November, three weeks after having established their base camp at 4,800m, Lacatusu and his climbing partner Ioan Torek made their bid to reach the summit from their third high camp at 6,200m. They climbed all day 300 meters up the right side of the tower and then gave up this line: they were now in a serac area with powder snow and impossible to fix with rope, so they returned to camp. The next day they attempted the tower's left side, moved up beneath overhanging seracs, and reached 6,400m only to find again impossible powder snow. They abandoned the climb.

Lacatusu summarized their attempt: "the first part of Janak was technical, and we climbed that, but the second half was dangerous and we didn't climb that." The technical part was "very nice" and he and Torek "would like to come back and finish what we started." Next time they would have more manpower and more rope to fix.

ELIZABETH HAWLEY, *AAC Honorary Member, Nepal*

Dome Kang (Domekhan) (7,264m), first attempt. On Nepal's border with Tibet, a six-member team of Spaniards were the first people to attempt a route on Dome Kang [see note below]. Its official name is Domekhan. Led by Carlos Soria, they made their base camp on April 18 at Pangpema, the normal base campsite for climbers going to Kangchenjunga's north face, and approached Dome Kang from the south via the Jongsang Glacier, working their way over a difficult unsettled rocky area, and pitched their first high camp 14 km from and 800m higher than base, at 5,350m. Their aim was to reach the summit via the mountain's east-southeast ridge.

They did gain the ridge, but were unable to follow it all the way to the summit. Their second camp was placed at a col, known as Jongsang La, on the ridge at 6,100m. They managed to move from there westward toward the summit, but finally stopped at 6,650m exactly one month after they had arrived at base. Now the clouds moved in covering the way ahead, and snow started to fall. And their time was running out.

From the Jongsang La the dge was a very complicated mixture of rock, snow, and broken pieces of ice, making it impossible to keep to the crest. They sometimes moved on the ridge itself, sometimes on its south side, and sometimes on the north side's big hanging glacier.

On May 18 they realized that they did not have sufficient time left to spend four or five days more to solve the last 600 meters up to a plateau. They want to come back in 2005 to solve this problem and finish the climb to the top. They plan to follow the same route, but they will give themselves more to time to do it.

Editor's note: In 1930, after reaching the summit of Jongsang Peak (7,483m), Gunter Dyrenfurth persuaded Lewa Sherpa to walk across the plateau and climb the south summit; 7,442m Dome Kang. Recently Dome Kang (officially opened by the Nepalese Government in 2002) appears to have been assigned to a lower (7,264m) snow dome east of the original Dome Kang, a little way down the latter's east southeast ridge leading to the Jongsang La. This difficult ridge above the La, attempted by the Spanish, was also visited in 1983 (Slovenians) and 1998 (Irish), who both noted it was far from straightforward.

ELIZABETH HAWLEY, *AAC Honorary Member, Nepal*

KUMBHAKARNA HIMAL

Jannu (Kumbhakarna), east face attempt and history. Jannu, also known as Kumbhakarna, not far from Kangchenjunga, has a forbiddingly precipitous east face, which Slovenians seem to have become obsessively determined to scale. Its main summit is 7,710m, while its east face tops out on the east summit at 7,468m. Nearly every team that has aimed to climb it has been Slovenian. None has yet succeeded.

Tomaz Humar, 35 years old, had demonstrated his exceptional abilities in earlier climbs in Nepal on Ama Dablam and Nuptse in Khumbu, Bobaye in the far west of Nepal, and—most notably—solo on the south face of Dhaulagiri I in 1999. This season his goal was to make the first ascent of Jannu's east face all the way—and to do it solo. But he had to abandon the effort at 7,000m where, in its present condition, the face had gotten "harder and harder, riskier and riskier as I went higher and higher."

Before tackling the face, Humar acclimatized to 6,000m on an east pillar with his Croatian friend, Stipe Bozic. Then to the face. But the face was "totally different" from what he had seen in pictures of the 1992 attempt: now there was black ice and above that many big mushrooms covered with powder snow, which made them very dangerous.

His ascent from advance base camp at 5,400m lasted for four days. On the first day, October 27, he crossed a high glacier shaped like an amphitheater where powder snow avalanches were falling constantly and depositing chest-deep snow, and where there were very deep crevasses, many at least six meters wide. But one was a mere two meters wide, and this he jumped across. Then to get out of this area of avalanche debris, he started up an ice and rock debris pillar at the southern end of the face, up 30 meters on an overhanging section with a series of dangerous and difficult obstacles where he was hit hard by an ice "candle" that luckily did him no damage. He bivouacked at 6,000m late that afternoon.

His second bivouac the next day was only 200 meters higher. Here he had to climb a system of overhanging rock cracks 20 meters high. He climbed up inside them and then over onto the outside. They were like polished granite and gave very little friction, and it was impossible to affix a rope. This was a "very risky" area, he said. Next came a number of mushroom ridges, a "nightmare" of ups and downs past mushrooms and avalanches. At 6,200m he found a narrow rock ledge and bivouacked there, half hanging over the edge.

On the 29th, Humar was finally able to climb very fast and in six hours had scaled a face of 80°-90° and then had to work his way up a very thin couloir covered with black ice under powder snow, which he laboriously cleared away. Each side was a huge balloon of powder snow and at the top of it were cauliflower cornices.

Here he fell three times but carried on, then traversed 20 meters to the right side on a mushroom to end up bivouacking at 6,850m in a snow hole that he dug deep into a mushroom on a ledge. He left his gear here and tried to find a route beyond, but he could gain just 25 meters in four hours. He returned to his snow hold and spent a very cold night there; 100 km/hour winds were blowing "very fresh air" into it and down his throat. But he was confident that next day he would be able to reach the shoulder on the southeast ridge, which leads to the top.

But "a nightmare came early in the morning [of the 30th] when I tried to reach this shoulder" only 20 meters above but "unreachable" through the mushrooms. He could find no way past them in five attempts up different couloirs and mushrooms. After four and a half hours of these futile efforts, he gave up at about 7,000m.

So at 1:00 that afternoon, he packed up his gear and headed down, found a way through fog, and after 4:00 p.m., through falling snow. He fell five times on rock pillars, and at one place below had to jump two crevasses. He could not follow his own tracks because avalanches had filled them in, but he managed to arrive safely at advance base camp after nightfall in six hours' descent. He spent the night there and was down at his base on the 31st.

He said that he has no plans to go back to Jannu's east face again. He would not declare the route to be impossible, but it is simply too dangerous in its present condition.

Like Humar, all of the earlier teams on the east face had no Sherpas or bottled oxygen with them, but not all actually did any climbing, two for tragic reasons. The Slovenians' first bid was made in the spring of 1991, when the two members attained an altitude of 7,050m, then gave up because of a combination of bad weather, frost-nipped toes, exhaustion, and no more gas for cooking. In the following spring, a three-member team moved over toward the left and reached 7,100m, at a point where the face meets the southeast ridge; they then turned back safely. But that autumn one member of a six-man party on their approach to base camp went for a swim in a river, slipped, and drowned; his teammates never went to the mountain.

In the autumn of 1993, two of a three-member group got to 6,800m, then abandoned the climb because of dangerous avalanching. In 1996 both members of a two-man team disappeared without trace during their acclimatization climb on nearby Kabru; fog closed in around them and they were never seen again. In the spring of 1998 eight members waited for weeks at the bottom of the east face for constant avalanching to cease, but finally abandoned hope and actually did no climbing. Four years later, four other Slovenes spent two weeks at advance base camp just beneath the face, where fog obscured the face and soon snow began falling; avalanching sent them home, too.

ELIZABETH HAWLEY, *AAC Honorary Member, Nepal*

Jannu, north face, new route summary. The historic climb in the Nepalese Himalaya during the pre-monsoon season was the successful ascent and descent by a direct route via the north face of Jannu by aRussian team (with one Kyrgyzstani member) led by Alexander Odinstov. This was the first ascent of the north face direct. A Yugoslavian (now Slovenian), Tomo Cesen, claimed to have accomplished this solo in one continuous push from base camp in the spring of 1989, but after his account in the following year of having summited the south face of Lhotse solo was discredited, there has been grave doubt about his Jannu success. In any case, by his own account, he did not descend the face but came down the less difficult northeast ridge instead.

Since 1975, nine expeditions had been on this extremely steep (80°-90° in places) face of 7,710m Jannu, which is officially known as Khumbhakarna, in addition to Cesen's one-man effort. The ninth was led by Odinstov himself last autumn, when his eight-member team reached 7,200m and then abandoned the attempt because of snowfall, strong wind, and the low temperatures found on the north sides of Nepalese Himalaya peaks in autumn.

This spring Odinstov returned with 11 members besides himself. Six of these men had been with him in 2003, and they now had more experience of the route, knew a better site for their base camp, and understood which places were especially exposed to falling rocks and ice.

Without using any bottled oxygen or Sherpa help, they moved slowly upwards, Odinstov reported, using a total of about 75 ice screws and 300 rock pitons to fix about 3,375 meters of rope; in some sections the rock was bad enough to require two and even three pitons at a single place. To make a place for camp 3 at 7,000m, they had to work in shifts of three members for eights hours per shift, working in relays cutting ice and removing stone, for four or five days. Their slow progress was also due to the impossibility of climbing this face with mittens on their hands, but going without them meant their fingers became very cold, so every two meters— or sometimes even less—they had to pause and rub their fingers to get them warm again.

They had arrived at their base camp on the Jannu Glacier at 4,700m on April 3. They pitched their highest camp, a second camp 4, at 7,400m on May 14. Now for a rest and then the summit push. But then Jannu was hit by a prolonged period of snowfall and strong winds, so it was not until the 26th of May that their first members reached the top.

Two members, Dmitri Pavlenko and Alexander Ruchkin, left the 7,400m camp at 5:00 a.m. on the 26th, finally gained the summit at 3:00 p.m. and returned to camp at 6:00 p.m. The final 70 meters was rock covered with dangerous powder snow, and the top itself was a difficult snow cornice.

Three more Russians, Sergei Borisov, Gennady Kirievskiy, and Nikolai Totmyanin, followed them on the 28th, and were able to move much faster since the way had been opened by the first two summiters. Next day, as they descended all the way to base camp, they cleared the mountain of all their tents and contents, plus as much fixed rope as they could recover— a lot of it was stuck in snow that had melted and then refrozen. [For a complete account, see "The North Face of Jannu," by Alexander Ruchkin, earlier in this Journal.]

ELIZABETH HAWLEY, *AAC Honorary Member, Nepal*

KANGCHENJUNGA HIMAL SOUTH

Kabru IV (7,318m), west face attempt. A Serbian expedition may have been only the third to make a serious attempt on the Nepalese flank of the Kabru Range. The team, led by Dragan Jacimovic, set up Base Camp at ca 4,600m on the moraines of the Yalung Glacier northwest of 6,682m Rathong and then fixed the initial, dangerous section of the previously unattempted West Face. This begins with a difficult rock barrier, which they climbed via an objectively threatened 500-600m gully. Camp 1 was placed above this section at c5,200m but in the unsettled weather of late April a large serac fall swept the bottom part of the route and destroyed the fixed ropes in four places. Just after the ropes were replaced another huge powder avalanche from high on the mountain hit a large rock, beneath which Camp 1 was situated, and rumbled on down the route. The following day, the 4th May, Jacimovic was pushing out the route to a proposed site for Camp 2 on the glaciated slopes above, when at around 6,000m he fell from a steep serac wall, hurting his shoulder. The Serbian leader was the driving force behind the expedition and with him out of action and the route obviously unsafe, the remaining members abandoned further attempts.

The first and only ascent of this peak occurred in May 1994, when Major A Abbey's Indian Army expedition repeated Reggie Cooke's route to Kabru III, and then traversed to both Kabru II (their Kabru III) and Kabru IV (their Kabru South).

Climbing fatalities in Nepal. Besides the seven deaths on Everest, two other climbers died last spring: American Jay Sieger and Ukrainian Vladislav Terzyul. They had gone to the top of Makalu together and were beginning their descent. Sieger apparently died when his head struck some rocks, but the body of veteran 8,000m summiter Terzyul was not found, so what caused his death is unknown.

No deaths occurred in summer, and remarkably few deaths occurred during the autumn: only one on Cho Oyu and two on Annapurna I. Cho Oyu has a history of very few fatal accidents: only 35 climbers have perished on it—an extremely small death toll considering the thousands of men and women who have been on the mountain and roughly 1,500 who have reached its summit. But this autumn a young Spanish Basque, Xabier Ormazabal, climbing independently and going for the summit alone, died while he was descending after having reached at least 8,100m and perhaps the top.

Another independent climber, Eloise Barbieri from Italy, had become acquainted with Ormazabal and was the only person who knew much about his movements. She watched him through binoculars as he went for the summit on October 13, a very windy day. He was entirely alone on the upper reaches of the mountain while the weather worsened. She saw him reach the summit plateau at about 8,000m, disappear out of sight for an hour and a half, and then reappear. This time span is fully consistent with his having reached the highest of several small peaks before coming back into sight, which he did at 1:00 p.m. Two hours later he had descended about 200 meters and then sat down for an hour, resumed his decent, but now moved down only a few meters at a time, intermittently falling over. At 5:30 p.m., when night fell, he had descended to about 7,700m. On the next day, falling snow made it impossible to see anyone or anything from afar; on the day after that, the 15th, when he had not come into camp, a searcher went up to look for him. His body was found at 7,550m.

The only others to die this autumn were two Japanese who were killed by avalanche on the notoriously avalanche-prone north face of Annapurna I, 8,091m and the world's tenth highest peak. The mountain has the worst ratio of deaths to summiters of any of Nepal's eight 8,000ers: 56 people, including this Japanese pair, have died on it, and more than half of these (29) were on the north face, while only 131 climbers have ever reached the top.

The Japanese who died were a four-member team's leader Michio Sato and teammate Hideji Nazuka, who were at 6,200m on October 10 when a big block of ice suddenly broke loose from the glacier on the feature known as the Sickle, fell onto to a sloping snowfield, and set off a major avalanche. This mass of snow and ice carried Sato and Nazuka 500 vertical meters with it. Their bodies were recovered an hour and a half later.

ELIZABETH HAWLEY, *AAC Honorary Member, Nepal*

China

Emerging trends among Chinese climbers.
China not only has the tallest mountains
in the world, it also has some of the
most technically challenging, least
explored, and most varied. What does
this all mean for a burgeoning Chinese
middle class that now has economic
means, a love of the outdoors, and a desire for a higher quality of life? They have an "infinite"
playground of incredible mountains and an immense backcountry to explore.

The Chinese are wasting no time in discovering their mountains and crags. In China, the
development of climbing as a recreational sport has grown rapidly in a short period and is
steadily gaining steam. In 1995, it is safe to say that all the serious Chinese rock climbers knew
each other. Now, climbing and outdoor-enthusiast clubs are springing up at a dizzying rate
across the country. It is difficult to judge how many climbers and want-to-be climbers there are
presently in China. One thing is clear: the sport is growing exponentially. There are several popular rock climbing areas in the south and north, most major cities have rock gyms, people are
starting to pursue alpine climbing, and Chinese are climbing Cho-Oyu, Everest, Mustag-ata,
and other peaks throughout all of China and Tibet. ISPO (the giant international sports trade
show from Europe) held its first show in China on March 14, 2005. One can now find all essential
equipment for climbing, and most major brands have entered the market. It is an exciting time
to be a Chinese climber.

This explosion in outdoor sports is clearly being driving by the private sector's new young
middle class. Traditionally, the focus among Chinese climbers was on altitude: climbing 7,000m
and 8,000m peaks siege or expedition style. Although this mindset is still prevalent, a new trend
is developing in alpine climbing: attempting 5,000m-6,000m peaks in a lighter, small-team
approach. Chinese climbers are starting to choose a mountain by what the route has to offer,
where style counts, and where the challenges of the line are the goal, rather than simply getting
to the top any way possible. This is a huge paradigm shift, and very well may be what makes
climbing a popular sport in China. Alpine-style climbing is more suitable for the working, middle
class climber who has economic constraints and limited vacation time.

However, alpine climbing is still in its infancy. In the past, Chinese overlooked their
"shorter" mountains. Foreigners, especially Japanese and Westerners, pioneered many of
the hard lines. For example, Mick Fowler and Paul Ramsden's award-winning ascent of
Mt. Siguniang's north face in 2002, Charlie Fowler's first ascents of unknown peaks in western
Sichuan in the mid 1990s, rock routes in the Jarjinjabo massif in the remote Kham region, and
Craig Luebben's ice lines in Shuangqiao Valley. We are now just starting to see Chinese climbers
attempt new ascents on technically challenging routes and really get into their own backcountry.
As a result, the Chinese have to learn a new set of climbing and backcountry techniques and
safety skills. The first climbing school dedicated to teaching such skills started two years ago
(AAIC—Arete Alpine Instruction Center—I am a co-owner with Ma Yihua, from Chengdu; the
website www.aaic.cn is currently only in Chinese, but it will soon be in English also and will
offer assistance to foreign visitors). In China, the scope of climbing is expanding along with the

rising number of people coming into the sport.

I see the Chinese climbing scene advancing in several areas: quadruple the number of people going into the mountains during the next two to three years, pursuit of alpine style climbing, and subsequent opening up of new areas and many new routes and peaks. The number of rock climbers will also continue to grow, with sport climbing being prominent. While official standards for guides are now nearly non-existent, the next five years should see a basic development of qualifications. It is safe to say that China's climbing scene is still in a pioneering stage. However, 10 years ago it was no more than a seed. During the next decade I am confident the development of climbing in China will surpass all of our expectations.

JON OTTO, *AAC*

TIEN SHAN

Kashkar, first ascent and traverse. In July a team from Moscow made the first ascent of 6,435m Kashkar (aka Koshkar or Kochkar Bashi), an isolated massif lying in the rarely visited Chinese Tien Shan ca 20km due south of Pobeda. The peak is thought to have been attempted by French in the early 1990s and members of the Moscow party made a reconnaissance in 2002. From a 3,400m base camp on the Chonteren Glacier Alexey Kirienko, David Lehtman, Vladimir Leonenko, Ilya Mikhalev, and Yury Strubtsov spent three days climbing through an ice fall and along a previously unnamed glacier (christened Morenny) to reach the foot of the north ridge of the mountain. The next day, July 11, they climbed up to the first summit on the ridge, Pt 5,550m and camped at 5,400m. The following day they crossed Pt 5,550m, the day after that Pt 5,620m and on the 14th 5,650m. Several days of bad weather pinned them down at 6,000m and at one stage a tent with three occupants was completely buried by avalanche but the summit snow dome was eventually reached on the 21st (from where they were able to contact Moscow by satellite phone). The team continued the traverse by descending the east ridge, a route they had climbed to ca 5,750m in 2002. In one and a half days they reached the Ladybird Glacier and were back at base camp on the 23rd. Climbing in classic style, the team used fixed rope on ca 2,000m of the ascent and 700m of descent, the total length of the route being nearly 14km and Russian 4B/5A. The team admits to being stretched, having taken food and fuel for a maximum of 10 days, rather than the 16 that it took in a round trip from base. They also note at least 20 unclimbed 6,000m peaks on this side of the range.

ANNA PIUNOVA, *mountain.ru, Russia*

KUN LUN SHAN

Kongur Tagh (7,719m), northeast ridge, new route. Kongur Tagh's summit is on China territory close to the border of two big mountain systems, the Pamir and Kun Lun. It is supposed to be the highest mountain of Pamir. In spite of its altitude, Kongur Tagh was unknown till 1900, probably because of its location inside a group of other high peaks. After the first investigation, 56 years passed before the first climb was attempted and 25 more years till four Britons (Peter Boardman, Chris Bonington, Alan Rouse and Joe Tasker) reached the summit in 1981. The summit is on a long ridge, stretching several tens of kilometers from east to west with an average altitude of about 7,000m. There are a few 7,000m peaks situated in the Ridge: Kongur East Summits 7,246, 7,126, 7,200, and Kongur Tube.

Kongur Tagh (7,719m), showing the new Russian route on the northeast ridge. *Alexey Gorbatenkov*

In 2004 there were five attempts to reach the summit. Three expeditions from the north side—from Saint-Petersburg/Riga, Moscow, and Krasnoyarsk (Russia) reached the summit. French and Italian expeditions attempted to make new routes from different directions. From the Saint-Petersburg-Riga expedition, the following people summited: Valery Shamalo, Kirill Korabelnikov and Latvians, Oleg Silin and Valdis Purins. Alexey Gorbatenkov turned back at 7,350m because of frostbite.

The north slopes of the mountain are not that steep, but extremely avalanche prone. The summit is surrounded with a few belts of hanging glaciers. They turned back many expeditions. Our route is not that difficult, the only technical places are a long ice slope at the altitude 4,900m-5,300m and an icefall around 6,000m. The entire route totally escapes rock climbing. Avalanche danger is more or less permanent on the route, but it is possible to find good places to bivouac. In the very beginning of the expedition our bivouac was blown down from the mountain by a fresh snow avalanche. Fortunately we were out of the tent at the moment and were just a bit covered with snow. This made us more serious about choosing good places for the higher camps. All in all, the climb required a lot of power. Probably because it is a long route with a big rise from base camp to the summit: more then 4,000m. Snowshoes are highly recommended between 4,600m and 6,900m. This saves you a lot of energy while breaking trail.

We suggest our route as the easiest way to reach the summit, but one has to keep avalanche danger in a mind. Our base camp was on green meadow at 3,500m. Kyrgyz nomads inhabit this valley. They were very friendly, and we felt comfortable leaving our stuff in the meadow. By negotiating with local people we had fresh meat, chicken and vegetables. They also provided us with donkeys for travel to BC. A few words about logistics: The best way to reach the northern side of Kongur is to start from Kashgar. This ancient city was a key point on the Silk Road. These days it is a big mix of civilizations. Local tour operators provide necessary permits, visa support, transport, and so on. You can buy most of the food you need here, but we did not find cheese or good sausages. You also can buy gas for the gas stoves here, but it's not that easy to find. Local beer bottles have a non-standard volume 0.63 L, which makes it difficult to calculate the total volume you need.

ALEXEY GORBATENKOV, *Russia*

Editor's Note: Japanese attempted the big north northeast ridge in 1981 and returned in 1989 to climb it from the East Karayalak Glacier for the second ascent of the mountain. In 1984 a four-man American team climbed the smaller rib of snow and ice to the right and continued direct to meet the upper section of the 1981 British Route on the west ridge at over 7,300m, where they retreated in deep snow. It was this rib that the St. Petersburg team climbed last summer, moving left onto the snow slopes above the lower north north east ridge, then finally reaching the summit from the left.

Later, another Russian team from Krasnoyarsk led by Nikolay Zakharov first appears to have attempted the north northeast spur (Japanese Route) to the left but then gave up and joined a third team from Moscow (led by Jury Hohlov), which was trying a variant to the St Petersburg line. Both teams summited, making the fourth and fifth ascents of Kongur. These two expeditions branched left from the American line at around 6,100m to reach the summit directly via the right side of the broad snow slopes above the lower north-northeast ridge. The Krasnoyarsk Route differed slightly from the Moscow line. The last Russian team of three reached the top on August 23. Despite attempts in 1998, 2000, and 2003, the Original British Route remains unrepeated.

Kongur East (7,300m), ascent to 7,300m and proposed name for highpoint on east ridge of Kongur (7,719m). Kongur is the main summit of the Kun Lun range, in the southwestern part of China. It is a complex massif with a long span of elevations over 7,000m running west to east. The only direct access to the main summit is from the north or the south. From the west or the east, climbing on Kongur tackles difficult and long ridges eventually leading to the top.

Kongur has been climbed only five times. The first attempt took place in 1981 by an English team led by Chris Bonington, which climbed a difficult ridge on the south side without reaching the top. A second effort led another strong party (Bonington, Boardman, Rouse, and Tasker) to the top via the west ridge, which is easily reached from the western slopes via the southwest rib but involves a long stretch at high altitude and a technical section on a sharp rocky ridge just before the summit. The second ascent was made by a Japanese team from the Kyoto Karakoram Club, led by Ryuichi Kotani, which climbed a prominent and difficult ridge in the center of the north face in 1989. In 2004 three separate Russian expeditions climbed from the north, as reported elsewhereSince the south face is huge and bordered by slopes prone to avalanche danger, what remained for us was the east ridge. Thus, during the 100th anniversary celebrations of the Club Alpino Accademico Italiano (1904-2004), an expedition was organized to climb Kongur via the northeast side of the mountain, where a prominent ridge (northeast) leads to an intermediate summit at 5,975 m, which is connected to the upper plateau by another long stretch of ridge (east) ending at an elevation of about 7,204m as marked on the Chinese map. We had a good picture from Daniel Waugh, who trekked a few times around the mountain. From this a relatively safe line was identified, although the first part was not yet clear.

The expedition team included Armando Antola, Donatella Barbera (doctor), Giovanni Ghiglione, Massimo Giuliberti, Carla Marten Canavesio, Claudio Moretto, Ezio Mosca, Beppe Villa, and myself as team leader.

We met our liason officer in Kashgar on July 20 and had a first look at the impressive east ridge of Kongur. What you see from Kashgar is only the upper part of our climb, above 5,800m. Base camp was set on a green valley bordering the Tugralkuluxi Glacier at about 3,850m, on July 22. Operations started immediately. In about one week we placed camp 1 at 4,600m, fixed ropes through the steep (60°) slopes leading to the ridge, and placed camp 2 at 5,600m. Weather condi-

Above the rock step on the east ridge of Kongur. *Mauro Penasa*

tions were strange, with high temperatures during the day, and usually snowfall during the late afternoon and night. The mountain was deeply snow-covered and in general conditions were wet.

A first attempt to reach the first peak at 5,950m was frustrated by bad weather. This waste of time forced us to climb in alpine style from camp 2.

On August 7 we camped at the foot of the east ridge of Kongur at 5,800m after descending the 5,950m peak; the 1,400m upper part of the ridge was impressive. The next two days were passed climbing relatively easy ridge slopes in deep snow, up to a rocky tooth at 6,600m. It took half a day to climb past this difficult section on rotten rock and unconsolidated snow. We could not fix more than one rope on the difficult stretch, thus there was no chance to place a higher camp. On August 11, at 17:00, Giuliberti, Villa, and I were at the end of the ridge, at about 7,300m on a small elevation that we called Kongur East, higher with respect to the point marked 7,204m on the Chinese maps. Having no experience with snow caves and in worsening weather we decided to put an end to our adventure.

This route, although long and challenging, is mostly safe and protected from avalanches. From BC it is 3,600m of vertical gain (due to a 200m loss below point 5,975m) with a much longer development. Unfavorable snow conditions were experienced regardless of the weather: almost every night a 10-20 cm snowfall kept the slopes difficult for climbing, and even during sunny days the snow was never transformed into more comfortable terrain.

From the highest point reached, that is from Kongur East, an additional climbing day would be required to reach the main summit at 7,719m. It is a long stretch (about 3 km), but only 400m have to be gained and snow conditions on the upper and windy part of the ridge are much better. We entitled the route "Ridge of the Centenario CAAI," in commemoration of this important event. We have asked the Xiniang Mountaineering Association to have the name Kongur East added to the official maps.

MAURO PENASA, *Club Alpino Accademico Italiano*

Along the east ridge of Kongur. *Mauro Penasa*

Kara Kunlun, Dolkun Muztag (6,355m), first ascent. The student mountaineering party of Tokai University Alpine Club was the first to climb an unexplored peak (6,355m) in the Kara Kunlun mountains at the westernmost end of the Xinjiang Kunlun in China. The Kara Kunlun mountains are about 15 km southeast of Mustagh Ata (west 75° 11' 18", north 38° 11' 29"). The summit is not visible from the foot of the mountains, so it was nearly unknown until our party reached the summit.

Our party consisted of climbing leader Yuka Komatsu (student), expedition leader Yoshitsugu Deriha, coach Kazuya Hiraide, Dr. Gen Sasao as our party doctor, and six other students (Taku Kojima, Tatsuya Aoki, Seitaro Ageta, Yusuke Hirano, Hidetaka Saruhashi, Satoshi Nomura). After the aptitude test at the Tokai University Medical School hospital, the low-pressure training at our laboratory of Sport Medicine Science, meticulous preparations were finished, and the party left Japan for the Kara Kunlun mountains on July 30.

On August 2, we arrived in the village of Takuman at the foot of the mountains. On August 4, our party completed setting up our base camp at the end of Cocoshir Glacier at an altitude of 4,500m. We set up the first camp on the glacier at 4,900m on August 7, where suddenly the sharp triangular pyramid summit of Kara Kunlun (6,355m) appeared. We started our real climbing of the mountain from this first camp. We went up higher and higher from the moraine on the glacier aiming at the snowy plateau toward the summit of Kara Kunrun. Our party built the second camp on the snowy field at an altitude of 5,600m on August 12.

The route to the summit was extremely difficult. We struggled long and hard, climbing the ice wall of a steep couloir and an ice/snow wall to get to the ridgeline. On August 14, we fixed the rope 600m up to the ridgeline.

At 6:30 a.m. on August 15, the three climbers of our party, Yuka Komatsu, Tatsuya Aoki, and Kazuya Hiraide, started to climb the peak as the first attempt team and fixed the rope 800m up to the top ridgeline leading to the summit. At 1:10 p.m., they reached the summit after a long and arduous climb. On August 16, the second ascent team, Yoshitsugu Deriha, Taku Kojima, and Hidetaka Saruhashi reached the summit. The weather was changing for the worse and we decided to be satisfied with six climbers in our party gain the top of the peak.

We cleared the second camp in a snowstorm. On August 19, when we got back to the base camp it was covered with thick fresh snow. On August 20 we cleared base camp and began moving down the mountain in heavy snowfall.

Yuka, our climbing leader on this expedition, was the first woman ever to lead a student mountaineering party of Tokai University. She led the entire route. It was an impressive and praiseworthy achievement for a student mountaineering party to reach the summit of an unexplored peak in a greater range of Asia. The main peak of Kara Kunlun mountains had not been named yet, so we named it Dolkun Muztag (Wave of Mountains), whose origin comes from the combination of Dolkun (Wave) and Muztag (Mountain) in the Uighur language.

YOSHITSUGU DERIHA, *Tokai University Alpine Club*

Adapted from Japanese Alpine News, TAMOTSU NAKAMURA, *Editor*

QINGHAI-TIBET PLATEAU

Qiajajima I (5,930m), first ascent. Qiajajima massif is the highest mountain in the headwaters of the Mekong River on the Qinghai-Tibet plateau. It is located at about N33° 28' and E95° 11' in the most isolated region of the Yushu Tibetan Autonomous Prefecture, Qinghai Province. The massif has two peaks, Qiajajima I (5,930m) and Qiajajima II (5,890m), which are indicated on the topographical map 1:100,000 of the China People's Liberation Army. They remained unexplored because the region had long been closed to foreigners. In 1997 the first special permit was granted to a foreign party, the Niigata Mountaineering Association, for entering the unvisited area and attempting the untrodden peaks. The association sent an expedition and that year succeeded on Qiajajima II, but the highest peak, Qiajajima I, was not scaled due to unexpected frequent onsets of snow in spite of the summer season. In 2004 came another chance. I joined as deputy leader for an expedition to re-challenge Qiajajima I.

One microbus and two jeeps carried all the expedition members from Xining to Hot springs (336km), Yushu (510km) along the Qinghai-Sichuan Highway, then Zadoi (231km), Zaqeg-Zaigela campsite (76km) in five days from July 15 to 20. There we employed six muleteers and pack animals of 18 horses and eight yaks. On July 22 the caravan marched up 10km along the stream to a campsite at 4,444m. On July 23, heavy rainfall, strong wind and increase of river water made us stop. On July 24, we went up 10km along the main stream. A large landslide blocked the trail before it entered a gorge. We were forced to set up Base Camp there at 4,690m. On July 25, as it was not possible to take advantages of yaks and horses from BC, loads were ferried up by porters. The advance base camp (ABC) was built at 4,800m on the riverbank of the upper stream. The Chinese members and muleteers waited at BC until the climbing was over. On July 26 two members went ahead to pave the route. ABC-II was placed at 4,900m, and C1 was built at 5,140m, as ABC was too far away from the wall. Loads were carried to the higher camp. On July 27, C2 was set up at 5,360m at the foot of the wall.

On July 29 an advance party of three members commenced an assault on the summit. As there was no space to pitch a tent, they bivouacked at 5,587m. On July 30, they started climbing in the early morning. After ascending a chimney, they reached the main ridge, where they made a second bivouac at 5,780m. On July 31 the knife-edged main ridge became steeper. They detoured around the ridge to the north side and then reached the summit of Qiajajima I (5,930m) at 15:15. GPS indicated N33° 28' 33" and E95° 11' 33". The summiters were Shin-ichi Abe, Katsutoshi Suzuki, and Miho Kakinuma. On the way down they were again forced to bivouac, at about 5,600m on the wall, roped together. A fierce snowstorm bothered them all the night, dropping 20cm of snow. On August 11 everyone returned to Niigata via Xian.

Expedition members from the Niigata Mountaineering Association: leader: Shin-ichi Abe (57); deputy leaders: Ryoichi Matsuzaka (70), Katsutoshi Suzuki (60); members: Norihiro Asano (64), Shizuo Sugai (52), Tatsuko Anno (58), Miho Kakinuma (25), Yoko Abe (28). Expedition members from the China Qinghai Mountaineering Association: Liaison officer: Lei Wang; cook: Haixin An; driver: Haichou Shou, Teiho Jang; interpreter: Takahiro Kakiuchi (Japanese).

JAN editor's notes: There are three outstanding mountain massifs in the source of the Mekong River. They form a watershed between the main stream of the Mekong River and a large tributary of the upper Yangtze River (Chinese name is Tongtian He). From east to west: 1) Qiajajima and neighboring peaks. 2) Sedari (5,770m) and 5,700m–5,800m peaks ranging to the west, where glaciers are most developed. This massif remains unvisited. No photographs of the mountains have been taken. 3) A massif at the true source of the Mekong River, where some 5,500m peaks were already climbed by a party of the Tokyo University of Agriculture, Japan, in 1994.

RYOICHI MATSUZAKA, *Niigata Mountaineering Association, Japan*
Adapted from Japanese Alpine News, TAMOTSU NAKAMURA, *Editor*

SICHUAN

CHOLA SHAN

Ganzi Tibetan Prefecture, Mt. Chola (6,148m), third ascent; correction to 1988 "Cheru" ascent and altitude. We made the third known successful ascent of Mt. Chola (Lat: 31° 48' 0", Long: 99° 7' 0") on July 22, 2003. Chola is located in western Sichuan province, Ganzi Tibetan Prefecture, Dege County, near the eastern Tibet border. Our team put the first Tibetan on the summit. It was also the second ascent by Chinese and Americans. The summiters were Yihua Ma, Terry Choi, Jin Zhu, Ying Liu, Ping Wang, and me.

We approached the mountain from Xinlu Lake. Our route followed the east glacier to camp 1 at 5,000m. We then followed a steep slope to the right of a sub-peak marked as 5,290m on our map. From our camp 2 at 5,450m (on a large snow plateau) we followed the north slope to the summit. The last 100-plus meters to the summit is along a ridgeline.

We believe we followed the same route as Charlie Fowler's alpine ascent in 1997. He listed Chola as 6,141m high (*AAJ* 1999, ppg. 210-213, and *AAJ* 1998, ppg. 353-357). We have listed it as 6,148m since that is what our GPS read at the summit. The latitude and longitude are

Pk. II
6168 m?

Pk. I
6148 m

Mt. Chola. *Jon Otto*

the same.

Correction to the joint China-Japanese 1988 climb: This climb is listed in the 1990 *AAJ* article (p. 300) as Mt. Cheru and is recorded as 6,168m (lat: 31° 30' 0", long: 99° 0' 0"). This is the height shown on Chinese topographical maps from the 1970s. This peak is about 500m (direct line) from the peak we summited. Comparing photographs from the China-Japanese 1988 successful ascent, we verified that we summited the same peak. Thus, they actually summited peak 6,148 (Lat: 31° 48' 0", Long: 99° 7' 0"). Peak 6,168 is still unclimbed. From the summit of Mt. Chola we looked across at peak 6,168m. We were unable to tell if it was higher or not. Both are very close in height. The elevations listed on the old topographical maps can be off by 20-30m.

Basically, this mountain has two peaks about the same elevation in close proximity to each other. This is confusing. The ridgeline out to peak 6,168m is much longer and sharper than Mt. Chola's ridge. One would have to climb both peaks with the same GPS unit to verify which is actually higher.

I suggest one name be chosen for this mountain—either Cheru or Chola. Then, each of these two peaks should be differentiated as I and II. Peak I: The peak that has been climbed (Lat: 31° 48' 0", Long: 99° 7' 0"). Peak II: The unclimbed peak listed as 6,168m on Chinese topographical maps from the 1970s (lat: 31° 30' 0", long: 99° 0' 0"). Note: We used a 1:100,000 scale Chinese topographical map from the 1970s.

The best time to climb this mountain is late July through August. During May the heavy spring snows melt rapidly due to warming air temperatures, which leads to unstable conditions. Late autumn should also be a good time but prepare for very cold temperatures.

Our climbing team consisted of: Jon Otto, USA (leader); Ma, Yihua, Beijing/Chengdu (leader); Terry Choi (Cai, Gantang), Hong Kong; Zhu, Jin, Jiangsu, China; Liu, Cong, Guangdong, China; Liu, Ying, Chengdu; Lin, Chao, Chengdu; Wang, Ping, Sichuan (Tibetan); Chen,

Gang, Shaanxi, China; Ding, Yinglu, Shanghai, China.

JON OTTO, *AAC*

SHALULI SHAN

Kham region: Jarjinjabo, Janmo Spire summit block, first ascent. In August Bernie Laforest, Ben Ditto, Jonathan Knight, Steve Cater, and I journeyed to the Jarjinjabo Massif in the Sichuan Province of China. With help from the American climber Jon Otto, we hired a translator and two 4-wheel-drive vehicles. From Chengdu, our drive took us three days over a route that has

Janmo Spire, Jarjinjabo Massif. *Tommy Chandler*

the reputation of being the highest and worst road in the world. The Chinese are on a paving frenzy, however, and the road is quickly being subdued. Our trip was similar to the American team in 2002 (see Pete Athans' feature article in the *AAJ* 2003) in that we traveled first to Litang en route to Zhopu Pasture, the gateway to the Jarjinjabo massif. Our stopover in Litang enabled us to acclimatize, as well as mingle with the Tibetans at the largest horse racing festival in the Kham region.

The dreary rainy weather began to clear as we arrived at our destination, and we quickly started outfitting our high camp and getting acclimatized. Ben and I were psyched for the main wall of Jabo, whereas Jonathan and Bernie were looking to the unclimbed spire atop Janmo, and Steve and Mark simply wanted to climb both formations and explore the surrounding walls.

Over three climbing days Jonathan and Bernie completed three different routes on Janmo Spire that reached a common highpoint. The highpoint positioned them at the base of a sum-mit block, which they began by climbing a short off-width to a ledge. From the ledge they reached the top by delicate face climbing, placing four bolts and one pin on lead from stances and hooks. Their complete route went at IV 5.11R and is reminiscent of a desert tower with a classic summit block pitch. After this they climbed a new variation to a route on the face of Jabo at III 5.11. Also of note were two excellent single pitches Jonathan put up on and near the base of Jabo, just above our camp.

Ben and I climbed one new route on the lower section of Jabo, which was four pitches at 5.10, and two new routes on the beautiful upper face. The first one of these followed cracks up and left towards the southeast buttress. It didn't quite make the summit, but was still excellent climbing on beautiful rock that went at III 5.10. The second went straight up the face, again with beautiful straight-in hand and finger cracks, and was probably III 5.10+ A1 (a few pulls through a wet section). We also repeated a route Jonathan and Bernie had done on Janmo.

Steve and Mark started out by summiting Jabo via the east ridge and climbing Janmo via a route on the right side. Their first day on Janmo was hampered by funky weather, but on their second attempt they made it to just below the summit block. They then made an attempt on another spire to the west of camp, but bad climbing conditions cut this attempt short.

We would like to express our gratitude to the AAC for supporting this trip through the Lyman-Spitzer climbing grant, as well as our friends and families for the support they gave. Not only did we make some great friends in China, we also came back as better friends than before. We were truly lucky to be able to experience a place as remote and unspoiled as this.

TOMMY CHANDLER, *AAC*

DAXUE SHAN

Haizi Shan (5,820m), east ridge, north summit ascent and main summit attempt. Known to Tibetans as Ja-ra (King of the mountains), Haizi Shan is a striking peak north of Kangding in a region that was formerly known as East Tibet. It is most easily approached from the north via Danba, allowing a drive up a rough track to base camp in a forested valley at 3,800m. An alternative is to trek in 1-2 days from the roadhead in the Yala valley, reached from Kangding. The north face is featured in Tamotsu Nakamura's article in *AAJ* 2003, page 155.

An Alpine Club (UK) expedition —consisting of Richard Isherwood, Martin Scott, Bill Thurston, and me— attempted the peak in spring. Haizi Shan had been attempted a few times before, notably by Neil Carruthers, who reached the lower north summit in fall 2003 (report on www.summit-post.com). We reached base camp on

Dick Isherwood high on the east ridge of Haizi Shan. *Geoff Cohen*

April 16, rather too early in the season, as the mountain was still plastered in deep soft snow. This made for slow and frustrating progress through thick rhododendrons followed by a twisting moraine ridge. We climbed up to an obvious snow shelf below the east ridge (very clear on Nakamura's photo) and left a gear dump there on the 25th. Poor weather and lack of food then forced us to retreat to base camp for a few days. On our return we camped at the gear dump, and on May 3 we climbed up the east ridge, getting excellent early morning views of the Minya Konka range to the south. The ridge was corniced and icy in places, but not technically difficult. Dick Isherwood and I reached the north summit about 11 a.m. and continued to the saddle below the main summit. We climbed the first of two steep icy steps, but reluctantly turned around before the second in order to avoid an unplanned bivouac. Our high point was less than 200m below the summit. On the descent from the north summit we took the glacier below the east ridge, as Carruthers had done. This necessitated a couple of abseils over short ice

Looking over at the summit of Haizi Shan from the high-point. *Geoff Cohen*

walls, and would not have been an attractive ascent route in the prevailing snow conditions.

Haizi Shan offers the possibility of many harder alpine-style routes. The valley around base camp is well populated in springtime by Tibetans collecting caterpillar fungus. We were very well supported at base camp by the staff of Sichuan Adventure travel (Chengdu).

GEOFF COHEN, *AAC*

Mt. Edgar and Xiao Pangwa attempts. During the spring a British expedition comprising Angela Benham, Chris Drinkwater, Titch Kavangh and Andrew Phillips gained permission to attempt Mt. Edgar (aka E Gongga: 6,618m), in the northern sector of the range (J. Huston Edgar was archaeologist with the China Inland Mission in Kangding and was important in the development of historical and topographical knowledge of the area). Unfortunately, due to the prevailing poor weather they were unable to find a safe approach to the mountain.

Until shortly before leaving the UK, the team only knew of one previous attempt on this fine pyramid: in 1982 Stuart Hepburn's British expedition first planned to examine the difficult north side but on finding the approach up the Nan Men Guan Valley impossible due to heavy flooding, macheted a route into the opposite side of the mountain and made attempts on both the south and west faces. Bad weather and poor snow conditions forced them down. However, last spring, just as the British team was about to leave for Chengdu, they learnt of an unreported ascent in 2000 by a Korean expedition, which, it is believed, climbed the mountain via the easier south face. Nonetheless, the British team decided it would keep Edgar as its primary objective and attempt to make the first ascent of the peak from the impressive north side. This would require possibly the first exploration of the upper Nan Men Guen, though the 1981 British Army Expedition had been some way up the valley during their reconnaissance of Jiazi.

After establishing Base Camp on April 2 below the snout of the glacier at 3,400m and two more camps in the valley at 3,800m and 4,200m, bad weather prevented much progress up the approach glacier to the foot of the north face. Finally on the 20th the team decided that the second serac barrier was just too dangerous and retreated, turning instead to two lower unclimbed peaks to the north on the opposite side of the main glacier. These were named Xiao Pangwa (5,630m) and Da Pangwa (5,910m). A 750m-high, east-facing snow couloir led to the crest of a ridge, which in turn ran first north west then north to the first summit, Xiao Pangwa. On the 22nd, Drinkwater, Kavangh, and Phillips reached the crest at 5,400m after climbing the ca 45° couloir through the previous night, then progressed along it to a suitable bivouac site. A little further on the climbing looked much more serious and time-consuming than they had expected and in the next two-three kilometers of ridge there appeared to be no suitable campsite. As the three were already weak and dehydrated, they decided to retreat.

Finding what they believed to be a sheltered site on the edge of the couloir at around 5,200m, they stopped to sit out a rapidly approaching storm. During the evening the site was battered by a shower of rock and ice, one large lump tearing right through the tent. It was a relieved trio that finally reached base camp the following day.

LINDSAY GRIFFIN, *Mountain INFO Editor, CLIMB magazine*

Longemain (6,294m) and Daddomain (6,380m), first ascents. The excitement started early on this trip. Originally heading to eastern Tibet, our permits were cancelled the day before we headed to Lhasa from Chengdu. Some parties had evidently annoyed the authorities by climbing illegally in the Nyenqentanghla East area—a warning to us all. Once we managed to get a smile back on our faces we refocused on the Daxue Shan Range in western Sichuan and in particular on the unclimbed peaks of Longemain (6,294m) and Daddomain (6,380m). Unfortunately, no one could supply us with a photo and we had no idea what the mountains even looked like until we woke up one fine morning in basecamp.

Longemain and Daddomain lie just north of the gob smacking pyramid of Gongga Shan (Minya Konka, 7,756m) and their western aspects drain down to the Moxi valley. We walked in from the village of Laoyulian over the Buchi La inr four days and set up base camp in a pleasant grassy meadow at 3,870m in the Moxi Valley. A few days later we established an ABC on the glacier under the icecliff fes-

The west ridge of Daddomain. *Sean Waters*

tooned west face of Longemain. We initially intended to reach the col between the two peaks, but a closer look revealed the prospect of scuttling back and forth under large unstable icecliffs. We changed our focus to the west ridge of Longemain. Access to the ridge was up a long couloir of depressingly unconsolidated snow and from there the route followed the main ridge to the top. We summited on October 20 in three days from ABC, after an earlier acclimatization foray to camp one, and an electrifying episode in which we were both hit by lightening. The route was about Alaskan Grade 4.

The route of Longemain's first ascent. *Sean Waters*

After a recce to check out the northern side of Daddomain we came back to our original ABC and, after sitting out poor weather, headed up a long rotten rock couloir, which boasted a lovely coating of loose snow. That deposited us on the west ridge, which we followed via two camps to a shoulder on Daddomain's subsidiary west peak. Once over that we dropped into a basin that led us around and up to the main summit on the 29th. This route was of similar grade to Longemain, although snow conditions were much more convivial.

The weather was mixed. Early in the trip we had clear mornings with regular afternoon thunderstorms. This gave way to a short period of settled clear weather, which in turn gave way to 10 days of unsettled weather with no discernable pattern. All weather came from the Tibetan Plateau to the west, and by early November had become very cold.

This is a great area with wonderful locals and plenty of new route potential on some big, steep faces. Longemain: 29 deg 39.110 min N, 101 deg 50.241 min E; Daddomain: 29 deg 40.503 min N, 101 deg 50.250 min E.

SEAN WATERS and JO KIPPAX, New Zealand Alpine Club

QIONGLAI RANGE

Lixian County, Bipeng Valley, Half Ridge Peak (Banji Feng) (5,430m), north face, first ascent. On May 4 our team made the first successful ascent of Half Ridge Peak (Lat: 31° 14' 41.1", Long: 102° 55' 39") via the north face. This is a semi-technical route of snow mixed with some rock (rock useful for placing pro but no actual mixed climbing required) and ice near the summit. We descended via the southwest ridge to the saddle with Peak 5,370m and then down. The climb starts at the ShangHaiZi parking lot in Bipeng valley. From the parking lot, walk back down the road about 400 yards to the first stream. You can clearly see the glacier from this vantage point. Turn right up the valley following the left side of the stream. The trail should be marked. The walk starts through a coniferous forest, which seamlessly melds into a rhododendron forest. At an

Summit Camp on Half Ridge Peak. *Jon Otto*

altitude of around 4,050m, you start to get above treeline. The trail meanders up a steep grassy slope to the left, then continues to camp 1 at 4,454m. The next day we trudged south through deep, wet snow and made camp 2 (summit camp) on the glacier at 5,026m. This glacier is split into two parts by a small rocky ridge that starts from the summit and cuts straight down the valley dividing it in half like a backbone. You must cross this backbone to reach camp 2.

On May 4 we went for the summit. On the lower part of the route at the base of the gully there was a short section of chest deep snow. We stayed to the left of the gully to avoid poten-tial avalanches, then followed the rocks around left and up. The steepest section is about half way up the rocks and may reach 45°. Near the summit is ice. The weather became continually worse, and by the time we reached the top visibility had dropped to 200 feet. To date, we have established four routes to the summit. They all start from camp 2 (summit camp) at 5,026m. This climb was run by the Arete Alpine Instruction Center (AAIC), a company I co-run based out of Chengdu. See www.aaic.cn for more information.

The team members were: Jon Otto, USA (leader); Ma, Yihua, Beijing/Chengdu (leader); Su, Rongqin, Chengdu; Ni, Hui, Chengdu; Liu, Qing, Chengdu; Sun, Ping, Beijing.

JON OTTO, *AAC*

Bipeng Valley, Peak 5,370m, first ascent. On April 27 Rongqing Su (China) and I (USA) made the first ascent of Peak 5,370 (so named because it is 5,370m) (Lat: 31° 14' 30", Long: 102° 55' 04"). This may be a sub-peak of Peak 5414.

Su Rongqin on the summit of Peak 5,370m. *Jon Otto*

Our climb started in the ShangHaiZi parking lot of Bipeng valley. We made camp 1 on a grassy field on April 25 at 4,450m. The next day we walked up through deep, wet snow and made camp on the glacier at 5,050m. On April 27, we walked up the glacier to the saddle between Peak 5,414 (to the west) and Half Ridge Peak (to the northeast, 5,430m). From the saddle, we followed the ridgeline west to the summit of Peak 5,370. The last 50m involved climb-

ing up a 50°-60° slope of loose snow on rock near the ridge and a small section of thin ridgeline to the summit, which can only stand one person at a time.

JON OTTO, *AAC*

Bipeng Valley Nature Preserve, background information. Bipeng Valley has at least 40 (maybe over 60) unclimbed 5,000+ meter peaks. In 2003 a paved access road was completed into the valley. This makes accessing this cluster of mountains easy and fast. The road ends in the heart of the valley at the ShangHaiZi parking lot (3,560m). There are two buildings, one a welcome center and restaurant, the other

Photo taken from the ShangHaiZi parking lot in the Bipeng Valley; this is the prominent peak on the southeast side of the valley. Unclimbed. *Jon Otto*

View of south-side peaks in the Bipeng Valley from near the parking lot. Unclimbed. *Jon Otto*

a guesthouse (at present you must pitch your tent on the guesthouse floor). The mountains range in difficulty from walk-ups to glacier climbs to world class vertical walls of rock and ice. The rock is good quality granite or a hard conglomorate.

Bipeng Valley is a Nature Preserve and you must buy an entrance ticket. Climbing is allowed and supported by the Valley's management company, although there are some bureaucratic details. There are certain regulations for climbing in China. My company AAIC works together with the Bipeng Valley's management and the Sichuan Mountaineering Association to encourage favorable policies and trouble-free access into these mountains. AAIC offers information to climbers, guided ascents to the mountains of Sichuan, and can assist with organizing any aspect of your climb into these mountains.

Access: The drive from Chengdu to Bipeng Valley is normally 6-7 hours. A highway will be completed in 2006 that will shorten the driving time by 1-2 hours. The route from Chengdu goes past Dujiangyan, Wenchuan, and Lixian County. If taking the public bus, buy a ticket to Lixian. From Lixian hire a mini-van to drive you up the valley, which takes just over an hour.

Unclimbed peaks at the head of the Bipeng Valley on the south side. Photo taken from summit camp (5,026m) on Half Ridge Peak. *Jon Otto*

Rental vehicles in Chengdu are also convenient and reasonably priced.

Seasonal climbing conditions: It is difficult to say what is the best time to climb in Bipeng Valley. Sichuan is semi-tropical and the weather changes rapidly. During the summer months you get longer stretches of alternating good and bad weather. There is little snow and the glacier is mostly ice. April is general nice but the heavy spring snows do not melt off until June, so snowshoes are recommended. Autumn is generally clear weather, but colder, and there is normally only moderate snow accumulation at the higher elevations.

At the higher elevations snow starts to accumulate in November and by the end of February there can be permanent snow at an elevation of 3,000m. There is a higher risk from avalanches during this period and potentially through May. By the end of winter there is a thick, heavy snowpack. By May the temperatures start to warm rapidly causing the snow to become thick and wet. During this time the snow line varies greatly depending on aspect. On north-facing slopes deep snow can start at 4,000m, while on south facing slopes it may not start until 4,600m.

Thus, there is snow at camp 1 (4,454m) on Half Ridge Peak into May, and the walk to camp 2 (summit camp) requires a lot of postholing. Over the next month or so most of this snow melts and in August this section of the climb is mostly dirt and rock, making the walk to camp 2 much easier and more straightforward. In October, camp 2, again, starts to get a permanent blanket of snow.

JON OTTO, *AAC*

Mt. Siguniang (6,249m), southeast ridge, second ascent. Mt. Siguniang was first summited in August 1981 by a Japanese team via the southeast ridge (*AAJ* 1982). We made the second successful ascent of this route, with six members summiting on November 17 and 18. The approach to this route is via Changping Valley from Rilong town, then up a side valley named GanHaizi to basecamp. The route follows the glacier to a 600m long (450m altitude gain) couloir up the west face of the southeast ridge. The route then continues along the southeast ridge to the summit.

We had attempted this same route in August of 2003. At that time, there was constant rockfall from all sides of the mountain, raining down pillow-size chunks of rock from several hundred meters above. The mountain has two obvious rock strata. The lower layer seems to be granite or a hard conglomerate of excellent quality, while the upper layer is a brownish, fragmenting, at places almost shale-like rock of poor quality. The dividing line between these two rock types is around 5,200m.

After almost being killed by this rockfall below the couloir, we went around the backside to the glacier between Siguniang's main peak and 3rd peak, climbing up 14 pitches on the southeast side of the southeast ridge to an altitude of 5,600m.

The "Pearl Necklace" stretch of Siguniang's southeast ridge, with high camp visible below. *Jon Otto*

It is clear that the mountain conditions have changed since the 1980s. Rockfall during the summer months make the mountain too dangerous. Whether subsequent summers will see as much rockfall as in summer 2003 is hard to say. Judging by that year's quantity of falling rock and reports from previous years, it is safe to say that summers will be unpredictable.

In 2004 we chose to climb the mountain in November, when the route is frozen, there tend to be more days of clear weather, and it is not too cold (though it was pretty cold). The first 15 vertical meters at the bottom of the couloir was good ice. The couloir was mostly snow and ice climbing. We secured the fixed line with pitons on the lower half of the couloir and with ice screws on the remainder of the route. There are no flat spots to put a tent on the entire route. For our high camp we had to shovel the loose snow off a section of the ridge at 5,834m to create a small platform. This platform was no more than five feet wide, just wide enough for a small tent.

Seasonal climbing conditions: I made my first visit to Mt. Siguniang's glacier in late April 1996. At that time there was a heavy, wet snow pack starting around 4,600m. Although April can be nice, the heavy spring snows do not melt off until May or June. During the summer months you get longer stretches of alternating good and bad weather, but due to potential rockfall, I do not suggest attempting Siguniang July through September. Autumn months are good because the weather tends to be clearer and there is only moderate snow accumulation, but there can be heavy winds and it is quite cold. Winter ascents are possible (very, very cold), and from December through spring be especially aware of avalanche danger.

Team members: Cao Jun, China (Leader); Jia Guiting, China. Summiters on November 17: Jon Otto, USA; Ma Yihua, China; Tim Boelter, USA (film maker). Summiters on November 18, all from China: Chen Junchi, Kang Hua, Chen Zigang.

JON OTTO, *AAC*

Siguniang, north face attempt; Siguniang North, attempt; Camel Peaks. The Siguniang Group was visited in May by UK alpinists, Tom Chamberlain, Dave Evans, Dave Hollinger, and Andy Sharpe. This team, which set up Base Camp in the Chang Ping, had as its aims the lengthy unclimbed southwest ridge of Siguniang and the uncompleted line on the north face attempted in 1981 by Jack Tackle and party. However, from the outset the mountains had a largely snowy appearance and the weather allowed no real improvement, being very unsettled throughout their stay.

In order to acclimatize the team turned to the humped Camel Peaks to the north. These are the two peaks on the northern rim of the valley, occupied by Pts 5,202m and 5,484m. They were both climbed from the col between the two summits by Charlie Fowler in 1994. First Chamberlain and Evans climbed Camel West from the gap and subsequently Hollinger and Sharpe climbed West and East peaks from the gap. Both peaks gave straightforward snowy climbing and were thought to be of equal height—around 5,510m. Chamberlain and Evans then attempted Pt 5,672m (dubbed Snow Goose), the next peak north of Signuniang North (5,700m: a subsidiary summit at the base of the north ridge of Siguniang) but retreated in heavy snowfall. They then set out for a fine rock tower on the west side of the valley dubbed Paine Peak, probably corresponding to Pt 5,422m on the map, but were again thwarted by the weather. A final attempt on Snow Goose reached the 5,200m col below the south ridge, then continued up snow on this ridge until a point estimated to be only 150m from this virgin summit. Here, the slope was so dangerously avalanche prone that the pair had no option but to retreat.

Meanwhile, Hollinger and Sharpe had attempted the north face of Siguniang. They swam up steep unconsolidated snow over granite to reach the crest of the spur tried by the Americans in 1981, then climbed several pitches of Scottish 3-4 mixed before realizing the route was totally out of condition and would prove far too time consuming for the very limited breaks in the weather. A few days later they went around to the col below Snow Goose and attempted the northeast ridge of unclimbed Siguniang North, carrying enough food so that if a fine spell materialized they could continue up the north ridge of Siguniang itself (descended by Fowler and Ramsden in 2002). They took to the right flank of the ridge and climbed about 200m of this 500m line, negotiating wet snow over very shattered rock, before deciding to bail in heavy spindrift. As if on cue a sustained blizzard moved in and accompanied them all the way back to Base. For the more ice/mixed climbing that the area offers, the team feel a return visit earlier in the year, perhaps from January to March when the weather is rumored to be more settled, would prove fruitful.

LINDSAY GRIFFIN, *Mountain INFO Editor, CLIMB magazine*

Siguniang National Park, Suang Qiao Gou Valley: Mi Mi Shan (5,018m), first ascent; Heart of Cow (Niuxim Shan) (4,942m), north face, first ascent. Giant pandas and Chinese acrobats swung the balance. After being inspired by Tomatsu Nakamura's splendid photographs of blank-looking granite and unclimbed walls featured in the Japanese Alpine News, we were inspired to find out more about this magical-looking area. No mega objectives presented themselves, but nevertheless we headed off in search of an Oriental adventure in the Suang Qiao Gou Valley, close to Mt. Siguniang.

Mick Fowler helped out by providing more useful information, as did Tanja and Andrej Grmovsek from Slovenia. With only three weeks to climb, arriving in Chengdu in July was a gamble due to forecasts for heavy rainfall. Our Chinese helper and cook extraordinaire Lenny was enthusiastic as we shopped for provisions playing the pass-the-parcel, guess-what's-in-the-packet game. The bus to Rilong called, and we set off on the six- to seven-hour journey through wooded panda-infested valleys. After visiting the curiously named "Tourist Service Centre" for our permissions and paying an environmental protection fee and park entrance, we set off on the tourist bus up the valley.

On this expedition we climbed two new peaks, one a subsidiary and one a main peak in the Suang Qiao Gou Valley. Setting up base camp at 4,100m, we took equipment to the base of the route near a stunning aquamarine lake and some fine three-pitch E6 climbing leading to the shoulder of Putala Shan. On the walls of a long rock ridge opposite Putala Shan we ascended right of a spur for 9 pitches, 350m at E3/E4 5c, to reach a sub peak we called Mi Mi Shan (5,018m). Should you be feeling particularly brave it may be possible to descend into a notch and then ascend a tricky loose and extremely narrow ridge from here to reach the main summit of 5,400m. We were in no fit condition for that. The granite intermittently formed rubble strewn ledges as we weaved our way up. Behind, the pointy snow-flushed cirque beckoned for another day. Many big walls and spires rise up and extend into the distance, as well as a feast of unclimbed peaks in the 5,200m-5,900m range.

The second objective we went for was "Heart of Cow" (Niuxim Shan), named by the Chinese. According to Lenny a Japanese team had attempted it the year before and reached

Anne Arran enjoying the view of unclimbed walls from the summit of Heart of Cow. *John Arran*

The route of the first ascent of Mi Mi Shan. *John Arran*

approximately half way. Rhododendrons repelled us from attempting the longest face, as swimming and wriggling proved unbearable without a machete. We set up the ABC bivi cave at 4,400m and spent a day hanging out, huddled, freezing, and surrounded by low-lying mist. During the night we recycled our last tea bag three times, unable to sleep without sleeping bags.

A sporting damp British 6a traverse led to a section of beautiful rock. The unclimbed Mt. Hunter and its rotten dark rock lay behind, still shrouded with stubborn cloud, and other unclimbed peaks behind winked at us in view. Just another couple of pitches and we emerged at 6 p.m. on the easy but occasionally narrow summit ridge. We climbed the north face and ridge to reach the summit. Heart of Cow (4,942m) became for a moment "our" peak and we realised looking at the descent why it had not been climbed before.

Many thanks to the Mount Everest Foundation, BMC and UK Sport for providing some expedition funding.

ANNE ARRAN, *United Kingdom*

Qonglai Shan, Nuixim Shan, northwest side, attempt. Shaluli Shan, Jarjinjabo Massif: Spank Peak (ca 17,500'), south face, attempt; Jarjinjabo, south ridge. Andy Bourne, Misty Tyler, Anitra Accetturo, and I traveled to western Sichuan Province, China on September 20. Our goal was to explore and attempt as many objectives as possible in the Qionglai Range, and later in the Jarjinjabo Massif.

We first went to the town of Rilong, in the Qionglai Range. We attempted to hike up into the Changping Gou to check out options there, but were disenchanted with the approach and our time constraints, not to mention we did not even get a chance to see the peaks through the clouds and rain. Next we drove into the Shuanqiao Gou, which is the next valley to the west of the Changping, to scope options, and faced with a decision on which valley to basecamp in, we decided to stay in the Shuanqiao. Camping next to the locals' roadside food and wares stands, we were treated very cordially, and were able to "eat out" for meals the days we spent in camp. The weather here at this time of year was abysmal. Rain and/or snow every night but one, yet clearing partially every afternoon. This weather pattern resulted in lots of acclimatization hikes and photographing peaks. One attempt was made on the northwest side of Nuixim Shan by Andy, Misty, and Anitra; it ended about 300 feet shy of the summit due to fresh snow and cold temperatures. The monsoon did not seem to end this year, but supposedly this is the time to come.

After returning to Chengdu and regrouping, we went to the Jarjinjabo Massif on the western edge of Sichuan Province. On October 16 we hired a jeep driver in Litang to take us to Zhopu Gompa, on the northern shore of Zhopu Lake. We basecamped upvalley from the gompa and made an attempt on Spank Peak (ca 17,500'). Spank Peak is located on the north side of the Jarjinjabo Massif about two miles up the drainage to the east of the Massif. Andy and I climbed four pitches up the south face, but were turned back as the dihedral pinched out to a bottoming seam. Still, climbing beautiful new ground up to about 5.10b was exhilarating. On October 26 Misty and I as one team and Andy and Anitra as another did two climbs up the east aspect of Jarjinjabo south ridge directly above the Gompa. Our climb topped out on the ridge after about 1,200' of climbing in a beautiful dihedral up to about 5.8. After 800' or so, Andy and Anitra's climb ended in bushwacking and lichened slabs to just below the peak we dubbed "The Asterisk" (a sub peak of Jarjinjabo).

The cold, short days during the month of November kept us from attempting anything higher than 17,000ft. in the Jarjinjabo Massif. Earlier is better. We then parted ways and went to Thailand to sport climb and Yunnan Province to sightsee. A bit of vacation is needed after seven weeks in China.

ERIK JOHNSON, *AAC*

Daxuetang-feng (5,364m), second ascent, new route. Daxuetang-feng is a well-known mountain visible from the road from Chengdu to Balang Pass (south of Rilong and the Siguiniang mas-

Spank Peak, scene of the spanking. *Erik Johnson*

sif). More than 10 Chinese teams have tried to climb this peak. On the 8th of October, five Japanese and one Chinese members of our joint party summited Daxuetang-feng. However, a pennant on the summit established that a Beijing mountaineering team had already reached it. Much to our disappointment, this proved that we were the second party to reach it. However, our route ascended the center of a glacier at a slope of more than 70°, and it will possibly become the standard route for this mountain. Therefore, we consider our climb very meaningful.

The team members of the China-Japan Joint Party: Japanese members from the Hakusan (Matto) Fuuro Mountaineering Club: joint team leader Rentaro Nishijima, assistant team leader Akira Hoshiba, climbing chief Masanori Kawamura, and members Yasunori Tanaka, Toshiaki Tamai, Sachiyo Manizaki, Shigeru Yasuda, and Takashi Suzuki. Chinese members: team leader Li Qing, members He Qin and Feng Yilong, and support staff Gao Yi, Qin Znenglin, and Tang Ping.

Ascent of Daxuetang-feng (October 1-11): We hire 35 porters for a total of 49 members, including 8 Japanese and 6 Chinese. Leaving Dengsheng in fog, we make our way to Yeniugou, a valley beneath Dengshen, cross a bridge and go along the left bank of a river flowing from Daxuetang-feng. A mossy path continues through a forest of conifers, rhododendrons, and bamboo where pandas likely live. After walking more than six hours, we reach Baishuitaizi Plateau (3,600m). The steepness of the place does not justify its designation as a "Plateau." Further up, we see that the north face of Daxuetang-feng is unclimbable due to loose rocks. We then climb along a valley from Ganhaizi, go around to the right where the east face of Daxuetang-feng becomes visible, and establish Base Camp at Heihaizi (4,700m).

The team decides on the ice wall route right in front of BC. The lower part of the ice wall is shaped like the bottom of a funnel. Two pitches are fixed, but snow begins to fall heavily in the afternoon, so we decide to cancel tomorrow's route operation. It snows all the next day. Route operation resumes on October 6 despite new snow accumulation of about 30cm. The fresh snow appears to be holding down falling rocks. Four members extend the route another two pitches from the previous spot. The porters who carried up the last of our loads shout with joy to see the top member of the operation team appearing from behind a rock after passing a difficult crux. The members return 200m short of the top.

October 7: Through binoculars, Suzuki can be seen standing only with the toe points of his crampons stuck into the ice wall, with almost the entire soles of his boots visible to us at BC. We see him inserting ice screws with one hand. This is quite a risky climb at high altitude and lack of oxygen. We hold our collective breaths as we fear he may not withstand the fatigue in his calves, or the toe points may not hold. We feel a sense of relief as his wheezing voice reaches BC by radio: "Belay removed. Climb on." At about 13:00, the three members of the operation team can be seen from BC standing on the plateau after climbing the 400m ice wall with a slope of 70°. They report by radio: "There are two peaks. We can't tell which is higher. We have time, so we'll climb the right peak today, and climb the left one tomorrow. The left one may need a lot of rope fixing."

The right peak is probably the pyramid-shaped peak seen from Balang Pass, and the left peak is the trapezoid-shaped, snow-capped one peeking on its left. In appearance and on the map, both peaks seem to be 5,364m. The team names the right peak Peak I, the left Peak II, and another peak, which is described as 5,354m on the map (hidden by Peak II) is called Peak III. Peak III is presumed to be the glaciated peak on the right side of Peak I, as seen from Balang Pass.

October 8: The advance team aims for Peak I and proceeds beside the walls of the crevasses and glacier. As the ground is relatively flat, no fixed rope is used. At the head of the glacier a gully 20m long, 1.5m wide, and 70° leads to a col. From there, a narrow 60° ridge of loose rocks crumbles easily with each step, making it impossible to hammer pitons to fix ropes. The Chinese member, He Qin, retires, saying, "It's crazy." At 09:36, Tanaka and Kawamura reach the summit, followed by Suzuki and the Chinese team leader, Li. The summit is only one square meter in size, so all of them cannot stand together. However, it commands a spectacular 360° view. Siguniang-shan and the Ganzi mountains can be seen. They find a relatively new pennant of a Chinese team with "Beijing" printed on it. Nishijima and Hoshiba come up after a while.

As I take in the scene while descending to the col from the summit, I have mixed emotions as the joint team leader. Looking up, I can see the massif snow-capped, trapezoidal Peak II on the left. It may be unclimbed, but there is no time for us to reach it. Satisfied with the second ascent of Peak I by a new route, we descend.

The team left behind a fixed rope in the gully after cutting close to 15m to be used for descent. Also left behind were two pitons on top of the ice wall. By using the 100m rope on those pitons, all the other pitons and ropes were recovered. Although not perfect, the team endeavored to leave the mountain as clean as possible.

RENTARO NISHIJIMA, *Hakusan (Matto) Fuuro Mountaineering Club, Japan*

*Adapted from Japanese Alpine News, TAMOTSU NAKAMURA, *Editor*

Tibet

Permit problems in East Tibet, what went wrong. Everyone asks me, "What happened regarding the permits to East Tibet in the fall of 2004?" According to the Chinese authorities, permits to visit unopened areas and climb in Nyainqentanglha East were suddenly cancelled because several Westerners had entered unopened areas and attempted to climb mountains without official permits.

Mr. Dou Changshen of the Tibet Mountaineering Association (TMA) explained the situation to me in Lhasa as follows: 1. Two Germans and two Americans entered Tsangpo Great Bend and crossed Doshong-La to the southeast. This was reported to the public security police by local people. For this illegal activity a travel agent that had taken care of the foreigners was fined US$5,000 and ordered to suspend their business activity for five years. 2. Two British climbers ascended peaks in an unopened area. 3. A Swiss mountain guide, Gabriel Voide, ascended Jieqinnalagabu (Namla Karpo) east of Lake Basong (photo: *AAJ* 2003, p. 134). This is the first ascent of the most famous and prominent peak in the region. A Kathmandu-based travel agent arranged for his travel. 4. An agent in Lhasa used by a Kathmandu-based travel agent for Mick Fowler's party intended to let their client climb the Matterhorn of Tibet—Kajaqiao [photo: *AAJ* 2003, p. 134]—with no permit. Finally the agent asked Mr. Dou of TMA to help in obtaining a permit for Fowler's party, but this request was rejected.

These cases stiffened the Lhasa authorities' attitude and resulted in prohibiting foreigners from entering unopened areas and from climbing the mountains in East Tibet. Sean Waters' New Zealand team's application to climb Birutaso (6,691m) and Chuchepo (6,550m) in the Lawa valley east of Punkar was rejected, and my own Autumn Plan of 2004 was turned down, too. The New Zealand team changed their objective and headed to the satellite peaks of Minya Konka in Sichuan [see report in China section of this Journal].

Mr. Dou mentioned, however, that this measure would last only about five months, and the ban would be lifted in winter 2005 (this appears to have taken place). It was hinted that my plan to visit Yigong Tsangpo and beyond would surely be given a permit in 2005. But, frankly speaking, there is always difficulty in communication with the Chinese since their information is insufficient in most cases.

As our Autumn Plan of 2004 (marching up Yigong Tsangpo from Tongmai to Niwu and beyond to the north crossing Shargung-la) was not allowed, I negotiated with the TMA and finally could enter the unexplored Bena valley east of Lake Basong. But my time was limited to only one week. So, after Bena valley we trekked along the Old Peking-Lhasa road from Gyamda. In mid-October we moved to Yunnan via Chengdu. The objective was to retrace French missionaries' trails and visit Catholic churches. We crossed Se La, a pass at 4,140m on the Mekong-Salween Divide with four days in a horse caravan from east to west; on the way we unveiled a little-known mountain in remotest Yunnan, which F. Kingdon-Ward and Joseph Rock had called "Kenichunpu." The members of our elderly party were my colleague Tsuyoshi Nagai (72) and myself (69). After Yunnan I continued alone with a trip to Sichuan, where I went to the Mt. Siguniang area and visited a valley of beautiful historical stone towers in Dangba

County of the Da Du River basin. [Details of these explorations can be found in the *Japanese Alpine News*, Vol. 6, May 2005.]

TAMOTSU NAKAMURA, *Editor, Japanese Alpine News*

Editor's note: We have heard that the Chinese authorities in Tibet are cracking down on tour operators in Kathmandu who apparently have been selling unofficial permits. In the autumn of 2004 there were also rumors about observers being stationed in remote villages in East Tibet to report on stray climbers. Expeditions that have been sanctioned by the Tibet Mountaineering Association in 2005 seem to be having no problems with permits.

WEST TIBET

NGARI PROVINCE

Nganglong Kangri (Kang Ngolok) (6,710m), first ascent. The British Nganglong Kangri Expedition consisted of Derek Buckle, Martin Scott, and myself (UK) and Toto Gronlund (Finland). We left London on the 28th of August, flying to Kathmandu and entering Tibet by road from Nepal on 1st September. The Nganglong Kangri massif lies in Ngari province in West Tibet at 81°00'E 32°49'N. The peaks lie 85 km east-northeast of Ali and 45 km north of the county town of Gegye. The massif consists of two sections separated by a deep valley, the northern section being the larger and higher. The massif covers an area roughly 24 by 16 km. It holds 37 glaciers, two of which are over 6 km in length, and more than 40 peaks above 6,000m.

Our land cruiser journey of 1,500 km from Kathmandu to Base Camp took a total of seven days. The route led via Zhangmu, Nyalam, Tingri, Lhatse, and Raga, then north on Route 22 via Tsochen to meet the Northern Highway at Dong Tso, and finally west past the saltpans

Approaching from the south. (1) Nganglong Kangri 1/Kang Ngolok (6,710m). (2) Nganglong Kangri 1 East Peak/ Kang Ngolok East (6,595m). Both peaks were climbed by the lines shown. *John Town*

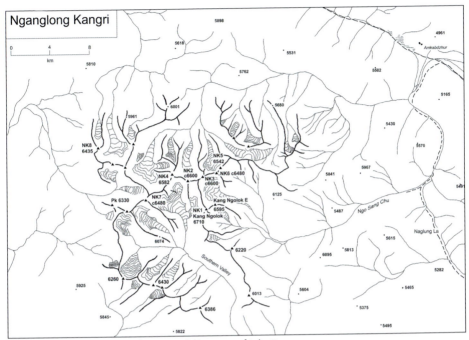

Map of Nganglong Kangri massif (Kang Ngolok) courtesy of *John Town*

of Tsaka and on to the back road, which runs via Chaktsaka toward Gegye. We knew of no motorable route for the final 36 km between the Gegye road and our hoped for base in the upper Ngo Sang valley. This valley leads west to the southeastern flank of the main summits and we had identified it as the best approach. The lack of a road did not deter the drivers of our lorry and two land cruisers, who plunged through a large river and set off cross country while demanding further guidance. Navigating by pre-programmed GPS and satellite photos we picked up a sketchy track, which took us over the Naglung La into our valley. The final section to our Base Camp was trackless and extremely rough with repeated river crossings.

On 8th September we continued up the valley on foot for several hours to where it turned right, opening out to reveal an impressive panorama of high peaks set back to the north. Initial impressions were that the largest and nearest of the big peaks must be the 6,542m Aling (Ngan-glong) Kangri marked on the Soviet 1:200K map. On the next day ABC was established at 5,400m on the glacial plain 3 km to its south. I had concerns that although the double-headed peak appeared higher than others, it was clearly well south of the marked location on the water-shed, and much else I could see did not fit the map or satellite image. On 11th September I descended to BC to conduct further reconnaissance while the others began our attempt on the peak by establishing a site for Camp 1 on a rocky promontory at 5,775m. The route then climbed over the lateral moraine and made an easy rising traverse of the southeast glacier to Camp 2 at 6,200m, which was occupied on the 13th September.

Meanwhile, I had ascended the steep valley to the northwest of Base Camp, bivouacking at 5,400m and then continuing up to Peak 6,153m, which gave a clear view of the southeast aspect of the massif. Our peak was clearly not the Aling Kangri of the map but another unnamed summit to the south of the watershed whose contour count of 6,600m made it the highest in the massif. The next day, 14th September, Derek, Martin, and Toto aborted a pre-dawn start because of cold and stove problems, but eventually departed from Camp 2 just before 10:00 am. Their route lay over a snow dome and up the southeast face toward a rightward slanting snow ramp at 6,600m. This proved unattractive on closer acquaintance and a more direct route was taken up the steep face to its left, which lead easily to the summit ridge and on to the summit. Readings from two GPS units gave the height as 6,710m. The peak, Nganglong Kangri 1, is known by local people as Kang Ngolok. On the 15th the party descended to the lateral moraine, where Martin continued the descent to ABC while Derek and Toto climbed the striking but easy southeast ridge of the 6,595m east summit. Between the 15th and 17th I conducted a further westward exploration, bivouacking at 5,500m before crossing a 5,900m pass and descending into the deep valley separating the northern and southern sections of the range. The pass gave excellent views of the two main southern peaks, ca 6,400m, but time ran out before I could gain a view from the opposite side of the valley of Nganglong Kangri 4 (6,582m) or the great southern glacier. The nearest permanent habitation is over 30 km from the main peaks and the area shows little or no signs of human presence. During our time in the mountains we encountered wild yaks, gazelle, kyang and a black wolf.

JOHN TOWN, *Alpine Club*

Editor's note: the GPS height of 6,710m for the main summit corresponds very well with the 6,708m given on a very recently published Chinese map to the region, not available to this expedition.

HIMALAYA

TATUNGSAKHU HIMAL

Pachyung Ham (6,529m), Gang Dzong Kang (6,123m), first ascents. The Kansai Section of the Japanese Alpine Club (JAC) sent an academic and mountaineering expedition to West Tibet in 2004 in commemoration of the JAC's 100th anniversary, which comes in 2005. The objectives of the expedition were to scale unclimbed peaks in the Tatungsakhu Himal of West Tibet, to retrace footsteps of a Japanese monk, Ekai Kawaguchi, who reached Lhasa a century before Sven Hedin, and to explore unvisited regions in the headwaters of Sutlej, Indus, Yarlung Tsangpo, and Mt. Kailas. The climbing record is briefly introduced below, while an article on Ekai Kawaguchi and explorations will be published as a separate volume of the JAC centennial issue of the *Japanese Alpine News* 2006.

In 2003 I led a party from the Osaka Alpine Club that took a picture of Gang Dzong Kang, a dominant rock peak that soars south of a highway connecting Lhasa and Kailas in the vast and arid Tibetan plateau. Since it can be viewed from the road, presumably many travelers would have been allured to the peak. An early explorer, Sven Hedin, sketched the mountain. However, no one had tried to climb it. The photograph, which was taken from the Nepalese side beyond a ridge, shows a rock face but does not cover the whole profile in detail. The challenging rock face on this 6,123m peak was estimated at 800 meters.

In 2004 I was again assigned to lead an expedition. The party departed from Kathmandu on August 13 and entered Tibet by road after having spent two weeks in the Khumbu area for acclimatization. Then the climbing leader, Satoshi Kimoto, and I headed to the first objective, Pachyung Ham, accompanying two sherpas after having seen a younger group off to Kung La pass, where they searched for the tracks of a Japanese monk, Ekai Kawaguchi. (A hundreds years ago Ekai had crossed the Himalaya and hurried to reach Lhasa in disguise with a mission to seek original scriptures of Mahayana Buddhism. His narratives are written in his book *Three Years in Tibet.*) We established base camp at 4,607m on August 20. Advance Base Camp was built at 5,216m between a current glacier and pasture in the upper part of a typical V-shape valley on August 26.

Our climbing route on Pachyung Ham follows the north ridge of this stunning rock and snow peak. A little before a younger team of six members arrived, an elder party of four members left the camp for reconnaissance, route paving (including fixing ropes), and ferrying up loads half a day in front of the younger team. After days of work, on September 3 we departed early from C1 at 6,167m. An unstable slate ridge became mixed with snow and then ended at a snow wall. A snow ridge then led all the members to the virgin summit.

A few days later after our success on Pachyung Ham, we returned to ABC to assault Gang Dzong Kang. We decided on the southeast face as had already been planned. The route opening work was conducted by two alternating parties. Senda's party took the lead first. In two days they gained four pitches that took them to where the ridge met the wall, which was very steep toward the large upper band. As the place was shaded and got colder in the afternoon, they wanted to move to the face on the left side, which received sunshine all the day. They gained only one 60-meter pitch the next day because the wind and snow were merciless. They hurriedly descended. The following day the face was found totally white with fresh snow. As it was obviously not a condition to climb, they returned to ABC.

They decided to extend the climbing period by three days. Senda's party reached the upper large band in a further three pitches in two days. On the third day, September 19, they stood on top of this unclimbed peak at 12:40. On September 20, Kimoto's party left ABC in deteriorating weather. Fortunately the snow that had fallen on the previous day did not much disturb the climbing. Despite snow and melting water in a wide crack, they reached the summit at 13:40.

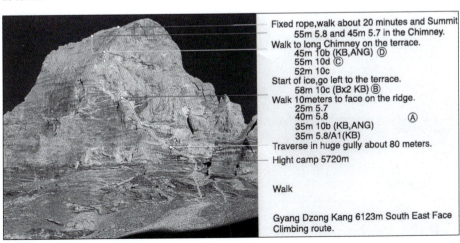

Fixed rope,walk about 20 minutes and Summit
55m 5.8 and 45m 5.7 in the Chimney.
Walk to long Chimney on the terrace.
45m 10b (KB,ANG) Ⓓ
55m 10d Ⓒ
52m 10c
Start of ice,go left to the terrace.
58m 10c (Bx2 KB) Ⓑ
Walk 10meters to face on the ridge.
25m 5.7
40m 5.8   Ⓐ
35m 10b (KB,ANG)
35m 5.8/A1(KB)
Traverse in huge gully about 80 meters.
Hight camp 5720m

Walk

Gyang Dzong Kang 6123m South East Face
Climbing route.

Gang Dzong Kang. *Tamotsu Ohnishi*

Members of the expedition: General leader: Kazuuki Abe (75); leader: Tamotsu Ohnishi (62); climbing leader: Satoshi Kimoto (48), and five climbing members. Academic party: Leader: Toyoji Wada (58) and one member.

Editor's note: this route involved approximately nine pure rock pitches up to 5.10d, with a short section of A1 on the first. Fixed rope was used and a few bolts placed.

TAMOTSU OHNISHI, *Japanese Alpine Club*

Adapted from Japanese Alpine News, *Tamotsu Nakamura, Editor*

ROLWALING HIMAL

Shishapangma main summit (8,027m), southwest face, solo in December with new variation. Over the years I had a simple idea in mind: to climb a big Himalayan route solo in the inhospitable conditions that typify winter in the Himalaya. During all my outings in the Alps and from when I first encountered the high Himalayan summits, I wanted to attempt such a project. Since my start in alpinism I have had one central belief: "Things always seem impossible when you haven't tried them."

The idea is simple on paper but difficult to realize. Even with all my experience at high altitude, I was still full of uncertainty as I flew to Kathmandu. Would I be able to make the needed effort in the cold and rarified air? Would I be able to climb fast enough on such a technical face to get up between windstorms?

I arrived at base camp on November 14, acclimatized until December 8, and left advance base camp (5,700m) on December 9. That day I reached a bivouac at 7,000m. Then I rested on "stand by" mode, climbing only a mixed section of the British route of 1982 until 7,200m, where I bivouacked. I started climbing again at 4:30 a.m. on December 11 and reached the summit (8,027m) at 11:30, Nepalese time. Despite my elation, I had to concentrate on the cold that lived in my feet and my entire body, and on the descent that awaited me. Four hours later I bivouacked at 7,000m. Bad weather hit on the morning of December 12. All the mountains were consumed by heavy black clouds. It snowed intermittently and blew violently. Very tired, I concentrated hard, alternating between rappelling and downclimbing while descending the thousands of vertical meters that plunge to the glacier. Around 6,600m my 7mm rope got stuck; it is still on the route. Finally I regained the security of the glacier and reached base camp that day (December 12). My project ended as it had begun, in infinite solitude. I had proven that I was capable of climbing a grand Himalayan route under winter conditions, alone, with no support, and without artificial oxygen.

JEAN CHRISTOPHE LAFAILLE, *France (translated by John Harlin III)*

Shishapangma, notes on the Lafaille ascent and winter season. When the Nepalese Government established a winter season for the Nepal Himalaya lasting from December 1 to February 15, their rules also stated that while camps could be established above Base during November, they could not be occupied until the start of the following month. Jean Christophe Lafaille began fixing ropes up the first section of the Corredor Girona on November 20. Only 300m of rope were fixed in total and on the following day he climbed to 6,500m and left some equipment before returning to Base.

He started up the face again on the 26th. Once clear of the fixed ropes he began to slant left up the great snow slope that lies between the Girona and British Routes. He camped the night at 6,500m and on the 27th more or less reached the British Route at 7,000m, having crossed the descent line used by Baxter-Jones, MacIntyre, and Scott in 1982, and the route climbed by Krzysztof Wielicki in 1993. Although Lafaille had hoped to install his top camp a little higher, he opted instead to erect his tent in a handily-placed crevasse. The following day he climbed 100m higher to establish a camp at an optimum height of 7,100m, then, with the wind forecasted to rise to 180km/hour at 8,000m, he descended to sit it out until the next break in the weather. All this took place prior to the start of December.

It is interesting to note that the first winter ascent of Dhaulagiri has been consistently credited to the Polish expedition that reached the summit on January 21, 1985. Japanese climbed the mountain on December 13, 1982 but their "winter" ascent was discounted as they had arrived at Base Camp in October with a post monsoon permit and did much work on the mountain during November.

LINDSAY GRIFFIN, *Mountain INFO, CLIMB magazine*

Editor's note: The original press release about Jean Christophe Lafaille's ascent of Shishapangma called it the first winter ascent of the mountain. This generated considerable discussion in the climbing community because he had reached the summit on December 11. The permit called the season "winter," however the calendar declared winter beginning 10 days later. Lafaille does not now report the climb as being "winter," but instead calls it "winter conditions." The following notes by Krzysztof Wielieki is being published not to refute claims by Lafaille, but to provide interesting commentary on the definition of winter ascents in the Himalaya. Wielieki, from Poland, has made more winter ascents of 8,000m peaks than anyone else—Everest, Kangchenjunga, Lhotse—and climbed a new route on the south face of Shishapangma. He wrote his comments not long after Lafaille's ascent. The first calendar winter ascent of Shishapangma took place on January 14, 2005 (see Simone Moro report, below).

Winter ascents of 8,000m peaks, commentary. Katia Lafaille, wife of the renowned Jean Christophe Lafaille, recently reported about the excellent achievement of her husband on Shishapangma, which took place on December 11. Much to my surprise the information called it the first winter ascent of Shishapangma. But winter begins on December 21 in our hemisphere. There is a need to distinguish between the season written on a permit and the real nature of the winter season in the mountains. The first one is an administrative decision only. It is possible to make the real winter ascent while breaking administrative rules, for example on February 28, after the administrative date. Simply speaking: no clerk can determine the real season of the year.

The formal point of view: The Nepal Ministry of Tourism established December 1 as the beginning date for winter mountain action (here understood as the day of establishing Base Camp) and February 15 as the day when Base Camp should be left. This last condition was a mere administrative reason. As we were informed in 1979 (before the Polish Everest winter expedition) the choice of the middle of February as the end of the winter season came because Sherpas wanted enough time to rest before the beginning of the spring expeditions.

The climatic point of view: From my personal experience—and I have participated in seven winter expeditions to the Himalaya and Karakoram—stronger winds set in at the beginning of November or some years at the end of October. At the end of November the winds quiet down and this relative silence continues to about Christmas (of course in high places winds are often strong anyway). The first snowfalls, usually moderate, follow at about Christmas (sometimes this snowfall is the last one until early spring snowstorms). Real winter winds strengthen after these Christmas snowfalls. Therefore, I think that Lafaille had rather excellent fall conditions rather than real winter ones.

KRZYSZTOF WIELIEKI, *Poland (translated by Grzegorz Glazek)*

Shishapangma, first winter ascent. I was sick and tired of the extra-European alpinism I was doing; I did not find it as enthralling as I had imagined when as a young aspiring alpinist I read of the big undertakings on the great mountains of the Earth. I wanted to stop that monotonous tramping through snow, lining up on the "normal" 8,000ers, and looking for the shortest ascent time or other slight improvements that should have filled me with satisfaction. Not even joining the club of aspiring collectors of the fourteen 8,000m giants lit my interior fire. By now I had sufficient experience in the Himalaya and in other mountain chains, and so there was no sense in following the same footsteps as someone from half a century earlier.

On the normal routes on 8,000m peaks there is no solitude, no adventure, no fantasy; everyone has the same problems, same complaints, and same hopes that someone else has already put up the fixed ropes, or that someone else set off a half hour earlier to make tracks after a heavy snowfall. If this person instead is us, we become the new champions in the base camp village, and we may receive the season's Hero Badge.

The history of mountaineering and of great adventures is on another wavelength, on values and difficulties hundreds of times better than this. For this reason in the last few years I had tried traverses, link ups, and ascents on new faces of mountains that were out of fashion. I had dreamed and often failed, but I had lived what I was really looking for, and even in my defeat I felt truly alive, the main character of my fantasies and able to write my daily achievements without any official approval. Still, I was becoming a high altitude hypocrite, and I absolutely wanted to find the cure before this bad habit became chronic.

In this spirit my Everest-Lhotse traverse attempts were born, as well as my ascents in the ex-USSR, winter attempt on Annapurna, a successful winter ascent on the Marle Wall in Tien Shan, a new route on Nanga Parbat (ruined by the missed summit). These experiences led to my successes on the north face of Baruntse [see Nepal reports in this Journal] and Shishapangma in winter.

Partners for winter ascents inevitably come from the East of the Old Continent where the cold seems to have frozen that part of us that was lost with our fathers' generation. A Will to work hard while cold and hungry motivates these people to follow difficult and rough roads; in alpinism this Will is indispensable for the great unresolved problems of the vertical world. With or without satellites, Gore-Tex, ice axes from outer space, and freeze-dried food, it is these men who make history. The men from the East seem to have kept their "manly" side in their every action. There are of course great men and alpinists amongst us Westerners who even with central heating, cars, and the Internet have been able to achieve their projects, but they are a minority.

Nobody had made a first winter ascent of an 8,000m peak in the past 17 years, and of the fourteen 8,000m peaks, only seven had ever been climbed during winter. This had been achieved exclusively by Poles, who had shown that it was possible to "violate" these summits even in winter.

There is a strict rule in the astronomical and scientific calendar that declares the 21st of December as the beginning of the cold season, which continues to the 21st of March. Our ascent had to be undertaken during the calendar winter, where no interpretation is allowed. Zawada, Berbeka, Kukuckzka, Wielicki, Pawlikowski, Cichy, Gaiewski, Haizer, and Czok made the first winter ascents of 8,000m peaks, and the rest of the mountaineering world has been an astonished spectator of their abilities.

Was winter climbing on the highest peaks only the prerogative of hard Eastern men? To answer this simple question I found myself breathing the freezing thin Shishapangma air in the winter of 2003/2004. Three hundred meters and the wrong strategy stopped me the first time from reaching the 8,027m summit on the "ridge of the pastures." On the 29th November 2004 I was full of energy as I headed off for my second attempt on Shisha. My partners were the same as the previous year, Polish. Denis Urubko, my Kazaki partner, had planned to join us, but financial problems and family obligations stopped him.

We wanted to respect the 21st December rule where you can only start moving on the mountain after that date. As soon as I had reached Kathmandu I found out about a French mountaineer who had set off at the beginning of November for Shishapangma; he had left orders to the few who had seen him to tell us absolutely nothing about his presence. The Frenchman had underestimated my contacts in Kathmandu after 35 expeditions. I understood straight away who they were talking about, but I did not change my plans and the rules of the game. 21 days separated us from the 21st of December, and anything that happened before would be in autumn. Even in alpinism there are rules to follow if you do not want to cheat.

After acclimatizing in the Everest valley we returned to Kathmandu, and on the 21st December we left the jeep that had driven us into Tibet. We started our approach trek and our adventure on Shisha strictly on the first day of winter. We still had not decided what route to climb because we wanted to see the face with our own eyes. I concealed my intention of a new route, which I had seen and jokingly had called "The dollar" due to a natural "S"-shaped cut in the summit rocky band visible from far away. Piotr Morawski accepted the idea straight away, while Jacek, Darek, and Jan preferred reaching the summit without complicating their already difficult lives. This is why we postponed my project on the mountain.

Instead we opted for the Yugoslav [Slovenian] route that in our eyes seemed to be the longer but more accessible route on the south face. I had brought from Italy 1,200 meters of thin Dyneema rope produced by a company in nearby Bergamo since it would be a light and enduring fixed rope. We then had to fix another thousand meters of rope made of 8mm plastic to fix the Yugoslav route up to the 7,350m ridge. We placed a camp at 6,500m and one at the end of the fixed ropes. It was a battle against the cold, the heavy backpacks, the wind, the snowstorm, and the snow that tested us for 20 days on the Tibetan mountain. In rotation the rope made up of me and Piotr was substituted by Jacek and Darek to be then substituted by us and then again by them. The last 300 meters of climbing at UIAA grade III and IV before coming out onto the ridge were a true battle against the elements, and it was almost dark when we finished setting the tent up at 7,350m and could see the last 700 meters of the mountain. We had not foreseen an attempt on the summit the next day, only a return to base camp. But so little separated us from the summit, and I was so afraid of a trick being played on us by bad weather or wind that could have torn through our camp where we were being sheltered, suspended over the abyss. "Tomorrow we will give it a go!" I said to Piotr, who in a surprised tone answered

"Ok, if you think that it is the best thing to do then we will. But at what time?" At 7:30/8:00, I responded, "as soon as the first rays of the sun come out. We mustn't f*** up like last year!"

What happened the next morning (January 14) was not a climb but a run to the summit. Without backpacks, harnesses, food, hot drinks, with nothing, and starved of oxygen, we isolated ourselves thinking about putting one foot after the other until we had reached the highest point of the mountain and of our dream. It was 1:13 p.m. when, with a dry throat and my lungs irritated by the cold, I shouted and cried out with joy for being up there, far from comfort and safety, at 8,027m! What joy something so apparently useless, so dangerous, and so stupid can give. Surrounding us was an infinity of mountains, powerful and silent. Marks that will disappear with the first gust of wind, cries that will be lost in thin air, stories that will never change the world. It seems to be so absurd to climb these peaks and so insane to do it during winter. Instead I felt terribly alive, logical, a direct protagonist of my life with that magical ascent. From a dead man I had become alive, from a slave I was free, just like the alpinism which had trapped me and from which I had managed to escape.

SIMONE MORO, *Italy*

MAHALANGUR HIMAL

Qow Xab (Palung Ri) (7,022m). I made a quick ascent of unclimbed [see editor's note below] Qow Xab via the northwest ridge in 9 days from BC (4,915m) on the Balung Glacier. This was accomplished by crawling up through innumerous hidden crevasses and wading through waist-deep snow. It was a miracle that eventually our party could find a feasible route up the crest of this ridge. The peak was considered a satellite peak of Qho Oyu because of the difference in height between them, but actually it is an independent peak isolated from the other. Our party consisted of my colleague Murakami, the high porter Pinzo, and myself, but unfortunately Murakami had to give up the top as he became exhausted while trapped in a hidden crevasse during our summit bid. We made base camp on July 27, and after reconnoitering the north wall in vain, we decided on the northwest ridge. We made camps at 5,960m on August 3, and camp at 6,350m on August 4, and after considerable snow fell, we reached the summit on August 7.

TADAKIYO SAKAHARA, *The Himalayan Association of Japan*
Adapted from Japanese Alpine News, *Tamotsu Nakamura, Editor*

Editor's note: This report is being published to clarify the record on Qow Xab. This was not in fact an unclimbed peak. It is generally known as Palung Ri and was certainly climbed in 1995 by Andrej and Marija Stremfelj, and has probably been climbed on other occasions by Cho Oyu parties.

Everest, north face, new route. One of the season's most important climbs was the ascent of Everest's great north face by a new direct line from a spot near their advance base camp at 6,200m to the 8,850m summit. During a month-long ascent, the leader, Victor Kozlov, and 14 other climbing members from Russia, faced nearly all the types of problems a mountain can involve. To overcome them the team employed three Sherpas to help carry supplies of rope, tents, and gear to camp 3 at 7,800m. From that point the members began their use of bottled oxygen and continued to use it almost all the way up to 8,500m, with some exceptions: not everyone slept on it, and no one used it while fixing rope above camp 3. Total amount fixed: roughly 5,000 meters from 6,300m to 8,500m.

They found problems from the very start of their climb. From base camp at 5,600m to advance camp at 6,200m, the concern was falling stones. Then came technical problems. Just below 7,100m, where they pitched their first camp on the face, they found a small, nearly vertical couloir. From camp 1 to camp 3 it was not very steep, but there were exposed rock slabs like slate roofing, alternating with patches of snow.

The face from camp 3 to camp 4 (from 7,800m to 8,250m), was steep gray rock followed by the famous yellow rock band; camp 4 was placed on a small rock ledge. The steepness continued for the first 200 meters above camp 4, then eased off to their final camp, also on a small ledge, at 8,600m. Above

Mt. Everest, upper north face. (1) North Ridge to Northeast Ridge (Gong-Qu-Wang, 1960). (2) Messner variation (Messner, 1980). (3) Great Couloir/Norton Couloir Direct (MacartneySnape-Mortimer, 1984). (4) Russian North Face (Mariev-Shabaline-Tukh-vatullin/ Kuznetsov-Sokolov-Vinogradsky/Bobok-Volodin, 2004). (5) Hornbein Couloir Direct/Japanese Route (Ozaki-Shigehiro, 1980). (6) West Ridge (Hornbein-Unsoeld, 1963). (7) West Ridge Direct (Belak-Strem-felj-Zaplotnik, 1979). Photo: www.mountain.ru; additional route information: www.planetmountain.com

this camp 5, the steepness resumed, and here they discovered a serious barrier: the climb became extremely difficult because the vertical rock crumbled, making it nearly impossible to fix rope. One of the team's four climbing leaders, Pavel Shabaline, gained only 50 meters' altitude in one day using a belay from camp 5.

To continue on this direct vertical line would have required at least two more days of very dangerous climbing to surmount the next 50 meters, so they decided to traverse left 100 meters, then circle back around to the top of this crumbly area to return to their direct line above camp 5. From here to the top there was no real difficulty and on three successive days, May 30–June 1, eight members arrived at the top. The two on June 1 were the only summiters from any Everest team that day and the last ones of the season [they were also the first ever to summit Everest in June—Ed.]. They had succeeded in forging a new line to the top of the mountain.

The Everest team made no attempt to descend the face. Another Russian expedition, led by Alexander Abramov, had summited on May 24 and 25 via the standard northern route; they left a tent for the face team with sleeping bags, food, gas, and oxygen bottles where that route's last camp is normally pitched, at 8,300m. The tent was, in fact, only used by the first summit party on the night of the 30th; they were exhausted from having fixed rope below their camp 5 and then trying to force their way up the crumbly rock section. The second and third summit groups descended past the tent all the way to advance base camp, and one member of the 3rd summit party even continued down to base camp.

Editor's note: The "Russian Everest Expedition Central North Wall 2004" summiters were: May 30: Andrew Mariev, Iljas Tukhvatullin, Pavel Shabaline; May 31: Piotr Kuznetsov, Gleb Sokolov, Eygeny Vinogradsky; June 1: Victor Bobok, Victor Volodin. Spellings vary; these were taken from the expedition's official website.

ELIZABETH HAWLEY, *AAC Honorary Member, Nepal*

Everest, north face new route, personal commentary on history and style. The expedition to Everest by the North Face was planned immediately after our ascent of Lhotse Middle in 2001 [feature article in *AAJ* 2002]. This plan was collective, and most team members welcomed it. Personally I had dreamed of this route since 1997 when I first saw a poster in the office of the Russian Mountaineering Federation of the North Face with the Spanish team's route. There were two test climbs in 2002 and 2003. I did not take part in the first one, its task was just to photograph. But I took part in the second one because at heart I expected project leader Victor Kozlov to get a permit and this test climb to become a full-fledged attempt. Kozlov organized the expedition and got a permit, but only up to 7,000m, and transferred to me the leadership of the test climb in Tibet. Then I planned a route, and three of us climbed up to 6,700m (to my mind there was no point in climbing higher because it was simple relief to 6,900m-7,000m, where our rights ended). Then we took all the equipment off the wall, took away all rubbish, and struck the camps.

Though my plan was not completely realized, nevertheless I was eager for a new route. I believed that as there had already been many worthy routes in good style on the North Face, it is not enough just to put up a new line in order to be an innovator on this massif. First you should do it without artificial oxygen, second you should use alpine style as much as possible, and third the team should be small—just five or six members. I joined the preparations for a new expedition. Once having said "yes," I kept my word. My plans for the climb and those of Victor Kozlov initially did not coincide. Being the leader, Victor needed only victory—to climb in the safest and most guaranteed style, with oxygen and a large team. But after all it is not the leader who climbs a mountain, so I expected to find support from the climbers themselves. Many of the members of the team had already been to Everest (five of them), so I thought that it would be interesting for them now to make an ascent without oxygen. Others were rather young but they had the experience of high-altitude ascents—some of them could support me. My expectations appeared idealistic. If in the beginning some climbers still thought "Why not?," then the further events developed the more the climbers inclined toward artificial oxygen. In this case, the tactic was clear and simple, it did not require additional risk, and there was just a pattern that was copied. Such an approach gave a very high probability of success. It was the effect of professional work.

We climbed, fixing ropes and establishing camps. The majority of the team felt well, and I hoped that in the final stage the advanced combined group of resolute climbers would try to make a fast push to the top without oxygen. I worked together with my friend Victor Bobok. Unfortunately he was out of form for an ascent without oxygen. Two of our climbers worked 20 pitches of the total of 63 up to 7,900m (this was not bad if you take into account that besides us there were two groups of three climbers and one group of four climbers). They established a high-altitude camp at 7,800m at the base of Hornbein's couloir. Staying in this bivouac, I offered our community the seditious idea of continuing the ascent from this point in alpine style and without oxygen via Hornbein's couloir. I considered it quite a logical course, the route would go without a traverse to the left. Deviating from a pattern and climbing a route without oxygen were important to me. This appeal met strong resistance from both the leader of the expedition and the group following us. Then my not very smooth relations developed into open opposition to the main idea of the expedition: ascent by the safest way strictly in the center of the north wall of Everest.

The team's opinion won. Two of our climbers fixed four ropes in the direction of the center of the wall. The next groups were already working with oxygen from 8,000m. The moment they started using artificial oxygen, the ascent lost the main sense for me, the adventure ceased to exist. In the final stage of the expedition began a struggle for who had priority for the oxygen carried up the wall, and in the end two of our climbers had to go down. The forthcoming work seemed like the usual rise with oxygen by a fixed rope up to 8,500m. Then the way out to Messner's route and the descent down the classic route. I felt I had obligations to my friend Victor Bobok because it was me who had involved him in this expedition as far back as the investigation, and Victor longed for Everest. Therefore, despite of all psychological troubles, we started.

At this stage Victor Volodin joined us. The quantity of oxygen in high-altitude camps was not clear. At 7,100m it became obvious that the oxygen was not enough for three climbers to make a safe ascent and descent. Then I decided to give my oxygen to my friends so they could be assured of a summit and descent. Our group was the last, and it could not expect any help from previous tired summit climbers in case of a force majeure. Besides, this decision was quite logical for me. I had dreamed of climbing Everest without oxygen. This did not mean a personal ascent without oxygen, it meant climbing such a route with a small team, ideally in alpine style. Certainly one should not consider the Russian route an absolute direct, but our team passed a new line on the North Face of Everest, and this is undoubtedly an achievement in the class of oxygen ascents in the Himalaya.

We left fixed ropes and camps with some equipment on the mountain because all groups came back on the classic route. During the fourth and fifth descents from the wall I managed to dismantle and lower downward the rest of the auxiliary camp at 7,000m.

YURI KOSHELENKO, *Russia*

Everest, search for Andrew Irvine's body. Amid much speculation about the fate of Andrew Irvine, members of the 1999 and 2001 Mallory and Irvine Research Expeditions joined the fray in 2004 to continue their efforts to locate the famous British climber (and hopefully his camera), lost in 1924. Unlike the several other well-publicized search expeditions on the mountain in 2004, our group this time took a novel "under the radar" approach. Our strategy in 2004 would be a closely targeted effort based on information from the 1960 Chinese climber Xu Jing, who told Everest historian Jochen Hemmleb and me of seeing a body high in the Yellow Band when we interviewed him in 2001. Operating under the guise of a commercial North Col team organized by my company IMG, Dave Hahn, Jake Norton, and Sherpas Tashi Tseri and Da Nuru were inserted into the climbing scene without anyone knowing their intentions. Over the course of their expedition they managed several days of searching in the Yellow Band, but

Mount Everest

Routes and findings of the 1999, 2001, and 2004 Mallory & Irvine Research Expeditions. 1999 (darkest), 2001 (medium), and 2004 (lightest). Image: © Swissphoto Group AG, Zurich, 2001; overlay: J. Hemmleb, 2004/5. A map of the search routes taken in 1999, 2001, and 2004, is available at www.cffiner.org; additional information on the current state of the research can be found at www.alpine-history.com.

unfortunately there was more snow on the ledges in the target area than they hoped for, which made it more difficult. A final push up high resulted in Hahn, from Taos, New Mexico making his fifth successful ascent of Mt. Everest, on May 20, 2004 climbing with Da Nuru Sherpa (also his fifth ascent) and Tashi Tseri Sherpa (his tenth ascent). Norton, from Golden, Colorado and a two time Everest summiter, chose to conduct additional solo searching on that day rather than going to the summit again. Jake now becomes the first individual to have visited all pre-modern era Mt. Everest high camps (British '24, '33, '38 and Chinese '60, '75). The expedition was organized by me and International Mountain Guides of Ashford, Washington, and was conducted under permit from the Chinese Mountaineering Association. We have attached a photo which shows the total searching now accomplished by our teams in 1999 (darkest), 2001 (medium), and 2004 (lightest).

ERIC SIMONSON, *AAC*

Makalu II (7,678m), new route and first ascent from Tibet. Jean Christophe Lafaille's ambitious and committing plan was a solo expedition to make the first ascent of Makalu II (aka Kangchungtse) from Tibet, traverse the summit to the Makalu La at 7,400m and continue up the Normal Route to the top of Makalu, so completing his 12th 8,000m summit.

Base Camp was established on April 21 at 4,950m on the Kangshung Glacier. On the 23rd, with his Sirdar and three porters, he took 65kg of gear south up the lengthy Chomo Lonzo Glacier, a difficult journey leading to the foot of Makalu II. Below the north face he established an Advanced Base at 5,750m. This is a very remote part of the world and only one expedition had traveled this way before: the Japanese expedition that in 1993 climbed Chomo Lonzo (7,790m) via the col to the northeast of Makalu II. Lafaille was now left on his own to reconnoiter and acclimatize on the mountain.

The logical line was a prominent north-facing spur, leading directly to the northwest ridge at a point approximately 7,100m in altitude. Conditions on the initial section of the spur, a snow/ice ramp of 50°-55° leading to the crest, proved to be good. Above, Lafaille progressed up the ridge to what he christened the Yellow Tower, a 60m icy granite step that gave considerably difficulties. He described the technicalities here as the hardest he had done at such an altitude and overcoming the pitch required a full two hours of difficult and delicate mixed climbing.

Lafaille made several forays up the spur, leaving a number of sections fixed and operating on the upper part from a camp at 6,600m, before reaching the crest of the northwest ridge and stashing some gear. The upper section of the spur had been in good condition and had an average angle of 45°-50° with some steeper sections. He then descended all the way to Base Camp for a good rest before the final push, knowing that on the northwest ridge he would be on previously trodden ground. Yasakawa Shuji's Seppyo Alpine Club expedition climbed difficult ridge from the Chago La in October 1976 to make the second ascent of the mountain. The route was repeated by three Koreans in September 1986.

On the 13th Lafaille set out alone for his final attempt and by the afternoon of the 14th had reached his pre-positioned camp on the crest of the northwest ridge at around 7,100m. Shortly above lay a vertical black wall, which he overcame at A1 and M5. This was followed by a vertical wall of snow detached from the rock to form a sort of tube, which the Frenchman likened to a caving pitch. Thereafter, the ridge was exposed, with a very steep mixed rock wall to his right dropping precipitously towards the Chago Glacier. Parts of the ridge still sported remnants of ancient fixed rope. Below 7,400m he left the crest and began to climb the left flank towards the summit. Another difficult wall barred progress. Hard mixed and dry-tooling on sound red granite at an estimated M5/M6 led to a small platform above 7,400m and a camp-site for the night.

On the 16th, in continuing good weather, Lafaille climbed 120m of mixed terrain, another steep step at M5 and then an 80° icy ramp before reaching the summit at 2:00 p.m. He had found the technical difficulties on this upper section harder than the South Face of Annapurna, and on the last difficult pitches decided to abandon a rope, pegs, and cams, rather than descend to collect them. After a telephone call to his wife in Nepal, he descended south ca 100m towards the Makalu La and set up his tent for the night.

The next morning he made the short, straightforward descent to the Makalu La, where he found tents occupied by climbers from expeditions climbing Makalu's Normal Route. Starting out next morning he realized he was tired and appeared to have a worrying chest infection. He returned to his tent and opted to descend the Normal Route to Makalu Base Camp, then attempt Makalu after a few days' rest. However, on the 19th he set off down the Barun to the lower Base Camp and then used the route over the col northwest of Peak 3 to regain Tibet. Seven days after leaving his Base Camp on the Kangshung Glacier he was back. Despite not completing his 12th 8,000m peak, the Frenchman had pulled off one of the most audacious traverses of the year.

LINDSAY GRIFFIN, *Mountain INFO, CLIMB magazine*

BHUTAN HIMALAYA

YADONG COUNTY

Chomolhari (7,326m), alpine style ascent. On 7 May Roger Payne and I (both British) made a rapid alpine style ascent of the south ridge of Chomolhari (7,326m) in Yadong County. We had been aiming to climb a new route on the northwest ridge of the mountain, but had to abandon this because of incessant strong winds. Base camp at around 4,500m below the west face was also exposed to persistent winds. We first made a reconnaissance of the northern and western flanks of Chomolhari and found a route from the glacier on to the crest of the northwest ridge (easy snow then mixed climbing up to TD). But on 2 May at 6,000m we abandoned the ridge in clear skies but ferocious winds that made standing difficult and the prospect of technical climbing impossible on the crux rock steps and towers above.

Back at base camp Roger and I decided to use the few days remaining before our transport pick-up to take a look at the south ridge. This ridge had been climbed in 1996 by a large Japanese-Chinese party using fixed ropes and was the third ascent of Chomolhari. The first ascent was a remarkable climb in 1937 by Spencer Chapman who followed the southeast ridge from Bhutan and which merges with the south ridge above 7,000m (the Indian and Bhutanese Armies repeated this route in 1970).

After negotiating an unstable icefall that was seriously threatened on either side by seracs, on 5 May we reached the col at around 5,900m, which marks the start of the south ridge. The strong winds continued at the south col and in the early hours of 6 May we had to prepare to exit our tent because of the risk of it being blown apart. However, we waited to the very last

The north sides of Chomolhari and neighbors, as seen from the road. From right to left: Chomolhari—the northwest ridge is on the right, the north face has few natural lines, and the couloir to the left is a big avalanche funnel. Nameless unclimbed peaks 6,972m and 6,706m (an easy looking northwest ridge/face begins at around 5,800m). The gap at left is called Tanggal Lunglha on the Tibet side (ca 6,000m). On the left is well-known Jitchu Drake, which has been climbed from the south (Bhutan) side. *Roger Payne*

moment before returning to base camp. Then, miraculously, on the evening of the 6th the winds dropped, the clouds parted, and a full moon appeared. By 01:30 on the 7th we were ready to depart from the col. A serac barrier had to be negotiated and parts of the summit ridge were excellent exposed snow crests (around AD). We reached the summit before midday and were back at the col by 17:00. On the 8th another early start was needed to descend from the col and get through the icefall to reach base camp. We arrived at base camp at the same time as the transport to take us back to Lhasa.

Chomolhari. The left skyline is the upper part of the northwest ridge, and the right hand skyline is the upper part of the south ridge. Fancy the west face? *Roger Payne*

JULIE-ANN CLYMA, *New Zealand, United Kingdom, Switzerland*

LHOZHAG REGION

Kula Kangri I (7,538m) (Künla Kangri, Main Peak), attempt. This assault on the main peak of Kula Kangri was combined with a training program for members of the Nihon University Alpine Club. Due to bad weather and an accident we were not able to mount an assault on the summit. On this climb we had planned to use the original route but, because of what appears to be likely avalanches from the west ridge, changed our route. This report introduces the first climb of the snow ridge on the lower side of the west ridge from the beginning of the west ridge to Camp Two.

Schedule of the expedition: September 5, Depart Lhasa for Zar village; Sep. 10, set up Base Camp (5,335m); Sep. 19, Set up Camp 1 (5,745m); October 4, Set up Camp 2 (6,200m); Oct. 5, Reached Camp 3 (6,900m); Oct. 9, Removed Camp 2; Oct. 10, Removed Camp 1; Oct. 13, Removed Base Camp.

Our new route from end of the narrow snow ridge of the west ridge to Camp 2 was able to avoid the danger of avalanches. For a while the ridge was fairly easy, but from the fourth pitch the slope exceeds 50°. On the ninth and tenth pitches the slope exceeds 70° and becomes a snow wall; beyond this it becomes less steep. We established this route in the middle of September and our movements were hindered every day around noon by clouds from the Bhutan side covering the west ridge and heavy snow with visibility under five meters. From Camp Two to Camp three, however, we retraced a route that had been already opened and paved by a French party that year. Although they were strong Himalayan climbers with years of experiences, time constraint forced them to give up an assault to the summit. For this year we felt it would have been best to have delayed our climb by two weeks.

Members: Susumu Nakamura (leader), Atsuo Sugiyama (climbing leader),Yoshitaka Omae, Takashi Suda (student), CTMA officer (1), cook (1), Chinese members (2).

Tamotsu Nakamura's notes on Kula Kangri [there is a photo of the Kula Kangri group in the *AAJ 2001*, p. 399]:

166km south of Lhasa (90°33'E and 28°13'N), the Kula Kangri massif soars over the greater Himalayan range in Tibet. Rising to 7,538m, the main peak (Kula Kangri I) has six neighboring peaks over 7,000m in Lhozhag of the Tibet Autonomous Region. To the southwest stand Kula Kangri II (7,418m, Central Peak) and III (7,381m, East Peak), while to the northeast are Karejiang I (7,221m) and II (7,045m). The above mountain heights are based on *A Guide to Mountaineering in China* (The China Mountaineering Association, 1993). A climbing chronicle follows:

Kula Kangri I (7,538m, Main Peak):

1985 April: The Alpine Club of Kobe University sent a reconnaissance party.

1986, March to May: The Alpine Club of Kobe University headed by Dr. Kazumasa Hirai made the first ascent on April 20 via the west ridge.

1994, April to May: An Austrian party made the second ascent on May 1 via the same route on the west ridge as the Kobe University climbed.

Kula Kangri II (7,418m) and III (7,381m) (Central Peak and East Peak):

2001, March to May: The Alpine Club of Tokai University made the first ascent of Kula Kangri II on May 2 and Kula Kanrgi III on May 4. A record of the expedition was published on the *Japanese Alpine News* Vol. 2 April 2002.

Karejiang I (7,221m, Main Peak):

1986, September to November: A party of the Himalayan Association of Japan made the first ascent on October 14 via the west ridge.

SUSUMU NAKAMURA, *Nihon University Alpine Club, Japan*

Adapted from Japanese Alpine News, *Tamotsu Nakamura, Editor*

Kula Kangri, west ridge attempt. A French commercial expedition jointly led by Jean Annequin and Ludovic Challeat attempted the west ridge of Kula Kangri from its base. Previous parties (there have been three ascents: Japanese in 1986, Austrians in 1994, and Spanish in 1997) appear to have followed the 1986 Japanese first ascent route, which short cuts the initial steep lower section of the ridge by climbing up the northern flank. However, this is more prone to avalanche and exposed to serac fall. The first section of the ridge to a camp at 6,200m (the point where the Japanese reached the crest from the left flank in 1986) had already been opened by the 2004 Japanese expedition [mentioned above] and the French added a few more ropes to those placed by the Japanese. Five hundred meters of rope were fixed on this section, which had one 20m step up to 80°. On the 6th October they occupied Camp 3 at 7,000m but more bad weather produced significant snow fall and the team abandoned their attempt, making a difficult and dangerous descent through the fresh snow.

This was a large expedition, half the members being trekkers with little in the way of altitude experience. They had official permission from the CTMA to trek in the lower Kuru Chu (valley) but when they arrived the Chinese Army would not allow them to do this, so all members had to trek close to their base camp.

LINDSAY GRIFFIN, *Mountain INFO, CLIMB magazine*

Kula Kangri, west ridge attempt. A three-man Danish team led by Claus Olsen also attempted the West Ridge at the same time as the French and Japanese. They gave up at around 6,500m.

LINDSAY GRIFFIN, *Mountain INFO, CLIMB magazine*

Monda Kangri (6,426m), attempt. Monda Kargri is located at 28.2°N and 90.6°E, 145km south of Lhasa. It is an isolated massif a little to the north of the mighty Ghula (Kula) Kangri, a 7,538m massif soaring to the west of Lake Phulma (Puma Yum Tso) in the Bhutan Himalaya. The Monda Kangri massif is independent from Ghula Kangri and has four peaks exceeding 6,000m. We have temporarily called these East Peak, West Peak, South Peak, and North Peak. The highest one is East Peak, 6,425m according to the 1:100,000 topographical map that we obtained from the Tibet Mountaineering Association. A photograph in *Immortal Mountains in the Snow Region* compiled by the China Mountaineering Association is not of the highest peak, but that of the North Peak (6,221m). No one, even the local nomads, knew the origin of the name Monda Kangri.

The approach to Monda Kangri is very easy. One can reach BC on the eastern bank of Puma Yum Tso in a one-day drive from Lhasa. Nevertheless, only one party had challenged the mountain before, that being the Montagne Alpine Club of Japan, which attempted the west face in July-August 1992. They set up BC at Monda La (5,266m) and climbed a very difficult rock face and ridge until ca 6,000m. Knowing that it has remained unclimbed, the alpine club in Sendai City of the northeastern region of Japan sent an expedition to Monda Kangri in June in commemoration of their 60th anniversary.

Our intended route ascended the west glacier to a col between the South Peak (6,250m) and the West Peak (6,291m). The ridge from the col leads to the summit of the highest peak in one kilometer. No reconnaissance of the east face of the main peak was allowed because the eastern side of the mountain is not open to foreigners.

On June 14 we gained the glacier at 5,400m, and we reached 6,100m on June 17, where we were blocked by large crevasses. We did not carry sufficient climbing gear to overcome such treacherous obstacles, and we were forced to give up the climb. The weather conditions were favorable throughout the activity. There was some thunder in the afternoon, and not much danger of avalanches because new snow was scarce. We strictly observed no trash mountaineering.

Japanese expedition members: leader: Tsuguyoshi Takahashi (62); climbing leader: Ryo Higasino (59); members: Makoto Saito (66), Sho Takeda (64), Zin Suzuki (60), Shigeru Suzuki (54), and Hitomi Kataoka (30). Chinese members: liaison officer: Zhang Jian Yuan, Vice-President, China Mountaineering Association; coordinator: Zhang Shaohong, Sichuan Earth Expedition, Inc.; high altitude support and guide: four Tibetans.

RYO HIGASHINO, *Japan*

Adapted from Japanese Alpine News, *Tamotsu Nakamura, Editor*

NYAINQENTANGLHA EAST

Jieqinnalagabu (Namla Karpa) (6,316m), first ascent. We met our staff and got our permit for Tibet in Kathmandu on August 16. The first plan was to go to Kajaqiao, but when we arrived in Lhari we had problems with the road, the yaks, and the yak drivers. So we returned to Lhasa and changed our plan. We started a new trip to the Basong Lake with the goal of climbing Jieqinnalagabu [also known as Namla Karpo]. We went by jeep to Zhonggo and then we put our base camp at the second lake at the base of the mountain (3,800m). For a week it rained. But we tried to find a way up to the base of the northwest pillar, and after a while we cut a way in the forest so we could put the ABC at 4,700m. And now we had to wait for good weather in order to summit. One morning the rain stopped but it was still cloudy. We started to climb, just one hour, to get an impression of the mountain. My two friends

Jieqennalagabu (Namla Karpo), showing its first ascent line. *Gabriel Voide*

decided not to climb to the summit. So we came down to the ABC. The next day the weather cleared and my two friends went down. I decided to try to reach the summit alone. I thought it's wrong to give up without seeing if there was a real problem in front of me. My goal was to climb until it would be too hard or too dangerous for me to solo. The plan was to climb the 1,600 meters to the summit in one day and then down to ABC: so it would be solo and alpine-style, a dream for me!

The next morning I started to climb at 1 a.m. I started so early because of the smooth and dangerous snow in the afternoon. The first 300-400 meters was easy, but then the difficulties began. The first 800 meters of the northwest pillar were rock and then 800 meters of ice. The first part of the rock was UIAA III-IV, not too difficult. On the last 200 meters of the rock I had to follow exactly the edge of the pillar because of bad conditions on the face. There where some difficulties in UIAA V and one bit of UIAA VI/VI+. To climb in this altitude in the night with this difficulty and solo, for me it was a big challenge!

After the rock it was definitely day and I could take off my headlight. The ice was at first 50° degrees and afterward 60°-70°. This part I could climb on the face to the right of the pillar. The last 200 meters became steeper and steeper and I had to traverse left across nearly vertical 85° back to the ridge. After a bad cornice I reached the summit. For me it was a great feeling to be the first on this mountain and to climb the first mountain in this part of the Nyainqentan-glha, but this feeling only lasted a short time because I was worried about the descent. My biggest problem was not having snow-stakes. So I had to climb backward down the steep snow. Once in the ice it was better—there I could use my ice axes. So I climbed everything down to the rocks and then I began with rappels. The easier rock-part I had to climb down, to win some time. At 6 p.m. I reached the ABC and I was very happy to see my friends. They decided to go down to the base-camp at 3,800m the same evening and so I went with them. I was very happy that they could help me to carry some equipment. At 10 p.m. I arrived the base-camp at the lake. I was very tired but also very happy!

GABRIEL VOIDE, *Switzerland*

New Zealand

SUMMER 2002/2003 – AUTUMN 2004

The Darran Mountains, Fiordland summary. The Darran Mountains are New Zealand's greatest multi-pitch alpine rock venue. With technical diorite slabs and faces, occasional glacier approaches, and peaks up to 2,700m, this region offers a diversity of climbing opportunities for the beginner and advanced climber alike.

Activity in the Darrans is sporadic and largely weather dependant—the range's coastal proximity and resultant high precipitation make climbing days precious. Limited flying-in opportunites make access difficult and progress slow on more technical climbs that require bolts. New routing in the Darrans requires time, commitment, and patience.

The 2002/2003 summer saw Craig Jefferies and visionary developer Paul Rogers complete an aid route on the isolated Sinbad Gully headwall. Their route, The Original Line, is rated 23 (5.11c)/A2+, 10 pitches, and was established over two seasons.

Long-time Darrans activist Dave Vass teamed up with Richard Turner and Rene Renshaw to make the first ascent of Mt. Mahere's south face (2,137m), in the Lake Turner area, Central Darrans. It's Alright—We Think is 10 pitches and grade 21 (5.10d). They also climbed a shorter route on the South Ridge of Mt. Milne (2,135m).

Also in the Central Darrans Keith Riley, Craig Jefferies, and Brigid Allan climbed the south face of Mt. Milne at grade 19 (10b), 5 pitches with 300m of scrambling to the summit, the east face of Tarewai (2,158m), 6 pitches, grade 18 (10a), and a short line on the west face of Mt. Milne.

Steve Carr, an active new-router and soloist from Otago made the first rope-solo of the ultra classic Labyrinth, grade 22 (11a), six pitches. Labyrinth is located on the north face of Barrier Knob (1,879m); a broad, steep face of glacier- and water-eroded diorite only a three-hour walk from the area's base hut, Homer Hut (NZAC). This face is growing in popularity and has seen a surge of quality new lines in the last three years. Murray Judge (active new router on alpine rock since the 1970s), Wayo Carson, Matt Squires, and Jamie Foxley have all contributed mixed bolts and natural pro lines at grades up to to 23 (11c).

Barron Saddle, Mt. Brewster region summary. This is a large and complex alpine region broadly covering the Southern Alps south of the Aoraki Mt. Cook region to the Haast Highway, north of Mt. Aspiring.

This region is a treasure trove of new route possibilites, a fact made apparent by the "number of new routes to come out of this area in the last two years. Ross Cullen (the area's guidebook author) and Bill McLeod tackled two peaks on the lower Huxley Range, climbing Waka Jumping, 13 (5.6), 13 pitches on the south face of Leaning Mount, and Zwieback on the Hunter Valley face of Peak 2,285m.

The Cullen and McLeod duo also continued to explore the South Temple Valley and pick off new lines, one of the best finds being the Grasshopper Wall on Peak 2,070m; this wall yeiled one line, and though not technically hard is a good contrbution to the area. Paul Hersey and Mat Woods established two new lines on the north face of Benross Peak (2,486m) from the

Dobson Valley (climbed with Derek Chinn and Dave Morgan also); the first ascent of the south face of Glencairn (2,499m), Neumann Range; and the eight pitch Zoe on Steeple Peak (2,207m), South Temple Valley. Derek Chinn and Paul Hersey also teamed up for a new line on the outlier slab of Steeple Peak, Love Me, Love My Zimmerframe.

Aoraki Mt. Cook and Westland summary. The Aoraki Mt. Cook and Westland region is a shadow of its former self as far as new climbs are concerned. The region of greatest focus for new routes and first winter ascents is now the névés west of the Main Divide, where shorter, more technical routes abound and are easily accessed. Hopefully this trend will bring another shift, with the refined techniques being applied to the bigger faces.

Boxing Day 2002 saw saw Jo Haines and Australian Adam Darragh make the first ascent of the North East Buttress of The Nun's Veil (2,749m), Mt. Cook Grade 4+, crux 15 (5.8). This route follows predominantly good rock for 17 pitches.

The Fox Glacier Névé has been the area with the most new route activity reported, mostly duing the winter. A well-iced north face of Mt. Haast (3,114m) made possible Natural Gas (5), by Allan Uren, Dave Vass, and Richard Turner. A couple of first winter ascents were made: the Atkinson Hall Route on Mt. Haast's north face by Craig Jefferies and Steve Eastwood, and the Moonshine Buttress by Allan Uren and Craig Cardie. On the popular south face of Douglas Peak (3,077m), Vass and Jefferies climbed some new pitches on the central rock buttress of the

face. Mt. Mallory (2,756m) saw a new route, Homeowners, by Uren, Craig Cardie, and Jeff Richards. A couple of first winter ascents were made on the south face of Mt. Barnicoat (2,800m). The previous November saw the addition of a new route by the female team of Anna Keeling and Laetitia Campe: Kiss My Axe is six pitches and grade 4.

The Balfour Face of Tasman, New Zealand's second highest mountain at 3,497m, was the scene of the most notable new route of 2003 with Surreal Insommnia, 8 pitches (6+) climbed on the extreme left of the face by Mark Sedon and Guy Cotter in April 2003. The route follows sustained and steep ice.

The Caroline Face of Aoraki Mt. Cook (3,754m), which rarely sees ascents these days, was climbed twice during the 2003/2004 summer, once solo by Nick Wall, and by a party of three including Pat Deavoll, Mike Brown, and Paul Knott. The south face of Mt. Hicks (3,198m) saw its second guided ascent when Heaven's Door (6) was climbed in November by guides Nick Cradock and Phil Penny, and client Neil Hickman.

Allan Uren on day two of the first ascent of God's Zone, Torres Peak. *Craig Jefferies*

The summer season at Aoraki Mt. Cook was sadly marred by a number of deaths, including a high profile tragedy involving the deaths of guides Paul Scaife, David Hiddleson, and David Gardner in an avalanche and resulting fall on Mt. Tasman.

Alpine rock in the Darran Mountains summary. After a quiet winter, some sustained periods of fine weather and a group of motivated climbers brought a surge of activity to the Darrans this summer.

Craig Jefferies and Martin Wightman made the most notable ascent of the season by getting off the beaten track and exploring the Llawrenny Peaks, situated in a seldom-visited tract of wilderness north of the Milford Track and southwest of Mitre Peak. The pair made the first ascent of the east ridge of the North Llawrenny Peak (1,925m). The route offered approx-imately 300-meters of quality rock climbing on a sharp ridge, with near vertical sections where the ridge merges with the north face.

Immediately north of the Llawrenny Peaks sits Sinbad Gully, where this summer Kester Brown and Sebastian Lowensteijn attempted to free The Original Line (mentioned earlier) on the upper cirque of Sinbad Gully. Established by Craig Jefferies and Paul Rogers in 2002, The Origi-nal Line has difficulties of 23/A2+ and was considered a viable free route —that is until Kester and

Sebastian were shut down on the seventh pitch of the ten-pitch route, having freed pitches up to grade 27 (5.12d).

Another route to have its free pitches eliminated, this time entirely, was Ram Paddock Road (23/A4) on the Little North Face of Mt. Sabre (2,167m). Derek Thatch-er and Jonathon Clearwater gave the route an overall grade of 24 (11d) and added a grade 25 (5.12) pitch called Rock Candy near the start of Ball And Chain.

On the south face of Tairoa Jonathon Clearwater and Thomas Evans climbed eight new pitches to create Liquid Toasted Sandwich (21).

Mt. Aspiring region summary. In terms of new route activity it has been a relatively quiet year for the Aspiring region. However, the fact that new route potential still exists was clearly illustrated when on the same day this summer two parties climbed new terrain on the south face of the classic "Matterhorn of the South": Mt. Aspiring (3,033m).

Howie McGhie and Chris Fox, believ-ing they were on an entirely new line due to

Torres Peak, northeast face. (1) God's Zone (Jefferies-Uren, 2004). (2) Denz-Gabites-Perry (1977). These are the only routes on the face. *Craig Jefferies*

The west face Mt. Tasman is on the left; the northeast face of Torres Peak on the right. The Abel Janszoon Glacier collects their avalanches. *Colin Monteath*

a mistake in the Aspiring Region guidebook, climbed the Whiston-Hyslop line (5+) for two thirds of its length and then took on new ground directly up to the upper Coxcomb Ridge. They have named their alternative finish Perspiring.

Forcing a direct line through the overhanging schist band at the base of the face, the U.K. team of James Edwards, Kevin Neal, and Oliver Metherell climbed up the center of the south face to join McGhie and Fox's finish, shortly after they had climbed it themselves. 24 Hour Party People is given 5+ and is possibly the hardest route on the face. Edwards had tried the route the previous spring with another ex-pat Brit, Dave Alderson, but the pair had failed due to a two-day wade through deep snow and difficult conditions on the route. The crux overhanging rock band featured "very dubious rock and thin blobs of plastic ice."

In March this year well-known guide Geoff Wayatt made his 80th ascent of Mt. Aspiring —a record for this mountain.

Sadly there were two deaths on Mt. Aspiring's Ramp this season. NZAC members Marc Freeman and Niklas Werner both died in separate incidents descending the Ramp, after slipping whilst unroped.

Queenstown region summary. The Remarkable Range continues to be a ice playground in winter with several new lines being establised this year. Most notable is Helicampers (M-something) by Mark Sedon and Lionel Clay at well-known ice crag Wye Creek. Mark aided and bolted the severely overhanging line and Lionel bagged the first M-rated "free" ascent, first shot. The route climbs a schist cave wall and links to a thin free-hanging icicle. This is the first true mixed line in New Zealand employing pre-placed bolts for protection and is no doubt a reflection of overseas trends, whilst being a staunch reminder as to how far behind New Zealand is in the development of sport mixed-climbing.

Hopkins Valley region summary. Exceeding the Aoraki Mt. Cook area for new routes, this accessible area continues to receive attention from a handful of motivated climbers. In the 2004 *New Zealand Alpine Journal (NZAJ)* Ross Cullen (guidebook author, and one of the area's leading first ascentionists) reported 20-plus new climbs in 12 months.

In May Paul Hersey and Mat Woods climbed the 500-meter rock route Tenderfoot, Grade 3, rock crux 13 (5.6), on Mt. Glen Lyon (2,050m) at the toe of the Neumann Range. The wall features some nice climbing with sections of good rock broken by ledges.

Later in the year a second route was added. Late Bloomer, by Mat Woods and Dave Morgan tackles more difficult ground, with a crux of 17 (5.9) and an overall grade of 4-.

In the Dobson Valley, Kynan Bazley and Yew-jin Tan made the first ascent of the east face of Mt. Glencairn (2,499m) via Hidden Treasures, Grade 15 (5.8), overall 3-. The route started from Sutherland Stream.

Ross Cullen and Bill McLeod once again teamed up for some new route exploration and after fishing around in the South Branch of the South Temple Valley the duo discoved and named the Salmon Slabs. This salmon-hued stretch of greywacke now has four multi-pitch routes up to grade 17.

The most notable first ascent of the winter was a new line on the southeast face of Mt. Ward (2,645m), North Elcho Valley, climbed in late August by Kynan Bazely and Paul Hersey. The route, named Great Dane, is a 12-pitch ice climb with an overall grade of 5-. Prior to this ascent the face had not seen a pair of ice tools for 23 years!

A handful of new ice routes were climbed at Bush Stream and a few other areas were explored for ice climbing potential.

This summer saw the Cullen-McLeod team active again on the Grasshopper Wall, Peak 2,070m, with the first ascent of Knees Up—grade 16 (5.8/5.9), nine pitches.

In the North Branch of the Huxley River James Edwards and Oliver Metherell made the first recorded ascent of Peak 2,072m, the 500-meter route is called Matinee.

A number of other climbers were active, completing new routes and repeating existing climbs.

Aoraki Mount Cook and Westland summary. There were a number of standout climbs at Aoraki Mt. Cook during the last year, with Allan Uren and Craig Jefferies' ascent of the northeast face of Torres Peak (3,160m) being the most significant. Climbed in early July, Godzone (14 pitches, grade 6+) tackles consistently technical terrain as it negotiates a more or less plumb line up the face. The 500-meter route was climbed with two bivouacs and is a definite contender for the badge of "hardest route in the country."

A few days later Glenn Pennycook and Tshering Pande Bhote tackled Mt. Haidinger's east face headwall via a prominent ice lead high above the Tasman Glacier. In a comitting effort the pair climbed the route from Pioneer Hut by crossing the South Ridge of Haidinger and abseiling and traversing steep slopes to access the direttissima. White Steel tackles 200 meters of ice from 65-90 degrees and is graded 5+.

Continuing with his penchant for soloing Southern Alps classics, Guy McKinnon upped the ante last winter with solos of the remote and difficult to access Hidden and Balfour Faces of Mt. Tasman (3,497m), both grade 6. The Balfour has been soloed in winter before, but not often and the Hidden (climbed via the Direct) was a first winter ascent.

In January this year Guy attempted a solo of the north ridge of Aoraki Mt. Cook (3,754m). Tackling the crux, the Beare Step, still shod in his big boots, Guy slipped, but his would-be fatal plunge was cut short after five meters by a small ledge that he was lucky enough to strike and remain on. The landing broke his left fibula and he remained on the ledge for 13 hours before being rescued by the Aoraki Mt. Cook SAR team.

Australian climber Gren Hinton also made some very impressive winter solos. On the south face of Mt. Hicks (3,198m) he made an ascent of the Yankee Kiwi Couloir (6+) and a mixed free- and rope-solo of Logans Run (6+).

Other winter highlights included a first winter ascent of The Balcony Line (4+) on the south face of Mt. Mallory (2,756m) by Tsering Pande Bhote, Johnny Davidson, and Glenn Pennycook. Pennycook also made the first winter ascent of Albino Merino (4) on the southwest headwall of Mt. Haidinger. Pete Camell and Nick Monteith climbed a three-pitch variation to the Valentine Gully on the Marcel Face of Mt. Haast and a new route on the south face of Mt. Barnicoat (2,800m).

Glenn Pennycook and Andrew Young also made the first winter ascent of the Gray-Williamson Couloir on the southwest face of Conway Peak (2,899m).

The readily accessible Murchison Face of My Aylmer (2,699m) was climbed in September by Paul Knott and Adrian Camm. Archbishop Of Canterbury is sustained 400-meters of ice with occasional rock steps, with an overall grade of 4/5.

Summer saw the usual throng of activity in the park, though few significant ascents were made. Early in the season Tim Billington and Paul Stephanus climbed a new line on the east face of Mt. Nazomi (2,925m).

In January Mike Madden made a solo ascent of the Direct (4+) on the east face of Mt. Sefton (3,151m). Vaughn Thomas and Thomas Evans made a quick ascent of the Central Buttress on the north face of Mt. Hicks—12 hours hut to hut.

The end of the season was marred by tragedy with the death of accomplished climber and guide Erica Beuzenberg. Beuzenberg was short-roping two clients on Ball Pass, just south of Aoraki Mt. Cook, when one slipped, dragging the trio over a 200-meter bluff.

SEASON SUMMARIES FROM MARK WATSON, *New Zealand Alpine Club*

BOOK REVIEWS

EDITED BY DAVID STEVENSON

When the Alps Cast Their Spell: MOUNTAINEERS OF THE ALPINE GOLDEN AGE. TREVOR BRAHAM. GLASGOW, THE IN PINN (NEIL WILSON PUBLISHING), 2004. 314 PAGES, COLORED PLATES. HARDCOVER. $30.00

When the judges gave the 2004 Boardman-Tasker Award for the best mountain literature to *When the Alps Cast Their Spell*, they knew what they were doing. It is a gold mine of scholarship about a critical period in the history of mountaineering.

Today, when mountaineering in all its many emanations, exploratory, alpine, rock, ice, bouldering, and even indoor, is practiced around the world by hundreds of thousands of climbers, it is hard to realize that the gym rat as well as the alpinist evolved from a single source, a group of Victorian Englishmen. Although a few people had climbed a few mountains in various parts of the world, giving a claim by their various countries to early mountaineering achievements, the sport itself was invented by the British in the 19th Century.

There have been many books on the Golden Age. Most of the scholarly histories are long out of print, and many recent ones are superficial reads providing an overview, but lacking the depth necessary to give the reader a feeling for the richness of mountaineering tradition. *When the Alps Cast Their Spell* does provide such a feeling. It is not an easy book, but it is smoothly written and well researched. As a mountaineer who has climbed in both the Alps and the Himalaya and as a former editor of the *Himalayan Journal*, who also has lived in Switzerland for many years, the author is one of the few persons who could write such a book.

Braham starts with a succinct but thorough chapter on the beginnings of mountaineering. The heart of the book is chapters on seven mountaineers, five of whom epitomized the Golden Age: Alfred Wills, John Tyndall, Leslie Stephen, A. W. Moore, and Edward Whymper. Braham then discusses subsequent developments through chapters on Albert Mummery and Emmanuel Boileau. As Braham says in his introduction, he chose subjects to illustrate the history of mountaineering, not explain it. Historians have considered Wills' ascent of the Wetterhorn in 1855 to have opened the Golden Age, while Whymper's ascent of the Matterhorn ten years later closed it. Mummery and Boileau represent the next stage of mountaineering, pioneering new routes of increasing technical difficulty in which the challenge is more important than the summit, an era Sir Arnold Lunn called The Silver Age.

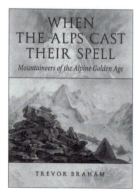

What comes through in the book is the similarity between these pioneers and modern climbers, not the obvious differences. They were on a pilgrimage and in their own way were overcoming difficulty, accepting risk, and pushing the envelope, as an extreme climber today does. And they were like us as well. As Braham writes, "There exist today mountaineers with Stephen's ethical standards, Moore's exploratory ardor, Mummery's pioneering spirit, Tyndall's taste for risk, Wills' trust in guides, Whymper's craving to predominate."

Those familiar with this history will recognize many of Braham's stories. But he has combined well-known material with original research, making this an important book even for those who think they know the history. By describing the lives of these men, he gives a compelling picture of why, as well as how, the traditions of mountaineering arose.

Besides relating the accomplishments of the five principal subjects, Braham discusses the contributions of others, making his book a comprehensive history, not just a collection of biographies. There is concise but good coverage of the importance of W. A. B. Coolidge, the mountaineer-scholar about whom it was said, "The only way he knew how to bury the hatchet was in someone's back." When necessary, Braham chooses detail over simplicity, thus providing an extra richness to his account.

The chapter I most appreciated was about Emmanuel Boileau and the first ascent of the Meije, the highest peak in the Dauphine. Prior histories in English have not given this story the attention it deserves. When mentioned, it appears to be an afterthought. I have always been curious about the elusive Meije, on which the famous Emil Zigsmondy died. This book does it justice.

Braham covers alpinists who may have otherwise been omitted in the chapter, "There Were Many Others," which includes Leading Ladies, Eminent Europeans, and Great Guides. Again, like the first chapter, it is concise, dense, and informative. There also is an excellent bibliography and a thorough, accurate list of Alpine First Ascents from the 13th through 19th centuries. If this is not enough, one can read the chapter endnotes, a treasure trove of obscure but fascinating information.

Besides facts, the book is infused with Braham's observations and judgments. He concludes, "Whatever might be the future of mountaineering it is to be hoped that certain essentials will remain. Such as the first spellbound moment of a youthful spirit stepping across the threshold into an awareness of the mountain world, and the birth of a desire to preserve what it has discovered."

While all forms of climbing have their own rewards, a knowledge of the heritage of mountaineering adds to one's satisfaction, as one becomes more aware of his or her relationship to the past. Braham's book is superb account of the pioneering era when mountaineering became a sport. Climbers unfamiliar with our rich traditions will obtain an understanding of them, and those who are well versed in the literature will gain new knowledge and insights. Every mountaineer should have a copy. It will almost make a rainy day seem worthwhile. Take it on your next attempt on Mt. Robson.

NICHOLAS CLINCH

High Rocks and Ice: The Classic Mountain Photographs of Bob and Ira Spring. IRA SPRING. FOREWORD BY JOHN HARLIN III. GUILFORD CT/HELENA MT: FALCON, 2004. NUMEROUS BLACK & WHITE PHOTOGRAPHS. 107 PAGES. $18.95.

In his introduction to this most essential volume in Northwest climbing history, Ira Spring acknowledges that "My twin brother, Bob, and I did not deliberately set out to chronicle the 'Classic Age' of Mountaineering." Nevertheless, that's exactly what happened—and everyone who loves those glistening peaks is in their debt.

High Rocks and Ice provides a retrospective catalog of the work of this pair of legendary alpine photojournalists, whose passion for taking pictures was first lit in 1930 when Eastman Kodak celebrated its 50th anniversary by offering every 12-year old in the United States a free Box Brownie camera. The brothers took the company up on its offer and headed off to the mountains. Over the long course of their professional partnership, the Springs moved on to bigger and better (not to mention heavier) camera gear, publishing their superb black-and-white photographs in a wide variety of places, including the *Seattle Times, National Geographic, Life, The Saturday Evening Post*, and more than 50 books. Completed just before its author's death in 2003,

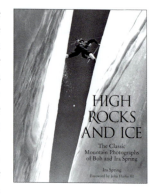

High Rocks and Ice includes photos taken on Mt. Rainier (the most frequently depicted location in this book), Glacier Peak, Mt. Shuksan, Mt. Challenger, as well as a few assorted sites in the Olympics, Canadian Rockies, and Alaska. As John Harlin III observes in his Foreword: "So ubiquitous were the camera lenses of Bob and Ira Spring…that most of us who loved the Northwest's mountains in the second half of the twentieth century have trouble separating our personal memories from the images we've savored on the printed page."

Surpassing the historical value of the photographs, however, is a powerful emotional charge that comes off these pages, which some may mistake for nostalgia but is in fact *memento mori*, a reminder of the inevitability that all things pass. In the section titled "My Teenagers," we find a picture taken on Mt. Rainier in 1951, when the Springs hosted a group of four teens who were eager to assist the photographers in the arduous work of setting up shoots in the difficult glacier landscape. There they are, sitting joyful around the cook stove in a camp perched somewhere near the clouds. In the foreground, we are given the very picture of youth fair and carefree; in the background, the lambent ranges of eternity. If we climbed to this same spot today, we should expect to discover these young people still lounging among the boulders, still happy, still vibrant, still *there*—or so the photo seems to suggest. But of course this response is based upon a dark and delectable deception, one inherent in the very nature of photography, especially in the documentary style black-and-whites that were the Springs' forte. As Susan Sontag expresses it: "To take a photograph is to participate in another person's (or thing's) mortality, vulnerability, mutability. Precisely by slicing out this moment and freezing it, all photographs testify to time's relentless melt." To reflect upon an artful documentary photograph only intensifies the effect. Nowhere is this more poignantly felt than in contemplating Ira's 1973 shot of Devi Unsoeld smiling in the immortal sunshine beside her father, Willi, on the slopes of Mt. Eldorado.

Near the end of the book is a 1950 image of the Quien Sabe Glacier in Boston Basin, North Cascades. In his commentary, Ira provides a sentence that could serve as the epitaph for what he calls the Classic Age of Mountaineering: "The last time I was in Boston Basin, the glacier was hardly there at all, reduced to a late-summer snowpatch, a vanishing memory of the Little Ice Age that began in the fourteenth century and pretty well petered out in the early twentieth." All things flow. Though the glaciers and climbers depicted in these pages may have vanished, something of them may yet be evoked by immersing oneself in the photos and vignettes found in *High Rocks and Ice.*

JOHN P. O'GRADY

Mount Everest , Khumbu Himal, Rolwaling Himal I Khumbakarna Himal, SATELLITE IMAGE MAP (1:1,000,000), JAN ZURAWSKI.

K2 and the Baltoro Glacier in the Karakoram, SATELLITE IMAGE MAP (1:80,000), GRZEGORZ GLAZEK. BOTH BY THE POLISH MOUNTAINEERING ASSOCIATION WITH GEOSYSTEMS POLSKA.

For all of us who have traveled to, or dream of traveling to, these crowning ranges of the planet, who read and write about them, or who simply enjoy images of the world's famous ranges, these two new publications are real gems. They cause one to sit and stare for long periods, as the eyes grow accustomed to the amount of detail found on these moderate-resolution satellite images.

Using fairly recent color imagery (Nepal Himalaya, 2000) and black–and–white imagery (Karakoram, 2001), these new satellite maps show details that were available only to those savvy enough to find and use Landsat and SPOT satellite images. They show us an unadulterated and surprisingly cloud-free view of the mountains, free of the interpretation and cartographic license used by cartographers in compiling their maps (often from these same type of images).

Few traditional maps can rival the detail found on the Karakoram sheet. (Brad Washburn's collaborations with the Swiss are the only ones that come to mind.) This is clearly a case where less is more, and the lack of color enhances the shadows and aids legibility. This sheet makes use of the higher resolution French SPOT imagery, which permits greater detail and a larger scale compared to the data used on the Everest sheet. Distinct medial moraines and access gullies on the Trango Glacier are clearly identifiable, as are sharp ridge lines and crevasse fields on the entire sheet. For those planning a trip to the Baltoro Glacier, or any other subrange portrayed, this map will prove an essential planning and visualizing tool. It fills a void for detailed current maps of the region north of the Baltoro Glacier along the China/Pakistan Border. Sources used in labeling this sheet are remarkably inclusive, from the earliest Italian to the most current Japanese maps of the range. The text elements are legible, tastefully done, and unobtrusive. [A 1:1 scale sample of this map can be found on page 16 of this Journal—Ed.]

The Everest sheet, while beautiful, is nonetheless not as aesthetically pleasing and of the two probably less essential. The spectral band combination chosen for its natural color look is over-saturated and makes the green of vegetation the dominant element on a sheet where the white of the mountains should be (including four 8,000m peaks). This is understandable for a product destined for the mass market, where colors mimicking nature are more likely to be understood quickly by casual observers. The multicolor typography, with a large number of serif-italicized river labels, is distracting and takes away from the imagery below it. There is also an abundance of transparent lines that, while not as prominent, are not useful enough to warrant their inclusion. For the Nepal region in particular there is an abundance of easily available maps that already fill that niche. Jan Zurowski, the cartographer, uses several of these as sources for his place names, including the Schneider and Washburn maps, yet does not make use of the more recent Finnish/Nepalese-produced National Survey Department's 1:50,000 maps. These were likely ignored because they introduce new elevations for peaks whose heights have been set for several decades from earlier maps.

Both sheets have illumination from the south, which in the Northern Hemisphere creates problems of cast shadows on the northerly aspects so favored by alpinists. Details on these faces lie in shadows and can be difficult to decipher. The southern illumination can also lead to an inversion of the terrain by some observers, with valley bottoms appearing as ridge tops. Fortunately, this can be fixed by rotating the map to show south at the top. The result is terrain relief that pops off the page.

The beauty of these images and the advantages of satellite maps lie in their large amount of unedited details. These are not traditional maps in that they do not contain enough navigational information (such as a coordinate grid and magnetic declination) to be used for taking measurements in the field, and the information has not been edited. When the cartographer obscures the image with superfluous information already found on traditional maps, it is to the detriment of the user. While text elements are useful for identifying peaks, they should in my opinion be minimized, as these images are best enjoyed as images, and are attractive enough to stand on their own merit. With the increasing availability of satellite imagery it is likely that more publishers will venture into this genre of map. They would do well to use Grzegorz Glazek's K2 and Baltoro Glacier map as a model.

MARTIN GAMACHE

Postcards From The Trailer Park. CAMERON BURNS. NEW YORK:
THE LYONS PRESS. 2004. PAPERBACK. 279 PAGES.

When I received Cameron Burns' book for review, I thought, "Piece of cake. It's 30+ short articles/stories/vignettes/essays about climbing. I can read a half-dozen, dash off 200 words, and I'm done." Well, *Postcards From The Trailer Park* is like that potato-chip ditty: "Bet you can't read [or eat] just one." I actually read the whole damn thing. PFTTP hasn't been off my nightstand in the two weeks since I got it.

While many of the essays are about the trips Burns has done and the people he's done them with, he is much more than an observer of the climber animal. He is a connoisseur of humanity and of his own surroundings. His descriptions of his surroundings, the recounting of conversations, and the ever-present exaggerations add up to very enjoyable reading.

Two of my favorites are his portraits of Fred Beckey and Warren Harding. Though completely different, both are presented with clarity, humor, and, yes, affection. "The Unbearable Greatness of Fred," is divided into two sections. The first, a scathing account of a '91 trip to Mexico with Beckey, presents a view unlike what those of us who have never met the man would have imagined. That said, in spite of a critical look at Beckey's personality, Burns's appreciation for Beckey's accomplishments is clear. The postscript, written three years later, after they became reacquainted and following several subsequent trips, ties things together in a way that resolves the bad taste from the Mexico trip. Here are two excerpts, the first from the third paragraph, the second from the last:

"Fed up with Mexican service, Fred Beckey stands up, grunts, farts, and heads for the door. Taken aback, Mike and I stare at each other. Beckey, a personal hero for both of us, is proving anything but a hero."

And, "…certainly, during these half-dozen or so other climbing trips, we didn't do a lot of climbing. But I'm incredibly glad I went with him. He is a genuinely great guy, and he deserves a prominent position in every climber's pantheon.'"

That's the tip of the iceberg. There are stories about climbing Aconcagua with a "hideous blue and yellow" $45 Wal-Mart Wilderness Trails tent, "hoopsticking" desert towers in New Mexico, his first outdoor climbing trip with his then-fiancé (now wife) Ann, a hilarious account of a '93 ascent of El Cap, and the ultimate tick story, "Ticking a Few Routes in Montana." Just when you think you can't laugh any more, he hits you with another line that lays you out. Example:

"Tell 'em I watched a dozen ticks crawl up your shorts while you were climbing," my wife pipes up as I poke the keyboard. "Remember those nasty, tiny Coq Sportif shorts you had? Ooooh. Dunno what was worse: the shorts or the ticks…."

My wife is glad I finished this book. I kept waking her up at 1 a.m. laughing. Burns reminds me of my favorite partners. No matter what happens, they manage to find humor in everything. Guys like that make climbing trips a lot more fun, and life on the edge more bearable.

AL HOSPERS

Ways to the Sky: A Historical Guide to North American Mountaineering, ANDY SELTERS. GOLDEN, CO: THE AMERICAN ALPINE CLUB PRESS. 334 PGS. 65 B&W PHOTOS, 15 MAPS. $24.95.

When Jeff McCarthy returned this spring from the "International Festival of Mountaineering Literature," he remarked that "the Brits seem far more concerned with history than we are." Hard to argue with that, especially given that the first comprehensive book-length history of climbing in North America was written by Chris Jones—a Brit—in 1976. Here in the States guidebooks and instructional books compete for climbers' attention, followed closely, I suspect, by website chat rooms and forums. History accrues climb by climb in these *AAJ* pages, in magazine reports, and in very condensed form in *some* guidebooks. My general sense is that here in the United States we find something admirable in Salathé's brief query: "Vy can't ve chust climb?"

Selters does a good job of explaining why it may not be quite enough to "chust climb." His Introduction begins with a line from Rita Dove: "If you don't look back, the future never happens." The Introduction bears close reading, for here Selters lays out his parameters, his vision, his questions, and even his definition of and "rules" of mountaineering.

Selters sets out to give us "the story of original-style mountaineering." He then asks what the phrase means. He lays out three admittedly broad parameters: one, the territory is the "higher peaks" of North America (so the Gunks and Yosemite, for example, are excluded). This parameter is also exemplified by references to particular climbers in the indices: in this tome Robbins garners six; in Jones' book Robbins gets 31; and in Roper's *Camp 4*. (Although I found it unavoidable to compare Selters' book to Jones', it's not fair, since each is indispensable.)

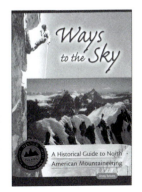

Second parameter: "Climbs that have been done predominantly free." Fair enough, I suppose, but he implies that climbs that did employ aid do not count as "progress." He adds that big-wall climbs in Alaska deserve a companion volume, but includes some anyway, all but ignoring their use of fixed rope, which, after all, is not exactly "direct aid from anchors to make progress." Thus, by his own criteria Selters probably should have left out the first ascent of Mt. Dickey by Roberts, Rowell, and Ward, but he rightly calls it "one of the most demanding climbs of the decade" (note the 30-year gap between its first and second ascent, just last summer!). Similarly, he mentions that on the first ascent of Mt. Kennedy's north ridge fixed rope was used between camps, but doesn't mention that an astounding 8,000 feet of it were placed on a route of about 6,000 vertical feet.

Third Parameter: He wished to understand "the progression of our mountain routes." This is really the issue he's grappling with: what is *progress*, "what yardstick do we measure with?" It's a charge he does not take on lightly, and despite my quibbles here, handles nicely throughout. Nonetheless, this concern with progress occasionally gets muddied: "the truest measure of mountaineering progress, then, is the evolution of the idea of mountaineering." Huh?

Selters does a good job of allowing chronology to structure the text. Logical enough you say, but easier said then done when you consider the importance of place and the force of personalities, either of which might compete with chronology as organizing principles. Chic Scott's *Pushing the Limits: The Story of Canadian Mountaineering* (2000)—a terrific book—suffers a bit from this; too often it's hard to be certain if you're traveling through time, space, or personalities—the book succeeds by its sheer thoroughness.

Particularly smart is Selters' breaking the book into four periods, which although tied to chronology are conceptual: I. "Discovery by Summiting," II. "Adventure Realized," III. "Better that We Raise Our Skill," and IV. "When 'Why' Disappeared." The introductions to these periods are fine essays and, coupled with the equally fine epilogue, comprise a thoughtful overview of our arena.

It's not just in the introductions and overviews that Selters' thoughtfulness is revealed. Smart, hard-earned observations abound throughout. For example, he remarks about Cheesmond and Freer's disappearance on their 1987 Hummingbird Ridge attempt: "For many climbers, their deaths peeled away a layer of denial that says, if you're good enough mountaineering is essentially safe. When climbers this good are killed, the core of the game is laid open, and we see all-too-mortal hearts perhaps playing the odds too many times."

Peter Croft notes in his Foreword that the book not only introduced him to "new chunks of history but also helped to fire up recollections of my own." I agree. One of the book's great strengths is that even though much of the early history ought to be familiar to me, I feel that I am being re-shown freshly through Selters' vision. One way he has accomplished this is by a terrific selection of photographs, clearly reproduced, that were new to me. Another way is through the closing section of each chapter: "mini-portraits" of representative climbs from the era. There I felt the book was at its freshest and most exciting. Selters chose these with "a bias to routes that haven't seen as bright a spotlight as our best known classics." I had done a few of the routes and knew of few others, but a surprising number were peaks that hadn't appeared on my radar screen—a gift, to be sure.

My only real complaint is that although Selters brilliantly chooses passages to quote, he rarely provides their sources. It's not that I doubt his accuracy; it's that the book doesn't facilitate further research very well. Not every reader will care, but people interested in history tend to be interested in the primary sources. Although Jones did not footnote his text (for which I'm grateful) he did provide a precise and thorough list of references at the end of each chapter.

To return to Selters' choice of Rita Dove's words as an opening epigraph, like most readers I am not personally pushing the future of our "life game" (Selters' term). But I am pushing (very gently) the future of my own climbing, and this book both helps me contextualize where I've been and gives me much to dream about in the years ahead.

If I had to choose a single volume as a cornerstone for a young climber's library, this is the book. *Ways to the Sky* joins Jones' *Climbing in North America*, Scott's *Pushing the Limits*, and the ubiquitous Roper and Steck's *Fifty Classic Climbs in North America* (1979) as the foundation for understanding where we've been, what we value, and what might yet be possible.

DAVID STEVENSON

Between a Rock and a Hard Place. ARON RALSTON. ATRIA BOOKS: NEW YORK, 2004. 354 PAGES, WITH 16 PAGES OF COLOR PHOTOS. $26.00

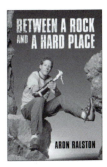

This is the book about the guy who cut his arm off, by the guy who cut his arm off. His name is Aron Ralston, and he's alternately gritty and dorky, inspiring and annoying. The fact that you already know the story is the first crux for this narrative: Aron goes canyoneering solo, gets his hand stuck and suffers, cuts off his arm, and walks out. The second crux is for the author to stretch this grisly incident into a book-length tale. How well the writing meets these challenges depends on the reader. If you've picked the book up for alpine adventure, you'll be disappointed, but if it's fortitude and resolution in the wilderness you seek, this is your book.

Ralston's first chapter describes the hike and then the tumble with a chockstone that shackled him to a remote canyon wall. The shock of not getting free is agonizingly well described, and we settle in with Ralston for a long, cold desert night in his "glove of sandstone." But now the writer reaches back into his past, stretching the incident into a full 300-page book, and it's here the reader begins to feel the washboard road rattling the suspension of narrative. He's in his mid-twenties, and while his life has been interesting, he's not exactly Ulysses. Ralston brings us through his youthful exploits in the mountains, including some rookie suffering we all recognize: postholing pointlessly for miles—and some we probably won't—chasing a bear who took his food in the Tetons. We travel with Ralston through various mini-epics, a major life change from an engineering career to living in Aspen, and arrive at his goal of climbing all Colorado's 14,000-foot peaks in winter.

There is much to like in this enthusiasm, and much to admire in his re-invention of himself as an endurance athlete. However, for you climbers there are apt to be some awkward moments, as Ralston stretches chilly days on basic peaks into long drama. He's hiking snowy summits, and rambling along ridgelines with one eye on his website and one eye on his stopwatch. Our narrator becomes that recognizable figure: the frenetic, gear-store geek, fixated on abstractions like "fourteeners," and painfully eager to share the video and the jpegs from his latest escapade. That gets a little old.

Of course, they say character is fate, and it's the very momentum of a young man's hyperenergy, an engineer's attention to detail, a neophyte mountaineer's bad decisions, an egoist's self-regard, and an endurance athlete's appetite for punishment that tumbles him into trouble and then enables him to survive. Ralston, you see, is his own perfect storm. That's what saves him and ultimately saves this book.

What I like about *Between a Rock and a Hard Place* is Ralston's strong writing skills, his self-deprecating humor, and his ability to share lessons from his accident without preaching. We have to tolerate the title as a pun too obvious for a publisher to forego. Ralston reminds me of Joe Simpson, without the technical ability but with the inclination for accidents, because he never presents himself as a hero, never shapes his story into a Christian allegory, and retains a sense of humor no matter the mess he's in.

Ralston's ordeal itself is strikingly well told, and the book becomes powerful as his frustration becomes responsibility, and ultimately psychological transformation: "You created this accident…you have been heading for this situation for a long time." The excruciating dismemberment is only part of his story. Ralston's sandstone prison is a venue for life-altering contemplation, and even if his guiding texts are lyrics from Phish or lines from *The Matrix*, the reader is privileged to witness a stirring change as this young man has the strength to learn about himself, about love for his friends, and about motivations for outdoor accomplishment healthier than altitudes and firsts.

American Alpine Journal readers will find this a Pop-Tart of a book: not really fresh or really filling, but tasty in the right spots and warming evidence of one person's ability to take a terrible situation and mold it into something constructive and uplifting.

JEFFREY M. MCCARTHY

Longs Peak: The Story of Colorado's Favorite Fourteener. DOUGALD MACDONALD. ENGLEWOOD, CO: WESTCLIFFE PUBLISHERS, 2004. 240 PAGES. PAPERBACK. $24.95.

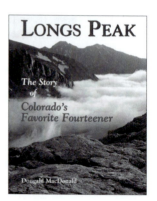

From a speeding airliner high over the American West you gaze down upon many mountains. But even the ones that should be familiar are flattened and can be devilishly hard to identify. Recently I flew from Oakland to Denver. Partway into our descent, probably around 25,000 feet, I looked out and spotted a highly distinctive peak. I blurted out: "God! Look at that!" My seatmate must have thought I was seeing an engine on fire. No, it was that massive, beautifully shaped mountain known as Longs Peak. It must have been 40 miles distant, yet my ancient brain cells had instantly recognized it.

Dougald MacDonald has produced a riveting book about Colorado's most splendid mountain. He begins with a step-by-step account of a hike up the "tourist" route, and we are swept along as if we had a guide hiking with us. This adventure, the Keyhole Route, is not exactly a stroll, as it involves a 4,850-foot elevation gain and a 15-mile round trip. This well-crafted introductory section makes the reader long for more. And you'll soon get it.

Most mountains have little recorded history. We may know who made the first ascent, or be aware of a few notes from this Journal, but let's face it: no book could be written about 99.99% of the world's peaks. But because of its prominence and height (14,259 feet) Longs lured many early adventurers, and their exploits have not faded into obscurity. MacDonald tells of the "discovery" of the peak in 1820, the controversy surrounding the first ascent, the explorations of Enos Mills in the early 1900s (he climbed the peak nearly 300 times), and the 1925 incident where Agnes Vaille died during a winter ascent.

Accounts of some of the famed routes on the east side of the mountain form the core of the book. The Stettner brothers and their 5.8 route in 1927. Bob Kamps and Dave Rearick's "sneak" ascent of the Diamond in 1960. Royal Robbins and Layton Kor climbing two routes on the Diamond in a four-day period in 1963. The first winter ascent of the Diamond, a five-day effort by Kor and Wayne Goss in 1967. The exploits of modern-day speed climbers (Tommy Caldwell and Topher Donahue did five Diamond routes in a single day!). A fact I was unaware of: there are 75 separate routes on the eastern escarpment of the mountain. Fascinating stuff!

Other sections of the book deal with accidents (54 dead so far), winter climbs, geology, and natural history. This last topic, though well done, seems out of place here, since little is specific to Longs Peak. Three full pages about quaking aspen and elk? Better to have omitted this and inserted more climbing history.

The many photographs are sublime, especially the ones by Topher Donahue. Some of the color shots are of startling definition, a far cry from so many cheaply prepared mountain books. Oddly, the photographers are not credited next to their photos; you must get this fine-print information at the end of the book. A minor flaw in MacDonald's near-perfect tome.

STEVE ROPER

IN BRIEF: NOTES FROM THE BANFF MOUNTAIN BOOK FESTIVAL 2004

Twelve years ago North America launched its first mountain literature event: the Banff Mountain Book Festival. Each November the festival celebrates the world's best mountain and adventure travel stories through readings, presentations, seminars, book signings, a book fair, and the presentation of internationally recognized awards for mountain literature.

Last year 137 books were entered in the 11th annual competition in Banff. A committee selected 32 finalists, which were then submitted to an international jury that included UK-based mountaineer and author Colin Wells; Lisa Christensen, a writer and curator with Banff's Whyte Museum of the Canadian Rockies; and writer, editor, and adventurer Donovan Webster.

The Jon Whyte Award for Mountain Literature, sponsored by the Whyte Museum, went to *Life and Limb: A True Story of Tragedy and Survival Against the Odds* by Jamie Andrew, Piatkus Books (UK, 2004), a book that jury members found had a "compelling and agonizingly suspenseful quality about it." It told the story of Andrew's rescue after five nights trapped by a storm on Mont Blanc. Frostbite injuries are horrible and debilitating. But what happened to Jamie Andrew in January 1999 transcended alpinists' worst fears. Storm-bound for six days in what proved to be a very effective wind tunnel near the top of the north face of the Droites, he developed injuries so serious that he subsequently lost his feet *and* hands to amputation. His climbing partner Jamie Fisher lost his life. It's a grim, ghastly tale and a scenario most climbers would file under "Nightmare." But what the jury found extraordinary about Jamie Andrew's book, which recalled his terrible ordeal and its aftermath, was that it wasn't depressing at all. Instead, it was gripping, intriguing, and often very funny.

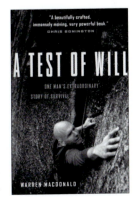

Nearly half the book is concerned with the climb on the Droites and the terrible situation in which the climbers subsequently found themselves. In Andrew's deft style, the tale has a compelling and agonizingly suspenseful quality about it. Andrew skillfully maintains a page-turning impetus by leavening the horror with retrospective vignettes from his climbing life.

What also distinguishes Andrew's book from most in what might be termed the "Triumph over Adversity" genre, are his insightful observations on life and society in general. And Andrew is not afraid to laugh at himself: "Tales of mastering the art of rolling your own fags without fingers, how to sup a spillage-free pint, or wipe your bum without hands are the kind of thing that rarely find their way into medical textbooks."

What shines through in this unexpectedly enjoyable book is the writer's extraordinarily positive attitude. It would have been all too easy to lapse into gushing sentimentality, but Andrew staunchly resisted this. Instead, like Joe Simpson, Andrew discovers a latent talent for writing that only a mountaineering epic seems to have allowed him to uncover.

Other books considered by the Banff jury and of interest to our readers include:

The Best Book—Mountain Exposition award went to Will Gadd for *Ice & Mixed Climbing: Modern Technique*, The Mountaineers Books (2003). A blend of step-by-step instruction and real-life stories, the book was described by jury members as "utterly bang up-to-date, as Gadd's still at the top of his game." The judges found the book to be well laid-out, accessible, and very thorough.

The Big Open: On Foot Across Tibet's Chang Tang, Rick Ridgeway (National Geographic Press) describes a journey across Tibet's northern plateau in search of the calving grounds of the chiru, an endangered antelope. Ridgeway was accompanied by Conrad Anker, Jimmy Chin, and Galen Rowell—Rowell's last big adventure. The jury commented that it was "a great story and cause." The cause is the group's discovery the Chinese government plans to create a national preserve.

The Fellowship of Ghosts: A Journey Through the Mountains of Norway by Paul Watkins (National Geographic Press) describes a solo adventure through the Rondanne and Jutunheimen mountains of Norway and makes connections between the landscape and mythical presences. The jury called it an "almost perfect blend of personal experience and historic reflection."

In the Ghost Country: A Lifetime Spent on the Edge by Peter Hillary and John Elder (Free Press) retraces Scott's epic but tragic journey to the South Pole as the backdrop for Hillary's own auto-biography. Jurists remarked that "weaving literature, adventure lore, and Hillary's experience achieves something remarkable."

Everest Pioneer, the Photographs of Captain John Noel by Sandra Noel (Sutton Publishing, UK) collects the official Everest photographs from the 1922 and 1924 expeditions. The panel found the photographs superb and were impressed by the excerpts from John Noel's own writing.

The 12th annual Banff Mountain Book Festival will take place in Banff, November 2-4, 2005. For anyone interested in submitting an entry into the competition, contact banffmountain-books@banffcentre.ca. A new Mountain Writing Program offers up to eight established writers an opportunity to develop a major essay, memoir, or book project on a mountain theme.

BERNADETTE MCDONALD, *Director, Banff Mountain Festivals*

IN MEMORIAM

BARRY CORBET 1936-2004

"Damn it," Barry said. I'd just shared my latest ruminations on heroes, and declared him one of them. He squirmed, didn't like it, said so. One thing that irks wheelchair users, he told me, is to be viewed by "normies" as needing their pity or admiration. "Hell, everybody's got their handicaps, even you, my friend, though it may not be so obvious." Touché. But it didn't change my view of Barry. Barry is for me a hero and *not* because he ended up paralyzed from the waist down in a helicopter crash.

Barry Corbet in 2004. *Muffy Moore*

After that crash Barry came to view his life, perhaps much like his new body, as divided into two parts: the 32 years before his spinal cord injury (SCI) and the 36 after. For many years following the accident he more-or-less closed the door on part one, trying not to look back.

Part One began in Vancouver, B.C. in 1936. Barry graduated from Prince of Wales high school and left Dartmouth in his junior year to settle in Jackson Hole. He was a superb athlete, a scholar without degree, and a mountain-dwelling alchemist who could turn dreams into golden adventure:

In 1958 he and three others (Bob French, Sterling Neale, Bill Briggs) pulled off the first ski traverse from the Bugaboos to Rogers Pass, now a classic known as *The Grand Traverse*.

The following year he, Jake Breitenbach, Pete Sinclair, and Bill Buckingham made the first ascent of the Southwest Rib of Denali, and he married an irresistible redhead, Mary (Muffy) French, a union that yielded three more redheads, Jonathan and twins Jennifer and Michael. Barry and Muffy divorced, remarried, and divorced once more. The lifelong relationship that followed proved to be more loving and nurturing than many marriages.

Barry entered my life during the 1963 American Mount Everest Expedition. We both cast our lot with a handful of others wanting to take the road "less traveled by"—Everest's West Ridge. On May 21 Barry and Al Auten pioneered the route to our final camp at 28,300 feet. At the time of our summit push, Barry was going strong. He relinquished a place on the summit team with the parting bit to Willi Unsoeld and me, "…you're both just about over the hump (36 and 32). This is my first expedition. I'll be coming back again someday."

Between 1958 and 1968 Barry guided for the Exum School, taught skiing in Jackson Hole, pioneered new routes in the Tetons, and started the area's first mountaineering store, The Outhaus. Corbet's Couloir at Jackson is one challenging, double-black-diamond bit of his immortality, though he points out that he was not the first to ski it. In 1968 he started Jackson Hole Mountain Guides.

On December 18, 1966, Barry, Pete Schoening, John Evans, and Bill Long became the first to stand atop Mount Vinson, Antarctica's highest point. A few days later, Barry and John pulled off what Barry later regarded as his finest climb, the first ascent of nearby Mount Tyree—a bold, way-out-there commitment.

In 1963, returning from Everest where his appetite had been whetted, he and Roger Brown started Summit Films, and Barry entered a whole new world of creativity. Most notable was his paradigm-changing film, *Ski the Outer Limits*, which touched new visual and spiritual levels in portraying the cutting edge of downhill skiing.

Part Two began May 2, 1968 when the helicopter from which Barry was filming fell to earth. In an instant his life was transformed. Much later he commented:

> As my life's turning points go…it was spinal cord injury that turned me inside out and spat me out a different person. My life was no longer the road not taken but the road yanked out from under…I still have trouble reconciling the life before with the life after.

His newfound disability thrust upon Barry a challenge the likes of which he'd never imagined. He had to learn to get along with a new, less compliant body. He continued to make films, focusing increasingly on the lives of those with SCI. Options: Spinal Cord Injury and the Future, a book to tell his fellow "gimps" and "crips" that there's still life after injury, is now in its tenth printing. For a time that life included white water kayaking until his shoulders would have no more of it.

In 1991 Barry became editor of *New Mobility*, a magazine devoted to the lives, concerns, and challenges of those living with SCI or related disability. Through his monthly Bully Pulpit editorials and other writings, he became a powerful voice for demonstrating that "wheelers" had some different needs but also aspired to loving and challenging lives with full opportunity for creative contribution to our world. Though it's the last thing he sought, he acquired guru status as guide, editor, and mentor. He was an inspiration to many, not only those among the SCI community. Which brings me back to Barry as hero. In a recent essay titled *Heroes: Personal Ponderings* I wrote:

> I have another type of hero where elements of selflessness and volition might seem less relevant at first glance, but it is just those aspects of the style of coping with adversity that defines the heroism of these ordinary heroes…. For me, though Corbet doesn't buy it—which adds challenging seasoning to our friendship—he is a model for my hero as survivor. Barry's been a paraplegic for the second half of his life, and it's never a life that's easy. But you get on with it…. What he has done is not unique, but he has pulled it off with style and creativity that adds to my admiration for him, even as I cannot truly imagine what it would be like to be in his place. When we talked recently about heroes, Corbet had this to say: "To me, a hero is someone who makes the world better or sacrifices his own interests for a greater, nobler cause. By that definition, we're all heroes some of the time, but almost none of us consistently. And by that definition, mountaineering is pretty much nowhere." Yes, Barry!

Over the years as a para, Barry's body began to wear down, wear out, and just hurt: pressure sores, bladder infections, compressed nerves, decaying shoulder joints. But the spirit grew even as the body shrank. He wrote in *New Mobility*:

> Disability shreds all our presumptions of freedom, authenticity or confidence. It writes its own rules. So my idle dreams of lofty mountain sanctuaries are nothing but that. Most

of us must find our adventures elsewhere.

And we do. Lionel Terray, a famous French mountaineer, called his chosen sport "the conquest of the useless." People with disabilities, I submit, are engaged in the conquest of the ordinary. We find adventure in reaching the unreachable object, in scratching the unscratchable itch, in making the impossible transfer. We find it every time our adaptive equipment breaks down or an attendant flakes out. We find it in confronting patronization and discrimination, in righting wrongs, taking stands and rousing the courage to be who we are. Adventure stalks us, insists that we participate. Like it or not, most of us get all the adventure we can handle.

Of course we don't often choose our adventures, but does anyone? We like to think we do, but the best adventures befall us, not we them. And there's no escaping the greatest adventure of them all--being part and parcel of the solar wind and the play of starlight, of the pull of tides and the convergence of hearts, of the splendor of life that is denied to no one. Once we accept the gift, the adventure has begun and cannot be abandoned.

A parallel trick of living with a disability...is to see all and everything as an adventure, one that endows every moment with all the most adventuresome qualities— uncertainty and risk, richness and joy, deliberation and derring-do.

But damn. Chimborazo, Cerro Torre, Alpamayo. The Annapurnas, the Karakoram, the Hindu Kush. Can't you hear the mermaids singing?

There were still mountains in the heart. Four years ago, Barry began to open the door to let part one of his life back in. This from the 25th Annual John Young Lecture at Craig Rehab Hospital, in which he inventoried a few of his life's missteps:

> Another mistake was this dumb division of my life into two separate lives. To a large degree, I rejected what I was calling my first life. I didn't maintain a lot of my best friendships. I dropped my old interests. I didn't exactly withdraw from life, but I did start over. I'll always be poorer for that.
>
> With the benefit of hindsight, it's easy to see that there is no first life, no second life. There's this life, and it's everything we ever hoped for. It's the brass ring we thought we had missed, the imperfect paradise we thought we'd lost.
>
> I just can't tell you how very imperfect it is, or how very tired I get of being disabled. Of all the crap that comes with it, of the constant financial drain. I can't tell you how much I wish I could take a vacation from all of that.
>
> But none of that matters. In spite of all the change and difficulty, life doesn't change. Life is still complete and terrifying and drop-dead gorgeous, and I have just as big a piece of it as anyone else.

Well, if Barry had any defense against being one of Hornbein's heroes, he sure blew it with his dying. He was living on the thin edge of having to give up the self-sufficient life he'd pulled off for most of those 36 years. Last August Barry was found to have widespread cancer. He elected to forgo dubiously helpful treatment. I've imagined that he saw this cancer as his exit permit. With his family and other loved ones tied into the metaphorical rope, a climber one time more, he started up that final pitch. On a sunny, mild December afternoon, with loved ones around him, he finished the climb with the same style and dignity with which he confronted all else in his life. It was the 38th anniversary of the day he had ascended to the highest point on the Antarctic continent. He left unresolved the mystery whether the white mountain he saw most days looking north from his bedroom window was Longs Peak or…?

A few days later a letter arrived in the mail:

> Dear Friends-
> …As many of you already know, my life is now over…. I'm a little saddened to be leaving a little earlier than expected, but feel no sense of tragedy. I've lived a lot longer than I ever could have or would have predicted thirty-six years ago after the helicopter crash…. I've had love overflowing, impassioned careers, a life of adventure and everything I've ever wanted. Nothing missed and no regrets. Live on in peace, health and happiness. Look for the meaning where you can, and cherish mystery when you can't.
> Barry

THOMAS HORNBEIN, *AAC*

WILLIAM PRESTON "BILL" ELFENDAHL 1914-2004

Bill Elfendahl, 89, Boeing engineer, one of REI's founders, mountaineer, skier, sailor, and Scout leader died June 7, 2004, in Seattle following a stroke.

He was born November 30, 1914, in Alameda, CA, the son of Gertrude Louise Baxter and Preston Henry Elfendahl. He graduated from Seattle's Garfield High School in 1931. In 1936, Bill earned a degree from the University of Washington in Mechanical Engineering and was a Lieutenant in the ROTC. Despite the memory of his cousin's death in a 1930 airplane crash, and resulting family objections, Bill pursued his dream to help people fly and to bring them together.

Bill was employed by The Boeing Company from 1936 until 1979—43 years—and retired third in seniority worldwide.

Bill Elfendahl in 1949. *Tom Miller*

He began as a draftsman in "The Red Barn." His first design job was for an airplane restroom door handle. He helped design the seaplane underbody of the Boeing Clipper. His first chance to fly came in 1940 over Spokane when he was assigned to assist with repairs on a Douglas UC-78 trainer. When he was sought by the War Department for WW II, Boeing intervened. Engineers were desperately needed to set up the B-17 Flying Fortress production line. After WWII, Bill was on the maiden flight of Boeing's Stratocruiser, directed Flight Test Instrumentation & Research Laboratories, helped design the 707 & 747, served as president of Boeing Supervisors' Club, and was a clown for Boeing's annual family holiday circuses.

Bill was very active with The Mountaineers, teaching, leading climbs, building lodges at Mt. Baker, Stevens and Snoqualmie passes, assisting Mountain Rescue Council, and sharing "Camp Crafter" trips with his young family. One of the founders of REI in 1938, he carried card #16. He and his friends began importing mountaineering equipment from Europe, which was unavailable in the US. His rock climbing tools are displayed in the Seattle store's entry.

An editor of the American Alpine Club's *Climber's Guide to the Cascade & Olympic Mountains of Washington* (1961), Bill yodeled from the summits of many, many mountains in the Northwest. He taught climbing at Olympic College. With Tom Miller, Dave Lind, Charles Cehrs, and Jay Todd, he shared the first ascent of the West Peak of Mt. Johannesberg (1949, North Cascades). He taught, "Nobody leaves the mountain until everyone is off safely." He sponsored the first minority memberships in both The Mountaineers and Seattle's Corinthian YC.

Bill was an avid downhill racing and alpine skier beginning in the 1930's. Long before chair lifts or rope tows, his favorite place to ski was Paradise on Mt. Rainier. A typical day was skiing down and over Mazama Ridge, then down and atop the Tatoosh Range and then back to Paradise. Another favorite ski destination was a remote valley near Rainier. He camped in the snow and skied there in the 1930s and '40s before anyone envisioned it as a ski resort—Crystal Mountain. Knowing the terrain, he helped design the resorts ski trails and had fun leading three generations of family in a sometimes terrifying game of follow-the-leader begun with the cry, "Through the Trees!" He skied there until age 85.

William P. Elfendahl was preceded in death by his first wife of 38 years, Florence in 1978; his brother, Major Elfendahl, and his grandson, Charles W. Elfendahl. He is survived by Sarah, his second wife of 25 years; two sons, Gerald W. and Lawrence E.

GERALD ELFENDAHL

RUSSELL O. HUSE 1908-2004

Russell Huse in 1973.

Russell Huse's roots are deeply embedded in the area of Ventura County, California, originally known as the Rancho El Conejo, part of which was named Rancho El Triunfo and later called the Russell Ranch. This 6,000-acre farming and cattle ranch owned by Russ's grandparents, Andrew and Abigail Russell, comprised a large portion of the area known today as Westlake Village.

Born in Los Angeles in 1908, Russ received part of his elementary education at the one-room Triunfo School located on the ranch. He spent summers and holidays living with his grandparents. Inspired by his love of the land, he began writing poems and essays in his early twenties. Russ began his career with six years as a park ranger at Yosemite National Park. In the 1940s he held positions in the aircraft industry as technical artist for publications.

In 1951 Russ began his 23 years of service at the Naval Center at China Lake, California. His position was supervisory technical report writer/illustrator for the Aviation Ordnance Department, preparing publications for the Navy's research and development programs.

Russ was a cofounder of the China Lake Mountain Search and Rescue Group and became an honorary club member. At age 49, while other people were beginning to look forward to retirement, he started mountain climbing in earnest.

Russ climbed most of the major peaks in the Sierra, the Tetons, the Cascades, Mt. McKinley, Mont Blanc, the Matterhorn, the volcanoes of Mexico, and several peaks over 20,000 feet in the Andes. Russ remarks, "At twenty thousand feet the air is always rare and the mountains ever there." He retired from climbing in his mid seventies.

Throughout his long life, he never stopped helping people where he saw a need. As a member of the Rotary Club, he was provided the opportunity to serve local communities and address global problems. Because of his dedication and service he has been awarded a lifetime

Honorary Club Membership in Rotary.

During retirement, Russ continued writing poems and essays, and perfecting his oil painting skills. In his late eighties, he began assembling his works for publication in this book and future ones. His last book of poetry was *From Sunlight And Shadow: Reflections at Age 95.*

Russ was blessed with a tremendous support, companion, inspiration, and Muse, his wife Edith. They were happily married for more than 67 years. The Huses made their home in Westlake Village overlooking the site of the old Russell Ranch. Russell O. Huse passed away in Thousand Oaks, California, on May 1, 2004, the day after turning 96 years in age.

MIKE WINICK

REESE MARTIN 1955-2004

Reese Martin was a true contemporary Renaissance man. Growing up, he was a constantly moving "Air Force brat," eventually expected to fill the shoes of his "Right Stuff" era test pilot father and his WWI pilot grandfather. Instead, as a teenager Reese developed a love for climbing and skiing in the Cascades when his family was living in Seattle, and continued those passions for the rest of his life in the Rockies, Sierra, Coast Range, Andes, and Himalaya. But Reese was not just a mountain sports enthusiast. He spent time surfing, and was involved in the art scene in Ventura, California, where he lived later for 16 years.

Reese Martin and Max in 2004. *Eric Hobday*

He was a Environmental Engineering consultant and political advocate there, also participating in the Big Brother program for five years, building a sports car in his garage, and staying involved in climbing, mostly by authoring new rock routes. He was a Southern California regional coordinator for The Access Fund from 1994-1998 and a member of their board of directors from 1998-2002.

In 1999 Reese moved to Aspen, Colorado, and the following year married me, a ski patroller, climber, and fellow Access Fund board member. Together we remodeled a home and at the same time built a "cabin getaway" at 10,000 feet on nearby Chair Mountain. Still, Reese found time to "clean up" bolts on Independence Pass rock climbs and add his own crag with me called "Reese's Pieces." And he learned to paraglide. The latter became a passion eclipsing all others, and so he was finally able to assume the role of heir to his family's piloting dynasty, in a rogue sort of way.

Though he took great pains to be safe and disciplined in his new sport, the stock phrase "I'd rather be lucky than good" unfortunately did not apply to Reese on July 9, 2004. When landing that day in a cross-country paragliding competition at Lake Chelan, Washington. Reese was caught in turbulent air and dashed violently to the ground. The "encyclopedic mind of useless information" (as he referred to himself) and the eclectic man of many interests and passions was suddenly gone.

Reese seemed likened to Iccarus, who fell from the sky while flying artificial wings too close to the sun in pursuit of deep insight and fulfillment.

Good night, sweet prince.

CHARLOTTE FOX, *AAC*

W. V. GRAHAM MATTHEWS II 1921-2004

I first knew Graham when I returned to Harvard College after World War II and found him enrolled at Harvard Law School. He had attended Exeter Academy ('38) and Harvard College (graduating early with the class of '42), where he was a classmate of Andy Kauffman and Mal Miller (both '43). He was already a mountaineer of consequence, having made the ascent of 18,603-foot Persian volcano, Mount Demavend, while stationed in Iran as an army cryptographer. Graham quickly became a loyal member of the Harvard Mountaineering Club and partook of all the usual New England climbs, both summer and winter.

Graham Matthews in 1959.
Irene Beardsley

Law school, even at Harvard, was not for Graham, and after one year he packed it in and took to selling the *Encyclopedia Britannica* door-to-door in South Boston. The futility of this practice dawned on him toward the end of 1948, when several of us were gathered at Pinkham Notch over the Christmas holidays. Joe Dodge needed a winter presence at the old (and well-equipped) Tuckerman Shelter (a.k.a. Howard Johnson's). We volunteered Graham for the dollar-a-day job, which he held down for the next five months, though he groused mightily at those of us who had talked him into taking the position, for the isolation of January and February was notorious. During that winter, Graham, mindful of the necessity for ski patrollers to have a quick access to the Gulf of Slides for rescue purposes, laid out the first of the two memorable trails that came to bear his name—this one across the mid-level, timbered part of Boott Spur. (The other trail marked with his name—which he laid out in 1978—runs west from Battle Abbey to gain access to the higher peaks of the Battle Range in British Columbia.)

Bigger mountains called him, however, and he left Tuckerman's in the spring of 1949. The next few summers found him almost everywhere—the Coast ranges of B.C. and Alaska; the Andes of Peru; Idaho's Sawtooths; the North Cascades; the Canadian Rockies; the Selkirks; back to Peru; and finally the Tetons, where he saw the desirability of a camping facility for climbers and campaigned for what later became the AAC Climbers' Ranch.

His first ascents (1947-1973) include Mt. Asperity and six other peaks in the Coast Ranges of B.C.; Grand Aiguille and West Peak of Heyburn in the Idaho Sawtooths; Trapper Mountain in the North Cascades; Mt. Shackleton in the Canadian Rockies; Mt. Salcantay and Yanapaccha in the Peruvian Andes; and Gibraltar, West Peak of Blackfriar, and Downie Peak in the Northern Selkirks. He was a member of the 1950 Harvard Andean Expedition that made the first ascent of Yerupaja (although he did not summit) in the Andes, and made numerous new routes and second ascents in the various ranges. Most of these climbs have appeared in the *AAJ*.

Graham taught school in several places across the United States, from Fessenden School near Boston, to the Robert Louis Stevenson School in Pebble Beach.

It was on a climbing trip in Yosemite that he met and married (on June 12, 1955) Mary

Ann Corthell, who presented him, in due course, with a daughter, Katharine Ilyeen (Kim), and a son, W. V. G. Matthews III (a.k.a. Weeg).

Graham retired from active climbing in the 1970s and took up the more sedentary task of volunteer weather observer in the upper Carmel Valley of California, and trail-builder from the Santa Cruz Mountains to the Northern Selkirks. He never did finish his magnum opus on Philippe Bunau-Varilla and the politics surrounding the construction of the Panama Canal, on the researching of which he had labored intermittently for more than 30 years. However, his heirs have retained his research material in case a future scholar wishes to take up the project.

WILLIAM L. PUTNAM, *AAC*

POLLY PRESCOTT 1902-2003

Polly Prescott's climbing career began in 1922 when she climbed Mt. Rainier as the climax of a Vassar College geology field trip. Her love of the mountains continued all her life. She spent over 40 seasons climbing and hiking in western Canada. Her first ACC camp was in the Tonquin Valley in 1926, and she came to most camps into the 1950s. In 1941 she was the first woman to receive the Silver Rope in recognition of her leading manless climbs with Marguerite Schnellbacher (Coveney). These included Mt. Louis and Edith Cavell. She also served as American Vice-President of the Alpine Club of Canada. She climbed extensively with Sterling B. Hendricks and Rex and Ethne Gibson.

Polly Prescott in the 1920s.

Among her best Canadian ascents were Hungabi, the northwest ridge of Sir Donald up and down, Forbes and the Lyalls, the first traverse of Louis, a new route up the north face with Edward Feuz and Hendricks. Others were a traverse of Assiniboine and the second ascent of Mt. Aye with Eric Brooks. She also climbed Freshfield and made the first ascent of Coronet. In the Coast Range she climbed Mt. Grenville, a first, with Don and Phyl Munday. She considered 1928 her best season when she climbed Bugaboo Spire, Howser Spire, and in Jasper the three snow peaks of Athabaska, and was the first woman to climb the North and South Twins, a third ascent.

In Europe noteworthy ascents in the Dolomites were: North Vajolet Tower (North route), Marmolata (South Face), Cima Grande di Lavaredo (via Dolfer, East Face). In the Alps were the Grande Charmoz and Grepon (traverse), and La Meige (traverse). Her last season abroad was 1957 when she climbed the Matterhorn, the Zinalrothorn, and a traverse of the Wellenkupper and Obergabelhorn.

A native of Cleveland, Ohio, she was active in civic affairs. During World War II she served with the American Red Cross in North Africa and Italy. After retirement in 1962, she joined the U.S. Peace Corps in Nepal. After her return to America in 1963 she continued her interests in gardening, needlework, music, travel, and world affairs. In 1993 she moved with her sister (me) to Kendal at Oberlin, Ohio, a continuing care retirement community.

KATHERINE PRESCOTT

Landon Gale Rockwell 1914-2003

Landon Gale Rockwell, known to virtually everyone as "Rocky" (including his very own mother; I asked him about that once) died peacefully at his home in Clinton, New York, on March 5, 2003, after an active and well-lived life.

Landon Rockwell in 1992. *Heidi Rockwell*

Rocky was born January 3, 1914, in New York City and grew up in Greenwich, Connecticut. He graduated from Dartmouth in 1935 with an A.B. degree in English and then studied politics at Princeton, where he earned an M.A. in 1938 and a Ph.D. in 1942. His service in the U.S. Navy during World War II included commanding a submarine chaser.

Starting in his early childhood, his family vacationed in Keene Valley, New York, and he grew up hiking and scrambling in the Adirondack Mountains. As an undergraduate, he worked summers as a hut boy at the Dartmouth Outing Club's summit hospice on New Hampshire's Mt. Moosilauke. Several times a week in June through August, he toted loads of up to 120 pounds of food and laundry up the 3,300-foot elevation gain to the summit. In the summer before his senior year, he served as hutmaster. In winter he skied all over the White Mountains, including many epic ascents and descents in whiteouts and ferocious winds in the Presidentials.

After teaching stints at the University of Cincinnati and Williams College, in 1950 he joined the faculty at Hamilton College, becoming in 1955 the James S. Sherman Professor of Political Science. He taught Constitutional Law and political theory until his retirement in 1979; his scholarly works were published in the *Yale Law School Journal, Cornell Law Quarterly, Vermont Law Review, American Political Science Review, The Journal of Politics*, and the *American Educator Encyclopedia*. Residing in Clinton, New York, just a few steps from the Hamilton campus, he was also within easy driving distance of the Adirondacks, where he built a sturdy second home in Keene Valley. The living room's picture window perfectly frames the view up the Johns Brook Valley, with Mt. Marcy in the center.

He was proud to be nominated for membership in the American Alpine Club in 1941 by Jack Durrance and Nat Goodrich.

While he climbed extensively in the Alps and Canadian Rockies from the 1930s through the 1970s, his "home range" was always the Adirondacks, which he knew intimately in all seasons. He was the first to explore the new slides on Giant Mountain following the tumultuous thunderstorm of June 29, 1963. Perhaps his favorite Adirondack route was the Trapdike on Mt. Colden, which he climbed dozens of times, in summer and winter. In his eighties and no longer able to take to the trails, he would nonetheless drive around after thunderstorms looking for new slide tracks ["slides" in the Adirondacks are where bare granite is exposed on the otherwise forested mountainside; they can suddenly appear after a landslide—Ed.]. He took up canoeing at about age 80, eager to keep getting outdoors.

Rocky served as an unofficial ambassador for the Adirondacks, starting in the 1930s when he brought fellow Dartmouth students for a "vacation" from the White Mountains; later he introduced Hamilton College faculty and students to the region and helped countless strangers along the trail. He admired Supreme Court Justice William O. Douglas's vigorous protection of the First Amendment as well as his mountain writings, and successfully invited him to visit the Adirondacks.

He derived a great deal of pleasure from intellectual pursuits. On a warm summer day you could find him on the summit of Gothics for hours, studying The Advance Opinions of the Supreme Court (because he wanted to stay current for his Constitutional Law classes) and The Oxford Book of English Verse "since Gothics is kind of a poem of rock and trees and light and air, and it's rather nice to read a poem while you're sitting on one."

Apart from mountaineering and skiing, Rocky loved classical music, *The New York Times*, and peanut butter.

Rocky is survived by his wife, Heidi; two children from a previous marriage, Sandra and Winthrop; three grandchildren; and scores of friends. Every one of them misses him every day.

ROBERT A. FORREST, *AAC*

PETER K. SCHOENING 1927-2004

Pete Schoening died at his home on Lake Washington shortly after dawn. As the day lightened, a lone bald eagle made one slow circle at eye level just outside the window, then rose into the morning sky. It was the 51st anniversary of Pete and Mell's wedding day.

Pete's lifelong passion for mountains never waned even as his physical capacity dwindled during his seven-year journey with multiple myeloma. To many of us who had the opportunity to climb with Pete in his heyday, he was the finest mountaineer of our time. His spirit continues to fill the empty space where once we walked and talked and climbed together.

Most of the obituaries appearing around the world focused on the moment that gave birth to the Pete legend—"the

Pete Schoening. *Bill Sumner*

belay." It took place on K2 in 1953. High on the mountain, within striking distance of the summit, Art Gilkey became critically ill. With the odds stacked against them, the team made the decision to try to get him down in horrendous conditions. Pete had anchored the makeshift litter with a boot ax belay, the pick braced behind an outcrop of rock. One member of the team slipped. As ropes entangled, one by one, four others were plucked from their perches on the steep snow. Somehow the ropes of the falling climbers became entangled with the litter. Their fall to certain death was arrested by Schoening's belay. The feat seems superhuman. A legend was born. The ax itself is one of the great artifacts of mountaineering history. Pete lived with this bit of inescapable notoriety with the same unassuming modesty that pervaded all aspects of his life.

That life played out in the Pacific Northwest. He graduated from Roosevelt High School in Seattle and joined the Navy near the end of World War II. He returned home to obtain a degree in chemical engineering at the University of Washington, where he taught mountaineering classes. Both the American Alpine Club and the Seattle Mountain Rescue Council felt the creative touch of his boundless energy and enthusiasm.

Pete began his climbing in the toughest terrain in the lower 48 states, the "green hell" of the North Cascades. He thrived on bushwhacking into places no one had been before and most would not want to go. He made many first ascents, not so much collecting new routes as new adventures. Pete's invitation to become the youngest member of the 1953 expedition to K2 followed pioneering climbs of Mt. Saugstad in the Bella Coola range of British Columbia in 1951 and of Mount Augusta and on King Peak in the Yukon the following year.

In 1958 Pete and Andy Kauffman reached the summit of Gasherbrum I (Hidden Peak), 26,470 feet, the only American first ascent of an 8,000 meter mountain. Combining superb technique and incredible strength with a ferocious determination, he stormed up the mountain, ignoring pleas of his teammates to save his strength for the final push. On summit day, he punched a trail through deep snow for 2½ miles, all above 24,000 feet, using food box lids impaled to his crampons as makeshift snowshoes.

The following year Pete, Willi Unsoeld, and Dick Pownall completed a one-day "enchainment" of Teewinot, Mt. Owen, and the Grand, unintended preparation for a three-day ascent of McKinley in 1960 with the Whittaker twins and John Day (and a resulting rescue that upstaged the climb itself).

In December 1966 Pete, Barry Corbet, Bill Long, and John Evans were the first to stand upon the highest point on the Antarctic continent, the summit of 16,880-foot Mt. Vinson. In 1974 Pete led the first AAC-sponsored climbing exchange to the Pamirs and was among those summiting 23,406-foot Peak Lenin. In 1985 he was part of the first joint Chinese-American Expedition to a remote mountain in the Kun Lun Range named Ulugh Muztagh. The expedition put five Chinese climbers on top of this frigid peak. Pete passed on an opportunity for the summit to instead evacuate two climbers who had experienced an accelerated descent down hard ice in the moonlight after their summit moment. Over the next few years Pete returned to China three more times to attempt peaks in the Kangkarpo Range between Tibet and Yunnan.

Meanwhile, here at home Pete was steadily picking off the highest points in each of the 50 states, learning new techniques of skill and diplomacy in order to negotiate cornfields, backyards, and irate domestic wildlife. He completed this odyssey in Wyoming in 1997. About the same time Pete, along with various friends and relations, was quietly ticking off some other high points—Aconcagua, Kilimanjaro, and Elbrus. That left only one of the seven continental tops to tease his fantasy. In 1996 at age 68 he and his nephew, Klev Schoening, headed for Everest, signing up with Scott Fischer's party. Pete was climbing as strongly as any of the young ones, but his famed snoring was now interfering more with his own sleep than that of others. He placed a satellite phone call to his friend Hornbein for some medical advice, then opted out of heading back up for the final push out of concern that if he were to have problems, he'd be putting others at risk.

Mountains were not the only passion in Pete's life. He met Mary Lou (Mell) Deuter in the late '40s. Their courtship was characterized by an anonymous spouse as brief encounters of the infrequent kind, taking place on those rare occasions when the Northwest's notoriously foul weather was more than even Pete could abide. Pete and Mell became engaged before he left for K2, and married when he returned. They built two houses and raised six kids. Pete took on a failing business and transformed it into a leading producer of corrosion-resistant fiberglass grating for factory flooring and other uses. He brought the same energy, integrity, and caring to his role as president of Chemgrate as to everything else he undertook, adding yet another notch to his status as legend.

Then there's Big Red, an overweight Schwinn one-speed bike with coaster brakes. Pete believed in one bike for all venues. He took to riding in the Seattle-to-Portland bike event each summer. Just imagine seeing this balding elder standing on his pedals cranking up a mile-long hill. In the beginning he did this 200 mile ride in two days but when this challenge paled, he and

Big Red just did it in one, which did little to mute his status as legend.

Pete's passion for his mountain world never waned even as his incomparable physical capacity dwindled. "Tuesdays with Pete" became precious "walks and talks" with friends, continuing until a couple weeks before his death.

Pete left behind a boundless pot of memories in the minds and hearts of those whose lives he touched. He was a superb mountaineer (he'd squirm if he read this). But his transcendent greatness was that radiant spirit with which some of us were privileged to warm our lives. He had the strength of a bull and the heart of a boy scout. Pete always did more than his share of the work and took less than his share of the credit. He worried about others and not about himself. His friends could count on him, and he never failed.

A few miles east of Seattle and almost 4,000 feet above the Interstate you can see an insignificant rocky pyramid on the skyline. His friends named it for Pete—Putrid Pete's Peak, *aka* P-Cubed. Pete liked having this bump named (irreverently) after him. Atop P-Cubed is a small, waterproof box. Inside the box is a book of poetry by Gary Snyder, *Turtle Island*. One poem in particular made Pete beam with delight:

Why Log Truck Drivers Rise Earlier Than Students of Zen
In the high seat, before-dawn dark,
Polished hubs gleam
And the shiny diesel stack
Warms and flutters
Up the Tyler Road grade
To the logging on Poorman creek.
Thirty miles of dust.

There is no other life.

NICK CLINCH AND TOM HORNBEIN, *AAC*

NECROLOGY

James Angell	Morgan Harris	David Robertson
Wilford Bucher	Pierre Juillerat	Sayre Rodman
Peter Cooley	Reese Martin	Peter Schoening
James Corbet	W. V. Matthews	William Siri
J. Edwards	Arne Naess	Jack Smith
William Elfendahl	Francis Olding	Johnny Soderstrom
Henry Everding	Brian Reynolds	John Woodworth
David Green	Dorothy Rich	

CLUB ACTIVITIES

EDITED BY FREDERICK O. JOHNSON

Because of space limitations, we have limited reports to those from AAC sections. We regret losing track of our sister organizations, whose activity reports have been a long and welcome tradition in these pages.

ALASKA SECTION. The principal activity of our Section continues to center around the monthly slide shows we offer from September through April. To begin the 2004 series in January, Thomas Falkenberry illustrated his trips to Afghanistan to help with the "schools-for-girls" building program. In February local guidebook author Kristian Seiling described his attempt with Dave Lucey on the Colton Leach route on Mt. Huntington, and Harry Hunt discussed his trip to the Cordillera Blanca. In March, Roger Robinson, the lead NPS Climbing Ranger on Denali, talked about the success of the Clean Can Program on Denali and showed pictures of hidden gems in the Alaska Range. April's last program before the summer break brought Rod Hancock to describe a first ascent on Mt. Nagishlamina, across the inlet from Anchorage. After a most glorious, unusually dry summer, the fall meetings resumed in September with Alaska legend Carl Tobin presenting images and entertaining us with stories of his many climbs in the Hayes Range.

In October John Tuckey described a past climb on Ama Dablam, then steered a discussion on the cultural aspect of climbing in the Himalaya. In November Danny Kost, our past Section chair, took us to the remotest corners of the vast Wrangell-St. Elias Park. Finally, in December, Ralph Tingey highlighted his many years of climbing with notable ascents from the Tetons to Yosemite to Alaska.

The Section thanks BP for opening its Energy Center for our meetings, and our many supporters who have helped with our fund raising raffles, including Alaska Mountaineering and Hiking, Talkeetna Air Taxi, and Alaska Denali Guiding.

HARRY HUNT, *Chair*

CASCADE SECTION. On April 8, with the Climbing Club of the University of Washington, we hosted a presentation by Hans Florine, speed climber extraordinaire, showcasing his record climb of the Nose of El Capitan in Yosemite with Yuji Hirayama (2hrs 49 mins) and his speed record climbing all legal California 14,000 footers (3 1/2 days). It was an impressive show, and Hans is an inspirational speaker. This was an opportunity for AAC members to meet student climbers and for us to let them know about the organization. Thanks to the UW Climbing Club for providing the space for this Section event and to Gary Ynge for his help in organizing it.

Later in the year we helped sponsor two events. The first was a film, *In the Shadow of the Himalayas*, featuring fifth-grade students at Hamilton Middle School, Seattle, who have a sister-school in the Kathmandu Valley, learning about Nepal. Throughout the film, the Hamilton students introduce different aspects of living in Nepal—geography, culture, religion, ethnic diversity, daily challenges, and play—while answering questions about their perceptions of what life is like in Nepal. The film's profits support girls' scholarships through www.room-toread.org. The funds are greatly needed since only 14 percent of girls over age 15 can read and write, and 50 percent of Nepalese students drop out of school by age six. After the film Stephen Bezruchka and others led a panel discussion about the current political conditions in Nepal and how they affect travel and work there.

The next event was a benefit slide show in Seattle by Steve Swenson to support the Central Asia Institute. The Institute is a non-profit, non-governmental organization based in Bozeman, Montana, which promotes and provides community-based education and literacy programs, especially for girls, in remote mountain regions of Central Asia. About 300 people attended this event and over $2,100 was raised for the Institute.

Steve Swenson is a well-known Northwest native who has climbed extensively throughout the world for over 35 years. He led and summited with the second American expedition to climb K2 in 1990, and in 1994 he made a solo ascent of Everest without the use of bottled oxygen. His December 2 show was about the past summer, when, following other first ascents in the Charakusa Valley of northern Pakistan, Doug Chabot and Swenson made the first ascent of the Mazeno Ridge on Nanga Parbat on August 12-18. It took two days of climbing to reach the crest of the Mazeno Ridge and then three more days along the ridge crest, which is 10 km long and almost entirely above 7,000 meters [see feature article in this Journal].

PETER ACKROYD, *Chair*

OREGON SECTION. During the summer a project was undertaken on Mt. Hood to search for highly adapted anaerobic organisms known as extremophiles. These sulfur-based bacteria thrive within boiling geothermal geysers and deep inside rocks. The study centered on the hydro-steam and sulfur percolating in the Coalman Glacier's terminal moraine, which produces steaming fumarole vents in the Devil's Kitchen in the Crater Rock area of Mt. Hood. The research was conducted by Ruth Hennebuger, a Ph. D. student from Macquarie University in Sydney, Australia, and biologist Dana Rogoff from NASA Ames and the SETI Institute. AAC members Tom Bennett and Robert McGown with Dr. Steve Boyer acted as sherpas/research assistants.

The Madrone Wall Preservation Committee (MWPC) , headed by Keith Dallenbach, continues to play an important role in advancing the cause for the proposed rock climbing park at the Madrone Wall in Clackamas County. The Committee launched a letter-writing campaign to the county commissioners, and Keith has written numerous articles for the local newspapers. A joint AAC–Access Fund presentation was given at the Climb Max climbing shop. The Vancouver Climbing Club, the Ptarmigans, constructed a 3-D topographical relief model of the Madrone Wall for display at presentations. Check out the Web site www.savemadrone.org. Because of the MWPC's efforts, Clackamas County is not planning to conduct any blasting or quarry development at the Madrone Wall site. However, its status as a park is still in doubt, and technically Madrone Wall remains off limits to climbers. The Section donated funds to the MWPC in support of its continuing efforts to open access at the wall to climbers.

The Section was one of several climbing organizations asked to set up a booth at the Smith Rock Climber's Carnival over the Labor Day weekend. Matt Brewster joined me to staff the booth. This first annual Carnival featured vendors and climbing shops from throughout the Western States. The well-organized event was situated next to Smith Rock State Park on private land. Portland's Climb Max, Mad Rock, and *Climbing* magazine were the main sponsors. Jim Bridwell and Brian McCray were two of the guest climbers. Jim shared stories about celestial navigation and his father. Jim, Brian, Heidi Wirtz, Timy Fairfield, Mike Volk, and Cartel Productions presented various slide shows. Throughout the event there were activities to display athletic abilities, such as climbing competitions, a tug-of-war (AAC vs the Access Fund), volleyball, arm wrestling, and pull-ups. The climbing competition featured climbing on three walls and slack lines of varying heights. A slack line was set from Panorama Point at the mouth of Monkey Face Pinnacle on which the best ropewalkers displayed their talents

Also at Smith Rock, the Monkey Face litter project was an interesting and successful one organized by Richard Bence, Matt Brewster, Robert McGown, Robert Speik, park ranger Thad Fitzpatrick, and Kellie Rice, western coordinator of the Access Fund. With advance planning and prefabbing, the project came together in a day. See photos at www.ors.alpineclub.org.

The work of Neale Creamer and the Friends of Silcox Hut (FOSH) was again noteworthy. In the fall the Friends assisted by Timberline Lodge continued to perform difficult maintenance on the Silcox Hut. The efforts of FOSH are appreciated by the climbing community for winter access to the 1933 WPA structure at 7,000 feet on Mt. Hood. The hut provides an excellent base camp for a southside emergency rescue location.

Another Section activity was a fund-raising multimedia program by speed climber Hans Florine. He presented an excellent program called "20 Classics in 20 Days." He also included an inspirational talk about his speed climbing ascents of the Nose of El Capitan. The Section hosts two slide/film presentations a year to provide funds for our activities, such as trail maintenance and support of local climbing organizations.

Section member and *AAJ* editor John Harlin completed a new line on the south side of Mont Blanc in the Alps in late September. "From Dawn To Decadence" (French alpine grade TD) was initially attempted by Harlin and Mark Jenkins in August 2003. After ascending the standard Innominata Ridge to 14,000 ft., the pair succeeded in climbing the crux pitches on a spectacular virgin 250 ft. dihedral (5.11-); the highlight was Jenkins removing a 10 ft. icicle on lead. A major storm blocked further progress. Harlin returned to the route last September with Julie-Ann Clyma (NZ) and Roger Payne (UK). The team climbed the dihedral and a further two buttresses, which included a bivouac and a 150 ft. (5.10-) corner crack near 15,000 ft. A few more pitches on ice, snow, and rock reached the Brouillard Ridge and the long traverse to the summit (15,702 ft.) and endless traversing across various Mont Blanc sub-summits to the French Cosmique hut, followed the next day by a spectacular gondola ride across the Vallée Blanche back to Italy, thereby completing a 4.5-day round-trip. For Harlin it was particularly meaningful, as his father had climbed two new routes nearby in the early 1960s, one with Tom Frost and the other with Chris Bonington.

ROBERT McGOWN, *Chair*

NORTHERN ROCKIES SECTION. 2004 was a busy and productive year in the Northern Rockies. We began the year in Boise with a video presentation by Dick Dorworth of the classic 1968 Funhog Expedition to Patagonia, which resulted in the third ascent of Fitz Roy. See *AAJ* 1969: pp. 263-269.

Also in January Brian Cabe represented the AAC at the Climbing Management Planning session at the City of Rocks and Castle Rocks State Park. He and other local climbers helped review the climbing rules and clarify/change those that were not working. Also, Brian has taken over as the Section's Salt Lake City area leader, replacing Mark Holbrook, who moved to Oregon.

The Boise group partnered with the Boise Climbers Alliance to complete the Black Cliffs Trail Project. In 2003 a flash flood washed out the trail and parking area for one of the more popular climbing areas at the Cliffs. Thanks to indispensable grants from the AAC Domestic Conservation Committee and the Access Fund, a project was underwritten to clean up existing trails, install new ones where needed, and sign each of the entry points with a kiosk. The kiosks provide trail maps and information for climbers and about the status of local raptors. On May 22-23 over 60 eager volunteers turned out to complete all of the planned trail reconstruction Brian Fedigan was particularly commended for his effective role as project leader.

In late September the Section hosted the annual Moondance at the City of Rocks National Reserve. The Section hosts the campsite with space available on a first-come-first-serve basis. We had over 75 people attending with the campsite completely full, which represents a large increase over prior years. Saturday night featured a gala BBQ and the telling of tall tales around the bonfire. We will continue the popular Moondance on September's harvest moon weekend.

The Barrel Mountaineering Ice Festival is held in Bozeman, Montana, and is sponsored by Brent Bishop's Barrel Mountaineering. In conjunction with the festival we set up an AAC display table for two evenings. Many existing and potential members stopped by to ask about the Club in the Bozeman area. Tom Kalakay has agreed to serve as the the AAC contact and try to establish the Club's presence there.

DOUG COLWELL, *Chair*

CENTRAL ROCKIES SECTION. Thanks to an enthusiastic group of CRS volunteers headed by Rick Casey, the AAC established a high profile presence among the vendors and organizations at the Ouray Ice Festival in January. The AAC tent was well positioned at the entrance to the vendor area Thursday through Sunday. Many visitors, especially younger climbers, stopped by for information about the AAC. As for the ice climbing itself, the competition event was covered by the major media. The two winners were from outside the U.S. Around 2,000 people were in town for the festival.

The Sixth Annual Cody, Wyoming, Waterfall Ice Roundup (www.southforkice.com) was once again a wonderful, quaint, and friendly event. Approximately 55 people from more than six states took part in the climbing and the festivities. Slide shows were given every evening, February 13-15. All three short presentations on Friday were given by Club members. Greg Sievers provided images of Bridalveil Falls and Keystone Green-steps (600'+, WI5), in Valdez, Alaska, from the mid-1980s including a "show-and-tell" display of a vintage Chouinard equipment, strap-on crampons, and Lowe Big Bird axes. Mark Jenkins, an *Outside* magazine writer, gave us a slide-show tour of remote unclimbed peaks in southern China, Tibet, and Burma. The third show of the evening was a brief overview of alpine climbing in Idaho by Dean Lords. Saturday evening's program was given by local fun hog Aaron Mulkey with an entertaining array of digital imagery and sound.

Quite a few new areas have been discovered and explored in the Cody area, many right in the South Fork Valley (Shoshone River basin). Many new and existing ice routes are having the rappel descents bolted because of the gathering V-thread waste in the drainages and rapid deterioration of cordage. Aaron Mulkey is the driving force in locating and climbing many of the new waterfalls. He and friends have also graciously installed many of the rappel stations. For current conditions, visit his Web site www.coldfear.com.

While our Section was the primary financial sponsor of the Cody Festival, thanks for support are also due to Mammut (Schoeller garments, gear, and free hats), Magicline.com, MSR, Trango, New Belgian Brewery, and Red Bull. Don Foote, the event organizer, did a great job keeping the happy crowd focused during the programs and touting the AAC and other sponsors. The dry-tool pull-up contest was a hit, and the "well-past-40" men took overall honors by a good margin. Bison Willy's Bunkhouse (www.bisonwillys.com), the adjacent AAC system hut, was full all weekend. Our thanks to Kenny Gasch for his undying support and partnering with the AAC for this fine wilderness facility. Nothing beats a hot shower and clothes dryer after a long, hard day of climbing in sloppy ice conditions.

The fourth annual Lumpy Trails Day held October 23 at Lumpy Ridge, was an amazing success, with nearly 60 volunteers attending. The Club hosted Front Range climbers, Club members, locals, and Rocky Mountain National Park employees to improve climber access trails to one of the country's most popular and photogenic rock climbing areas. This year we were joined by nine students from the Adams County School climbing team and their coaches. The Park provided 10 NPS trail crew employees to guide the group to the Twin Owls Rock access trail. The group gave a "face lift" to over 400 vertical feet of extremely rugged mountainous trail. Over 40 wood water bars were installed to help check runoff, control erosion, and act as stairs Dozens of huge stones were moved to build new steps and armor against further erosion.

GREG SIEVERS, *Chair*

NORTH CENTRAL SECTION. The North Central Section has about 165 members spread out over an area of roughly 600 miles x 600 miles. The membership has two pockets, one in Minneapolis/ St. Paul, Minnesota, and the other 400 miles away in Omaha, Nebraska. The Omaha group has a spring membership drive with dinner and slide show. The group in the Twin Cities has two service related projects that also include membership drives. The first of these was on June 26 at the Taylor's Falls crag, about 50 miles north of St. Paul. It was the annual AAC clean-up day, which focused on the Wisconsin side of this popular climbing spot. Technically speaking this side is not within our Section boundary, as it is across the St. Croix River that separates Minnesota from Wisconsin. It is nevertheless an integral part of the destination. A small but dedicated group of seven members showed up for early morning climbing, afternoon clean up, and an early evening barbeque. On August 7-8 we had a similar clean-up day at Blue Mounds State Park in southwestern Minnesota. Blue Mounds is about 250 miles from the Twin Cities and is roughly the geographic center of our Section. The day was similar to that at Taylor's Falls, with 12 people in attendance for climbing, clean up, and the barbeque.

The North Central Section Web site is not presently operational, and this Chair is eagerly seeking a webmaster.

SCOTT CHRISTENSEN, *Chair*

NEW YORK SECTION. While the New York Section, now a record 750 members strong, hosts a variety of outdoor and indoor events, both winter and fall, it is perhaps best known for its annual black tie dinner. This year was especially significant as it marked the 25th Anniversary of what has now become a national institution of sorts with members and guests from all over the country regularly traveling to New York specifically to attend the event. In addition we were pleased this year to see long time members Friedel and Helke Schunk join us from their new home in Germany.

With David Breashears, Emmy Award Winning High Altitude Cinematographer, as the star attraction, the Silver Anniversary Dinner was held before a record crowd on November 20 at Manhattan's Union Club. Honored in a special way were those in attendance with 25 or more years of continuous membership. President Mark Richey presented each with a special pewter membership badge, reserved for senior members, as well as a scroll acknowledging their contribution and years of dedicated support to the Club and its mission. Included in the group were two members of 50 or more years standing: Fred Golomb and Gibson Reynolds. Both also received a specially engraved memento in addition to the above. The ceremony will be repeated at appropriate intervals in future years as a new crop of members reaches the quarter century or higher mark and to accommodate those who were unable to attend this year's dinner.

The list of senior honorees is as follows:
- 50 Year Members: Fred Golomb, M.D., Gibson Reynolds
- 35 Year Members: Jan Arnet, Ted Church, Bill Fix, Jim Henriot, John Reppy, Sam Silverstein, M.D, Olaf Soot
- 25 Year Members: Vic Benes, Phil Erard, Bob Hall, Jack Reilly, Mark Richey

Youth was also served as a record 20 new members were also introduced and presented with their membership pins. Among these were Dan Lochner and partner Dan Meggitt. Lochner, a Connecticut native and college student, narrowly missed becoming the youngest climber to have completed the Seven Summits. This honor went to Britton Keeshan, who completed his record-setting quest last May. While Lochner and his partner summitted Everest a couple of weeks before Keeshan, they missed their opportunity to journey to Vinson last winter placing them one season and one summit behind Keeshan. Included in the group of rookie members was Intesar Haider, who became the first Bangladeshi national to summit in Antarctica in 2003 in an expedition which forged a new route on Vinson. A colorful group was led by Judge Barry Feudale from Pennsylvania accompanied by lady climbing judges. We're not sure what verdict the judges gave this crowd and this event!

Breashears, who is directing the cinematography and climbing sequences for a new dramatic film on the Everest 1996 disaster, relived the drama of that tragedy and the rescues in which his IMAX climbing and film team played a key role. Last May he made his fifth ascent of Everest to capture footage for the new film.

As in the past, proceeds from the Dinner benefited the AAC Library Fund. Over the years this event has raised well over $125,000 for Club related causes.

On the weekend of January 22 and 23, many of those in attendance swapped their tuxes and gowns for ice axes , crampons and skis to participate in our traditional Adirondack Winter Outing in Keene, New York. As usual the weather was bitterly cold but the atmosphere was warm and inviting particularly at the Saturday cocktail hour and dinner.

Special thanks go to our indispensable volunteers: Vic Benes, our webmaster, Bob Hall and Fritz Selby who put on slide shows for us at our Winter and Fall outings, John Tiernan, who led a number of hikes for us in the region and Martin Torresquintero and Bob Barker, who are our new membership chairmen. Richard Ryan provided indispensable technical support at the Annual Dinner as well as organized lectures for us at the North Face Store in Manhattan. Our outings benefited enormously from the culinary contributions of Chris and Mim Galligan and Jonathan Conrad.

Stay in touch with AAC events in New York by logging on to: http://nysalpineclub.org.

PHILIP ERARD, *Chair*

NEW ENGLAND SECTION. On March 6 the Section hosted its first "Old Timers Day" on the ice and in the rain at Willey's Slide at Crawford Notch, New Hampshire, displaying and using ancient garb and ice gear from the 1970s and earlier: 10-point crampons, manila hemp rope, wood-shafted ice axes, and weird protection devices ("coat hangers," snargs, army tubes, and wart hogs). Several parties actually "Frenched" their way to the top. In the evening we repaired to a local inn, where the gear was on display and where Randy Chatterjee presented an edited video of the day's events, which had been organized by Bob Plucenik and Dale Jancic. The audience was also delighted with Ken Henderson's recently restored film of the first ascent of Pinnacle Gully and Woodrow Wilson Sayre's film "Four Against Everest."

Eighty-five members and guests attended our 8th Annual Black Tie Dinner, at which Henry Barber offered an overview of "Significant Climbs of the Seventies" following a reception amid an exhibition of the 1930s Chamonix cartoons of Samivel. A cartoon auction netted the Section $1,000. Karen McLaughlin organized the elegant "tasting menu" meal and Steve Weitzler, as usual, organized the awesome door prizes.

In June we enjoyed a cookout and social at Nancy Savickas's place in Albany, New Hampshire, which drew a record 30 souls. Among them were AAC President Mark Richey and family, fellow Everest summiter and former Section chair Barry Rugo, and 1972 Mt. St. Elias expedition leader Malcom Moore. Malcolm had a few stunning slides of the St. Elias East Ridge, and Joe and Judy Perez some images from Namibia, South Africa, and the Dolomites.

In September Sam Streibert joined parties on the Northeast Buttress of Higher Cathedral Spire in Yosemite. Sam says that his partners actually climbed the route, while he just "made it up." In any event, we were impressed. Bob Wadja spent a week in Canada doing two routes on the north face of Mt. Fey and Yamnuska (7,349'), a limestone peak near Canmore in the Canadian Rockies.

We gathered again at Nancy's on Halloween, but were able to materialize very few ghosts of climbers past. Henry Barber and Jack Reilly of the New York Section were among them.

BILL ATKINSON, *Chair,* AND NANCY SAVICKAS, *Vice Chair*

INDEX

COMPILED BY RALPH FERRARA AND EVE TALLMAN

Mountains are listed by their official names. Ranges and geographic locations are also indexed. Unnamed peaks (eg. Peak 2,340) are listed under P. Abbreviations are used for some states and countries and for the following: Article: art.; Cordillera: C.; Mountains: Mts.; National Park: Nat'l Park; Obituary: obit. Most personnel are listed for major articles. Expedition leaders and persons supplying information in Climbs and Expeditions are also cited here. Indexed photographs are listed in bold type. Reviewed books are listed alphabetically under Book Reviews.

Submissions Guidelines

The *American Alpine Journal* records the significant climbing accomplishments of the world in an annual volume. We encourage climbers to submit brief (250-500 words) factual accounts of their climbs and expeditions. Accounts should be submitted by e-mail whenever possible. Alternatively, submit accounts by regular post on CD, zip, or floppy disk. Please provide complete contact information, including e-mail address, postal address, fax, and phone. The deadline is December 31, through earlier submissions will be looked on very kindly! For photo guidelines and other information, please see the complete Submissions Guidelines document at the American Alpine Journal section of www.AmericanAlpineClub.org.

Please address all correspondences to:
The American Alpine Journal, 710 Tenth Street, Suite 140, Golden, CO 80401 USA; tel.: (303) 384 0110; fax: (303) 384 0111; aaj@americanalpineclub.org; www.AmericanAlpineClub.org

INTERNATIONAL GRADE COMPARISON CHART

To download the complete "American Alpine Journal International Grade Comparison Chart," including alpine and ice grades, go to: www.americanalpineclub.org/knowledge/aaj.asp

This chart is designed to be used with the *American Alpine Journal* to help decipher the difficulty ratings given to climbs.

Seriousness Rating:

These often modify the technical grades when protection is difficult.

R: Poor protection with potential for a long fall and some injury.

X: A fall would likely result in serious injury or death.

YDS	UIAA	FR	AUS	SAX	CIS	SCA	BRA	UK	
5.2	II	1	10	II	III	3			D
5.3	III	2	11	III	III+	3+			
5.4	IV- IV	3	12		IV-	4			VD
5.5	IV+		13		IV	4+			S
5.6	V-	4	14		IV+	5-			HS
5.7	V V+		15	VIIa		5			4a	VS
5.8	VI-	5a	16	VIIb	V-	5+	4 4+	4b	HVS
5.9	VI	5b	17	VIIc		6-	5 5+	4c 5a	E1
5.10a	VI+	5c	18	VIIIa	V	6	6a	5b	
5.10b		6a							
5.10c	VII-	6a+	19	VIIIb		6+	6b		E2
5.10d	VII	6b	20	VIIIc	V+	7-	6c		E3
5.11a	VII+	6b+		IXa			7a	5c	
5.11b		6c	21	IXb		7	7b		E4
5.11c	VIII-	6c+	22	IXc	VI-	7+	7c		
5.11d	VIII	7a	23					6a	
5.12a	VIII+	7a+	24			8-	8a		E5
5.12b		7b	25	Xa	VI	8	8b		
5.12c	IX-	7b+	26	Xb			8c		E6
5.12d	IX	7c	27			8+	9a	6b	
5.13a		7c+	28	Xc			9b		E7
5.13b	IX+	8a	29			9-	9c		
5.13c	X-	8a+	30	XIa	VI+	9	10a	6c	
5.13d	X	8b	31				10b		E8
5.14a	X+	8b+	32	XIb			10c	7a	
5.14b	XI-	8c	33			9+			E9
5.14c	XI	8c+		XIc				7b	
5.14d		9a							

YDS=Yosemite Decimal System; UIAA=Union Internationale des Associations D'Alpinisme; Fr=France/Sport; Aus=Australia; Sax=Saxony; CIS=Commonwealth of Independent States/Russia; Sca=Scandinavia; Bra=Brazil.